LOOKING BACK

LOOKING BACK
Never Explain, Never Apologise

JOHN OSBORNE

faber and faber

This edition first published in 1999
by Faber and Faber Limited
3 Queen Square London WC1N 3AU

Typeset by RefineCatch Limited, Bungay, Suffolk
Printed in England by Mackays of Chatham plc, Chatham, Kent
All rights reserved

A Better Class of Person was first published in hardback in 1981 and paperback in 1991 by
Faber and Faber Limited
© John Osborne, 1981

Almost a Gentleman was first published in hardback in 1991 and paperback in 1992 by
Faber and Faber Limited
© John Osborne, 1991

'Bad John' by Alan Bennett first appeared in *London Review of Books*, Vol. 3, Issue 22/23,
3–16 December 1981. © Alan Bennett, 1981
'A Lifelong Satirist of Prigs and Puritans' by David Hare first appeared in the *Spectator*,
10 June 1995. © David Hare, 1995

John Osborne is hereby identified as author of this work in accordance with Section 77 of
the Copyright, Designs and Patents Act 1988

A CIP record for this book
is available from the British Library

ISBN 0–571–19649–7

2 4 6 8 10 9 7 5 3 1

I do not have the least pretension to 'appear before God, book in hand', declaring myself the 'best of men', nor to write 'confessions'. I shall tell only what I wish to tell; and the reader who refuses me in his absolution must needs be harsh to the point of unorthodoxy for I will admit none but venial sins.

Hector Berlioz, *Memoirs*, 1848

Contents

Illustrations, ix
'Bad John' Alan Bennett, xii
'A Lifelong Satirist of Prigs and Puritans' David Hare, xviii

VOLUME I A Better Class of Person 1929–1956

1 No Pride in Real Gentry, 5
2 Uncalled-for Remarks, 8
3 'I Don't Want to End Up in a Dead-and-Alive Hole', 30
4 'A Better Class of Person', 49
5 O Wall!, 68
6 Bugger Bognor, 81
7 Too Young to Fight and Too Old to Forget, 100
8 Deathaboys, 112
9 Tomorrow, the Empire, 125
10 'Must Leave Now to Take Down the Front-room Curtains', 144
11 Hold the Front Page, 150
12 Kindly Leave the Stage, 165
13 Dead-and-Alive Holes, 182
14 I'm Forever Blowing Bubbles, 193
15 Holy Ghost for Four, 209
16 Fall of a Sparrow, 218
17 'Great Hatred Little Room', 234
18 On the Pier at Morecambe, 251
19 'Let me Know Where *You're* Playing Tomorrow Night and I'll Come and See *You*', 264

VOLUME II Almost a Gentleman 1955–1966

1 A Palpable Miss, 277
2 Camp Following, 286

3 May 8th, 293

4 'Take it Orfe', 305

5 'I Have a Go, Lady. I Do. I Have a Go', 315

6 Barwick's Suit, 324

7 'All Russia is my Garden', 335

8 The October Bonfire, 342

9 Broadly Speaking, 353

10 American Panic, 362

11 'His own Worst Enemy', 373

12 'Not at his Best', 384

13 'Letting down England', 393

14 A Night to Remember, 403

15 Surprised by Joy, 416

16 Viva Mexico!, 426

17 Pushing Thirty, 434

18 Off the Peg, 444

19 Never to be Seen Again, 455

20 'Do your Nuns Decline?', 466

21 Holy Moses, 476

22 Grey-haired Youth, 486

23 'Don't Cry for Me, Nicaragua', 497

24 Crimson Twilight, 506

25 Bad, Sad and Mad, 515

26 Then Whom Have I Offended?, 525

27 All the Day Long, 536

28 Vale Nora Noel, 551

29 Philadelphia Story, 556

Envoi, 569

Index, 571

Illustrations

1 John Osborne, aged three.
2 Mother – Nellie Beatrice.
3 Father – Thomas Godfrey.
4 Grandma Grove on her hundredth birthday. Photo: Salisbury Journal.
5 At Hampton Court, 1946: John Osborne with Grandma Grove, Uncle Jack and Nellie Beatrice.
6 Sister Fay.
7 Auntie Queenie, aged twenty-four.
8 Auntie Nancy and Uncle Harry in 'The White Man's Grave'.
9 At St Michael's.
10 In rep: at Kidderminster. Photo: Lisle Haas. At Derby with Pamela Lane. Photo: Raymonds News Agency.
11 Pages from John Osborne's notebooks: the original title page and draft of *Look Back in Anger*.
12 George Devine © BBC Hulton Picture Library.
13 Kenneth Haigh as Jimmy Porter, Alan Bates as Cliff, and Mary Ure as Alison Porter in the original production of *Look Back in Anger*.
14 *Look Back in Anger*, Royal Court Theatre, 1956 © Mark Gerson.
15 Pamela Lane. Photo: Somers and Smith.
16 John Osborne, 1950.
17 At the Royal Court: writers, actors and directors. Condé Nast Publications Ltd. Photo: Tony Armstrong-Jones.
18 John Osborne, Woodfall Street, 1957 © Mark Gerson.
19 Kenneth Tynan © Universal Pictorial Press, from the collections of the Theatre Museum, by courtesy of the Board of Trustees of the Victoria and Albert Museum.
20 Tony Richardson, Oscar Lewenstein, Margaret 'Percy' Harris and John Osborne in discussion about the set for the Russian production of *Look Back in Anger*, by kind permission of Lindsay Anderson.

21 The golden couple: John Osborne and Mary Ure, 1957. Photo: Associated Newspapers Ltd.

22 Mary Ure in New York's Vegetarian Restaurant, 1957.

23 Elaine Tynan and Mary Ure, Sandy Wilson's flat.

24 Brenda de Banzie and Laurence Olivier in *The Entertainer*, Royal Court Theatre, 1957. Photo © Tony Armstrong-Jones.

25 *The Entertainer* at the Royal Court Theatre, 1957. Photo © Tony Armstrong-Jones.

26 Laurence Olivier and Dorothy Tutin in *The Entertainer*, Royal Court Theatre, 1957. Photo © Tony Armstrong-Jones.

27 Laurence Olivier as Archie Rice in *The Entertainer*. Photo © Tony Armstrong-Jones.

28 Cover of the original programme for *The Entertainer*.

29 Oscar Lewenstein. Photo © Universal Pictorial Press & Agency Ltd.

30 Neville Blond. Photo © Universal Pictorial Press & Agency Ltd.

31 Joan Plowright, George Devine and John Osborne in *The Making of Moo*, Royal Court Theatre, 25 June 1957. Photo: David Sim, from the collections of the Theatre Museum, by courtesy of the Board of Trustees of the Victoria and Albert Museum.

32 John Osborne and Mary Ure at home. Photo: *Lilliput* magazine, April 1959.

33 John Osborne and Mary Ure arriving at London Airport after the New York success of *Look Back in Anger*. Photo: *Lilliput* magazine, April 1959.

34 John Osborne, Jamaica, 1958.

35 Francine, 1958.

36 Richard Burton and Mary Ure in scenes from the film version of *Look Back in Anger*. Photos: *Lilliput* magazine, April 1959.

37 *The World of Paul Slickey*, discussions at the Café Royal, 1959. Photo © Alec Murray.

38 Rehearsals for *The World of Paul Slickey*, 1959. Photo: © Alec Murray.

39 Vivien Leigh in *Look After Lulu*, Royal Court Theatre, July 1959. Photo © David Sim, from the collections of the Theatre Museum, by courtesy of the Board of Trustees of the Victoria and Albert Museum.

40 Jocelyn Rickards, 1959. Photo © Islay Lyons.

41 John Osborne, Lower Belgrave Street, 1959. Photo © Alec Murray.

42 John Osborne, Nuclear Disarmament Week, September 1959. Photo © Euan Duff.

43 The first Aldermaston March, by kind permission of Lindsay Anderson.

44 Tony Richardson, Rita Tushingham and John Osborne at the première of the film *A Taste of Honey*. Photo © Hulton–Deutsch collection.

45 The 1961 protest at the Royal Court Theatre against the arrest of Wesker, Bolt and Logue, by kind permission of Lindsay Anderson.

46 Penelope Gilliatt and Nolan, 1965. Photo: *Evening Standard*.

47 Jill Bennett. Photo © Camera Press Ltd from the collections of the Theatre Museum, by courtesy of the Board of Trustees of the Victoria and Albert Museum.

48 Jill Bennett in *A Patriot For Me*. Photo © Zoë Dominic.

49 Ferdy Mayne and George Devine in *A Patriot For Me*. Photo © Zoë Dominic.

50 John Osborne the day after the opening of *A Patriot For Me*, 1965. Photo © Zoë Dominic.

All photographs not otherwise credited are courtesy of the author.

Bad John

A review by Alan Bennett of *A Better Class of Person*

One of John Osborne's Thoughts for 1954: 'The urge to *please* above all. I don't have it and can't achieve it. A small thing but more or less mine own.' This book does please and has pleased. It is immensely enjoyable, is written with great gusto, and Osborne has had better notices for it than for any of his plays since *Inadmissible Evidence*.

Books are safer than plays, of course, because (unless one is a monk at lunch) reading is a solitary activity. A play is a public event where, all too often these days, for the middle-class playgoer, embarrassment rules, oh dear. Especially where Osborne is concerned. Nor does reading his book carry with it the occupational hazards of seeing his plays, such as finding the redoubtable Lady Redgrave looming over one ready to box one's ears, as she did to a vociferous member of the audience at *A Sense of Detachment*. The book as a form is safe, even cosy, and I suspect that critics, who have given Osborne such a consistently hard time for so long, heaved a sigh of relief at this autobiography, since it was something, to quote another John's spoof of Dorothy L. Sayers, 'to be read behind closed doors'. Though without necessarily taking Orton's other piece of advice – namely to 'have a good shit while reading it'.

Osborne, like Orton, had a bleak childhood (or would like us to think so). Both had weak chests, and both spent a brief period learning shorthand at Clark's Colleges. There the resemblance ends. At the outset of his career Orton changed his name from John to Joe, lest the public confuse him with Osborne – and tar him with the same brush. For Joe, unlike John, did very much want to please. But do playgoers mind very much if they're *pleased*? I never do. Boredom is my great terror. 'All I hope is that the dog hasn't been sick in the car' is the epitaph on too many a wearisome evening in the theatre. I have never been bored by Osborne – well, by Bill Maitland a little, but that was meant. I often disagree with his plays, but I invariably find his tone of voice, however hectoring, much more sympathetic than the rage or the patronizing 'Oh dear, he's at it again' he still manages to provoke in an audience. (At Brighton, the stage carpenter used to greet him in mock-despair: 'Oh blimey, it's not you again!'). I actually enjoyed the frozen embarrassment of the glittering house that packed the Lyttelton when his *Watch it Come Down* opened the National Theatre, and at *A Sense of Detachment* was told off for laughing too much (or laughing at all) at the catalogue of pornographic films, recited in nun-like tones by the said Lady Redgrave, her title an important ingredient of the audience's resentment, their fury fuelled by a touch of class.

Osborne thinks those days are past: 'Most of my work in the theatre has, at some time, lurched head on into the milling tattoo of clanging seats and often quite beefy booing. The sound of baying from dinner-jacketed patrons in the stalls used to be especially sweet. Nowadays one is merely attacked by a storm cloud of pot and BO.' Another way of saying that the audience is (Gr-rr-r) young.

It's hard to see who made Osborne a writer. In working-class childhoods the Curtis Brown role generally falls to the mother, but not apparently in this case. A colleague of his mother's, Cheffie, cast him as a future 'thousand-a-year man'. This was in Surrey in the forties. In much the same class and period in the North aspirations were approximately half this. My mother thought £10 a week the salary of a successful man in the profession she had picked out for me, the unlikely one of 'gentleman farmer'. Osborne's mother had no aspirations for him at all: 'My mother always made it clear to me that my place in the world was unlikely ever to differ from her own.' Nellie Beatrice was a barmaid, almost an itinerant one she changed her job (and their accommodation) so often – thirty or forty times during the first seventeen years of the boy's life. Flitting flats, changing schools: Osborne's life was like a rep long before he became an actor.

The name Nellie Beatrice seems odd. It took me some time to get used to the fact that this was his mother, not his aunt. It is an aunt's name, and, according to him, an aunt was pretty much what she was – unsmiling, given to sulks and Black Looks, not at all the jovial lady smiling, if Osborne is to be believed, an almost unique smile in her picture. Other people's mothers are always easier to swallow than one's own, and Nellie Beatrice is funnier than her son will allow. He conned her into going to see him in *Hamlet*: 'I've seen it before,' she remarked to her companion. 'He dies in the end.' Osborne lovingly records her make-up:

> Her lips were a scarlet-black sliver, covered in some sticky slime named Tahiti or Taboo . . . She had a cream base called Crème Simone,

always covered up with a face powder called Tokalon ... topped off
by a kind of knickerbocker glory of rouge, which ... looked like a
mixture of blackcurrant juice and brick dust. The final coup was an
overgenerous dab of Californian Poppy, known to schoolboys as 'fleur
des dustbins'.

She lives on, Mrs Osborne, 'hell-bent' on reaching her century.

Osborne's father, Godfrey, was the more sensitive of the two, living apart
from his mother, though Osborne does not remember why ('I have a vague
remembrance of them hitting each other'). A copywriter in an advertising
agency, he died of consumption when John was about twelve. (I say 'about'
because dates are quite hard to come by in this book: nowhere, for instance,
is Osborne's date of birth plainly stated.) His father came home to die at
Christmas 1939:

> I was sitting in the kitchen reading ... when I heard my mother
> scream from the foot of the uncarpeted staircase. I ran to see what was
> happening and stared up to the landing where my father was standing.
> He was completely naked with his silver hair and grey, black and red
> beard. He looked like a naked Christ. 'Look at him!' she screamed.
> 'Oh, my God, he's gone blind.' He stood quite still for a moment and
> then fell headlong down the stairs on top of us. Between us we carried
> him upstairs. She was right. He had gone blind.

This gentle wraith had some literary ambitions, writing short stories, two
of which his son submitted as his own work when taking a correspondence
course at the British Institute of Fiction Writing Science. The stories were
extravagantly praised, but when Osborne started his own work the reaction
quickly became 'reproachful, impatient and eventually ill-used and sorrowful'. It's a progression he must have got used to since. But if one were to ask (as
presumably his multitudinous relatives did and do ask), 'Who is it Osborne
"takes after"' or 'Where does he get his brains from?' then I imagine it is his
father who would take the credit. His father was born on 8 May 1900. And it
was on 8 May 1956 that *Look Back in Anger* opened at the Royal Court.
Osborne notes that it is the one unforgettable feast in his calendar.

I generally assume that childhoods more or less ended with the First
World War – halcyon childhoods certainly – and that most of them since
have been the 'forgotten boredom' of Larkin's poem 'Coming'. Anyone
born after 1940 got the Utility version, childhood according to the Authorized Economy Standard. But Osborne (unexpectedly) seems to have had a

childhood of Dickensian richness and oddity, divided between his mother's relations, 'the Grove Family Repertory', based in Fulham, and his father's, who made up 'the Tottenham Crowd'. There are relatives and relatives of relatives, and Osborne remembers them all, together with their small claims to fame: his grandfather's Uncle Arthur, 'said to be a director of Abdulla' (of 'cigarettes by'); his grandmother's sister, 'Auntie Min', whose life revolved round milk bottles; her husband, Uncle Harry, with his ferocious cockatoo. His great-grandmother, Grandma Ell, was laid out in the front parlour. The undertaker, who doubled as her son, Osborne's great-uncle Lod (the *names*!), lifted up the baby John to see his aged forebear lying in her coffin 'in what seemed unthinkable luxury'. Another uncle threw himself under a tube train *en route* for the cobblers, and a grandma chucked Marie Lloyd out of the pub she ran, the Duncannon, off St Martin's Lane, with the first lady of the music-hall screaming, 'Don't you fucking well talk to me! I've just left your old man after a weekend in Brighton.' All these, not to mention a strong supporting cast that features a proper quota of nancies and at least one of what in our family used to be referred to as 'them man-women'. 'Oh,' one is tempted to exclaim with the Radlett children, 'the *bliss* of being you!' Or at any rate the bliss of being him now, remembering (and being able to remember) it all. Of course, it wasn't much fun at the time. 'There was no cachet in youth at that time. One was merely a failed adult. I sought the company of people like my grandparents and great aunts and uncles: they were infinitely more interesting. And I was an eager and attentive listener.'

I said his childhood was 'unexpectedly' rich, because to date there's not much hint of it in his work. He quotes examples from *The Entertainer* and *Hotel in Amsterdam* that draw directly on members of his family, but not much of the personnel or atmosphere of his childhood has hitherto found its way into his plays, even on television. Speaking as one who has recycled his only two serviceable aunts so often in dramatic form they've long since lost all feature or flavour, I'm sure his restraint is to be commended.

When he does start drawing on his later experience for the plays, it's nice to find that the relation between Art and Life doesn't unduly exercise him. In this narrative the real become the fictional almost in mid-sentence: characters are dragged struggling out of Life, allowed a quick visit to Wardrobe before being shoved breathless on to the stage. And no *Brideshead* rubbish about 'I am not I: thou art not he or she: they are not they.' His first wife, Pamela Lane, becomes Alison at her ironing-board, and her hapless parents leap on to the stage with her. She is she: they are they: and he himself makes no bones about coming on as Jimmy Porter – in 1956 anyway. Newspapers won't believe he's come on as anything else since.

Much of his childhood was spent in the more run-down bits of suburban Surrey, with spells at umpteen schools where he grew to expect to get beaten up as a matter of course on the first day. He was sent away to school at various times because of his health, the bills being paid by the Benevolent Society that had looked after his father. The account of the cold convalescent home in Dorset where he was sent at the end of 1942 makes grim reading, but for all that he doesn't come over as ever having been desperately unhappy in the way sensitive boys sent away to school are supposed to be (if they have an eye on Art, that is). One has no sense of his looking for affection, though there is a beautiful account of his friendship with a self-assured and decidedly eccentric boy, Mickey Wall. 'When he introduced me to his sister, Edna, a nice but slightly irritable nineteen-year-old, she was bending over the fire grate. "This is my sister, Edna," he said . . . I was prepared to be impressed both by her seniority and attractive appearance, but not for his comment. "Hasn't she got a big arse?" he said thoughtfully.'

There is something of Richmal Crompton's William (and his more than slightly irritable sister Ethel) about Mickey Wall, and also of Saki's Bassington – a boy too self-assured and finished ever to turn into an adult. I've no doubt there will be some research student, maybe one of those paid-up, card-carrying members of the London Library that figure on Osborne's hit list, who will one day sift the plays for evidences of Wall. But on to sex.

Convalescing in Cornwall after an operation for appendicitis, he finds himself alone on a beach. 'I took off my bathing suit and began to cauterize my appendicitis wound with a stick, rather like a crayon, which I had been given for this purpose. It was six months since my operation but my scar had refused to heal and was still partially open with patches of wormy flesh protruding from it.' The naked Osborne, poking away at his stomach, is espied by a handsome middle-aged man sunbathing in the next cove. He turns out to be a writer and asks him back to his cottage. They drink china tea out of nice cups, listen to a record of Arthur Bliss's *Miracle in the Gorbals* and the author, J. Wood Palmer (that initial says it all), suggests Osborne stay the night. At the same time, he cheerfully warns our hero that a bit of the other is quite likely to be on the cards. Exit the author of *A Patriot for Me*, hot and confused. But the scar, the writer, the nice cups make it all straight out of the last writer one would ever associate with Osborne – Denton Welch.

Mind you, this sort of thing is always happening to him. He's able to drop his guard temporarily during a brief (and glorious) stint as a reporter on *Gas World* – not, one imagines, the most epicene of periodicals – but no sooner does he give up journalism than the word goes round and the forces of pederasty are on the qui vive. No rep does he join but at the first read-through the resident Mr Roving Hands is giving him the glad eye. One is even observed fumbling him under a café table by a private detective specially hired (in Minehead!) by his fiancée's parents. Nothing ever comes of these approaches, despite the assertions of colleagues like Gerald at Ilfracombe that 'I didn't know what I wanted'. Osborne knew what he wanted all right, and he'd been wanting it for years.

'Sex was the most unobtainable luxury in the winter of our post-war austerity.' What passed for sex in 1947 was 'a few snatched pelvic felicities during the quickstep, what I came later to know as a Dry Fuck on the Floor'. For the boy who, at school, did not know what a twat was, opportunity finally knocked in Llandudno, on tour with an actress called Stella. Knocked and knocked and knocked. He was nineteen, and to read back from Art to Life (*A Sense of Detachment* again), he 'could do it nine times in the morning'. And, what is nice, five wives later he still thinks it a very worthwhile activity. 'If I were to choose a way to die it would be after a drunken, fish-eating day, ending up at the end of the Palace pier . . . To shudder one's last, thrusting, replete gasp between the sheets at four and six o'clock in Brighton would be the most perfect last earthly delight.' Even this last, putative, fuck is due for a matinée performance.

Little mothered but much married, Osborne has a complicated relationship to the opposite sex, pointed up by a happy printer's error. For his first performance with Stella he had invested in a pair of yellow poplin pyjamas from Simpson's. Stella, however, jumped the gun and 'began to make love to me with alarming speed, but I was still sober and self-conscious enough to insist on going to my own room to get my pymamas.' Once in his 'pymamas', he came back to bed and Stella, and burst into tears. It was some considerable time before he ceased crying, took off the pymamas and got down to the serious business of sexual intercourse.

This is a lovely book. It has jokes ('Handing over the Hoover to my mother was like distributing highly sophisticated nuclear weapons to an underdeveloped African nation'). It is not mellow. And it constantly brings alive that remotest of periods, the recent past.

Alan Bennett. First published in *London Review of Books*, Vol. 3, Issue 22/23, 3–16 December 1981.

A Lifelong Satirist of Prigs and Puritans

David Hare's eulogy for John Osborne, given at his
memorial service in London
2 June 1995

'I've an idea. Why don't we have a little game? Let's pretend that we're
human beings and that we're actually alive. Just for a while. What do
you say? Let's pretend we're human.'

It took the author's sudden death last Christmas and his burial in a Shropshire churchyard, just a few miles from the blissful house he shared with his
beloved Helen, to wake his own country into some kind of just appreciation
of what they had lost. It is impossible to speak of John without using the
word 'England'. He had, in some sense, made the word his own. Yet it is no
secret that latterly John had imagined the local eclipse of fashion that is
inevitable in his profession to be sharper and more hurtful than ever before.

However, in the flood of heartfelt and often guilty appreciation which
followed on his death, he would have been astonished to see publicly
acknowledged what he most surely knew all along: that the world is full of
people who feel strangely rebuked by those who dare to live far freer, more
fearless, even more reckless lives than the ones we are able to lead ourselves.
Of all human freedoms the most contentious is the freedom not to fear what
people will think of you. It still shocks people when you claim the right to
hate with the same openness with which you love. But even the stage carpenter at the Theatre Royal, Brighton, who liked regularly to greet the
visit of each of John's plays with the words 'Oh, blimey, not you again',
would have admitted that the man who wrote 'Don't be afraid of being
emotional. You won't die of it' had all along been possessed of an enviable
courage.

'It's deep honesty which distinguishes a gentleman,' he wrote on one
occasion. 'He knows how to revel in life and have no expectations – and fear

death at all times.' On another: 'I have been upbraided constantly for a crude, almost animal inability to dissemble.' Or, as his mother, the famous Nellie Beatrice, put it, after watching him act: 'Well, he certainly puts a lot into it. Poor kid.'

Central to any understanding of John's extraordinary life – five marriages, twenty-one stage plays and more flash clothes than anyone can count – is the striking disparity between his popular reputation as a snarling malcontent, the founding member of the Viper Gang Club, and the generous, free-spirited man that most of us in this church knew and loved. What he called his 'beholden duty to kick against the pricks' concealed from public view a man whom we all adored as an incomparable host, an endlessly witty and caring friend and one of the best prospects for gossip and enchantment I have ever met in my life.

He had, in Dirk Bogarde's happy phrase, a matchless gift for 'uncluttered friendship'. His postcards alone were worth living for. To a man writing from America to ask him the meaning of life, his typically courteous reply ran, in whole: 'Wish I *could* help you with the meaning of life. J.O.' To me, a colleague consoling him on some routine professional humiliation, he wrote from his beautiful home: 'Never mind. I lift my eyes to the blue remembered hills, and they call back: "Shove off."' To an Australian student, astonished to get an answer to his card saying he wanted to be a playwright: 'All I can say is trust your own judgment. Don't be discouraged by anyone. The only ally you will have is yourself.'

It is hardly surprising that right until the end of his life students and young people continued to write to him. The whole world knew that it was John who established the idea that it would be to the stage that people would look for some sort of recognizable portrait of their own lives. It would not be from this country's then weedy novels, nor from its still shallow and mendacious journalism that people would expect strong feeling or strong intelligence, but from its often clumsy, untutored living theatre. Free from the highbrow pieties of the university on one side, and from the crassness of what came to be called the media on the other, the theatre alone could celebrate John's approved qualities of joy and curiosity. It could also affront his deadly enemy, opinion.

And for many years, ridiculously, this central claim of John's, his ruling belief in the theatre's unique eloquence held and kept its authority. 'On that stage,' he said, of the little space behind the proscenium arch at the Royal Court Theatre, 'you can do anything.' John knocked down the door and a whole generation of playwrights came piling through, many of them not even acknowledging him as they came, and a good half of them not noticing that the vibrant tone of indignation they could not wait to imitate was, in John's case, achieved only through an equally formidable measure of literary skill.

John was too sensible a man to make extravagant claims for what he achieved. He knew better than anyone that the so-called revolution attributed to him was on the surface only. The counter-revolutionary enemy was waiting, preparing to send relentless waves of boulevard comedies, stupid thrillers and life-threatening musicals over the top, in order to ensure that the authenticity and originality of John's work would remain the exception rather than the rule. Nobody understood the tackiness of the theatre better than John. After all, he had played Hamlet on Hayling Island, not so much, he said, as the Prince of Denmark, as more like a leering milkman from Denmark Hill. Yet behind him there remains the true legend of a man who for some brief period burnished the theatre's reputation with the dazzle of his rhetoric.

'I love him,' he wrote of Max Miller, 'because he embodied a kind of theatre I admire most. "Mary from the Dairy" was an overture to the danger that [Max] might go too far. Whenever anyone tells me that a scene or a line in a play of mine goes too far in some way then I know my instinct has been functioning as it should. When such people tell you that a particular passage makes the audience uneasy or restless, then they seem (to me) as cautious and absurd as landladies and girls-who-won't.'

There is in everything John writes a love for the texture of real life, a reminder of real pleasures and real pains. 'I never,' he wrote in what I once claimed was his most characteristic statement, 'had lunch in Brighton without wanting to take a woman to bed in the afternoon.' When he heard that my own theatre company, Joint Stock, had gone on a mass outing to Epsom races to research a play about Derby Day, his scorn was terrifying. He said that when he was a young actor everyone he knew went to the Derby anyway, to enjoy it, not to bloody well research it.

It is fashionably said of John's work that he experienced a decline in the last twenty years of his life. There was nothing he resented more in later years than being asked what he was writing at the moment. Nobody, he said, asked an accountant whose accounts they were doing at the moment. Nor indeed did they ask, 'Done any accounting lately?' As he himself remarked, it is invariably those who have detested or distrusted your work from the outset who complain most vehemently of their sense of betrayed disappointment at your subsequent efforts.

Yet in making this familiar observation critics ignore or take for granted the two outstanding volumes of autobiography, which prove – if proof were needed – that his celebrated gift for analysing the shortcomings of others was as nothing to his forensic capacity for making comedy from his own failings. If he could be hard on others, he could be almost religiously brutal on himself. They also omit to mention what it was John declined from: a ten-year period, the last ten years of his great friend George Devine's life, in which he wrote *Look Back in Anger*, *The Entertainer*, *A Patriot for Me*, *Luther* and *Inadmissible Evidence*. Oh, yes, John Osborne declined. He declined in the sense that an unparalleled, mid-century period of dramatic brilliance remains precisely that. Unparalleled.

'A real pro is a real man, all he needs is an old backcloth behind him and he can hold them on his own for half an hour. He's like the general run of people, only he's a lot more like them than they are themselves, if you understand me.'

The words are Billy Rice's, and yet they apply as much to John – more like us than we are ourselves, if you understand me – as to any music-hall comedian.

'Oh, heavens, how I long for a little ordinary human enthusiasm. Just enthusiasm – that's all. I want to hear a warm, thrilling voice cry out "Hallelujah! Hallelujah. I'm alive!"'

It is, if you like, the final irony that John's governing love was for a country which is, to say the least, distrustful of those who seem to be both clever and passionate. There is in English public life an implicit assumption that the head and the heart are in some sort of opposition. If someone is clever, they get labelled cold. If they are emotional, they get labelled stupid. Nothing bewilders the English more than someone who exhibits great feeling and great intelligence. When, as in John's case, a person is abundant in both, the English response is to take in the washing and bolt the back door.

John Osborne devoted his life to trying to forge some sort of connection between the acuteness of his mind and the extraordinary power of his heart. 'To be tentative was beyond me. It usually is.' That is why this Christian leaves behind him friends and enemies, detractors and admirers. A lifelong satirist of prigs and puritans, whether of the Right or of the Left, he took no hostages, expecting from other people the same unyielding, unflinching commitment to their own view of the truth which he took for granted in his own. Of all British playwrights of the twentieth century he is the one who risked most. And, risking most, frequently offered the most rewards.

For many of us life will never be quite the same without the sight of that fabulous whiskered grin, glimpsed from across the room. Then John heading towards us, fierce, passionate and fun.

David Hare. First published in *The Spectator*, 10 June 1995.

VOLUME I
A Better Class of Person
1929–1956

To Helen

1. No Pride in Real Gentry

May 8th is the one unforgettable feast in my calendar. My father, Thomas Godfrey Osborne, was born in Newport, Monmouthshire, on May 8th. Had he lived he would now be the age of the century. The Second World War ended on 8 May 1945, a date which now passes as unremembered as 4 August 1914. On 8 May 1956, my first play to be produced in London, *Look Back in Anger*, had its opening at the Royal Court Theatre. This last particular date seems to have become fixed in the memories of theatrical historians.

In the summer of 1938 my father was compelled to give up his job through ill-health. He was a copywriter in an advertising agency in Shoe Lane, right beside the *Daily Express*. I was not sure what a copywriter was as my mother always insisted that he was an 'artist'. He had been given an imitation-oak clock and twenty pounds, which he spent taking us to his favourite seaside resort, Margate. A few weeks later the three of us stood on the Continental platform at Victoria Station waiting for the train to leave to take him on his way to a sanatorium in Menton. We stood there, in the way of these lifetime farewells, each impatient to see it over quickly. My mother was biting her long-gone finger nails, dressed in one of her all-one-colour 'rig-outs'. He leant out of the railway carriage, gave me a ten-shilling note and said, 'Take your mother to the pictures, son, and then go to Lyons Corner House.' The train drew out, and his head soon vanished into the carriage. Even I knew that the trappings of glamorous departure were taking him to an exile of pain of some sort and little hope or comfort whatsoever. My mother and I went to Lyons Corner House and then to a West End cinema for the first time, the newly opened Warner in Leicester Square. The film was *The Adventures of Robin Hood* with Errol Flynn. It banished the sight of my father's disappearing head for the rest of the day and some of the next.

I forget faces quickly, often alarmingly so. The images of people with whom I have spent long, intimate months, years even, become easily blurred, almost as if a deliberate act of censoring evasion takes place either through me or by some strange agency. But my father's appearance, even at this remove of forty years, is as clear as if I had seen him only a week ago.

His hair was almost completely white (at this time he would have been thirty-eight), but it had been that colour since he was in his early twenties. His skin was extremely pale, almost transparent. He had the whitest hands I think I have ever seen; Shalimar hands he called them. ('Pale hands I love beside the Lethe waters', of Shalimar. It was one of his favourite Sunday ballads.) The fingers were very long and, in contrast to the whiteness of the rest of the hand, the tips of every one were stained burnt ochre from years of Players Pleasing. His suit – as I remember he had only one, blue-striped suit – was usually unpressed but he was meticulous about the state of his cuffs and particularly his collars. The rest of his costume was unvariable: a rather greasy bowler hat and a mac which, on his insistence, was never sent to the cleaners although my mother once threw it, to his distress, into the dustbin. The edges of the collar and sleeves were an ingrained, shiny, mourning black, but his papery shoes were always brightly polished. In all, he must have seemed a little like a Welsh-sounding, prurient, reticent investigator of sorts from a small provincial town.

'As each of us looks back into his or her past, doors open upon darkness.'
E. M. Forster

In an essay on racial purity, Forster puts down this challenge:

> Can you give the names of your eight great-grandparents?
>
> The betting is at least eight to one against. The Royal Family could, some aristocrats could, and so could a few yeomen who have lived undisturbed in a quiet corner of England for a couple of hundred years. But most of the people I know (and probably most of the people who read these words) will fail.
>
> . . . Two doors at first – the father and the mother – through each of these two more, then the eight great-grandparents, the sixteen great-greats, then thirty-two ancestors . . . sixty-four . . . one hundred and twenty-eight . . . until the researcher reels.
>
> 'Racial Exercise', 1939

Most of the detail of my family background comes from hearsay. From dropped remarks, endlessly repeated anecdote, a roundabout of jokes, songs, moral stories, hints, gossip, conspiracies, implication, hymns. Just as children demand your instant familiarity with what is known only to them, you were expected at an early age to be able to identify members of the family – on both sides – even the dead. There were dark places in the filial landscape where figures would appear in a blazing memory of innuendo. This was especially so with my father's family, the Osbornes. There were my grandfather's brothers, all thrashed regularly with a cane in their night-shirts by my great-grandmother. A widow, with four sons, she seemed to have come from what my mother called 'moneyed people'. 'There's no pride in real gentry,' she'd say. My great-grandmother was clearly proud, not Gentry but definitely Trade.

I spent years of unforced, curious listening in my boyhood, trying to establish hard details about what any of them actually *did* or were, but information was difficult to come by. It was rather like saying to a singer of ancient ballads, 'Yes, but what were the real *facts*?' Their memories were fixed in a chain of images, scraps of conversations, swift allusions to people or occasions which were dangled before you in the deft way of someone who has access to things you will never know nor understand. They were enjoined to their own past and a little with the present, in so far as it affected their comfort and prospect. Recall was minute, examination perfunctory. They were like actors in a long run. The past held little mystery, the present only passing interest. As for the future, it was something to be dismissed with some holy satisfaction. 'I shan't be here to see it.'

Throughout my childhood no adult ever addressed a question to me. When I was at boarding school, when I went out to work, until the day she died when I was thirty, my father's mother never once asked me anything about myself. I think she had a glancing fondness for me. If I volunteered information, she would smile a thin winter of contempt and say nothing. Or change the subject firmly. To how well my cousin Tony was doing at Sand-hurst. How her niece Jill was engaged to such a nice young man. Who had been to Blundells School and had a very high position in Lloyds Bank in Lombard Street. I was convinced that her dismissive smile was aimed only to chill my father's coffin yet again.

2. Uncalled-for Remarks

PHOEBE: I remember once my Mum promised to take us kids to the pantomime, and then something happened, she couldn't take us. I don't know what it was, she didn't have the money I expect. You could sit up in the gallery then for sixpence. Poor old Mum – she took us later, but it didn't seem the same to me. I was too disappointed. I'd been thinking about that pantomime for weeks. You shouldn't build things up. You're always disappointed really. That's Archie's trouble. He always builds everything up. And it never turns out.

The Entertainer, 1957

Fulham Palace Road was the first identifiable landscape of my life. A lady to whom I was once married described me without humour or affection as a Welsh Fulham upstart. I must say that I didn't mind the description at all. For one thing, it seemed accurate enough even if meant unkindly.

Fulham in the 1930s was a dismal district. It sprawled roughly across an area, at least as far as my territory was concerned, from Hammersmith to Chelsea to Walham Green – as it was then called, it is now Fulham Broadway – to Putney Bridge at the other end. It was full of pubs, convents, second-hand clothes shops, bagwash laundries and pawnbrokers. Everything seemed very broken down.

I was born at Number 2 Crookham Road off the Dawes Road, which is between Lillie Road and Fulham Broadway. Even today, with the odd Italian restaurant and boutique, the area is gloomy and uninteresting. The boundaries of my earliest territory extended from Hammersmith Broadway with its clattering trams and drunken Irishmen to the Fulham Palace Road, a long road leading to Putney Bridge. On the left there is a huge cemetery (containing first my sister and then my father), a stonemason's scrapyard of broken tombstones and dead daffodils in milk bottles. It stretches as far as Fulham Broadway, where my mother would walk past my sister's grave on her way to pay the bill at the Gas, Light and Coke Company and my father took me to the old Granville Theatre or dropped in at Lyons for his favourite black coffee and brown bread and butter on the way to his regular visits to Brompton Hospital.

On the right of Fulham Palace Road is a succession of identical streets, Victorian terraced houses with strange little gnarled cigar stubs of trees lining the pavements. A most depressing red-brick church stands on the right and here, in Harbord Street, my mother's mother – Grandma Grove – lived for some forty years. When I last visited this street it was to go to a party given by a successful young actor. He had just moved into a house a few doors away from where my grandmother had lived for so many years. He is very like most of his neighbours who now live in that resolutely unprepossessing area, backing as it does on to the Fulham Football Ground and Bishop's Park, which still has a little green Victorian bandstand. My mother, living apart from my father, and I lodged in a succession of digs in some seven or eight streets by the Fulham bank of the Thames: Harbord Street, Finlay Street, Ellerby Street, Donerail Street. She was always moving because the house was 'a dead-and-alive hole', and she would inevitably have had a row with the landlady.

The actor's house was just round the corner from my first school, Finlay Road Infants, where, as was my experience at every new school, I was casually beaten up in the playground on the first day. The actor had paid £15,000 for it. My grandmother paid eight shillings a week rent. She had no bathroom. The corridor from the front door into the kitchen was cold and gloomy and covered in a very metallic claret and gold linoleum. I could just make out the inscription on the wall of an illuminated address presented to my grandfather: 'To William Crawford Grove with All Best wishes and Gratitude from all His Customers at the Marquis of Granby, Peckham Rye.' The front parlour was even less inviting, looking on to Harbord Street with the blank walls of the Football Ground visible at the far end and tall cranes from the barges stooping over them like iron giraffes. Sometimes, when I was staying there, I would have to sleep in this alarming room with its musty smell of a disused sanctuary for small animals. On the wall above the mantelpiece was a picture of my grandfather's Uncle Arthur. It looked rather like a Gothic Spy cartoon. He was regarded with great respect by the family and was said to be a director of Abdulla cigarettes.

My grandfather's background was fairly misty, like the rest. He claimed that he and his brother had gone to Dulwich College. Whether it was true or not I don't know. My grandmother might or might not have told me. Below Uncle Arthur's picture was a gilt ornamental clock in a glass case and, beside this, photographs of soldiers with fierce moustaches, relatives too, possibly. There were lace mats everywhere, an aspidistra in the window, which was shrouded with heavy lace curtains keeping out what little light ever filtered in from the cold length of Harbord Street. The dining-room was a different matter. Although it was shrouded in the same curtains, it hardly mattered as there was no light to come through from the view of the wall of the house next door and electricity burned all the winter and summer. The table in the centre was cheerfully lit with a low red-tasselled lamp, the chairs were old and comfortable, particularly my grandfather's which no one else ventured to sit in. The gas fire, with its saucer of water set before it, burned almost continuously, drinking innumerable shillings and coppers fed into it from a most imposing gas meter sited on the top of a cupboard. My grandmother, who was a tiny woman, fed this god by perching on a chair like a watchful acolyte. My grandfather would never have got up to do it, even if it went out when he was alone in the house. The scullery was a grey-green brown, the sort of thing one might associate with a Victorian mortuary. There was a bare table and, of course, a gas stove. The room was almost empty and scrubbed clean.

Grandma Grove's past was shadowy, too. Her maiden name was Ell. Her relatives were referred to somewhat contemptuously as the Tottenham Crowd. It was hinted – as everything was *hinted* – that old Mr Ell was a Wesleyan minister. But, in the face of such theological vagueness and innuendo, it was impossible to establish anything beyond approximate truth about these matters. The Tottenham Crowd, or some of them, lived beside the fire station in a row of villas long since demolished. They were dominated by my grandmother's eldest sister, Auntie Min. She was a very gloomy woman who appeared to spend much of her time collecting milk bottles, putting out milk bottles and complaining about the milkman. Her husband, Uncle Harry, was retired and had been a stoker in the Royal Navy. He said very little but was friendly enough, encouraging me to talk to his ferocious cockatoo. Then there was Grandma Ell, my great-grandmother, who was extremely old, something like a hundred. My mother's family seem to achieve great age. My grandmother lived to be 103 and my own mother seems appropriately hell bent on a similar score.

Before my great-grandmother's funeral, her coffin was placed in the middle of a table on trestles in the front parlour. On another table were the funeral baked meats of ham salad and sandwiches. One of her sons, Uncle Lod, was an undertaker. He was very tall, thin, taciturn and had a reputation for getting wildly drunk at the weekends and becoming involved in

fights. It was he, I think, who lifted me up – I was four or five at the time –
to look into the coffin where my great-grandmother lay in what seemed
unthinkable luxury. Then there was Auntie Rose, who had the reputation of
being some sort of ill-used beauty, but was very sullen and not very beautiful. She, too, had a husband who said very little, just like Uncle Harry.
There was Uncle Henry, who, as far as I could make out, was Auntie Rose's
father. The same story about him was repeated to me like all my family's
anecdotes, and my mother's in particular, endlessly. It seemed that he was a
well-known musician in Tottenham and played the piano with such loudly
proclaimed feeling that crowds used to assemble outside his house to hear
him. In the evenings, policemen had to be called to disperse them. He was
said to have been one of the resident conductors at the Crystal Palace. His
story, which made clear that he was a mysteriously unhappy man, was that
one evening his wife asked him if he would deliver the children's shoes to be
mended on his way to the Crystal Palace. He took them with him and they
were later found on the line of the tube station. Uncle Henry had thrown
himself in front of the train. No one ever questioned why he should have
committed suicide in this way. The legend was enough.

Auntie Winnie, another of my grandmother's sisters, lived and worked all
her life in a north London hospital. She was friendlier than any of them and
I can remember her always sitting with a glass of stout or port. Most of
them did. She called everyone 'mate', men and women. I don't know why it
struck me as odd. She had very little hair and never married. Her affectionate nature didn't seem to be returned by her sisters who dismissed her with,
'Poor old Auntie Winn, she'll never leave that place.' No one made any
effort to see that she might. They were all pushy in their way, tolerating one
another peevishly rather than having any actual exchange of feelings. If one
of them died, fell ill or short of money it was something to be talked about
rather than experienced in common. It was as if they felt obliged to live
within the literal confines of their emotional circumstances. The outlet for
friendship or conviviality was narrow in spite of the drunken commiser-
ation, endless ports and pints of beer and gin and Its. This may in part
explain my mother's stillborn spontaneity and consistent calculation that
affection had only to be bought or repaid in the commonest coinage. 'He
doesn't owe you anything', or 'You don't owe him anything.' 'What's she
ever done for you?' These were the entries that cooked the emotional and
filial books. They were chill words, flaunting their loveless, inexorable
impotence.

My grandfather would talk at great length and vehemently about Oscar

Wilde and Lord Alfred Douglas without ever revealing to me what the whole affair was really about. For some reason, Lord Alfred Douglas seemed to escape censure. Possibly being a lord helped. In this obsession, my grandfather was of course a stock figure of the time. There was a similar scandal involving the Duke of Clarence and messenger boys which also intrigued him. In my father's family identical waxen figures were brought out and maintained unchallenged by mere curiosity, to be left intact in the common memory, sometimes not much more than names – like the Princes in the Tower, or Auntie Margery; like the Lady of Shalott, or Uncle Ted; like Horatio Bottomley, or Lord Alfred Douglas. They were all, public and private, creatures of personal legend.

In Harbord Street people were nailed to the edges of public events. For example, my grandmother had some knowing significance contained in the fact that she had been a waitress at the Franco–British Exhibition. It fixed her into a place in history rather as one marks out one's life in terms of Coronations or Royal Weddings or Churchill's Funeral or moments of national ritual. Perhaps most people check their private memories against such occasions just as I tally my daily life with the dates of plays I have had produced. I know, for example, a little of what I was doing in 1961 because *Luther* was produced in that year. Events match themselves.

> She is a tough, sly old Cockney, with a harsh, often cruel wit, who knows how to beat the bailiffs and the money-lenders which my grandfather managed to bring on to her. Almost every working day of her life, she has got up at five o'clock to go out to work, to walk down what has always seemed to me to be the most hideous and coldest street in London. Sometimes when I have walked with her, all young bones and shiver, she has grinned at me, her face blue with what I thought was cold. 'I never mind the cold – I like the wind in my face.' She'd put her head down, hold on to her hat and *push*.
>
> *They Call it Cricket* ('Declaration'), 1957

As a result of this, as I thought flattering description of Grandma Grove, some of her family threatened to sue me on the grounds of libel. An extract had been published in some Sunday newspaper like the *People* and did perhaps appear patronizing. In her early sixties she was very small and very round-shouldered, which made her little more than about five feet tall. Her movements were quick, unlike Grandma Osborne who was tall, straight-backed and moved slowly and with schoolmarm precision. Like both her sisters, and, indeed the rest of the Tottenham Crowd, she was dressed at that time during the thirties almost exactly as she must have been thirty years before: her straw hats, the flowers, her wispy hair long and resting up above her head, the very long skirts almost to the ankle, and the boots, the smell of lavender water and moth balls, a brooch at the high neck collar – all these were Edwardian, which I accepted as part of her character.

She was born Adelina Rowena Ell. At eighteen she married my grandfather who was nineteen, and they quickly had two children. The first, my aunt, Queenie Phoebe Adelina Rowena Grove. Then, eighteen months later, my mother Nellie Beatrice. There were hints of deaths in childbirth which I indeed believe were true and talk of puerperal fever, or 'prooperal', as they called it. Eight years later my Uncle Jack – John Henry – was born. My grandfather, as young William Crawford Grove, was said to be the Smartest Publican in London, becoming manager at an early age of a pub in Duncannon Street, alongside St Martin-in-the-Fields. The name of the pub was simply the Duncannon and it is still there, a rather anonymous fluorescent place clearly quite unlike the fashionable hostelry it had been during my grandparents' tenure. It was frequented by theatrical folk a good deal, including Marie Lloyd. A central part of the folklore of this period of their life was that my grandmother, pregnant with my mother, came down the stairs of the Duncannon one morning to find Miss Lloyd reeling around the sawdust-covered bar swearing and shouting. My grandmother drew herself up and ordered the doorman to escort Miss Lloyd out and hail her a hansom cab. Whereupon, the story continued, Miss Lloyd screamed up the stairs at the young mother-to-be, 'Don't you fucking well talk to me! I've just left your old man after a weekend in Brighton!' I don't know whether this part of the Ballad of Grandma is true, but it has an encouraging ring of tinsel fact about it. Anyway, it makes a nice family tableau, and is also the only recorded link I have with anything to do with the theatrical profession.

Profligacy seems to have been a strong characteristic with both my grandfathers, although Grandpa Grove was a far stronger, flamboyant personality than Grandpa Osborne, who lost the jeweller's shop entrusted to him by his mother because he 'Played cricket all day' when he 'Should have been in the shop'. When I knew him he had retreated into the role of unpaid family retainer, gardener and odd-job man, despised openly by his family for not getting work, and doing menial tasks about the house, like packing his daughter's trunks for her trips to Africa. He was goaded into perfunctory trips to the Labour Exchange but his heart was never in it. Hurt, I am sure he was. Grandpa Grove would never have been hurt. No one would have dared to jeer at him in the first place.

When I first knew her, Grandma Grove worked as an office cleaner in the main office of Woolworth's, which was then in Cork Street. She had become head cleaner after a few years and was in command of some thirty or forty women, her 'girls' as she called them. I don't think she did a great deal of actual cleaning herself, but acted as a sort of motherly sergeant major, reserving the top directors' offices with their flaming turkey carpets and heavy furniture for herself. She held this lob until shortly after the war, often walking to work in the early hours of the morning when the Blitz had been particularly fierce, threading her way through rubble and glass, almost like a cartoonist's Cockney: 'We can take it!' Sometimes she took me up to Cork Street and I would sit in the staff room with its faded rattan chairs, surrounded by her admiring 'girls', who would feed me on all kinds of cakes, buns and sweets. They also gave me money, from pennies to threepenny bits and sixpences. By the end of the day my reward was considerable. Why they gave it to me was mysterious. They all had kids of their own. I must have been a mascot or something. Anyway, I was pleased if unsurprised.

This friendly, rather cloying treatment from young women as well as middle-aged ones, may have been partly due to the way that my mother insisted on dressing me for such public occasions. My uniform consisted of a suit, silk in summer or some kind of artificial silk which was extremely uncomfortable and seemed to be perpetually wet, and in a self-proclaiming bright colour like pink, yellow, or what my mother insisted on calling 'lemon'. All ensembles like this, including her own, she declared to be 'rig-outs'. She planned them down to the last detail, going through phases of passionate attachment to certain colours or materials. She would have, for example, a coral and nigger-brown period, or a blue and lemon period. Everything matched inexorably. There was one period of tan mania. The seven ages of tan. 'I'm going to get myself a tan hat, tan shoes, tan handbag' – tan *everything*.

The snooking badge of bohemianism in my own rig-out was the black beret that she insisted on my wearing. This had originally been a practical innovation when I had a mastoid operation and my head was almost entirely shaved. The beret did indeed cover up what she called 'my unslightly head'. She regarded almost everything about me as irredeemably unsightly, bald or not. However, the beret did attract attention, and it appealed slightly to my early rather coarse, dandyish instincts. I may have consciously cultivated what I thought of as a kind of quiet, serious-looking charm. A lot of people must have seen through it as a mere fawning wish to impress. I always wanted to get on with adults, to have access to the mysteries and excitements of their lives, which held out so much more promise than that of children of my own age. There was no cachet in youth at that time. One was merely a failed adult. I sought out the company of people like my grandparents and great-aunts and -uncles; they were infinitely more interesting. And I was an eager and attentive listener.

> Billy Rice is a spruce man in his seventies. He has great physical pride, the result of a life-time of being admired as a 'fine figure of a man'. He is slim, upright, athletic. He glows with scrubbed well-being. His hair is just grey, thick and silky from its vigorous daily brush. His clothes are probably twenty-five years old – including his pointed patent leather shoes – but well-pressed and smart. His watch chain gleams, his collar is fixed with a tie-pin beneath the tightly knotted black tie, his brown homburg is worn at a very slight angle. When he speaks it is with a dignified Edwardian diction – a kind of repudiation of both Oxford and Cockney that still rhymes 'cross' with 'force', and yet manages to avoid being exactly upper-class or effete. Indeed, it is not an accent of class but of period. One does not hear it often now.
>
> *The Entertainer*, 1957

Indeed, one does not. This description (I used to shower my scripts with irrelevant stage directions; *Look Back in Anger* is full of them) is a part-portrait of my grandfather.

BILLY: We all had our own style, our own songs – and we were all English. What's more, we spoke English. It was different. We all knew what the rules were. We knew what the rules were, and even if we spent half our time making people laugh at 'em we never seriously suggested that anyone should break them. A real pro is a real man, all he needs is an old backcloth behind him and he can hold them on his own for half an hour. He's like the general run of people, only he's a lot more like them than they are themselves, if you understand me.

> *The Entertainer*, 1957

Grandpa Grove certainly had his own style, but unlike Billy Rice he could not be regarded as having been a star, except in a very small way at the height of his career as a publican, when there were hansom cabs, cigars and his famous breakfast which was said to have consisted of half a bottle of 3-star brandy, a pound of porterhouse steak, oysters in season and a couple of chorus girls all year round.

Under the mantelshelf in Harbord Street there was one of those fringe-like curtain arrangements which failed to conceal his trusses, or 'trusts' as my mother called them, which I would gaze at while he talked about Henry Irving in *The Bells* and bawled various bits of the Old Testament at me. He was always dressed, apart from a well-worn cardigan, as if ready to go out at any moment. His patent shoes, cleaned by my grandmother, gleamed as did his hair and watch chain. He would sit toying with his sovereign case or buffing his carefully attended finger nails. He was the only man I met until I was in my late teens who habitually used a cigarette holder, usually containing Abdulla Egyptian cigarettes, doubtless cadged from Uncle Arthur.

He was most impressive, and convincing, in the way he would roll out names: names of stars as if they were either personal friends or members of his club – which he said was the National Sporting Club – Sir Edward Carson or Rufus Isaacs. Like so many people at that time he took as much interest in law-court proceedings as people do nowadays in football or pop singers and indeed the success charts of lawyers were followed in awe by the British public. It was not a matey, familiar business but a show laid on for the common people by their superiors and masters. His account of Carson's cross-examination of Oscar Wilde was one of his specialities. So it was, too, with King Edward, admired for his flash friends and racehorses and, later, the next Prince of Wales, once admired and then to be reviled after his disgrace with Mrs Simpson. There was constant invocation of the Lord Chief Justice, almost greater than God in his infinite wisdom and power; the Aga Khan ('Mum always likes me to put a shilling on the Black Man's horses'). Lord Beaverbrook was a particular favourite because Grandpa had seen him once emerging from his Rolls Royce: 'One of the finest men in England today.' He seemed to know everything about him. 'When I was with Beaverbrook during that time . . .' he would say. He had worked as a canvasser in the north of England for the *Daily Express*, a miserable commission job which only the most desperate unemployed took on. Flushed with port and excitement, I would listen as he told me that he would live to see the day when one of two things would happen: one, I would be the Prime Minister of England; or, two, I would be the next George Bernard Shaw. His reverence for Shaw was almost as extreme as his hostility to Gandhi. As he disagreed grandiloquently with almost everything that Shaw ever uttered on any subject, except the benevolence of dictatorships, this was confusing.

When we visited the Groves the rest of the family would be literally yelling news to each other. My grandmother would come in and out of the kitchen, picking exactly the wrong moment to interrupt my grandfather. I would be the only one listening to him, but then I was the only one who seemed to listen to anybody. They didn't talk to each other so much as barrack themselves. He would yell some humiliation or, if she were sitting near enough, kick her, imperceptibly but expertly, under the table. He was most adroit at this. Beside him on the dark red tablecloth would be the Bible, the *News of the World* and the *People*, the *Empire News* and, in later years, the *Watch Tower*. He would read from these aloud and everyone was expected to listen. 'Now, hold your bloody noise while I'm talking and put the wood in th'ole.' He had an obsession with draughts and none of the windows was ever allowed to be opened. The gas fire was on summer and winter and often it was quite difficult to breathe through the haze of Abdulla, as he boomed his police-court rhetoric, invariably berating some Draconian judge for not giving a severe enough sentence, especially in cases concerned with sex. 'Bloody rogue, dirty bastard, rogue! Fourteen years! Men like that should be hanged. Worse!' Worse than hanging was God's word to Grandpa in such matters.

When I was dismissed from his presence or he was bored or tired, I would follow my grandmother into the tiny scullery and get a slice of 'dinner' (called 'chaw'; she was particularly good at dishes like braised heart, stewed eel and faggots). There would then be a lot of winking and whispering. 'Dirty old bugger,' she'd say. 'I don't like to think what *he'd* get. Do you know he has women in here every day when I'm at work? At *his* age.' He was then about seventy and was constantly seeking out and finding the rent money, insurance money or gas money that my grandmother had hidden away, to spend on taking one of his 'women' out for stout and oysters at the Clarendon in Hammersmith. Grandma Grove was ingenious in the way she discovered the addresses of these ladies and took a great deal of pleasure in hunting them down to their various houses. They all called themselves Mrs Grove when she confronted them at the door. I don't think any of them lasted for very long. She was understandably keen on recounting her triumph over Marie Lloyd and of casting her into the outer darkness of Duncannon Street. 'Of course, *he* doesn't know *we* know about it,' eased the pain in her shin bone. Happy recrimination and ill-feeling were never very far below the surface.

Religion was rather baffling. Auntie Queenie was very High Church, my father professed sickly atheism, and my mother never went to church at all. I was rather mystified by the meaning of all this, but it appeared to be something very exclusive and beyond the grasp of most. It was my mother who was the main antagonist in these matters, particularly during the brawls of Christmas, when she reacted fiercely to Auntie Queenie's over-heated and sentimental religiosity. Queenie assumed a royal, wounded aspect when these periodic fits came upon her. Even at that age I sensed that it was a very bogus performance indeed. In her most gushing periods of zealous charity she would use theatrical convent language, calling everyone, people like bus conductors and shop assistants, 'Dearest Heart', in the way that some priests matily invoke the Sacred Heart of Jesus.

Certainly, Auntie Queenie never felt any pernickity Anglican constraint. Over her bed there hung not only a large cream-coloured crucifix but an even more prominent figure of the Virgin Mary. Also beside her bed was a white Common Prayer Book. Whether she used another one for her visits to church I don't know, but it was certainly new and unthumbed-looking. The basis of her belief seemed to consist of what she believed to be her capacity for more suffering than others and, in particular, the coarser members of her family. She had been brought up by a doting aunt and this apparently contributed to her feeling herself well above what should have been her natural station of Harbord Street. My mother was particularly resentful at this show of swank travail. The two of them would match suffering for suffering, pain for pain, blow for blow, strolling down separate memory lanes on to rival vales of tears. My mother pointed out that her sister's privations were nothing compared with her own. *She* had none of the advantages of being educated properly but of going out to work at the age of twelve to scrub a dining-room floor for six hundred orphans at the Found-ling Hospital. This was no doubt true, and certainly no one ever contra-dicted her. She, my mother, had by her own efforts become head cashier at the age of sixteen of Lyons Corner House in the Strand. Queenie, on the other hand, had been levered by her pious, protective Auntie Phoebe, into an undemanding ladylike job, first in a milliner's then as a draper's assistant, becoming under-buyer and then head buyer at D. H. Evans. It was a com-mon secret that she had been dismissed from this appointment when she was discovered taking home the firm's latest models and wearing them, not always temporarily it seemed. Later, at Peter Robinson's, she was similarly apprehended. She ended her career working in a small Jewish Madam shop in Richmond High Street. It was a cruel blow to her pride and most enjoy-able for my mother to visit her there, taking hours to make up her mind what she might buy from her sister, now that she was no more than a small-time head assistant.

Comfort in the discomfort of others was an abiding family recreation and my grandmother shared her barmaid daughter's satisfaction. After all, she too had come down in the world, relegated to head cleaner of Woolworth's from being Mistress of the Duncannon and the Hammer of the Marie Lloyds of this world. Coming Down in the World was something the Groves had in common with the Osbornes, except that the Groves seemed to feel less sense of grievance, looking on it as the justified price of profligate living or getting above yourself, rather than as a cruel trick of destiny or a creeping army of upstarts Getting the Better of their Betters. Still, getting above yourself is a hazard open to many of us still and can be chastening. 'But there's no pride in Real Gentry – that's what I always say.' And they always did. They had a litany of elliptical sayings, almost biblical in their complexity, which, to the meanest mind or intelligence, combined accessibility and authority. Revealed family wisdom was expressed in sayings like, 'One door opens and another one always shuts' (the optimistic version – rare – was the same in reverse). 'I think I can say I've had my share of sorrows.' Like Jesus, they were all acquainted with grief. 'I can always read him like a book'; 'I've never owed anyone anything' (almost the Family Motto this); 'You can't get round him, he's like a Jew and his cash box'; 'Look at him, like Lockhart's elephant.' This meant someone was being inordinately clumsy, and apparently referred to a popular large bun that was sold in an establishment called Lockhart's in the Strand, long since disappeared and forgotten even then.

There were lots of references to Jews. One of my mother's favourites was, 'Listen to him, John Lawson's son. "Thank God, I'm only a Jew."' This was a reference to a very famous music-hall sketch called *Humanity*, performed by John Lawson at a time when, according to serious historians, music hall was well on the way down its pristine path to revue and 'variety'. My only link with this famous sketch was provided for me by my mother, whose memory was always definitively faulty. It was, according to her, about a highly reputable, rich and – it seemed – wholly virtuous Jew who struck up a full-hearted, passionate friendship with a Gentile who became his Best Friend. The wholesome Jew leaves home for some reason, the war perhaps, and his lovely wife in the care of Best Gentile Friend. Adultery, Close-Thing, but, most of all, Betrayal takes place before John Lawson reappears. My mother thought it good for a quick laugh to call me John Lawson's son – 'Only a Jew!' As she was anti-Semitic in the sense that she thought all foreigners were Jews, it was meant unflatteringly. But she described in detail the roof-rending scene in which the Good Jew Thrashed his Best Friend.

Quite apart from the horror of such untidy destruction, was the principal character – the Set. This, as she described it, consisted of a superb sitting-room, furnished in Taste-Beyond-Which. Which being mostly breakable – like ornate and irreplaceable chandeliers. Glass, blood, antiques, teeth, hair, tailoring all exploded everywhere. A ruined palace of a place, a disgraced wife, a treacherous friend, destroyed virtuous Jew. After the vicious fight between Gentile Snake and Jew, the virtuous one, bleeding in mouth, mud and spirit among all the despoil sang his song: 'Only a Jew'. Twenty years later it was this shaky fragment of theatrical memory that was to nudge me towards *The Entertainer*; not, as I was told authoritatively by others, the influence of Bertolt Brecht.

Sic: if one were looking for a word to describe the argot used generally by my mother's family and friends one might call it this; Sic – a self-conscious, disorderly babble, perhaps like Peter Brook's Orghast except that Sic is presumably more lucid and spontaneous. But only just. I grew up believing that there was a language one read in books and another one spoke, and that the divide between the two was impassable. I was in my early twenties before I realized that 'long' words could be inserted quite freely and natur-ally within ordinary conversation without remark or derisory comment. Talking expressively to strangers and more often intimates was perhaps the beginning of the long gritty road to addressing God Himself without hob-bling embarrassment.

Queenie or, as she preferred to be called, Queen shared a flat with a friend known to me as Auntie Caddie, although her name was in fact May. Why she was called Caddie I have no idea. Perhaps it was something to do with golf as there seemed to be numerous snapshots of them together in what were then called sporting clothes. Auntie Caddie looked born to wear plus fours. She even referred to herself as a John Blunt woman ('person' hadn't occurred to her), and although most people poked fun at her, very few of them did so to her face. She always wore a tweedy suit or, rather, a 'cos-tume', with a high collar and beefily knotted tie. She also wore Henry Heath hats which carried some authority in the name alone.

Anyway, Auntie Caddie would stand with her legs wide apart, her plump hands behind her back and boom questions at me, usually about why I wasn't at school. This was a hard one to answer and one repeatedly asked by probing adults. My mother for years kept me away from school as often as she dared on the pretext of my poor health; in reality, it was because she was bored with being on her own and needed even my childish company. Caddie and Queenie shared a Key Flat in Blythe Road, a plaster Virgin above their double bed, an Airedale and, of all unfamiliar things to come, a white telephone. There was also an intimidating porter. On the other side of Blythe Road was Cadby Hall, which was the headquarters of J. Lyons and Co., as well as being their biggest teashop. My mother and I used to have tea there before having to face the porter and Auntie Caddie. These visits were always uneasy and overpowered by the magnificence of Lyons Biggest Teashop, where I usually managed to faint, greatly to the annoyance of my mother.

These 'blooming fainting fits', as she called them, persisted for years. They nearly always seemed to happen in public places like cinemas or restaurants or where they would create the maximum of irritation and embarrassment for my mother. I was constantly taken into the offices of cinema managers after witnessing fairly innocent but distressful scenes on the screen. One, I remember, was a childbirth sequence in a film called *The Citadel*, starring one of my father's favourite actors, Robert Donat. The climax involved the doctor holding up the newly-born child and slapping it into life. The spectacle was too much for me. Blood seemed to drain out of me and in no time my head would be between my knees and I would be sipping water from a kindly usherette or, in the case of Cadby Hall, waitress, who was certainly more sympathetic than my mother.

It was not until I was about sixteen that I was to have much contact with Uncle Sidney. During these Fulham days he was not much more than one of the Smaller Players of the Grove Repertory Company. As always, what little information I had was by implication and elaborately vague. Auntie Queenie, Caddie and Uncle Sidney took numerous holidays in Sidmouth together, where they all dressed in tennis clothes, consisting of white trousers, blazers and white pleated skirts. I think little tennis was played but there was a great deal of dressing up and snapping away with the Box Brownie. Even to me they presented a rather bizarre trio. Auntie Caddie with her dark flecked Eton crop, striped blazer and carefully starched collar and tie. Uncle Sidney with his Silverkrin crinkled hair, large flannel bags and very sheepish expression. And, finally, my Auntie Queenie who looked remarkably like the carefully posed theatrical photographs of Ivor Novello, with the same thin, rather accusing mouth. The first time I saw Ivor Novello in his Tyrolean *unterhosen* he immediately made me think of Auntie Queenie. She, not surprisingly, thought he too was wonderful.

The general verdict on Uncle Sidney seemed to be that he was a pretty decent sort but a bit of a cissy boy. He had his own flat, which he shared with his friend John and which was furnished almost entirely by coupons they both collected from Carreras cigarettes. After about seven years of courtship, Queenie and Uncle Sidney were married. I was later to grow quite fond of Uncle Sidney and his letters in particular.

'*Dear John*, Do so hope you have a very nice Christmas. Gosh how I wish I was with you all. I just hate the thought of it, all alone. Just had the Coalman deliver, another Bill £5. 6s. Ah well why worry. It's a rotten day here, very dull and raining . . .

'*Dear John*, Queen seems about the same. Looks well in herself. They get her up for a while each day now, so that makes a break from Bed all the time . . .

'*Dear John*, A few lines in haste. Don't get much time for letters these days. Was home on Spring Holiday last week, but busy with spring cleaning the home. Gave it all a good clean, Curtains down in all rooms, Windows clean, fresh Curtains put up, Ceilings, Walls cleaned, and Furniture polished, Pictures and Ornaments washed . . .

'*Dear John*, Queen keeps about the same, looks well in herself, but leg no better. Grandma Grove is supposed to come with Jack today to see Queen. Of course his Lordship would not write me to ask the best way. Queen has been in hospital now 6 months and he has never written me a line . . .

'*Dear John*, Just been doing some washing, so shall have to Iron when its all dry. Going out after that to have a little Drink, just feel I need it. Begin to get a bit fed up at home with no one to talk to, and all the work . . .

'*Dear John*, I used to think Mother a dear ole soul, but now realize she is as bad as the rest. Don't want to see any of them anymore. Queen goes on about the same, but tries to be the big I am, and the Sisters and Nurses have not much time for her. I've had a rotten cold in my head. Have to go to the Dr. tonight 6 pm, as my ear is bad with Wax. Hope he can get it out, and not have to go to Hospital the same as last time to see an Ear Specialist. Been busy since I've been home. My Lunch to get, then washing for Queen and myself. Just going to have a Cup of tea, then the Dr and Ironing when I get back. I feel so fed up today with it all. Do hope you are well . . .

'*Dear John*, Sorry I did not write you as usual on Sunday, but I felt so tired. Queen seems to be getting on quite well with the Walking Aid. She looks so well in herself, but I have to be so very careful what I say, otherwise she takes things in the wrong way. I've just been busy in the front garden, now broke off for a little rest. Have the Back to do later. Such a lot turns up to do in Gardens . . .

'*Dear John*, Have washing on the line, must be dry now, so have that to Iron. Nightdress, Knickers etc from the Hospital. Do hope you are keeping well. I'm alright – except for a little tired, but must get the Ironing done . . .

'*Dear John*, I can manage alright, just a little tired at times . . .

'*Dear John*, We shall be thinking of you at Christmas Day and no doubt have a little drink to your health from the Bottle of Gin we bought with your kind remittance, say 12 O/c.

All my love,
Sidney   xxxxxxxx'

They were already self-parodies before they were popped in the box to me. I made a passable pastiche in *The Hotel in Amsterdam*, when they were singled out as being snobbish and anti-working class and apparently confirmed I did not know or understand my own background.

DAN: What are they?

LAURIE: Retired rotten, grafting publicans, shop assistants, ex-waitresses. They live on and on. Having hernias and arthritic hips and strokes. But they go on: writing poisonous letters to one another. Complaining and wheedling and paying off the same old scores with the same illiterate signs. 'Dear Laurie, thank you very kindly for the cheque. It was most welcome and I was able to get us one or two things we'd had to go without for quite some time, what with me having been off work all this time and the doctor sends me to the hospital twice a week. They tell me it's improving but I can't say I feel much improvement. How are you, old son? Old son? We saw your name in the paper about something you were doing the other day and the people next door said they thought you were on the telly one night but we didn't see it, and Rose won't buy the television papers so we always switch on to the same programme. Rose doesn't get any better, I'm afraid. I bought her a quarter bottle the other day with your kind remittance which served to buck her up a bit. Your Auntie Grace wrote and said she'd heard

Margaret was having another baby. That must be very nice for you both. We send our best wishes to you both and the other little ones. Hope you're all well. Must close now as I have to take down the front room curtains and wash them as Rose can't do it any longer, but you know what she is. Bung ho and all the very best. Excuse writing but my hand is still bad. Ever. Your Uncle Ted. P.S. Rose says Auntie Grace said something about a letter from your mother which she sent on but I'm afraid she sent it back unopened. She just refuses to pass any comment. She told me not to say any thing about it to you but I thought I'd just – *PASS IT ON TO YOU*!

(*He gestures towards them.*)

Pass that on!

                                        The Hotel in Amsterdam, 1968

My Uncle Jack, eight years younger than my mother, might occasionally drop in at Harbord Street bringing with him an unusual feeling of dash and optimism. He appeared to take little part in the continuing story of Harbord Street, distributing generous presents and always leaving early with his son, Peter, a huge amiable boy who became a successful steward on the *Queen Elizabeth*. He rarely brought his first wife, Auntie Vi, known because of her swarthy appearance as the 'Gypsy queen'. She made it quite clear that she didn't want to be mixed up in family 'squibbles'. Uncle Jack was what my mother called 'a bit woman mad'. He certainly seemed more cheerful and reassuring than either Auntie Queenie or Uncle Sidney, always bent on despondency and the theory that nothing good in this world, even if you should get it, ever lasted.

Nothing, indeed, is more revolting to English feelings, than the spectacle of a human being obtruding on our notice his moral ulcers or scars, and tearing away that 'decent drapery', which time, or indulgence to human frailty, may have drawn over them: accordingly, the greater part of *our* confessions (that is spontaneous and extra-judicial confessions) proceed from demireps, adventurers, or swindlers: and for any such acts of gratuitous self-humiliation from those who can be supposed in sympathy with the decent and self-respecting part of society, we must look to French literature, or to that part of the German, which is tainted with the spurious and defective sensibility of the French. And all this I feel so forcibly, and so nervously am I alive to reproach of this tendency, that I have for many months hesitated about the propriety of allowing this, or any part of my narrative, to come before the public eye, until after my death (when, for many reasons, the whole will be published): and it is not without an anxious review of the reasons for and against this step, that I have, at last, concluded on taking it.

Guilt and misery shrink, by a natural instinct, from public notice: they court privacy and solitude: and, even in their choice of a grave, will sometimes sequester themselves from the general population of the churchyard, as if declining to claim fellowship with the great family of man, and wishing (in the affecting language of Mr Wordsworth)
> – humbly to express
> A penitential loneliness.

Confessions of an English Opium Eater, Thomas de Quincey

According to my mother's shaky testimony she met my father when she was working as a barmaid in a pub called the Essex on the corner of Essex Street in the Strand: 'All the Press boys used to come in there.' Perhaps, to a young man recently up from South Wales, with no friends at work and only digs to go home to, the atmosphere of the Essex was comforting. Pubs are more than tolerable places in which to be lonely. My mother would throw bottles in the air, two bottles sometimes, catch them, throw up two more, catch them again, and pour off four bottles into four glasses at once with one hand. Soon he began talking to her about his work in the advertising agency, bringing in his drawings to show her, and they would go on to the all-night Lyons Corner House in the Strand, where she had worked as head cashier.

Living the first years of my life in Fulham meant mostly living with my mother. My parents saw little of each other. What had happened between them I have no way of knowing. My father, when he was not in Brompton Hospital or in Colindale Sanatorium, seemed to stay in digs a long way from us in Harrow or Hounslow on his own, and my mother would occasionally deliver a clean shirt and socks to his landlady. He would come over to see us when he was able and I have a vague remembrance of them hitting each other. They seldom took me out together. Apart from visits to the Shepherd's Bush Empire and walks in Bishop's Park and by the river, my father and I mostly visited pubs – the Spotted Horse in Putney High Street and the King's Head in Fulham Palace Road. Although he was frail (by this time he had only one lung), he enjoyed walking, saying very little. His own father was a great walker and taught him what was called the

Countryman-Tramp's Walk, which consisted of putting all your weight on your forward foot, rather like wearing a surgical boot, and enabled you to walk for thirty miles a day, as he said he often did, without any discomfort. I practised this strange gait for years, much to the amusement of passers-by and sometimes catch myself experimenting with it now on long walks.

But most of the days in Fulham were spent with my mother, forced into bored idleness by having to look after me, and biting her finger nails to stumps. Heaven knows what she was living on. I was either too young or too sickly to go to school to give her some respite, not that she wanted to be on her own. I did spend a short time at Finlay Road Infants and was given the cut eye on enrolment. I still have the scar. My mother walked, too, not because she liked it but because she had no other alternative. Willis Road, King Street and Hammersmith Broadway are hardly tourist attractions even forty years on, and her walks were aimless expeditions to escape from digs with nothing to do in them and no one to talk to, pushing a small boy up to Fulham Road for his regular check-up at Brompton Hospital, or 'shopping' with no money in Kensington High Street.

The Brompton Hospital visits would take all day, from about nine o'clock in the morning to the end of the afternoon. For days before we set out my mother stoked my apprehension by telling me what they had done to my father, who had been shown off to the students like the prize pig at Skipton Fair. 'If only this man had come to us before,' said the house surgeon. I could imagine those eyes on my father's white, marble-veined body. 'Of course, they're very kind and *good* to you,' my mother would say. They didn't seem particularly kind or good to me, frightening certainly. This feeling established itself the moment we entered the door and passed the porter who acted like a policeman. I felt I had been arrested and was there because of some unknown transgression. The overpowering smell of the place reinforced the sense that it was like no other. We sat on long, dark, refectory-like benches and prepared to wait for the rest of the day in this dim, bustling crypt.

'They're all Scotch and Irish in here.' The Sister, who usually took charge of me, was indeed Scots. She wore a dark blue uniform with white dots on it and was about the only friendly face I could ever make out. But even she would make me take off my shirt almost immediately on arrival and I would be forced to walk without dawdling around the monastic corridors to my various X-rays and tests, and return to our bench wearing only my shorts with my braces chafing my salt-cellar shoulders. We had nothing to eat all day, as my mother obviously thought that to bring sandwiches or something of the sort would have been a little like munching away during Evensong. She had a reverential, almost mystical attitude towards medicine, an attitude very common at the time, and believed, for example, that doctors, exclusively, were the people who drove their own motor cars. If we saw one in the street, she'd say, 'Oh, look, there's a car outside. Must be the doctor.'

Shivering, hungry, largely ignored for hours, it was a little like waiting for the jury's verdict to come in, and the last visit of the afternoon was rather like being arraigned before the judge. In this case it was always Dr Henderson, another Scot. She thumped away at my tinny, inadequate body impatiently. Would I be reprieved? How squalid had I really been? Had it shown up on the X-ray screen? Eventually, throwing me a barley sugar, she would sit and write her report. The barley sugar seemed to indicate that I was on parole and soon would be let outside into the grey, free air of the Fulham Road. My mother, doubtful and bewildered, would lead me off to the dispensary to the next inevitable wait. At last, like the prisoner having his watch, keys and money returned, I was allowed to put on my clothes and cover myself up from any further fear of accusation. My release was not complete until the final interview with the Lady Almoner. I did not mind this so much because by this time I knew that I had got my ticket, at least for the next three months. My mother was having to go through it now, only she had it with smiles and nods of understanding and all from a very posh lady in overalls.

Kensington High Street was the Appian Way to the West End. The border ended at Barker's store and we rarely ventured beyond it except for visits to Woolworth's in Cork Street, which was scarcely going Up West. Going Up West was something we didn't do until the later years of the war, when my mother was working full time and, with the aid of generous tips from GIs and Allied Servicemen, she was able to take me up with her on her days off. Up West in the 1940s was a very different affair from Kensington High Street in the thirties. For one thing, my mother seemed to have a great deal of money. The routine was almost always the same: lunch at the Trocadero, when she would complain about the menu being unintelligible and I struggled to explain with my inadequate French the concealed identity of the dishes. We invariably ended up having fish and chips. Her technique with waiters, as in life, was to either bully or fawn upon them. 'Oh, you really are very kind.' 'Oh yes, we *did* enjoy that very much. Very tasty. Really nutritious.' 'You *are* busy today, aren't you?' If this ladylike charm got no response from the waiter she would then resort to her usual domestic bad temper giving both the waiter and myself Black Looks. The waiter would be indifferent, or downright rude and unimpressed by my mother's current rig-out. If anything went wrong with the meal the blame was heaped upon me. The rest of her day off could be ruined almost at the outset in this way and if we could get through lunch without one of her Black Looks, when dark rivulets of rage and disappointment spread across her face, it was relief indeed. If I summoned up enough bravado I would sometimes – at the age of fifteen – order myself a cigar, choosing at random from the box ('That looks a nice one, dear'), looking around me as if my mother were not with me or even as if I were alone. Like Lyons Corner House, it seemed just the sort of place a gentleman would take a beautiful woman, but the Trocadero seemed unquestionably classier.

My mother's hair was very dark, occasionally hennaed. Her face was a floury dark mask, her eyes were an irritable brown, her ears small, so unlike her father's ('He's got Satan's ears, he has'), her nose surprisingly fine. Her remaining front teeth were large, yellow and strong. Her lips were a scarlet-black sliver covered in some sticky slime named Tahiti or Tattoo, which she bought with all her other make-up from Woolworth's. She wore it, or something like it, from the beginning of the First World War onwards. She had a cream base called Crème Simone, always covered up with a face powder called Tokalon, which she dabbed all over so that it almost showered off in little avalanches when she leant forward over her food. This was all topped off by a kind of knicker-bocker glory of rouge, which came in rather pretty little blue and white boxes – again from Woolworth's – and looked like a mixture of blackcurrant juice and brick dust. The final coup was an over-generous dab of California Poppy, known to schoolboys as 'fleur des dustbins'.

Tea Up West would be cream cakes at the Regent Palace, gin and It for my mother, and then on to The Show! Ivor Novello, *Dancing Years*, *Perchance to Dream*, *Lisbon Story*, all of the George Black shows at the Hippodrome. Vic Oliver was my mother's favourite comedian. She thought he was marvellous. It was during these Black shows that huge chorus girls came down into the stalls and invited members of the audience to dance with them. My cream cakes almost churned as I thought one of them might approach me. I was about thirteen when I saw a revival of an old twenties' musical comedy, *The Lilac Domino*. I was overwhelmed by the beauty of the girls in it, longing to be on stage with them and take every one of them in turn to dinner at the Trocadero. It was the night before I went back to school and on my return I discovered that my headmaster had also been in the audience. I felt passionately that he had no business to be prying on such a world; one in which, unlike me, he could not possibly have any place.

But before these affluent, wartime days, we would come up the stairs from the District Line and walk straight into Ponting's, a superb store which preserved its *Kipps'*-like draper's atmosphere for many years. Going next door into Derry and Toms was like stepping from one century into another. Here there were blue carpets, everything looked very modern, rather like Auntie Queen's flat, white telephones and the girls behind the counter were not only as lofty as the Lady Almoner but all seemed to be casting smiling, seductive glances at me, just like the ravishing giants at the Hippodrome in later years. Any one of these creatures would surely be quietly flattered to sit beside me at a discreet table at the Trocadero.

Glorious Ponting's, Derry and Toms and Barker's. We would walk around these stores, hardly venturing anywhere else for almost the whole day. We went through miles of departments, floor by floor, my mother unable to buy anything, saying little except to complain about her feet aching. Often I felt that my own legs were going to drop off, something I dreaded in case I were to faint from fatigue, which occasionally I did. This meant coming round in a public place and looking up at a clouded, furious face and an aggrieved silence all the way back to the District Line, without even the consolation of baked beans for tea at Lyons at the end of it.

My sister, Fay, had died of TB and meningitis when I was two. She was reckoned to be a starry personality. 'Like a little fairy on top of the Christmas Tree'. My father had managed to get her christened at St Martin-in-the-Fields by the Reverend Dick Sheppard, then a very popular star himself. She was spoken of as if she were some exquisite prodigy, but she exists to me only as a description of the last moments of her life, and my mother and father walking down the steps of Westminster Hospital afterwards with Big Ben chiming as they did so. This is really the only image I have of my sister at all. The remembrance was small, and later, as an adult, I often resented her wilful departure, leaving me alone to carry the burden of our mother. Perhaps she might have been some help and support, I thought. She was older, appeared to be beautiful and, from all unreliable accounts, affectionate. An ally, an affectionate one, and a woman, might have been helpful. Instead of making such a pious exit, so lovingly and medically described by Nellie Beatrice, so relished by Auntie Queenie, together we might have been an inseparable team on those aimless trips along the Appian Way to High Street, Kensington. There were no Black Looks in Heaven.

3. 'I Don't Want to End Up in a Dead-and-Alive Hole'

By 1936, my father's health had recovered enough for him to go back to his work as an advertising copywriter. Some kind of reconciliation must have been effected between my parents as they now set about living together under the same roof. We moved out of London, away from Fulham, the beginning of a change in things for all of us.

In the mid-1930s the Waterloo to Effingham Junction line fingered its way as so many others did into the Surrey countryside. Although it was still possible to keep sheep and cows in the East End during the Second World War it seemed to me that the railway led into an open, light and muted world without trams, with few buses – and those green instead of red. During the next ten years I grew to know almost every house and building and factory, the signs on them, the sheds in the back gardens, on the thirty-minute ride to our new house. Clapham Junction, home of Arding and Hobbs; Wimbledon with its stuffed St Bernard railway dog in his glass case on the platform (the grave gaze of this heroic animal made the change worthwhile); next, Raynes Park, with Carters Seed factory on the left, where my mother was later to work for a pittance during the early days of the war; Motspur Park, small factories and houses gathered round a pub, the Earl Beatty; then, Worcester Park, the village Neasden of its time. And Stoneleigh, where we came to live. The developers' fingers hesitated briefly before ploughing onwards, and paused to spread haphazard speculative tentacles. Beyond Stoneleigh were Ewell West and Epsom, a rather unappealing Victorian town being changed into a new, bright, brick-and-cement dormitory like others that became Reigate, Redhill, Leatherhead and Dorking. But beyond them lay the Downs; Effingham Junction nudged countryside which still had a few secrets left.

Stoneleigh itself was a station surrounded by groups of housing estates. Coming off the concrete railway bridge on either side were 'Shopping Parades'. In the middle was the Stoneleigh Hotel, which was not an hotel at all but a by-pass Tudor pub where my mother was to work throughout the war and for several years after. The Parades consisted of a small Wool-worth's, the dry cleaner's, newsagents and a twopenny library, butchers, florists and empty shops which had not yet been sold, gaps in the town-scape, corners which had not yet been built on, patches of fields and stubble between houses and shops. It was not Stockbroker's Tudor but Bankclerk's Tudor. The ribbons of streets were empty most of the day except for occasional women on their way to the Parades, pushing prams along the clean pavements with their grass verges, fresh as last week's graves.

Grandma Osborne had been settled into this Byzantium of pre-war mediocrity by my father's sister Nancy. Aunt Nancy reminded me of Sister Ethel in the *William* books. She was flattered, fawned upon, almost beati-fied. To me she seemed affected, rude, snobbish and vain. She complained constantly that my cousin Tony might pick up my cockney accent. She had married Uncle Harry, who worked for the Unilever Company in Lagos, Nigeria. This meant that she spent a year at a time with him there, this being the span then allotted to wives in the White Man's Grave. Someone had to look after cousin Tony, and the obvious person was my grandmother.

Grandma Osborne's house was at the end of Clandon Close, a long cul-de-sac of pebble-dash counter clerk's Tudor with a back garden leading on to a large field encircled by exactly similar houses. At this time, houses in places like Stoneleigh cost something in the region of £300 to £600 to buy, but many were rented. My mother was insistent that we should not enter into buying because she didn't want to be 'tied down'. Thirty or forty times during the first seventeen years of my life we wrapped up dozens of china dogs and picture-hatted ladies with straining borzois – bought or won from fairgrounds like Dreamland in Margate – to move into another house or new digs until her snarling, raw-nailed boredom and dissatisfaction exploded again, driving her to make a dash for another lair. 'I'm fed up with this dead-and-alive hole.'

It was a just description of Stoneleigh and all other places like it. How-ever, to a seven-year-old boy it could hold out promises of freedoms and discoveries that were not to be found in the streets of Fulham. Following the elder Osborne's exodus from South Wales, my parents moved into Number 68 Stoneleigh Park Road. What decided my father to forsake London, which he enjoyed as a true provincial, revelling in its variety and its mysteries and vastness, for the rolling acres of suburbia, upon which no countenance divine or otherwise would have shone, in ancient or any other time? His mother would certainly never have encouraged him to feel his proximity would give her any pleasure. She was incapable of communicating such a thing and to her son above all. Filial guilt must have been uppermost, or perhaps the inner and physical fatigue that had led him to his healthless marriage.

Number 68 was half way down a very steep hill leading from the station. It must have been a patch of miniature downland before the concrete blotted it out a few years before. The descent on a bicycle from the top was thrilling. To hurtle down the switchback length of Stoneleigh Park Road without applying the brakes until it flattened out into the Ewell by-pass at the far end was heart-stopping. The chances of an accident were unlikely as cars were rare, vans few and the only regular traffic was the horse-drawn United Dairies cart or the Walls Ice Cream man on his bin bicycle. The house was similar to my grandparents' in Clandon Close but brighter and more airy, more toy box than Tudor. Instead of burnt oak there was an unlovely stab at modernity with black and cream for the almost uncarpentered woodwork and the staircase. Cream, not white, like Queen's crucifix. Cream was sophistication, like coloured telephones, telephones at all, as lemon to yellow. It had been, as my mother pointed out, a Show House, and some sales talk had been slapped on to the nasty edifice to make it look as though it had just been uprooted from the Ideal Home Exhibition. The estate agent had rubbed his hands and the dream descended. I liked the show house, and I hoped my mother's patience would hold out longer than usual this time. My father was now working regularly and seemed in better health and they appeared friendly to one another. Rows and silences were fewer.

Nellie Beatrice spent an inordinate time cleaning and polishing what was quite a small house for three people who didn't and were not allowed to create the merest untidiness. She had no reason to complain for my father was almost spinsterish in this respect, but every Friday was Black Friday for me, the day when we had what was called the Spring Clean. Sheets were draped over the furniture and chairs were piled on tables. Mattresses would be ripped from their beds, curtains taken down, washed and ironed. In the winter, when it was not possible to go outside, the Black Look clouding over the billowing dust bag of the Hoover was inescapable as it thrust its way into every corner, every bed or cupboard, bellowing and bullying a filthy uncomprehending world for hours. Handing over the Hoover to my mother was like distributing highly sophisticated nuclear weapons to an underdeveloped African nation. By the early evening she would be almost babbling with fatigue. A breathless interval at midday allowed us to bolt down an egg on mashed potatoes, frenziedly washed up so that she could 'get on' for the rest of the afternoon and a final burst to clear the field of this spotless battle and return everything to its gleaming, dustless place, raped by Mansion Polish and elbow grease, before my father returned home from work.

He soon came to prefer spending Friday evening in my grandmother's Fulham scullery rather than listen to my mother gibbering with irritability, as she shuddered with her life's bad back to prepare his evening meal. This fractious, jangling, indomitably Hoovered world was not a welcoming one. He always brought back a half-pound box of Terry's plain Brazil nut chocolates but it hardly placated her. No reward or show of gratitude would recognize her effort sufficiently. Besides, her attitude was that presents are given only either to buy affection or to make it clear that you are unbeholden. In this way you could alone face the world and say, 'I don't owe anyone anything.' So, if he hadn't decided to avoid coming home by drinking port with Grandma Grove at the Clarendon in Hammersmith, or with the 'Press boys' in Fleet Street, he would return back to all this with *Mickey Mouse, Rover, Hotspur*, the *Gem* for me and, after supper, and doubtless full of Waterloo buffet whisky, Guinness or Moussec, would sit down at the upright piano and sing. His piano playing was self-taught. He had a very pleasant light voice and would sing a few hymns, and songs like 'There's an Old-Fashioned House in an Old-Fashioned Street', 'It's My Mother's Birthday Today', 'Friend o'Mine', 'On the Road to Mandalay', 'On the Isle of Capri', 'Red Sails in the Sunset', Layton and Johnstone favourites, as well as a large repertory of music-hall songs: Harry Champion, George Robey, George Formby even, Paul Robeson, Peter Dawson, Melville Gideon, Jessie Matthews, Richard Tauber, Arthur Tracey – the Street Singer, who would have been smartly turned away from the forecourt of the Stoneleigh Hotel.

On Sunday mornings, braced by a visit to the Stoneleigh Hotel, he would take me around to Clandon Close. This weekly visit to his mother was something he dreaded and it was not difficult to see why. Her dismissive skill was subtle and brutal; sometimes no more than a thin smile, a watery upward look or an amused intake of breath, a scanning cauterizing instrument which rendered any endeavour puny or extravagantly indulgent. Her son was her prize victim.

There was one incident which she resurrected constantly with controlled, unabating bitterness. In the course of the Sunday lunchtime catechism of his present employment, preferably, or unemployment, his health and myself, she always struck back to her true course – Money. In particular, the money he, as a child, had cost his parents through wilful ill-health and some kind of applied original sin. The high point of this bitter retrospect was the South African Incident. She would take as her cue something like a glance at my new overcoat or pair of shoes, and say to him, 'Of course, when you had that trip to South Africa it cost your father and me a great deal of money . . . a great deal.' When he was about twelve my father had won the first prize in a drawing competition sponsored by the *Daily Mail*, a small sum of money and a round trip by boat to Cape Town. The prize was regarded as an outlandish and impractical one for him to accept because of his frailty and chronic asthma. Eventually and reluctantly he was allowed to board the steamer bound for Cape Town. A few days out in the Bay of Biscay he suffered a violent attack of asthma and was sent ashore to a hospital in Lisbon for some weeks before being shipped home with the bill of several hundred pounds. It was a mishap he was never allowed to forget. The account of the family borrowings and scrapings inflicted by his unhappy prize was repeated to him until he died and still recalled afterwards. Like a mark of inner folly the prize caught up with him in death, as she always knew it would. I never heard her say a kindly word to him or of him. When both her children died, both in their thirties, she spoke only of the bitter injustice of her daughter's early death.

If the pebble-dash house in Clandon Close was not exactly a dead-and-alive hole there was little activity inside or around it. It led nowhere, a terminus of semi-detached inertia. The houses in and around were a uniform standard, scattered in their ribbon millions all over England between the wars. There were occasional attempts at exotic variations such as extra bow windows in odd places or patio-type entrances which seemed to be useful for nothing but umbrellas. Bungalows, with concrete front gardens, had a sort of jaunty independence, inhabited by a somewhat younger set, often without children. My grandmother's house was not typical because it was the type itself. The hall was a small, unusable area flanked on one side by a tiny lavatory and bathroom and on the right side by a room which was usually called, for some reason, the Playroom. In most houses it was used as a cloakroom or for storing old toys and golf clubs. A few self-important husbands might even call it the Study or the Den, but there would be few books there, just *News Chronicle* give-away editions of Charles Dickens or the Waverley novels gathering dust behind the golf clubs.

Novels were read in other rooms, borrowed from the twopenny library in the Parade. Biographies of statesmen or soldiers came from the public library. Few letters were written except at Christmas and Easter, few dens contained a desk. Letter writing was a practice which was foreign to the people who lived here. They were immune or indifferent to contact, past or present, as if they came from nowhere and wanted to keep it that way. Routine was Stoneleigh's altar, its liturgy Radio Normandy, its mother's milk a nice quiet hot drink as usual after yet another nice quiet evening. Casual entertaining or informal hospitality were like tolerating a smell on the landing or a blocked-up sink. Conviviality seldom went beyond planned visits from relatives. Whim or sudden impulse was unthinkable and blasphemed against the very idea of the God Routine. The litany read: 'I just have to have my routine. If I don't have my routine I don't know where I am,' or 'Well, before we start anything we've got to work out a routine.' I think Routine. Therefore I am Routine.

Spontaneity was bad breath to them. Certainly Grandma Osborne's conviction of her son's wanton instability would only have been confirmed if she had seen my maternal grandmother sitting long into the night with my father, my grandfather swearing over the *Watch Tower* and the *News of the World*, eating eel pie and faggots, drinking port and Guinness, disregarding time, health and tomorrow. What little social contact took place in Stoneleigh was mostly on the station platform and from the high-fenced back gardens on summer Sundays, when the air was broken in the early afternoon by repeated cries of 'Come on, it's getting cold; it's on the *table*', as if some sick or dying patient needed attention or the kiss of life. The few telephones, always beside the front door next to the coatstand in the hall, like an unwanted ornament or vacuum cleaner, can seldom have been used for idle conversation. Sited by the coldest draught with nowhere to sit, it was an instrument for discouraging communication, forbidding it in the interest of frugality of pocket and spirit, only to be used in the reporting of sickness, disaster or death.

Apart from the offensive notion of outside interferences like casual friendly visits, there was a similar attitude to religion which was looked upon largely as an intrusion from outside, better kept out of the house, like a muddy dog which would mark the furniture with its paws. The nearest church was up in the shopping parade by the railway station and the Stoneleigh Hotel. I can't remember what denomination it was but it looked like a steepled garage, less assured than the Great West Road factory Papist style, so it was probably Non-Conformist, a religion more suited to Stoneleigh, itself no place for Sunday drunkenness and large families. I had no contact with church at all until we went to live in Ewell Village, which had a reasonably ancient parish church where I became a choir member for a short time, purely for venal reasons. We were paid one and sixpence a week, plus funeral and wedding fees.

Although Grandma Grove had been brought up as a Wesleyan by her minister father, she had given her daughter no religious instruction at all and never went near a church herself. 'We worked too hard to go to church.' As for the Christmas disputations between my mother and her sister, these were conducted on the Cavalier–Roundhead level of hypocrites versus the really good guys. My grandfather's religiosity was held to stem entirely from getting over the DTs and as a method of atoning for a lifetime's sexual voraciousness. It was accepted without question that Grandma Osborne, an ordinary Welsh Anglican, never went to church. God would not like her to risk her health by going out in the cold. Even in the height of summer her frailty demanded dispensation and was gladly given in His divine understanding of her. Instead, she would lie back in her chair, eyes closed, legs crossed and her high-heeled shoes tapping, as she listened to the Sunday evening hymns on the wireless. She seemed to know them all by heart. For all her show of austerity and undefined self-sacrifice, she was an incomparably lazy woman, as comfort-loving and selfish as a cat. Her husband did all her shopping for her and the wireless did her churchgoing.

My father was particularly contemptuous of clergymen, even more than civil servants. It must have had something to do with his experiences in hospital, when he never allowed them near him. His mother, too, had not bothered to give him any religious encouragement, possibly thinking he was unworthy of the effort. Grandma Grove didn't go to church because she worked too hard; Grandma Osborne didn't go because she hardly worked at all. Sponging off relatives was her God-given burden and her only daily toil.

The Bible was almost unknown to me until I later attended the Church of England school in Ewell. What distinguished this place was that more boys were caned more often during Scripture lessons than others. Sometimes it was for giggling at the salacious parts of the Old Testament, but often the result of divine, random whim of its instrument, the headmaster, Mr Jones, a fierce Welshman, whose lips would glisten with excitement as he swept around the classroom – all eyes lowered – looking for the next victim of unjust wrath. It was said that Mr Jones was very religious indeed because he was Welsh, and very Welsh at that. As the only other excessively Welsh person I knew was my grandmother with her feet-tapping and meticulous hymn singing, I assumed that being Welsh and believing in God were the darkest heart of religion. It was easy to imagine God with a firmament

South Wales accent, whereas Jesus might easily come from Surrey; if not from Stoneleigh then from one of the larger houses in the better-still rural parts of Ewell, in the nice fresh air and certainly well away from any satanic mills.

There was something almost relaxing about the God Routine as practised with such ruthless self-containment by Grandma Osborne. It made a comforting change from the chaos of my mother's irritability and snarling boredom. By comparison, she was kindly, blessedly consistent in her entrenched detachment, and unknown to lose her temper. A strange thing. To have lost her temper would have been a breach with routine and not to be countenanced. Through all the Family Rows I witnessed I never once heard her raise her voice. She withdrew like a Judo Black Belt, using the weight of her opponents' bluster and shouting to throw them over her shoulder with that watery smile.

Supported by her son-in-law for looking after his child, my grandmother ruled over their two up and two down as if it were a country house while my grandfather played the role of the docile retainer. I liked the old man very much, but he was a shambling, shy figure who said little. Throughout the day he made breathy whistling sounds as if he were talking to himself. The only thing I ever remember him saying to me was pointing out someone in the street. 'Do you know who that man is?' 'No,' I said. 'That man is a Socialist. Do you know what a Socialist is?' 'No.' 'Well, a Socialist is a man who never raises his cap to anyone.' It didn't occur to me then that no one in Clandon Close ever wore a cap except to play golf at weekends: caps worn in the pretence of golf playing. My grandfather wore the cloth sort, with a white muffler. His daughter, as if in conspiracy with her mother, gave him one for Christmas. He wore his badge gratefully. Perhaps it reminded him of the land of his mothers, where it would have gone unnoticed. Like my grandmother he was terminally lazy. He had not worked for many years and a fiction was kept up that he went to the Labour Exchange regularly to find odd jobs and gardening, which he may have done. No one took this very seriously, including my grandfather. He made occasional impassioned pleas that he was doing his best. He probably was; Stoneleigh, being little more than a settlement by the railway line, was not the kind of place where people employed jobbing gardeners or handymen. Self-containment was the rule. Self kept resolutely unto self. It was not merely a matter of income. Even a jobbing gardener in the shed or cleaning woman in the house would have threatened unwanted intimacy. His failure was doubtless genuine and his relief, too. He was allowed pocket money by my grandmother from Uncle

Harry's allowance, which he was permitted to spend on an odd pint of beer and a packet of Woodbines.

Treated contemptuously as a servant, he managed to behave like a dignified one. Even my mother patronized him, something she could do to none of the other Oṣbornes, gleefully pressing the odd shilling into his hand. He was shown scant affection and I had the rarest pleasure of feeling sorry for an adult. The most responsible task he was given was packing his daughter's trunks when she was going back to Nigeria, and his skill in doing this was acknowledged even by my grandmother. Apart from his brief lessons in Socialism, a demonstration of the classical straight left in boxing, and of packing, the only other thing he tried to teach me was his Countryman-Tramp's Walk, the one my father had already inherited.

Disarmingly, in these four rooms his wife behaved like Mrs Danvers in *Rebecca*, keeping a firm eye on her tiny kitchen as if it were the butler's pantry. Although there was little to do apart from cleaning the fire grate, getting in wood and coal, Grandpa Osborne was not allowed to sit down or even light up a cigarette before lunch. He would often wait standing in the kitchen until he received his shopping instructions, which were small enough ('drop in at the Co-op ... bakery up on the Parade') for three people, but were planned as if for a country-house weekend. Almost his most important errand was changing Grandma's library book at the twopenny library. She admitted that this was an extravagance but maintained that the public library didn't have the sort of books she liked, implying she had a special, refined taste. The truth was that she thought her husband incapable of even choosing a book for her whereas at the twopenny library they knew, of course: Ethel M. Dell, Netta Muskett and, that pre-war Dickens of them all, read and re-read again, Warwick Deeping. She didn't really want new books, rather the same books again. And, of course, she was also too lazy to either make the choice herself or walk a quarter of a mile to the Parade. Books had to be offered to her like an afternoon sweetie.

When the old man was finally given his instructions he would stay out for the rest of the morning. The shops were only ten minutes away and his list filled a small piece of paper. He was never asked what took him so long. He was out from under her feet. The Stoneleigh Hotel was not a place where unemployed old men are offered drinks, however long they sit in corners with near-empty glasses. Apart from going to the public library a mile or so away, he would sometimes mumble that he had been up to the Labour Exchange, knowing he was disbelieved. I think he just went for walks in Nonsuch Park on his own.

They never got up later than seven o'clock, breakfast was eaten and washed up by eight-thirty. The only reason it was necessary to keep to these spartan hours in such an otherwise indolent household was in order to have an Early Dinner, which was essential to the living of a Proper Normal Life, supposedly in the interests of my cousin Tony. The God Routine had to be obeyed even if, as in their case, it was to countenance sloth rather than endeavour. Its Prime Hours were as fixed as Sext, Nones and Compline, being Early Breakfast, Early Dinner, Early Tea, Early Supper and Early Bed. To have even considered Late Breakfast or Late Supper would have broken the rule of Grandma's enclosed order. I'm sure she never had either in her life. Had she been there she would certainly have made sure that the Last Supper was an Early one. Whatever the old man pretended to be doing he was back in time for dinner. By saying Dinner rather than Lunch, she did not, like my mother, categorize the rich and privileged as people who had Dinner at Night. She regarded them as Late instead of Early, staying up Too Late and eating Too Much. Their own Early Dinner would be ready at half-past twelve or a quarter to one at the latest and would be washed up by one-thirty.

It was then time for grandfather to go upstairs to bed for his afternoon sleep, where he would lie down on his own in his long underwear until it was time for him to come down and make the tea. Meanwhile, she would have her Rest. One was supposed to make as little noise as possible during this, although she affected to be indulgent about it. She would read out from the *South Wales and Newport Argus*, the only paper she ever read at length, mostly the names of those in the Births, Marriages and Deaths columns.

Death received first attention. Birth announcements were a matter of counting months on fingers. A few marriages produced a sniff of respectful approval but most a sceptical intake of breath. It was as if almost everyone at home had committed some predictable foolishness, like the girlish mistake of her own marriage. My mother in one of her occasional prurient confidences told me that Auntie Annie, as Grandma Osborne was known, had only allowed Grandpa to touch her twice during their marriage. This was when they were both managing the King's Arms in Newport at the turn of the century, and she submitted herself to this unroutinelike ordeal solely after secret tippling while working behind the bar, a job she despised and held to be far beneath her. It rang true. Nancy was born in 1903. Grandpa Osborne, poor neutered old dog, was to die in 1941, going without his oats for thirty-eight years. I thought of them in their feather bed, of the old man lying upstairs alone every afternoon, Annie downstairs reading the

South Wales Argus. What were his thoughts? Denied affection, sex, respect, even the work he shunned. Years later, George Devine told me a story about his own father. George's uncle was dying when he confided to him that George's mother had only allowed his father to approach her once. 'Only the once, George.' The result was George. Innocent of calculation, his father would sometimes give her presents of flowers or chocolates. Her response was always the same: 'Oh, I see. I know what you want. Well, you're *not* going to get it.' I always used to call him 'One-shot George.'

After the *South Wales Argus* my grandmother would flip through the *Daily Mail* which she thought a Good Sensible Paper and which contained her favourite journalist, Collie Knox, and her daughter's intellectual choice, Beverley Baxter, who she thought wrote wonderfully on the theatre. She said it as if it were self-evident, in spite of the fact that, apart from the pantomine, she had never been to a London theatre in her life. Beverley Nichols was another great favourite with both of them. Then, sinking her court shoes into the leathery squash of the pouffe, she would settle into her latest Warwick Deeping. Every afternoon for forty years the rigour of her daily regime was proclaimed by her uplifted court shoes. No one dared point out to her that she spent more than half the day sitting or snoozing in them.

The sitting-room itself (unlike my mother she knew better than to say Lounge) was shabby and dark, with a mixture of old sub-standard Harrods furniture and threadbare Victorian relics of middling monstrosity. The floor was covered with ancient Indian carpets, drained by time of any of their original colours. On the walls were aged Pre-Raphaelite prints, and the mantelshelf was littered with a selection of trophies from Nigeria – brass boxes in the shape of iguanas and monkeys, the sort of thing you see nowadays at African airports. The only thing of any possible value was a handsome carriage clock. A large turtle shell stood in the fireplace, a shield against anyone who might ever think of lighting the fire before the statutory seven o'clock. A huge walnut sideboard dominated the whole of one wall from floor to ceiling. It was the altarpiece, always covered with offerings contained in silver bowls, filled with a selection of nuts, fruit, tangerines, and her own home-made treacle toffee, which had its own silver salver and a silver toffee hammer. Quite delicious it was too. These luxuries, never available to me at home, were always to be had however hard the times were said to be. She had that masterly talent of the middle classes for complaining bitterly about her financial condition with no palpable change in her way of life. She must have achieved almost exactly what she wanted: a nice Early

Night, a nice Early Life. It was certainly easy, easy and empty of spirit. She personified the terrible sin of sloth at its most paltry. Not the sloth of despair in the face of God. Despair would be like staying up spiritually too late. Every afternoon of this replete lifetime of self-conceit and cosseting, a bit of toffee or butterscotch went down a treat with Warwick Deeping.

After twenty minutes or so her head would fall back rather as if she was going to break into hymn singing. Her mouth would open, her teeth start sucking in the air and she would begin snoring lightly. I often sat with her during these afternoons, watching this unfailing event. Not daring to move, I would turn over the pages of my book or comic as carefully as possible. It was accepted without question that Grandma did not go to sleep in the afternoon. To have woken her would have broken the spell for me as well as for her, like rousing some mythic animal in a dark cave, and she would have had to go through the irritable charade of pretending she was still reading old Warwick and miss the rest of her frozen snooze. She thought that she could melt unobserved into something resembling a stone abbess prone upon her tomb.

The only person who ever had malice or nerve enough to challenge this delusion was my mother. She would watch in sneering anticipation waiting for her to wake up. When my grandmother did so, slowly rising like a lounge Lazarus, she would get her punch in before the old lady had time to come up from the count. 'Well, Mother, did you have a nice sleep? Nice sleep?' 'Sleep? I've not been asleep!' 'Oh, come off it, Mother, of course you've been asleep. Don't be silly, we could all *see* you. You had your mouth wide open and you were snoring.' 'I was not snoring.' 'Everybody heard you.' My mother would look at me appealingly, but she got no help from my corner. 'I *never* go to sleep in the afternoons.' 'But you *do*, mother. Everybody knows that.' 'I was *not* asleep.' 'Then what were you doing?' Contemptuous pause. 'I was just closing my eyes.' They were the few occasions my mother ever managed to score, almost her only satisfaction until her triumphant coup the day, years later, when she pitched the old lady from her pouffe into a local authority home.

Cousin Tony was also supposed to have his afternoon rest. Being a year older and the baser part of her son, I was allowed to sit and read. I had no wish to join him as I detested him. He was one of the few children in Clandon Close who used the Playroom as a playroom, but the only game I remember playing with him was that of King George's Funeral. This was done by arranging his vast army of toy soldiers on the floor of his room and into a procession leading to his toy fort which served as Westminster Abbey.

He even had a magnificent gun-carriage. Behind it he placed the king's horse, with boots reversed and his little dog behind him. We were, at the ages of five and six, both well instructed in the minute details of that occasion. But when I say 'play', Tony ran a commentary and he moved the pieces about. I was a patronized spectator.

Tony was an ingenious and malevolent schemer, proudly encouraged by his grandmother, to whom he was undoubted heir apparent. No one, child or adult, was allowed to challenge his domain or his tantrums, flagrant lying and dwarfish bullying. Nurturing him, imposing him on any company, Grandma Osborne alone seemed to be aroused to excitement by him. I was repeatedly instructed by my mother never to retaliate whenever he surprised me with his armoury of kicks, finger twistings or rabbit punching. Having disabled me with one of these, he would howl off to Grandma, accusing me of his own offence. He was always believed. Later, of course, I found it to be a common technique among adults, particularly in marriage. After his father finally took him away from Clandon Close he went to a Welsh public school – Christ's College, Brecon – then to Sandhurst, where he contracted TB and was invalided out. As a schoolboy, he became very solemn and priggish. I had an argument with him one day about the advisability of free love. He looked at me sternly and said in a comic, Clive Jenkins-type Welsh accent, 'If God had intended men and women to have sexual intercourse together without marriage he would never have invented venereal disease.' When I met him years later, he had become a probation officer in Macclesfield, rather mild and thoughtful. It was hard to think of him as the odious child who had plotted to get me into trouble at all times. His name, incidentally, was Tony Porter. Perhaps it was a wry remembrance of his persecution to borrow his surname for a character in a play.

At almost exactly four o'clock my grandfather would come down the stairs, making his soundless whistle like a despairing kettle and go to the kitchen. Hearing him, my grandmother would slowly arouse herself like an alerted cat to resume her upright Deeping position, pushing her spectacles up on her nose and sucking the plate of her false teeth back into place. She would take the cup of tea proffered to her without thanks and without looking at him, avoiding the sight of the bare feet underneath his combinations. She would then go into the bathroom to rearrange her hair, which was a strange substance when dressed, like a saucepan scourer made of white spider's web. She belonged to the generation that boasted of sitting on its own hair, and indeed she could as I saw – rarely – in her bedroom. How she managed to gather up this strange filmy mass into what looked like a bearskin hair-net was most baffling. I was convinced that in the mildest breeze it must surely blow off and reveal a bald skull. As she hardly ventured out, even into the garden, I was never to know.

An elaborate tea followed, however delayed or inadequate Uncle Harry's monthly cheque might be. There were nearly always two kinds of bread and butter, two kinds of home-made jam, possibly a sponge cake, Dundee cake, rock cakes, eggs perhaps; soused mackerel was one of her specialities, as were her pickled onions, mussels and cabbage. *Children's Hour* was put on *exactly* at five o'clock – she wasn't going to waste electricity – and, while Grandpa puffed his first evening Woodbine in the kitchen, the three of us would sit down and listen to it until it was time for Tony to go to bed and for my grandfather to take me home, leaving Grandma to a nice play on the wireless or *Monday Night at Seven* before Early Supper – Marmite sandwiches or biscuits and cheese – then bed, Warwick Deeping and an Early Night.

When we grow too old to dream . . .

Jim and Annie Osborne were what my mother would call the 'wash outs' of the family. The old man's profligate days of playing cricket and rugby instead of looking after the jeweller's shop in Newport had come to a dead end in a pointless green circle of suburban grass. The Countryman-Tramp's walk had led to the cul-de-sac of family handyman, with little family and little to hand. His brother Harry, once the mayor of Newport and chairman of the Conservative Association, was long since dead. His older brother Tom had prospered moderately in the small ironworks that their mother had left him and was now retired to an hotel in Bournemouth with his wife, Lottie. They paid very occasional visits to Clandon Close, rather as if they were visiting an ailing relative in the workhouse. Grandma became skittishly attentive on these occasions and intent on pleasing Auntie Lottie, a huge woman like a balloon of flowered wallpaper in an enormous hat, who talked about her own money and her own bridge game. Trying to remember it, I feel that Auntie Lottie's heavily veiled message to the assembled company was that if there was ever anything to come, Jim and Annie must learn to live with little expectations. Jim said little, staying in the kitchen, preparing the tea and serving it while Annie admired Auntie Lottie's immense jewellery and the huge car outside. The two brothers said little to each other, possibly because Uncle Tom was almost stone deaf, although my mother, in one of her rare perceptive moments, told me that he exaggerated his deafness in order to avoid talking to Auntie Lottie.

Large, pink-faced, white-haired, Tom could have been a General's orderly. Lottie's common, boastful silliness was apparent even to me and enhanced her husband's dignity, if that's what it was and not deafness or stupidity. His deafness may have been a shield but it was worn with authority. His eyes seemed to be on me throughout the visit. I was unused to scrutiny from adults even in reproof. Grown-up boredom was most embarrassing when adults invariably feigned interest: 'And how are you getting on at school? . . . What subjects do you like best? . . . Want to be when you grow up?' Mercifully, Auntie Lottie was as uninterested in children as other grown-ups and ignored me, though she might acknowledge my cousin. But the old man's eyes stayed with me, disregarding Tony who whined, screamed and demanded, unchecked by his grandmother. It was hard to look away, so I looked down. If he had some message for me he would give it to me in a secret manner. When they got up to leave, he would hang back at the sitting-room door, nudging his brother ahead of him and turn round to me. Staring down at me he would press a half-crown in to my palm, close it hard and say, 'Not a word to anyone', and go quickly. Tony Porter never got so much as a good-bye. It was a sweet conspiracy between the deaf and the silent.

Apart from Grandma's sisters from Newport there were other occasional visitors. There was Auntie Lulu, my father's cousin, who lived in, of all places, East Cheam, some four or five miles away. Stoneleigh was a world away from East Cheam's leafy roads, detached houses and surrounding gentle pastures. Lulu's husband, Uncle John, was an accountant, a pale weedy figure who looked obscenely exposed without his bowler hat, like a turtle without its shell. Somehow, my father made his own bowler seem degenerate, defiant and bohemian. I don't know how he managed it. Perhaps because his own hat had seen many a lovely Late Night. Uncle John's bowler was extra work, hung on the hook of Early Night forever. My father despised him: 'whey-faced, wormy little bank teller'. He usually concealed his rages with unconvincing politeness to contain his sparse energy, an instinct I may have inherited. He was a reluctant and poor dissembler, but his contempt for Uncle John was fearsome, even to an eight-year-old. John had a black saloon car, a telephone and 'such a pretty daughter', Jill, who was the first vaguely middle-class little girl I ever met. Twice I was asked to her East Cheam birthday parties. I had known nothing like it and had no idea of how to behave. Few little boys were invited and those that were ignored me. The little girls seemed quite vicious, their favourite word being 'spiteful', as they inflicted some physical or verbal nastiness on one another. I was prepared to be impressed by pretty cousin Jill in the same craven way as my grandmother with Auntie Lulu. When I arrived at the front door she was receiving her guests in a dress which was a cross between a velvet nappy and a tutu. My grandmother would obviously have thought it perfect for such a pretty little girl. She had an enormous velvet bow in her hair and looked like a slightly indecent ice-cream salesgirl at the Odeon. She stared at me so coldly I wondered if I had been invited.

I was never to go to any other of these children's parties, which were and are apparently such an unenviable feature of English middle-class life. Like most grown-up parties they seemed competitive gatherings planned to promote as much noise and ill-will as possible. I had never seen so much food, though I ate little, feeling that there must be some unwritten rules to break. The one rule I did absorb was that you must eat lots of bread and butter before your jelly or anything really delicious, so I obediently ate my bread and butter while the good things disappeared. Then came humiliating Pig in the Middle, the Farmer's Wife, Ring-a-Ring o' Roses, Musical Chairs, none of which I had heard of, let alone played. When the overseeing mothers decided these revels were becoming more like a frilly tribal riot we were ushered into a room to watch *Felix the Cat* and *Bonzo the Dog*. The projector stammered and the little girls screamed and punched and kicked the boys. In the future, only the school air-raid shelters were nearer to mayhem. I didn't like Felix or Bonzo anyway. Most comedy films that delighted other children disturbed and distressed me. Laurel and Hardy, Chaplin and later Abbott and Costello and the Three Stooges; circus clowns, Punch and Judy shows, all filled me with sick premonitions. I even sat gloomily through Cowboy films, before they were elevated into Westerns, while all around were cheering and stoking my dislike for them and what I was watching.

At Jill's party there was worse to come, that Strolling Player of the Nursery, the Party Uncle. His assumption that all children at heart are retarded four-year-olds was correct, for that was how he made his howling audience behave with scarcely any effort. His absurd tricks and, 'Come along, children' seemed like an invitation to Hell on Earth. I had scarcely ever felt such panic and loathing. I longed to get to the door, say good-bye to cousin Jill if she would speak to me, collect my bag with its orange and banana and remember to say thank you very much to Auntie Lulu and wormy Uncle John. For some reason, my mother forced me to go again, implying I was a lucky boy to be asked. The third year I refused. This time my mother didn't bother to argue.

Passing looks at Christmas

I remember some Christmases very vividly and some not at all. My early Christmases were spent between Harbord Street and Clandon Close. Christmas Day in one and Boxing Day in the other. When I was twelve I was in a nursing home for sick boys. When I was twenty-one I was drinking evaporated milk and eating brown bread and peanut butter on a camp bed in a theatre on Hayling Island.

The highlight of Christmas at both houses was the Family Row. The common acrimony and bitterness of generations would claim its victims long before the Christmas wrappings had been thrown away. It was impossible not to be caught in some cross-fire or stray flack at some points during these festive manoeuvres. I would be attacked through my mother for her profligate spending on the new clothes I might be wearing. You could be made to feel very foolish indeed standing in your new jacket or trousers which suddenly seemed to sprout pound-note signs all over them.

The Osborne Row differed from the Grove Row but they had their similarities. With the Groves at Tottenham or Harbord Street the atmosphere would be violent, even physically, and thick with accumulated melodrama. Religion was a favourite launching pad, even though only Grandpa Grove and Auntie Queenie seemed to have any religious beliefs at all. The Osborne Family Rows, in spite of the fact that they were unheedingly Christian, were centred on the related subject of money. Their disputations were on wills, testaments, entails; who had been left out, what some loved one's real intentions had been and how subsequently thwarted after death.

The Osborne Family Row was more reticent, subtle, bitter and less likely forgotten. It was stage-managed by my grandmother, like a child who alone knows the rules of a new game so that it is assured of winning. About four o'clock on Boxing Day, the appetite for muscatels and almonds and Chinese figs would begin to pall. A dawdling disappointment hung in the air. Into this let-down lull, Grandma would make the first throw. The game was hers and the name of the game was money and property. The property was mostly of a very small kind: a reference to some diamond engagement rings foolishly pawned at the wrong time; pawn tickets lost or unredeemed; fur coats handed on to the wrong recipient; wills misinterpreted; wills wrongful; unintended; insurance policies not taken out or allowed to lapse; stocks withheld; shares pledged. Nothing was beyond recall or valuation. Even my father's notorious Lisbon hospital bills were itemized yet again.

Having started the game rolling, the old woman would sit back in her hymnal posture, the corners of her mouth tucked into a smile and wait for all the other players to make wrong moves. My mother said little and when she did was ruled out of order and, by implication, stupid. My father seemed to become whiter and thinner than ever, watching his mother as she sat back, her eyes half-closed like a smug fakir. I could swear she was singing in her head contentedly, 'Say not the struggle naught availeth', or one of her favourite self-loving songs, which sucked up to the innocence of brave old age, like 'When We Grow Too Old to Dream' or 'Little Old Lady Passing By'. She regarded these songs as some kind of personal tribute to her own geriatric divinity. They were only two of the many Battle Hymns praising a world made in the image of Grandma.

The Grove Family Rows were not masterminded but emerged from a port-wine haze of unsated disappointment. Grandma Grove was a stoic rather than an optimist. What the two families shared was the heart pumped from birth by misgiving. Not a proud misgiving of the spirit but a timid melancholy or dislike of joy, effort or courage: 'I don't suppose it'll last.' . . . 'I knew it wouldn't last.' . . . 'How do you know it'll work?' . . . 'But aren't you worried?' . . . 'Well, there's nothing we can do about it.' . . . 'No use crying over it.' . . . 'Can't expect too much, go too far, only get disappointed . . .'

Disappointment was oxygen to them. Their motto might have been *ante coitum triste est*. The Grove despond was all chaos, shouting and tearful rebukes. Their battle cries were: 'You've always had it easy.' . . . 'You didn't have to go out to work like I did when I was twelve.' . . . 'You were always Dad's favourite.' . . . 'What about you and Mum then?' . . . 'I've worked hard for everything I've ever had.' The Osborne slough was full of sly casual strokes, all the more wounding to my mother because no one said openly what they meant, not about money and certainly not about property, but about emotional privilege, social advantage, hypocrisy and religiosity against ordinary plain dealing. The Osbornes appeared to preserve calm while being more succinct and specific. Their bitterness and sense of having been cheated from birth were certainly deeper. If my mother tried to wade in to an Osborne Row she was soon made speechless by the cold stare of Grandma and the passing looks of amusement between her and Nancy as my mother mangled the language and mispronounced words and became confused at their silences. 'Did you see that?' she'd say afterwards. 'They were *passing looks*.' She would flush through her flaking Tokalon powder, bite her nails and turn to my father for support, which seldom came.

For Boxing Day, Grandma Osborne had perfected a pumpkin trick which turned all the cold Christmas pudding and mince pies suddenly into funeral baked meats. She did it almost on the stroke of five and in one wand-like incantation. Lying back in the Hymnal position, she would close her eyes, smile her thin gruel of a smile and say, 'Ah, well, there's *another* Christmas over.' I dreaded the supreme satisfaction with which she laid the body of Christmas spirit to rest. In this one phrase she crushed the festive flower and the jubilant heart. On New Year's Eve she used less relish in confirming that there was little reason to feel good about the year passing and certainly less about the coming one.

Two days of bewilderment, betrayal, triumph and, above all, irredeemable and incurable disappointment ended. My parents gathered up our presents. A redemptive after-battle calm settled over the sitting-room strewn with wrapping paper and ribbon. We shuffled out in near silence back to Stoneleigh Park Road and my father's whisky bottle. Another Christmas Over. And in the beginning God created Grandma. To her the Inferno was as unthinkable as Paradise.

4. 'A Better Class of Person'

Early in 1938 we moved from Stoneleigh Park Road to a flat right beside Ewell by-pass, almost in Ewell itself, Number 8 Homedale. My mother was delighted. She liked the drudgery of moving for its own sake anyway, but she soon became bored when the move had been made and as soon as the new place was 'straight and nice' she wanted to push on. However, Homedale was a flat, which she regarded as being 'more modern' and less stuffy than a house. Not yet as chic as a bungalow but a step up from the dead-and-alive cul-de-sac.

My father was spending more and more time at home in the new flat. His employers at the advertising agency must have been patient, especially for the time, but after six months of almost constant absence he was sent the cheap High Street clock and a month's salary. He seemed relieved and grateful. 'We'll have a week at Margate,' he said. 'But don't tell your Grandma. She wouldn't understand.' We stayed in digs by the station. Morning breakfast was huge and delicious, the landlady as friendly as the best of barmaids, the weather was warm, even the sea. We spent half the day in Dreamland or on the beach, waded under the pier and went to nightclub-like entertainments in the evening, sitting at tables which seemed very grand and grown-up. When I first went to Las Vegas I immediately thought of those evenings in Margate and my parents, of fish and chips and Guinness. And the streams of girls. I had never seen a chorus line before. As they tap-danced and swung their legs they would sing 'Lullaby of Broadway' and 'Shuffle off to Buffalo', which seemed to be that year's most popular show numbers. I never tired of hearing them. They stayed in my head daily for months. It was the happiest week I can remember with my parents. They were friendly to one another. There were no moods and few black looks. I was unused to adult adventurousness, and it was exciting. Walking along the promenade towards Cliftonville under the coloured lights it felt as if all the songs belonged to Margate rather than Broadway or Buffalo, wherever or whatever they were. We would look up at the large hotels of Cliftonville. My father might suggest going in for a drink. But my mother would hurry on ahead. 'This is where all the posh people stay,' she would say. 'You can't go in there.' 'Rich Jews,' my father added, following on behind with me. For a week, it was indeed Dreamland. For me, at least.

Homedale was a row of detached houses, each divided into two flats, set below an embankment beside Ewell by-pass. Ewell Castle School was beside it and opposite was the boundary of Nonsuch Park. The school was a Victorian-Tudor building and looked as if it had been built as a set for the film about Greyfriar's. It didn't seem to figure very largely in the life of Ewell Village. Whether it was a prep school or a private school masquerading as a public school I don't know. Homedale was flanked on its other side by yet another shopping parade which linked the surrounding suburbia like forts in a Roman wall. This particular Parade was just a curved corner consisting of a dozen small shops overlooking the busy roundabout at the junction of the roads to Kingston, Ewell Village, Epsom, North Cheam and London. On the other side of the roundabout was a pub similar to but even nastier than the Stoneleigh Hotel, oddly named the Organ Inn. Was it some Borough Architect's joke to call these shop-blocks Parades? Or did some Councillor think that the word itself would invest their dismal rows of newsagents and hairdressers with gaudy pomp, flaunting display and 'fond ostentation of riches', promenaded by prosperous Rotarians and Freemasons?

Some time ago I watched Michael Frayn on television describe his child-hood in Ewell at what must have been roughly the same time. Although I recognized much of what he said, his experience of it seemed rather different from mine. He described it accurately and eloquently as the typical suburban outpost. However, to me, coming from Fulham and then Stoneleigh Park Road, it was a small rural island. On my way home from Heathrow Airport to Kent I have peered down at Homedale and wondered what it is like now. In 1938 it had a few remnants of charm, but the 406 bus to Kingston every twenty minutes and the frequent Green Line to Morden had ended its life as a village. It had become a timetable on a bus shelter, not lived in so much as passed through. Such places, however remote once, seem reluctantly on the move themselves. Stillness never returns to them. They are reduced to being thoroughfares, platforms for getting on and off. By the main bus stop there were a spring well and pond, backed by a large girls' school, Bourne Hall, which was surrounded by parkland. Its pupils, pouring out of the gates in boaters and swirling purple gym slips on sum-mer afternoons, made the wait for a 406 an adventure. There was always the possibility of following one or two of them upstairs on the bus.

Opposite there was a church and in the churchyard a tomb commemor-
ating the man who invented the aeroplane propellor. Facing this was a
blazer-and-tweed pub, the Spring Hotel, where my mother was to work
after the war, although its unfamiliar gentility subdued her and she didn't
stay long. 'Nice class of customer and the guvnor's a real gentleman. But a
bit morbid – well, *quiet*.' In a narrow lane, rather like prints I had seen of
nineteenth-century Eton, was Glyn House. I imagine it was eighteenth-
century and it was occupied by a Sir Arthur Glyn who everyone spoke
about as if he were the squire. Whoever he was or had been, he was pointed
out as if he were a retired Prime Minister. Whether he was Ewell's last link
with politics, empire or commerce, he was its last surviving Grand Old
Man. The High Street was full of small grocers, the Gas, Light and Coke
Company, a corn chandlers, the Olde Oake Chest Tea Shoppe and another
1930s pub. My school, Ewell Boys, lay back in Church Street in what
seemed to be perpetual shade. Next to it was a sweet shop which sold
liquorice sherbet and aniseed balls at a farthing for twenty, the best buy for
an afternoon's reading aloud from *Pilgrim's Progress* or *Nicholas Nickleby*.
Farther up was the recreation ground, the Rec., not to be entered alone and
best avoided.

We left Homedale, either for financial reasons or because of my mother's
restlessness and moved into Ewell Parade, another promontory of small
shops with flats above, green iron railings at the back and tiny yards below.
The 406 stopped outside on its way to the by-pass and to Epsom. Epsom
had only recently been widened, scythed through and turned from a pokey
country town into a municipal concourse able to accommodate traffic, with
a new Woolworth's, pubs, and a brand new Odeon. I went there the week it
opened with *A Star is Born*. Janet Gaynor, of course. I remember the title
outside though, for some reason, not the film. Opposite the Odeon was the
market place. Later I used to go every Saturday to buy books, old records
and very early copies of the *Magnet* and *Gem*, which were links to my father.
Number 2 Ewell Parade was above the twopenny library which was in the
charge of two spinsters. Ewell was scattered with little shops run by single
ladies or widows, often in pairs, selling confectionery, toys, tea and cakes,
woollen goods, a milliner's with two hats and a handbag in its undressed
windows. As a display of commerce it fitted the meagre imagination of a
Parade perfectly.

Quiet tributaries led from what remained of the village, Drives, Ways,
Avenues – Laurel Drive, Firtree Way, Linden Close – where you might
stumble on a tiny footpath or green gap revealing a patch of the Old Ewell

overlooked for a short while in the developers' haste. In between the new houses and beyond there were still steamy woods, thick with nesting birds, and ponds full of frogs. Only ten yards or so from Conway Drive or Edith Way I might pass in a few steps from suburbia into thick, silent copses, from civilization into the jungle, like passing from the palms and greenery of a florist's shop into a backroom of great primeval forests. The glimpse and plunge from the trim pavement to untrodden undergrowth was startling. For me, at least, Ewell had its scattered White Rabbit holes for the imagination, popping up all over the place, to follow obediently and headlong behind the stockade of fences and garden sheds. I suppose secrecy is childhood's great eroticism. These woods invited you to give yourself up to unimaginable private excesses. The depravity lay not in what you were doing – watching a toad or coupling rabbits – but the orgy of concealment itself. 'They can't find me. However hard they try.' Lying beneath a sea of fern the tumescence of brute secrecy triumphed and subsided only on the return home down Conway Drive and Edith Way.

It was a handy mixture of sport and perversion to be unseen, flat in the grass, and observe a group of tadpoling boys as if they were a hostile tribe. Or to track some unsuspecting District Commissioner of a grown-up who was walking his dog and unaware of your contemptuous scrutiny. Close by was Nonsuch Park, Henry VIII's hunting lodge, with huge oaks and elms strung across its parkland, empty most of the week except for elderly dog walkers. In the middle of it stood a Victorian-Tudor house where council employees served tea from urns on trestle tables, and buns and sweets from its empty rooms. Nowadays the whole place would probably be policed as a Leisure Area with play parks, sports and picnic facilities, information booths and every kind of organized amenity dear to the municipal imagination. No doubt it is. The glory of Nonsuch Park then was that there were no amenities at all, apart from one lavatory which was concealed behind the house. There were a few park-keepers, presumably there to see that small boys didn't chop down the oaks. I don't know how large it was, but to an eight-year-old boy it seemed the size of a county. In the dull flower gardens by the house women sat on benches with prams and in the parkland there were children but, astonishingly, never more than a few dozen. Surrounding it was a fortress of trees where I could actually get lost, and did occasionally. Not so many yards away the 93 bus passed on its way to Putney and Fulham. To see or hear it meant penetrating right up to the edge of the Park and peering through to the road beyond.

My father's parting gift at Victoria Station – sending me off to *The*

Adventures of Robin Hood – paid off in months, years of excitement improvising the film which I knew almost frame by frame after two visits. Nonsuch Park and its turreted house were Sherwood Forest and Nottingham Castle and the park-keepers unmistakably the Sheriff's Men. Armed with a bow and arrow made from garden cane and string, I crouched on thick branches ready to drop on any arrogant Guy de Gisbourne who would pass below. What I lacked was a Band of Merry Men. There were advantages to this. First, there were no arguments about casting. My role as Robin was as unchallenged as the scenario. I had bought a Victorian edition of the legends with Doré-like coloured illustrations which I knew almost by heart. There was a particularly poignant one of Robin, Christ-like, supported by Little John, aiming his final arrow into the air, from where it fell to mark his final resting place. It must have been familiar to almost every schoolboy although I thought it only revealed to me. Occasionally I did come upon groups of boys, Cubs or would-be Scouts who were curious rather than hostile. My costume consisted of little more than a dagger and belt at the waist, my bow and arrow, and cycling gauntlets, which made accurate aiming difficult but established the character. After a little explanation of character and plot, I could sometimes assemble my Merry Men for a day's outlawry. I tried to select younger boys who would not dispute my authority as casting director. Will Scarlett and Mick the Miller were pretty nondescript roles and could be distributed at random. There was usually someone taller than the rest who would be glad to revel in his superior height as Little John and a fat boy who could hardly turn down Friar Tuck.

Older boys often contested the leading role and disputed that it was My Game. If they were aggressive enough and clearly more powerful physically than myself, I would concede my rights as producer and consent to playing Sir Guy. It was a cowardly compromise but I decided that as Robin's adversary I was on an almost equal footing. Villainy had a sense of wicked superiority about it and I had a sneaking feeling that sometimes old Robin was a bit too good to be true. Perhaps I already had a vague sense that courting and, what's more, achieving popularity was not a gift I possessed. Sir Guy was contemptuous, feared and solitary. It was a close-run thing between him and Robin and he died bravely. Furthermore, Basil Rathbone, lean and lofty, spoke inevitably in a posh voice that was a good cut above Errol Flynn. It was pleasing to know that I must be the only acceptable aristocrat. Even if I were to be defeated by some bully from North Cheam or Ewell Village, I could despise Robin and his Band of Merry Louts, I could look down on them openly without challenge.

Maid Marion was the problem. What girl would let herself become lone hostage to a gang of rough little boys charging all day through inaccessible undergrowth in the Park? To almost every mother, Robin's exploits would have seemed like an adventure that must end in medical evidence about her daughter being read out in the Police Court. 'And where have you been all day, Gloria? I've been worried stiff. Where have you been?' 'Oh, to the Park.' 'On your own? Who with?' 'Oh, some boys.' Few girls could afford to be so daring, even if they had the inclination. Tomboys of independent mind were hard to come by. When I did discover my Maid Marion, she soon asserted her superiority by natural right. She also insisted that she should be Robin.

I don't know whether it is possible to identify early sexual quickening at particular moments. I dare say not. But the image of a young woman bending over a cot and taking out a baby lingered with me like the detail of a dream. I don't know who she was, only that the child was called Malcolm. Her skirt was black, her bare legs white, and it was exciting. I was about five. Then, the blur of twin girls called Daphne and Gloria and their plump younger sister, all four of us, smacking and touching on a cold leather sofa which stuck to our bare limbs, somehow stayed in my head and became vivid when I met my rebellious Maid Marion. She was no infantile mirage. She was present and became increasingly pressing. I was nine.

Joan Buffen lived at the far end of Ewell Parade. Mrs Buffen, a widow, ran the wool shop below the flat with her sister. Joan was an only child. The flat was small and cramped like all the others but its interior was very different. It was chintzy, comfortable and similar to the parlour room at the Olde Oake Chest Tea Shoppe. My mother thought Mrs Buffen was a bit stand-offish, but could never find anything specific to complain about. She was polite, rather abstracted and not one to stop and chat or borrow a cup of sugar. Running a wool shop implied that she had come down a few rungs, if only a few. But her puzzling other occupation lifted her above her admittedly genteel trade. She bred Staffordshire bull terriers, which even my mother realized was the kind of occupation pursued by people who most probably had dinner at night. She kept these unlovely, dangerous creatures in a yard behind the shop. Her daughter acted as full-time kennel maid when she was not at school.

Joan was three years older than myself, taller too, and dark. She usually wore a tweed divided skirt, a mean fashion which swathed her effectively from curiosity. When she climbed trees, which she did often, there were no fleeting rewards, only a coarse protective crotch. Joan and her mother were unmistakably different from the other residents of Ewell Parade. When I compared them with Auntie Lulu and my cousin Jill I began to see East Cheam differently. My mother had conceded that there was 'not much swank about her'. She dressed in old tweeds and heavy brogues or gumboots, striding in and out of the wool shop as if she had come in from the cow shed. They had no car like Uncle John. If they needed one to go to a dog show, they borrowed it from a relative. But I saw that compared to Mrs Buffen and Joan, Auntie Lulu and Jill were perceptibly Common. My grandmother would have been horrified at the suggestion. Mrs Buffen worked and was still undeniably a lady. Auntie Lulu was certainly full of swank. The frivolity of Jill contrasted with Joan's practical skills, grooming her charmless Bulls, cleaning them out, walking and training them.

It was weeks before I approached her about Maid Marion. I watched her every day from the end of the iron gallery, returning from school, walking her clutch of dogs like a circus performer. I ventured up to her flat. Being at the end, Mrs Buffen had been able to construct a wire fence to prevent her one domesticated dog, an old but still savage brindle, from mutilating the postman or other residents. Peering over the railings, I watched Joan carrying large buckets of food and sawdust, hosing out the kennels. They were big enough for me to stand up in. It occurred to me then that Joan and I could have lived in one together. If only she would look up at me, but she didn't. She must have seen me. But her attention never turned from the dogs. My mother soon noticed my absorption impatiently: 'I shouldn't bother trying to make friends with her – stuck-up little thing.' Besides, she thought that I had no business wanting to play with a girl, and an older one at that. Also, although she thought Joan was stuck-up, she might surely have reason to be. My mother always made it clear to me that my place in the world was unlikely to differ ever from her own. There was no reason why Mrs Buffen or her daughter should care to speak to me. I had nothing to offer people like the Buffens, therefore why should they bother to acknowledge my existence? It was consistent with her view of affection or friendship as a system of rewards, blackmail, calculation and aggrandizement in which people would only come off best or worst. Nothing ever strikes me with such despair and disbelief as the truly cold heart. It disarms utterly and never ceases to do so. I wish it were otherwise. Grandma Osborne's barrenness had some unyielding dignity. At least she didn't poison it with the unction of sentimentality.

But I was spared making the first move. One day, for the first time, she looked at me across the wire gate. 'Hello, do you want to come in?' She hardly looked at me. It was as casual as a stranger offering to light a cigarette. I was aware of a slightly impatient air – 'Oh, well, he's been hanging about looking so stupid. I suppose I'd better ask him in.' When I hesitated, she unbolted the gate and held back the brindle beast beside her. Compared to the young dogs in the yard, he was almost benign. 'Don't let them see you're frightened.' I entered Buffendom prepared for anything. But at least I was inside. I had been noticed if not welcomed.

From then on, and for the next year, I spent hours sitting with Joan. We cooked meals of boiled sweets, fried with bananas, molasses and dog biscuits over a small fire, burning a hole in Mrs Buffen's saucepan. She accepted this with a calm that set her apart for me. At home, Nellie Beatrice would have sported a Black Look for a week. The dogs were constantly fighting, particularly the piggy-eyed White Staffordshires. They seemed to spend half the day, when they were not being fed, tearing each other to pieces. I have rarely encountered anything more terrifying but I determined not to show my fear in the face of their keeper's coolness. Mother and daughter shared this easy practicality in everything. Their assurance was enviable. I was bitten, sometimes quite badly, and began to take it as a matter of course and the Price of Love. Mrs Buffen would bandage my bites with such calm and lack of fuss that when she escorted me the few yards home my mother's ready hysteria was immediately deflated. It was like being given safe conduct by the Lady Almoner. I was saved the days of abuse and recrimination I ordinarily suffered if I returned bruised or bleeding from some encounter with boy or nature in Nonsuch Park. I relied on the uncomplaining aid of strange mothers or sisters. It softened the resentful onslaught when I got home, but none had Mrs Buffen's authority. She made no excuses for me like the others, 'It wasn't his fault. It was only an accident. Don't be *cross* with him.' And when we were left alone together my mother wasn't cross, she just hoped I was grateful to Mrs Buffen. I was, though not for being savaged by her dogs; but at least their bite was no worse than Nellie Beatrice's bark.

Joan went out of her way to draw my attention to sex. She was tantalizingly mysterious, refusing to be explicit and inflaming my bafflement. She had a narrow repertory of infantile jokes, mostly variations on the theme of a small boy and his sister being bathed by their mother, and the boy asking if he might put his train into the girl's tunnel. My father had once attempted to give me a very straightforward account of the whole reproductive process. He drew two detailed male and female figures and began explaining the functions of both at length but simply. The diagrams and the unlikely enormity of it all were too much for me. To his amusement, I rushed out of the room to be sick before he was half-finished. 'What did you want to go and start telling him all that for?' said my mother. 'You know what he's like.' He never brought the subject up again. One day, waist-deep in bull terriers, Joan made me look up the staircase at the enormous figure of Mrs Norman, the butcher's wife, who must have weighed about seventeen stone. Mr Norman, although not a particularly small man, was certainly half his wife's size. Joan's eyes watched me, smirking as she sometimes did when she gave me an unexpected punch in the back. 'What do you think of that?' 'What?' I said. 'What about Mr Norman getting on top of Mrs Norman?' she demanded. I had never thought of it. It was still difficult to imagine when it was put to me. I had only ever seen Mr Norman in his bloody apron and hard as it was to see him on top of Mrs Norman it was unthinkable without his apron. It took some time for me to make sense of the connection between the train and the tunnel.

On rare occasions, she would ask me up to her small, comfortable bedroom. It was more of a sitting-room, a place to talk and read. The lounge in our flat was like a doctor's waiting room without the magazines. Even the wireless was usually in the kitchen. Joan's room had hockey sticks, a well-used armchair, her toy animals, mementoes of holidays, school, jodhpur boots, pictures of flowers, animals and, of course, horses. All our walls at home were bare. There was hardly any evidence of a life already lived or being lived, a solitary enlarged snapshot of my sister hung on the walls of the lounge with a few china heads and flowers. A scattering of glass animals and swans from the Dinky Shop littered the mantelpiece. Magazines and books were cleared away as soon as read. The only permanent books in the house were *The Doctor's Book*, a popular encyclopaedic guide to all sorts of arcane and alarming ailments which could befall the average family, my father's copies of the *Boys' Own Annual* from 1908 to 1915 and Priestley's *Angel Pavement*. A large green volume was kept on the top shelf of the airing cupboard where I was unable to reach it. Years later I came upon it hidden beneath some blankets. It turned out to be *Contraception* by Marie Stopes. I spent days reading it, staring at the photographs, until my mother missed it. 'You haven't seen a big book around, have you? It's a *medical book*. One of the girls lent it to me.'

Joan had her own bookcase, and a full one. Anyone going into my bedroom would have had to guess who its occupant might be. Apart from the teddy bear allowed on my pillow it could have been a room reserved for the odd lodger rather than a child. My few books and comics were 'put away' in a cupboard along with toys. Meals were things prepared with the principal aim of being 'cleared away', washed up; beds, rooms, cushions existed for the sake of being 'tidied up', 'put straight'. The whole process reached its state of pristine perfection if we went on holiday and all hint of life or comfort was covered in immaculate sheets and clean newspapers. Joan's bookshelves contained the kind of things which, unknown to me, were cherished by most little girls of her class. There were girls' annuals, fairy tales, some poetry (Walter de la Mare I think), a few classics, Dickens, Stevenson, Lewis Carroll, Kipling, the *Jungle Books*, *Swallows and Amazons*, *Winnie the Pooh*. I had heard of few of them and read less. There were rows of books with titles like *Smokey – the story of an Exmoor Pony*.

In the holidays she was allowed to come with me to the pictures at the newly built Odeon in Epsom. Her family used the astonishing French pronunciation *O-Day-On*. It did seem a bit affected. Together we saw *Robin Hood* (yet again for me), *Sabu the Elephant Boy* (a particular favourite, this one), and *The Four Feathers*. As with *Robin Hood*, these were all re-enacted by us whenever we could find a willing cast. This was difficult because the nearest kids were a rough, uncooperative lot, but Joan could manage to intimidate a small group of usually younger children into taking part. I was allowed to be Sabu, a prince but a coloured one and therefore Other Ranks.

Before long, during our wanderings in Nonsuch Park alone together, she came to insist that I undo my fly buttons in front of her and achieve as big a trajectory stream over a bank of stinging nettles as I possibly could. I made feeble protests at first but she was able to blackmail me by threatening to refuse to let me come up to her bedroom ever again and read her books or even put my life at risk beside her in the kennels. Besides, I was flattered by her uncharacteristic curiosity. I tried to extract a promise from her that if I followed her command she would perform a similar service for me. Eventually, she agreed, but invariably went back on her word after having watched me with a kind of mocking encouragement. When she did at last relent and take her knickers down and crouch impatiently, I felt none of her exultation. It was a disappointing spectacle. Her demand had been triumphant, a sort of victory. Mine seemed childish and dirty. She allowed me into her room and to expose myself to her only when the caprice took her. Sometimes she would simply refuse without giving any reason. She could be spitefully snobbish, correcting my pronunciation of words. I was unhappy for days when this happened.

Joan was a girl, and I had accepted the role of her NCO, therefore I had to accept her whims. But dismay began to grow into resentment. When her cousin, who went to Epsom College, visited her in his grey shorts, school tie and striped cap, she would usually refuse to let me go out with them on the dogs' twice-daily walks. When I gave up pleading and probably looked abject enough, I would be allowed to accompany them, while they ignored every attempt I made to gain their attention. Such glee in the discomfort of others is one of the many contemptible aspects of childhood. I have encountered it in some adults and once, most overbearingly, in marriage. To look for generosity in a child is like expecting gratitude from a cat. Happily, this predatory gloating usually passes from us as our own frailty becomes more evident than that of others. But the sight of Joan in jodhpurs, her boots gleaming as she strode around the kennel yard like an eleven-year-old Hunter Dunn was inflaming and unbearable. The gulf between us became only too clear and complete. Whenever she swung up on to her piebald pony she was lost to me. It was hard to know which was more hateful, the piebald pony or her cousin. The pony had Joan's thighs around his back. Her cousin was too wholesome and scrubbed to think or have any physical connection with Joan. *He* would never allow himself to be bullied by a girl into exposing himself in front of her. Nor would she have asked him.

I began to see that my longing for any scrap of affection, friendliness or even tolerance would come to nothing. The crumbs would diminish and be given with less and less grace until they were withdrawn altogether. I was a makeshift, and a poor and fleeting one at that. When her cousin left, I would be reprieved. For a day or two she would smile on my enthusiasm until her patience broke again. Seeing my misery only urged her on to throw me back to whence I came, like an amusing mongrel who quickly proves his dull breeding, untrained, untrainable and ultimately unrewarding.

My mother, her indifference melted by unkind curiosity, got the picture with unusual – if blind – accuracy. 'What do you want to go on moping about after Joan for? You just make yourself look silly. She's only laughing at you the whole time. They all are. What do you think a girl like that could see in you? Even if she were the same age, she's not ever going to be interested in someone like you. She'll get fed up with you in five minutes. You'll see. They're all the same. Time you learnt it now. Before you get *really* unhappy.' The prospect cheered her up for a little. The Black Look flaked its powdery surface and broke into a yellow grin.

Before the year was out, Joan told me that she was going away to Boarding School in September. It was 1939. She tried not to sound excited and I tried not to sound impressed. I had learned to protect myself a little. Later, I watched her pack. She showed me her new uniform, books, lacrosse stick.

I had nothing to say, but it was unnecessary anyway. What existence I had been allowed was already discarded. When the day came for her to leave I went out of the flat before breakfast and went for a walk in Nonsuch Park. When I came back she was gone. My mother caught my red eyes at once. 'Joan came to say good-bye. I said I didn't know where you'd gone. She looked ever so nice in her posh uniform.'

In time I grew to convince myself that I could become ill with grief. Stricken with Sickness unto Death, I only waited for it to pass. It was vain to resist the excess of a faulty nature. It had to be endured along with the inheritance of a weak body, a blemished skin, ugly limbs, teeth and dandruff. Leaning against Robin's favourite tree in Sherwood that day, the tears falling into my mouth tasted as bitter and surprising as those that were to come. As I spluttered against a tree in a suburban park, an ordinary middle-class English girl in a gymslip was happily making her way most willingly to school. A girl very like my own daughter now.

If Joan was my first girlfriend she was also for some time my only friend. The boys in the village were a hostile bunch, probably the remainder of what was once Ewell. Their encampment was bounded by the new by-pass on the one side and the growing collection of council houses in West Ewell on the other. The Rec. was their reservation. I dare say their tiny tribe was soon to be defeated by the London homesteaders. Ewell Boys' School, tucked away in its dark lane, was very much as I had dreaded. Like Brompton Hospital, the faded brick and tall windows held out nothing but the promise of harshness and pain. It was damp, dark and cold, even in the summer. The School Inspector – a figure in my life rather like the Income Tax Man in Archie Rice's – who was to follow me around for years to come, finally caught up with me. I don't know why my mother connived in absenting me from school. She was not protective when she protested that I was 'over-sensitive' or 'delicate'. It was as if I were a rather prestigious cripple. There was no question of tangling with authority on my account. Having drawn attention to herself she would have despatched me anywhere. My first day at Ewell Boys' School was much as I expected. Like hospitals, I knew that they were places where pain and humiliation were the rule. Every school and hospital I went to proved me right. With my packet of sandwiches deep in the pocket of the too-new raincoat which my mother insisted on my wearing, I attached myself to a file of boys who looked like prisoners but acted like eager recruits. A huge-chested man in a polo-necked pullover, running on the spot, blasting the whistle between his teeth, shrieked and chased us into the morning assembly. Mr Jones, the Welsh terror himself, already wet-lipped, cane dangling beside his hymnal, herded us through a couple of Ancient and Moderns. There was whipped-up retribution in the air, baiting everyone into a kind of happy expectant impotence.

Almost all the lessons in the class I'd been assigned to seemed to be taken by Mr Blundell, the polo-necked drill sergeant. He told us that he was a superb footballer and that he weighed thirteen stone. He had the instinct of the nerveless for putting his bullying finger on the quaking nerve. He constantly barked out my name, as if it were itself some damn silly bugger's attempt at deceit. The dread time for me at all these council schools was Playtime. What I remember above all is the constant clash of boots on gravel. Most boys wore huge boots, gaping above the ankle, passed on from their brothers or even their fathers. Some wore no socks. Only a few of us wore shoes. I asked my mother if I might have a pair of these boots, second-hand preferably. They were the accoutrements of war, without them you were unarmed, unprotected. They had a war-like sound and a powerful look. The wearer of such boots had a clear advantage over an adversary wearing a light Freeman Hardy and Willis shoe. Walking the Barratt way was not for these warriors.

The classrooms may have been purgatory but the playtimes were undoubted hell. I always spent the whole twenty minutes longing for the bell which would rescue me back to the comparative safety of the classroom. Apart from physical timidity I was also rather girlishly fastidious. I was, and am still, almost spinsterish in my distaste for noise and personal disorder, although I am capable of initiating both. Because of my mother's instruction not to disturb my father and because of her 'nerves', I was always constrained to close doors with a surgical accuracy so that the lock went into its place without making a sound, or of taking my shoes off in the house and padding about in slippers or even stockinged feet. Creaking stairs had to be negotiated like minefields. These restrictions did not apply to my mother who could make the kitchen reverberate like a firing range. However, I did know that my father, trapped and sore in bed, could be reduced to fulminating pain by a carelessly slammed door or some beefy doctor slumping his carcass on his bed, even by a noisily folded newspaper.

Milk bottles in particular were anathema to my mother; the sight of one half empty on a table would bruise her face into the blackest of her looks, and she would sweep it away out of sight if she didn't actually pour the seamy liquid down the sink. This had a lasting effect on me. Playtime was the festival of the Milk Bottle and I thought it squalid. The smell of milk and the sight of small boys straining at their bottles with or without straws made me feel very queasy indeed. Most of the boys had free milk. I dare say I might have been entitled to it, but my mother gave me the few pence it cost to buy my own, which I pocketed. Apart from my absurd primness, I didn't like milk and loathed taking part in this headlong scramble.

She talked about germs always as if they were like ants that could be made to writhe in a miserable death, gasping on their backs, in the cauldrons of her fortress home. Whenever I emptied my money box she would insist on putting all the pennies, halfpennies, sixpences and threepenny bits into a large bowl, pouring boiling hot water and Dettol over them. They were, she said, full of 'germs' from other people. She was the same about my father's germs. He had 'dry TB' and not 'wet TB', she explained, so Dad's germs did not buzz around in the air like filthy moths. They stayed, presumably snugly, inside him in little sachets like dried cigarette tobacco, almost hygienic germs. Using anyone else's cup was as deadly as handling coins. She hurled pints of scalding water over any cups, plates or forks left behind by the rare visitor. Even the doctor's tea cup was sterilized. His patients' germs must have been jumping like fleas from it. The sight of children sharing the same bottle of Tizer or, worse, milk, made her almost delirious. If ever, afflicted by raging thirst, I was driven to share a bottle, I was to wipe the top of it as vigorously as possible, but only if boiling water were unobtainable.

From this induced aversion to the milk bottle, germ-ridden lucre and the healthy animal noise of everyday life, I developed an overwrought distaste for anything which might become a group or a crowd or threatened confusion. As for orderly groups, like queues, whether outside cinemas and bus stops or martialled, eager lines in the playground, they aroused me to a frenzy of helpless and bigoted malevolence. Later, I always refused, on principle, to buy duty-free goods on aeroplanes or at airports. It must seem a mincing kind of snobbery to those others set on an easy bargain. In any scramble for the best seats, rate of exchange or even for survival itself my prig's foot would be the first to step back. I would insist on the feeble dignity of being at the tail end of the bus queue, and be the first to fall back on the right to watch others pile into the lifeboat. It is neither courage nor politeness. Perhaps it is what is meant by *hubris*. If so, I am afraid it has displayed itself in more petty than heroic gestures. *Hubris* or morose misanthropy, it has been constantly and indeed continues to be tested, just as it was on that first day in the playground.

For a short while I was able to conceal myself behind the wash-house but

I knew there was no escape, at least not from the ritual interrogations and trick questions like, 'Does your mother keep dripping?' Smart replies to this kind of cross-examination were more dangerous than silence or stupidity. In my new raincoat with its bourgeois room-for-growth, I was a conspicuous target in that pit of milling boys. The sound of boots on gravel, pitching limbs and shrieks was like nothing I had ever known. Suddenly I found myself watching an earnest, determined-looking boy about my own age who could almost have been cast as William in one of Richmal Crompton's books. He was at the head of a long line of careering boys. Behind him, a chain of them hanging on to coats and jerseys followed on an unsteady rampage all over the playground. Yelling with triumphant ferocity, they hurtled and snaked round, a little like the huge electric Caterpillar Ride in Dreamland. The point of it was to hang on to the boy in front and not get thrown off the chain. The game was called, simply, Trains, and its inventor turned out later to be the boy at the front. He looked too solemn to lead, let alone enjoy, this kind of demented power. Later I came to realize that by diverting others into excitement, he could escape being manipulated, coerced or bullied himself. He could baffle a brutish little world with clowning, grapeshot energy. It was my first glimpse of Mickey Wall. I came to admire and envy his difference, his wholesome eccentricity which he managed to make acceptable even to the stampeding, booted herd of Ewell Boys' School.

Mickey Wall or, as he preferred, M. Geoffrey Wall was certainly odd if not, as it turned out perhaps, remarkable. For a boy of nine, he had an icy brain, quick and disarming. Such youthful shrewdness often betrays a calculating heart. There was little affection in him but it was to take years for my importunate spirit to realize this. As I watched him, I had no idea of the light-hearted contempt he felt for his companions. When he was about fourteen, a pedantic socialist and professed democrat, he enjoyed quoting Horace about the common herd of men and holding them at bay. *Odi Profanum Vulgus*. 'I loathe the uncouth, vulgar throng', he translated for me. Unlike me, with my patrician pretensions and genuine loathing, he was merely dismissive of meagre intelligence. Hatred would never rush that cool head. For the next five years he was to be my only friend and nobody's fool. Nobody's fool was what I aspired to be, though with little confidence. It was difficult enough to avoid becoming anybody's victim. The herd was about to strike.

Absorbed in watching Mickey Wall's progress across the playground, I was suddenly aware that I was surrounded by three boys. They were dirty, ragged and huge-booted. Their eyes were narrowed with curious hostility. This fixed look scarcely moved when they spoke, their lips and face muscles wired up into a mask of threat. Foolishly, I was slightly reassured by their height. I towered over them. They looked unhealthy, either hard but underfed or flabby and germ-ridden. My spirit stiffened very slightly; a little gasp of home-made *hubris*. One of the boys spoke. 'D'you want a fight?' I knew that there was only one answer to this question. Refusal was impossible and would lead to unending torment instead of isolated bouts of pain. 'All right then.' 'All right then. Take your pick.' I looked at the three of them and immediately chose the smallest. He was a good head shorter than myself, rather plump and unhealthy-looking with a closely shaved head (later I was told he had been a bad lice case). Nowadays he would be identified as a lesser punk. He was slug-like. A swift tap and he might spill slime. Certainly a wet-germ carrier. My mistake was apparent within seconds.

Looking down at the suddenly contemptible slug, I stabbed at him with the classical straight left taught to me by Grandpa Osborne, who had sworn it was the ultimate defence and, with a long reach like mine, a safe, effective attack. Immediately, his fist, which seemed almost as large as his head, hammered into my stomach and ribs. I could see my own blood through the corners of my eyes, tear-like streams pouring down into my mouth, tasting thick and warm. I had no idea of what I was doing but mechanically went on jabbing my ponderously executed straight left well past his right ear. Perhaps twice I contacted his head, hurting my knuckles. The speed and power of his short fat body and bobbing asphalt head were astonishing. I had no idea that such physical strength might exist. It was an astounding experience.

Within seconds he had given out more energy than had escaped from Grandma Osborne for probably a whole half-century. I had lived for eight years without knowing that such animal power roamed the earth around me. Here was Robin Hood all right, cruel and pitiless. In a black and red swirl of faces, boots and asphalt, I looked down at the weaving scrub of the slug-head as I went on blindly miming Grandpa's South Wales amateur middle-weight instructions. His fists, like tight pebble bats, pounded into me from forehead to groin. I don't know how long this went on, but presently I heard a voice saying, 'Had enough?' In the blood and darkness I managed to shake my head. He relaxed his speed and began to punch me casually, like a painter adding touches to a canvas. He fell back, just filling in the empty spaces in a diagram of pain. Then, like some cheeky circus dwarf, he butted me in the stomach, not so much with his head as with his whole body.

Suddenly it stopped. I could just make him out. He looked puzzled but not triumphant, then turned away with his two lieutenants to the sound of muted cheers. Such an abject match must have been disappointing, even to those who found the sight of blood its own reward. As a contest it was comparable to a blind-worm faced by a terrier. An older boy led me to the lavatory basins and washed my face clean with water from one of the dreaded milk bottles. My whole body seemed raw and inflamed, within and without. Indeed, all those furious blows seemed buried in my body, unseen. The pain was eased slightly by a glance at my face, which felt as if it had been scrubbed with a pumice-stone but which was not badly marked. I looked at myself, almost grateful for the slug's skill at inflicting inner damage. I needn't expect much more than a medium Black Look and suppertime sulk of sighs and reproach before I escaped early to bed.

The following morning I woke up wondering whether to feign one of my fainting fits or nervous attacks. I decided reluctantly that this would be a strategic mistake. I was right. The iron-headed slug never approached me or even glanced in my direction again. His lieutenants occasionally smirked and bumped into me deliberately in the corridors, but for the rest of the time I was at Ewell Boys' School I was never challenged again. My humiliation had been so complete it was a guarantee of safe conduct. What the slug had done with such ease needed no repetition, even if anyone cared to bother. I made neither friends nor enemies after that first day. Other playgrounds later were to be more dangerous, when my status was not so immediately fixed. I had been tested, found totally wanting and unfit even for occasional persecution. Perhaps the paralysis of shock and pain that had immobilized me had disguised my fear and even been interpreted as dumb courage. Everyone, including the staff (who never interfered in fights until the participants had all but killed each other), had watched the incident and no one ever referred to it. I was surprised and relieved. The slug had established my lowly place in the herd without fuss or feeling. There was a civilized constraint implicit in leaving the humiliated or vanquished alone which I found wanting in later adversaries, both men and women. It was a closed incident and natural to the primitive, tribal mind. To the cultivated mind, the closed incident is often too sophisticated and unacceptable to accept graciously, particularly in the face of love or ambition.

For the next year or so my life at Ewell Boys was glum, anonymous and uneventful. Scarcely anyone spoke to me directly, staff or boys, for which I was grateful. Boredom and ratty apathy prevailed from nine till four. Enduring Mr Blundell's jokes and jingles ('When we all go to Chelsea, we shall all see what we shall see, shan't we?'), the present passed, hour by long hour. The extent of pleasure seemed a boiled sweet, excitement was the four o'clock sprint past the church to tea with my father if he were home in bed. Mr Jones continued to rumble during Assembly and Scripture classes, looking like Elijah and sounding like Clive Jenkins having a mild fit. I learnt nothing. We recited the twelve-times table endlessly and memorized Imperial measures, rods, poles and perches. Mr Blundell found I had not been taught either multiplication or short division so he mercifully ignored me. I think we must also have been taught Sellar and Yeatman history, King Alfred and the Cakes and King Canute, and we read Bunyan, Dickens and, of course, the Bible. Those who could read at all did so aloud. The majority, those who couldn't or barely, were left to stare at the pages unaided and in silence. I longed for Nonsuch Park, where Robin Hood was still a kindly soul, and the tales of Joan's Exmoor ponies. Even the treacherous bull terriers were preferable to the inferno of two Playtimes a day. It seemed madness to be doing literally nothing nearly all week when I could have been reading, listening to the wireless, even walking in the empty park or, best of all, talking to my father, Black Looks permitting.

Mickey Wall, the dashing driver of the Train Game, had not yet spoken to me. I would certainly not have approached him. He seemed very cheerful and friendly to everyone in an abstracted way. He had no particular comrades and usually read or carried a book at Playtime. No one bothered him so he had obviously secured his position in the school as surely as I had mine. One morning, going back up the stone stairs to the classroom, I looked behind and saw Mickey Wall making his way alone across the playground. It was a strange sight. He waddled forward, flapping his arms vigorously up and down against his sides like a penguin about to take impossible flight. His concentration was fierce and exhilarated. His palms pumped against his shorts in a deliberate, slow-motion rhythm. 'Wall, what do you think you're doing, for God's sake?' Mr Blundell's parade-ground bellow was startled. Mickey Wall's r.p.m. increased as he swooped downwards. 'I'm just flapping, sir.' 'What d'you mean, you're flapping?' 'I'm *flapping*, sir. I do it all the time.' Mr Blundell's sneer turned to distaste and then discomfort as if he had seen something very nasty indeed. 'Well, whatever it is, stop doing it. You're just looking bloody silly.' 'Yes, sir,' came the cheerful reply. If Mr Blundell hoped for a note of insolence there was none to detect. I had never witnessed such spontaneous and self-assured behaviour. Seemingly unaware of anything but his own joyful release, he did look as if he was having a thoroughly enjoyable time all to himself. Others might have suggested that he was merely acting daft but he seemed to wander the school and even the streets determinedly flapping, happy and unmoved. Here there must be an unusual spirit. He was certainly unique in Ewell Boys' School in 1938. The sound of one hand flapping.

It was forbidden to talk in the school corridors, but one day I found myself beside him as he was singing 'Some of These Days', and quite loudly at that. He gave a passable imitation of what was to me then an unknown Sophie Tucker. Turning, he said, 'D'you know I think that's my favourite song?' 'What is it?' I asked. (Listening to the smart, rented shilling-a-week Ekco wireless was only possible when my mother was out. Music, even turned down to the lowest volume, was too much for her nerves.) His gaiety was startling. ' "*Some of These Days*". *Sophie Tucker*,' he said and whooped away into another verse. That afternoon we arranged to have a long talk during Playtime the next day. I wasn't sure I was yet ready to walk beside him in the street; besides, he lived in the opposite direction, off the Kingston Road near the Rembrandt Cinema. Talking was hard to sustain during those dreadful twenty minutes. Shouting, yes, kicking, milk-gurgling, pinching, hurtling and lurching. Conversation was inconceivable. In the event, we were ignored. I might have thought that his petty eccentricity was a splint to support someone hobbled with shyness like myself. I was quite wrong. His extrovert oddity was simply the happy expression of an oddly uncomplicated spirit. He used it to his advantage as a tactical device against parents, relatives, teachers and other boys. For a nine-year-old to invent an enjoyable and acceptable persona cannot be a common achievement. For an Oxford graduate it is a commonplace path, but in a sprouting suburb of South London, eccentricity, like irony, is ineffective or resented. However, he was harmless and cheerful, neither rebellious nor conformist, nothing disconcerted or alarmed him. Polite, almost courtly, he seemed as modest as he was opinionated. Practical, full of cheeky mockery, he might have been dull, but he never seemed so to me. What he lacked in imagination he compensated with the bubbling enthusiasm of his confidence.

Most of the characteristics were ones that I came to suspect or despise in others. It was impossible to think of him brought down by doubt or regret. Doubt could be ignored as a technicality, and regret unlikely to a life conducted without risk. Experience was a series of fairly proscribed certainties and all the more enjoyable for that. He was blessed with the gift of painless accommodation. He would never be happy. It set him apart, and it did seem a rare gift for a boy rather than a common adult flaw. I knew none of these things then about M. Geoffrey Wall. I knew only one thing. I had found a friend. Mrs Buffen could feed the bull terriers herself.

5. O Wall!

Mickey Wall's flapping must have made a strong impression on me. Some thirty years later I found myself struggling to stand on a chair in a rather staid restaurant, the Hotel Metropole in Beaulieu. I then, I am told, for I remember very little of it, gave the assembled diners, English and French, a detailed lecture on how to take physical flight unaided except for a Nietzschean Concentration of the Will. I demonstrated the exact curve, the amount of pressure required, aided by the correct arm movements and supreme resolution needed to inch your feet from the ground, flapping ever more powerfully until you were triumphant astride the air, like a seagull resting on the wind. The next day the waiters were all smiles, and the English visitors cool. I had done it often enough in dreams.

Mickey Wall's technique of containing adults was the pre-emptive strike which left his victims instantly trivialized. With the patience of a sniper, he would pick off an unheeding grown-up with some tangled *non sequitur* or inscrutable nonsense that defused retaliation. Even when he gave voice to what seemed to me the unsayable, his gravity ensured that his reward was never more than a half-hearted cuff or brief banishment from the meal table. It is hard to convey the impact of these sallies, which certainly did not rely on wit but on transported cheekiness. Rude, naughty or invented words exploded with inevitable shock but his blandness belied mischief, let alone wickedness. Propriety and dignity had a whiff of shot and shock, as if innocence, in the form of Mickey, was keeping them on their toes. For those with sufficient style, he had compiled a nine-year-old's manual *pour épater le bourgeois*.

For example, he was ever ready to coin a meaningless phrase or invent a word by the mere addition of a letter. During a long, fiery afternoon in Mr Jones's pit of Scripture and whacking, he was challenged about the contents of a toffee tin under his desk. 'What is that you are playing with, Wall?' 'It's my gzoo.' 'What's in that tin?' 'My gzoo, sir.' 'And what's that?' Mickey, looking eagerly helpful, held up the tin and took out the various toy animals, elephants, giraffes, lions, antelopes. 'These, sir. This is my gzoo.' Mr Jones looked upon Mickey's Ark as if it were of the Covenant rather than Noah. The creatures of the pit waited for the fork of Welsh flame to strike and consume the blasphemer. Mr Jones stared, nostrils flared for the whiff of evil. Instead of dragging Mickey to damnation by the ear he flung down his palsied cane and mumbled, 'Well, put it away again. We don't want to see it.' Elijah's chariot wheel had lost a small spoke.

His little guerrilla sorties weren't to be beaten off with retorts like, 'Can't you stop being so *childish*?' 'Why don't you grow up?' When he introduced me to his sister, Edna, a nice but slightly irritable nineteen-year-old, she was bending over the fire grate. 'This is my sister, Edna,' he said. She turned round politely and acknowledged me, all of ten years between us. I was prepared to be impressed both by her seniority and attractive appearance, but not for his comment. 'Hasn't she got a big arse?' he said thoughtfully. Edna aimed a token blow at him. She was used to his solemn insults but they still disconcerted her. Once, returning in his parents' car from a day trip to Eastbourne, he winked at me, as he usually did before he was about to take aim and, leaning forward to his mother's ear, yelled, 'Ma!' 'Yes.' Pause. 'You've blown off.' The consternation that resulted from this grenade slung into the front of the car was furious. Mr Wall almost stopped the motor as if some damage needed inspection. We all rode back in silence, Mr and Mrs Wall like the victims of a bomb attack and Mickey and I exploding with our easy rout. On our return he was packed off to bed without supper and I was reproachfully sent home.

On another occasion during a visit to his aunt's in Saffron Walden, we had been particularly instructed to be quiet and well mannered, as Auntie was going through a difficult time. 'Don't play her up, lads,' said Mr Wall confidentially. 'She's a bit on the sensitive side. Anything'll bring on the old waterworks.' Then, man to man, he added, 'You know – woman's troubles.' We didn't know. I doubt if it would have stopped Mickey, winking at me over the tea table as she moved into his sights. She was a kindly woman, taking great pains to give us a huge, country tea with hams and unfamiliar delicacies. 'You're quiet, Mickey. What are you thinking?' There was the usual pause as he despatched yet another piece of cake or trifle before he lobbed over his reply. 'I was thinking . . .' he turned to her husband. '. . . I was thinking she's an old cow.' I sat appalled at this gratuitous assault. Perhaps he'd expected the waterworks to explode but his aunt took it calmly. He must have realized his mistake as he almost immediately sent himself to bed. He was not so much willing to wound as unafraid to strike.

No reference was made to it during the rest of our stay and if Auntie had been hurt she concealed it, pushing on to us all the good things we could carry when we left. Our fears that she would report the incident to Mr Wall were dispelled.

Mickey's father was a genial man, a minor clerk in some government department in Whitehall. He had a dry line in humour. When I proudly showed myself in my first pair of long trousers he said, 'Nice fit under the armpits.' Grandma Osborne and others had been insultingly scornful: I was too young for them. It was a relief to have them regarded so lightly and not as a social blunder. He was also about the only person I knew who drove a car, a 1938 Ford. My mother's insistence that cars were driven almost exclusively by doctors led me to believe that he must be well-off, although his appearance and way of living seemed unremarkable. He walked to the station and the car was mostly used for Bank and summer holidays. There was a telephone in its proper place behind the front door but, like those belonging to carless residents, its use was monitored and not encouraged. Mickey said his father earned eight pounds a week, which was the same as my father. However, as my mother pointed out bitterly, *they* hadn't got doctor's bills to pay. Added to this, Mickey's mother worked as a secretary in a newsagents and stationers in Epsom.

She seemed immeasurably older than her husband and Mickey was pleased to embarrass her by telling any company assembled that he was 'a change of life baby'. He surely must have been because she had been Lord Robert's secretary during the First World War, and her life must have changed especially late for she looked as if she were his grandmother. She was a busy, impatient woman, constantly typing in the otherwise unused front parlour, but she was always absent-mindedly welcoming. It was a relief to be accepted unthinkingly as just an extra place setting, without the resentful preparation of 'dainty' sandwiches, expensive shop cakes, and with no recriminations afterwards about the bother of it all. If Mickey or Joan came to tea they were fawned upon and then reviled after their departure. Hospitality was as unknown to Nellie Beatrice's nature as friendship. Her attempts at it were simply more excuses to put someone in her debt so that her social rent book was paid up and in credit. But then if you've never felt welcome in your heart for anyone, sharing a meal is no more than taking in Extra Catering. If my mother asked you to break bread with her she was only thinking of how long it would be before she could start clearing up crumbs after you.

I was soon spending almost every evening at the Walls' home at 39

Bradford Drive. There were no invitations at teatime. It was assumed I was staying. Even during the war, with rationing pinching hard, such a hungry family (unlike my mother, they would never have resorted to the Black Market or the favours of spivs and GIs even if they might have had the opportunity) fed me as lavishly as they could. Nellie Beatrice could neither understand nor admire this behaviour. It was baffling, unmotivated and suspect. Like their house, which was untidy, shabby and none too clean, it paid no heed to her rent-book accounting. The kitchen at Ewell Parade was as bare as an empty operating theatre. The dishcloths were as sparkling as clean sheets and the scrubbing brushes looked scrubbed themselves. It would have taken a strange strain of germ to have entered there. The Walls' kitchen smelt of fat and burnt greens eroding the walls and woodwork, the saucepan enseamed and blackened like an industrial antique. What the bottom of the sink was like I never knew, as it was buried at all times beneath a cold greasy sea of floating china. If Ewell Parade was Auschwitz to germs, 39 Bradford Drive must have been Butlins with special terms for cockroaches.

Big-arsed Edna was a good-natured girl, rather plain and anxious. Saturday was the big night of the week at the Walls', though little happened except for a long and lavish tea when Edna's anxiety about the coming evening sometimes became oppressive. She and her friend would have a bath after tea and then rush up and down the stairs in curlers, half dressed for hours, in preparation for a dance at the Stoneleigh Hotel or the Toby Jug at Tolworth. It was a frantic, enjoyable event to watch. Few people I knew had a bath more than once a week. It was a fixed feast in the calendar, usually Friday or Saturday, and everyone took their turn. During the war it was unpatriotic and impractical to soak in more than the prescribed four inches, which barely covered the nether parts. It was a hardship easily borne. Most people shared Grandma Osborne's belief that immoderate bathing was 'weakening'. But before the demands of the war effort there were the claims of economy, health and even, in the Walls' case, a hint of morality – Mrs Wall insisted that Mickey bathed in a pair of bathing trunks to cover up what was known in that family as your 'tickle pot'. I was never sure whether this was one of his flights of flapping fancy. However we were not allowed to play cards on Sunday so it might have been a dark aspect of his mother's otherwise free and easy bearing. Similar Saturday-night fever must have been disrupting tea in lower middle-class households all over Britain, but at the Walls' it was simply rowdy and good tempered and Edna was a forgiving butt. After several hundred tantalized Saturdays Edna got married in the early part of the war to a French-speaking aircraftman from Guernsey. He left her after six months and nothing was said about the circumstances. I don't know whether or not she remarried. I hope so.

Mickey's brother, Alan, was a pupil at Tiffins School in Kingston. He was studious, amiable and looked uncritically upon his younger brother and even myself as temporary lunatics. The Walls were not, as my mother described them with sham admiration, a close-knit family. They were quite loosely knit, with dropped stitches all over the place, but as comfortable as an old pullover. To me, their trust seemed almost like indifference. The Osbornes and the Groves, with their common mistrust and carping, suspicious spirits, were neither close-knitted nor comfortable. The grudge that was their birthright they pursued with passionate despondency to the grave.

I had Saturday tea at the Walls', on and off, until I was nearly eighteen and went off to the provinces. Even at that age, even then, possibly from habit, Mickey and I behaved like a variety act, like giggling schoolgirls rather than teenagers who were curious about books and politics for no identifiable reasons. 'Come on, old man, out with it. If the joke's that good why don't you share it with everyone? Either that or get down from the table.' We would invariably have to 'get down', when we retreated to an emergency meeting of the Viper Gang in Mickey's room. The occasional cloud of disapproval or, even rarer, disgrace, was always preferable to hushed evenings at Clandon Close or the Old Black Look of Home.

M. Geoffrey Wall was president of the Viper Gang Club, membership two, myself being the secretary. The objects of the club were implicit in its name. It was formed to strike. Its targets needed no specification. It created a deterrent, although, as its existence was unknown except to us, its value in this respect was limited. We tried to remedy this by posting cards bearing an ill-drawn viper about to pounce above the words 'The Viper Gang is Watching You'. The teachers, schoolchildren and parents who received them can hardly have been alarmed. It was also frustrating, since no one could respond to the anonymous challenge, so postage was pointless as well as wasteful. However, the existence of a secret society can be sustained by the pursuit of pure secrecy itself like some abstract discipline. It was enough to be secret about being secret. The newsagent who refused to sell you five Woodies, even though you swore they were for your Dad, would have no idea that henceforth he was under permanent and clandestine malign scrutiny. Actual consumption of tuppeny ha'penny packets of Woodies, Weights or De Rezkes was indeed not only secret but subversive, risking deprivation of supper, privileges, pocket money, a possible thumping for Mickey or the Black Look of the Month Choice from my mother.

Soon I, too, became J. James Osborne, and survived for a while as the signature on the fly leaf of my school books. Later, when I began writing poetry and short stories I omitted the initial J. It sounded too American. John was a boring, commonplace name. James was forthright and adult-sounding. We both came from homes where books and music were almost completely disregarded. Although no one said as much, people who went out to work every day had no time for such luxuries. Even in the Walls' house there was little to read apart from the dusty Waverley novels, a complete Dickens and an incomplete encyclopaedia. When I see the junk books on my sixteen-year-old daughter's shelves and hear the exclusively pop music she plays, I wonder at the catholicity of the Viper Gang's taste in music and literature. I find it hard to understand what influences made us cast our cultural nets so haphazardly. Our earliest reading, with grown-up encouragement for once, was the *Magnet* and the *Gem*. We became early archivists in this later rich field, acquiring the first issue of the *Magnet*, 1908, and of the *Gem*, 1912, for a few pence in Epsom and Kingston markets. Later, when I was out of work, I sold the whole collection, with its Nelson Lees, Sexton Blakes and Schoolboy's Own Libraries, for £8. It would be worth many hundreds more than that now. We read comics: the *Dandy*, *Hotspur*, the *Wizard*, clung still to Mickey Mouse and had a fondness for *Chips*, a pink comic beloved of my father. This featured two especially likeable characters in Weary Willy and Tired Tim, who glorified good-hearted laziness and friendship, unharassed by teachers threatening not only work but extra work, and adults demanding stints of weeding or burdensome shopping, and were the very ideal of friends. The *Dandy*, with Keyhole Kate, Desperate Dan, Homeless Hector and Ivor Clue, was popular with everyone. Possibly, for this reason, I decided it was rather coarse. Popularity didn't affect my taste for *Film Fun*, I had spent too many hours in the cinema to resist its spell, its cramped little drawings with its regular final tableau of two comedy heroes – Laurel and Hardy or Arthur Askey and Stinker – sitting down in triumph to a blow-out in a posh restaurant surrounded by attentive waiters. Diamond tie-pins as big as pebbles sparkled above napkins tucked into their collars, as they brandished knives and forks in front of a gorgeous mountain of mashed potatoes studded with sizzling sausages pointing outwards, like batteries of guns on a battle cruiser.

This dish, which no one ever seems to have seen in life on a real plate, was the ultimate metaphor of wealth and success. It was the still-life subject of ultimate poshness. I once tried to persuade my mother to create it for me but she refused. I tried it myself, but the potatoes were neither mountainous nor gorgeous and the sausages, limp and bready, sagged pathetically. The tie-pins and the waiters were missing. Lacking, too, was the essential ingredient of this fantasy dish – success. Secret celebration is all very well, but when the reason for it is inaccessible, even to its participants, it must taste unsatisfying.

Beside Mr Wall's unread Waverley novels, there were a few books that must have been bought by someone in the family in the last century. Together with these, we read or skipped and delved into the books Mickey was later introduced to at Tiffins. We puzzled over and sometimes enjoyed Harrison Ainsworth (*The Tower of London*, particularly) and Bulwer Lytton, both dusty Victorian historical novelists, *Gulliver's Travels*, *Tale of a Tub*, *Rape of the Lock*, Everyman editions of Tacitus and Suetonius (odd chapters), and *The Faerie Queen* (his set books). I still have a lot of the books we read then. Apart from politics, histories of the world by Wells (*Crux Ansata* was a favourite) and Winwood Read were popular. I suppose they were the common popular self-educational coinage of the time. Wells seemed a bit too much like a scrimping schoolteacher for me. I goaded myself through Shaw's dull novels once, when I was convalescing in Penzance, but we enjoyed the Prefaces to the plays almost more than the plays themselves. They were both frowned upon, unread, by most adults which made them essential to the Viper Gang. Also on our shelves were *The Scarlet Letter*, *Alice in Wonderland* – read many times – Edgar Allen Poe, Dumas, Hugo, Stevenson, Kipling, Belloc for some reason, but not Chesterton. We had a sneaking regard for Grandma Osborne's Warwick Deeping and despised what were probably the most popular of boys' stories at the time, the Biggles books.

A device common to many of us, even in later life, is that of appraising the character of others by their tastes in literature, films or art by marking them against your own. It is a superficial guide to personality but can be surprisingly accurate in the case of early allegiances. Or so it seemed to me. Biggles readers were unspeakable, as were admirers of the Three Stooges, a film comedy trio universally popular with schoolchildren at the time. But partisanship about comedians seems to lose little of its intensity with the advance in time. The schism between Chaplin men and Keaton men remains abiding. Most of us revere our comic angels and denounce the devils of others. It is possibly as well that we each take our stand on laughter, which is founded on our confusion. We only compound the chaos it expresses for us by dissembling, because we fear to confess that we may sit unhappy and baffled, unable to be coerced by the laughter of others.

I don't know why we were both intrigued by books as musty objects as much as ciphers to something that was being concealed from us. Mickey certainly had a complacent, academic nature, an immunity to imagination (in spite of his near-Surrealist, almost Lewis Carroll swoops) that pointed unmistakably to his ending up a polytechnic pundit or at least a school-teacher of sorts. As it turned out, he became a clerk in the Transport Department at County Hall. He probably did the crossword in four minutes on the 8.17 to Waterloo, but the *Telegraph* not *The Times*. At the age of nine he had all the blandness and inability to be aroused of the fully paid-up London Library card-carrying pedant, all characteristics locked into life-long combat with my own ungovernable choler. Our temperaments could hardly have been more dissimilar.

In spite of my admiration for Mickey's awesome curiosity, I developed a distaste for crossword wizards. Apart from envy of such indisputable cleverness, I also felt perhaps unwisely that intellectual facility of this order must be the mark of an impassive, untroubled spirit – a justification for my own inadequacy which persisted. A few years ago in the south of France, I was joined by a group of young, rich, successful men and their wives and girlfriends. Their bronzed bodies glimmered with health, wealth and a muscley, animal yet urban confidence. The men were the kind of lawyers, accountants, brokers or property dealers who were being tipped to become millionaires before they were twenty-eight. One of the girls noticing me, asked me with over-polite indifference, 'What did you do for 17 Down?' My brain, dimmed more than usual by several morning Ricards and sunshine, slowly concluded that she was referring to that day's *Times* crossword. 'I don't do the *Times* crossword.' 'You don't!' Her surprise, if that is what it was, seemed more hostile than curious. 'But how do you exercise your mind?' Discarding the coarse reply that sprung to mind – 'I fuck intel-lectual girls' – possibly thinking it was too subtle for her and her com-panions, I mumbled something about letting my mind out for a swift turn round the block only when absolutely necessary.

When he was barely thirteen, Mickey declared he might become a philologist and walked about with two heavy works under his arm or in his satchel. One was Hogben's *Loom of Language* and another was by a Dane called Jespersen about the science of languages, and from these he would quote passages about the roots of Finnish or Icelandic verbs. Early on I had a rather morose taste for Grimms' tales and Oscar Wilde's fairy stories.

Perhaps because of Grandpa Grove's prurient obsession with Wilde, I read all I could find about him, as well as the plays, *The Ballad of Reading Gaol*, *De Profundis* and *Soul of Man under Socialism*. Even then this last was surprising and intriguing and seemed to contradict the flabby voluptuousness of the fairy tales or my grandfather's judgement of his life. Later, before 1945, we both became intrigued with Socialism and the Labour Movement, reading indelibly dull books about people like George Lansbury and J. B. Thomas, books about the General Strike, the Jarrow March and, of course, every available word of Orwell. We bought Strachey's *The Theory and Practice of Socialism*, *The Road to Wigan Pier*, *Guilty Men* and many another Gollancz orange-covered edition.

Somehow the excitement of the 1945 General Election filtered down to two schoolboys, possibly because it was the first Election we had experienced. The end of the buoyant days of the war was in sight and we must have looked for something to replace it. A new eager divisiveness was snatching in the air, increasingly evident in the *Mirror* and the *Daily Worker* which began to throw startling light for us on the attitudes of the *Mail* and *Telegraph*, and all the adults we knew read nothing else. We chortled over Quintin Hogg's book *The Case for Conservatism*. The case for Socialism appealed less to idealism than to the crude subversiveness of the early Viper Gang. We could acquire a populist chic with little more than slogans about the means of production, statistical runes about 1 per cent of the nation owning 90 per cent of the nation's wealth, and mere graffiti like 'Joe for King'. The practical mood of the country, sensed so accurately and crusaded by the *Mirror* with its Servicemen's readership, must have attracted an army of similar cheeky boys, to whom 'Jane' was not only a handmaiden to randiness but an Angel-General leading us out of the land of adolescent bondage.

Among such boys was Hugh, who later became a lecturer in politics at Keele. His was more of a Damascus awakening than our anarchic dissidence. At the age of thirteen or fourteen he was a passionate Christian Socialist and devotee of the works of Conrad Noel, whom he would quote almost word for word at great length, interspersed with long passages from Isaiah and *Prometheus Unbound*. Shelley and Isaiah were his twin Messiahs. Although we might have regarded ourselves as the Apostles of Ewell, there was little affinity otherwise between us and Hugh. His cleverness and the devoutness of his conversion were impressive but his solemnity clashed with our taste for cheap ridicule rather than systematic argument. There was a whiff of nocturnal emissionary zeal about the chap. We had the instincts of pillaging soldiery rather than missionaries.

Hugh's memory was prodigious, even by Mickey's standards. To me, having no gift of memory, it was miraculous. Our giggling Godlessness, bent on petty vexation rather than fierce vision, seemed and was shabby in the face of his Christian Socialism. Baring-Gould was another of his heroes. I got a little pleasure reading a passage from *Point Counter Point* in which the character based upon D. H. Lawrence suddenly reviles Shelley for canoodling with nauseating love-sick angels, ending up, 'I wish to God the bird [the skylark] had had as much sense as those sparrows in the book of Tobit and dropped a good large mess in his eye.' Hugh winced at my delight in Huxley's coarseness. 'You're so superficial,' he'd say. 'You sound just like Noel Coward.' I wasn't quite sure how to react to this. All I knew about Noel Coward was that he wore dressing gowns all day, played the Captain in the film *In Which We Serve*, which Mickey and I had enjoyed immensely, and had written the awful 'I'll See You Again', beloved of my mother. We made it clear that Baring-Gould gave us the pip and that Shelley was the victim of wanker's doom, without a decent limerick in him. Our ribaldry was doubtless the unthinking exuberance of commonplace minds. Whatever the truth of this might have been – and it could be justified – Old Hugh was mightily lacking in the salt of human scepticism. We all attended the local Labour Party meetings and Hugh was shocked at our mocking of the chairman who kept saying that the People had been Misled, a word that he pronounced as 'mizzled'. It was another example of our purblind failure to confine ourselves to what no doubt, in later years, Hugh would have called the Broader Issues.

Mickey and I were always joining, usually for a very short time, various societies or organizations. He persuaded me to join the Epsom Choral Society, which was affiliated to the Goldsmiths' Union. We both went for an audition. He read hardly any music and I none at all. Somehow we duped Mrs Ralph Vaughan Williams, who was in charge of the choir. We even took part in a concert in the Albert Hall and I found myself among a regiment of huge baritones struggling to make sure that I turned the pages over in the right place during the *Messiah* and the *St Matthew Passion*. Mickey joined something called the Linguists' Club for which I at least couldn't bluff my credentials. He discovered Bradlaugh, the Victorian atheist militant, and I subscribed to the Rationalist Press Association which published a monthly magazine, the *Freethinker*, which we read aloud eagerly, selecting the most offensive passages, to Hugh. Later, the office in which I worked in Fleet Street overlooked their headquarters in Johnson's Court and I could gaze down at the very temple of my unbelief. Another publication, *The Thinker's*

Library, featured contributions by a renegade Catholic priest calling himself Father McCabe. As I remember, his tales were almost exclusively concerned with the lewd activities apparently raging in monasteries, and the depravities of nuns.

The BBC was our sole music mentor, or mine certainly. For almost a year when I was in bed with rheumatic fever, I listened all day to both Forces and Home programmes, discovering how to pronounce Dvořák and Dohnányi and what the mysterious 'Köchel' might be. During the war, gramophone records had a punitive Purchase Tax imposed on them, being classed as luxuries, along with furs and jewellery. Perhaps it was some gaggle of sour egalitarians protecting the people from elitists who clamped a higher tax on Mozart than Glenn Miller. Anyway, one twelve-inch scarlet-label record of a symphony (usually six to eight sides) cost nine and elevenpence three farthings, 33⅓ per cent of which was tax. Collecting under these proscriptions was difficult so we pooled our money and saved for months to buy a symphony or concerto. We vowed to have a complete set of Beethoven and Vaughan Williams, all seventeen symphonies. We never achieved it partly because it was too tempting to buy single records rather than wait for weeks. The first one I ever bought was a Beecham recording of the 'Entry of the Queen of Sheba' and then Prokofiev's Classical Symphony.

The cinema was my church and academy. From about the age of four I went at least twice a week. In those days of double features I must have seen over two hundred films a year. It was the kind of thriftlessness that made Grandma Osborne and her tribe swear as indignantly as she did about the Welsh miners at home throwing legs of mutton to their whippets. When the insurance man, the clothing-club man or the milkman called and my mother was hiding in the bedroom, I would as often as not be sent to the front door to mumble, 'Mum's out'; but she could always lay hands on Money for the Pictures – the mainstay cultural benefit of a generation of children from similar backgrounds to my own. Picture Palaces, as Grandma Grove still called them, were aptly named. The warm luxury of Eastern or Egyptian Art Deco, the ascension of the cinema's organist like a matey angel, were preferable to a cold room with a mantelshelf lined with unpaid bills from doctors, coalmen and the Gas Light and Coke Company. To the profligate poor or near-poor, the priority of the Picture Palace was an unanswerable case.

Hollywood bit-players, now known by name only to cineastes, the elevator boys, gangsters, cab-drivers, bar-tenders, cops, butlers, Italian chefs and foreign counts were, I suppose, as real to us then as the characters of *Coronation Street* today. The difference lay in the kind of familiarity. For one thing, it was unmistakably foreign and beyond our reach. We had to learn to translate intuitively what Confederate money was, a sawbuck or even a hundred bucks, convert a dime or a nickel into something comparable, or the meaning of being behind the eight-ball, taking a rain-check or over and easy. These were elementary steps but they had to be mastered at an age when the grasp on your own language and birthplace was meagre enough.

But foreign, and specifically American, their very strangeness made the dreams of Hollywood accessible and open to identification and fantasy in a way that home-grown films were not. Surely few *Coronation Street* diehards could want to live there. The luxury and privilege of, say, living in Manhattan held more promise of imaginative fulfilment than the more familiar but remote English equivalents. The American model was unreal but attainable, the English model slightly more real but ultimately unattainable. A world of large gardens, tennis parties, housemaids, college scouts and Inns of Court might seem pleasant and comfortable enough but there was little impulse or point of dreaming yourself into it. You would watch it from without but never enter it even if you were inclined. What was not unimaginable or close to you was Eric Blore opening the door to your apartment, having William Powell recover your wife's jewellery for you, being made vice-president of a corporation by your father-in-law, Edward Arnold or Eugene Palette, handing your topper to the hat-check girl at the Stork Club as you escorted Carole Lombard or even, at a pinch, Gail Patrick into dinner, wearing a black shirt and white tie and black pin-stripe with a white carnation like Dan Duryea, or maybe taking a cab driven by Frank Jenkins to Penn Station. There was no need to have passed your Common Entrance, let alone have been to Eton or Oxford. It was available, to be admired, envied and even coveted, and most of all to those of us in the front seats who had sneaked in through a carelessly unbarred exit door.

Madeleine Carroll was my earliest favourite star, but then there were scores, year after year, never replacing, only enriching each other. Robert Donat reminded me of my father, although they were unalike. I saw *Thirty-Nine Steps* whenever I could and there was a time when I knew the dialogue of *The Four Feathers* and *The Prisoner of Zenda* by heart. The Rembrandt Cinema in Ewell was almost always full every evening during the war. On Fridays and Saturdays there was certain to be a queue. A Bette Davis film was almost impossible to get into all the week. Even Grandma Osborne was known to leave her Warwick Deeping for the afternoon and walk a hundred unaided yards to the Rembrandt to see *Now Voyager* or *Mr Skeffington*.

I can only remember one occasion when the Rembrandt was almost empty the whole week – apart from Mondays, which were unpopular. The word of mouth about the film showing around Ewell and Stoneleigh was resentful and indignant. In the Parades and saloon bars, there was talk of Speaking to the Manager, even of Writing to the Film People themselves. Later in the week, undeterred by those who said we were wasting our pocket money, Mickey and I went to see *Citizen Kane*. We came out afterwards from looming Gothic darkness into the bright Kingston Road, silent, uncomprehending and deeply depressed. At tea the Walls asked if we had tummy ache. It had been nothing, even for two such eleven-year-olds as we were, to giggle about.

6. Bugger Bognor

My father was away in the sanatorium in Menton for a few months, leaving me without even a silent ally. I went home as little as I could, spending days or the short evenings first with Joan Buffen and later with the Walls. I avoided going back to the certainty of the Black Look, the reproach for being late when I had scrupulously made sure I was on time, the whine of complaints about selfishness, what was so special about the Walls? They were nobody; he was only a government clerk; worse than a guvnor's man; only with a pension. That stuck-up kid in her riding breeches, who did they think they were? Anyone could run a wool shop if you'd got the money; morbid job; no life; so bloody quiet; no one to talk to; dead and alive; nowhere to go; seen all the pictures on; walked to Epsom; just enough for a cup of tea and a bun; can't remember when I last had a drink.

Ewell, 1964

Dear John,

They say if one can live here one can live anywhere, as one might express it: the English weather is always pulling down the blind on beauty. I would like to have a small cottage near the sea: and shops – *not* too remote as I have been so used to noise and lots of cars and people, when one is old and lives alone one does not want to be shut up at least, I don't; after all you're a long time dead. I like life and people and I think a change from this place and Stoneleigh would be rather nice. Please *don't* think I am discontented: *far from it*. Treated myself to a pair of curtains: cost nearly £2 gosh everything is a price: you could get the same ones for 10/- a few years back: but it will brighten it up a bit. Had a dam depressing letter from Queenie: so sent her £1 to cheer her up. What an unhappy woman she is.

Always in my thoughts,
Mother

p.s. Sorry ree the mistakes and writing – must get some more glasses my sight is not too good.

Fortunately, she let my room to a commercial traveller and spent hours preparing huge meals for him in the evenings with the result that she had a lodger *and* was well out of pocket at the week's end. When he offered to pay more she refused, saying to me, 'I can't help it. I'm just good hearted that's all. There it is – that's the way I am. Always have been.' This preposterous conviction was reward enough for her and she smiled at me knowingly when she gave Mr Evans his dinner, telling him what a quiet, good boy I was. However, it was more than worth my sleeping on the sofa and I hoped he would stay until my father returned.

I got regular postcards from the south of France with his drawings on one side of them, very detailed and spidery. They were mostly jokes constructed around current catch-phrases, using me as the principal character. He sent one of a 'skipper', which was his name for me, in a sou'wester and vast oilskins, staring up at an enormous giraffe, quoting Mae West, 'Come up and see me sometime.' 'Can't. I'm no angel,' replied Skipper. I had dozens of these with laconic messages in his tiny but legible handwriting, always in green ink and with a postscript for my mother. 'Dad's had his bum shot full of gold today so he's never been more valuable. The nurse is German and a proper Hun she is. Must be Mrs Hitler.' I kept them for twenty years until they were stolen from me by a vengeful lady of too intimate acquaintance who refused to return them.

Early in 1939 he returned, relieved to be free of the Hun's tortures. Sitting around the flat, fully dressed but always wearing his Sherlock Holmes-style check piped dressing gown and large carpet slippers, stroking the cat and reading, he said little but his presence silenced my mother somewhat and the atmosphere and tension calmed considerably. Occasionally he would venture out to a nearby pub and go for a short walk, but by the spring he was again spending most of the day in bed.

During that summer the Walls took me in their dinky claret and black Ford to Felpham near Bognor. It was their custom to rent a little semi-detached house in this seaside suburb which has now become an exclusively geriatric watering place. It was pleasant enough, a little like the leafier environs of Clandon Close with identical shopping parades catering for its mostly regular annual visitors. Nellie Beatrice reluctantly agreed to let me go after tactful pressure from my father. He was not yet so ill that she dared to ignore his fleeting will. As ever she was determined not to be beholden to anyone or tricked into making preparations for suspect favours. Naturally, the Walls thought nothing of it. The only money I needed was the price of a cheap bathing costume – one and sixpence – which I bought at the H. G. Wells draper's in Epsom with its smell of calico and overhead cash trolleys. When I showed it to her, she said, 'Well, there goes my Sunday Guinness.' I decided the best course was to disbelieve her. She was to remind me of this sacrifice from time to time, probably in imitation of Grandma Osborne and the Lisbon Hospital bills. Immediately I returned she waited sullenly for me to finish my blurting account of Royal Bognor before she attacked me for not having brought back a present for her or my father. My father told me not to think about it, which is exactly what I had done. Eight days of Black Looks could not blow away the sunny freedom of those two weeks.

I had been to Bognor before in the winter of 1934. Bognor, made legend by the last words of the recently dead king. Three years ago I returned with my daughter. It seemed very much the same – pleasingly small, shabby and unassuming – with the same arcade of shops and stalls, the pier (now irreparably storm-damaged), a first-rate bookshop, Queen Victoria's comfortable old hotel. Apart from a huge Colditz Butlin's complex on the eastern shore, some concession to fashion and dress, a collection of foreign students hanging around the Victorian station and more traffic, it could almost have been 1939 again.

On my first visit I had been sent to recuperate from a mastoid operation, subsidized entirely by my father's charitable association, the National Advertising Benevolent Society, which was to steer both of us through the fiscal waters of repeated illnesses. Then, with my right ear smothered in one of my mother's absurd black berets, specially sent from Paris she boasted, we stayed in a very cheap boarding house where welcome was unknown, particularly during the day. Forbidden to return to our cold bedroom till high tea, we trailed around the town, a small enough place, in the March wind and rain waiting in cafés and promenade shelters for the cinemas to open. Munching ham rolls from Woolworth's, we would shiver until it was time for us to be allowed back for our soup, pink salmon and salad. I came out in a series of large ugly blisters which burst like watery boils and were extremely painful. The local doctor insisted that the only cure for them was to stand in the icy sea up to my knees. I was also to conceal them from the landlady in case she turned us out. Neither of us wanted to stay but my mother was afraid that we might be reported to Mrs Ure, the kindly secretary of the benevolent society, who had made our holiday arrangements for us.

My visit with the Walls was very different. We went for long drives in the black and claret Ford into the countryside for picnics, to Chichester to look over the Cathedral, empty and uncluttered by German tourists, unlike when I visited it some forty years later. We spent the long sunny days on the beach tucking into piles of tinned salmon, sardine and ham sandwiches, shivering in the cold sea, sustained by Tizer, blessed Tizer, the orange champagne bubbly of thirties' children, and the cooler mornings in amusement arcades, with fish and chips for tea, the end-of-the-pier show and then back to Felpham, as friendly and familiar as Bradford Drive. We could go back when we liked and stay up as long as our happy, tired bodies would allow us.

Only one incident marred my second visit to Bognor. For years I suffered the humiliation of being a fairly regular bed-wetter. I had not yet discovered that this was a common affliction and that the lone unfortunate bed-wetters themselves conspired unknowingly in their own isolation, each one intimidated into believing that he or she was a toad-like creature who made a swamp of beds in defiance of all that was decent. If it was hinted that a child had 'filthy habits' everyone knew at once what it meant – and it wasn't picking one's nose. To be exposed as one of these was hideous degradation, and left you permanently under threat of blackmail, revenge or gratuitous cruelty from any child or parent who might be privy to the sinful stream that insistently gushed forth from your possessed body. Certainly a majority of children at the schools I attended were such sinners, but working-class clothes smelt anyway and stale urine was little more than an ammonial additive. Parents and children from Bradford Drive and Clandon Close, with at least one ritual bath a week and neat washing lines, were more fastidious. Occasionally, some especially nasty boy – a customs officer, Inland Revenue Inspector or letter-writer to the *Daily Telegraph* in the making – would yell, 'Pooh! Blimey! Don't go near him, he's wet his bed!' And a few more inspectors, town hall toadies and form-serving bullies-to-be of post-war Britain would hold their noses and perhaps dance around the flushed-out victim. But some of the tormentors would be aware of the shame beneath their own noses.

Naturally, my mother was hot on to this gaping weakness, and it stoked her ingenuity to theatrical excess. She would settle for nothing less than an auditorium for my arraignment. She would expose me before the assembled school, the Headmaster, the lady teachers, the girls, indeed the entire world. Grim tales abounded about children forced to stand with their shameful sopping shrouds covering their bowed heads. It must have been a fairly common ritual, especially in institutions, but observed in lower middle-class homes as well. As usual, my father, when he was at home, came to my rescue. When he discovered this reign of blackmail he immediately and angrily put a stop to it. Brushing aside my mother's aggrieved self-righteousness, he took me to a doctor, who discussed the problem, all smiles, and diagnosed a general state of anxiety, which sounded more encouraging than wilful sloth. The doctor gave me a monthly diary in which I was to mark the dry days with a red pencil, rather like a church calendar. My father checked it with me regularly, but for months there were no red-letter days, High or Holy, and we quietly gave up the experiment. Nothing was said. Nellie Beatrice was not yet secure enough in my father's frailty to challenge him but she gave the clear impression of having been vindicated of cruelty.

So, I was unsurprised after a night's blissfully fatigued sleep in Felpham to wake early and find myself wet, cold and immediately awake and trembling. I was sharing a bed with Mickey but his place was empty. I lay wondering whether I had overflowed on to his side. Hoping it might dry up under the heat of my own body I got up and found that the guilty overflow seemed to have stayed in my own territory. I took off my wet pyjama trousers and looked up to find Mickey and his brother Alan staring at me and at the bed. Almost immediately, I ejected another pounding flood on to the bare floorboards. The sound of it seemed to splutter all over the small house and go on endlessly. Finally Alan said, rather calmly, 'You seem to have a weak bladder, old man.' I stared at the ragged grey stain, defeated. When they had gone to breakfast, I managed to approach Mrs Wall alone in the kitchen and began to explain the terrible event. She interrupted me almost at once, telling me to have my breakfast and not let it spoil my holiday. I knew the boys wouldn't have told her. They seemed no more than mildly curious about my bladder. It must have been Big Edna. To my unbelieving gratitude it was never referred to by anyone. I was especially appalled at the idea of Edna knowing about it and I was excessively polite to her, not only for the rest of the holiday but from then on.

On our last day Mickey and I became very gloomy at the prospect of returning to Ewell. Our lugubrious depression must have been comic for it amused everyone else. We packed up our buckets, spades and the toys bought for the beach and I put my collection of tiny crabs into a bucketful of stinking sandy water. I later emptied them into my frog Horace's tin bath. Whether it was the foul water that killed him or the crabs I don't know, but he only survived the creatures of the sea for a few hours, which added tragedy to the sorrow of my return home. We went down in the early September sunshine and looked out at the sea, hurling pebbles skilfully across the tops of the waves, bouncing out to the darkening, golden sea. 'Good-bye Bognor. See you next year . . .'

'No such undertaking has been received . . .'

I know the place to within a foot where I was standing when the material for countless comedians' later scripts incorporating Chamberlain's words came from out of my mother's kitchen into the air at eleven o'clock on that still Sunday morning. She was having her Sunday Guinness and I was standing on the green-iron landing waiting for Joan to come back from church. My father was in bed reading the *Sunday Express*. As the words came out from the window: 'No such undertaking has been received and we are now at a state of war with Germany', I had no idea that I would come to know them as well as the Lord's Prayer. I rather liked Mr Chamberlain, especially his butterfly collar and umbrella. He looked like the sympathetic headmaster of a posh school.

Almost immediately after Chamberlain's thin voice faded away and before the BBC launched into one of its fits of national solemnity with an orgy of Elgar and elegy, the air-raid siren sounded. It had begun. Herr Hitler hadn't wasted any time. This was the week when my father had read out the *Daily Express* banner headline: 'THERE WILL BE NO WAR'. My mother was saying something about it not being like the last time and thanked God Dad was too ill to be called up and I was too young. If I were to be left later on my own with my mother the prospect of going into the Army or, preferably, the Navy offered escape but not for almost nine years – my age over again. I think my father said the words which we were all to hear so often in the next few months that it would All Be Over By Christmas, but I was determined to be unconvinced. I looked out the pamphlets about what to do in the event of an air-raid and took my Identity Card from its drawer. I would doubtless need it when stopped in the street by suspicious policemen. I had already memorized its number – EPHA/64/3. Like so many official things at the time it was blessedly more simple than such a document would be today. An Identity Card number now would have at least forty digits instead of the mere seven. Some lunatics have recently advocated the reintroduction of these Identity Cards. It is certain they would be impossible to remember.

A whistle sounded from the road and I rushed to the window to see what was happening. It was like the beginning of an early Ealing Comedy. An elderly, blue tin-hatted policeman was labouring up the hill from the village on a bicycle, occasionally pausing to blow his whistle. His progress was extremely slow and breathless. Hanging around his neck was a placard with the message: 'TAKE COVER'. Take cover? Where? Stay indoors, I supposed he meant. Presently, he disappeared over the hill and the All Clear went. A false alarm or a trick of the enemy? Or Whitehall, whatever it was. Mickey's father, Mr Wall, worked for Whitehall. Perhaps he might know.

I resisted all this adult talk about it being all over by Christmas. It was rather the same attitude, I felt, as my grandmother's Boxing Day spoil-sporting. I don't know whether my father believed it. In the circumstances he can't have cared very much. Anyway, I was determined not to believe it. I didn't want to believe it. The war was like an extended Christmas, a festival of carolling warriors, or it might be with any luck. Invasion seemed like the idea of Christmas to me, better than the brawling, carping Christmases in Clandon Close or Harbord Street. My father seemed to know a great deal about the Great War. After all, it had only been over for twenty years. Of course, he had been like myself, too young to fight. He was fourteen years old when *the* great war was declared. I besieged him with questions about anything he might remember.

Mrs Ure wrote to my father saying that the Benevolent Society would make arrangements for us all to move to Ventnor in the Isle of Wight where we would be safer and the climate would be more suitable for his health. There was a famous sanatorium in the area where he could be looked after if and when it became necessary. On a bright September day, the 28th, a huge Daimler ambulance drew up at the back yard behind the shops and my father was lifted on a stretcher down the steep iron steps into it. It was enormous inside with great windows, and looked like a very comfortable upholstered hearse. My mother and I went in afterwards and sat down. It was thrilling. I would miss Mickey, but he was buoyant to flapping point at the new drama of our various lives. Everyone said I would make New Friends, but I didn't set much store either by their judgement or by the likelihood of meeting anyone as stimulating or amusing as M. Geoffrey Wall.

I had only been in Mr Wall's car before and the majestic trip across Surrey, over the Devil's Dyke, Hampshire and the New Forest was luxuri-ous. It was enjoyable being stared at by people as we drove through towns and were observed like the Royal Family going up The Mall. We made Royal Progress to the ferry at Southampton. The sea looked dark and dangerous and we were surrounded in the harbour by grey, whooping des-troyers. Would we be torpedoed? We arrived at Ventnor in the late sunny afternoon, going on a mile or two to a place called St Lawrence Halt where there was a tiny railway station and a gloomy, grey Victorian hotel called the Carfax, which I was to get to know well. Below the country road leading on to Black Gang Chine and Niton, a small village, was a little 1930-ish house with a large derelict garden and orchard that went down almost to the sea itself. From my bedroom I could see out into the Atlantic for miles. I went for a walk almost immediately in the fading autumn sunlight. The downland on the upper cliff was full of places to explore and trees to climb. There were a great many cattle and hardly a sign of anyone except the occasional dog walker on the beach far below the chalk cliffs. I hurried back into my father's bedroom to tell him what I had seen.

Soon there was very little to be seen as a few days later a black mist and enveloping fog settled over the whole island, only to be pierced by the flash of gunfire from the convoy attacks in the Channel, which took place frequently during the next few months. That unyielding icy mist must have bitten into my father's remaining lung immediately. No cars, let alone trams. I spent days wandering along the cliffs between Ventnor and Black Gang Chine, ancient shrine of smugglers, where I was soon to play constant truant from school. My introduction to the school was much the same in every detail as my initiation at Ewell Boys, only it seemed colder and more alien. Again, little work was done and we seemed to spend most of the time practising gas-mask drill and preparing for an air-raid. Air-Raid Drill in any school I ever went to was conducted with the same grim bullying tactics, although most children found it difficult to take seriously. The most popular use of the gas masks themselves was as megaphones for farting sounds made from within. They steamed up immediately when donned and it was almost impossible to see, let alone breathe. The possibility of surviving long inside one of these smelly, steamy rubber things, with or without a gas attack, seemed unlikely. Apart from this, the straps hurt your head.

My mother managed to get a few medical certificates from my father's sympathetic doctor, saying that I was too delicate to attend school during the island winter and the four-mile walk every day was too harsh for my health. This was untrue, but the walk itself was indeed long and bitterly cold and, in the almost black wintry evenings under arches of overhanging trees, rather frightening. I settled down to following the course of the conflict in the newspapers and on my own cheap portable wireless. My bedroom began to resemble a briefing room with photographs and drawings from the newspapers of anything to do with the war. On one wall was a map of Europe and the Western Front, with the Maginot Line and the Siegfried

Line clearly marked, and Swastikas, French flags and Union Jacks dotted all over such places as Latvia, Lithuania, Estonia, Czechoslovakia. One of my particular favourite photographs was of Finnish soldiers looking like white-hooded monks on skis poised to fight off Russian troops. It was about this time that the P&O liner, *Rawalpindi*, sank. My father seemed affected by it. 'Look,' he said, 'the old *'Pindi*'s gone down.' There was a wonderfully dramatic drawing of it sinking, guns blasting the sky in the *Daily Mail*. 'Gone,' said my father, 'the old *'Pindi.'* It seemed to upset him.

A new schools' attendance officer, more zealous than the previous one, discounted my mother's certificates and insisted that I go to St Boniface's School in Ventnor. Again, it was very like the one before. Coming home after the first day with blood on my collar there was a Black Look intensified by the island's chill to greet me. I managed to keep away as much as possible from the small enshadowed house and explored the beach which stretched for miles, and hardly anyone in sight. It was in this way that I met Isabel Sells, and fell in love for the second time. She was a tall, pretty girl, much taller than I, and had just had her twenty-first birthday. I met her as she was walking her dog along the beach and she was so immediately friendly and easy that a wave of happiness overwhelmed me, as I had not felt since first crouched on the kennel floor with Joan. Here, I was sure, I had found a true friend and one who would allow me to love her. She told me that her mother ran the Carfax Hotel, but because of the war there were hardly any visitors. They lived there alone with her grandmother. The bad news was that she had just become engaged to a young man called Raymond. He was twenty-eight and wasn't in the Army because he was in a Reserved Occupation. In the event, he turned out to be a very jolly, companionable young man who always seemed astonishingly pleased for me to join them. At weekends the three of us would set out enthusiastically along the beach and over the cliffs together. For some reason I insisted on calling him Professor Huggem. Perhaps it was because a lot of kissing and cuddling went on between the two of them, which caused me to feel much more than envy. Still, my distress was worth witnessing such trusting pleasure so easily passing from one to another. I had the occasional consolation of holding Isabel's willing hand when they finished.

She invited me to tea every Sunday and it became a regular occasion. Sometimes I even went during the week when Raymond was claimed by his Reserved Occupation, which was even more enjoyable. Her mother was a warm woman – motherly, I would have called her, if the word did not have a specific meaning for me. The third member of the Sells' family was the grandmother who always dressed in black bombazine with a toque and a huge black overcoat. She also had a black cane and a smelly black dog. She was like a mixture between Queen Mary and Giles's cartoon Grandma. She sat beside the fire in a vast, Spanish ebony armchair, never moving except to say something disapproving, principally of Isabel but also of her daughter. They took no notice of her and Isabel laughed openly, if kindly, at her. She whispered in my ear, 'She hasn't had a bath for months. I don't think she's taken her clothes off for *years.*' Certainly the old lady was more polite to me than she was to her own relatives. In fact, she seemed to almost look forward to my visits, as she always asked me lots of probing questions about myself and what I was doing. This adult curiosity was most unusual, so I felt she couldn't be all that bad.

The Carfax was not as boisterous a retreat as 39 Bradford Drive, but it was a happy escape from the tiny kitchen down the road at our house, inappropriately called *Mon Abri*, My Refuge. The whole family seemed interested in me and treated me as if I were an equal, even the formidable old Giles woman seeking out my boyish opinions about anything. For example, when discussing the progress of the war or the state of the nation, I was able to find my voice and use it to some length, as I read the newspapers from cover to cover and, of course, there were the exhibits in my briefing room. I must have seemed oddly well informed on developments in every theatre of war and thoughout the Empire. During a discussion about when it would all end, the Sells and their friends had all agreed with my father about it being 'All Over By Christmas'. I confounded them with my firm opinion that it would last at least five years. Unknown to me at the time, it seems that Lloyds were offering odds in late October that the war would be over by Christmas. The national obsession with Christmas seemed to be very like my own.

The island was shrouded in silence apart from the whooping destroyers passing the island in convoy, out of sight in the thick mist. Something was going on out there and, whatever it was, I was missing it. Whenever their guns roared, the whole island seemed to shake as if it might disappear into the sea. I think my mother would have wished exactly that. She complained even more bitterly about her loneliness and this deadest of dead-and-alive holes. As far as I remember, the nearest cinema was a considerable bus-ride away in Shanklin. Ventnor seemed hardly as lively as Ewell Village, especially out of season as it was now. No doubt in the summer it was very different, but I was not to find out.

As my mother bit her nails to purplish stumps, my father grew weaker, and I was able to spend more time with him in his bedroom as she huddled over the kitchen grate. We read aloud from the papers to each other and, while his strength lasted, long adventure yarns from his old copies of *Boys' Own Paper*, 1908–12. When he grew tired I would read to him. November came and I began to become excited at the prospect of Christmas. I don't know why, because there seemed little to become exercised about, just the three of us together. However I was sure that lovely Isabel would ask me over, possibly on Boxing Day as I knew my mother wouldn't allow me out of the house on Christmas Day. She would say that I was leaving my father and her all on their own. It was, of course, only half a mile down the road. I think she also suspected that my feelings for Isabel were not just those of childish friendship. Anyway, she was disapproving of the Sells family, thinking that if they ran an hotel they must be rich and privileged, which they clearly were not. She soon developed an overweening jealousy of the family, Isabel in particular, and was always discouraging my visits. 'You're not to go down there and worry Mrs Sells. She's got quite enough to do looking after that hotel. I'm sure that they don't want you round the place – kid like you.' As much as I protested that they *liked* me being there, she wouldn't believe it. Well, Boxing Day would at least be free of Grandma Osborne's annual Christmas message.

Round about the end of November, an ambulance, an ordinary white one this time, took my father on a stretcher to the sanatorium between Ventnor and Shanklin. My mother and I accompanied him, helping him out into his wheelchair when we arrived there. It was a huge Edwardian affair, like a Continental hotel, with grand verandahs facing out to the sea, where patients coughed in their beds overlooking the black mist. I waited in a corridor while my mother and father went up to see a doctor. They were not away very long and we returned home in silence. While the ambulance men carried him back up the stairs, my mother said, 'Well, your father's only got six weeks. Six weeks to *live*, do you understand?' Would he be alive at Christmas? '*I* don't know, do I? Don't ask bloody silly questions.'

I didn't quite believe my mother. She was not to be trusted. I was determined to give him a nice present, something to keep him going, even alive. I scarcely bothered to think of what I might get for her. One evening I asked him what he would like for Christmas. He told me that there was a new series of books called Penguin Books that could be bought at W. H. Smith's and he said, 'I'll give you a list. They're only sixpence.' He gave me a selection, which included *Ariel* by André Maurois, a Pelican book in fact, and I think the first. The other two were *Death of a Hero* by Richard

Aldington and *A Safety Match* by Ian Hay. I had saved some money from Ewell days, there being little to spend it on anyway on the island and went out and bought the three of them immediately.

Mon Abri, it turned out, was to be a very poor refuge from death and Christmas Day, when it arrived, was a morose affair. Money seemed to be shorter here than it had been in the suburbs and my pillowcase was limp, barely a quarter full. I never had the customary stocking. My mother did not have the thrifty middle-class imagination to attempt filling an inexpensive stocking with makeshift surprise delights. But there was a splendid model yacht, which I stupidly tried to convert into a three-master schooner, making it top-heavy and impossible to sail, a few odds and ends, comics and, best of all, *Boys' Own Annual* and the *Greyfriars Annual*. I gave my father the three books from his list. 'But I didn't mean you to get all three of them, Skipper. I only meant you to get me one.' But he seemed pleased with them.

Christmas dinner was fretful. My father put his dressing gown on and came down the few stairs into the sitting-room, where he hardly ate anything at all except his favourite bread sauce, saying that he would prefer to have the bird cold. He left nearly all of it while my mother scowled with heavy-breathing and pique. We listened to the King's Speech and toasted him sitting down. My father said this was a traditional custom in the Navy. The King himself was obliged to give up the Christmas 1939 forecast and said: 'We cannot tell what it [the New Year] will be. If it brings peace how happy we shall be.' Eating my own dinner eagerly, I was suddenly overcome with a panic sense of loneliness that I felt had descended on me for good. Sitting between my father and mother I burst into tears as he struggled to fan the tiny blue flame on Grandma Osborne's Christmas pudding. 'What's he grizzling on about?' said my mother. 'Leave him alone,' my father replied. 'The boy's upset. It's not surprising is it?' Or something like it. I left the remains of my dinner while my mother cluttered our plates noisily back into the kitchen. As I went up the stairs to my room I could hear her muttering about all the trouble she had gone to and nobody bothering, not so much as a bloody thank-you, at least she wouldn't have to spend another dead-and-alive Christmas in *Mon* bloody *Abri*. The following day she allowed me to go down to the Carfax and I almost forgot the sense of inescapable desertion I'd felt the previous day, consoling myself with kissing Isabel underneath the mistletoe, albeit egged on by laughing Raymond. I longed to enfold her passionately.

January 1940 came and I managed to keep away from school more than ever, although the attendance officer was a constant visitor. He was surprisingly friendly but kept pointing out with uncommon official tact that school could not be put off for ever. It was at least a temporary reprieve. However, I was legitimately unwell for a while with a bad cough and often feverish, which prompted my mother to tell the attendance officer convincingly that I was going to be just like my father.

I was sitting in the kitchen reading about two weeks after Christmas, when I heard my mother scream from the foot of the uncarpeted staircase. I ran to see what was happening and stared up to the landing where my father was standing. He was completely naked with his silver hair and grey, black and red beard. He looked like a naked Christ. 'Look at him!' she screamed. 'Oh, my God, he's gone blind.' He stood quite still for a moment and then fell headlong down the stairs on top of us. Between us we carried him upstairs. She was right. He had gone blind.

A day or two later my grandfather arrived. The old man's presence seemed to restrain even my mother, although she still contrived to treat him as a begging tramp at the door, overfeeding him as if he were some wandering supplicant. My father seemed to recover and brighten up in his own father's presence and they spent some time talking to each other. I was curious to know what it was about but never ventured in when they were alone together. Grandfather was rather shyly apologetic about Grandma Osborne's absence, saying that she was, *of course*, not strong enough to make the journey. Besides, it was far too cold for her. Together we went for a few long walks up on the cliff. He said very little to me except to murmur about how I should have to Manage On My Own in future, putting ponderous emphasis on this fact. He was obviously thinking of my mother, who was already making no secret of her relief that it would all be over soon, when she could get out of this dead-and-alive hole and back to London or, at least, to the blacked-out lights of Ewell.

My father's condition soon deteriorated. When I saw him he croaked incoherently and the doctor suggested that it would be a good idea if I were to spend the next few days down at the Carfax with Mrs Sells and pay a short daily visit to my father. I found myself occupying a bedroom next to Isabel, full of dread for the time when I should soon have to leave it. The day my father died my mother came down to the Carfax and told Mrs Sells. She tried to insist on my immediate return but she was gently coaxed back. I threw myself into the arms of Isabel for the comfort I felt I would never receive again. The following day I was reluctantly sent back up to *Mon Abri*. My mother would need looking after. She was waiting excitedly for me and at once insisted that I go into my father's bedroom to look at him in his coffin. The smell in the room was strong and strange and, in his shroud, he was unrecognizable. As I looked down at him, she said, 'Of course, this room's got to be fumigated, you know that, don't you? Fumigated.' Frumigated was how she pronounced it. With my father's body lying in the bedroom across the landing, I had been obliged to share my briefing room with my mother, who spent hour upon hour reading last Sunday's *News of the World*, the bright light overhead, rustling the pages in my ear and sighing heavily. For the first time I felt the fatality of hatred.

A few days later, after hysterical hours of packing up and my grandfather being abused for his meticulous slowness, we left the house taking my father in yet another Daimler ambulance. The journey back to Southampton was unlike the journey out. I was going back to Ewell but nothing could be the same. Mickey Wall had won a scholarship to Tiffins Boys' Grammar School. Joan Buffen was lost for ever. The funeral in the crematorium in Southampton was unremarkably eerie. From the faded pages of a pencilled diary I can read: 'January 31st. Father's funeral today.' And then a description of the coffin rattling on its rails, disappearing behind the purple curtains. 'I met the clergyman who is one of the nicest individuals I have ever met.' Who could I have been addressing so self-consciously?

We returned by train to Clandon Close where Grandma Osborne received us rather as if we had been obliged to cut short an unwise holiday. When her daughter Nancy had died two years before, she had worn a black armband in the house for twelve months. She wore no mourning sign now, even in her face, which looked as if the wafery skin had tightened with a repressed vindication. Her eyes seemed brightened and not by grief. My mother and I shared the second bedroom at the top of the stairs. During the next few months we paid constant visits to the headquarters of 'Dad's Society' in St Paul's Churchyard to discuss our future with Mrs Ure, what work my mother could do, and my schooling, followed by incessant talk of wills and insurance on the train home and in the bedroom. My father had taken out a life insurance policy with the Sun Alliance and Insurance Company of Canada for £400. It emerged that he signed a letter, under clear duress from his mother on one of his Sunday morning visits, stating that his entire estate, such as it was, was to go to her in repayment for the Bay of Biscay incident some thirty years before. He was finally to settle his debt.

My mother made as much show of resistance to this as she could. Letters to and from the Osborne family solicitors, Monson and Petty of Newport, Mon., dropped through the shared letter-box. After weeks of morning races to catch the postman first, my mother gave up and the old lady pocketed the money without a word said. Routed and intimidated, Nellie Beatrice smarted silently while Grandma's bearing quickened more brightly than ever. It was clear that we should have to find digs. The Grove pride, incapable of accepting kindness let alone charity and in spite of protests that it 'was unnecessary and a waste of money' to leave our room in Clandon Close, made a hasty, defiant move inevitable. I would have preferred to stay. Although I was in an exposed, neutralized position, my grandmother offered me some protection that would vanish as soon as I left the seething calm of the cul-de-sac.

Finding digs was disappointingly easy. The newsagents' boards in Stoneleigh Parade were full of cards offering accommodation and the ambiguous 'use of kitchen'. There were fewer bowler hats and more battle-dresses on the station platform in the early mornings. The 'business' trains became crowded with ex-filing clerks, shop assistants and senior storemen in khaki, often standing where they had once sat unchallenged. Army boots scraped the polish from City shoes and crisp *Telegraphs* and *Daily Mails* were ruffled by hoisted kit bags. Street after street of two-ups, normally in siege against friends, let alone strangers, suddenly sought out occupants for their spare rooms. Confronted by paybooks and uncertainty, housewives who had scarcely ever nodded at next-door-but-one from the fastness of their latticed stockades openly touted for well-behaved hostages. Rarely, the motive was a desire for discreet 'company' and fear of being alone in the house surrounded by blacked-out deserted streets. Usually it was a reluctant concession enforced by the meagreness of Privates' pay. Like all amateur landladies, and many professionals, they sought the Invisible Lodger with visible rent books filled in unfailingly every Friday.

In her fury to 'get away from the Osbornes' my mother was in no mood to be discriminating. Taking with us little more than a suitcase of clothes, we were soon settled in with a Mrs Williams, at 120 Worcester Park Road. This was on the north side of Stoneleigh Station where the ribbon development at its highest looked back out upon the metropolis. On a clear day you could see the gasholders of south-west London. We had a double room and share of the kitchen. The sitting-room was theoretically at our disposal, but although Mrs Williams was quite a genial woman, it seemed implicit that we were not expected to ever take advantage of this amenity. Besides, my mother pointed out that we liked to keep ourselves to ourselves and John was a very quiet boy.

At this new address, I had no choice but to go to Elmsleigh Road School, which was some five minutes' walk away and near the north side of Sherwood Forest. My mother soon got a job working at Carters Seed Factory at Raynes Park, two stations away. This was piece-work, picking seeds, demanding a mechanical dexterity to achieve even a starvation wage. She would often come back with only twenty-two and sixpence a week. As our rent was something like twelve and sixpence excluding a shilling a week for the bath plus her fares, it was not adequate. After she had left, at about six o'clock, I would get up, listening to Billy Tennant on the radio and Freddy Grisewood *On the Kitchen Front*, before setting out with my sandwiches and gas mask for Elmsleigh Road. The school, which was mixed, was only different from the others in its modern buildings. The effective *Gauleiter* was a girl called Daphne, who held the balance of power between timid pupils and indifferent teachers. Tall and muscular, she wore a heavy stained gymslip and a great sash, which came in useful for bondage. She was always surrounded by her cohorts, usually all girls, who would select random victims for her, sometimes at mob whim, sometimes at her own unpredictable caprice. The victim, almost always a boy, was dragged to a suitably public place like the middle of the playground or playing field and, spread-eagled, he would have to endure the humiliation of Daphne lifting up her skirt and placing her navy blue gusset firmly on his head. She would sit like a conquering hunter for as long as it suited her, with the cold frenzy of a goddess on heat for sacrifice, while her prey gave up the struggle against asphyxiation. She might even urge her slaves to remove the victim's shorts. It came close to more than ritual castration, averted only by the bell for class. I witnessed these mass tribal seizures from the safest of distances. It was an all-girl exercise and even the toughest boys kept well away from the scene whenever it unexpectedly erupted, but there seemed no avoidance of the degradation once it had been decreed by Daphne. By some fluke, I was successful although I knew I was certainly on the goddess's list. The eyes of her warriors missed no one, particularly lone new boys. I fled their hounding scrutiny term after term, sniffing the air for some cunning ambush until the day I left the school two years later.

There was no black mist here to escape into or downland to wander over. The open roads back to Worcester Park Road offered no protection. The system of education differed little from what I had experienced before. The only thing I can remember learning at this school was a rude version of Thomas Moore's ballad 'The Harp that Once through Tara's Halls'. Again, lessons seemed drowsy interludes between the real business of Playtime, an underworld made more satanic by Daphne, its princess of Darkness. The blasting of whistles was louder and the gas-mask practice and air-raid and shelter drill consumed the day increasingly.

Sometimes I slept through *On the Kitchen Front* and was late. The punishment for this was a statutory caning of six strokes upon the hand, boy or girl, although the girls were sometimes overlooked. This took place almost daily, sometimes in front of the assembled school, sometimes in the headmaster's room. Mr Cotter looked, in retrospect, rather like a King Street Communist with a beret and pebble spectacles, and spent all his time doing woodwork and caning small boys. On being sent to him he asked your name, then enquired, 'Late?', or whatever the offence might be, and administered three strokes of the cane on each hand. They were delivered with abstracted intensity as if he were driving a rivet. It was particularly painful in the winter and some boys were foolish enough to yell – to the delight of the assembled girls. It was also regarded as an invitation for more. The slash of bamboo aimed at the tips of cold, mitten-clad fingers in the early morning was like the shock of an electric current, so much more telling than the palm, where presumably it was meant to be directed. If he was disturbed at his woodwork, the punishment was summary and quick, without need to play to the gallery of Assembly. He would relight his pipe afterwards and go back to the carpenter's bench without a word. Sometimes he sent you out to the corner shop to get him a fresh supply of his favourite tobacco. This seemed to be regarded as a favour. 'Say it's for me,' he would say, putting down his cane. 'They know what I smoke.'

Playtime was unavoidable; but I usually managed to escape the midday meal by running home, eating my sandwiches by the wireless and rushing back in time for lessons. A torment even worse than Playtime was the Shelter Drill which began to take up more time than anything else. More than the dead stretches in the classroom, I remember the shouting, whistling columns of children in corridors steaming with cold air, bobbing balaclavas and woollen helmets, being swept into the black hole of the dripping shelter. It was a pit of unwashed, stinking boys and girls, fists, bones on shins, their inescapable flailing in crazed screaming darkness as you crouched for the All Clear that might never come. When the air-raids did in fact come with daily regularity, the penalities for running away from the shelter and going home as I did so often were made to sound unspeakable. Even this seldom prevented me from taking the risk. Mock or real raid, the terror was palpable. I spent hours running between home and school, once almost being machine-gunned by a low-flying German aeroplane; better to be mown down with some lone dignity out there in the open ribbon development than buried alive along with that mass of struggling young bodies, shrieking 'In the Stores' and 'Roll out the Barrel' till the kingdom might not come. 'In the stores, in the stores, in the sergeant major's stores/ My eyes are dim I cannot see/I wish I'd brought my specs with me.' The school shelter was my only brush with fear in the war. My battle shock was puny enough but staged by Bosch and abetted by Daphne, its effect lingers enough after forty years to make me shun discos or nightclubs or football stadiums.

It was in the summer of 1940 that Mickey and I visited his aunt ('you're an old cow') at her small farm near Saffron Walden. Watching our balsa Hurricane gliders hovering above the open, flat fields, looking at sides of ham and eating more eggs, cream and butter than I had ever seen, even in the Home and Colonial window, it was like nothing I had known. We went on to a transformed, fortified Bognor, where it was impossible to go anywhere near the beach. It was sprayed with barbed wire and signs saying: 'KEEP OUT – MINEFIELDS'. Even the road from Felpham into Bognor was pitted with concrete tank traps and all approaches to the beach had sprouted pill-boxes, already sandy and grassy. The town was almost empty, cafés closed, whelk stalls and gift shops shuttered, the few remaining dodgems attended by glum youths hanging around waiting to stack them away before season's end.

Wartime and weather drove us into the cinema in Chichester to see *Pinocchio*, which featured a character, a very raffish fox, who was an actor and sang a song called 'Hey-diddle-de-dee, an Actor's Life for Me'. I took to him at once and when we came out into the High Street looking vainly for egg and chips somewhere, I felt elated by the spry fox and his song. We must be two of a special kind. Later, they were called spivs. Suddenly we heard the air-raid siren, still an unfamiliar sound, and we ran aimlessly down the street. There were few people around and Mickey and I gave up running and stood to gawp hopefully up at the sky. Some cellar doors opened in the pavement outside a pub like a pantomime trap and we followed a small crowd lowering themselves unhurriedly into the vaults. The doors overhead thudded behind us and we sat among the barrels of sweet-smelling beer, waiting. Everyone looked up straining their ears but nothing happened. After about twenty minutes the All Clear went and we climbed back disappointedly into the street. When my daughter and I walked up this same street in the evening it was as quiet as it had been thirty-seven years before. There were one or two people going home from work and some foreign tourists trailing up to the Cathedral. Standing on the same cellar doors Mickey and I had crouched beneath, I thought of Bognor in 1940 and Elmsleigh Road. The trite tune of 'Hey-diddle-de-dee' sounded in my head like a snatch of enduring joylessness. I needed an immediate drink.

On the last day in Bognor we said our muted farewell to the beach, unable this time to cast our pebbles into the sea although we repeated the incantation of the previous year, 'Good-bye Bognor. See you next year!' Neither of us voiced our unbelief. We returned home in silence. Even Mickey was unmoved to rudery. The future held nothing more than endless Playtimes, Sirens and Black Looks. There was no imaginable relief. It was hot, mid-August and after only a few days it came.

7. Too Young to Fight and Too Old to Forget

Mickey and I were eating Victoria plums in the Walls' tiny orchard when the aircraft appeared out of the opposite ends of the sky, streaking high above us towards each other. Theirs shimmering black, ours silver. Or so it must have been. The blinding blue silence. Then the hurtling formation and symmetry exploded.

Throughout that autumn of 1940 we were charmed, privileged spectators at the most thrilling spectacular we could ever have imagined. Day after sunny day, I ran over to Bradford Drive to take my front seat in the moist shade at the bottom of the garden. We had the house to ourselves so there were no teachers or policemen to force us below ground. The sky was all ours and we were enclosed by it. Edna would come in for her dinner and scream hysterically at us to take cover but we ignored her. There would probably never be anything better than this at any time, ever, and no one could take it from us. We lay on our backs, spinning in the world, chomping on pounds of Victorias, secure and happy in our grassy cockpit, suffering no more than sore lips, stained teeth and stomach pains. The Battle of Britain exhausted everything, especially our appetite for tea. We knew our Dorniers from our Heinkels, and in the evenings in Mickey's briefing room we listened to the day's tally and moved our pins on the map of southern England. It seemed that those long days of blasting sunshine must go on until we dropped into something indescribably different, obliterating inert Stoneleigh and Ewell, inglorious cities of England's Southern Plain.

It ended with the shock of its beginning. The rush of blood was staunched, we looked up into the sky and saw only the unwarlike flab of barrage balloons. Numbed, we strained at the silence and longed for the day before yesterday and every bright minute. The darkening evenings of September, then the weeks, drew in and closed over us like the cellar doors in Chichester. Very soon they dwindled away into the flight from the school shelter and nightly prostration in Mrs Williams's Anderson, imprisoning dark, searchlights, ARP torchlights flashing in windows and irritable cries of, 'Put that light out!'

Mrs Williams spent much of her time at her daughter-in-law's house and as my mother was at work behind the bar at the Stoneleigh Hotel I passed most of these nights, which began unremittingly almost on the dot of six o'clock, on my own in the Anderson, listening to the plodding hum of German bombers. They were confined, uninspiring hours, very different from the free-for-all of being part of visible earth and sky. At least I was alone. When a bomb did shiver the darkness, the heart only faltered. It didn't overflow. The last crouch was not suitable for sharing. A rat has no comfort. My mother had refused to go into the Anderson anyway. 'I'm not going in that thing. Catch your bloody death of cold, you will. Rather get bombed.' Every evening for the next few months I would get into my pyjamas and dressing gown and take myself down to the Anderson with my copies of the *Magnet* and the *Gem* or some book like Mickey's *The Black Out Book* or *101 Things To Do In The Black Out* and the portable wireless, to lie in my narrow bunk until seven or so the following morning. On my mother's evening off, she insisted that we lie in a tiny triangular cupboard under the stairs, where we would read by the light of a candle. The wireless was forbidden as she believed that it might attract the attention of the German bombers.

Late into night in the cupboard, my mother, in her curlers and dressing gown, would read the *Daily Mirror*, hunched upright in a thick swirl of cigarette smoke, while Black Looks pierced the haze of the four or five feet of space we shared, daring me to sleep and leave her to hear the unremitting hum of the Hun. She fidgeted and kicked me awake until morning. Many nights passed without a bomb dropping. When they did it was difficult to guess how near it was to Number 120 Worcester Park Road. Sometimes the little cupboard would blur and seem to stretch and float an inch or two. On one particular evening she had hardly been able to glance at the *Mirror* 'for want of a gin'. The candle flickered, she stared and fidgeted me back to wakefulness:

MOTHER: Listen! No, listen. There. It's gone all quiet. Get me a drop of that gin. No, I'd better get it. I want to go anyway. Listen. D'you think it's quiet for a bit?
ME: They'll be back soon.
MOTHER: Oh, bloody cheerful as usual!
ME: Well they always are.

MOTHER: Well, I'm going to risk it. Don't you want to go?
ME: No.

She hesitated, possibly wondering whether to shove me out instead, then dashed up the stairs. No sooner had she closed the lavatory door than there was a shattering whizz and the house trembled as a bomb began its fall. The candle went out at the impact, followed by a scream from my mother. Deafened and groping I emerged from the cupboard into the mist of dust and plaster, found the matches and relit the candle. All the doors and windows had been blown out and the ceilings had collapsed. My mother was just visible, frozen to the lavatory seat. She moved forward to the head of the stairs bent at the knees, like a crazed gymnast, arms outstretched. I thought of my father's apparition at the top of the stairs a few months earlier. Her face sagged, powdered and gaping black, her mottled sloped chest heaving with her moans. Her knickers were flounced below her knees in a collapsed silky bag. The lost days of summer were recompensed for a few joyous moments as I looked on at the funniest, most enjoyable sight I had ever seen. When she tottered down to the hall, I was still laughing. Nothing could have stemmed my exploding delight. The Black Look had been blasted into a blob of stupidity and fear. Too shaken to aim a clout at me, she crawled back into the cupboard, curled up into a heap and left me to sleep undisturbed until the cold air from the rising dust of the street woke me and a neighbour in an ARP helmet appeared at the jagged porch. Everyone had their Best-Night-of-the-Blitz stories. I couldn't wait to tell mine to Mickey.

We spent the Christmas at Harbord Street. Grandma Grove, like thousands of others, had spent weeks walking to work through devastated streets, picking her way among rubble and broken glass to make her way up to the head offices of Woolworth's in Cork Street. She always left about four o'clock, long before the All Clear sounded, dodging posses of wardens and policemen to be sure of arriving on time, at six o'clock. A landmine had destroyed the nearby convent in Hammersmith and there was no gas or electricity. The festive chicken took hours to cook in a bucket over a cluster of candles. It was smoky but delicious, like Joan's kennel cooking. Even Grandpa was uncomplaining. The Dardanelles were to blame.

In 1941 I sat my Common Entrance examination. I knew it was hopeless and was astonished to get through the preparatory paper. Perhaps it had passed unmarked. But there could be no doubt about Part Two. Another four years of Elmsleigh Road loomed ahead, dull, unrelenting and unprofitable. The long, snug warren nights of the Blitz subsided. I had made no friends, seeing Mickey only at the weekends, which were interrupted by his increasing homework at Tiffins. Joan Buffen was gone, although I sometimes hung around Ewell Parade, looking up for a glimpse of her. Once, Mrs Buffen spotted me, and waved but, as she started to beckon, I ran round the corner. Once I saw Joan going into a sweetshop with her cousin. Later, she came towards me in the Village High Street. There was nowhere to hide. She was riding her pretty piebald pony and was flushed with strength and energy. I thought she wouldn't see me in her glow of concentration but, as she came alongside, she looked down with a brief, unsurprised smile, raised her cane and trotted on. I avoided the Village. It had never seemed a friendly place.

I wrote regularly to Isabel. If I could only live with the Sells at the Carfax, I would have willingly gone back to St Boniface Secondary School in Ventnor. I had never seen those beaches in the summer. Isabel and I could walk for hours along the open sands. The Germans wouldn't want to invade Ventnor. It wasn't Bognor. She wrote an affectionate letter in reply, full of questions about myself. She had got married to Raymond. Grandma had died at last and they were going to live near Southampton. They all sent lots of love and were always thinking of me.

'Don't you know there's a war on?'

By 1942 the Osborne–Grove family had shrunk. Aunt Nancy had died in 1938, of peritonitis it was said, but, according to my mother, really of 'Dad's complaint'. Grandpa Osborne died in 1940 shortly after my father of cancer of the bowel and Grandpa Grove followed soon after, possibly brought down by his youthful breakfast regime of porterhouse steaks, half-bottles of 3-star brandy and chorus girls. Grandma Grove emerged exhilarated and bustling from her adventurous Blitz into widowhood and was shortly pensioned off by Woolworth's with the unlooked-for sum of eight pounds a week for the rest of her lifetime, which was to span nearly another forty years. She was to be seen photographed in the local newspapers on her hundredth birthday brandishing her telegram from the Queen.

When I was first aware of Grandma Osborne she can scarcely have been much older than I am now, but she had already settled determinedly into iron-clad, impassive old age. After her husband's death, she left Clandon Close for a small flat above Tesco's store (more like a cheap-rate village shop then) in yet another Parade, Ewell Court, only five minutes' walk from Bradford Drive. Cousin Tony had moved on to Christ's College, Brecon and then to Sandhurst, his father having decided that he should be a professional soldier, no doubt to have undone the damage to his manly fibre wrought by his grandmother. Boasting loneliness, she graciously offered room to her sisters. After all, they were two widows and a spinster with little more than their pooled pensions to support them. Besides, with Grandpa gone, she needed someone to do the shopping and heavier housework. All of which was, of course, quite beyond her.

Auntie Bessie was a round, cheerful woman. She had married Great Uncle Frank, who was some kind of Cad or Bounder, having been obliged for unspoken scandalous reasons to emigrate hurriedly to Canada, leaving his wife and four sons to follow him later. She was kindly in a twinkling sort of way with a streak of Welsh deceit and petty vindictiveness which were harmless enough. She shocked her sisters by indulging in flights of nostalgia for the way she and Uncle Frank had enjoyed their sexual life, not in detail but revering an experience once enjoyed wholeheartedly and still, incredibly to them, at the age of seventy-one, relished. She was a tiny woman, a little over five foot. Uncle Frank had been six foot four inches and weighed some sixteen or seventeen stone, which might have fired the sisters' puzzled imagination whenever they cast their eyes upon her tiny round form.

Auntie Daisy was like an emaciated dwarf, a quick-moving cripple with a hunched back. She was a spinster, having lost her fiancé during the First War, in the way of the fact and legend of the time. She soon became the only sister left to look after their mother, and thoughts of marriage, if they had ever been, quickly receded. For twenty years she attended the old woman, heaving her deadly weight out of bed and into chairs. This was said to be the reason for her present condition, but it seemed more probable that when she entered this world it was as the perfect crabbed creature she was now. There was no hint from her sisters that her sacrifice, if indeed it was one, might have been wasted on what sounded like a charmless, unrewarding old bully. On the contrary, her grim frailty and intransigent character were admired as the acceptable scar of a Godly life. Now, humped off by a stronger hand, the ancient matriarch was gone, leaving Auntie Daisy with nowhere to live in Newport. Auntie Bessie's four sons were unable or unwilling to take her in, so both sisters winged back to their last days with sister Annie over Tesco's stores.

There were only three small rooms in the flat, including the kitchen, and the two younger sisters, Annie and Daisy, were soon ganging up on the once-nubile Bessie. She confided to me that they made sure that she had less rations, mixing margarine into her butter and watering her milk. Such low practices, true or not, would cloud whole days for her, driving her out walking for hours on her own. She did all the shopping while crippled Daisy did the heavier work. Annie cooked one meal a day of the lighter kind. Surprisingly, Bessie died several years before her two apparently frailer sisters. Her four giant sons – Dallas, Percy, Cecil and Basil – were either abroad or living somewhere in the provinces. Uncle Dallas was still in Canada, Cecil and Percy in Sheffield and Belfast, and Uncle Basil, who Annie seemed to imply had inherited his father's caddish tricks, was now a flight lieutenant in the RAF which, oddly, didn't impress her. Basil's wife had had a baby somewhat less than nine months after their marriage. Annie, a dab at counting on her fingers, tried to shame her sister with this fact but it only puffed her up. Perhaps it confirmed the continuity of Uncle Frank's vast prowess, something that cold, haughty little Annie could never have matched.

Meanwhile, back at the Groves, my Uncle Jack had suffered a motoring accident while he was working as a salesman for an ice-cream firm in Southend and had lost his right arm. Awarded over three thousand pounds, which in 1939 seemed a vast sum of money, he adapted himself to one arm with great ingenuity and dabbled with some style in what were always called 'risky ventures' by his family, mostly in catering and with small success. However, he always had a cigar to press on you carelessly. I never heard him complain about any of his unsupportive wives and mistresses or his falling circumstances. Today he lives in a council house in Salisbury, over eighty and with a back like a board, he looks like a retired sea-captain, cheerfully waiting for his next command. Ignored by his sisters, he seemed sweetly free of their malice and envy.

Stoneleigh

'*Dear John*, What a nasty jealous undesirable brother he has turned out to be. Frankly Johnnie its Mothers own fault. She has always made too much of him. Oh no he could do no wrong. He has caused those upsets with Mum and Dad for years. Thank God he is miles away from me. I could not stand his nonsense now; and cannot stand upsets of any kind . . .

'*Dear John*, Regarding Mother I have written and asked Jack's permission for me to go and see her and if I went there would he allow me to go upstairs to see her if only for an hour, its no use me taking a chance going there and he refuses to let me see her, don't you agree, am standing by for a reply – *if* I get one shall go right away – but the mood he is in – I have my doubts . . .

'*Dear John*, I don't want to blame my poor Mum too much: but it looks as though his Lordship [Jack] *did not* let her have my letter saying I was waiting for his Consent for me to come along and see her – or *maybe is* afraid to say anything frankly I can't make it all out, have registered a letter to her this morning – I wonder if she will have it. I explained the position of things. I just let things stay as they are. I thought I must tell you and let you know everything. Such things: there will never be a cure for bitterness.

Always in my thoughts,
Mother'

As for Auntie Queenie, 'gone down in the world' as my mother had it, in the Richmond Jewish madams' shop, she was living in her pristine flat in a new mansion block overlooking Turnham Green with poor Uncle Sid, a clerk in a City firm of ribbon-makers which he had first joined at the age of fourteen until he became Aircraftman Bates in 1942. It was then that he met again his pre-war flat-mate and love-of-his-life, another aircraftman, John. Sid and Queen were married during a weekend leave in Queenie's church in Turnham Green. He was forty-two and the bride was fifty, wearing a new blue costume and veiled hat, wholesale price, from Madame Leons of Richmond. John was the best man.

'I don't know what I was doing when I asked her,' Sidney said years later, in a snatched simpering confidence. 'I must have been ever so tiddly. She made me go out and get the ring the first thing next morning. Bit of a cheek, I thought.' Technical manuals on *Married Love* and *Sex within Marriage* by a Mrs Renee McAndrew were left by the side of their twin beds next to the white-leather prayer book. During my lightning peeks into these manuals I learnt, amongst other things, that it was possible to achieve enormous satisfaction by being on top of the eiderdown as well as underneath it. Knowing Auntie Queenie, who could not bear the sight of even a creased cushion, I found it very hard indeed to imagine her contemplating crispy stains on her expensively dry-cleaned eiderdowns. 'She left these soppy books out while she was off in the bathroom for bloody hours. Sid Muggins supposed to be reading them. Have you read them? Well, *I* wouldn't. Lot of piffle. I tell you, I had half a bottle of gin while she was in the bloody bathroom –

pardon my French – silly cow!' He looked around the pristine lounge. 'John and me had such a lovely flat pre-war. You'd have liked *that*.' It was not a welcoming place. 'More like a showroom,' as my mother said enviously.

Once married, Auntie Queenie became less like an Ivor Novello cast-off than a relentless home store-detective, steaming open Sidney's letters and monitoring his telephone calls to his friend John. She wrote to his commanding officer about their friendship and even went to the lengths of consulting their family doctor about his inadequacies, unimproved by the counsel of Renee McAndrew. At Chiswick she presented a package of letters from LAC2 John to the desk sergeant at the police station. But, we all learnt in disbelief, 'There was nothing the Police could do about it. Nothing.'

Auntie Queenie put great onus on her rare guests, demanding incessantly what they wanted to *do*. Did one want to read a book or the paper or why did one look bored or why didn't one go out for a walk – anything to get them off the furniture. The Chiswick Empire on the other side of the Green was the only lure to visiting Sid and Queen. Sid sometimes timidly slipped me a shilling. I could get Black Looks at home.

After her disastrous weeks at Carters Seed factory my mother threw all her frayed energies into her job at the Stoneleigh Hotel, earning a basic four pounds a week plus a great deal of overtime for Masonic dinners and Ladies' Nights. I saw less and less of her, sometimes only while I was trying to listen to *On the Kitchen Front* before school. When I got back she gave me my tea, to be eaten and washed up before going back to the pub. While the Blitz continued she often spent the night under the saloon billiard table with the rest of the staff. When she did attempt to get home and burst in on my candle-lit solitude in the Anderson, she was often thwarted by the air-raid warden. 'But my little boy's on his own down the shelter.' 'I can't help that, madam, you should have made some arrangements.' Fortunately for me, she never did.

For many people like her, the war was a free-wheeling, careless time of opportunity and relatively easy money. Tips flew fast and foolishly across the bar from GIs impervious to English currency, and what she called her 'Dutch Boys', mostly sailors. At weekends she would come home with a purse gaping with half-crowns and ten-shilling notes. She had, after all, worked as a barmaid since the age of eighteen, when she left her cashier's job at Lyons Corner House and went to work, 'living in', in a pub in Eastbourne. The 'guvnor' there, Charlie Farrell, had attempted and perhaps, she hinted, succeeded in seducing her. Mrs Farrell, who had apparently treated her almost like a daughter, giving her her cast-off coats and hats, became hysterical and Grandpa Grove was sent down to East-bourne with an army pistol from his Dardanelles days, threatening to shoot Mr Farrell. However, he was immediately recognized as the one-time smartest publican in London, all three of them got happily drunk together and my mother continued work there until Charlie died and she came back to Harbord Street.

With her long experience in the trade, including such lost arts as fining spirits, breaking down port with gold instruments (so she said) and other mysterious things that had to be done to barrels of beer in the cellar in those pre-keg days, she established herself as the Stoneleigh's star turn. Quick, anticipative with a lightning head for mental arithmetic, she was, as she put it, a very smart 'licensed victualler's assistant' indeed. '*I'm* not a barmaid I'm a victualler's assistant – *if* you please.' I have seen none better. No one could draw a pint with a more perfect head on it or pour out four glasses of beer at the same time, throwing bottles up in the air and catching them as she did so. New customers would watch her juggling skill with wonder and regulars with some pride. I always hoped she'd drop one. She never did. Tired and abstracted when I occasionally saw her for a few minutes, she seemed almost content, never enquiring after the course of my own day; her mounting self-absorption left me thankfully ignored and unobserved.

Five years of comparative plenty and activity opened up for her after the blundering misalliance with my father and the apathy and discontent of digs in Fulham and Ewell. No more dead-and-alive holes, lots of laughter, a great deal of noise, less time to squander on Black Looks. When she did turn her attention to me it was usually after she had a barney with Cheffie or one of the girls, never with the customers. Cheffie was always getting riled and took it out on my mother, niggling her for no reason. When I was still at school or, later, going out to work and leaving early in the morning, she would wake me up in the small hours to listen to her account of these endlessly sustained bouts of ill-feeling and resentment. When I yawned, usually unwittingly, at the third or fourth recount she would slam out of my room complaining that I didn't care what happened to her. The catering trade is largely given over to neurotic self-servers, as I was to discover during my brief experience of it later when I worked in hotel still-rooms and kitchens in Brighton. Arnold Wesker's metaphor of *The Kitchen* is an uncanny realization of that hopeless, unhappy world.

So, Nellie Beatrice, or 'Bobby' as she was known to her admiring customers, spent the next twenty years, lunchtime and evening, behind a succession of bars, shrieking at half-grasped jokes, bawling out her unvarying catch phrases: 'Get up them stairs' (the battlecry of the barmaid and indeed of the whole war it seemed); 'The second thing he did when he come home was to take his pack off'; 'One Yank and they're off'; and, when she could single me out as a target, 'He's like John Lawson's son. Only a Jew.' 'There's no separating a Jew from his cash box.' 'I couldn't laugh if I was crafty.' And so on. Uncurious though she was about me, my disclaiming attitude in front of others was irksome and she repaid it with mockery. After my father died, I addressed her obliquely, and never as 'Mum'. 'It's funny, you never call me "Mum" or "Mummy". People have remarked on it. Just "she" or "you". I'm not the cat's mother, you know.' Mickey Wall grinned, 'Perhaps you're what the Yanks mean by Sonofabitch.'

We had never eaten so well. Unlike the Walls and Grandma Osborne, my mother had no scruples at all about dealing openly in the Black Market for coupons, points for sweets and ration books. Throughout the war we always had more than enough butter, sugar, bacon and clothing coupons which cost, as I remember, three and sixpence each. These were peddled in the bar by Eric, who must have been one of the earliest spivs, for he began his operations at the beginning of the war, running a fruit stall in Berwick Market. I had all the oranges and bananas I could eat. Grandma O, who would not turn on the wireless if the licence was a day out of date, was appalled and refused to accept them even for frail Daisy or hungry Bessie. For once, I wholeheartedly approved mother's blinkered morality. It seemed stupid and goody-goody to go without for fear of reprisal from above. It was the attitude I later took in school towards the code of owning-up, telling the truth or being put on one's honour. The adult world was already over-endowed with prying privilege and all the aids to blackmail. If it was expedient and a reasonable gamble, I chose to lie in my teeth rather than be honest in the gutter.

Christmas 1941 came and went much as usual. Grandma Osborne's Boxing Day message was addressed to a depleted audience. The religious and moral debate raged more tepidly at Harbord Street, though Auntie Queen turned on me during a doctrinal thump-up when she discovered that I had finished reading the book she had given me for Christmas, while she was still in the middle of a mournful outburst against her sister. It was all about dogs – my passion at that time. Partly from my lingering love and loyalty to Joan, I had spoken of becoming a veterinary surgeon, at best, or a dog breeder at worst, a suggestion which was ridiculed by all as silly, and worse, presumptuous. 'Don't tell me you've read that book already. Not right the way through. That book cost seven and sixpence.' She snatched it away from me. I was a selfish, greedy little ingrate, who gobbled up expensive presents. 'Seven and sixpence,' she screamed and stuffed it into her shopping bag. The crumbs of *The World of Dogs* spattered all over me.

Early in 1942 we shunted from Worcester Park Road to Stangrove Road. The ceaseless discord about bath times, charges, petty nuisances like the late whisper of my wireless or the stairs creaking after midnight had come to a head, and we moved into the upper half of yet another semi-detached on the other side of the railway line. The landlady's name was Mrs Dawson, a woman in her early thirties, whose readiness to take offence matched that of Nellie Beatrice. Her husband was in the Western Desert with the 8th Army, and she made it clear that she abhorred company. With the true suburban charity of the wartime landlady, her rooms were urgently for rent and unwelcome to lodgers. Mrs Dawson seemed altogether sharper and tougher than Mrs Williams and I had little hope of us staying as long as we in fact did. She acknowledged our existence on rent days and contrived to be close behind her own door whenever we came in or out. The house was silent except for the howls coming from her naked three-year-old son as he received his daily caning. Apart from knitting, it seemed her solitary relaxation. Whenever Corporal Dawson returned on leave she would invite him to join in with her. Upstairs, I turned up the wireless volume to drown the frightening cries. But not for long. She would somehow hear it above her own uproar and scream up the stairs at me, cane in hand.

Some of the houses in the street had been bombed and had grown over to become miniature recreation patches for the less restricted children and, in particular, those of the Woman Opposite. She had seven children, which caused the neighbours to avoid her. Men had been observed coming and going by the whole street, and it was certain none of them was her husband. Apart from descriptions of the condition of her son's bottom, the Woman Opposite was the only subject which tempted Mrs Dawson into conversation. 'Someone should Write to the Council about her, get on to the school inspector, the police.' If her Les wasn't out in the Desert, he'd do it. That bombed bit should have barbed wire round it. In full view, some said, and without hindrance of police or barbed wire, the eldest daughter, a scornfully pretty girl, became pregnant. Pushing their cartload of shopping, the family seemed unaware of mounting scrutiny as the girl's shameless girth increased. My mother muttered blackly about what my father would have thought of any boy who did anything like that with a girl. I viewed the Woman Opposite with fresh respect. She had a cheerful look on her face, and her seven children, beaten or unbeaten, as far as one could see were ragged, dirty and happy.

8. Deathaboys

One evening I was kneeling on the floor of the sitting-room, listening to *Hi Gang* or *ITMA*, my ear pressed to the wireless so as not to disturb Mrs Dawson's evening relaxation. Thinking I heard her stirring downstairs, I tried to get up from the floor to listen at the door. I couldn't move. My legs seemed paralysed and I was just able to lever myself up on to the uncut moquette of the three-piece suite. I couldn't ask Mrs Dawson for assistance, so I turned the wireless up and waited for my mother to come back from the Stoneleigh. When she returned after midnight I told her what had happened. She was seething with Cheffie's latest infamies. I'd got cramp and it wasn't surprising, sitting in a draught all evening with that damn wireless. The next morning I was unable to get out of bed and she called the doctor. By this time I was running a very high temperature, which was to continue for months to come. I had rheumatic fever.

We had a 'lady' doctor who was kindly and overworked. I settled down with some curiosity to lying in bed twenty-four hours a day, my legs swathed in thick rolls of cotton wool throughout a very hot summer. I followed the course of the newly opened Russian Front, recording the difference in my temperature between morning and evening and accustoming myself to the exhausting sound of my heart, which hammered every time I moved my position, however gently. It was uncomfortable but had advantages over the pounding of Elmsleigh Road School. For ten months, I read all day and listened to the wireless. The lady from next door lent me the entire set of a 1919 edition of a children's encyclopaedia. She brought them in one at a time every week, so that I didn't skip through the lot at once. In the evenings I used to hear her throwing plates at her husband.

Apart from her and Mickey I saw no one, except for my mother after work. For a short while she insisted on giving up her job to 'look after me' during the day. Making and remaking the bed she thumped around the room, telling me that I was too much to look after and should rightly be in hospital. The idea appalled me, but I agreed. Anything would be preferable to her presence. Presently, she decided to go back to work and left me to myself. I became absorbed in the observable processes of my body. The texture of my hair began to change from being smooth, silky and very slightly wavy to becoming harsh and brittle and unpleasantly coarse and, in some places, falling out; I began to notice an unpleasant odour from my finger nails and toe nails which stayed with me for years. Later came boils, and dandruff cascading from my head, powdering my neck endlessly. It was as well that neither Joan nor Isabel could see me.

After some nine months, a wheelchair was obtained so that my mother could take me out. It was a cold November, the chair was flimsy and even painful to a body sore and bony from lying. I tried to discourage these outings but she persisted on showing me to the world, pushing, or rather, aiming me reproachfully at the shopping parades. She had the consolation of having the sympathy and admiration of her customers. I felt like a discarded litter basket or an old pramful of coal, waiting for her to stop chattering in the warmth inside the shops. People asked after her health rather than mine, which was a relief. There seemed to be an implicit feeling among her saloon-bar confidantes that a twelve-year-old boy bundled in a wheelchair must be either a malingerer taking advantage of his hard-working, indulgent mother or some sort of shameless cissy. Fortunately, her appetite for the pity of the Parade was soon overcome by the pointlessness of jolting me past streets of identical houses. There was Nonsuch Park, but I thought better of it.

She did agree to take me to see *Gone with the Wind* at the Rembrandt. This was a big event. For one thing, the fame of the film was such that it was hard to believe it would be shown in Ewell. However, here it was at last, with increased prices and bookable-only seats. Apart from sitting outside Tesco's in the perennial wind of the Parade window-blind, it was my first outing for almost a year. I was assigned a place at the end of an aisle in my chair. There were a few old people similarly positioned in the packed cinema so I didn't feel as conspicuous as I had anticipated. Once the auditorium darkened, I gave myself up to the film. The excitement became so intense that I felt myself sweating and cold tremors rushing to my head. I gripped the chair, knowing that I was going to faint, which I did, once during Olivia de Havilland's labour (before the hot water had boiled or the ritual sheets had even been torn up) and again when the young Confederate soldier had his leg amputated without anaesthetic. Each time I came round, my head dripping and fallen on to my knees, I looked up to see if my mother had noticed. Fortunately, her eyes were on the screen. She wasn't able to complain afterwards that I had spoilt one of her few precious pleasures once again.

After my visit to *Gone with the Wind* I recovered quickly, although I was only able to move slowly. I think it must have had a blood-letting effect in its excitement, after being so long in confinement. I longed to be in the world again. School must surely be out of the question. A letter from Mrs Ure told us that arrangements had been made for me to be sent to a convalescent home for boys in Dorset. Even Stangrove Road and Mrs Dawson were preferable. My father knew these places. They were all prisons, he had said. But my mother insisted that after all the Benevolent Society had done for my father it would be selfish and ungrateful to refuse to go. On 23 December 1942 I arrived with my mother at Shaftesbury and looked over the iron stairs across the deserted platform. In the empty station yard we were met by an unsmiling nurse wearing pebble glasses. 'Osborne?' she enquired impatiently. 'That's right,' said my mother, almost grovelling. 'This is him.' 'I see.' 'He'll be a good boy.' She stared down at me, her eyes embedded pebble, and grabbed my hand. 'He'd better be,' she said, as if I'd been arrested already for trying to escape. 'Well, you'd better say good-bye.' My mother hugged me, in her usual ear, nose and throat crunch hold. Unsure whether I was more glad to leave her loveless clinch or loath to let myself be dragged off by Nurse Pebble Head, I found my suitcase dragged from my grasp as I was pushed into a tiny car.

My father had been right, as I knew he would. The convalescent home was more like a Borstal for sick or dying boys. As she drove to the house itself, Nurse Pebble Head grew less fearsome but made it only too clear that she regarded the boys in her care as little less than criminals who had fallen sick. There were about seventy of them, ranging from six to sixteen years old, all from the East End or the poorer parts of London, though not from Fulham. The home itself was a large mid-Victorian house off an almost traffic-free Dorsetshire road. The atmosphere within might not have resembled Borstal but it was cold, institutionally quiet and watchful as if one were taking part in a silent and endless Morning Assembly. If I had heard of such places then, Elmsleigh Road would have seemed like a holiday camp in comparison. A sparse tea was served from trestle tables by very slow moving, clearly local-yokel nurses. The bigger boys took almost all of the little jam on the tables to go with their bread and marge, unchallenged by staff or inmates. It was quickly despatched in silence. The new matron announced her arrival, striding into the middle of the room, her red and blue cloak swishing behind her. She had a distinctly martial, or rather nautical, manner, having just left several years' parade-ground experience behind her at the Royal Naval College in Dartmouth. There, she pointed out, the sons of gentlemen and officers were beaten regularly for the merest misdemeanours. Surveying her new rabble of skinny, unhealthy, underfed urchins with distaste for the contrast they must have made to the future officers of the Royal Navy, she made it clear that we were all to expect similar if not the same treatment. If healthy, decently brought-up boys could take this discipline why shouldn't we sickly, weedy mob of little street Arabs be treated with equal severity? We had lapsed into illness only through lack of discipline and could all regard ourselves as under close arrest. A good hiding was as likely to make an unhealthy boy healthy as not. She would surely spot me as a lifelong malingerer.

Pebble Head bustled with respect at this address from the bridge and took me tightly and unnecessarily by the arm up to my dormitory which I was to share with another thirty or so boys. One of the local-yokels shouted at us to hurry up cleaning our teeth and then put out the light without warning. I waited for something to happen, possibly unpleasant. After a while one or two of the younger children called out for their Mums and were told to shut up. One boy could be heard weeping. It soon became quiet. Like the others, overcome by cold and tiredness, I fell asleep before I could puzzle more over the word 'convalescent'.

I was wakened the following day very early. The small boy opposite me aged about eight, suffering from malnutrition, and looking like a wizened old man, had, as was apparently his habit, wet the bed and was ordered by the matron to stand with his wet sheets over his head until breakfast. He shivered like this on the bare linoleum, but after ten minutes Miss Pebble Head relented and took the sheet away from him allowing him to dress, forgoing a bath before breakfast. Matron didn't seem to notice. It was hard to believe she would have thought it better to smell than to starve.

It was Christmas Eve 1942, the first time I had ever been away from home apart from Bognor. In the evening some children from the local church came to sing carols and the following day I was presented with a small pencil box by the vicar. He and Matron had taken an immediate evangelical shine to each other. They reminded me of Mr and Mrs Squeers as they herded us from food and presents to carols. The strains of one of my least favourite, 'Star of Wonder, Star of Night', seemed to fill the gloomy house most of the evening. A few desultory games were attempted by the fitter children but were soon abandoned as too rowdy and physically taxing for convalescent boys or their bored overseers. Cousin Jill might have got a few old favourites together. Come to think of it, middle-class party games had not been much nicer or quieter than the shove-and-kick encounters of these sickly street Arabs.

The daily routine was unchanging. I was, according to my mother, 'a finicky eater', but I soon found myself thinking of little else but Eric's Black Market goodies and the Walls' lengthy, easeful fry-ups. Food was sparse, ill-cooked, cold and for the most part commandeered by the bigger boys who were unchallenged by the young, frail and feeble. During the morning there was PT for those capable of taking part, which seemed to include the sick, crippled and near unto death. Matron would probably have considered physiotherapy a pretty cissy option for anyone. Mornings were supposed to be given over to lessons. We sat at desks while a young woman we called 'Miss' or 'Teacher' encouraged us to use the few writing or drawing materials. Most were unable or unwilling to do either and she read aloud to us – few of the boys could read themselves (I pretended to be unable to for fear of being penalized for suspect superiority, a deceit she kindly accepted) – or simply encouraged us to talk about our homes. This was unpromising as the common experience had few accounts to tell beyond Dad blacking Mum's eyes, getting bloody good hidings from Dad's belt, visiting him Inside, the Probation Officer, Cops and how the other kids at home thought *we* were lucky to be where we were. Everyone, including the teacher, thought this was funny. Even to me, the germ-ridden streets of Stepney sounded like teeming alleys of joy compared to Matron's antiseptic ship-shape brig. An early, quickly consumed lunch was followed by a compulsory rest period of a couple of hours, lying down on the school-room floor covered by a blanket, while a girl nurse tried with difficulty to read from Kipling's *Jungle Books*.

A Family Row would have been welcome that Christmas and I even missed the Boxing Day valediction from Clandon Close. On Christmas Day I was sent up to the dormitory to lie down properly on my own bed with a blanket. Pebble Head told me this was necessary because of the condition of the valves of my damaged heart. My stay was to be for at least six weeks, she warned. There were no short cuts, which meant being *good*. The only other occupant of the dormitory during my afternoon rests was a boy called Fiske. He was in a bed at the far end. We never spoke. I used to watch him shamble to and from his bed like an old man negotiating a park bench. Soon he took to walking with a stick. I asked Pebble Head what was the matter with him. 'Oh,' she said, 'he's got heart disease. He won't last another six weeks.' Sure enough, shortly afterwards, he was confined to his bed and then disappeared during the night. I didn't like to ask what had happened.

We went for long walks along the deserted Dorset roads. After weeks of this, I still found myself struggling up hills with some difficulty, my heart pounding in the rear of the bored, unruly crocodile of young recidivists. Soon, however, I was reluctantly playing football. Feeling stronger, I began to count the days to my release. This prospect was delayed by a boy picking a fight with me in the usual, familiar playground manner. As before, his appearance was misleading. Three or four years older and more powerful than myself, he looked as if he were dressed head to foot in his father's oldest clothes, and he may have taken a dislike to what Eric's clothing coupons had contributed to my own appearance. Anyway, he decided to call me a twat in front of my fellow convalescents. I wasn't sure what a twat was but I knew it must be perjorative. His casual aggression was a relief after weeks of lethargy and I found myself pitching into him with some sense of relief. He seemed to be on the verge of giving in and I was feeling a literally pulsing sense of triumph when Pebble Head came between, holding us apart like a couple of Mrs Buffen's dazed Staffordshires. Waiting outside Matron's office, I heard her talking to the other boy and then shouting at him. I wondered if we would both be flogged. Perhaps we were well enough for the yard-arm by now. However, when my turn came to see her, her manner was milder but unmistakably gloating and cryptic. I would have to see the doctor the following day and the consequences would certainly be unpleasant.

She was perfectly right. The penalty for my scuffling little victory was to have my stay lengthened by another month. I was like a prisoner losing remission. Pebble Head explained that it was not a punishment but treatment I had brought on myself by undoing the results of enforced rest, routine and good food in a foolish fight. On 27 January, the anniversary of my father's death, I felt very sorry for myself indeed. Pebble Head became quite chatty, confiding how bored she was and that she didn't approve Matron's unselective strictures. Still, unlike me, the other boys were all a right rough old lot. She said she had been down on me at first, thinking that I was 'a bit of a cissy', so she had secretly approved the violence of my unwise fight. My twathood and cissiness remained unproven.

This was not the first time I had been accused of being a cissy – a heinous tag in those ungay days. I was accustomed to my grandmother saying to me that I looked like a street-corner nancy boy, but I took this to be part of her general puritanism and disapproval of my fugitive flamboyance. It was a time when drabness was synonymous with maleness. I was once jeered at for wearing a new yellow pullover given to me for my twelfth birthday. To the shouts of 'Tweet Tweet' and 'Blimey, there's a blooming canary', I hurried red-faced along the streets of Fulham and even sophisticated Ewell.

Shortly before I was to be released, a plot was laid in my dormitory by half a dozen boys bent on getting away from this hated place at any cost to health or comfort. It was entered into in no spirit of fun or adventure but despair. They asked me to join them but it was too late. Six weeks earlier I would have accepted immediately. The day of the great escape arrived and I helped them with knotted sheets and climbed out of the window on to a roof, taking the sheet back and lumping up the pillows in their beds to make them look occupied when Pebble Head came round to make her midnight inspection, or in case Matron made one of her unscheduled checks. This she did later, snapping her torch on each side of the empty beds while I pretended to be asleep. When she questioned me about the boys' absence I enjoyed lying to her. She deserved it. Perhaps *she* would get into trouble. Besides, even she couldn't keep me for ever. The following afternoon, six exhausted, ill-looking boys were brought back by the police. It seemed impossible that I could have thought they might succeed. Still, by some remarkable chance, hitch-hiking on those ever empty wartime roads they had managed to get as far as Hemel Hempstead, a distance of at least two hundred miles. Perhaps the sick urchins' determination to escape from her care reminded her a little of the Dartmouth Spirit. They were in Matron's office for hours and the air was thick with speculation about them being sent to the Real Borstal or even prison. Whatever did happen was concealed from us, even Pebble Head refusing to discuss their eventual fate. Anyway, *my* convalescence was over. For the next few days of my stay the atmosphere relaxed. Even Matron called out 'Good-night Boys' as she turned the lights out. Instead of, 'If I have to come in here again tonight, you won't be very happy to see me.' To her, the war on malnutrition was not to be conducted against the disease but its victims.

Don't fence me in

After my convalescence I returned home uncertain whether or not I would be going back to Elmsleigh Road. I had known that any chance of passing the Common Entrance examination was impossible, but the thought of another two years of running errands for Mr Cotter and dodging Daphne's gusset was dispiriting. My mother was absorbed in Cheffie, Eric and the Guvnor. She gave me a sick note when she wanted me for company on her day off. If I mentioned school, she responded as she had done about the daughter of the Woman Opposite, muttering at me not to do anything that would have upset my father. When I did go back to Elmsleigh Road I found that Daphne had left and was working in Woolworth's. Even that luring excitement had gone.

Some weeks later we were summoned by Mrs Ure to 'Dad's society' in St Paul's Churchyard. She explained, like a Scots magistrate delivering balanced judgement, that it had been decided that I should go to a boarding school where I would be able to work hard and try to make up for my non-existent education. In view of my poor health they had decided to send me somewhere with only moderate academic prestige but which put special emphasis on clean country air, wholesome food and a healthy, specifically Christian life. The St Michael's brochure showed pictures of rows of boys happily hoeing in the huge kitchen garden. I loathed gardening instinctively. I looked on amateur gardeners and, later, golfers, as people impossible for me to love.

I felt divided and uneasy about St Michael's. It was undoubtedly many steps up from any school I had known. It might even be grander than Tiffins, Mickey's school, like Greyfriars even, but it was clear that I was not being presented with a choice. The decision from above ('Dad would be ever so pleased. It's what he'd have liked for himself. But he was always so poorly') had been made. My mother was delighted and expected me to look abjectly grateful. Joan was gone, Isabel married, Mickey taken up with Tiffins and his arcane studies. I had made no friends. Perhaps St Michael's might not be such a bad place, more comfortable than the Convalescent Home and happier than nights with Mrs Dawson and the black days off with Nellie Beatrice. I did my best to smile gratefully at Mrs Ure. It was a perfunctory performance and my mother punched me in the back on the way out. We then went to celebrate with tea at the Regent Palace and on to the first house of a George Black show at the London Hippodrome, and there again were the ranks of huge chorus girls swarming into the auditorium to scoop up male members of the audience and dance with them in the aisles. Would one of these gorgeous plumed creatures swoop down on me? The merest brush from their long gowns promised some animal scented power from beyond. Far, far beyond Stangrove Road, and Daphne, a pasty lump of a schoolgirl in a Woolworth's overall.

I went to St Michael's for the summer term in 1943. My mother saw me off at Waterloo on the reserved coach with its bold St Michael's reservations on the window. The platform was filled with figures in black and yellow piped blazers with black and yellow caps, some wearing short trousers, some long. I had not thought to put on my own new uniform and I looked with some envy at those who had clearly ancient blazers, grubby, stained and unclean, feeling conspicuous in my mufti: a red, black and grey checked suit which aroused instant scorn, it being regarded as the sort of suit only a bookmaker would wear. The suit was a clear tactical blunder. Their handy snobbery had made me blush already but I tried comforting myself with the thought of their slavishness. Eric would have approved of my suit, so of course, and above all, would Max Miller. If only I could have a suit like one of his. I had seen a ukelele on display in W. H. Smith's on the platform and I decided on the spot to buy it for seven and sixpence. Armed with the sheet music of 'Don't Fence Me In' I determined to set about learning it when I got to St Michael's. This was another error. The uke was dismissed as a joke and I never got further than learning the fingering for 'Deep in the Heart of Texas'. I was reminded of it later, reading the account of Kipps being politely asked at tea by his demure hostess if he was interested in music and his reply, 'Well, I *am* learning to play the banjo.'

The headmaster, Mr Eric Pepper, was shepherding his boys on to the train. He looked like a solicitor's clerk, or something similar, with slightly stained striped trousers, black jacket and waistcoat, and an Anthony Eden homburg dented and most unrakishly worn, which made him resemble the popular figure of the time, Billy Brown of London Town or Mr Strube. Together with a yellow toothy smile, topped by a dense moustache my mother would have suspected of culturing germs, he could have been a bystander in a George Formby film. Unlike Mr Cotter, who seemed more like a grim shop-steward than a teacher, Eric Pepper's braying, pedantic vowels and dowdy, prissy appearance sniggered rather than proclaimed his calling. With more individual style, he might have made an unsavoury, unloveable Will Hay. Even then I had the notion that I could unerringly smoke out the prigs, hedgers and dissemblers. Eric Pepper looked at a glance to be all of these, a guvnor's man who happened to be also the guvnor. It was, of course, a glib judgement but schoolboys, especially new ones, need to invent fools gladly for their own protection. I may have felt already that if I had talent it was to vex rather than to entertain. Unlike Noël Coward's, it was not to amuse but to dissent, although I possibly thought I could do both.

Eric (or Little by Little as he was shortly to be christened by me), like so many teachers, understandably sought at all times the Easy Way Out. The technique was the simple one of appealing to the craven instincts, apparent in most boys and girls, of overweening, paltry ambition and desire to please. If I shared these instincts, as I undoubtedly did to some extent, they were thwarted by some sort of cynical defeatism that spared me the effort of competing. In the most wayward child there is often a snivelling conformist struggling to get out. Eric had a nose for this worm of cupidity within and thinking himself a Fisher of Boys he had become an efficient and respected Prig Farmer.

St Michael's had been evacuated from north London, with a skeleton staff and a depleted number of pupils to its present primitive village. From the top of the playing fields one could see a great stretch of the Taw and Torridge estuary. The school itself was a pleasant early nineteenth-century, long, low house, approached by a drive and surrounded by parkland which served as playing fields. There were large vegetable gardens, a piggery, and outbuildings later to be converted into Eric's most cherished dream, the School Chapel. In appearance, comfort and amenities, it was certainly an advance on anything I had experienced before, possibly superior to the Gothic pretensions of Ewell Castle School. To my relief, none of the boys seemed to come from what might be called a posh background, although most of their fathers owned cars and telephones.

I soon became very friendly with a boy slightly older than myself, Greville Pelham Monserrat Watson. In spite of his Lord Snootyish name, his father was a civil engineer from Belfast. I told everyone that my father had been an artist, that is to say a painter, which seemed less dull than civil engineers, dentists or bank managers. The father of one of the prefects was a police inspector, which would have been impressive in Elmsleigh Road but not, I decided, at a school with its own colours. Perhaps Dad's Society had been duped by the school prospectus. Or, more probably, they had carefully chosen what was most suitable for me, like the Convalescent Home. I had been accurately placed for the cut-rate. St Michael's, I decided, must be well among the lower depths of boarding schools. Anyway, I certainly felt more comfortable with these boys than Daphne's bandits and the carpentering shop-steward. They were also less brutal. The ages ranged from about eight to seventeen and, once again to my surprise and relief, there seemed to be scarcely any bullying. For my own protection from various assaults I relied on my Viper Gang tongue, modelled somewhat from my father's but mostly from my grandmother's, more than willing to wound and rarely afraid to strike. A negligible athlete, I showed a certain muscle with my mouth which could disarm most lustreless spirits and even appear to belittle certain of the guvnors and their men. To those who might have bothered to subject me to any scrutiny, I was affected, self-regarding and striving after eluding style.

BILL: No, but I never seriously thought of myself being brilliant enough to sit in that company, with those men, among any of them with their fresh complexions from their playing fields and all that, with their ringing, effortless voice production and their quiet chambers, and tailors and mess bills and Oxford Colleges and going to the opera God knows where and the 400, whatever I used to think that was. I can't remember at the time. I have always been tolerably bright.

JUDGE: Always been?

BILL: Bright. *Only* tolerably bright, my lord. But, to start with, and potentially and finally, that is to say, irredeemably mediocre. Even at fifteen, when I started out in my profession. Oh no, before that. Before that. Mark. I have never had any but fugitive reasons – recurrent for all that – that this simple, uncomplicated, well, simple, assumption was correct.

Inadmissible Evidence, 1964

If vanity led me into actorish posturings, I was not helped by my physical appearance. After almost a year in bed, I felt myself to be what my mother called 'a bit unwholesome' within and without. My hair had become crinkly and wiry, almost Negroid. I tried to straighten it with careful applications of Vaseline and water and, when I could afford it, Brylcreem. I developed a hideous acne not only over my face but on my back, which persisted well into middle age. Any dandyish pretence was spoiled by these glowering pustules which later made shaving such a painful, bloody, morning exercise. Apart from the dandruff which fell in itchy scabs on my close-shaven neck, I cannot have been an engaging sight, with salt-cellar chest, elongated face, too long upper lip – I had what my mother termed a 'gummy smile' – eyes set deep but, as pointed out to me by a kindly young scholar, possibly too close together. And squinny-eyed, like Henry VIII. My only asset was fairly long legs. I longed for a barrel chest and a big head like the police inspector's son. I was a poor sort of whippet among bulls. Thinness was not then admired, but largeness, in men particularly, was regarded as the mark of health, manliness and affluence. Men who would nowadays be dismissed as overweight and misshapen were respected as 'a fine figure of a man'. Compared favourably to Edward VII, the caddish, embezzling Uncle Frank, had been grudgingly acknowledged in my grandfather's eyes as, 'a

1 John Osborne, aged three.

2 Mother – Nellie Beatrice.

3 Father – Thomas Godfrey.

4 Grandma Grove on her hundredth birthday.

5 At Hampton Court, 1946: John Osborne with Grandma Grove, Uncle Jack and Nellie Beatrice.

6 Sister Fay.

7 Auntie Queenie, aged twenty-four.

8 Auntie Nancy and Uncle Harry in 'The White Man's Grave'.

9 At St Michael's: John Osborne (*top*) back row, far right;
(*above*) fourth row up, far left.

10 In rep: (*left*) at Kidderminster;
(*below*) at Derby with Pamela Lane.

11 Pages from John Osborne's notebooks: the original title page and draft of *Look Back in Anger*.

12 George Devine.

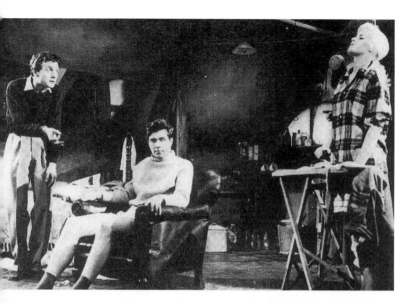

13 Kenneth Haigh as Jimmy Porter, Alan Bates (*sitting*) as Cliff, and Mary Ure as Alison Porter in the original production of *Look Back in Anger*.

14 *Look Back in Anger*, Royal Court Theatre, 1956.

15 Pamela Lane.

16 John Osborne, 1950.

1 Joan Plowright, 2 Anna Manahan, 3 Jacqueline Hussey, 4 John
Osborne, 5 Frances Cuka, 6 Tony Richardson, 7 George Devine, 8 M
Ure, 9 Alan Tagg, 10 A. L. Lloyd, 11 Alan Dobie, 12 Alex Jacobs,
13 Tom Maschler, 14 Miriam Brickman, 15 N. F. Simpson, 16 Willi
Gaskill, 17 Michael Hastings, 18 Robert Shaw, 19 Anthony Page, 20
John Arden, 21 Margaretta D'Arcy, 22 John Dexter, 23 Wilfred Laws

fine figure of a man'. At least my father had had a power of silky straight hair, unlike my new kinky stubble, and a superb flawless pale complexion. No one suggested any remedy for my scrofulous appearance and I could find none.

St Michael's was probably not much seedier or inefficient than many other schools of its kind, offering the merest, timid trappings of a fake public school for the minimum expense. No one from Dad's Society ever visited the school to see what a poor investment they had made in their choice of a bargain-basement education for me. The emphasis was not, as the prospectus claimed, upon lots of good food and healthy living but upon the vague but rigorous code of the time – Patriotism, Religion and Athleticism. Only in patriotism did it prosper. As for its academic standards, they were surely makeshift and erratic even by the standards of cheap boarding schools in wartime, rural England.

In spite of this, a small proportion of boys took the General School Certificate, as I did myself in six subjects after less than two years at the school. In recollection, it was a bloody-minded achievement on my part, pursued to show that I could prosper unaided and without the indignity of appearing to try, which was the very reverse of the truth. Boys could go on to Higher School Certificate and even, rarely, to the Redbrick or White Tile universities and colleges. Except those on the run from the police or recruiting officer, few teachers could have been so reduced as to accept Eric's pittance and posting to this remote corner of North Devon. Only the quiet desperation of both teachers and pupils can have sustained the day-to-day existence of the place at all. In sport there was barely enough aptitude among the whole school to raise teams in any game, even to play each other. Whenever we ventured out to play local boys' clubs the results were so humiliating that Eric was often moved more to pity than reproach. We were surrounded by schools, even humble preparatory schools, which were uniformly more excellent.

It was an isolated place which gave us little hope for the future and no possibility of pride. In spite of Eric's efforts, torpor took hold of the building like dry rot. As a school we were a collection of wash-outs, staff and pupils alike, which may have given us some uneasy sense of community. It was unpopular to point out, as I sometimes did, our patently wretched estate, but I doubt if many boys ever boasted of their St Michael's days in the years to come.

Eric was the only abiding vitality of a genteel sort amid this sea of inertia and indifference. It was hard not to award him nine out of ten for Effort, except for those hard-minded spirits like myself who were too ungenerous in our youthful cynicism to grant him even that. The effort showed increasingly in his shop-soiled appearance, his frayed shirts, the paper cuffs he wore until they were almost black with grime and ink. His accent was widely imitated, especially by me when I discovered I had a pretty good ear for such things. It was strangled and over-deliberate, pronouncing words like 'Boogie-Woogie' as 'Bogey Wogey', 'chance' as 'charnce', and a school was always a skol, a little like the lager of the same name. He came from Bungay in Suffolk which, for some reason in our determination to find him even more ridiculous than he was, we found funny. If he was aware of this concerted flimsy derision, thinly disguised in my case, he wisely ignored it, relying on some outlying remnants of loyalty. After all, we were all adrift in the St Michael's boat. Parents were unlikely to thow us any lifelines whether their money was profitably spent or not. They were those kind of parents, careless more than uncaring. Still, I was keenly disappointed at having been sent to such a third-rate establishment and not to a decent school like Mickey's. I knew I had been fobbed off with a specious and pathetic imitation.

9. Tomorrow, the Empire

THE
MICHAELIAN

Being the Official Organ of St. Michael's College

Vol. 1. No. 1. APRIL, 1944. Postage Inland 1½d. Price 1/-

Donna è mobile

Arse holes are cheap today
Cheaper than yesterday
Little boys are half a crown
Standing up or lying down.

There were two 'Houses', but these had no separate physical existence. Boys were selected by what appeared to be Eric's whim to be in either School House or Gray's. He was the head of School House which had the implications of his authority over it and reflected his own taste and moral attitude in the selection of boys who were without exception, in my opinion, the most conscientious collection of future customs officers, civil servants or teachers. Gray House, on the other hand, to which I was assigned, was raffish and anarchic in comparison or, at least, so its members chose to believe.

For example, all the day boys – about a third of the school and despised heartily by the boarders – were allotted to School House. They were certainly a dull lot of dogs, suspicious North Devonians, an unforthcoming bunch, and two Jewish boys, the first I had ever met. One of them learnt Hebrew, which seemed a pretty exotic thing to be doing. Eric's attempts to establish separate identities and rivalries for the House were frustrated by a minority, including myself, which took pride in never making any competitive effort or caring about its results. Our motto might have been: 'Strive not for the laurels are not worth the blooming candles. Leave them to the Suckers.'

Gray House was in the charge of the senior maths master, a lanky Welshman who spoke with such lisping, donnish speed that he was almost impossible to understand. In the face of my near refusal to grasp mathematics, even simple arithmetic, he soon accepted the truth which was that I was by now unteachable. After a few dogged weeks, he graciously gave up and ignored me. St Michael's had its advantages, especially for the stubborn and indolent. Mr Ronald Furness-Bland, who had taught at a school in Bishop's Stortford and always walked around in a rather gamey blazer, took the lower-school boys for maths and sciences. However, the main burden of teaching fell upon Eric himself which, to be fair to him, he did amiably enough, taking us in French, English, modern English history, Geography and Latin. It was a full day for him.

The English literature was taught to us by an old toad-like man, Mr Prentiss, who called his lessons 'Literature and Living'. Most of the boys poked idle but open fun at him, paying little heed to his watery stare and encouraging his old dog to fart under the desk. He had been persuaded out of retirement to engage us in a course of moral improvement rather than literary appreciation. Eric heralded it unmistakably:

Character-Forming

> The Headmaster of Ardingly, in a recent letter to "The Times', writes: 'Public Schools regard the training of character as of more importance than the training of either mind or body.' In our course, 'Literature and Living', we follow the Public School tradition. Voltaire said: 'We shall leave the world as foolish and wicked as we found it.' But shall we? We believe that our L. and L. students will prove the great French cynic wrong. May we be right.

In spite of this Mr Prentiss made a strong impression on me and I looked forward to and enjoyed his growling passion for Dickens, Thackeray, Richardson, Fielding, Tennyson, Matthew Arnold. He read long poems, *In Memoriam, The Return of Eugene Aram*, doggerel poets like Barham, Thomas Hood and minor Victorians. He always carried the same two books in his pocket. One was the *Meditations of Marcus Aurelius* and the other Plato's *Republic*. He said that whenever he was out for a walk or on his own, he would have something to occupy him in the event of sudden injury or, I fancied, approaching death. He did little more than appearing to think aloud. If you wished, you were quite welcome to listen. His method was not as openly proselytizing as had been suggested by Eric. He hardly spoke to any of us directly, leaving us as abruptly as he arrived in class. In my first year he gave me a prize for my Literature and Living papers which I still have, a huge, dull book about the Austro-Hungarian Empire. I dipped into it later when I was writing *A Patriot for Me*. I wondered if Eric thought the course might yet be character-forming.

THE CHAPEL FUND CONCERT, MARCH 3rd.

> We had a great treat on March 3rd when the Choir, assisted by a bevy of local talent, gave its very first concert, of sacred, classical, and traditional songs, in aid of the Chapel Fund, which has benefited in consequence to the extent of £22 16s.
>
> Miss Edna Friend (soprano) delighted the audience with 'Love's a Merchant' (Molly Carew) and 'The Pipes of Pan' (from Lionel Moncton's 'Arcadians'); Miss Maria Beer (contralto) contributed 'Still as the Night' (Carl Bohm) and 'Spirit Song' (Haydn) in a voice of haunting richness; and Miss Dorothy Prideaux set everybody chuckling at her monologues, 'Speech Day' and 'The School Concert.'
>
> Mr. Richard Russell, who so kindly organised the concert for us, was unfortunately indisposed, and Mr. Sydney Harper,

M.B.E., efficiently deputised for him at the last moment, receiving a hearty ovation.

All these, and Miss Dorothy Shutler, L.R.A.M., who assisted Miss Tunks at the piano, contributed to a memorable evening's entertainment, and we are indeed grateful to them for so generously giving their services 'in the cause.'

The main part of the concert was, of course, undertaken by the Choir; who sang with a quality of tone, clarity, and power of contrast that were thrillingly beautiful. Their interpretation of 'The Border Ballad' and 'King Charles' was positively exciting, and that of the Bach Chorale, 'Jesu, Joy of Man's Desiring,' delightful in its soothing peacefulness. A two-part arrangement of 'On the Banks of Allan Water' was another gem, whilst a highly original arrangement of the hackneyed 'The Campbells are Coming' fairly brought the house down. 'Life's Short Tale' and 'The Lord High Executioner' (soloist, J. Osborne) were very well done, and D. Hammett sang 'God's Garden' and 'Swing Low, Sweet Chariot' with much feeling and command of tone and volume.

Music, an extra subject which I didn't take except for choral singing, was taught by a hunched, white-haired lady who reminded me of Auntie Daisy, and who looked as if she had incontinently wandered in from the Home for Distressed Gentlefolk. She had only a few piano pupils and would seek me out and encourage me to sing Peter Dawson-type ballads like 'Friend o'Mine' and 'The Story of Alkazaar' for our frequent patriotic concerts.

A group of songs entitled the 'River Scene' contained 'Swing Low Sweet Chariot' and 'Old Man River.' The solos here were taken by Miss Friend and Osborne. The finale was a tribute to the men and women of England who during these difficult years have kept alive the spark of liberty; the heritage for the coming generation. This tribute was borne out by pupils representing members of the Armed Forces, Civil Defence Units and Workers, and in a moving speech by Hornsby.

Ronald Furness-Bland would have made a passable Captain Grimes in *Vile Bodies*. It was obvious to us that he brought some unease to the staff room. He was a gin and tonic rather than a sherry man, someone Nellie Beatrice would have respectfully identified as a sporting type. Far from resembling this Edwardian paradigm he personified Metropolitan Man, awesomely to us unhappy, exiled boys and disconcertingly to his colleagues. Some of them might have imagined him more at ease in a Frith Street drinking club than in the rustic bareness of the Bell in Market Street, or that he might have preferred the stand at Kempton Park to sipping tea in the School Pavilion wearing knife-edge flannels and pristine boots. Quickly aware of this attention, he assumed an air of swaggering reticence which led to constant speculation about his certain criminal past. Somehow, he also managed to communicate an aura of prodigious sexual power. This was soon confirmed when Eric employed a rather effeminate male secretary, Mr Wilson, and his wife who acted as matron. She was an attractive girl to me, like Madeleine Carroll of holiday memory. From the moment she arrived, almost the entire school was bent upon the wild but intent dream of having an affair with her or, at the very least, a fleeting stolen embrace. Fantasy tottered between chastest passion and mass rape. It was generally agreed that she was completely wasted on Mr Wilson, who was supposed to be a painter and looked far too much of a cissy to have such an attractive young wife. No one who seemed to be such a willy-wet-egg would possibly have served this lady as well as any one of the older and adventurous boys.

O Mores, O Directoires!

Sure enough, one day in one of the passages, I came upon Furness-Bland, his arms around Matron, crisp and crackling in her white overall. They glanced at me absently as if they were only intent on not becoming unstuck. My interruption may have amused rather than alarmed them for they both treated me with surprising un-staff-like friendliness. I felt like a privileged conspirator, the silent witness to full-throated adultery under Eric's own monkish roof. Sex filled our days if not our nights. Even the bovine Devon maids who waited on us in the dining-room were coveted itchily under the tablecloth as they bent over us, revealing the elastic Plimsoll line of desire. As far as I discovered there was no evidence of homosexuality. I may have been deceived as I thought little about it. Sex meant masturbation or girls, women, older women and, most coveted of all, married women like Mrs Wilson. This was the ultimate prize of the swashbuckling fornicator. There is an obvious piquancy in cuckolding seniority, power and privilege which recedes as one grows older. Grown-up cuckolds could excite little pity from deprived schoolboys. If Mr Wilson was aware of his wife's blatant infidelity, he must have recognized the contempt in a hundred young faces.

I did once witness a somewhat girlish boy being held down and summarily masturbated but it seemed more of a young animal lark than bestial assault. One boy, inexplicably named Juicy Lemon, used to make regular evening visits to Ronald Furness-Bland's room for extra tuition. This was

Soloists:
>   D. Adams: **Keep on Hopin'.**
>   J. Osborne: **Cobbler's Song** (Chu Chin Chow).
>   N. King: Piano—**To a Wild Rose and Sur la Glace.**

Sketch, THE HARE'S SCUT (by permission of H. S. Joyce, Esq):
>   The Husband: M. Gordon.
>   The Wife: J. Worthington.
>   The Gardener: J. Osborne.
>   The Maid: F. Glover.

Sketch, THE STOIC:
>   Lord Bunstead: J. Osborne.
>   Lady Bunstead: A. Burn.
>   Their Daughter: F. Glover.
>   The Butler: A. O'Dare.

puzzling as he was one of Ronald's prize pupils and there was some doubt as to whether Mrs Wilson alone could satisfy the Furness-Bland brand of sexual versatility. However, no one put the question to Juicy himself who, if he was aware of our curiosity, was blithely unforthcoming about his mysterious cramming. I recognized him in an interval at the National Theatre thirty years later. He introduced me to his wife before I hurried to the bar. I wish I had asked him why we called him Juicy Lemon.

One or two local girls were said by some boys to be obliging. 'Give her a shilling and she'll be willing.' I fancy it was mere speculation. It's been my experience that only a minority of men, or boys for that matter, venture willingly beyond cautious innuendo into clinical sexual confidences. I have, however, been expected to listen with pleasure to tales of the calculated male conquest, inch by monstrous inch, of a multitude of last night's guardsmen or waiters. Garrulous or not, the cold, cruising stare of the marauding gay seeking to inflict or invite violation and defilement, often masquerading as love, is pretty unlike the wry gaze of the Male Quest for Crumpet. Homosexuals seldom acknowledge close seasons or protected species. Adultery, after all, is more often a matter of survival than sport.

Imprisoned in this dream of girls and married women, of looking up skirts on tennis courts and lying beneath hedges, each new term brought its challenge, recharged, more urgent and impatient. Its call came across the playing fields, a grassy sea of refuge for unhurried delights, longingly from across the Estuary and sea front at Ilfracombe, smothering the very air above the cricket pitch, mingling with the muddy pain of the scrum, its sinewy legs trampling blasphemously on the vision of the thousand plump thighs wrapping us around from the world only just outside.

> The programme was interspersed with sketches entitled
> 'Nature Abhors a Vacuum.' 'The Way to Ware,' 'The Cure,' and
> 'Props.' The leads in these were taken by E. Platt, J. Worthing-
> ton, J. Rose, S. Rose, Spittle, Hillman, Osborne, and G. Watson.
> Watson and Osborne deserve special mention for their playing
> in 'Props' and 'The Cure.'

Habitual possession of Durex was essential to sophistication and the
rubber badge of courage. These could only be obtained from the barbers in
the town and, for some strange reason, the corn chandler's. Sometimes a
group of boys would approach a friendly looking GI or sailor in the street.
There were thousands of them stationed in the district preparing for the
Normandy Invasion. Hundreds of landing craft lay in the estuary and were
visible for miles. We knew that the Yanks, pampered in all things, had their
free issue of French Letters. These could be seen, stretched out on countless hedgerows like spidery cobwebs from a midsummer night's dream of
permitted ravishment of the locals and of what were then called Officers'
Groundsheets, in other words, any girl in the services. We had no uniforms,
nylons or gins and orange, barely a shilling for even the most willing. We
could usually run to a packet of heavenly delight between half a dozen of us
– 'like sucking a sweet with a wrapper on' – but incomparable to the guerrilla hand beneath the dormitory sheet. A few puritanical young warriors
refused us, but we could occasionally persuade one to go into the barber's
on our behalf and get three for two and sixpence. Failure meant a group of
us drawing lots to go into the corn chandler's and risk being challenged in
our school uniform and reported back to Eric, which would have been
unthinkable and have led to almost instant expulsion – or at least so we
believed.

It was Eric's custom after Evensong on Sunday to treat the school to one
of his homilies about Christianity and how we should apply it to our everyday school life. Once, unaware of our coarse sophistication, he even treated
us to the famous cautionary tale of the little Dutch boy who bravely kept his
finger in the dyke. One dull Sunday, assuming our ignorance and innocence
even more, in the course of familiar calls to uprightness and truthfulness, he
made elliptical but identifiable reference to a scandal which had been
reported in the local newspaper. All of us knew about it from kitchen and
servants' gossip even if we had not read it. It was a stock *News of the World*
type story, dear to Grandpa Grove, involving a scoutmaster and several local
boys in a rowing boat on the River Taw. The scoutmaster, known to us as a
fairly wet but decent, friendly sort, had been sent to prison for sexual

The Michaelian

MAY THE TWENTY-FOURTH.

As we write, the most ruthless enemy civilisation ever knew reels brokenly across the rocking landscape, thankfulness and hope fill the national heart.

Countless people, who include our own parents, have been called upon to face times of unprecedented trouble, and they have faced them. Some have endured privation and loss, some have exposed themselves to appalling peril, some have made the sublime sacrifice. These were the care-free, irresponsible youngsters of a handful of years ago, through whom our Empire has survived, and whose ardent hope is that the coming generation may never be called upon to face such trials as they have known.

Now, soon it will be our turn to take a hand in the destinies of Empire. To-day, scholars; to-morrow, the Empire. It is a solemn thought.

offences against them. It was the kind of thing we were all familiar with in the Sunday newspapers, and the general feeling was that the sentence was inordinately harsh. Why hadn't the silly little bastards whipped off his shorts and pushed him into the river?

Devon was not yet the hub of national sexual scandal that it was to become thirty-five years later and this particular case had caused frenzied reassessments in some genteel quarters, especially as the scoutmaster was an active churchman. Whether or not he was an active Liberal in that traditional stronghold I can't remember. Outside the grounds of St Michael's, the locals soon lost excitement and returned to their age-old peasant pursuit of amassing wealth beneath their goose-feather mattresses. Eric's references to the affair were so delicate as to be quite mystifying to the younger boys who had little idea of what he was talking about, except an uneasy feeling that it was unwise to go out on to the river at all and so get your name into the newspapers. Incantations to manliness, proudest and most watchful of virtues, rang out for weeks afterwards. During this solemn warning against sodomy stalking abroad, G. P. M. Watson whispered in my ear, 'What's he talking about? Some silly bastards being buggered is it?' 'Looks like it.' 'D'you think Eric's a bugger?' 'Don't know. He's not married.' 'No, but neither is Furness-Bland.' 'What about Juicy Lemon?' 'Well we don't know, do we? Not for certain.' In our beginning, manliness was the word and the word was manliness.

My first term at St Michael's was largely spent in the sanatorium, as after barely a week or so I was found to have measles and for the next six weeks was the sole patient. During the first few days I had been horrified by the high standard of the work in the third form where I had been assigned along with other boys three or four years younger than myself. They answered easily questions about English grammar and mysteries of parsing, Latin declensions and French verbs, things of which I had never even heard let alone understood. This public academic humiliation so casually administered on my first day by these little boys was incomparably more bitter and astonishing than any of my past playground initiations. Like the bullet-headed slug at Ewell Boys' School who had butted me contemptuously from below, my classmates barely reached my looming salt-cellared chest. Their fretless confidence, like his, was invincible. Unchallenging or gloating, they seemed merely apologetic or embarrassed on my account. Physically, each would appear to have been a match for Daphne. It was hard to imagine them cravenly avoiding her path.

Accordingly, confined to bed again, I set myself unhopefully to catching up. By the end of my confinement, I had managed to get myself up to a shaky Fourth Form standard in French and to have covered most of the period in history which was set from 1688–1815. The text books were surprisingly clear and I began to enjoy the unaccustomed daily rigour, forcibly feeding them into myself. It was the Latin and, in particular, the mathematics – algebra, geometry – which made the empty room almost spin with defeat. The geometry theorems, for example, I was obliged to learn parrot fashion without understanding them in any way. Algebra eluded me completely and I could never accept that two minuses might make a plus. Bellicose defeatism told me that it was all too much too late.

Eric did pay me occasional encouraging visits, talking to me rather warily but quite kindly. It did not change my first scratch assessment but relegated him to the natural role of adversary rather than tyrant. He lent me a copy of *The Good Companions*, and as Priestley was one of my father's heroes, *Angel Pavement* being one of his favourite books, I read it twice, casting myself as the young penniless graduate, Mr Jollifant. Tinkling the ivories in the care-free company of the Dinky Doos seemed to beckon paradise from Hall and Knight's tormenting incarceration by equations.

> One of the earliest events of the term was a meeting of the St. Michaels Brains Trust. This consisted of Mr. Prentice, D. Roberts, K. Reynolds, J. Osborne, R. Spittle, and R. Mellor. The proceedings aroused the greatest interest, and it is regretted that lack of time prevented further meetings. We will just give

one specimen question and answer as some illustration of the discussion: –

Q. What is the best way to convert the heathen to Christianity?

A. To live the true Christian life as General Gordon did. Nothing can be more convincing; that is the way to command others to be Christians. As Pliny said, 'We do not want precepts but patterns, for example is the gentlest and least invidious way of commanding.'

It was a hot summer again and as I sat surrounded by books I could hear the friendly clack from the practice nets every evening. After weeks at St Michael's, I had not yet been able to establish my place, however distasteful it might turn out to be. Curiosity, even envy, slowly overcame my apprehension. I began to wonder whether my friend G. P. M. Watson had found another friend or had perhaps teamed up in some way with T. B. Williams, who seemed to have a stamp of tough-looking stardom about him. When I did return cautiously to my dormitory the term was almost over.

> The fathers opened the batting, Mr Adams and Mr Friend staying in for three-quarters of an hour, and scoring a fine 45 between them. They both very sportingly retired. The rest of the team scored 10 between them, and with one wide and two byes, were all out for a total of 58.
>
> The two opening St Michael's batsmen put up a good show, but when Gordon was dismissed for 11 things began to look black when Osborne went in at seventh wicket down. Together with M. Bird, Osborne put up a fine stand at the wicket, scoring 19, and enabling the school to draw with the fathers.
>
> The fathers also gained a distinction, it being the first time they have not lost for many a long year.

The school doctor had told me that my heart had still not fully recovered from the strain imposed upon it and I would therefore have to be excused games for quite some time, certainly until the following term. This was some relief, although cricket attracted me slightly as being less given to physical risk than other games, and for its grace and style which I unaccountably believed I possessed in greater quantity than most others. I still found my heart pounding unexpectedly, immediately summoning up the image of purple curtain swallowing up a rattling coffin. Only swimming seemed to be untaxing, but as this involved a compulsory early-morning dip in the outside pool throughout the year it had its drawbacks. In winter it was often necessary to crack the ice before entering. Boys who were unable to swim were obliged to walk across the width, a sure-fire incentive to learn.

Perhaps because of my supposed sickliness, I seldom joined the band of malingerers and found myself among the hardy, foolish few who were eventually left still able to endure this first light shock in mid-January or February. I had no enthusiasm at all for football. The freezing mud and certain prospect of injury didn't suit my spinsterish instinct at all. My object was always discreet avoidance of both ball and the opponent whenever it could be done without detection or derision. Boxing, to my dismay, became compulsory. I found that my grandfather's tips were surprisingly successful in the more orthodox arena of St Michael's, where we were coached by the ex-amateur boxing champion of South Wales and the Royal Navy. He decided that I had the right sneaky speed, and my straight left, which had proved so inadequate in the playground, was now greatly admired for its classic accuracy and deadliness. What I feared was finding myself entered in tournaments and pitted against the certainly superior local boys of any half-decent school. There was no doubt in my mind that I would be ignominiously thrashed. So I again used my tactics of the football field, but with less success.

> M. Hill (Gray) boxed S. Mellor (School) in a most determined match, in which both received considerable punishment. Breakell (Gray) v. A. Davis (School) proved an evenly contested match. Breakell attacked hotly, but in the end Davis's steadiness won him the points. Osborne (Gray) then met K. Reynolds (School), delighting the spectators with a really good straight left and winning on a technical knock-out.

It became the only activity in which I was forced to take the offensive and denied retreat. It was a question of getting in there first and saying, 'All right, *do* it to me.' It was a rat-like narcotic strategy, dicing on the swift collapse of a more powerful, impressionable opponent. By a quixotic barrage of desperate contumely, over a short distance, it could often dupe superior weight and skill. It could later be applied over longer distances to hostile audiences in the theatre. It was a creative tactic I later employed consistently, to my own satisfaction at least, in a play, *A Sense of Detachment*. Inviting punishment and fuelled by it, a bloody technical knock-out could result with negligible injury to oneself. 'You're really hating this, aren't you? Why don't you walk out?' Most of my work in the theatre has, at some time, lurched head on into the milling tattoo of clanging seats and often quite beefy booing. I must be one of the few playwrights to be barracked by an audience led into attack by a phalanx of standing theatrical knights bent on utter rout. I was also chased by a whooping mob down the length of Charing Cross Road. The sound of baying from dinner-jacketed patrons in the stalls used to be especially sweet. Nowadays one is merely attacked by a storm cloud of pot and B.O.

Whenever I went to the Theatre Royal, Brighton, the stage carpenter used to look at me in mock despair, 'Oh blimey, it's not you again!' One Thursday matinée I was booed by a few old ladies and what seemed to be a dog. Those were the *fin de siècle* funk days of Binkie Beaumont's lily empire with its praetorian guard of Godfreys, Terrys, scuttling agents, managers, poison bum-boys and their hacks. The lordlier ones, spinning down from town in their Rolls Royces for a ringside place at one of my preview exhibitions at the Theatre Royal, held out certain hope for them of retaining their divine title. One week, over at the Hippodrome, they were there in such number and so drilled that the manager was convinced that any bout in which I was billed was now the most popular royal bloodsport of following queens. It is one of the many reasons I hold Brighton in such affection. Once, during a performance of *A Sense of Detachment*, a lady got up and threw her boots on to the stage, triumphantly unaware that she had trodden accurately on one of the many devices sown in the minefield of the text. 'How can you do it, Lady Redgrave?' she bawled. Audiences were tricked astonishingly by a series of booby devices and would often blow them roof-high into explosions of, 'Rubbish. Take it off!', almost exactly where the script indicated it. Participants felt themselves blooded, regrouping joyfully against a flailing, weak enemy until the realization came to them that they had been sold a dummy. Their slow rage could be terrible. Not only ladies of Esher and Golders Green fought back, but their hairy *Time Out* sisters with their agit-prop weaponry of participation and improvisation joined battle in the common cause of democratic banality.

The pursuit of drink was more practical than that of sex, and this led us to the town's main station where a usually dim girl behind the bar would serve us unquestioningly all the strong cider we ordered. We made these trips fairly frequently, my friend GPMW being absorbed by British rolling stock, which he stared at rapturously from the empty platform. Still, it enlivened some blacker dog days of the term, especially when followed by egg and chips at the Ice Cream Parlour, where a kindly GI might sometimes treat us to a second portion. It was essential to establish an alibi for these forays: practising at the nets or at some game or other, badminton, swimming. It was difficult for a complete check to be kept on every boy's

'They gave all'

D. BEATON, Private, R.A.C.
 Killed in Action, Libya, April, 1942, Aged 25.

H. F. BLUETT, Corporal, R.A.S.C.
 Killed in Action, North Africa, Dec., 1942, aged 27.

I. A. S. MOORE, Pilot Officer, R.A.F.
 Killed in action, Germany, Feb., 1945, aged 21.

M. A. MORGAN, Signaller K.O.Y.L.I.
 Killed in Action, Italy, April, 1944, Aged 19.

R. RUTTER, Pilot Officer, R.A.F.
 Missing, Presumed dead, the North Sea.
      Oct., 1941, aged 25.

J. C. SIMPSON, Sergeant, R.A.F.
 Killed in Action, over Europe, 1944, aged 20.

'At the going down of the sun and in the mornings,
we will remember them.'

whereabouts during an entire evening. The stakes were fairly well in our favour, but depended entirely upon everyone interrogated sticking to his story in the face of threat, bluff or blackmail, the stock arsenal of authority.

One evening several of us reeled back from the station through the school gates rather tipsily and unwisely singing. Suddenly confronted by Eric, who stepped out of the darkness surounding the school building, we scattered immediately. Dashing into the changing room and locking myself in the lavatory, I soon heard Eric rounding up the others and ordering them to his study. Cold, and rumbling with sweet cider and chips, I sat on the seat wondering whether I should make a tactical dash to a different vantage, when Eric knocked on the door. 'Where have you been?' he asked. 'Oh,' I said immediately, too loudly and clearly in reply to his quiet enquiry. 'Oh – well – I've been practising up at the nets.' 'Was anyone with you?' 'Yes, sir, Watson.' Or was it Mellor? Anyway, it was too late for correction. 'Very well. Go upstairs and wait outside my study.' I did so to find the others standing there, unwilling to speak. Looking at them, I knew at once that they had broken the contract to a man and that only I had kept to the story. My outrage and gaping betrayal were sponged up by the tiring, distending effect of alcohol. Let them wallow in the vomit of their manly honesty, a quality I had manifestly and dramatically disowned by keeping to our sacred pact. Their instinct for mitigation was correct, as I guessed. Last in to bat, I had been left not only to carry the can but to stumble into Eric with my head in it. We were all confined to the school grounds until half term and I received nine strokes of the cane.

The discomfort of this was muffled by my writhing at the perfidy of my sometime comrades. When I confronted them they were apologetic but not contrite, taking the view they had acted on impulse and improvised intelligently to a surprise situation whereas I had misjudged it, and events had proved them right. From then on I made a private vow that I would never enter into such agreements with others, knowing that few had my determination to outwit those already over-armed. I would certainly never own up like a man but practice every deceit which might reasonably result in outwitting any adversary. These guvnor's men might intimidate with their corrupt cant of manly honesty but not with my cowed connivance. Eric would occasionally drop little sneering parentheses into remarks during class. 'Well, of course, we all know Osborne's reputation for the truth. So perhaps we should take that observation with a pinch of salt.' And, sure enough, some arse-creeping little hack conformist would cackle back at him for reward.

> Oh, Directoires of the world unite
> In one great gusset of delight

The boys in the Upper School were allowed to go out in groups of not less than two at a time. GPMW and I would take a train to Ilfracombe, eating in the equivalent of the Ice Cream Parlour, braving the breakers over the open beach with ever an eye out for likely girls who might spend an afternoon with a couple of impressive-looking boys from some unimpressive but unknown school. We always ended up at the pictures, with wet socks hung steaming on the radiators and a bag of buns and cakes. Deprived of the pictures after a boyhood of constant exposure, I had suffered severe withdrawal symptoms at St Michael's where we were only occasionally allowed to see propaganda films like *Western Approaches* or *One of Our Aircraft is Missing*. In the tiny cinema at Ilfracombe I was reunited with the best of the outside world with films like *Double Indemnity*. Deep in wartime Devon, Southern California with Barbara Stanwyck and Fred McMurray was like a sinister blow-out, a forbidden tuck-in. One couldn't imagine Eric cheating for monkey nuts let alone murdering for sex or money.

To our short-lived delight, a few day girls were allowed to attend the school as an apparent gesture to the exigencies of war, apart from those of Eric's pocket. I found myself sitting beside Jane Gregg, a rather vapid girl who lived with her sister Betty nearby, and who was said to have been screwed by T. B. Williams fairly regularly in the playing fields and even in her house before she transferred her attention to the GIs. The pleasures of inserting my hands deep up into the silky recesses beneath Jane's dress, and staring out at Eric while doing so and risking her denouncement, slowly palled in the face of her sulky refusal to acknowledge me.

However, Eric had also admitted several of his nieces, the most interesting of whom were two sisters, Jenny and Sheila. Jenny was a fine swimmer, stronger than many of the boys, and on the tennis court she blacked out my fading image of scrawny Joan Buffen. Jenny and her younger sister were no callow tomboys. We lay on the ground watching their defiant underwear flutter in the wind as they pulled down their skirts with useless modesty. Sheila, with her red hair and green knickers, was the more voluptuous and popular of the two, but Jenny who seemed more modest surely promised more. When I found myself playing one of the young lovers from *A Midsummer Night's Dream*, Demetrius, opposite her, only my irritation with the undimmed manliness of the character could conceal my confusion.

We exchanged a few implied intimacies and notes, but this was clearly something that would have to be conducted strictly according to the code I had adopted since the drinking betrayal incident had all but outlawed me. To my surprise, Jenny's mother made an application to Eric for permission for me to go to Sunday tea at their fisherman's cottage in Instow, where row upon row of craft were lined up in preparation for the Normandy landings. Even more to my surprise, he readily agreed. It became a fairly regular idyll and I would walk over on Sundays meeting Jenny half way, walking across the fields and looking out at the estuary, holding hands and saying very little. I was certain that she was surely consumed with the same kind of feeling as myself. We both seemed to have the patience of prone certainty and it would soon express itself extraordinarily.

During the next holidays I wrote her long passionate letters, starting early on 'Dear Jenny' and ending later, finally, 'My dearest darling'. She was worryingly slow to respond to this show but when she did it seemed to tally unquestionably in identical passionate coinage. After the separated fervour of the holiday, the following term progressed confidently as far as I'd hoped, mostly in silent walks and punctuated with occasional ear-flushing kisses and probing embraces. For the present I was happy, almost palpitating, as I had as a convalescent prisoner, on the way to meet her on our regular Sunday walks and tea at the little cottage by the harbour. Weeks passed with little thought beyond the next Sabbath's clasp of palms. I had never felt such physical fever and I was certain it was flowing back to me with the same exhausting fire. Her silences couldn't conceal indifference let alone treachery.

Suddenly, our shared furnace silence blew up into wreckage and her abrupt, complete absence. Without explanation she didn't appear. Was she ill? Should I write to her at home? I daren't ask but the explanation was soon coming. I had been sufficiently flushed into carelessness to drop a wallet full of Jenny's letters somewhere in the school. Eric presented these to me as damning evidence of my unspecified sin. The letters were absurdly innocent. My almost tearful request for their return was refused with what passed for relish in Eric. He had spoken to Jenny and her parents, he said. They all agreed with him that it was best that Jenny should leave the school at the end of the term and in the meantime she and I were not to communicate with each other in any form. I said, as bravely as I could, that I could not find it possible to agree with this. But that bit of unmanly bravado be as it might, Jenny had already agreed to the conditions without any pressure being put upon her. It was not to be believed, but Eric observed his own ludicrous code. He may have been a sworn dissembler but he was no liar. For the next few weeks until the term ended I stared at her miserably, willing even a whisper of regret or farewell from her. She never glanced at me. For the first time existence itself seemed deliberately pumped out from my being.

I heard little from Mickey. He was deep in exams, and while I was preparing for my General School Certificate, distracted by the bitter wreck of my love affair, he was preparing himself for the Higher School Certificate, something which seemed well beyond my reach. I was soon beginning to wonder where indeed the path from St Michael's was going to lead. One

day I approached Eric, who seemed now to have banished the Jenny incident from his mind and was prepared to be polite to me, as to what he
thought my possibilities were after I left school. What did I have in mind? I
asked if he thought there was a remote possibility I might get a place at
Oxford. Might I, for instance, perhaps become an historian? He smiled at
me curiously and pointed out my virtual ineradicable academic inadequacies. Perhaps, with my enthusiasm for English and my father's background,
a career in journalism was practical. However, it required a skill in shorthand and typing and, above all, the capacity for self-discipline without
supervision. Did I have that? He implied that it had not yet shown itself.

Despising him as I did, I don't know why I was disappointed at his
lighthearted lack of interest. One way and another, the approaching end of
St Michael's for me was going to be, in Nellie Beatrice's words, A Proper
Let Down.

After the School Certificate exams were held and over, we were three-
quarters of the way through the summer term in 1945. In a way, it may have
matched the weary, impatient mood of the country at the fading stage of the
war. There was a general air of restlessness throughout the school and of
longing to get back home and be free from the results of the exams and
Eric's routine, which he however seemed determined to keep up until the
last possible moment, overloading us with more and more provocative regulations. VE Day, 8 May, seemed frantic, disconcerting to me anyway, neither
celebration nor sorrow. No more pins on wall maps. Victory in Europe: was
it the glad end or a possibly bad beginning? I remember little of the events
of the day, but they don't seem to match the hindsight description in the
Michaelian. I do remember helping to drag a piano from the music room up
to the playing fields and setting fire to it, the sight of its red-hot strings
twanging and snapping back into the rising flames, a strange noise breaking
over the shimmer of the summer air. There was a free holiday the following
day which was slightly clouded by the piano incident, especially for those
who had taken part in it. But Eric, in the wisdom of his patriotism, was
lenient and decided magnanimously to let us off with a reprimand. However, he added that although the war in Europe had ended, the war itself
had not yet come to its close and that anyway the school and its work must
go on until its allotted span.

It was fair warning but I was in no mood to stay still. For once, my own
poised impatience was generally shared. About a week before the end of
term tempers worsened throughout the school. Eric was evidently feeling
the strain and I thought I could detect a rabbit-twitch of apprehension

VE DAY AT ST MICHAEL'S

VE Day was celebrated fittingly at St Michael's, which had somehow become gaily beflagged with decorations from unexpected and mysterious sources.

After a preliminary speech, in which our Headmaster touched on the historic nature of the occasion, the boarders found their way to the gaily decorated streets of the town, where, we understand, a rousing trade was done at the Ice Cream Parlour!

Lunch was followed by a treasure hunt with plenty of prizes (and not a few surprises!), after which the school assembled to hear the Prime Minister's Declaration of Peace in Europe. During the day full advantage was taken of the glorious weather to make good use of the swimming pool.

The College attended the crowded and moving Service of Thanksgiving and of Dedication at the Parish Church, returning in time to hear His Majesty's speech, and then gave itself whole-heartedly to the construction of a bonfire, which should out-shine all the other beacons now twinkling merrily on surrounding hill-tops. And with the memory of that blaze in our minds we crept tired, but triumphant (for our bonfire **was** the biggest and best) to bed.

The second day – the first day of peace and the very first day of peace in the lives of our youngest – was a day of excursions, and many boarders attended The Gaumont Cinema as the guests of R. Perplow, Esq., whose generous treat was greatly appreciated.

Footnote. – A very small boy wanted to know if Monday's holiday was given for the end of the war of Europe, how many days would there be to celebrate the end of the whole war! A nice problem in proportion! Anyway, he should know now!

coming from him. As he became more bland and affected, I took to watching him for weakness. One night a large crowd was gathered round the radio listening to Frank Sinatra, then a baffling phenomenon with his armies of screaming girls and the uncertainty of whether or not he actually dropped his trousers to engineer this incredible hysteria. Evening cocoa was being handed out from huge chipped aluminium jugs, cold with skin on top. Eric suddenly entered and most voices lowered somewhat except for mine. He strode over to the wireless and turned it off, looking round, defying a response. Seeing my upturned, smirking scorn he lunged forward and slapped me very hard across the face. This shocked me, as I had never seen him do anything so unconsidered and spontaneous. My own reaction was equally spontaneous. I drew back my fist, not a straight gentlemanly left this time, and smashed my wild right into his moustache. He went flying over two trestle tables, which collapsed in a pile at the far end of the room, spilling the cloudless cocoa all over the place. Slowly, dripping blood and cocoa, he rose to his feet, to my infuriated dismay, helped by several boys. He swayed and quivered. 'Go to the sanatorium,' he said.

I was to stay in the sanatorium for the next day or so, visited only by the new matron. Eric telephoned my mother saying that it was essential that I should leave the school, as it was in a rebellious state after what had taken place. His implication, as she later reported it to me, was that the entire school was united in my support. True, a few braver spirits did manage to slip notes of encouragement and gratitude under my door. But the shifting St Michael's code would soon reassert its old shaky, despised self. My bag was packed, I was refused cider by an unfamiliar girl before getting on the train back to London. I stared out of the window at the huge placards by the track: 'You are Now Leaving the Strong Country'. I wasn't entering it for sure. All I could be sure of seeing was the Black Look of Waterloo. Behind me I had left nothing.

EXCELSIOR

And how time has marched on since our last issue. VE-Day, VJ-Day, a Socialist Parliament, the Atomic Bomb. What next? Has the world sufficient moral intelligence to withstand the temptation to unleash the forces of destruction it now commands? It seems incredible that it should not . . . And in 1939 it was incredible that Germany would deliberately encompass the organised destruction of millions of innocents. It is doubtful if any of us realise the extent of the horror that has occurred. Perhaps it is a mercy we do not. But even the blindest of us must see the utter necessity of holding on to decent ideals and humane principles, each and every one of us, as never before. May we ourselves never fail in the humble part we play as units in this fantastic world-embracing scene.

10. 'Must Leave Now to Take Down the Front-room Curtains'

My mother was quite unprepared for my return, foresight being unknown to her kind. It was easy for us to avoid each other. When she was not at work, I could visit Mickey Wall or the Rembrandt Cinema or join Grandma Osborne listening to *Saturday Night Music Hall*. An advantage of her refusal to enquire about my life was that she ignored the bad as well as what might have been the good. The news came from Eric that I had passed my School Certificate – a passport to nowhere as it turned out. More important, the matter of Jenny came out. 'Oh my God,' said my mother, poring over the letter. 'There's a *girl* in it! He says something clan- . . . something was *going on*.' 'Clandestine,' I said. 'What's that mean?' 'It means he didn't know. Except that it's not true because he let me go to tea with her.' 'Oh dear,' she looked at me with some bitter satisfaction. 'How upset your father would be.' No, he wouldn't, I thought to myself, he might even have said Jolly Good Luck.

Mrs Ure also seemed uncertain as to what should be done with me. Prompted or not by Eric, it was decided that journalism was my only hope and I should be sent to Clark's College, where I would learn rudimentary shorthand and typing. It was made to seem both prosaic and unattainable. I cycled every day some five or six miles to the college, a large Victorian house in a leafy Surbiton street, where I was the only boy in the class of some thirty or forty girls. Day after day passed and no one, including the mild little teacher, addressed a word to me. After three months I had mastered enough shorthand to get me through an official 100 words a minute, which I was unable to read back, and an unverified typing speed. Mrs Ure provided me with introductions to local newspapers in Croydon, Sutton, Cheam and Barnes, but it was soon made clear to me that my chances of reporting a wedding in Norwood were as unlikely as phoning in an exclusive account of a military coup from some unheard of trouble-spot. 'He'll be a thousand-a-year man, he will. You'll see. He'll be a thousand-a-year man', even Cheffie put in a word for me. A thousand a year was more than twice the amount my father had ever earned.

During this period of charade interviews, I woke up one morning with violent pains in the stomach and complained to my mother, who gave me three brimming tablespoons of castor oil. When she came back from work in the afternoon, I lay sweating on the bed, doubled up and she sent for a doctor. He was encouraging but did nothing to ease my agony and insisted on 'A Second Opinion', which seemed to be something available, like the Second Coming, even to the humblest like myself. The Second Opinion confirmed that I had a twisted burst appendix and peritonitis, urged on by Nellie Beatrice's castor-oil chaser. A few weeks later I had an appendectomy at the Epsom Cottage Hospital, a cosy little place which nevertheless could do little to ease the ordinary unpleasantness of operations at that time, most of all the administration of the anaesthetic. This sensation, like being held down on a table and slowly stifled to death by numbers, was ineradicable. Even the painful abdominal after-effects were almost a reassurance of out-raged life still within me. For once, my grandmother ventured out, as she had failed to do for my father's funeral, and came to see me.

Convalescence seemed inevitable but the NABS had either lost interest or felt, understandably, that they had done enough for my career. I embarked instead on a two-week trip to Penzance with Uncle Sid and Auntie Queen who had unaccountably visited me in the Cottage Hospital. They seemed to have decided to adopt me like bemused foster parents, taking me to the theatre, visiting third-rate opera companies and concerts at the Albert Hall. Queen's employer, Captain Leon, had a drawerful of free tickets amassed for charity by the theatre-loving customers of Richmond, enabling me to sit in ten-guinea seats and watch *Don Pasquale* or *Crime and Punishment* with John Gielgud. Queen and Sid found it all a bit too 'high-brow', until the time would arrive when he urged her to go on and be a sport, snap out of it and have another drink.

Sid and Queen booked rooms for their week's summer holiday in Penzance. Before the war they had always gone to Sidmouth with Auntie Caddie, in their tennis-playing days. Now, with Auntie Queenie, bride of a few years standing, in her early fifties and Sid in his mid-forties, they seemed frightened that Caddie might catch up with them. I enjoyed myself tremendously. Penzance was a cosy place, not boisterous like Margate or sleepy like Bognor, but what I imagined Ventnor to have been like in sum-mer – hot, palmy and drowsy – like Isabel. Queen scrutinized every move Uncle Sid and I made together, although the three of us were almost always in company. Occasionally Sid would come into my room in the evening, sit on the bed and try to talk about what he called 'highbrow books and things'. Listening outside, her ear placed to the door as she had done on my mother's wedding night, Auntie Queen could have heard nothing compromising, only what she regarded as an excess of attention to a young boy.

At the end of the week they had decided to go home. It had been 'very nice' but they had had 'quite enough'. The high spot had been a visit to the film *The Bells of St Mary's*, with Bing Crosby and the adulterous Ingrid Bergman as a nun, which possibly appealed to Queen's nostalgia for Renee McAndrew. I said good-bye to them, excited at the prospect of a whole week without their bickering and hourly disappointment with Penzance, and a world loured over by Auntie Caddie. I longed for them to go, leaving me to explore the fishing villages and rocky beaches on my own. Sid dared not show his regret. Queen was impatient and their preparations to leave were like disassembling a siege. I had not had such a sense of freedom since walking on the beach in the Isle of Wight and there was no Black Look to return to at teatime.

I wandered among the rock pools, perhaps thinking of Isabel or Mickey and the undisclosed future, but only slightly missing a companion. At least the circumscribed tedium of St Michael's was over. Towards the end of the week, feeling stronger after long walks to Mousehole and Lamorna Cove, my acne dried up and improved under the burning sun. I found myself on what seemed to be a deserted beach, and in the shelter of a huge pile of rocks I took off my bathing suit and began to cauterize my appendicitis wound with a stick, rather like a crayon, which I had been given for this purpose. It was six months since my operation but my scar had refused to heal and was still partially open with patches of wormy flesh protruding from it. The cauterizing was not painful but the sight of my exposed abdomen was depressing.

Scraping away at a piece of hanging flesh, I noticed that I was being watched and quickly hoisted up my trunks. I went to make off in another direction where I could carry on undisturbed. I looked towards the figure on the beach, a handsome, grey-haired man, possibly in his late thirties, who was lying on the sand near the sea. He looked extremely relaxed, rather amused and very brown. Covering myself up, I tried to hurry past him, but he stopped me and spoke in a very confident, educated voice. He asked me about myself and what I was doing on my own. His name was J. Wood Palmer and he had just come out of the army, a major in the Army Educational Corps, 'trying to bash a little poetry into the heads of squaddies'.

He asked me what was the book I was holding in my hand. It was Shaw's forgettable novel, *An Unsocial Socialist*. He too was a writer and had had several short stories published in international collections. He invited me to have tea at his cottage.

The cottage was small but very comfortable, lined with books and exactly what I imagined a writer's cottage to be, lacking only the spaniels and a wife. 'This village is called Sheffield,' he said. 'Rather piquant I think, don't you? There's only one small post office and a pub. You might think of it next time you buy something inscribed "Made in Sheffield".' I was puzzled that someone so worldly should find something barely remarkable so amusing. Unsure how to react, I studied the books on his shelves, while he made tea. He was indeed a famous writer; there were editions of proper books, no Penguins, inscribed *International Short Stories of the World*, a great many volumes on history, poetry, novels, first editions. There was more to read in his small sitting-room than I had seen outside my favourite bookshops in Bognor and Kingston, only here everything was covered in the scent of flowers from the open doorway.

As he made the tea, he sang pleasantly in a baritone voice from something I identified as being from Italian Opera though not precisely. He sounded happily occupied and the sounds of his preparations were very different from the noise of impatient, resentful drudgery I was used to hearing from kitchens. His kitchen was clearly a retreat, a place to put up your feet in, rather than a coven of grease, elbow grease and bad temper. Presently, he put on a record of *The Miracle in the Gorbals*. 'Listen to this,' he said. 'The first thing is the theme of the lovers which in the next scene is played as the theme but in a different key as that of the prostitute's. Rather interesting I think. Amusing. Don't you?' I wasn't sure what he meant, or, rather, just how really interesting it was. Perhaps there was more to it than an obvious musical trick. As it was I had actually heard of *Miracle in the Gorbals* and of Arthur Bliss. There had been a long article about him in *Picture Post*. After a week with Queen and Sid it seemed amazing that I should strike up an acquaintance with a cultured and apparently famous writer so easily.

During tea he talked a little about himself, about his own experiences teaching young soldiers about civics and politics. He asked me about my own politics and my friends. He was so courteous, casually encouraging me to tackle his effortlessly prepared tea (my mother would have taken heavy-breathing hours over it). The delicious scented tea, the pretty china cups and bowls, the silver trays and flowered knife-handles were friendly and obviously used every day and not mummified in serviettes among new-smelling drawers in the lounge sideboard. His ease and attentiveness, the absence of any sense of hurry, behind or to come, was heady. There was no washing-up to be got out of the way before you'd finished, no summoning bell or waiting landlady. I soon began to feel that if I did say anything foolish, he would generously find it 'interesting', like the lovers' theme. I told him about Mickey Wall, Eric, trying to be a journalist. 'Perhaps you're really a poet,' he said. Could he be serious? Yes, he was. I said little about Queen and Sid and nothing about my mother. I didn't want to be found *too* amusing.

The light was beginning to fade and, clearing the table, he suggested that I might like to stay the weekend here at the cottage. My heart stopped. I was quite unprepared for invitations so lightly offered. Such things were usually mulled over suspiciously like will-readings. I was due to go back the following day. What could I do? 'Why don't you ring up your mother?' To the famous writer it was quite clear, but I knew there was no point in doing that as she would only raise difficulties. A cloud of changed plans was unthinkable to her wellbeing and would be proof of my selfish caprice. I explained that we had no telephone. 'In that case, why don't you get me to send her a telegram from the Post Office? We can do it in the morning.' It seemed worth the certainty of a week's Black Looks for the chance of a few days in this civilized man's company. I agreed eagerly. 'Very well then,' he said. 'It's all fixed. I have a young friend coming at the weekend. I think you might find him quite amusing. He's a poet, too, but sometimes he gets very sulky and goes outside and sits by himself, so you and I can talk together if necessary.' It was all fixed. Short-stories and their writers seemed very important then. My father had written them sometimes and read them constantly.

Before it got quite dark, I was sitting comfortably, reading one of his contributions to *International Short Story*. 'Before I send a telegram tomorrow I do think that I must tell you that I shall almost certainly try to seduce you.' This time I could think of no reply at all. He was smiling but he was also serious. The back of my itchy neck and chin were wet and burning. I felt immediately transformed from a welcome visitor to an oafish shoplifter. Above all, I felt pitiful gratitude for his honesty and good manners. It was what I knew to be *Good Behaviour*, a rare sight in myself and others. I mumbled a few excuses about my mother after all really expecting me and that she would be cross. He took me across the fields and showed me the quickest way back to Penzance. 'If you ever change your mind – remember Wood's Ha'pence and Made in Sheffield.' Unable to express my mixed feelings of admiration and relief, I escaped back to High Tea and my cheerful, unlettered landlady.

I looked later for the works of J. Wood Palmer without success. He had told me that he was a descendant of the famous Wood in Ireland, he of Wood's Ha'pence, the subject of Swift's *Drapier's Letters*. It was the one reference he had made over tea which I had instantly recognized. Eric had taken me over it a few months earlier. That afternoon was the first time I had ever felt indebted to him.

11. Hold the Front Page

In January 1947, Dad's Society sent me to work for Benn Brothers, which was a glum building, grey outside and white tile within. However, the *Daily Telegraph* offices were only a few yards farther down so it was better than being sandwiched between Kennard's and Dorothy Perkins in Croydon High Street. Benn Brothers was a subsidiary of Sir Ernest Benn Ltd. Sir Ernest, it seemed, was a near Fascist Evangelist who principally published educational and religious works and, through his other companies, a host of technical journals like the *Electrician*, *Nursery World*, *Engineering World* and so on.

Benn Brothers was controlled by his sons, Mr Glanville and Mr John. Perhaps this identification by Christian name was to give it the feel of a family firm, implying a filial, cosy atmosphere which it certainly did not fulfil. Benn Brothers was an old-maidish, anonymous organization and its employees, doubtless most of them failures in the mainstream of journalism, were rather like the boys at St Michael's, aware of the drab hopelessness they had settled for so defeatedly. Defensive and prickly, they were scornful of the big stars on the Street, implying that they were casting-couch upstart scribblers and inferior to real 'working journalists'. I never understood this phrase but I took it to imply seriousness and permanence. The big by-liners, like myself, probably couldn't read back their own shorthand outlines and were unlikely to bother, as I saw it.

Mr Glanville, who seemed rather like a cleaner and more prosperous Eric, sent me to Mr Silcox, the Editor-in-Chief of the *Gas World*. Mr Silcox had a very high opinion of himself and immediately and eagerly gave me long lectures on the ethics and responsibilities of journalism. He would occasionally take me pottering around to conferences or to the offices of the British Gas Corporation in Hyde Park Corner in his rotund little Austin with a huge placard on the window proclaiming: PRESS. The Editorial staff numbered four, including myself. His daughter, Primrose, acted as his secretary, fawning on him with the admiration of an ambitious wife rather than a daughter and was seldom away from his side. I was soon given the impression that every lurking eye in the building was after Primrose's body. It was clear that I was not yet a serious candidate, but Mr Silcox was on the look-out for a suitably serious working journalist son-in-law who might one day step into the Editor-in-Chief's chair at the *Gas World* and display PRESS on the window of his baby Austin.

I was assigned to a tiny desk in the adjoining room, which was even smaller than the Editor-in-Chief's. This contained the Assistant Editor, a large gloomy man rather like Mr Prentiss, who said little but wheezed and grunted on a running sewer of a pipe all day. By the end of the day the little room was almost black, like a railway tunnel in mid-winter. Apart from myself the only other occupant was the Chief Reporter, a foxy-faced man who wandered in and out on various assignments which he increasingly handed over to me. These 'assignments' included summonses to press conferences at Ministries about anything that had to do with industry, engineering or the Gas Council. At first I enjoyed these expeditions, especially when I found myself sitting next to some scruffy authoritative expert, like the Industrial Correspondent of the *Daily Herald* or the *Daily Telegraph*, watching Sir Stafford Cripps or Emanuel Shinwell conferring with their Eric-like heads of departments, trying to answer cheeky questions from the back-of-the-class Press. They were hugely unlike smarmy Silcox with his hair parted in the middle and Primrose's hand on his working journalist's shoulder. The only man who later reminded me of him was Ernest Marples, a most famous Minister of Transport, which must be the Working Journalist's idea of a plum political appointment. I have no son and am unlikely to father one now but it is more than passing comfort not to have begotten a future Transport Minister, Golf Club Secretary or Royal Court actor.

Even Mr Silcox found it hard to conceal how little work there was for me to do. There was little enough for anyone except the Assistant Editor, preserved like a sweating kipper in his own pipe smoke, who hardly ever looked up from his proofreading all day long. The Editor-in-Chief spent most of the day out of the office. He would announce half way through the morning that he was going out on an assignment, confirmed by the commissionaire who checked all our movements, in his Press car. Primrose was kept busy typing letters which her father dictated to her first thing in the morning, and the Chief Reporter opposite me was also out most of the day. He would come in for about an hour, type up his little bits of copy and then disappear.

My first task of the day was to read a large selection of provincial newspapers, the *Glasgow Herald*, the *Scotsman*, the *Yorkshire Post*, the *Liverpool*

Post, the *Manchester Guardian* and one or two others to see if there was anything about the gas industry that might startle some of our readers. I could make this enjoyably last the morning with ease. There were never more than a few buried column inches about gas, and provincial life seemed vastly richer than Ewell's or, indeed, Fleet Street's. Mr Silcox had given me a book on how to proofread and I got through this without much difficulty, although I was never entrusted with any proofs to actually read. All the copy was of such a highly technical nature, mostly by experts in the world of gas that it would have been difficult enough to understand let alone correct. The only two contributions made by the staff were Mr Silcox's weekly leading article, almost always inveighing against the Labour Government, its nationalization of the gas industry and the coal mines, and the Chief Reporter's column called 'Round the Showrooms', which was supposed to be bright and snappy stuff giving information about how to evangelize the gas cause in showrooms, cinema foyers and restaurants. He fobbed this off on to me, with the Press Conferences, but it helped to release me from Primrose and her father. I became 'Round the Showrooms, by Onlooker', and it offered me new scope for going past the commissionaire without explanation. I spent almost a week wandering round the Ideal Home Exhibition, sampling healthful drinks, midday drinks, sleep-inducing drinks, fruit drinks, along with dozens of different breakfast cereals. Stuffed in the cheeks with honey, milk, malt and wheat I watched demonstrations of cleaning, sweeping, beating, stain removing and polishing available to the ingoing tenants of Attlee Buildings and Stafford Cripps Estate.

During my twelve months' spell in bed with rheumatic fever I had subscribed to a correspondence course conducted by the British Institute of Fiction Writing Science. I received weekly lessons on thick blue paper. The syllabus was mostly concerned with disciplines like How to Choose Your Market, the Correct Size of Your Margins, Spacing, Letters to Editors, Dealing with Rejection Slips, Essential Information, and so on. When it came to the art of fiction writing itself this turned out to be a simple matter of observing a narrative pattern which was something like 1a), 1b), 1c), 2a) and 2c). This iron formula was inviolable and simple, based on self-evident principles of exposition, conflict, exposition of second conflict, conflict and resolution of both conflicts, or variations on these. One's efforts were tolerated only by the most slavish adherence to these scientifically proven standards of fiction writing.

Not daring to send in anything of my own, I submitted two short stories written by my father. One was called 'Crawshay-Bailey Had an Engine', a story about a small boy's obsession with a Great Western steam engine, and another one called 'Mouse Pie', which I read after his death and was obviously about me and the problem of bed-wetting. Eating Mouse Pie was a traditional old Welsh cure for this habit. I submitted these under my own name and waited. The replies of the Fiction Editor were fulsome in their praise of my promise, but he made it plain that without the expert tuition of his Institute my chafing genius would never find an 'outlet', even in the 'class' market that I was aiming at, like *Argosy*. I was already aiming too high to affect a sale. When I started sending in my own efforts, the response from the Head Fiction Editor soon became reproachful, impatient and eventually ill-used and sorrowful. I was quickly disheartened, gave up sending my five-shilling subscription to the British Institute, grateful that no more was demanded of me than my original ten guineas deposit. Now, with an empty desk facing me all day, I decided to take up my writing again, wondering if I had retained any of the craft that could make a success out of fiction untutored by scientific method.

Silcox and Primrose kept a sharp eye on me and there was not much opportunity for me to persevere with my British Institute of Fiction Writing Science training at my exposed desk. However, the Editor was often away for days at a time to attend some conference vital to the future of the gas industry, and I could then invent some showroom exhibition far enough away to get a chit for my two-shilling bus fare and go off for the rest of the day, wandering about the City lanes looking at churches. I seemed to be installed in the St Michael's of Journalism and Mr Silcox was its Eric, the *Daily Telegraph* a closed fortress like an Oxford college or the Inns of Court. But already thoughts of a huge office rattling with telephones and delivering copy to order were unattractive. I didn't fancy being yelled at as a copy boy. My spirit was cheeky certainly, but my irreverence was not the pushy, imperturbable kind necessary to a young reporter. Even at the highest level, it seemed a striving, unrelenting pursuit, untroubled by inner life or dignity. It was a priggish response but accurate enough about my own deficiencies.

In spite of these gloomy conclusions during my afternoon walks in the City lanes, I was soon to become the Ace Reporter of the *Gas World*, following up a scoop which led to my almost immediate promotion. The winter of 1947 was an historically harsh one, ushering in the first post-war fuel crisis. Everyone, particularly at the *Gas World*, blamed every bleak succeeding day on the Labour Government, Mr Attlee, and our own office villain, Mr Shinwell. Mickey Wall took his *Daily Worker* without incident to Tiffins, but on the 8.17 up to Waterloo there was no avoiding unfriendly

stares or the brusque reception when I arrived at the office, particularly
from Primrose. Silcox would have me in his office on some pretext and give
me more lectures about the ethics of journalism and what a fine profession
it was, making it clear that the Royal Road to Working Journalism did not lie
through the columns of the *Daily Worker*. He also made it blandly clear that
if either Mr Glanville or Mr John were made aware of the existence of this
publication in the building the culprit would probably be summarily dismissed. Sir Ernest would come down from Leatherhead or somewhere and
strike fire into our little corner of the building.

In February there were heavy floods in the Home Counties and I was told
to take a train to a hard-hit region and report on the situation as it affected
the gas industry. I set out idly enough, regarding the 'assignment' as a day's
paid holiday. However, I had not yet abandoned the ethics of Working
Journalism and took a ticket to Windsor, where flooding had been reported
to have been especially heavy. I got out with very little idea of what to do
with the rest of the day. Being near the river, even I was easily able to
acquire a boat and, astonished by my own enterprise, found myself rowing
enjoyably down a main street in Windsor, asking people from upstairs windows where I might find the local gas works. I soon found it and made for
what I took to be the coke ovens, where I was welcomed enthusiastically by
Mr Shinwell's New Army. I took down a lot of technical details about what
had happened to the ovens, knowing that it made no sort of sense but that
when I tidied it all up it might become A Story. By this time I had so
enjoyed my own undiscovered, untapped resourcefulness that the outcome
was unimportant anyway. Benn Brothers seldom sacked anyone. They
didn't employ sackable people. Rowing myself back to the station I telephoned the Assistant Editor, telling him what had happened, saying that I
was more or less stranded and would have to go home. The next day I wrote
up my story and gave it to Silcox, who was delighted at my enterprise and
immediately gave me a special recommendation to Mr Glanville. I decided
then and there that he must be a bigger prick even than Eric. I couldn't
believe that even a reader of the *Gas World* could be interested in my rowing
trip to the gas ovens of Windsor. Within a few days I was summoned by Mr
Glanville and told that my weekly salary of forty-five shillings was going to
be raised to four pounds. He asked me how I was getting on at the *Gas
World* and I replied warily something to the effect that there was not enough
writing to do. He said he would look into it.

Encouraged by my huge rise of almost 100 per cent I decided to buy
myself a typewriter. These were not very much in supply just after the war

and I could find only one within my price range at a second-hand shop in Fleet Street. It was a pre-1914 government model which had been rehabilitated. The keys clanked down in a sideways, lurching motion. It was £14 and I borrowed the money from my mother, promising to repay her out of my new rise. It seemed to be built of iron for use in an Austro-Hungarian fortification, and I almost ruptured myself carrying it across Waterloo Bridge to the station. When I staggered into the house, my mother said, 'That's a funny-looking thing to spend all that money on'. Ace Reporter or not, I now had the basic equipment for a writer.

I seldom went into the staff canteen which was always full of typists and boys of about my own age, dull sub-Silcox men and women all incestuously working on the various journals. Often I ate sandwiches in one of the Inns of Court or the Temple. But one figure at Benns' struck me at once as being quite different from the rest. He would occasionally stride into the canteen. Tall, with a bushy moustache, reddish hair, very athletic looking, he was about thirty and was the only man in the building who wore what was then considered to be long hair – in other words, nearly down to his collar. He was extremely handsome, I thought, a little like an American-footballer version of my father. I was very curious about him, and asked the Assistant Editor who he was. He was the editor of a magazine called the *Miller*, he said, and volunteered no more.

After a short spell with the *Nursery World*, where I was treated very coldly by the female staff, I was summoned to Mr Glanville again who told me that Mr Silcox felt there was not enough work for me to do on the *Gas World*, especially as it was even more technical than most of the other journals published by Benn Brothers. He asked me if there was any other journal I would like to join. I couldn't think of one that held any remote interest to me. 'What about the *Miller*?' I suggested. He seemed puzzled. 'Well, I was brought up in the country, you see,' I explained. 'We'll see what we can do.' After a few days I was transferred with Mr Silcox's benign blessing and slight puzzlement to the *Miller*.

Arnold Running, the editor, more than lived up to my expectations. For one thing he was Canadian, racy and quick-witted. Apart from this he used the dirtiest language I had ever heard. At first he seemed slightly unfriendly, and suspicious. Later he explained that he was sure I was a bit of a 'panty-waist'. After the circumlocution of one of Silcox's Weybridge lectures, the delight of hearing, 'Jesus Christ, Osborne, more horse shit comes out of your mouth than out of a horse's ass' or 'You fucking stupid little ass-hole', all delivered with utmost, unfamiliar friendliness and a broad grin was more encouraging than anything I could remember. Arnold's candour was gruff, overwhelming and delightful. On my first Monday in his dark little office, which overlooked the white-tile well of the building and received little light, he looked at me appraisingly and said something like, 'Jesus Christ, this firm really makes my balls ache. There's sweet fuck-all for anyone to do here and I get paid forty quid a week for that and then they send me some shit-head ass-hole like you to help me do it.' Forty pounds a week! He was only twenty-nine it turned out, and already he was a thousand-a-year man. 'Well, as long as you don't get restless, give me any bullshit or generally get up my ass you can stay. But no bullshit. I can't stand bullshit. That's why I keep away from everyone here. Too many panty-waists and ass-holes. Just when anyone's around look as if you're doing something, for Christ's sake.' 'Yes, sir.' 'And for Christ's sake don't give me that Sir bullshit. My name's Arnold. Right?' It certainly was more than all right.

The contrast with Eric and Mr Silcox was total. There was probably even less work for me to do on the *Miller* than on the *Gas World*. Arnold's job as editor simply consisted of reading long articles on milling, correcting proofs and giving them to me to recorrect. He also typed a few letters to subscribers and contributors which were taken down by his secretary, Josie, a very plump, nubile and provocative girl quite unlike most of the silly gigglers up in the canteen. Arnold was open in his contempt for the *Miller* ('Just a load of horse shit'), and for Benn Brothers and everyone in it. Everyone there was just 'a horse's ass'. He was impressively educated, having a degree in English at the University of Saskatoon. The document testifying to this was framed on his sitting-room wall at home – 'Universitatas Saskatooniensis'. ('Quit your laughing, you fucking little shit head.')

I had scarcely anything to do most of the week except assist him make up the pages and go down to the printer's in Liverpool Street and help him put the paper to bed on Thursdays, something I had never been allowed to participate in on the *Gas World*. The work of the *Miller* could have been done by one man in about two days, including the day spent at the printer's. It was a Time and Motion nightmare. The routine was simple. Josie came in to do Arnold's letters which should have taken about ten minutes but stretched into an hour-long exchange of sexual repartee. We talked of little else. Josie was as different from Primrose as Silcox from Arnold, who kept calling me a 'horny little bastard' in front of her which seemed to please everyone, including her. She dressed in very short skirts in defiance of the recently introduced New Look, slavishly worn by the girls in the canteen. Over-painted with vast eye make-up, deepest black red lipstick and lurid finger nails, she seemed the perfect, sophisticated, lecherous, sublimely common barmaid the heart could imagine. Her favourite colour was a particularly whorish dark green, which she wore with over-reckless insistence like Wilde's carnation. Some of the staff, particularly the older women and those on the *Nursery World*, had complained about her wanton appearance. How she ever got past the commissionaire let alone Mr Glanville or Mr John was inexplicable. But Arnold would listen to no one, including Mr Glanville. 'So what the hell! She just looks like she's a good fuck.'

Arnold's snorting, effervescent spirits, which sparked over the office all day, were soon dampened when he got home. Mrs Running even contrived to make his moustache, which seemed so sprightly in the white-tile corridors of Benn Bros, tame in her presence. They lived in a mansion block between Cheyne Walk and King's Road, which felt extremely smart to me, but she had no liking for it and wanted Arnold to go back to Canada where there was a better life, with lots of 'fancy gadgets', as he put it, and modern kitchens and Chevvys with automatic gear shifts. England had none of these desirable things then. Arnold was reluctant to go until he had written his novel, which he felt could only succeed if he stayed in London. There was a lot of open bickering between them about it and a few years later he gave in. He wrote to me from Toronto in 1957, where his wife had decided they should live: 'The ass-hole of Canada,' he said, adding, 'Come to that, it's the ass-hole of anywhere. Always knew you were a clever little prick, pantywaist or not.' He was working on some newspaper and now had a couple of novels published. He didn't sound very cheerful and kept referring to being middle-aged, missing London and no longer being able to 'horse around'.

I knew him for less than a year but I grew fond of him and dependent on his advice. No one had shown me such consistent, energetic kindness. His locker-room gaiety was melancholy, touching and encouraging to me and probably no one else. He was all for me going into the theatre and turning my back on Ace Reporting for Mr Glanville. 'Get the hell out of it while you can. I *have* to stay in it. I'm married. You're too full of highbrow horse shit for Fleet Street. You better get rid of it someplace else.' His soft, attractive Canadian accent was reassuring in itself and there was no doubt about its seriousness or considered concern. He was to be trusted. It became clear that there would be pricks like Eric and Silcox in the world, and men like Arnold. From then on it was a beholden duty at all times for me to kick against the pricks.

Slow quick quick slow

Arnold would work for a token hour or so during the day (he had a most puritan conscience), while I made a pretence of correcting proofs, which he would do himself later anyway. He gave me the less technical articles to go through which were mostly scientific arguments for and against certain ingredients used in the process of milling going on at that time, like the wheatgerm itself, riboflavin and Vitamin B. Then there was the weekly article on windmills, of which there still seemed to be hundreds in those days, particularly in East Anglia. These articles, too, were highly technical as well as historical. Unlike the *Gas World* no one ever seemed to come in snooping, except for the advertisement manager, who was no match for Arnold. There was no Mr Silcox or Eric to make us mime a day's work, so we spent most of our time talking about politics, sex and writing. I told him of my attempts at the short story and he seemed to think that I would have better luck trying, as he was, with a novel, which might easily become a best-seller. Short stories were mostly written by highbrow shit heads.

His taste in literature was almost exclusively American and he lent me his favourite books, including Melville, Hawthorne, Thomas Wolfe, Elmer Rice, Eugene O'Neill, John Dos Passos and Hemingway. I had read some of these already, but he also gave me books that had been on the American best-seller list, such as *Anthony Adverse*, *Gone with the Wind* and *King's Row*, all of which had made huge sums as successful novels, vastly enjoyed by Mickey Wall and myself. Arnold, too, had his idea of getting to know one's market and his choice seemed shrewd. He was also very interested in philosophy. I had been reading popularizers like C.E.M. Joad and knew the identities if not the doctrines of Locke, Berkeley and Hume. He was very keen on Schopenhauer and Nietzsche. I had just tried to read *Thus Spake Zarathustra*; Hugh had presented it as a challenge to my suspect intellect. *The Decline and Fall of the West* by Oswald Spengler was very popular at the time and Arnold lent me this too. In his view, Spengler was borne out by present events and I was prepared to take it on trust from him. It was impressive to me at the time.

National Service lurked beyond the *Miller*'s friendly den. Boys like Hugh, who certainly had none of Mickey's inventive resilience, told tales of lads driven to suicide. The spirit of Shelley and Baring-Gould had proved an ineffective protection against the corps of crop-headed NCOs who seemed to have been recruited from the Gestapo to administer a system of misery for National Servicemen. To make it worse, it was a system that was gleefully endorsed by secure middle-class adults, the kind who nowadays talk yearningly of short sharp shocks. Unfortunately, National Service seemed neither short nor sharp but two years of unremitting, abject misery. The prevailing sour climate of austerity encouraged these attitudes, and its shortages often seemed to extend to ordinary human patience, sometimes even kindness. Wartime dreams of being a Jolly Jack, obligingly serviced by a fleet of randy Wrens, being entertained by concert parties of Hollywood Stage Door stars and flattered and cosseted by a grateful nation, had died with the twang of burning piano strings on 8 May, gone with the matey Churchillian past. Mr Attlee's cowering recruits were the forgotten army of post-war adolescents, despised outsiders with no glorious recent past to distinguish them, a shamble of nuisances, irrelevant to the present and of no particular account to the uninspiring future.

They were not to know the privilege or status of Teenager, an American word and a foreign concept like 'Mother's Day'. They were certainly not a market for goods. There were no goods and they had no money. No one fawned upon them, feigned affection for them or, above all, feared them for their one irrefutable, unattainable gift – youth. Rarely did the nation's leaders ask, as they do now, with toadying anxiety, 'What about the *Young* People?' If they ever did, the hostile inflection would have read, 'What *about* the Young People?'

We had heard comforting but unlikely stories of lads successfully convincing blimpish psychiatrists that they were undesirable homosexuals, but I knew that this was a fantasy I had neither the talent or nerve to explore seriously. So, like thousands of other displaced, pimply youths, I waited, dimly hoping that a Labour Government, surely dedicated to libertarian compassion, would dramatically abolish conscription before my number came up, or even that a short, glorious war would turn us overnight from disregarded, snotty-nosed little erks into Our Gallant Boys in Uniform.

There was no doubt that I was indeed marking time, not only at Benn Brothers but waiting to undergo my Army medical and enter another period of undefined expectations. Mickey Wall had gone into the Army Educational Corps and seemed to be enjoying himself, but he, after all, had a cheerful, improvisational spirit. As I had often seen, his spontaneous eccentricity could disarm the most rigid imagination. His bland apparent conformism would protect him from the ugly harassment to which the National Service seemed dedicated. This was regularly confirmed to me by highly coloured, alarming accounts of basic training in places like RAF Padgate. In the meantime, life with Arnold was pleasant, a pocket of

subversive idleness in the very crypt of Sir Ernest Benn's temple of industry, dedicated to the ethic of Hard Work is Good for all the Others. Often he
would say, 'Fuck off, you little bastard,' in the middle of the still afternoon
and I was able to wander around the City. I usually chose the City rather
than go home early and disturb my mother's afternoon rest and hear about
Cheffie's latest iniquity. I also had an arrangement with the commissionaire,
whereby I and a few others were allowed to sign the book after the rest of
the law-abiding staff and get in a half an hour or so later in the morning.

One lunchtime, having been told to fuck off early, I was walking down the
Strand and passed the Vaudeville Theatre, where a play called *Now Barabbas* was being presented. It was by William Douglas-Home and I was aware
that it had created something of a stir as being a very 'serious' play, a
description which in those days would inflame the Gallery First Nighters
and give a boost to those box offices where it was not playing. I can't
remember the name of the leading actor, but outside was a photograph of
the leading actress, Jill Bennett.

Walking further along, a girl emerged from the Halifax Building Society.
She smiled shyly, waved and hurried down the Strand. All I knew about her
was that her name was Renee, that I saw her on Tuesday and Friday evenings and that she lived somewhere in Elmsleigh Road, almost opposite the
school. I had seen her regularly waiting for the 8.17 at Stoneleigh, when she
would smile at me in the same shy way before she got into the same carriage
every morning a few yards down the platform from my own.

One of the reasons for not returning home early was to avoid my
mother's parting accusation when she left for work, 'Why don't you get out
of the house of an evening instead of sitting around being a bloody misery
just reading and listening to that bloody wireless and records. Bloody good
thing when you do get in the Army if you ask me.' I was not bloody
miserable doing these things but was eager indeed to get out. The thought
of my having the room to myself, even without much likelihood of putting it
to immoral purposes, irked her increasingly. Mickey was by this time promoted to sergeant, posted to Norwich and his leaves were infrequent. I went
on my own to a few Saturday-night dances, but soon left early discouraged
by the lines of sulky, scornful-looking girls, the usually empty floor separating them from gangs of strutting Brylcreemed boys. Also, I seemed to have
unaccountably ignored one fact – I couldn't dance. I must have felt that you
went to a dance and then, with luck, the social process took over technicalities like where to put your feet while you were thinking of what to say or
of whether the bathroom mirror had let you down.

I left the dance hall of the Victoria Inn at North Cheam one evening, having danced with no one, spoken to no one and after hastily drinking one beer. Staring into a shop window framed with lace curtains and displaying photographs of young women, some dressed in ball gowns, some in *tutus*, and young men in dinner jackets or white tie and tails, the answer seemed clear. It was the premises of the Gaycroft School of Music, Dancing (Classical, Exhibition and Modern Ballroom), Speech, Elocution and Drama, proprietor Mrs Elizabeth Garrett. The following week I enrolled in the beginners' course. Arnold allowed me to fiddle about ten shillings a week on bus fares and miscellaneous expenses. With my train fare costing fourteen shillings a week, twenty-five shillings a week handed over to my mother, I had a little over two pounds a week left to pay for dancing lessons at two and sixpence an evening, and the odd private one thrown in. My freezing sense of foolishness left me within minutes of my first lesson. I could see that I was quicker-witted and more adroit than most of the pupils, a pretty clumsy, dullard lot mostly in their late twenties, older and crippled by lack of rhythm, instinct and ineptitude of bearing and character. Week after week they struggled with their joyless, fumbled formations and I soon became snobbishly encouraged by the sight of proclaimed mediocrity concentrating such mountainous effort on so little. Among the few of my own age was Renee Shippard of the Halifax Building Society.

She seemed to be a quiet but open, affectionate girl without any of the whining inert suspicion that marked so many girls like the ones at Clark's College or in Benns' canteen, trusting yet responsive without being avid. However, the light-on-her-feet prurience of Mrs Shippard, the black suspicions of Nellie Beatrice, and the English winter hampering brief experiments in Nonsuch Park, reduced us to snatched pelvic felicities during the Quickstep, what I came later to know as a Dry Fuck on the Floor. Slow, slow, quick, quick, slow. But soon we were seeing each other almost every evening even if only for a few short minutes on her doorstep. (Mrs Shippard: 'Perhaps you should have a little rest from each other sometime, dear. You don't want to get tired of each other too soon, do you?') She didn't mean it. Her enthusiastic, prying coyness was too obvious. But what we so simply wanted was denied to us. Apart from Mr Attlee's weather or watchful park-keepers, more vigilant than the Sheriff of Nottingham in keeping Maid Marion off her back in the ferns and bushes, sex itself was the most unobtainable luxury in the winter of our post-war austerity. Even Eric the Spiv couldn't help me. As for 120 Elmsleigh Road, there was nowhere to go except the sitting-room, Renee's bedroom being open only to a glimpse on the way to the toilet. After a short evening listening to the wireless or my classical gramophone records, which the Shippards tolerated in polite boredom while Renee and I held hands, we were left a statutorily timed ten minutes as Mr Shippard 'turned the lights off', an exercise which in such a house could take not more than two minutes. What we both wanted was buried not in a waste of grinding shame but of perfervid fumbling.

Nellie Beatrice did not welcome the idea of a girl being alone with me in 'our' house. She said the word 'girl' as if it were synonymous with prostitute, although she was unable to fault Renee's respectability. Her father had a 'good position' in the Strand branch of the Chase Manhattan Bank, something Grandma Osborne could approve, if pressed. My father, I knew, would have despised Mr Shippard, a non-smoker and a Christmas-only tippler, and his wife for her importunate lower middle-class gentility. My own abiding snobbishness emerged: I wanted Renee's body, her friendliness and uncapricious affection, and I had begun to cherish the idea of her daily, fleshy, unfailing comfort. But what about the misty goal of a thousand words a day before lunch, home to the wife and children for lunch and walks with the spaniels before tea, revision of the novel, then maybe a few friends for dinner at *night*, perhaps even in dinner jackets? Renee didn't quite fit in with that picture, even if she were allowed to contemplate it. The dream was insubstantial and silly enough as it was but it would need her blind devotion if I was to set out somewhere in my undefined, uncharted future to achieve it. At present, the only certain prospect I could anticipate was that of National Service squalor, followed by almost certain unemployment.

Seeing Renee in the suburban, frantic neatness of Elmsleigh Road was one thing, but spending a darkened Sunday in a terraced house in Westcliff with her relatives was discouraging. The Shippards had unbelievably raised themselves upwards. But her Uncle Jack lived in Westcliff, the dispiriting 'over-spill' of Southend, a word not yet invented; the sort of place where incipient Thompson and Bywaters might have once been trapped by the gods who look down upon the godless, and drove them to front-parlour madness – all before the days of housing estates and wife swapping over Bacardi and Chinese Take Away. The front-parlour gloom was the same I had known at Tottenham and Fulham, with the odour of anaemic self-righteousness, the lifeless whine, the lack of rigour or gift of even petty decision. Union with Renee soon appeared a consummation more devoutly to be escaped than contemplated and the Royal Road to Mere Content between Renee's legs looked less inviting after a high tea in Westcliff with relatives even duller and more commonplace than my own. Even a dutiful escape to the Odeon in Southend to hear the *Messiah* and then a windy fruitless fumble on the beach back to Westcliff were not reassuring.

In spite of this December storm warning, clear even to my muddled, protective sense, I found myself being encouraged by Renee and her mother to willingly buy her an engagement ring, a solitaire diamond, if that it was, for £12 from Bravingtons, celebrated in every tube train like Tiffin chocolate. Bravingtons in the Strand, a few yards from the site of Miss Bennett's debut in the West End. My mother disobligingly lent me the money. However, it was mildly gratifying to feel that if I was pledging myself to the most untrue marriage of unlike minds I was at least being seen to give in my notice to Nellie Beatrice for good and all. Renee and her mother were kindly, good tempered and agreeable, virtues as remote from my mother's crabbed nature as dog shit and fag ends to the daily discontent of *Guardian*-reading women. Mr Shippard seemed prepared to go along with his wife's rather flighty fancies, even if they presented him with an eighteen-year-old prospective son-in-law earning four pounds a week in a job with no clear prospects. Mr Silcox, in a good mood, might have reassured him, but Arnold would have taken care of that: 'Jesus Christ, your daughter must be some kind of ass-hole to want to marry a fuckin' panty-waist like little Osborne.' Arnold's admiration for me was genuine but impossible to call upon in Station Road, Westcliff.

Somehow, the Shippards became protective of my alleged intentions towards Renee in the circumspect, cautious way of the Ratepayers' Association of Elmsleigh Road. I was at once titillated and alarmed by the pattern of events I had so blithely set in train. Mrs Shippard became more girlish and flirtatious, her Sunday teas more lovingly elaborate and her daughter's engagement ring was the table centrepiece. She emerged as a lifelong Bride, born a Bride, a practising Bride. Nuptials were a garment she drew on every day, like underwear, never the bridesmaid always the bride. Her attention was centred forever on the Central Act of the wedding feast as if it were regular Holy Communion. Impregnation, live issue and age were consumed in the transubstantiation of Holy Matrimony, endlessly administered until they spotlessly reached happiest descent in a girl's life into the grave, where Virgo was for ever Intacta.

As for Renee, her hesitant, rather maidenly affection looked already 'contented', precipitately sated into matronly tenderness. Instead of browsing round the stalls and bookshops of Kingston and Epsom, I was being led gently to gaze into High Street furniture shops. I had not dissembled my doggy, lecherous, sentimental feeling for Renee, but I knew also that it was fired by a wholly selfish desire for comfort and flattery. Perhaps RAF Padgate or Catterick would provide an escape route after all. My snobbery and embarrassment made certain that I confided in neither Arnold nor Mickey Wall. The Shippards were kindly, simple, attentive and I had no reason to despise or hurt them, but I knew that I would have to, and with the least cost to myself.

Two things changed this headlong turn of events for me. My engagement lasted three months into 1948. In October 1947 I had gone to Kingston upon Thames to undergo my Army medical, quite certain that in a few weeks I should be wearing a uniform malevolently designed by the authorities to proclaim to the world the patent inadequacies of mortals like myself or lesser breeds from nowhere. The only law we were to know was that imposed upon us by our betters. It was not to be. My mother's careless castor oil, the possible imprecision of the Epsom Cottage Hospital and my sustained jabbing with the purple cauterizing stick paid off. Pressed for details by the doctors about my medical history I found myself enjoyably reciting the list of ailments I had in all truth endured, if not suffered, from childish diseases, glandular fever to the dreaded TB, father and sister both having been struck down by the White Plague, and so on. After a couple of hours of standing – a naked postulant – peered at, mumbled about, pulled and poked painfully in what seemed like clinical rape, I began to be alarmed. It made me wonder if my refusal to keep up my regular visits to Brompton had not been a mistake. Was I a physical wreck? Did I have the Osborne Plague? That might be worse than RAF Padgate where, even if I were certain to suffer, I was unlikely to die.

Clutching panic about me I faced the medical officer for his verdict. I was Not Guilty. It was not merely a reprieve but an unconditional dismissal. Because of the abdominal damage I had sustained I would be unable to engage in any of the likely tasks that the Army might call upon me to do. In no circumstances of National Emergency would I ever at any time be called upon to serve in His Majesty's Armed Services in any capacity. With this terse pronouncement I was free not only to leave home but to choose my destination, to be neither a military nor a suburban hostage.

12. Kindly Leave the Stage

The three greatest lies in the world.
I hate money.
I'm glad I'm a Jew.
I'll only put it a little way in.

Preserve me from the carping spirit. I say it almost daily now when the captious refusal to be pleased or assured by ordinary modesty or reticence is general. Charity is hard to come by, certainly in youth and was missing in me then. I hope I extended little to myself. No doubt I did, but, in flight from what I feared as defective imagination, supine passion, I was at least aware that the snobbery of my feelings towards the Shippards was not only unworthy but a reflection of my own inadequacies.

Existentialism was the macrobiotic food of the day and Mickey Wall and I were 'into' the impenetrable brown rice of Heidegger, Kierkegaard, Jaspers and, of course, Sartre. Uncomprehended concepts of freedom, will and choice floundered to act in the face of concrete possibilities like two-up-and-down in Stoneleigh with Renee and Mrs Shippard. My untutored understanding told me that I was standing at a crucially Existential cross-roads. The problem was simple: how to get rid of Renee without causing her too much pain and me too much guilt, and how to leave home and my mother and manage to support myself. I suspected that any resistance Nellie Beatrice put up would be counter-weighed by her pleasure in my broken engagement. My calculations were vulgar but shrewd in knowing when to strike to the most disadvantage to others and the greatest benefit to myself.

One of the older, more serious pupils of the Gaycroft School of Dancing had encouraged me to join an amateur dramatic society in Leatherhead. It was directed by a young lady called Terry Tapper, which had a merry theatrical ring about it, like the Dinky Doos. She accepted me eagerly and we began rehearsals for one of J. B. Priestley's 'Time Plays', *I Have Been Here Before*. The rest of the cast were not only maladroit and unenthusiastic, but bewildered by the play, a gloomy affair which no one could understand. I suggested that we do a production of *Blithe Spirit* instead. Everyone agreed thankfully as they had seen it as a film and enjoyed it. Seeing the film myself about half a dozen times, I gave what I thought was an astonishing reproduction of Rex Harrison's performance. However, after a few short weeks rehearsals were abandoned. I was the only one who seemed to have any instinct for walking round the furniture or learning any of the lines and the production was shelved to everyone's relief except mine.

But the fumbling of others had given me some confidence. I knew that my impersonation had been an accurate one which everyone agreed was professional. In fact my aptitude seemed to have confirmed them happily in the knowledge that they could never become even amateurs. Added to this, Mrs Shippard insisted that I looked and sounded exactly like Rex Harrison, her favourite actor, in spite of the fact that she had not even seen my performance. I had no respect for her taste but I felt she could represent a popular opinion which might help overlook my natural deficiencies. But real encouragement was to come from within the outlying fringes of the profession in North Cheam. My dancing teacher, Betty, took a very flattering fancy to me, especially in view of the fact that she was twenty-nine. While she put me through the parade-ground drill of the Quickstep, Foxtrot, Samba and Pasodoble, she would thrust her heavy erotic frame against me and talk of her husband's inordinate sexual demands. Her mother, Mrs Garrett, said I looked like Leslie Howard and should certainly go into films. She was certain that it could be done. Leslie Howard was indeed a little like my father but I suspected he had a certain wet-egg appeal to middle-aged ladies. My father was no Rhett Butler, but he was no Ashley either. With the right wardrobe, Rex Harrison was nearer my style. Better still than any, but for age and accent, would have been Conrad Veidt.

Renee and her mother were impressed by Mrs Garrett's ambitions for me but disconcerted. Reaching for the stars might mean lifting one's dedicated gaze from Renee's flowing bottom drawer. In the meantime, Mrs Garrett seemed benignly confident about my future. She made no attempt to thrust drama or elocution lessons on me. Her belief was astonishing. My star was to be ripped most timely from Gaycroft's by a few sittings with a reputable wedding photographer in Sutton High Street. My studio portraits were mounted and displayed in the Gaycroft window and sent off to whatever agent might be looking out for failed aircraftmen from the suburbs of South London. I was to be put up for the leading part in a film, *The Blue Lagoon*, starring a girl called Jean Simmons, a romantic story about two innocent teenagers alone on a desert island. It was patently unthinkable, but whatever grafting Mrs Garrett may have done on my behalf must undoubtedly have been undermined by my photograph. The part went to a hefty young man called Donald Houston.

An audition for pirates in *Peter Pan* followed and then I was sent for an interview with a Mr Michael Hamilton who was a producer for a management called Barry O'Brien. He was moving into a large Edwardian block of flats near Harrods and, with the aid of a young man, capriciously and irritably directing a cast of removal men to arrange an enormous selection of antique furniture. He was the first man I had ever met who was openly camp, and in the unblinking, self-travestying tradition of the time. The subtleties, degrees and form of camp had not yet been revealed to me. This was the everyday, cooking camp of actors and hairdressers which I soon found myself half-consciously imitating, leading to a lifetime of random misunderstandings. Mrs Garrett had told him all about me so he asked me no questions. She had only seen me perform a passable Quickstep and a flashy Pasodoble, but it was enough to get me the job of ASM, touring in Hamilton's production of *No Room at the Inn*.

Barry O'Brien Productions specialized in what were then called Number Two Tours of West End successes. *No Room at the Inn* was a melodrama about wartime evacuees being farmed out to unscrupulous foster-parents. The wartime memory was still vivid enough to make it seem topical, and there was a bravura part for a leading actress, of a tart in a provincial town, which had been played three years before with great success in the West End by Freda Jackson, then an unknown actress from Nottingham. (Its author was a woman called Joan Temple.)

The likeable villainess, Mrs Voray, was a readily identifiable archetype. A careless, rather than wicked foster-mother to a bunch of irrepressible East End evacuees, she was a figure of melodramatic tragedy rather than a calculating, depraved monster. Although she neglected and railed at the foul-mouthed urchins she had taken in for a few shillings a week, it was hard not to sympathize with her. Harassed by smug clergymen and social workers with posh voices, priggish school teachers and overworked billeting officers, she seemed more put upon than the repellent charges she was supposed to be exploiting. When she pulled on her old 'Sailor Beware' hat with its limp, bright feather, her slit black skirt and garters, jeered at by strident child actresses, her drunken ignoble death was more pitiable than morally justified, which the script seemed to imply.

Anyway, given a roistering performance by the doomed Mrs Voray,

cheered on to her destruction by cute kids who said 'bleeding' every few
minutes (led by fifteen-year-old Rita Garnsey, the dramatic star of
Gaycroft) to the excitement of their elders, it struck the theatrical gong
squarely between Moss Empires and Shaftesbury Avenue. With its short
scenes of melodramatic information, sentiment and broad humour, it was a
skilful example of music-hall drama. It is sometimes overlooked that the
halls relied so much on undiluted drama, where laughter was interrupted
perhaps for twenty minutes at a time by very simple appeals to emotions
like jealousy, crude patriotism, lost love, poverty, death. John Lawson had
done it, obviously, so did the embarrassing Wee Georgie Wood and Dolly
Harmer, Elsie and Doris Waters, ventriloquists with their surreal dummies,
Thora Hird in her second-act silent monologues and curtain calls, Hylda
Baker in her working-man impersonations.

No Room at the Inn was a series of broad sketches mounted on a ninety
minutes' narrative with time for two intervals. It let the orchestra go to the
pub while getting the second house in and effecting the simple but necessary changes of scenery. I say necessary because they were, essential to the
succession-of-sketches formula which distinguished its style from most
three-act plays. Even a nude backcloth with new actors every ten minutes or
so provided the driving rhythm of dramatic 'turns' and changes of mood
and response. My mother, for instance, always asked in advance of seeing
a play or show, 'How many scenes are there?' A play with one set offered
no renewed hope every few minutes. As with Shakespeare, if one set
of characters or action bored you, there was the certainty of something
different forthcoming shortly while you ate an orange or studied the rest
of the programme.

The tour was to last for six months going first to Cardiff, Southport,
Cambridge, Lewisham and Wimbledon. If I proved satisfactory during that
period I would stay on with the company until the tour ended the following
Christmas. My duties were to be Assistant Stage Manager, understudying
the five men and teaching the children. Mr Hamilton didn't make it very
clear to me what this task required except to say that it was the company's
responsibility to see that they were – unlike the children in the play – not
morally deprived or improperly fed. The company chaperone was Mrs
Garnsey, mother of the child star. I was to tutor them during the mornings,
except Mondays when I would be doing the 'Get-In'. It sounded daunting
but more exhilarating than being Ace Reporter for Benn Brothers. I was
being offered the almost certain guarantee of a year's work with no qualifications or experience needed and seven pounds a week. It was explained to

me that I would be able to live comfortably in digs for about three pounds a week. I was determined to believe him. I could and would.

The Shippards were not quite defeatist about my offer, as I knew my grandmother, Nellie Beatrice and even the Walls would be, but they were certainly dubious. Mr Shippard seemed even more shrewdly suspicious. His daughter was unmistakably cast down and looked for comfort to Mrs Shippard who fluttered and brought out the sherry decanter. I pointed out irrelevantly to my fiancée that if I had passed my Army medical, I would have had to leave her anyway, and told her of the dates when I would be in London and able to be with her.

The real problem would be my mother, so I decided to enlist Arnold's support in by-passing her objections. She insisted on believing that Arnold was an American, a gentleman, and one who possessed a quaint foreign wisdom about big decisions. Arnold artfully managed to strike the right note, pointing out that I would be able to send her home two pounds a week, which was what I had been giving her up till now, except that I would in future be self-supporting. He even tried a sly appeal to her vanity. 'Well, you see, Mrs Osborne, the little bastard's a kind of genius in my humble opinion.' This homely verdict may have been a reassuring explanation of why I was so unrewarding to have around except to accompany her ungratefully to the pictures on her days off. 'Oh, Daddy would have liked to have heard you say that, Mr Running,' she simpered. And it was fixed.

Stoneleigh

Dear John,

    Mother is so disappointed in Queenie as she always thought she would be a great Some body: as she was clever as a child and so liked by everyone. I was not very pretty like her, and Mum said I was always crying and got hurt very quickly. Well, as my Dad always told me I turned out to be a real gem: although at times I had a bitter tongue which was not always my fault. So you see one must never have great expectations or demand so much from one's children.

Always in my thoughts,
Mother

I began rehearsals on 5 January (her birthday) for *No Room at the Inn* at the Winter Garden Theatre. 'Just my luck,' she said. 'On my birthday and my one day off.' In my diary for the month an entry reads: 'Monday 5th: Started rehearsals. Tuesday 6th: Gaycroft. Wednesday 7th: Write for an hour or so. Thursday 8th: Writing.' I don't remember what I can have been writing. Perhaps it was just a resolve not to break faith with the future novelist and his spaniels now that I had left Fleet Street behind. Two weeks later Renee and I spent a tearfully flailing evening on the floor in front of the fire in my mother's sitting-room. The following morning, Sunday 18 January 1948, I joined the midday company train call for the first date of the new tour, the Theatre Royal Cardiff. Instead of getting a train up to the Big Smoke, I was getting into one and Away From It.

> *Brutus and Cato might discharge their souls,*
> *And give them furloughs for another world;*
> *But we, like sentries, are obliged to stand*
> *In starless nights, and wait the 'pointed hour.*

Dryden

1948, January 20th: Cardiff. Not good digs. Getting good address.

    ,,   ,,   21st: Letter from Renee.

    ,,   ,,   22nd: Matinee.

    ,,   ,,   23rd: Letter from Renee.

    ,,   ,,   24th: Letter from Renee.

    ,,   ,,   25th: Cardiff depart 12.40. Crewe. Liverpool for Southport. Arrive 6.45.

Diary

Apart from the leading lady, Diana King, I was the only new member of the company. The young Irishman who played a sailor client joined us the following day. There were four second-class carriages reserved for the company. I was claimed on arrival by Bert, the stage carpenter, and his wife, the wardrobe mistress, and bustled into one of the two carriages that appeared to be reserved for the staff and stage management – wardrobe mistress; stage carpenter; two ASMs, including myself; stage director; Mrs Garnsey, mother of the leading child actress; the three older girls and a small boy. The actors had their own carriages and it was soon clear that there was an accepted system of Officers and Other Ranks in the operation of company train calls. Bert made it obvious that my place was among the Ranks, with the *News Of the World*, *Sunday Pictorial* and Mrs Garnsey's charges, who reminded me of the most deprived and appalling inmates of the convalescent home. Apart from the star, Rita, they too looked as if they were plagued with lice, bed-wetting and malnutrition, like the inmates at Deathaboys Hall.

The actors' carriages were littered with folded copies of the *Observer* and the *Sunday Times*. The young juvenile, Sheila, a twenty-two-year-old who played the leading evacuee with elfin Elstree winsomeness, swooped in during the journey. With her Joan Buffen accent, unteased schoolgirl's hair, above all her enthusiasm, goshing rather than gushing, she was almost a shock after the memory of Renee, hair carefully rolled, her corsage – for that is what it was – flattened on what was already a bosom. It was a shape I had found exciting as well as comforting, but it would soon burgeon into what was then known as a roll-top desk; not something to be despised, but Renee was still barely eighteen. Sheila was twenty-two and her own roll-top seemed some more careless years away. Childhood still beckoned to her from behind at a time when the word 'gamin' was popular with film publicists.

Bert was quite agreeable, although his wife, Lily, was a very bad-tempered crone. He was a dedicated Tory voter ('*You* put them in, *you* get them out,' he would intone every time he read something about the Labour Government in the papers). He sucked up to the actors shamelessly. The stage staff were itinerant forelock-pullers, and lucky to be so. Bert would rush out on to the platform on our frequent stops offering one of the more haughty actors a choice of sandwiches or tea. 'Can I get you something more, Miss Atkins?' he would wheedle. 'No thank you, Bert. That's very kind of you.' Miss Atkins turned out to be a particularly churlish actress given to waspish tea-shop outbursts, which she may have intended to be Mrs Patrick Campbell gestures to style.

One of my jobs as ASM was to act as call boy, not only calling the half-hour, quarter, five and Beginners, but giving individual calls throughout the play. It was undemanding enough, simply requiring the actor's acknowledgement. This established, he had no excuse for missing his cue. An ASM, I was told, should always wait for the acknowledging 'Thank You' or accept responsibility for a missed entrance. However, actors rarely blamed dozy lads for their own unpreparedness. Calling the artists seemed a gratuitously servile and unnecessary tradition to me but I soon found it was a friendly, bantering business. Not so with Miss Atkins. She had a trick of occasionally ignoring the most insistent knock, deliberately missing her cue, hurling insults like stale scones at the Prompt Corner and demanding abject apologies in her dressing-room, when her artistic sensibilities had recovered. She was extremely cunning about when and how often she chose not to answer the call. Someone should have warned me against her for I soon discovered that a couple of ill reports to the company manager could, in theory, cost me my job. The only remedy was to knock relentlessly until she was forced to snap back a reply. I won this war of attrition at the Hippodrome Theatre, Bristol, by knocking on the door and entering immediately as she was inserting a Tampax. She never tried the trick again. I once found myself needing to provide an actor with a prop fountain pen. Asking him at the dress rehearsal if he could do this for me, he replied, 'I have eight fountain pens. But it is your job to provide me with one.' It was this sort of actor's kitchen *hubris* that nowadays would bring subsidized companies to a standstill.

The rest of the company were not so irksome, all secretly thankful to be working in a third-rate but long-running tour. The leading lady, Diana, was as friendly as her billing permitted. There was a rather vain and vague old queen who had worked for Martin Harvey and sounded like him; a neurotic, chain-smoking Christian Scientist, a Welshman called Davis; a gloomy hypochondriac Jewish character actress who carried a huge and heavy suitcase full of medicines and pills which I found myself obliged to carry for her; and an amusing, morose young Irishman who had me full of envy with his tales of very different travels with the famous Irish actor-manager, Anew McMaster, which made the *No Room at the Inn* company seem about as carefree and adventurous as Mr Shippard. It was difficult to understand how anyone could have thought me capable of understudying five actors aged between twenty-one and seventy. However, it was never questioned and, fortunately, only twice put to the test. Besides, the actors, selected on the principle of being the cheapest and most replaceable, were reliably immune to accident or caprice almost unto death.

Number 18 Tudor Street, Cardiff, was depressing. Thirty-five shillings a week, bed and breakfast. It consisted of a bed in the front parlour in a back-to-back street, with a white stuffed fox terrier staring down from a glass case on the sideboard. The landlady insisted on payment in advance. This, it turned out, was against all theatrical custom but she had a drunken merchant seaman in the kitchen to encourage her aggression and I paid up without hesitation. I was guided through my Actors' Church Union and Equity lists of theatrical lodgings and consequently did much better the following week in Southport. Bert was my most reliable authority in this essential knowledge, always aware of the cheapest and usually the best digs in all the forty-eight different towns we were to visit. It was hard to grasp that there would be so many places eager to watch Mrs Voray's downfall six or often twelve times a week.

Three pounds a week breakfast, tea and supper after the show was a fair average price. Fifteen shillings a week could get you bed and breakfast in places like Glasgow, but you might find yourself enacting the old gag of leaning against the wall in your overcoat to feel the warmth from the fire in the house next door. Three guineas a week usually guaranteed warmth in Victorian comfort, plenty of proudly prepared food, especially in Lancashire, Yorkshire and Scotland, and served with a gaiety to coax the most weary, beery stomach. The cook's confidence and concern made supper especially seem like a hungry hero's welcome home. They were very unlike Mrs Shippard's or Nellie Beatrice's formal meals, drudged over deliberately and eaten in polite anxiety. There were, of course, exceptions: the sullen amateur landladies unused to the ways of theatricals' late-night eating and midday rising were resentfully tolerated at such addresses and were struck off by those unworthy enough to spend an unwelcome week at them. A week in these circumstances would be ultimately expensive as well as dispiriting, so the matter of digs was crucial.

I found the best bargain of all was something called Room and Service. This meant paying thirty shillings a week for a bed sitting-room, providing your landlady with a list of your requirements for the week, which she would buy and cook for you provided it was 'nothing fancy'. If you chose wisely, it was easy to live very cheaply indeed. Grimsby was my first attempt at this experiment. Arriving, wet and tired, with aching arms from carrying my case down the dark streets from the station, I found my recommended address. The door was opened by a startled woman who looked as if she might burst into tears. Wondering if I had gone to the wrong house, I followed her into the front parlour where I was to eat my meals. Once again, a stuffed dog stared at me forsakenly from the sideboard while she silently made a list of my requirements for the week.

The following day I was too busy and lazy to look elsewhere. Throughout the week she served me sumptuous meals obviously beyond the budget of the list I had given her. Shy, watchful, she could hardly have been more attentive or different from what I had come to expect. Midnight bravura and eccentricity were customary in most digs but her silent stare, enjoined with that of her frozen fox terrier, sent me to bed promptly, wondering about my bill for the week. When I came back from Treasury Call at Friday lunchtime and asked to settle up, she refused to let me pay for my room but only for the food I had ordered. When I pressed her, she said she had been unable to speak to me all the week because I reminded her of her dead son. On the following Sunday she brought me a lavish breakfast. My train call was early, the parlour was damp and still and I was anxious to be away. The dog's stare from its landscaped glass booth and her silence discouraged lingering. I looked for her in the kitchen, but she must have gone back upstairs. I was about to call out when I realized I might wake her husband. I assumed she had one. There was a man's coat in the hall. Husbands in digs were often elusive creatures, carefully kept out of sight from embarrassment or diplomacy. Leaving a note, I let myself out as quietly as I could and walked quickly up the street, empty except for a couple of Salvation Army bandsmen assembling their instruments. I felt I had done right to leave without seeing her but it seemed unkind to have left most of the elaborate breakfast.

Every Sunday morning I hurried past houses, the moist curtains in their windows drawn behind limp grey lace, hearing only the sound of my dragging footsteps. My suitcase was always heavier than I had remembered. By the evening, in another town, I would have passed through an almost exactly similar darkened porch into what I came to feel was the domestic back parlour of Music Hall itself, full of laughter, coarse comfort and the defeat and melodrama of stuffed fox terriers. Some streets were given over almost entirely to the profession, like the dreaded Ackers Street in Manchester. Actors rarely wasted their salaries on hotels and the big stars especially had their favourite addresses where they stayed unfailingly. Every other place I stayed at had a signed photograph of G. H. Elliott or George Formby Senior on the piano. A line or two from them, hardly varying from year to year, in the Visitor's Book was the equivalent of five spoons in the Michelin Guide. 'Thanks again Rosie for a grand week. Usual lovely grub, lashings of it and plenty of good old giggles. Here's to the next time!'

Theatrical landladies were usually stage-struck, parlour performers, discriminating on the whole, and their opinion after the Monday performance carried some weight. The landladies' thumbs down could make itself felt at the box office the following day. Praise would be warm but cautious. 'Ooh, you were a bugger in that. I said to Albert, "He's a real *bugger* in that."' This would be her husband or fancy man who lurked collarless in shirt sleeves reading the racing papers in the only armchair in the kitchen. A fiction was sometimes maintained that he was head of the house, particularly in matters of morality. If you contemplated nocturnal bedroom visits or discreetly sharing a room, it was rash not to consult or be advised by your landlady. Deprived of her conspiratorial rights, she might become very ugly indeed, not by turning you out of the house but by displaying her contempt in the contrasting treatment received by her undeceiving favoured guests. However, a circumspect approach made, married protocol was observed. 'Well, I'll have to ask Albert. *I* don't mind, you see. But Albert is a bit on the religious side.' Albert might spend Sunday and most of the week at the dog track or with the local tart. Out of the house during opening hours, his approval, if it was ever sought, was invariably confirmed. Rarely glimpsed or heard, he was given respectful precedence by everyone.

Once, in Kidderminster, a few of us wanted to watch a Sunday night play. The television set stood in the front parlour and, like the room itself, was seldom in use, kept silent for some unique occasion. Our request for permission to switch on was considered politely as if it were connivance at a night's adultery. 'Well, it's perfectly all right with me, but I'll have to ask Archie.' She went out into the kitchen where she could be heard shouting at Archie in a crisp Welsh voice. 'Archie, the boys want to stay and watch the television tonight, so you'll have to get out and bugger off to the pub.' We heard a grunt and Beattie returned. 'Yes,' she smiled, 'Archie says that'll be perfectly all right.'

Some were shy women wanting company, others high spirited ex-pros, frequently battened off by their men folk. Their gentlemen or 'boys' – preferred to girls, with their dripping 'smalls' – were lifelines to a world which, shared weekly, might seem less desperate and more companionable than that just beyond the terrace. Feelings were open, often raw, and most frailty smiled on or laughed away. The cast of *Soldiers in Skirts* were universally popular. ('Oh, they're such fun. They all call each other Elsie and Doris and Ada.') This show toured for seven years, subsidized by its exploitation of a company of hard-worked, underpaid queens. With their special but commonplace talents, they were hard put to refuse a guaranteed unrising pittance, less than my own. Cheap digs and loving landladies might have been their only comforts on those often cottageless provincial nights. After a fry-up supper and beer, the family might bring ukelele, violin, accordian, guitar into the parlour and another evening would begin for us, fired with the actor's late-night expectation of reprieve from dull sleep and the bonus of energy returned in full payment. The road into England might have been the noblest prospect that a Scotsman ever faced, but in my case it was the railway line that led out of Euston.

Nowhere in England seemed willing to feed a stranger on Sundays except the local Odeon in the late afternoon. On Monday morning at seven-thirty I went down to the railway yard to see the scenery and props unloaded, transported into the theatre and set up. In time, I managed to get some nightly changes down to twenty-one seconds from thirty-eight. Miss Atkins's behaviour was untypical. Rough democracy ruled, notably between sexes – equal pay, billing and no favours asked, shared expenses. Twice-nightly dates were tiring but the Variety Pit sparked the Prompt Corner into another life. Percy, the stage director, hardly ever bothered to have under-study calls. He locked up the prompt copy after each performance until the next. I had to rely on scripts then known as 'Sides' to learn my lines. These were the size of a pub menu and contained only the last few words of your cue followed by the speech. I was often given these later in weekly rep and they were nightmarish for someone with no special gift for memorization like myself. Admittedly, I heard the play word for word every night and knew the moves, but I had lighting, music cues and changes to distract me. I discovered *répétiteur's* skill with the prompt book, knowing the how and when of helping an actor deserted by memory or improvisation. I enjoyed presiding alone over the Prompt Corner, umpire and captain in one.

I was surprised, elated and eager about almost everything except going through the farce of giving lessons to Rita Garnsey and her pals each morning. No one seemed concerned except Mrs Garnsey, who, having bullied her sleepy, quarrelling charges into the dressing-room, settled down to knit, make tea and chat till lunchtime. I had bought several text books including some I had used at school, all equipped with answers at the back. Thinking that I might be asked at some stage to provide evidence that I was doing my job, I made perfunctory efforts to persuade them to at least copy out passages from books that were familiar. They were barely literate, but knew instinctively that I had no competence let alone real authority and I soon gave up. I was scarcely credible as an ASM. Besides, no one seemed to be concerned about even the pretence of observing the regulations, which varied bewilderingly from town to town. The children's education was a more onerous and pointless task than calling Miss Atkins. Proven inadequacy seemed the only way I could look forward to lying late in bed after the long, happy nights with the landladies. But if I were exposed by the authorities, would the company manager, Miss Dalton, be obliged to fire me?

However, apart from occasionally checking that we were all assembled with our books in the dressing-room at 10.00 a.m., she showed no interest in what we were doing. The problem was solved precipitately a few weeks later in Newcastle. Walking into the dressing-room on Tuesday morning, hand-ing out my ancient text books, I was confronted by an official from the local educational authority who politely asked me to carry on with my tuition. If I had been asked to go on for one of the five actors without the book, I might have been forgiven for failure. I knew I could expect no indulgence from Newcastle. I made some sort of mime show of instruction for a miserable hour or so under the inspector's eye, while Mrs Garnsey's needles clacked in silence for the first time. The children were loyally attentive, sensing that my job might be at stake. Certain that my theatrical career was about to be destroyed by a council official, my gratitude to them made our charade possible only by its solemn absurdity. The Education Officer rang me the following day and asked me to go and see him. 'You see,' he explained, 'we don't teach children in that way any longer. Besides, you have no qualifications and no aptitude. I'm afraid your employers will have to make some fresh arrangements.' Astonishingly, arrangements were made immediately that Mrs Garnsey should take her children to the local school every week. More important, my job and salary were unthreatened, my amateur standing gone. By the end of the tour I would be a full member of Equity. I was free to explore unknown heartlands after all. The future was now open. There remained the matter of Renee.

I had made no arrangements the following week in Cambridge. University towns, Cathedral towns and seaside towns in season were traditionally ones where actors could expect small comfort or welcome. By about nine in the evening I was still stumbling around with my huge suitcase. It was the beginning of the Lent term and even Bert had been discouraging about finding a bed for the night. Almost in tears with the thought that Mrs Shippard might yet be serving me tea, hand held by Renee beneath the table, I was suddenly aware of a tall don in a dog collar striding towards me. Perhaps I was breaking some ancient statute with my vagabond presence. 'Are you a member of this university?' 'No, sir, I'm not,' I said, putting down my suitcase. If only I had been. 'Have you nowhere to go? That case must be very heavy for you.' 'It is. No, I can't find anywhere.' 'Well it is the beginning of term and it's sure to be difficult.' He introduced himself as Duckworth. He looked me up and down smilingly and said, 'Well look here, if you don't find anywhere by 11.30 you're welcome to come over and stay on my sofa if you care to.' He turned away quickly into the crowd without waiting for me to reply. 'You'll find me at St John's,' he said. 'I'm just off to speak to the heathen at Peterhouse.'

Two hours later I managed to find the police station, where I was given the address of a doss house in Portugal Street. I stood outside, contemplating the choice between St John's and Portugal Street. The college would certainly be warm, interesting and I could be sure of some sherry or, with any luck, whisky. I wondered what the Reverend Duckworth's opening preamble would be, possibly not *Miracle in the Gorbals* but something more recondite. My head throbbed and the thought of his tall, athletic, healthy frame and manner led me wearily to Portugal Street. I had a feeling that the Rev. Duckworth would be less frank than J. Wood Palmer. I paid one and sixpence for my bed and groped in the dark towards it, cursing my lack of foresight and undoubted timidity in shunning the comfort of St John's.

On Monday morning I left my suitcase at the stage door and went to the station to load the scenery for the Get-In. There was no sympathy for my digless condition except from Sheila. I was working all that day and evening and would have no chance of finding an alternative to Portugal Street. Her concern welled over as I told her and she promised that she would fix me up with her own landlady. That night I fell asleep exhaustedly in a room beside hers. The landlady was not the theatrical sort but almost as solicitous as Mrs Shippard. Sheila and I shared a late, delicious breakfast, while she chatted away with gamin laughter and welling eyes to match. Elmsleigh Road, a memory of refuge in the arm-aching hours outside St John's the night before, had to be exorcized after breakfast with Sheila, quilted and flowery from the nursery warmth of her landlady's bed. Something clearly had to be done and fairly soon. Even my sluggardly resolve had been fixed by Sheila and the remembrance and steamy promise of tales of Exmoor ponies.

Renee had written to me every day, sometimes twice. Even a few weeks before I would have been touched by her letters, no less simple or trusting than my own had been to Jenny. Now I thrust them quickly into my pocket at the stage door before Sheila could see them. The following week it was back to the Smoke, to Lewisham and Wimbledon. My job was apparently secure. I needed to dissemble for three weeks until it was back to the Heartland, to the Empire, Sunderland. I had no qualms about Mr Shippard's feelings. He was the kind of man I knew my father would have despised out of hand from his deathbed. My panicky determination to get the train from Euston and take myself off to the care of Mrs Ellis of 21 Turnstile Lane, Sunderland, was increased by the knowledge of my calculated treachery towards two people whose affection, however it might be dismissed, I had sought in my friendlessness and then abused. Guilt and some sense of my headlong absurdity warned me a little against Sheila's Elstree overflow. As with Renee, my eagerness and talent for unscrupulous compromise outfaced my own mean and common spirit, but I could not quite shake it from its course.

Renee and her parents came to see the play in Wimbledon. They could find little to say about it. I knew that the next week I would be safely in Sunderland.

GEORGE: Oh, don't be so innocent, Ruth. This house! This room! This hideous God-awful room!

RUTH: Aren't you being just a little insulting?

GEORGE: I'm simply telling you what you very well know. They may be your relations, but have you honestly got one tiny thing in common with any of them? These people –

RUTH: Oh, no! Not 'these people'! Please – not that! After all, they don't still keep coals in the bath.

GEORGE: I didn't notice. Have you looked at them? Have you listened to them? They don't merely act and talk like caricatures, they *are* caricatures! That's what's so terrifying. Put any one of them on a stage, and no one would take them seriously for one minute! They think in clichés, they talk in them, they even feel in them – and, brother, that's an achievement! Their existence is one great cliché that they carry about with them like a snail in his little house – and they live in it and die in it!

RUTH: Even if it's true – and I don't say it is – you still sound pretty cheap saying it.

GEORGE: Look at that wedding group. Look at it! It's like a million other grisly groups – all tinted in unbelievable pastels: round-shouldered girls with crinkled-up hair, open mouths, and bad teeth. The bridegroom looks as gormless as he's feeling lecherous, and the bride – the bride's looking as though she's just been thrown out of an orgy at a Druids' reunion! Mr and Mrs Elliot at their wedding. It stands there like a comic monument to the macabre farce that has gone on between them in this house ever since that greatest day in a girl's life thirty-five years ago.

Epitaph for George Dillon, 1958

In the dressing-room at the Empire, Sunderland, I began writing my first play, a melodrama about a poetic Welsh loon called *Resting Deep*. It had nothing to do with my own experience and certainly none of what might be occasionally found in the drab world of George Dillon. Thick envelopes came daily from Renee. There was no Gaycroft gossip, the Halifax and the 8.17 unmentioned, even her parents seemed unbelievably to have given place to me, *our* future, when I returned to London and got another different sort of job. Her speculation and plans put the Pasodoble back in its rightful place. The following week on Good Friday, in front of Mrs Coleman's gas fire in Number 70 Dudley Road, Wolverhampton, after an evening lying on the rug with Sheila's welling Anglo-Catholicism and our reading of Aldous Huxley, I began to compose the letter that must be sent off to Elmsleigh Road.

I had told no one of my dilemma. It was unthinkable to write to Arnold or Mickey Wall. I decided to confide in the young Irish actor, Sean. He was sympathetic but gloomy. The callous indecency of what I was proposing to do to a nice girl, who had acted towards me in good faith, was inexcusable. However, he made a characteristically morose suggestion. He had decided to go to Spain after the tour was over and enter a monastic order until such time as he might return to Ireland and Anew McMaster's touring company. I could accompany him. I didn't take the suggestion about the Spanish monastery very seriously but the possibility of entry to McMaster was convincing. Religious conversion as a provision against marriage, like homosexuality against conscription, looked too difficult to sustain, but more worthy of a try. After all, Mr and Mrs Shippard were not Army psychiatrists who were authorized to poke me about in the nude and interrogate me about my failed attentions to Renee. Also, I had no intention of mentioning Sheila, who was already proving to be neurotically frigid – which possibly accounted for her constant Anglo-Catholic welling-up at the sight of my tumescent belief that being an actress she was likely to be even more responsive than my fiancée.

After a few days I received Mr Shippard's reply to my letter. He was not impressed, nor was he disappointed but quite unsurprised at my behaviour. He had always suspected something of the sort from the outset and regretted ever having agreed to his daughter becoming engaged to someone like myself. The tone became even clearer. 'The country's well rid of the likes of you and the sooner you get out of it the better and leave girls like Renee alone. Naturally, in the circumstances, we will not be returning your engagement ring. Never try to communicate with her again. Yours faithfully, D. Shippard. P.S. Renee has been crying her eyes out ever since she got your letter. It's a disgrace. Your mother must be ashamed of you.' Or something very like it.

My mother could only have been consoled by an incident that had ended in distress for everyone involved. After a few readings of the letter, I told myself I was puzzled by the rather vulgar reference to the returning of the ring. My letter, long-winded, dishonest and evasive, larded with banalities about Life, Art and God, had been lost on Mr Shippard. But lying to myself was no comfort. My reprieve left me in no need of it.

Wednesday, March 31st: Sheila's 22nd birthday.
Thursday, April 1st: Letter from Mr Shippard.
Saturday, April 3rd: Act II *Resting Deep* finished.

The following Saturday in Leeds, there is a note reading: 'The play should be finished by now. If not, why not?' And, underneath, a memo: 'Start on comedy.'

13. Dead-and-Alive Holes

CHAP: Then there was Rosemary.

GIRL: (*To the* INTERRUPTER) There's Rosemary for *you*.

INTERRUPTER: We don't know who any of these people *are*. What they're *doing*. Where it's taking *place*. Or anything!

OLDER LADY: Give the boy a chance.

CHAP: What? Oh, Rosemary.

GIRL: Yes, Rosemary.

CHAP: Ah yes, well, she had the rags up all the time.

GRANDFATHER: Well, they can't help it, you know.

CHAIRMAN: Well, he's got a point there.

CHAP: No, but she had it all the bloody time. I mean like all over the graveyard in Norwich Cathedral.

GIRL: Norwich – you mean like –

CHAIRMAN: Yes. (*Wearily*) Knickers off ready when I come home.

CHAP: I mean, Women's *Insides*. I've been walled up in them and their despairs and agony ever since I can remember.

GIRL: Perhaps you should try it yourself.

CHAP: I'm not strong enough.

GIRL: No, you're not.

INTERRUPTER: I think this sort of talk is highly embarrassing. My own wife is in the audience and I may say that she is undergoing what I can only call to someone like you, an extremely difficult –

GIRL: Period –

INTERRUPTER: No. I would say more than that. Expected but dramatic experience in her life.

GIRL: You mean she's got the Hot Flushes?

CHAP: Well, let me tell you mate, *I've* had them for forty years.

GIRL: And you look it . . . So we've got to Rosemary.

CHAIRMAN: Yes.

A Sense of Detachment, 1972

OLDER LADY: Thank you. May I say first that I have no particular personal complaint. In some ways, I was born into a good time. And because of my natural intelligence, have managed to cope with what to most *men* would be an intolerable situation. My young friend here has complained, if I heard him correctly, of one of his earlier girl friends being sick in the grounds of Norwich Cathedral. However, I would just say to him and others like him that it is a mere fact of life that women at all times and at all ages have suffered from, and in many cases died from, not merely childbirth but from what you would no doubt call the inbuilt tedium of organs such as the cervix, the vulvae, the vagina and the womb.

BOX MAN: Disgusting.

OLDER LADY: If men had to undergo what they so cheerfully call 'the curse' –

BOX MAN: Period pains –

OLDER LADY: – They would have long ago invented some alleviation.

BOX MAN: Invent it yourself. Sing us a song.

OLDER LADY: I'm afraid our young friend here has let him delude himself into dreaming about something he thinks of as 'Eternal Woman'.

BOX MAN: Who doesn't?

OLDER LADY: That is because she is only valued by the excitement she may or may not arouse.

BOX MAN: Get off out of it, you old bag.

OLDER LADY: In short, she has to be desirable.

BOX MAN: Well, it does help, lady.

OLDER LADY: In the case of men, it appears not to be necessary. We women can be put down, if that is the expression, by the flimsiest physical or intellectual failing. We have been eternally abandoned from the Old Testament onwards. All I say to you now is that we may all probably totally abandon you. Men, I mean.

A Sense of Detachment, 1972

Nearly every town we visited until the middle of the summer had, if not a cathedral, a famous or commended church or churches. With Sheila, I explored the ecclesiastical wonders of Norwich, Peterborough, Liverpool, Leeds, Manchester, Newcastle, Aberdeen, Edinburgh, Plymouth, Coventry. Her mind stuffed with Pugin and Perpendicular, Sheila's spirit was made tranquil in transept and cloister in a dozen cities, as I thought of the coverlets in our digs crinkled and crying out for an afternoon turn down. When the rain washed us out of the deserted Close we would take our Equity cards to the nearest cinema for a free seat, where I could enjoy the warm darkness instead of the afternoon chill of nave and apse. Incense was to warm her spirit more than the steam of damp unfamiliar sheets. By the mid-summer our score for the tour was: Burnes Oates: 9; Oats: Nil.

Apart from bouts of light, sparrow melancholy, Sheila seemed happy with our weekly progress through English cathedrals. I had no way of knowing whether her fluttery chill was merely wilful boredom, but I began to wonder whether her vague languor and spasms of terror might have once been dismissed in the novels she admired as 'the vapours'. She was not content and neither was I. My Welsh melodrama lay untouched since Wolverhampton. Once again, Mrs Garnsey's girls were helpful, mocking me ungently but playfully about Miss Tight-arsed Bossy-drawers having got me where she wanted. Their dirty-minded derision seemed kindly and sensible as I faced Sheila's outbursts in and out of the dressing-room and back into our digs. Her flaunted helplessness and demands fuelled from misty recollections of Exmoor, an ideal of Elstree, were becoming resistible. After nine cathedrals we were back on what now seemed home ground at the Empire, Kingston. We began rehearsals for replacements for the next stage of the tour. For no reason, I felt open to new confidence and any kind of possibility.

Barney and the yellow pyjamas

You should choose your theatre like you choose a religion. Make sure you don't get into the wrong temple. For me the theatre is really a religion or way of life. You must decide what you feel the world is about and what you want to say about it, so that everything in the theatre you work in is saying the same thing. For me the theatre is a temple of ideas and ideas so well expressed it may be called art. So always look for quality in the writing above what is being said.

George Devine

BARNEY: This the first play you've written?

GEORGE: My seventh –

BARNEY: Dialogue's not bad, but these great long speeches – that's a
    mistake. People want action, excitement. I know – *you* think you're
    Bernard Shaw. But where's he today? Eh? People won't listen to him.
    Anyway, politics are out – you ought to know that. Now, take *My Skin*

is my Enemy! I've got that on the road at the moment. That and *Slasher Girl!*

GEORGE: *My Skin is my* – Oh yes, it's about the colour bar problem, isn't it?

BARNEY: Well, yes – but you see it's first-class entertainment! Played to £600 at Llandridnod Wells last week. Got the returns in my pocket now. It's controversial, I grant you, but it's the kind of thing people pay money to see. That's the kind of thing you want to write.

GEORGE: Still, I imagine you've got to be just a bit liberal-minded to back a thing like that.

BARNEY: Eh?

GEORGE: I mean – putting on a play about coloured people.

BARNEY: Coloured people? I hate the bastards!

*

BARNEY: You spend your time dabbling in politics and vote in some ragged-arsed bunch of nobodies, who can't hardly pronounce the Queen's English properly, and where are you? Where are you? Nowhere. Crushed down in the mob, indistinguishable from the masses. What's the good of that to a young man with talent?

*

BARNEY: To get back to this play of yours. I think it's got possibilities, but it needs rewriting. Act One and Two won't be so bad, provided you cut out all the highbrow stuff, give it pace – you know: dirty it up a bit, you see.

GEORGE: I see.

BARNEY: Third Act's construction is weak. I could help you there – and I'd do it for quite a small consideration because I think you've got something. You know that's a very good idea – getting the girl in the family way.

GEORGE: You think so?

BARNEY: Never fails. Get someone in the family way in the Third Act – you're half way there. I suppose you saw *I Was a Drug Fiend?*

GEORGE: No.

BARNEY: Didn't you really? No wonder you write like you do! I thought everyone had seen that! That was my show too. Why, we were playing to three and four thousand a week on the twice-nightly circuit with that. That's the sort of money you want to play to. Same thing in that: Third Act – girl's in the family way.

Epitaph for George Dillon, 1958

I wrote that scene with Barney Evans, the entrepreneur, one winter evening in a Hammersmith flat seven years later. As usual, with better things that I have done, it was written quickly almost without pause, my pen tripping clumsily behind swift memory. It was a scene which pleased me to write but left audiences slightly baffled. They were not familiar with the Barney Evans type, which is unsurprising. Self-caricature is so general that it makes the task of the writer very difficult, particularly in the theatre. Barney was probably unacceptable in a play, being so likely in life, embodying the cliché, 'If you put him on the stage, no one would believe it.' Improbability is writ large over half the nation, making restraint almost the first necessity of art, defending the truthfulness of drama against the distortions of documentary and social realism. In the face of life – notably English life with its cultivated eccentricity and anomaly – reticence is almost the first discipline a writer must assume. Theatricality is an elusive refinement which may be why Dickens adapted to the stage seems invariably gross, with character overwhelming landscape. Barney Evans was the hybrid of a type I was to meet constantly. The first of this species, ranging from Barney to Binkie, I was to meet through one of the new replacements. Her name was Stella Linden and her husband was indeed very like the whale of Barney, Patrick Desmond, sometime producer, actor, agent, theatrical entrepreneur and play doctor.

The next few weeks were all London-based, Moss Empire, music-hall dates, where my idols had trodden the boards, soon about to creak away for good. I contrived to stay in digs instead of going home to Stoneleigh where I felt the Shippards might be lying in wait for me. I was also able to see less of Sheila, saying that I was living with my mother. Stella was about thirty, very dark with a large, handsome head and a very fine striking nose. To me, she had the appearance and authority of what was thought to be a Leading Lady. Even in adolescence, she could never have strived as an eternal slip of a girl, which was Sheila's pride and forte. Stella was a woman, all right, with a pelvic arch like the skull of an ox, a slippery slope of hips and the shoulders of a Channel swimmer. It was a body which looked capable of snapping up an intruder in a jawbone of flesh. In the phrase of a friend, 'She could draw you in and blow you out in bubbles.'

During rehearsals I scarcely followed the prompt book. Fortunately, she knew her lines and moves from the first day. She was taking over the role of the earnest social worker. Like all the parts in the play, it was small but vital to the tale of Mrs Voray's downfall, with one showy scene where she pleaded the evacuees' case for them. Mr Hamilton came in once briefly and left bored but apparently satisfied. There was no attempt to redirect the scene or bother with interpretation. It was not required and would have irked the other actors. Only the children had been called in to run in the replacements. I read in for the rest of the cast. By now I knew the entire play almost word for word but fumbled even as I carried the book. Stella's effortless, instant polish suggested that she was more familiar with the text and production than I should have been. Unsurprisingly, it must have been pretty cold and mechanical. The previous actress had been competent and seemed to have gushed unnecessarily for sympathy. This performance had, to my eager eyes, a firmness which must come from intelligence rather than a chill spirit.

I convinced myself that here was an almost masculine, stalking power. She was no walking wounded woman, pleading for love like Sheila or weaning tamely like poor Renee, but arrogantly lubricious. Already no slouch at whistling up enigma, I was impelled to pursue whatever it might be. A weakness for pursuing siren sphinxes without secrets was already in full flight. I had an unfortunate tendency to regard instinct as merely a trick of reversed hindsight revealed only to myself. It was to produce fewer particular insights than rollicking blunders.

This overvalued instinct may have led me to the ploy of the Yellow Pyjamas. Free from Sheila, Shippards and Black Looks for the five London weeks, I wandered into Simpson's in Piccadilly. The basics of my Rex Harrison wardrobe were there but the weekly deposits I had made in provincial post offices, confined me to one agonized choice only. It was a pair of silk poplin pyjamas. They were yellow, not Nellie Beatrice lemon but yellow, the colour of the pullover that had been mocked in the street. Thinking I might soon be charged with loitering with intent, I asked the price. They were a week's salary and more – eight pounds. Having asked the price, there was no hanging back. I paid for them and went out into the sunshine of Piccadilly, to get on the bus for the first house at the Hackney Empire, clutching my new investment. Unlike some of my pushy impulses it was to pay off.

Stella had said little during the rehearsals, refusing proffered cups of tea politely and unsmilingly. The first night of the new tour with the replacements was at the Kingston Empire and I could think of nothing but her looming presence at the theatre. Besides, by this time I was no longer intimidated by the simple technical requirements of the show and had more or less taken over from Percy, who spent the evening reading in the staff room. I had got the changes down to a fine turn and knew how to get the stage staff to perform with only token disinclination. Unlike the printers at Bishopsgate they were unable to foul me up by exploiting my ignorance even in fun. I 'knew' the show and they didn't.

I called Miss Linden in good time, went back to the Prompt Corner and waited for her to tiptoe her way past the gloom of counterweights and prop tables towards her entrance. I waved encouragingly but she was intent on edging her way over to the dim outline of the knob just visible from the cracks of light from either side of the door flats. She stood poised, minutes early and, instinct and commonsense both awry, I crept up to her. 'Good luck,' I said, 'you're going to be smashing. Much better than the other.' She seemed to nod. I went back to my corner and waited for the flat to rattle exactly on cue, as it did. I hardly glanced at the book, knowing anyway that she would never look to the corner for aid. If only she had it would have been our first shared secret.

During my flash scene change immediately after her exit she brushed me aside among the charge of stage hands. Throughout the rest of the play I thought of the hours in the coming months which I would spend isolated in my corner watching that jaw bone of desire sit and stride across the stage. The set had to be changed back to the first act and I was unable to approach her until I called her for her entrance in the second house. This time I put my head in eagerly. Her own dark powerful head turned and the lubricious jaw bone opened over me from six paces. 'Don't you ever dare to do that to an actor again and don't you dare do it to me.' What did she mean? Her contempt was terrible. 'Don't you ever dare do that in any theatre again. I *mean* going up to an actor and talking to him just before he is about to make his entrance. And I don't just mean on a First Night. I mean now, at any time. Here or anywhere you may ever happen to find yourself in the future. I should get back to your corner.' I was snapped in two. My crass blunder was ineradicable.

I watched the second house in misery, the prospect of the next six months in what should have been Pleasure Corner destroyed. I knew that flowers or a contrite letter would only stiffen that stern nature. Appeals to sentiment from such a quarter might be won by honest graft but not feeble obsequiousness. The instruction was fierce and unmistakable. I had broken a self-evident theatrical rule. It was like a soldier dropping his rifle. I had dreaded calling her for the line-up but she anticipated it. Ignoring Percy, she slipped behind me on my stool and whispered, 'Forget it. I don't think you'll ever do it again. If you do, you won't last for very long.' Gratitude cast out everything but the thrill of her chastening. Schooled as I had been within a lifetime ethic of reproach, her unaffected forgiveness was startling.

Instead of banishing me to certain nonentity, she then seemed to seek me out. She came into the theatre long before the rest of the cast and sat reading in her dressing-room while the stage management prepared for the performance. Getting in early, she explained, was one of the hallmarks of professionalism, and I was anxious to believe her, collecting and delivering props to her long before necessary but with time to be encouraged to linger. She became quickly confidential without the condescension I might have felt deserved but with a needling curiosity about myself. Her low opinion of the company, the management and, to some extent, the play itself was disarmingly casual (actually her husband would have been only too pleased to have had such a rattling money spinner on the road as *No Room at the Inn*). It was, she said, a tatty production but she had agreeed to do a six months' tour because she and Pat needed the money either to start their own company or to put a similar show, of better quality, on the road. Neither their talents nor the prospect seemed in doubt.

She insisted proudly on her husband's prescient gift for the theatre. His flair was phenomenal. I was unclear what either of them had been doing in the three years since the war. He had been in the RAF until 1946 and she had been a teenage housewife in Coventry with a child before she had been divorced by her upper middle-class husband. Directness is more invigorating than the ambiguity of truthfulness, the jawbone of an asp more plausible than the jawbone of an honest ass. When you are eighteen, hedged in by evasion and timidity, it is exhilarating, at the least. Whether directness, or deception, combined with unassumed sexual pride, Stella's theatrical sales talk was irresistible. She catechized me about Sheila, my feelings for her, and inability to contain her elfin tantrums and self-absorption. Like a television interviewer, her opinions were masquerading as questions, although I was unaware of it. She seemed to know more about my predicament than I did myself. She turned my groping game with Sheila on to its beetle back of callow posturing, exposed and futile. It was fortunate that she had not witnessed me floundering with Renee on her back. As it was, I said nothing about my enforced trail around England's premier cathedrals with the walking-wounded juvenile, disabled for eternity by Anglican menstrual mysticism.

I did tell her about *Resting Deep* and she asked me for the script as if it were a menu. Like a waiter, I gave it to her. Her verdict was no sterner than I had expected. Directness prevailed. Speeches were too long; wordy scenes; slack; audiences left hanging in the air; ending unresolved. Then there was the matter of characters being discussed who never appeared, leaving the audience wondering, 'Who are they talking about?' This critical trip-wire was one I was to encounter many times. Could wondering ever lead to wonderment? I was too gratified to ask. She went on a great deal about construction. Had I read *The Second Mrs Tanqueray*? I had not. There was the key. What I needed was a short sharp lesson in Pinero.

I had not been too cast down by Stella's verdict on my play. I knew there was little merit in it although I thought she had disregarded its flashes of poetry. As *The Times* was to say of *Look Back in Anger*, it did, I was sure, 'contain some good passages of violent writing'. 'Fine writing' is no doubt what they were. Besides, intimations of poetry in the theatre was pornography to her. If she were to nose it, she would eliminate it as gleefully as Mrs Whitehouse would crush a smutty innuendo. Quick to offend, she not only believed in Dr Johnson's ruling that the drama's laws the drama's patrons give, but that they were to be administered without mercy and favour to any. Like all agents and managers of the time, she had no doubts that her own perception of public taste was a working primer for any form of dramatic activity. If I had said 'art', she would have reached for her hatpin.

When such powerful people talked about immutable theatrical laws, they gave the impression that their divine conformity was about to be outlawed. Nothing is noisier than a philistine in pain. If they despised the original imagination, they worshipped nebulous rules. These were almost elevated to a metaphysic in Moss Hart's *Principia, Act One.* The Broadway system still thrives scarcely troubled by the schisms and heresies that have split the rock of established theatre in England. But in New York the articles of theatrical faith are rarely challenged. Dissident murmurs may be heard from aggrieved dramatists, but few, even of these, would court excommunication. They cannot plead creative conscience and disown the faith they were born into, which means adherence to what might be called the Hart of Mystery. To some it might seem to be the Hart of Commercial Darkness but it survives as the only true faith. Its doctrine is unmodified and is expressed in the litany that includes 'Being Bombed in New Haven' and 'Getting the Second Act Right' – night-long vigils in hotel rooms with coffee and typewriters. The frenzy of these ceremonies conducted in semi-secrecy; producers, directors, writers, actors are locked out from the gaze of the world (except New Haven or wherever has been chosen) like disputants in an electoral college. They cannot emerge until the puffs of smoke rise from the printed reviews rushed to the tables of the waiting faithful in Sardi's. Half an hour after midnight the celebrants in the theatre will know the public's edict, whether they have toiled and brought forth a palpable hit or a flop. Thumbs up light the Broadway sky while their downward thrust can make the sidewalks tremble. The world between is grey and lonely.

West End managers were and are charged by the same beliefs and motives but they have never been so systematic and efficient in putting them to work. Stella, with her regard for creaky, Edwardian melodrama, was more literate than most, her husband certainly, who regarded Frederick Lonsdale as a cerebral taste. Artifice concealing any art could be whipped out by what critics often called the 'director's judicious [that is to say, butchering] scissors'. Construction was the centre of all their faith and was invoked like the Resurrection or Redemption. To me it has always been far more elusive than either. In Pinero's case and possibly Rattigan's it appeared to mean the construction of an artefact like a carriage clock, which revealed its beautiful precision to all, particularly for the benefit of those who were obliged to write and explain its workings to their readers. This made an otherwise tiresome task easy and even enjoyable and didn't apply only to critics but to those who were unlikely enough to read the plays themselves in the first place. Agents and managers like their popular models to be annually unchanged. If the new Ayckbourn or Stoppard is too unlike the last one there will be complaints from those who had got such reliable mileage from previous makes.

I mucked about on the drawing board with Pinero and soon accepted – without saying so to Stella – that if I would never make it as a theatrical draughtsman, I could never be so dull either. I was not even dismayed by the thought that I might not have the right kind of mind for writing plays just as I lacked the right one for doing crossword puzzles. The spaniels would be as happy walking beside a novelist as a playwright. An irate agent once ordered me to get out and about and learn by heart the Newtonian principles of theatre embodied in *The Winslow Boy*. The most perfect play ever written, he roared. I was also, oddly, directed to the feet of the Master; but Coward on Construction seemed pretty wobbly. Yet playmaking, a home craft like fretwork or pottery, demanded kits and models. It was hard to understand why Stella was intent on encouraging me. She still assured me that I needed a crash course in Playmaking at Home as urgently as anaemic girls were said, on railway hoardings, to need Virol.

She went on to tell me what possibilities might become open to me. She and Pat were both determined to return to Actor–Management and were negotiating an almost certain takeover of a theatre called the Granville at Walham Green. This was a famous music-hall theatre which had been floundering for many years and a lot of people had tried without success to revive its fortunes. If anybody was capable of doing it, she assured me, it was Pat, and then went on to give me an explanation of how it could be done, with a breakdown about the rent, percentages, house charges, salaries and all kinds of unfamiliar things. If I was willing to sit down with Stella and start to rework the play from scratch they would be prepared to include it in a new season which they projected. Was I willing to agree? I most certainly was. For the next few months I would not be merely peering at Stella from the Prompt Corner but Home Playmaking with her. The close confines of digs shared with her was certainly preferable to the gynaecological agonies of the cathedral close.

Stella was emphatic that we should spend all possible time together from now on. There was no telling when the Walham Green deal might come through but not before the tour's end at Christmas. Sheila's insides would certainly protest as violently against making plays as love. I knew I could look to my new mentor to sort out these troublesome trifles for me. As an ambitious actress, Sheila must be moved by the plea, 'My Career Must Come First.' I was to hear it often enough in future. As a career person I may have lacked all passionate intensity, but this time I would get it in first – albeit something different from the nature of my first intention. The next stage of the tour looked like being a considerable improvement on the first.

14. I'm Forever Blowing Bubbles

During the weeks in London I had wondered if I might one evening find Mr Shippard waiting for me at the stage door. Already I felt I could put Stella on to him too. I was able to visit my mother only once and was rewarded with a couple of pounds. She was surprised and relieved that I was still in work and, for some reason, she had decided that I was safely away from 'girls'. Actresses, even young ones, were not girls, but likely ladies at least. Also, there was no need to leave out the warmed-up leftovers from one of Cheffie's lunchtime ruckings.

I visited Grandma Osborne, who pretended she didn't know what I was doing and asked me no questions at all. She talked about the news from Newport, who had died, Auntie Daisy's back, her own aching eyes particularly and her inability to sleep; Mr Attlee, horrible Bevan (a disgrace to Tredegar), *The Archers* and Warwick Deeping. Cousin Tony was doing very well at Sandhurst and Cousin Jill had entered a very nice secretarial school in preparation for getting a good steady position with her father's firm until such time as she got married. The room over Tesco's contained the furniture from Clandon Close, the same huge walnut sideboard, the silver bowls still full of home-made toffee and nuts, the props of many a Sunday night. Visiting her now in the suburban afternoon it was hard to believe that I had ever found her company comforting. Still with no reference to how I was spending my life, we said good-bye on the iron staircase. She wiped her eyes, as she would put it, discreetly, and kissed me, barely brushing my acne. 'Oh dear,' she said. 'Life seems to be full of good-byes.' Which is what she always said when I visited her.

She watched me for several minutes before I disappeared behind the Rembrandt Cinema. I went inside to see if any of the girls were there. Only one was left. Lily in the box office with her dark ringlets and strawberry lips and green dresses, who had allowed me in for nothing and let me take her home, had left to get married. The girl who had replaced her looked at me coldly, barring me the privilege I had known before. There were no occasional free Cambridge steaks to be had in the restaurant upstairs and only the one usherette left to sit beside you cosily among the old-age familiars before the ice-cream interval.

Grandma Grove, Auntie Queenie and Sid came to see the play at the Chiswick Empire. Grandma thoroughly enjoyed herself, especially the bits with the sailor ('Your grandfather would have liked that'); Queenie thought it was a bit suggestive and Uncle Sid said it went too far. I toyed with the idea of taking them round to see Stella, and immediately abandoned it. The beginning of the tour consisted mostly of seaside dates – Margate, Eastbourne, Bournemouth, Torquay. It was back to familiar territory but no less exciting than the first time around and offering new promises. There was still a gazetteer of Midland and Northern towns to follow. We seldom progressed logically from one southern seaside town to another, but would go from Torquay to Hanley to Eastbourne to Sheffield, making for long, wearisome Sunday train calls.

Stella proved to be serious about the playmaking which I soon found irksome and unrewarding. However, I was not prepared to oppose her at this stage. What did concern me was that she seemed unaware of me except as a likely journeyman in dramatic construction. Sympathy among the company for Sheila's abandoned plight was general and Stella was regarded as a cynical older woman, spoiling whatever they thought a young girl like Sheila possessed to be spoilt. Even Bert became more churlish than ever, forgetting to chide me with having Put Them In and Not Getting Them Out. In Sheffield, I was summoned after Treasury Call to the room of the company manager, Miss Dalton. She was a huge, taciturn Australian and like all that recidivist race not given to praise or the willing expression of pleasure. She had never spoken to me about my work except over the school inspector incident, which she had thought of no importance. I had assumed that everything was satisfactory. I knew that my playmaking had not interfered with my professional work. With Stella's eyes upon me in the Corner I made sure of that. I had become a passable stage manager, a lowly calling which I despised and longed to leave behind. It required a bland, conscientious temperament that expected abuse and never admiration. The best stage managers are usually women, who bear indignity for the historical necessity of continuity itself.

Miss Dalton handed me my wage packet, letting out a deep sigh as if from some lonely marsupial pocket, saying that certain things had been passed on to her about my conduct, from the company. She didn't have to tell me what they were, et cetera. But she would just like to point out, although she, of course, had no jurisdiction, as such, over my moral behaviour, she would like my attention drawn to the fact that it had been noted. Was she going to write to Mr Hamilton? Or Barry O'Brien and Jack Hylton? From what I had heard of Jack's reputation it could scarcely have been of any interest to him. Or perhaps Barry O'Brien and Michael Hamilton had a policy of discouraging heterosexuality within their touring companies? Surely she wasn't threatening me with the sack? Miss Dalton looked at me wearily. I found myself blushing beneath my acne, thinking that she must be wondering how an attractive and mature actress like Stella could even consider dallying with an unprepossessing eighteen-year-old ASM. Perhaps she would think that the stories were possibly idle rumour after all, because she ended rather lamely, 'Well, I just suggest you might think about what your mother might feel if she knew that there was any kind of truth in this kind of goings-on. None of my business, but I felt I had to say something.'

There was as yet no truth in her suspicion, that most Australian of all traits, and anyway I felt unthreatened. Obviously my job was not at stake and it was flattering to have been the object of gossip, but exasperating that someone in the company could be so suburban as to draw her attention to what must surely be a way of theatrical life. Here was the manager of a touring theatrical company talking to me about moral lapses like Eric or Mr Silcox. I had two prime suspects. One was Beatrice, the character actress, who was Jewish and therefore might have prompted concern for my mother's feelings. The other was Davis, the Christian Scientist, whose Welshness and puritanism made him a likely double dealer. Had he been more shifty than usual, glancing anxiously at my acne, muttering that he was working on it and fumbling all the while with his cigarette packet? Mrs Baker Eddy might have attributed my worsening condition to the turpitude of mortal mind.

Whether or not it was Mary Baker Eddy's reproof to his own mortal mind, Davis was too ill to go on as the billeting officer a couple of days later. I wished fervently that I were making the calls instead of listening to them as I made up. Stella came in, gave me a small whisky, and didn't wish me luck. I went through the performance mechanically, following the moves to within an inch and shouting the lines to the back of the auditorium. I made a slavish imitation of Davis's boring Welsh trades union lilt. I had discarded any idea of trying on my Rex Harrison as risky and inappropriate, and the billeting officer was not Leslie Howard material. Little was said afterwards. Percy gave me an absent-minded pat. Sheila said I was wonderful and Stella said I hadn't done badly for an amateur. I played it twice more and began to enjoy it. Miss Dalton beamed her spade-like chin in my direction. Viewed upside down it might have been antipodean approval. My job must be safe, immorality or not.

The physical possibilities of mutual playmaking were still unexplored. In Llandudno, I had the chance to draw on my investment in Simpson's. Sean and I were asked to leave our digs on Saturday. The landlady had some holidaymakers arriving early, and her Welsh cupidity delighted in turning out a drunken Irishman and his friend without argument. We protested but she was adamant. Stella came to the rescue. She was staying in a vegetarian hotel at great and unthinkable expense, but she could get us both in for one night at ten shillings. After the performance I struck the set and got the show out on to the waiting lorries in particularly quick time. Miss Dalton could not have complained. Getting back to the vegetarian hotel I found Stella in her bedroom eating chips from a newspaper, with Sean. I was worn out as usual after a Saturday get-out and looked, I hoped, appealingly at Stella, too tired to pretend about my needs. Sean seemed bent on reminiscences of Anew McMaster for the rest of the night, but by this time I had heard most of them several times over. The three of us lay on the bed drinking Irish whiskey. As if she were challenging the billeting officer, Stella said very firmly, 'Sean, do you think you could go to bed?' Sean looked baffled and a little hurt. She went on patiently. 'Can't you see that John and I want to be alone together.' He flushed almost angrily, as if she were revealed to him like a flasher in the confessional. I could never have been so direct.

He stumbled out and Stella began making love to me at alarming speed, but I was still sober and self-conscious enough to insist on going to my own room to get my pyjamas. I went into the bathroom down the corridor and put on the yellow rig-out for the first time. When I came back I got into bed, Stella turned out the light and I burst into tears almost immediately, not stopping for what seemed to be hours. The pyjamas peeled away like clothing cut through before surgery. I had never known anything like it.

CHAP: Then there was Jean, I suppose.
GIRL: (*Dances and sings*) 'Jean, Jean . . .'
BOX MAN: You'll get no awards for *this* lot.
CHAP: She was really good and big and well-stacked and knew how to –
GIRL: Get you on the job.
CHAP: Christ, I was only nineteen! I could do it *nine times* in the morning.

CHAIRMAN: Nine times. Could you really?

GIRL: There's not much impressive in that.

CHAP: (*In bad Scots accent*) 'Oh, there's not much impressive in that.' We've all had *colds*.

GIRL: And then there are all those dreary wives of yours.

CHAP: That's right. Those dreary wives of mine . . . They all think I'm a pouve.

GIRL: I'm not surprised.

A Sense of Detachment, 1972

After Llandudno Stella and I became more or less official company lovers. Even the burly Dalton seemed intimidated by her, everyone treated me respectfully and Sheila took on a paler shade of piety, treating me in the theatre more like a wayward younger brother than a would-be lover. Like so many awesome decisions, once taken, the subsequent mechanics were bewilderingly simple. Outside the theatre, Stella and I spent all our time together. For a long time to come lovemaking preceded and often took the place of playmaking. Banished one afternoon from our landlady's bed-springs, we broke our way into the dressing-room floor of the Theatre Royal, Hanley, which burned down the following week. Stella dealt with all the landladies and the scruples of their husbands with no trouble at all. We often spent whole days in bed with the connivance of some landladies who attended to us like trainers sustaining their athletes. 'You're only young once, love!' For three months my play was almost forgotten as we progressed to a different town each week, Treasury Call every Friday, cheap delicious food, northern beer, sleeping in till noon, feather beds, free films and fucks.

I dreaded the end of the tour in Wood Green in December. The Granville theatre project had come to nothing. However, Pat had acquired a basement flat in Brighton and he would promote his theatrical productions from there. It would not interfere with Stella and I living there together. The marriage, explained Stella, was a mutual benefit based on their professional compatibility and affectionate friendship. They did seem fond and tolerant of each other and with respect for the other's fragile qualities. Pat's personality was less like Barney Evans than Ronald Furness-Bland, but his aspirations and opinions were Barney's exactly.

Stella and I had finished work on *Resting Deep*, which had now been retitled *The Devil Inside*. Stella had given it a Pinero uplift and added a few coarse jokes, one of which I remember was someone coming on and singing a song called, 'I love to play with your snowballs. There are no balls like your snowballs'. How this got past the Lord Chamberlain at the time is a mystery. However, it did, as Pat was determined to get the play presented, putting it on at the Theatre Royal, Huddersfield, later the following year. I couldn't think why.

Genius and cheek

'He was a popular hero more than a comic. He was cheeky because he was a genius. All genius is cheek. You get away with your nodding little vision and the world holds its breath or applauds. Max took your breath away altogether and we applauded. When I was at school he was popular only with the more sophisticated boys, and girls seemed bored by him altogether although I suspected that the girls I longed to know – big, beautiful WAAFs or landgirls – would adore an evening with him. I loved him as fiercely as I detested the Three Stooges and Abbott and Costello. He was not a great clown like Sid Field nor did he make me laugh so much. The Cheeky Chappie was not theatrically inventive in any profound sense. His fantasy was bone simple, traditional, predictable and parochial.

'It is said that he hit his insolent peak during the early forties at the Holborn Empire. I saw him there only twice, but during the next twenty years his style slackened very little and he never looked less than what he was – the proper champion of his type.

'What type?

'He was the type of flashiness. He was flashiness perfected and present in all things visible and invisible. The common, cheap and mean parodied and seized on as a style of life in face of the world's dullards. Maxie would have been in his element in the Boar's Head. Just to begin: his suits were superb. My favourite was the blue silk one with enormous plus-fours and daisies spluttered all over them. With his white upturned hat on one side and correspondent shoes he looked magnificent, perfectly dressed for bar parlour or Royal Enclosure. In those days of clothing coupons, I longed to wear such suits, although a weakness for clothes was likely to get you called nancy boy. Someone called out after me in the street once because I was wearing a dull but yellow pullover. No doubt he grew up to be a customs officer or on the staff of the *Daily Telegraph*. No one would have dared to jeer at anyone who could wear a suit like Maxie's. He was constantly being banned by the BBC, then the voice of High Court Judges, Ministries and schoolteachers. Sometimes he was fined £5 for a blue joke which became immediately immortal. I knew the truth was that Max was too good for the BBC, and all the people like it. But this was just.

'He went on telling them from the *Blue Book*, wearing his smashing clothes, looking better than anyone else, and smelling of sea air, the open doors of public houses and whelks. He talked endlessly and with a fluency that made me spin. He was Jewish, which made him racy and with blasphemy implicit in his blood. He sang his own compositions in an enviable voice and with a pride I thought both touching and justified. "This little song . . . this little song I wrote . . . you won't hear anyone else singin' it. No one else dare sing it!" Nor would they.

'He seemed to talk supercharged filth and no one could put him in prison or tell him to hold his tongue. He appeared to live in pubs, digs, race-courses and theatre bars. Naturally, he never worked. On top of all this, he had his own Rolls Royce and a yacht, and was rumoured to own most of Brighton. I discounted stories about his alleged meanness and never buying anyone a drink. He was simply holding on to what he'd got and he deserved it more than anyone else in the world.

'Above all, he talked about girls. Unwilling girls, give-her-a-shilling-and-she'll-be-willing girls, Annie and Fanny, girls who hadn't found out, girls on their honeymoon, fan dancers minus their fans, pregnant girls and barmaids the stork put the wind up every six weeks. You always felt with Maxie that he didn't go too much on birth control, but if anything went wrong the girls would be pretty good-tempered about it. As for their mothers, he could always give them a little welcome present, too. In the same way, the wife was complaisant, just another cheerful barmaid at home, reading the *News of the World* till Max felt like coming back for "coffee and games". Except that Max could always do without the coffee.

'One always acknowledged his copyright to a joke. You could do nothing else. Some of his jokes are still school folklore. There's the immortal story of the man on a narrow ledge and didn't know what to do about it. That one cost £5 and worth every penny of it. There are incomplete lines like:

> "When roses are red
>   They're ready for plucking.
> When a girl is sixteen,
>   She's ready for – 'ere!"

'You could repeat the line but not the master's timing over his swivelling grin of outrage at the audience. "You can't help likin' him, can yer?" They couldn't. They daren't. He handled his rare shafts of silence like – a word he would have approved – a weapon. When he paused to sit down to play his guitar and watched the detumescent microphone disappear, he waited till the last bearable moment to thrust in his blade with "D'you see that, Ivor? D'you? Must be the cold weather!" He was a beautiful, cheeky god of flashiness who looked as if he'd just exposed himself on stage. "There'll never be another!" There wouldn't, and he knew it and we knew it.

'As soon as the orchestra played "Mary from the Dairy", I usually began to cry before he came on. And when he did appear, I went on doing so, crying and laughing till the end. Even his rather grotesque physical appearance couldn't belie his godliness. You could see his wig join from the back of the stalls and his toupée looked as if his wife had knitted it over a glass of stout before the Second House. His make-up was white and feminine, and his skin was soft like a dowager's. This steely suggestion of ambivalence was very powerful and certainly more seductive than the common run of manhood then. He even made his fleshy, round shoulders seem like the happy result of prodigious and sophisticated sexual athletics – the only form of exercise he acknowledged.

'Some people have suggested to me that I modelled Archie Rice on Max. This is not so. Archie was a man. Max was a god, a saloon-bar Priapus. Archie never got away with anything properly. Life cost him dearly always. When he came on, the audience was immediately suspicious or indifferent. Archie's cheek was less than ordinary. Max didn't have to be lovable like Chaplin or pathetic like a clown. His humanity was in his cheek. Max got fined £5 and the rest of the world laughed with him. Archie would have got six months and no option.

'I loved him because he embodied a kind of theatre I admire most. His method was danger. "Mary from the Dairy" was an overture to the danger that he might go too far.

'And occasionally he did, God bless him, and the devil with all nagging magistrates and censors and their wives-who-won't. Whenever anyone tells me that a scene or a line in a play of mine goes too far in some way then I know my instinct has been functioning as it should. When such people tell you a particular passage will make the audience "uneasy" or "restless" they seem as cautious and absurd as landladies and girls-who-won't. Maxie was right. And hardly a week passes when I don't miss his pointing star among us.'

Max Miller – The Cheeky Chappie, 1965

Brighton meant Max Miller to me as well as licence and liberty. Hardly a month goes by when I don't spend at least one whole day there, but 1949 is, to me, the year of Brighton. I was not looking forward to the prospect of Christmas with Grandma Osborne and Auntie Daisy or the Yuletide Dance at the Stoneleigh Hotel. Leaving Wood Green, I moved with Stella into Number 7a Arundel Terrace. It was at the far end of Brighton, opposite Black Rock swimming pool, then unblighted by the Marina. The flat was the basement of a huge Regency house the size of an embassy, clean, newly painted and the rent was £8 a week. In the flat above was a very successful actor, Robert Flemyng, and his South American wife. Now it's owned by a waiter from Wheeler's in Market Street.

We were living in Brighton, Terence Rattigan was around the corner, stars were above and around us. In Kemp Town there was a tiny theatre called the Playhouse. They were putting on *Treasure Island* for Christmas and urged on by Stella I reluctantly went to see the director who gave me a job as one of the pirates. At least I was not in stage management and I could truthfully tell my mother that I was working over the holiday. Apart from the sick boys' Borstal, it was my first Christmas away from home. After the tour, *Treasure Island* was dull and amateurish. It also took me away from Stella when I wanted to be with her. However, we were sharing a flat, we had a vegetarian Christmas dinner of nut cutlets and vegetables and I was happier than I had ever been before.

'A memory of Mondays'

In January, we were both out of work and content. Pat offered to subsidize our playmaking by letting us live rent-free. Food was our only requirement. We ignored heat and light. Stella, for some bureaucratic reason, was unable to collect her unemployment benefit, having an almost unheard-of record of non-contributions. However, with my dole money and an occasional ten shillings from my mother we improvised exultantly. I went to Stoneleigh every Friday, eating as much as I could while there and returning with a selection of mostly tinned foods which helped to keep us going for the rest of the following week.

'I think of those who worship the physical side of life, but whose bodies have betrayed them.

'Lawrence took the 1914–18 war personally. And if train travel in Mexico was made difficult because of bandits, he took it as a personal affront. So it is with the bus that does not arrive at precisely the

moment she starts to wait at the stop, or, which should be so overbearingly thoughtless as to overrun her destination: and so it is with the
sun that fails to appear on her day off, and the umbrella that has to be
lost because it is hers. There is always a scene, shouting and bullying,
the vicious sulking and gratuituous insults. And, above all, the terrible
blackmail of her remorse. That is the worst of all. For she owes the
world nothing, it is gasping with humiliation, self-convicted, grasping
all it can from her. It owes everything to her.

'My grandmother's apothecary: Dutch drops, Beecham's pills and
peroxide. With these, she too can reject any approach from a sympathetic world. "I owe nothing to anybody. I have always paid for everything I have ever done or received. I have accepted no gifts from
anyone. And if I have, at any time (and I am quite sure I never did),
picked up sixpence, I have never failed to lose half a crown shortly
afterwards."

'He has no curiosity, and is a terrible bore.'

Notebook, July 1953

I would return on Tuesday, having to spend Monday with my mother on
her day off as the price for our stocked larder. My mother resolutely
shunned friendship in spite of being the life and soul of the bar. She hinted
to me about men who had asked her to go out with them and even some who
had offered to marry her. No one, she said, would ever take the place of dear
old Dad. I found these offers difficult to believe. Perhaps some lonely soul
might have been deluded by her bar-room gaiety and mistaken her ful-
someness for generosity of spirit. These Monday excursions were held
sacrosanct. She grumbled about my being out of work, but no one else was
acceptable to accompany her. I suggested that one of the girls at work might
like to share the day with her. The company of a stranger was like an
indecent suggestion. God had indeed always paid debts without money, or
whatever she meant by that. What it meant was never to be beholden to
anyone for the smallest favour. 'You don't owe them anything.'

Stoneleigh

Dear John,
I live here on my own: think well of those I love so dearly and it helps
to make my life worth while. I would rather live on an island all alone
than have any more upsets, all my life I can remember nothing but
trouble. Tottenham people, the Osbornes. There was always jealousy

of some kind; none of it was nothing to do with me at the time: but there was always this dam family bickering about who said, who or who done what: if Mother wants to get away from Jack (which Queen says she does) she is welcome to come with me: but it must come from her. I have asked her and she doesn't even answer – so there is nothing I can do now. You bet your life if he goes too far Sid will let Jack have it: but he does not want to upset or hurt Mother as he said her life is hell as it is.

Always in my thoughts,
Mother

For the next six or seven years I gave myself up to these Black Mondays. It was a guarantee of two meals in Joe Lyons and the reprieve from having to speak to each other in the cinema or music hall. We got on the bus to Epsom, Kingston or on the train to Wimbledon, trailed a while through Bentall's or Kennard's, looking, as we had once done in Kensington High Street, like foot-sore eunuchs in a brothel. An early lunch was followed by the pictures. We would then come out, have tea and perhaps ice cream before going on to another film. Often she would stare into windows, planning her next rig-out. Sometimes she insisted on buying me a jacket or a pair of trousers, saying that I looked like a 'down and out'. 'What a pity you couldn't have been something like a barrister or a doctor,' she said in front of some smirking salesman, 'instead of an actor.' There was no doubt about who was paying. Even if the day had offered up a couple of enjoyable pictures and a meal, the journey home, the queue for the bus, the bad back or headache, would obliterate the memory until the following Monday.

As the word Brompton was to pain, Brighton was to pleasure. If I were to choose a way to die it would be after a drunken, fish-eating day ending up at the end of the Palace Pier. Brighton is like nowhere else. No other resort has its simple raffishness. At that time in Brighton and Hove there were nearly forty cinemas and eight theatres. Two unemployed actors with Equity cards could keep themselves entertained constantly at no cost. It was still the Mecca of the dirty weekend. Before the Arundel Terrace days, Stella and I had spent a whole week in a place called Moss Mansions, which was a temple reserved entirely for this purpose. The whole building smelt of salty sex and frying pans. The stamping ground of Binkie, Terry Rattigan, Cuthbert Worsley, an entrenched outpost of the theatrical homosexual prevailing cadre, Brighton had randiness hanging in the air throughout the year. There was no close season on sex; sex was all year round. There was no drowsiness in the air as in Bournemouth, only randiness. Ozone in East-bourne was spermatozoa in Brighton, burning brightly like little tadpoles of evening light across the front. Whenever I have lunch in Brighton, I always want to take someone to bed in the afternoon. To shudder one's last, thrust-ing, replete gasp between the sheets at 4 and 6 o'clock in Brighton, would be the most perfect last earthly delight.

Stella and I were supposed to work on our next venture from Tuesday until Friday. She had decided that we should write a play which was to be called *Happy Birthday*. It was to take place in a middle-class house and concerned the events during the birthday celebrations of a middle-aged woman. Using a family celebration where people gather and are reunited was a favourite device in the playmaking manual. Weddings (not funerals), birthdays, weekends, Christmas, even honeymoons, had all been used suc-cessfully as a dramatic structure from Dodie Smith to Coward, Priestley, Ben Travers, N. C. Hunter. The form solved a lot of dramatic problems. For instance, characters could confide themselves, explain their pasts under the duress of a special occasion and react quickly and, with their bourgeois emotions usually well under control, it could all be expressed in short, 'effective' (instantly grasped) scenes. Strangers or families who had seen little of each other for years could bare their hearts at a rattling speed during the preparations for weddings, birthdays, Christmas, the New Year, which provided lots of useful stage business with packages or plates. These plays with their meals, drinks, parcels and decorations, were repertory stage managers' nightmares.

Stella had fixed the formula for us immediately in her choice of title, *Happy Birthday*. Now that sounded like a comfortable evening with a nice, instantly recognizable family, a long, busy part for a middle-aged star organ-izing everything and everyone all the evening, sweeping the stage with flower arrangements, giving instructions, reading lists to cook and house-maids. She could commiserate with adulterous daughters or love-lorn undergraduates, upbraid returned family cads, unearth unsuitable affairs, listen to confessions of wasted, wicked or empty lives, dispense smiles, forgiveness, understanding, innocence and bestow her ultimate great gifts of overbearing middle-class decency and tolerance all round.

The models for the play itself were numerous. Some playmakers had even used Stella's trick of embodying the formula concretely in the title: *Quiet Weekend*, *Quiet Wedding*, *Spring Meeting*, *The Fourth of June* or, impli-citly, *Autumn Crocus* and *The Holly and the Ivy* – all identifiable class gather-ings. *Dinner Dance*, for instance, would have been unsuitable. *Saturday*

Knees Up or *Dinner at Night* would have been playmaking folly. T. S. Eliot got the idea perfectly, beckoning audiences to watch Greek Furies enter from French windows, in tweed skirts, gardening gloves and brandishing trugs and secateurs by shrewdly calling his play *Family Reunion*. That didn't sound like an evening of myth and theology at all – just a Nice Play.

The leading woman in *Happy Birthday* was to be based on Stella's mother, a vain, complaining woman with an older, sponging lover. She, too, was an evangelistic vegetarian as well as Christian Scientist, and examined my spots as badges of animal toxins and mortal mind. She could hardly criticize her daughter for living with me except for my youth and distasteful unhealthy appearance. She was puzzled by Stella's description of me as common-camp. So was I, and none too pleased, either. Pat was eccentric and a bugger, according to her lover, but he was middle class in a remittance man sort of way. Stella, however, refused to let her mother patronize or bully me. 'You'll be hearing a lot of him later on,' she said. 'For the moment he's my fledgeling.' I had never heard the word used before, certainly not about myself. She said it so carelessly that my heart almost stopped again.

Her mother's life was sustained by Mary Baker Eddy, Gaylord Hauser and a substantial private income. Fearing neither death nor illness, she lived in terror only of the Labour Government. For someone who dismissed mortal mind, she was most addicted to mortal money. She seemed packed and poised to fight her way on to the next boat to escape the Socialist holocaust. It was a state of deepest dread very common among people like herself at that time. Stella wouldn't permit any Viper Gang jeers at her mother, saying, correctly, that I was incapable of understanding her feelings. Besides, Stella herself had no time for youthful Socialism. Her vegetarianism was of the most self-interested kind. My own motives in this respect were similarly funk, dictated by a desire to fend off the White Plague and clear up my skin. Stella had pointed out that I should make myself attractive to other girls, something which was not then on my mind, being so preoccupied nine times a day. But I did become more dismayed by our playmaking. Collaboration was making us both impatient and tetchy. My disinclination and Stella's growing irritation at my wilfulness and sulky bouts of pride made it easy to find excuses not to work. In Brighton there seemed so much to do.

Sometimes Stella would spend the weekend at Pat's flat in London and we would catch the last bus from Victoria back to Arundel Terrace. This cost five shillings, a considerable saving on the train fare. Underneath the rugs provided, we also contrived yoga-like postures between Crawley and

Brighton that could have earned us founder membership of the Southdown Mile High Club. From Tuesday to Friday we spent drowsy marathon mornings in bed before wandering through Kemp Town to Joe Lyons in Old Steine for coffee and a fruit bun. In the early afternoons we attempted work on *Happy Birthday*. I disliked everything about it including the meaty but inaccurate, sentimental portrait of Stella's mother. I favoured characterizing her as slothful, selfish, grasping, snobbish, true to her class; a shameful anachronism and traitor to her country. This was pitching it a bit strong for a play with such a homely title. It would be like going to a sale of work and being faced by abusive WI pickets. Besides, creating a middle class monster defied every rule of playmaking. No audience would tolerate or believe in such a creature or accept its authenticity.

Above all, no character who was unsympathetic could ever dominate a play. It was a point to be made to me endlessly, even when, years later, I and others seemed to have long since disproved it. A captive minority audience was to emerge, which was induced to come in to the Playhouse so that they might enjoy walking out. The playmaker's manual had no entry for 'Walking out'. Leading ladies loved being lovable and their public insisted on it. There was nothing like a dame and an unlovable dame was nothing.

Stella accused me of amateurism and inexperience, of poeticizing instead of dramatizing. They were fair criticisms. Aggrieved, I hinted insolently that she was an untried commercial hack, tone-deaf to literary sensibility. These nagging discontentments were becoming patently plain to both of us. Every time we tried to carry on with the play, we began berating and patronizing each other. Accusation and disappointment sent us to bed for relief but even that unfailing well of comfort became poisoned by such bitterness. The harshness of her resentment alarmed and angered me. Everything I did or said seemed to provoke her to venomous impatience. If I had ever seemed to possess some tender promise, it was no longer youthful or touching but the trite posturings of a tetchy, spotty teenager. I was, she said, lazy, arrogant, dishonest and ungrateful, particularly to Pat. Again, she was right in everything. Even my gratitude was backsliding. Regular sex had not dimmed desire but had ceased to make me feel beholden. Nine times and nine times nine must earn its due. Furthermore, she was anxious about having nothing to show Pat in return for keeping us rent free, in some comfort and, in my case, in blissful sexual affluence for the first time.

By the middle of summer we had produced little more than one act which was unsatisfactory as both matter and output. I knew almost at the outset that collaboration was abhorrent to my nature. As she had said, I was too arrogant. Besides, I was over-absorbed and distracted by my feeling for her. I dreaded that having lost heart in our work, her interest in me would wane. If I were a fledgeling I had turned out to be a disappointing, wayward one, flying tiresomely in all the wrong directions. For my part, her playmaking was more onerous and absurd than the formulas of the British Institute of Fiction Writing Science, being neither science nor art. A little later, it bore into me that Pat and Stella were only, if kindly, interested in my contributing vehicles for their seedy ventures. If I were to issue a challenge of my own to Binkie it was evident that it would never come from the lower depths of Kemp Town.

The summer visitors intruded beyond Black Rock, and Brighton seemed less of a friendly fortress than it had been when we had felt protected by the empty front and the wind across the beach. Stella was restless, constantly reminding me that we couldn't go on exploiting Pat's good nature. They were both overdrawn at the bank. Mr Attlee had made a loan from her mother unthinkable. We would have to do something. She had no doubts about her own ability to get some sort of job, but was discouraging about my own chances. Pat had promised to see what he could do but it was clear, even to me, that he was in no position to help anyone, including his wife.

Pat had shown no enthusiasm for what he had seen of the play. There was little doubt that it was to be an abandoned enterprise. My relief was tempered by justified apprehension. Stella was brutally realistic. One day, watching the trippers alight from their tiny train on the beach, she said to me, 'You know, the day will certainly come when I have to get up and go. It will be painful, possibly more for me than for you because you will recover more quickly. But I can be ruthless in these things if it's necessary and I will do it without hesitation, like discarding a limb. I can always grow another one. I've proved it to myself.' Her words struck at me, baffling my reluctance to believe her.

After returning from one of my Black Mondays I was dismayed to find that Stella had taken a job in a Greek restaurant just beyond the Palace Pier. Her employers were vile, the hours long, but she seemed exhilarated. It would help to feed us, she said, and put something towards the rent. An unmistakable barrier of honest self-help had been put down between us. At her suggestion there was no escape from the course of enforced endeavour. I went around to the kitchen entrance of the Hotel Metropole and was immediately taken on as a temporary dishwasher. Thankfully this lasted barely a week, when I was dismissed by the restaurant manager who said curtly that they were overstaffed. There were vacancies for the unemployable elsewhere and goaded by Stella I got a job, again as a washer-up at an hotel in Rottingdean. It was called something like Fitzherbert Court, catering particularly for Pinewood-based adultery. Film stars like Margaret Lockwood or Pat Roc, however, spent chaste, pruriently observed weekends there. Cameramen, in blazers during the day, danced the night away with continuity girls, as I loped home wearily after midnight.

15. Holy Ghost for Four

DIMITRI: They all wanted to fight. Listen, you put a man in the plate room all day, he's got dishes to make clean and stinking bins to take away and floors to sweep, what else there is for him to do – he wants to fight. He got to show he is a man someway. So – blame him!

The Kitchen, Arnold Wesker, 1959

Arnold Wesker's metaphor was accurate, although Fitzherbert Court might not have recognized itself. It was inadequate in every respect. The staff were all seasonal or casual labour like myself. Hysteria, neurosis and bad temper dominated, and guests were despised above all others. It was a hell's kitchen of Black Looks, hypochondria, an eternity of whining self-aggrandizement. My mother would have been the goddess of such a place and Cheffie could have rucked the fires of hell cheerfully for ever. Human kindness or concern must melt in a steam of heat and frenzy. I had no choice but to stick it out. Stella received a telegram offering her a job as leading lady in Kendal. She left suddenly with disconcerting enthusiasm. I was to keep the flat as clean as possible and not incur bills of any kind. As I was now out all day and half the night there was little time even to switch on the light or answer the telephone. She would 'send for me' as soon as she could.

'They eat what they want, don't they? I don't know what more to give a man. He works, he eats, I give him money. This is life, isn't it? I haven't made a mistake, have I? I live in the right world, don't I?' Nearly twenty years later I heard these words of Wesker's restaurant proprietor uttered in the famous clipped vowels of Noël Coward when we were both playing in a bizarre charity performance of *The Kitchen* at the Old Vic. One thing was certain – I was not living in the right world.

I became staff waiter, laying out the meals in the staff room and waiting on its members. A supposed soft option, it turned out to be as disagreeable as sweating in the grease and steam of the kitchen sink. The staff, to a person, were as bullying, churlish, capricious and impossible to please as

Nellie Beatrice on her day off. When they were not complaining about my inadequacies or slowness ('You'll have to do better than that, my lad. Look sharpish'), they wailed about their ailments and spouses. Most of the waiters spent their afternoons at the races where they would lose several hundred pounds of their tips. They chafed peevishly about the rest of the staff, the management and, above all, about health. They all had bad backs or some faulty-functioning organ, were 'bags of nerves' and perpetually 'run down' and 'in need of a tonic'. The staff room was like a squalling warehouse stacked with bags of nerves, longing to be moved elsewhere.

I was soon found to be quite unsatisfactory and was demoted to the still room. This was lorded over by a proudly self-confessed psychopath – who had spent most of the war in the Glasshouse – and his chubby, benign wife. They only spoke to issue orders to me at first, having decided I was both their personal slave and too snooty for the job anyway. She spent most of the day doing undemanding tasks like cutting sandwiches by the hundred as she sang 'Ghost Riders in the Sky'. Her husband's attitude to me was hostile if not downright frightening. He muttered about Rampton, which I knew to be a famous bin for the very likes of him. On the rare occasions he spoke it was to tell me the number of military policemen he had despatched with his bare hands. 'Bare hands mind.' Between them they ensured that I had scarcely a free minute during the day, without even a flop on the beach for respite. I now had to be in at six in the morning in time to prepare the early breakfasts, and as there was no bus service between Kemp Town and Rottingdean at that hour I had to leave at four-thirty and walk the four miles. Breakfast was like the beginning of the day in *The Kitchen*. Life seemed in tatters and violence and despair hummed in the air as waiters began screaming, 'Holy Ghost for Two', 'Holy Ghost for Four' until it exploded and receded by about nine-thirty. The rising, frantic tempo was exactly the same as in Wesker's play. My simple task was to provide toast demanded from the bedrooms, where the famous occupants were hungry after the delights of the night and screamed for instant attention. As I lit my oven, using my new dexterity to extract hundreds of slices of Holy Ghost and thrust them at the shrieking line of waiters, my lie-abed mornings in Arundel Terrace seemed irrecoverable.

I felt ill-used by Stella, but too physically tired to think of much except sleep. With the flat to myself I had toyed with the idea of going into Edlin's or an equally inviting pub, getting drunk on five-penny cider and picking up someone. However, on my one day off a week, my willing flesh and spirit were both too tired and too downcast to leave Stella's bed. There was a most attractive redhead who had served me in the chemists' when I had gone in to buy Stella's spermicidal jelly, an errand which I loathed but which she sometimes insisted I do for her. My lower middle-class discomfiture seemed to give her some amusement as a required part of my training for life as well as the theatre. The redhead had always smiled at me with what I thought was intrigued sympathy whenever she handed over the tube. In Edlin's, when she was always accompanied by an older man, I had thought her eyes were picking me out. One evening I followed her when she was alone but I failed to approach her.

Before the end of the season everyone working at Fitzherbert Court seemed to collapse with inertia at the prospect of the winter and their departure to the lower depths of some other catering underworld. There was talk of bankruptcy and closure and I was dismissed without explanation and given my cards peremptorily. The Still Room Terror and his wife said goodbye to me, saying that I hadn't been such a bad lad or so toffee-nosed as they'd thought. They gave me their address in case I should ever want a job in another still room with them.

My cards were insufficiently stamped so I was ineligible for the dole. I had been earning about £14 a week and had saved enough to see me through the next month or so. But this depended on my being able to continue living rent-free at Arundel Terrace. After a few nights hungrily watching the redhead in Edlin's and going back to my empty bed, I received a telegram from Stella. It read: 'Pat closing up flat. Please turn off electricity, close all windows, lock all doors. Writing. Love Stella'. I decided to wait until Pat turned up and see if he had anything to suggest. When he did, he was characteristically vague about the future in general and mine in particular. He only seemed interested in talking about *The Devil Inside*, saying that he thought he had found a theatre in which to open it in the provinces and an exciting new actor to play the leading part. By this time, I realized that this would be someone inexperienced and cheap, like myself. But as usual he was engaging, and infected me with his ferrety, genteel enthusiasm.

He took me to a bar where he insisted on buying pints of draught Bass. It was, he explained, like Archie Rice, impossible to get in Canada, one of the reasons for getting himself discharged from the RAF by truthfully inform- ing the Commanding Officer that he was a practising homosexual. He had, he confided over Bass, become a vegetarian and now a Vegan not because of any high falutin' moral or health reasons but because the irrefutable attraction and logic of vegetarianism was that it enabled you to get pissed quickly and cheaply. Your system, uncoked by toxins, thrust you into drunken over-drive miles ahead of any poisoned meat-eater. That evening he told me Archie Rice's story about being caught up with by the Inland Revenue after twenty years, when he had been ambushed in a hospital while being treated for a hernia, by two men in bowler hats who appeared uninvited from behind the screens.

He had a list of projects, including the tour of a play called *Because I Am Black*. He talked about the author enthusiastically and I felt that I had been superceded. *Because I Am Black* was a sure money-spinner according to Pat. It was about black people who had come to settle in England. He soon dispelled any idea that this might be a liberal treatment of a new social problem, but insisted it was sensational stuff and really good theatre. Perfect for the twice-nightly music-hall circuit. He showed me a grubby copy of the play and I could see that although the principal character was drawn more or less sympathetically, according to the playmaking precept, the appeal of the piece lay in rattling bones of hatred and envy all over the place. He had already tried it out at somewhere like the Q Theatre and the production was triggered for the rightly selected dates. The author had agreed that the uppity leading man should be replaced. Blacks in *Because I Am Black*, like the queens in *Soldiers in Skirts*, were poorly placed to negotiate with the likes of Pat Desmond.

After closing time, he piled a few things into some newspaper and a brown carrier bag and rushed off to catch the last train to Victoria, saying that I'd be hearing from him as soon as he'd got something fixed. I decided to hang on at Arundel Terrace and see if anything happened. *No Room at the Inn* had only just finished its last tour and I decided to write to Michael Hamilton. Apart from looking in the *Stage* there was little else I could do. Mrs Garrett belonged to my amateur past. Besides, Nellie Beatrice told me that she had died. The North Cheam School of Music, Dancing, Speech, Elocution and Drama had drawn its lace curtains finally and for ever.

A few days later a letter came from Stella. She reminded me of her words about being able to cut herself off from me like a wasted limb. She had, after all, decided to do this. She had also been unable to find me a job in Kendal. There was a little gossip about the work and a casual reference to the fact that she was sharing a caravan with a young man in the company. For the next few days I walked about Kemp Town and Brighton with her letter in my pocket reciting it to myself and trying to salvage comfort between the lines. I knew she was speaking the truth. Her warning to me had been made in good faith and possibly out of hurt regard, a reminder of my obvious lack of enterprise or conviction. I certainly felt neither, only that both Stella and the theatre itself had turned their backs on me, that the Shippards, Grandma Osborne and Nellie Beatrice had triumphed, and so soon.

There was no alternative but to go back to the Black Looks. I sent what was surely a self-righteous, reproachful letter to Stella. When I left Arundel Terrace I took great care to see that the electricity was still turned on and that the windows and door were not locked. It was the only sweetness I could find in my farewell to my Brighton year. Michael Hamilton had nothing for me and the *Stage* produced nothing either. With my lack of experience or contacts I had little to offer. Stella wrote back unsympathetically, scornful about my complaining letter, but most of all enraged by my failure to follow her instructions about leaving the flat. Rightly, she never forgave me for that spiteful, graceless little act, infecting some little pain with most puny revenge.

For adults only

My mother had had one of her 'flare ups' with the tenants where we had been living before. In other words, as usual, she nursed minuscule grudges against the people living there. She was now living in an almost exactly similar house with Yvette, an amiable, volatile Frenchwoman who worked in the kitchen of the Stoneleigh Hotel. She was friendly, with two attractive teenage children whom she used to threaten with the cat o'nine tails, and was certainly a relief from the dull bank clerk and his wife we had left around the corner. Furthermore, she turned out to be an amused ally in the face of Nellie Beatrice's darkening temperament.

If Arnold had been still working for Benn Brothers I would certainly have gone back, if only to escape for the present, but by this time he had returned to Canada. Apart from Stella, he was the only adult who had befriended me, and I missed them both. It was not until the New Year that anything turned up, when Pat, good as his non-toxic word, sent me a telegram saying that he had arranged a job as ASM at Leicester. The pay was only six pounds a week and I was to start at once. It didn't sound like an advancement, but I accepted immediately. Yvette thrust a few pounds on me, which she made clear were a non-returnable loan as long as I said nothing to Nellie Beatrice. Between them I collected enough for my fare and first week's rent.

Arriving in Leicester I went straight to the theatre management, Mr and Mrs McTaggart, a depressed couple who ran the Theatre Royal's weekly repertory company. They reluctantly gave me the address of the room that they had booked for me and asked me to come back as soon as possible and start work. I dragged my suitcase to a back street, fortunately not far from the railway station. The landlady pointed me to a bedroom and washbasin. Needless to say, Mr and Mrs McTaggart, with the stubborn defeatism of lives nurtured in the Midlands, had seen to it that meals were not available, nor was food to be brought in.

The theatre itself was pretty and the market lively, but the McTaggarts were palpably unattractive and bent on ill-feeling. I was to discover that there were three kinds of repertory companies to be avoided: those which were twice-nightly; those run by married couples; and the local amateur dramatic society. Both the last almost guaranteed an unappreciative parsimony and this also often went with the first. The company itself was as despondent as the management. As always, with theatre companies, the prevailing climate emanated from those above. The leading man was a bald, morose actor called Wilfred Brambell, who managed to acquire some kind of star status from having been the standing understudy to Robertson Hare. The rest of the company also seemed smugly drab and particularly the women, who would have looked familiar on the 8.17 to Waterloo every morning. They were *Daily Telegraph* readers to a person and easily impressed by the prevailing atmosphere of unease which came from the knowledge, consciously encouraged by the management, that they were at all times replaceable by any one of an army waiting in the wings.

The first production was a play called *The Wind and the Rain*. In addition to my duties as stage manager, I played the small part of a student who comes on at the end of the play, which is about the life and love of a medical student in Edinburgh. It was identical to another role I was to play later, more than once, in *White Cargo*. Such parts seemed to have been written with stage managers specifically in mind. In *The Wind and the Rain* the leading man, the young student, appears in the first minutes of the play, which is devoted entirely to him until the last five minutes, when another young medical student comes on uttering almost exactly the same stock lines the audience has heard two hours before. It was consummate play-making but demanded an entire evening spent waiting to make a derisory appearance in the dying minutes. It seemed also to be a measure of lowly status, like being the hind legs of a pantomime horse. In *White Cargo* the exact formula is used again. In that play the character is a raw young chap sent out from the Old Country to the White Man's Grave. In this case there was one guaranteed laugh, which was, 'Gosh [mopping brow and taking off topee], damn hot, isn't it?' This had been repeated by some buffoon throughout the play and even the most hardened amateur could hardly fail to get his rewarding laugh.

The season's programme at Leicester consisted of the staple repertory diet of the time: Home Counties comedies and murder mysteries; plays with maids and middle-class girls compromised in their cami-knickers; and the occasional northern comedy. Many of these northern comedies were written in a northern house style which hardly ever penetrated below Nottingham. They had titles like *Jobs for the Boy* or *Jack's the Lad*. Whoever wrote them knew their audience. Lines which were uttered by RADA-trained actors at rehearsal in utter disbelief were greeted in performance with howls of happy recognition. One I remember particularly involved a character getting his hands stuck in a vase. After struggling with it for long minutes, his line expelled itself into the audience: 'Eeh, I've got me 'and stook in't jug . . .' Wait thirty seconds for laughter to swell and subside . . . 'Come 'ere lad, get t' Vaseline . . .' Instructions: stare at scenery for at least one minute, while the audience recomposes itself.

The management soon decided that I was incompetent and unwilling. They were right. I had put most of the day-to-day burden of collecting props and furniture from unfriendly shopkeepers, sewing curtains and repairing scenery on to my girl ASM who was unaccountably grateful. Leaving Leicester I would have welcomed 'Ghost Riders in the Sky' at six o'clock in the morning and the cries for 'Holy Ghost!'

Pat Desmond had had predictable problems with his coloured actors. I guessed that his scruffy, patronizing air, which was tiresome enough to ordinary theatrical white trash like myself, would probably be inflaming to some ill-paid black actor. Consequently, *Because I Am Black* was postponed until a more slavish replacement was found. Until then, another money spinner was to be set on the road in its place. This was a stage version of the *Blue Angel*, which had been adapted by a florid old actor rather like Robert Atkins, called Edgar K. Bruce, as a vehicle for himself in the original Emile Jannings part. The Marlene Dietrich role was bravely played by an attractive young girl married to the actor Jack Watling. There was little scope for her apart from showing her legs, as the play was a *tour de force* for Mr Bruce, whose acting style was not so much Regent's Park as Hyde Park Corner. Pat offered me a part as a student and ASM which I gladly accepted. It was clear from the outset that Pat himself had very little faith in the show, and for all the right reasons. He had only become involved in the venture because Mr Bruce had supplied the investment in the hope of recapturing his supposedly popular loyal following between Carlisle and Huddersfield.

After a few weeks it was clear that his following was no longer loyal or popular. Few people had heard of the film, there was no Marlene and very little sex at all. Mr Bruce spouted whole passages of Shakespeare *ex tempore* for no reason except to prove what a fine neglected actor the tiny audience was privileged to see. Pat lost interest in trying to drum up support, and the end came like a damp dawn execution, swift and expected.

In the meantime, he had managed to mount a production for one week of *The Devil Inside* at the Theatre Royal, Huddersfield. There was to be one week's rehearsal which I was unable to attend, being still with the tour. However, I was to go there for the opening the following week in case of rewrites. I had played Huddersfield before, although I had yet to be bombed in New Haven. Stella was in the theatre when I arrived. She seemed enthusiastic and confident. Rehearsals had gone well. The young actor playing the lead, Reginald Barrett, was a real discovery. Bookings were thin, but we were assured of at least a couple of good nights, it being Easter week. I sat through the dress rehearsal in a confusion of feelings, trying to relate what I was watching not only to myself but to Stella and our months in Brighton together. It seemed to have only dismembered resemblance to what I dimly remembered having written in Sunderland or even after. I thought the 'real discovery' was disastrous, but was too timid to say so, thinking how much better I would have been in the part myself.

On Easter Monday 1950 I sat in the stalls of the Theatre Royal, Huddersfield, watching the world opening performance of my play, holding hands with my co-author. Surging gratitude, excitement returned, I relented with myself as well as with Stella. After less than eighteen months in the theatre, I was watching my own play – or a version of it – being performed in a professional theatre. I was getting paid and I had an ex-mistress saying affectionate encouraging things to me. Stella's coarse jokes worked, as she said they would, but my remaining wastegrounds of poetry palled even for me. However, the reception at the end was friendly and the character actor brought forward the young man playing my part and said something like, 'I think, ladies and gentlemen, you will agree with me that tonight we have discovered a new star.' This absurdity was applauded politely, which I knew must be a recognition of the power of the role and not its feeble interpretation.

Afterwards both Pat and Stella were optimistic and there was talk about who they would bring over to see it during the week. The business had been good, nearly £400, but then of course it was Easter Monday. As it turned out, it was a little more than we took the rest of the week, and my share of the royalty was just over nine pounds. Stella tried to persuade me to stay until the Saturday night performance but, protecting myself from further disappointment and demands for pointless rewriting, I returned to Stoneleigh. I was pleased that the play had been performed but some pain had been expended for small reward. I had had one minimally gratifying evening in Huddersfield as an author with an ex-mistress and collaborator. And there was nine pounds to show for it, a week's salary.

16. Fall of a Sparrow

Wanted: Scarborough twice nightly
one leading M one F two juv char M
one char. Own wardrobe evening
clothes. Start immediately. No
Fancy salaries and no queer folk

Discouraging advertisements of this kind appeared regularly in the *Stage*. Only desperate folk, queer or not, could have felt bold enough to answer such an intimidating invitation. Even as an escape from Nellie Beatrice it sounded like self-immolation. Shortly after the *Blue Angel* tour I saw another advertisement, cautiously worded but almost matey in comparison. It read something like, 'Saga Repertory Company, llfracombe. Wanted: enthusiastic young actor to muck in with co-operative company. No salary but expenses, accommodation and sharing.' Instead of threatening no fancy salaries, it disarmingly offered none at all. But it sounded as if any folk sufficiently cast down by penury and despondency to accept such terms might expect some sort of welcome. Enthusiasm could be dissembled if necessary, unless circumstances were truly intolerable. Also, the word 'Saga' had an optimistic sense of epic. I sent off a photograph with details of my experience, some discreetly invented. A telegram arrived the next day telling me to go to Ilfracombe immediately. It was signed 'St George'.

Unsure whether it might be some facetious code, I got on the train from Waterloo quite hopefully. The idea of an incompetent co-operative was preferable to some end-of-the-pier bully. The Saga Repertory Company might be a little like the Dinky Doos. I wanted to be back in the provinces. Ilfracombe hardly matched my idea of what they might be, but it was familiar from my half-terms with G. P. M. Watson and must be nicer than Leicester in any conditions. I found the company in the little theatre on the front, pounded by the sea from the promenade. They were dress rehearsing the week's play, Rattigan's *Flare Path*. It had to be abandoned during the second act as darkness descended on the box office and the remaining wintry light bulbs showed the way to a few dozen bent figures clutching blasted umbrellas. I sat among the sparse audience like a happy dog-owner watching its pet's ill-performed tricks. The piece was performed with such earnest sentimentality that its groggy honesty seemed to overcome its unpreparedness and deserve the respect and attention it undoubtedly received. The audience was unexcited but content.

The Saga Repertory Company was run by two young men, Anthony Creighton and the sender of the telegram, Clive St George. Clive was sandy-haired, balding, in his mid-thirties and the business manager and publicist. Anthony was the Artistic Director. The sentimental excess of *Flare Path* was clearly imposed by him. Short, stocky, he seemed a little like a gushy Battle of Britain pilot or a slightly spastic Auntie Queenie. He welcomed me as if I had bailed out only after dropping a couple of bandits in the drink first. He had, in fact, been a Bomber Navigator and won the DFC for gallantly saving some crew members in a Halifax over Hamburg. After the war he had gone to RADA but, apart from this, appeared to have no professional experience, unlike myself. The average age of the company turned out to be about twenty-one, all of them almost immediately out of RADA or the Young Vic. Stella would have dismissed them all as amateurs.

Anthony, unable to find work after leaving drama school, had borrowed money from his mother and started the Saga Repertory Company with the vaguest intentions. Clive, his partner, was openly intent on making money with minimum effort. A corpulent, uncanny waxwork Terry Thomas, proffering his flair like a temperamental cigarette lighter, he was already a failure as a kind of used-play salesman. My short experience told me that he was a dedicated bankrupt, long set on a drifting, good-humoured, absent-minded course to the Scrubs, if he had not already made the trip. Addressing himself to some tricky matter of transport or publicity he would mutter darkly, 'Don't worry, we'll fix it. Don't forget *I've* got Coptic blood.' I thought this was some vague claim to fortune's destiny until I accompanied him on a visit to borrow money from his father, who was indeed a dignified and polite rich Egyptian. Clive's theatrical experience was less evident than his Coptic blood. Anthony, however, had toured extensively in an RAF drag show directed by Terence Rattigan. It was called something like *Boys in Blue* or *Things in Wings*. Anyway, it must have been a precursor to *Soldiers in Skirts*, the wartime makeshift of the Kenneth Clarks of drag. He showed me a photograph of himself with Rattigan, dressed in a *tutu*, carrying a wand, accompanied by a line of aircraftmen, during which Terry had sung his own show-stopper, 'I'm just about the oldest fairy in the business. I'm quite the oldest fairy that you've ever seen.' He had told Anthony to go and see him after the war when he said he would be able to do something about his future. I wondered why he hadn't. Or perhaps he had.

The company consisted of three men, including myself, and three girls. There was a plump girl called Veronica Wells, who seemed physically flushed, or rather, mottled by her devotion to Marcel Proust. She had been trained at the Young Vic, George Devine's school, and, like all its students I had encountered, seemed tutored in solemnity, making one relish coarse pedlars such as Pat and Stella. A sour, nubile girl called Liz played most of the leading parts, allotted to her by Anthony to distract her from her pre-occupation of being publicly in love with him and rousing and caring for his resistant needs. She fawned on him unaccountably, frantic, voluptuous and disturbing – to me, at least. She seemed over-ripe for violation, even defile-ment, from Anthony, who curled his own voluptuous lips with the disdain of a pantomime dame playing her Apache partner. The third female mem-ber of the company was Lynne Reid Banks – later author of a book and film called *The L-Shaped Room*, and fearless campaigner against dog shit in public parks. I already had some nose for such women, and her own oil met the iced water certain women draw from me. Not to be mixed, I became a poisoned well; charity was mutually and immediately interred.

The size of the company meant presenting only plays with casts of six or less, but they seemed to have found enough of these to keep them going for weeks past. Liz painted the scenery and there was no distinction or privilege between the actors and stage management. Business was treacherous and the weekly shareout was never more than a few shillings each. Liz was absorbed in Anthony and the other two girls, particularly Lynne, were given to continual carping about what they considered to be artistic as well as moral improprieties. Fresh from the sixth forms of Kenneth Barnes and George Devine, unexposed to the streets of Hartlepool or Grimsby, fornica-tion on dressing-room floors in Hanley, the abiding scrutiny of grief stuffed into fox terriers, they enabled me to feel patronizing of others in my profes-sion for the first time.

We lived in a large Edwardian hotel flanked with palms called the Grove Park. I remembered it from my half-terms at St Michael's. It never seemed to have recovered from the war and its occupation by the US army, and still appeared from the outside to be derelict and unoccupied. Clive had made a deal with the proprietor for which we all stayed at a cost of about four pounds a week each. Whether we got our negotiated breakfast and late supper depended on both the caprice of the proprietor and our box-office return. The men slept in a large dormitory room and the girls in a similar one. We had the run of the entire place to ourselves, including a dozen bathrooms. The only other occupants were Gerald, the proprietor, always clad in the same dressing gown with a cigarette hanging out of the side of his mouth, in a state of laconic catatonia. Contributing to his iron inertia was Eric, his boyfriend, who worked in the kitchen with Calpurnia, an elusive crone who might have been incarcerated by Mr Rochester but was allowed instead to run the hotel and ease Gerald's nervous exhaustion.

Eric, too, was a figure of speculation, made more mysterious by Gerald's urgent confidences. 'Ooh, I can't tell you the trouble I had with Eric last night.' He would blink stoically, as the smoke from his drooping fag end invaded his eyeballs. 'I thought he was going to go crazy, my dear. Had to tie him down with ropes. Ropes! Silken ropes, my dear. Wanted to throw himself out of the window. I don't know why. He's such a sensitive boy. He's too good to be a kitchen boy. I keep telling him. Come into my room. He's such an artistic boy, he shouldn't be in the kitchen. Come and look at his underwear. Look at that!' He would open a drawer of Eric's tallboy to reveal rows of underpants, all ironed and wrapped individually in blue and pink tissue paper. 'Look at that. He does all that himself in his spare time. You can see – he's definitely artistic. Like you, my dear. Just like you.'

He was indeed convinced that I, too, was definitely artistic and was quick to notice that I was weighing up my slim chances among the three girls. Liz had eyes for no one except Anthony; Lynne was unspeakable (she may have unconsciously prompted me years later when I wrote a line in *Watch it Come Down*, describing an indiscriminating lecher: 'Some people will put it in a brick wall'); and Veronica was plump and motherly. On her back she might well cast out the spirit of Proust with a mask of Young Vic sexuality.

Whether or not he had been tying up Eric with silken ropes, Gerald would sink unexpectedly on the edge of one's bed for a chat at any time of the night. Anthony would have often disappeared into the town, while Clive wandered around the hotel in his long underwear with a glass of whisky in his hand like a sleepwalker to no unclear purpose. One night he, too, sat on the bed, frowning as if startled by some unsought pleasure. 'D'you know, I went down to the kitchen just now for a sandwich and as I was eating it, d'you know what happened? That old cow, Calpurnia, that dirty old cow, she came into the kitchen, took out my cock just while I was eating and sucked me off. What about that? What about that? Right in the middle of my sandwich.' The girls, too, wandered a little, but I could see that Lynne had cast herself as chaperone to the others, and my designs on either of them would be hurled aside like dog shit in the park threatening the frail children of *Guardian* readers. Gerald eyed me from the end of the bed, 'You should watch yourself, my dear. I've been watching you. You've got your eye on those young girls, you mark my words. You be careful. You don't know *what* you want. I think you know what I mean. At *your* age you just don't know.'

The first play I was to appear in was a melodrama called *Duet for Two Hands* by Mary Hayley Bell, the wife of John Mills. The part was that of a young pianist whose hands are severed at the wrist, replaced by the brilliant skill of a malevolent surgeon who sews on a natty pair of murderer's mitts, which have a nasty uncontrollable twitch to place themselves around the neck of haphazard victims. Clive drawled his scoundrelly way through the part of the surgeon while I clawed my way through the part of the pianist, thankful that Stella was unable to watch my confusion. I knew that I couldn't blame my lamentable performance entirely on the absurdity of the play. Clive was getting away with his part without apparently trying or caring. The company seemed relieved that I had got through it at all, implying that most weeks were far worse. Unlike Pat with his, 'No, laddie, you don't stand like that on the fucking stage in the professional theatre,' Anthony was even fulsome. By Friday I had become almost confident and the company manager from Minehead, who was in the house, came round to see me, saying that if ever I wanted a job I was to write to him at any time. My first week's share of the takings was something like ten shillings. I reckoned that I had done rather well.

The nights became more black and the sea hurled itself across the street on to the front of the theatre itself. Neither Rattigan nor Mary Hayley Bell could continue to compete with the warmth of the bridge rooms tucked away from the ice and spray of the front. Clive wheedled and Anthony pleaded. If we could get through the winter there would be pickings for all the following Easter. I was sceptical but happy until something better turned up. There was no word from Pat, most likely in full flight from the Inland Revenue or Equity. However, the girls were becoming sullen, particularly Lynne Reid Banks who disapproved of this wayward life as she would later of dog faeces and fag ends. Veronica, less aggressively, was yearning for the emotions she had kindled in herself at the Young Vic with Obey and Chekhov instead of Mary Hayley Bell. Lynne disapproved of each one of the men. She could detect the smell of male squalor in either cock-happy Copt or free-crapping labrador. Some time later at an improbably posh party in London I offered her a sandwich. I had taken some trouble to insert among the smoked salmon and cream cheese, like a worm in the bud, a used French letter. The unbelieving repulsion on her face, the prig struck by lightning, was fixed for ever for me, like Kean's Macbeth. Liz remained loyal to Anthony, and seemed to relish the idea of wintering through a rent-free nervous breakdown at the Grove Park Hotel. Finally, Lynne and Veronica made the decision. We must disband.

Disappointed, I went back to Stoneleigh, but before I had time to write to Minehead, Clive rang me to tell me that he had arranged a tour of one-night stands. 'All *fixed*, old boy.' We were to be based in London using his second-hand car, with a trailer to transport our twelve-foot flats. We would be the same company, minus Lynne, playing towns and villages near London, all unserved by professional theatre, like East Grinstead, Hartley Wintney, Saffron Walden and Epsom. He was to prepare for our coming with saturation publicity for two of our biggest Ilfracombe successes, *Night Must Fall* by Emlyn Williams and *Springtime for Henry* by Benn Levy. The first which was, and still is, a classic thriller of its kind was a shrewd choice. It was most certainly what Pat and Stella would have called cracking good theatre and was almost actor-proof. Not so shrewd was Clive's Coptic saturation. In Hartley Wintney eight people turned up and in East Grinstead none at all. However, there is still something mysteriously wrong with that town. Perhaps, like the Royal Court, it should now be sold off to Sir Freddie Laker. Clive was as baffled as he must have been when he looked over his sandwich at the top of Calpurnia's thrusting head. 'Can't understand it, old boy. *Saturated* the whole town.' The eight people of Hartley Wintney were subjected to a pitiable presentation. Anthony Creighton played Danny, the psychopathic killer, investing every unlearned speech with the remembered vigour of a Night over Hamburg and enlivened by too much whisky. I was little better as the Inspector. After my experiences with *Duet for Two Hands* I was determined to try to avoid juvenile parts. I, too, had not bothered to learn my lines very well and relied on the script concealed in a hefty notebook which I carried all over the stage.

We were disgraceful, inexcusable and boring, as well as pleased with ourselves like a trio of saloon-bar drunks. Veronica played Mrs Bransome competently and was at least chillingly DLP (Dead Letter Perfect) as the phrase was then. Liz was creditable as a jealous wife (possibly thinking of Anthony) in *Springtime for Henry*, a modest but enjoyable farce, and I gave a passable imitation of Sid Field for no valid reason. For weeks we travelled from town to village in Clive's rusting Hudson, playing to never more than a dozen or so people. Clive's advance strategy had been as ineffective as the saturation bombing of Hamburg by Flight Lieutenant Creighton. There was no panic shift from cocktails and evening bridge. Even Anthony conceded that the Saga Repertory Company must disband yet again. Clive was anxious to join his father in scrap metal or something similar. Veronica had got herself a job at the George in Hammersmith and Liz seemed to have retreated into a withdrawn stage of depressive nymphomania.

Anthony, with a deficient sense of enterprise, would not consider alternatives. He still had some scenery and equipment and all he needed was the money to continue the course of his muddled indolence. This soon came from a young man called David Payne, tall, sandy-haired with a fanatic Papist smile. He was evidently eccentric, if not dangerously downright dotty, and was a lunchtime regular at the Salisbury in St Martin's Lane, at that time the Rialto for loud-mouthed actors and lounging fairies. Anthony came back one afternoon from the Salisbury with a cheque for £1,000 illegibly inscribed by David Payne. We went to the bank first thing in the morning and it was honoured without question. We emerged with money in our hands and went straight to the Builder's Arms in Hammersmith, dropping in later to see Veronica at the George.

Looking down the columns of the *Stage* we had noticed that the lease of a theatre was available at a place called Hayling Island. It appeared that the Victoria Theatre could be acquired for a weekly rental of only twenty pounds. Like the cheque, it seemed too good to be true and we went down immediately to see it. It was hardly recognizable as a theatre, being, in fact, the rear end of a small hotel. However, it had a sizeable auditorium, enough room to seat about 300 people, a proscenium with a twenty-foot opening and a reasonably deep stage. There was no flying space, but with our equipment that was not necessary. There were three sizeable dressing-rooms, one lighting batten and a set of floats. A monthly contract was drawn up for the lease of the theatre and David Payne's money was handed over for the first month's rental. We lunched lavishly in Portsmouth, toasting Dotty David in champagne. We even offered Veronica a job, which she refused. She felt more secure dipping into Proust with her Irish customers behind the bar of the George.

Hayling Island is not an island but an isthmus, a leafy, tight suburb with a long, empty beach, obscured in a blur of cold wind and sand. Adjoining it was Hayling Island Holiday Camp, a few windswept, exposed chalets, hemmed in by kiddies' roundabouts and pedal-driven trolleys for the campers to trundle themselves a few hundred yards to the tiny dodgem rink and ice-cream and doughnut hut. This was our literally captive audience. The nearest cinema was at Havant and the nearest place of any entertainment, Portsmouth. Car-owning democracy had not yet liberated campers from the confines of their site, and the motorcycle and sidecar were still the dream only of backyard ingenuity. In London we reported back to Dotty David who was vague, unsurprised and pleased. We made a list of available small-cast plays and set about getting a company together.

Clive was no longer available, so I became company manager. We would start from scratch. I would be able to ensure the selection of agreeable, uncensorious girls and Anthony would handpick the actors. His pipe-smoking, Johnny-head-in-the-air self-caricature concealed from almost no one that he was one of those luckless homosexuals, like J. R. Ackerley, who only fall in love with heterosexuals. I was quite fond of him, but his frequent references to 'the rough kiss of male Hamlets', made me eager for him to find some young actor who would command his whole attention. I had no taste nor aptitude for jealous melodrama, especially one like this, based upon a sexual fiction. My role in Sheila's soap opera was clear enough. I wanted to sleep with her. She didn't want to sleep with me but demanded chastity from me and the fervid pleasure of jealousy for herself. I had made it repeatedly clear to Anthony that rough male blankets had nothing on white bodies, like Stella's, in black silk sheets. The coarse prospect of the stubble of female armpits around my own bed sickened him, but it was one which he had to be made to accept if we were to work together with any harmony.

We placed a friendly-sounding-out advertisement in the *Stage*, like the one I had responded to myself. I had suggested we might employ Patrick Desmond's virtual confidence trick, which was to advertise for what were called 'students'. This meant that you could get your stage management at least to work for nothing, and in some cases someone dumb enough might even pay a premium of £50 for the privilege of working for an unscrupulous management. It was a practice frowned on by all respectable branches of the theatre and by the drama schools in particular. However, we decided against it, thinking, correctly, that we hadn't the sort of bravura and experience to get away with it. In the circumstances, we decided to offer £4 a week within the profit-sharing democracy of the company. For this kind of money, it was certain to me that no experienced or intelligent actor would be tempted. Anthony's sentimental faith was rewarded like a smug, supplicant cripple. The response was astonishingly enthusiastic. There seemed to be dozens of young men and girls eager to work for these wages, an unknown company and an unspecified vision.

We hired a studio in West Kensington and enjoyed ourselves hiring actors, as if we were furnishing a new house or buying a string of race horses. We went through what we judged to be the pick of the left-over flowers of RADA, Central School, the Webber Douglas and, of course, the Young Vic. Each drama school proclaimed its tenets. The St Denis–Devine graduates were still the most earnest and tiresome, especially in their criticism of our choice of plays, which were commercial and provenly popular. We still had some £900 to play with, enabling us to get Anthony's scenery out of store, buy ourselves a few clothes, which we thought was a legitimate company expense, including a £10 dinner jacket for myself, an essential for a weekly repertory actor, and a few other personal presents for each other. We were in business.

A nice drop of cider

CHAP: Woman is dead! Long live Woman! . . .

I do not believe it. She has always triumphed in *my* small corner of spirit, just as I have failed *her* image—my broken, misty, self-deceiving image you may say – during most of my life. And, remembering it, what a long time it has been. I believe in Woman, whatever that may be, just as I believe in God, because they were both invented by man. If I am their inventor, they are my creators, and they will continue to exist. During most of my life. What made me think of it? Watching a couple in a street late at night in a provincial town. Being in love, how many times and over such a period. Being in Love! What anathema to the Sexual Militant, the wicked interest on free capital.

Anathema because it involves waste, exploitation of resources, sacrifice, unplanned expenditure, both sides sitting down together in unequal desolation. *This* is the market place I have known and wandered in almost as long as I indecently remember or came to forget. Being in love, quaint expense of spirit, long over-ripe for the bulldozer; of negotiating from the strength of unmanning women's liberation. Those long-shore bullies with bale hooks in bras and trousers seamed with slogans and demands . . . Being in love. Desolation in the sea of hope itself. Sentimental? False? Infantile? Possibly. And infantile because my memories of the phenomenon, if there be such a one, is or ever will be, start *so young*. From three, yes. I know it was three, even till the only twenty-one, there were so many girls, girl-women, women of all ages, I loved. Very few of them were in love with me, alas. Being in love blunders all negotiations and certainly differentials. I have been sometimes indecently moved to tears and if there were a court of justice in these things, I would have been dealt with summarily as a persistent offender, asking for innumerable, nameless and unspeakable offences to be taken into account. However, if I have been such a villain in this manor of feelings, I have tried to be as clever as I know how. Knowing, as we all know, that there is no such thing. If I have used blunt instruments and sophisticated gear, I've tried to avoid soft risks and only go for the big stuff. Naturally, I've made mistakes. In fact, when you look at it, the successful jobs have been far fewer than the fair cops. But that is the nature of crime itself, of *being in love*; you are incapable of adding up the obvious odds against you, unlike the law abider with his common sense and ability to discriminate between his own needs and that of the rest of society . . . *Girls past.* If I ever yearned for a figment of England, so I yearned for *them;* for girls' past, fewer in the present and sadly, probably in the future. Who *were* they? All I remember most is their names, what they wore, sometimes what they looked like. Not very much.

A Sense of Detachment, 1972

We opened in June with *Springtime for Henry* and *Night Must Fall.* They were sound choices and saved us both the labour of having to learn lines, although in Anthony's case they rarely ever returned. Dotty David noticed but didn't seem to mind. He admired us like the new MG he had also bought out of his recent inheritance. He never enquired about how the money was being spent or about the receipts, which at first I insisted on presenting to him and then gave up gladly. During the next three months business was good, especially on Fridays and Saturdays when we were usually packed out. We played from Wednesday to Wednesday, which theoretically enabled holidaymakers, who were only staying one week, to see two plays. I used Patrick Desmond's trick of marking the posters 'For Adults Only'. Even plays like *Rookery Nook* or *Candida* could be hawked abroad in Hampshire as salacious.

With a weekly rental of twenty pounds and a company of eight, our get-out net figure was low and we managed to lower it still more by performing plays without licence, thus paying no author's royalties. We also avoided the entertainments duty which should have been levied by affixing Customs and Excise stamps on the back of each ticket that we issued from the tin box on the card table in the foyer. As a result, we were operating on a small profit almost from the opening of the season. The company became suspicious. I kept the books and issued no returns for them to check but distributed small, equal bonuses on Fridays which seemed to satisfy all of them except for one militant, who had also declared himself elected Equity representative, something I had not anticipated. Like all Equity representatives he was assuredly the least talented and most voluble member of the company. It is a job for failed guvnor's men which all but the most mediocre shun. I was determined to get rid of this particular actor before he aroused too much support or demands for investigation of our finances. He suspected, accurately, that we had not deposited the statutory two weeks' salary with Equity on behalf of their members. Although I was a full member, I had no more regard for Equity than authors' agents and the Customs and Excise. Besides, none of them had worked the forty-eight weeks necessary to obtain full membership as I had done. Their drama school privilege was a badge of snooty amateurism to me. I had to teach them how to cleat up a flat and adjust a counterweight. So much for Michel St Denis.

The company safe was a large tin box which I kept beneath the camp bed on which I slept in my dressing-room. We had no bank account. I regarded cheque books with as much suspicion as my mother did garlic. Anthony and I decided to sleep in the dressing-rooms, saving us the expense of a room in the adjoining hotel with the other actors. For several weeks we had House Full notices up outside the theatre almost every night. One particularly surprising success was a play called *Love in Albania* by Eric Linklater, which we put on solely because I wanted to play the part of an amiable, dumb GI, played originally by Peter Ustinov. But by the first week in September the holiday campers had almost gone and business dropped alarmingly. It was certain that we had made no impact upon the local elderly and retired residents. I pleaded with the company to be patient but they were all overtired, disillusioned and understandably unconvinced of our good faith. They were in no mood to be persuaded by a twenty-year-old Pat Desmond. Feeling was not good. Anthony was discounted as amiable and quite inadequate. I was aware that they looked on me resentfully, in some cases with a kind of revealed dislike, as an unteachable theatrical barrow-boy, to whom mask, mime or Copeau were the drama's despised Dinner at Night. The girls had turned out to be dull and I was encouraged by the certainty that every one of them was a lifelong prig. Better a spiv than a prig.

In defiance of them and in a bout of self-indulgence, I decided that we should finish the season with *Hamlet*, playing the Prince myself. I cut the play down to a running time of a little over two hours and threw myself into the part in manic defiance of the other dismayed actors and their mincing theorizing. It was a superb opportunity to express my contempt for them through Shakespeare. The women I taunted with vindictive relish, attacking them in the play with my own mind's eye of them. Ophelia, a vapid virgin from Leicester, no less, who had won prizes at RADA, asked me to leave her bedroom. As for Gertrude, I had quite capriciously decided to my own satisfaction that she was a prying lesbian who had prevailed on Ophelia to reject my attempts on the body she coveted herself. In the closet scene, I mauled her as lewdly as her costume allowed, which still gave me some clinical opportunities. She had a residual taste of the rank sweat of Claudius's enseamed bed and of all the monstrous regiment of women. My kisses were reeking with whisky as I paddled in her neck, and other places, and pinched wantonly on her low-slung cheeks.

As a Hamlet, it was a passable impersonation of Claudius after a night's carousing. I looked forward to Gertrude slapping my face during the scene or at least walking out afterwards. She would have been eagerly supported by the other actors on artistic if not moral grounds but, like them, she seemed almost intimidated by the low, lunging coarseness of the Osborne Prince, a leering milk roundsman of Denmark Hill, full of black looks rather than nighted colour. Seldom can a Hamlet have exemplified so wholeheartedly the vices mocked in the speech to the Players.

Anthony managed to remember a smattering of the Claudius I had left to him. I was almost unaware of the others. They were interruptions of a huge euphoria I was certain never to be allowed again. I persuaded the local schoolteacher to send some children, and about a dozen bought half-price tickets. Some of the retired folk from the Victoria Hotel and their friends walked the few yards into the theatre. There could never have been more than thirty altogether. They were patient and possibly too infirm to hobble out. One old gentleman told me I reminded him of Frank Benson but that I was much noisier. Mrs Creighton came proudly to watch her son's valiant attempts to drop his lines on some random target. She had somehow persuaded my own mother to see the last performance. Understandably, she was bored. She had accidentally seen the Olivier film, not knowing in advance it was Shakespeare. 'I've seen it before,' she said to Mrs Creighton, meanly giving away the plot. 'He dies in the end.' She thought my peroxided hair made me look a bit of a nancy boy and too thin. Watching the home audience and the surly embarrassed actors at the one scrambled curtain call, she said loudly, 'Well, he certainly puts a lot into it.' And, with a sigh, 'Poor kid.' It was unusually prescient.

The company broke up, jeered at and unchallenged from the stage by a Hamlet in a brawling, alcoholic stupor. The girls were gratifyingly acrimonious and genteel. They might have even said something like, 'Men are all the same – only after one thing' if they had the memory or perception to know what that might be. Savouring my defeat as a rogue actor-manager, their contempt was sweet, heady and welcome. The vengeful commissar from Equity was less comic but could never distrain on my godlike moments. I had resolved early not to dissipate my frugally displaced energy kicking against small pricks.

We were left to find two more girls and a list of four-handed plays. The girl stage manager loyally decided to stay with us but she was unable to act at all. We continued until Christmas, never playing to more than a few dozen people every week. Our reserve profits were soon absorbed in paying the new girls their literal subsistence expenses. Anthony and I lived largely on evaporated milk and boiled nettles. We congratulated ourselves on discovering this reasonably agreeable diet. Our gypsy resourcefulness contrasted significantly with the bourgeois expectations of drama-school townies. The owners of the hotel seemed unaware of our presence in the building and had no interest in the matter of rent, even when I pointed it out to them. Anthony had rented his flat in Hammersmith, so apart from going back to Stoneleigh there was nowhere for me to go. Then the local Customs and Excise man caught up with us after months of profitable evasion. In the foyer, I handed him an unstamped ticket, along with maybe ten others. When he asked to see me privately, I knew I had been ambushed as surely as Pat Desmond behind the screens. The Excise achieved what Equity could never have done. The remnants of any godlike imaginings were hurled aside as my criminal activity was ransacked.

Within seconds, the Excise man seemed to be teetering with triumph at my discovered perfidy. The sounds of his conquest scarcely disturbed the other ticket holders as the curtains trickled apart for my entrance. His hysteria became reassuring, perhaps because of its familiarity. I wasn't able to make out a balance sheet but I thought I could smoke out a bully without looking up. He thought of himself as a personal servant of the King and accused me in the same terms as an Enemy of the King, which was flattering but was a clear sign of overheated impotence even to my unpreparedness. I pleaded the Nuremberg principle of obedience to orders from above.

I had taken the instruction of my absent partner, David Payne, who had failed to supply me with the necessary stamps I had meticulously requested.

In fact, Dotty David had disappeared weeks before, on his way to Oberammergau. He had said something about being engaged, but Anthony and I decided that he had gone into some Retreat or a kind of Catholic holiday camp. The Excise man began to be protective, in the way of policemen and gaolers. I said something idly about his interest in the theatre and was rewarded by confession. His daughter was a pupil at the Hayling Island School of Dancing. I said immediately that we would be wanting to cast the star role of the Good Fairy in our Christmas pantomime, *Aladdin*. His gratitude was as startling as his rage. The following day he brought her round for an audition. Anthony and I conferred, as if we, too, were servants of His Majesty, and told His Majesty's man that his daughter had been graciously given the job. For a while, I hoped, I had bought a blind eye.

On 12 December 1950, I spent my twenty-first birthday in Havant Magistrate's Court. Mr Cherry, the local grocer, had taken out a summons against us for a bill for fourteen pounds. We had begged him not to proceed, trying to persuade his never-festive spirit that the pantomime would bring in the locals where all else had failed. But he was eager for litigation as a career woman for alimony. We later based the character of Percy Elliot in *George Dillon* on him. Percy's lifetime ambition was to get the park gates closed long before dark so that no one could have any illicit pleasure. I denied any responsibility for these bills, saying that Dotty David was answerable for all company expenses. I believed this, thinking that just as I had provided work for actors, I had realized his own off-hand theatrical ambitions and my obligations were discharged. My own effort must be surely evident and my small reward undetectable. Convinced that no one would challenge me, except possibly Equity, I was disabused. Dotty David appeared in court, and was called into the witness box with his bank statements improbably to hand, which showed the sums of money he had paid out to us since the original £1,000. The magistrate was impressed by his vague but authoritative upper-class manner and his attitude changed at once. 'You are the company manager?' 'Yes,' I replied. 'I take it that you do keep properly audited books?' I hesitated. 'Yes.' Dotty David was dismissed from the case and Anthony and I were ordered to pay Mr Cherry's fourteen pounds as well as his legal costs.

The first and last night of *Aladdin*, was a cloud of unknowing nightmare. Through the innocent support of H.M. Customs, we had enlisted some volunteers to play small parts, a pianist and a dozen or so pupils of the

Hayling Island School of Dancing. I had written the script and doubled as Abanaza and Dame. Anthony played Wishee Washee, ad-libbing enthusiastically and incomprehensibly throughout. We both sang 'J'attendrai' in the style of Flanagan and Allan, and attempted a comic lyric which I had written to the tune of 'Sabre Dance', which was then in Hayling Island's Top Ten. Barely rehearsed and unremembered by Anthony, it was a lot put by me into very little. I had a frontcloth act without front cloth, wearing my hat from *Springtime for Henry*, and I told all the cleaner Max Miller jokes I had ever heard. Most disastrous of all, we improvised what I could remember and Anthony had forgotten of Sid Field's golfing and painting sketches. Those who have never appeared on the stage will never know the living presence of silence. But that is familiar ground testified by more hardened pilgrims.

For someone who had scorned the sanctimonious conformity of Pat and Stella, I was fiercely derivative and plagiarist by now. The evening actually began to rouse feeling. Anthony's balding head was streaked with perspiration as I bullied and shouted at him through our halting charade. Our only hope of forgiveness from the audience lay in the girl playing Aladdin. She had quite beautiful legs and sang in an uncajoling, unpantomime, thin, apologetic way. She even persevered after our act which only the most true believers could have followed. She stood alone with a song-sheet lowered behind her trying to coax a few scattered rows of pensioners and parents to sing 'Hey, Little Hen' and 'Rudolph, the Red-Nosed Reindeer'. There was no doubt about their refusal or ill-feeling. I wished that she would kindly leave the stage, for my sake at least. It was magnificent or war even.

The opening of the second act was the Dancing School's big number, led by the Good Fairy. In the interval, His Majesty's man came round in the frenzy of the man moved only by the mole of his bureaucracy. The outrage he had suffered in watching his daughter taking part in such a disgraceful spectacle matched the perfidy of the King's unstamped tickets. 'I have never seen anything like it,' he screamed. 'You shan't have her.' He grabbed the Good Fairy and took her off like a snatched bride from the theatre. A dozen other angry parents followed, with their howling, protesting offspring. The Big Spectacular number of the show was cancelled. I took an uncaring look out front and saw that the audience had disappeared with the exception of the old man who had compared me to Benson. I explained to him that the performance was cancelled and he returned understandingly to the hotel's television room.

Anthony's flat was now available. Mr Cherry kept coming round at all hours to make sure that we were still there to be harried. H.M. Customs and Excise must surely pounce. We ordered a van from a friend of Clive's and a few days later, with our scenery, our belongings and Aladdin herself, we did a one a.m. scarper to the Big Smoke. When we got to London in the early hours of the morning, Anthony's flat proved to be occupied after all and we had to point the van towards Stoneleigh, where a triumphant Black Look greeted us.

I wrote immediately to the manager from Minehead and received a telegram by return telling me to go to his company which was now at Bridgwater in Somerset. My embarrassing performance in Ilfracombe had paid off. I was sorry to leave Anthony to Nellie Beatrice but enthusiastic about the prospect of an actual salary again. Any instant escape must be better than tunnelling out from under that wooden horse in the suburbs. For the moment, she affected to like Anthony. She would not have been so welcoming to dear, brave little Aladdin.

17. 'Great Hatred Little Room'

The Bridgwater company was run by a couple called Diplock. They were a smugly uxorious pair who had cast themselves as civic figures of theatrical respectability. They were keen on crèches, children and actors who were clean-living and time-servers of the community. Diplock was thirtyish, like a costive slug, wore a grubby beret and an open-necked shirt as worn by the Outward Bound of the time. On holiday he might have relaxed in the healthy mufti of an aertex shirt and knee-length shorts. As he ran the company like a Scout troop trained to rub plays together to make community bonfires it was an appropriate uniform. His wife was similarly open-necked, eager and odious. The company was mostly inexperienced, stupid or corrupt enough to accept Diplock's theatrical scouting ethic. Ivor, the leading man, an amiable lecher, was protected from paying much lip-service to the Diplocks' bob-a-job thespianism by his proven box-office pull with the Mendip maidens. Bob, the character man, like Mr Wood Palmer had been a major in the army, which impressed Diplock, who had spent the war in a reserved occupation. He was the kind of man for whom reserved occupations were created. Partly because of his wartime rank and fulsome eccentricity, Bob's pre-war clowning camp was tolerated, along with his mocking adoration of Maisie Gay, Jessie Matthews, Naomi Jacobs and Mary Ellis. He was almost forty, did the work of three men for six pounds a week and shone like a naughty deed in an unctuous world. Within days he had declared his hopeless love for me. It was a discouraging beginning.

Bargaining with my instinct, I decided I could cope with scouting actors, matinée queens and hostile yokels. Bridgwater was a small market town and I had no idea of the kind of scrutiny the Diplocks' troops aroused among the locals. I had inherited the previous juvenile's digs. Apart from Ivor, he alone seemed to have won Bridgwater's flinty heart. My landlady said he was a lovely boy, which also meant that he must have been a pretty good Scout to the Diplocks. A bustling bundle of non-theatrical motherliness, she told me that I reminded her of her son, which took me back to the fox terrier in Grimsby. Fortunately this son was alive and working in London. Less fortunately, he had spurned his mother's advice, upset all the plans she had made for him and got married to a girl. The wording might have been Nellie Beatrice's own. The tautology was an exact one. Married – he was – to a girl. I had the impression that I too might develop into a fairly lovely boy, though not as lovely as the last one. For a start, I wouldn't get so many badges from the troop. The costive slug would see to that.

I was made welcome to the camp fire. It was evident that I was considered an acquisition to the troupe. It was puzzling. The first play I had to rehearse was a family comedy called *My Wife's Family*. I had naturally been cast as the lovely boy who opens the play being discovered with his arms round the housemaid and kissing her. This actress turned out to be a local girl who had been to RADA and returned to become one of the two ASMs in the company. Her home town was suspicious of her and resolute that she must only prove herself in Bridgwater under the fire of local ill-will. I was aware that I had left behind the sophistication and tolerance of the true provinces. Sprung from Fulham and Stoneleigh, where feelings rarely rose higher than a black look, the power of place, family and generation in small towns was new to me. In the suburbs, allegiances are lost or discarded on dutifully paid visits. The present kept itself to itself. In such a life there was no common graveyard for memory or future. The suburb has no graveyard.

Bridgwater's undoubted feelings about this one actress were muddled but obviously strong. My landlady hinted that she was wilful, even the kind of girl mother's sons went off and married. Renee's misery or future would never have aroused interest or speculation on the 8.17. In Stoneleigh you could be jilted in daylight and no one would come to your assistance. In Bridgwater it would still be discussed in your dotage. Local feeling was complicated. As professional players, even the Diplock company were interlopers living off the parish. Pamela Lane, even as a housemaid, had to be seen to excel over outsiders. Cravenly aware of the town's combined expectation and suspicion, the costive slug was cautious about giving her opportunities. There was a focus upon her that almost excluded the rest of us.

I was reminded of this by a story about Richard Burton. Wales is the well-guarded reserve of its natural and principal species, the amateur. Someone suggested that Burton be invited to lead a National Welsh Theatre. A distinguished leader of the principality asked what were Burton's qualifications. It was explained that he had played Henry V at Stratford and a Hamlet at the Old Vic applauded by Churchill. The reply, which evoked no surprise, was, 'Yes, I see that. But what has he done in Wales?'

*

Pamela's refusal to be drawn was the power of her sphynx's paw. I had not then realized it. She had just recently shorn her hair down to a defiant auburn stubble and I was impressed by the hostility she had created by this self-isolating act. I was unable to take my eyes from her hair, her huge green eyes which must mock or plead affection, preferably both, at least. I was sure of it, whether or not it was directed at me. She startled and confused me. The herd casting her out, as I saw it, drew me to her. There was no calculation in my instant obsession, no assessment, thought of present, future comfort or discomfort. I knew that I was in love as if the White Plague had claimed me earlier than I had calculated. I resigned myself to it, certain that indifference, including Pamela's own, would put out any smouldering excess of nature I might have thought my flesh or imagination heir to.

I waited for the curtain to go up, holding in my arms this powerful, drawn-up creature, dressed in a green maid's uniform of all things. Life was unimaginable without her matching green eyes. Pamela's emotional equivocation seemed so unstudied that I interpreted it as ineffable passion. It was as if she had once known a secret divinity that, in time, would reveal itself and her. With both of us rehearsing every morning and Pamela collecting props or furniture during the afternoon, we had little opportunity to be alone together. Rampant mystery would show itself like a blessed virgin to be taken into unfailing voluptuary. I began waiting for her to clear up the prop room before going back with her to the Lane Family Drapers. She made no excuses about my being uninvited beyond the door and I asked none. I had seen her parents and rugby-playing West Country brothers. I expected no gestures and looked for no quarter. What did surprise me was the tide of dislike that I had been able to attract and sustain so soon. The Diplocks, who could see pillars of salt in the desert of a Dorothy Perkins display window, became visibly cold. They put on disapproval like balaclavas, and with homely wartime style.

JIMMY: There is no limit to what the middle-aged mummy will do in the holy crusade against ruffians like me. Mummy and I took one quick look at each other, and, from then on, the age of chivalry was dead. I knew that, to protect her innocent young, she wouldn't hesitate to cheat, lie, bully and blackmail. Threatened with me, a young man without money, background or even looks, she'd bellow like a rhinoceros in labour – enough to make every male rhino for miles turn white, and pledge himself to celibacy. But even I under-estimated her strength. Mummy may look over-fed and a bit flabby on the outside, but don't let that well-bred guzzler fool you. Underneath all that, she's armour plated – (*He clutches wildly for something to shock* HELENA *with.*) She's as rough as a night in a Bombay brothel, and as tough as a matelot's arm. She's probably in that bloody cistern, taking down every word we say. (*Kicks cistern.*) Can you 'ear me, mother. (*Sits on it, beats like bongo drums.*) Just about get her in there.

Look Back in Anger, 1956

Pamela had her twenty-first birthday party in April and prevailed upon herself to prevail upon her parents to invite me. I am certain I said very little. Pamela especially said little to me. I had been asked for provocation and offered none. I was not to be tricked into kicking against the heavy scrum of heavy Somerset pricks. Pamela had said almost nothing to me about her parents or brothers and I still assumed her support if I should be tackled. Still, I had an aptitude for charging down the ball while avoiding it altogether. It meant I need rely on no one, least of all the love of the one I meant to rely on most.

JIMMY: Let me give you an example of this lady's tactics. You may have noticed that I happen to wear my hair rather long. Now, if my wife is honest, or concerned enough to explain, she could tell you that this is not due to any dark, unnatural instincts I possess, but because (a) I can usually think of better things than a haircut to spend two bob on, and (b) I prefer long hair. But that obvious, innocent explanation didn't appeal to Mummy at all. So she hires detectives to watch me, to see if she can't somehow get me into the *News of the World*. All so that I shan't carry off her daughter on that poor old charger of mine, all tricked out and caparisoned in discredited passions and ideals! The old grey mare that actually once led the charge against the old order – well, she certainly ain't what she used to be. It was all she could do to carry me, but your weight (*to* ALISON) was too much for her. She just dropped dead on the way.

Look Back in Anger, 1956

The Lanes hired a private detective to follow my movements after it had been reported that they had seen Bob fumbling with my knee under the table in a teashop. I don't know where the detectives might have come from. Minehead now seems likely. But the report was true. The more I insisted on my passion for Pamela, the more he insisted upon his own for me and, like

Gerald in Ilfracombe, tried to persuade me that at my age, 'I didn't know what I wanted'. Mr and Mrs Lane were much coarser characters than Alison's mother and father, but their tactics were similar. They were certainly farther down in the class scale, firmly entrenched in trade for generations, and all the family had Worzel-Somerset accents. Pamela herself still retained traces of a thick burr which RADA had not completely erased.

I began to feel surrounded and outflanked by hostility. I might have told myself that it emanated from Pamela's parents or even the Costive Slug but I had set off a crest of anger that had not been much more than drowsy before my arrival. Plainly I would not be able or allowed to stay in Bridgwater much longer. The Diplocks were touting for the merest grievance within the company to allow them to dismiss me as non-scouting material. This proved difficult. In spite of my general unpopularity, my coarse acting style had a perverted minority-following. Each actor had their band of admirers who helped to fill the theatre every week and even I had mine. The Diplocks couldn't discount or explain it. It surprised everyone, myself especially. It was scarcely important. Pamela was the battlement I was determined on.

HELENA: Oh for heaven's sake, don't be such a bully! You've no right to talk about her mother like that!

JIMMY: (*Capable of anything now*) I've got every right. That old bitch should be dead! (*To* ALISON.) Well? Aren't I right?

(CLIFF *and* HELENA *look at* ALISON *tensely, but she just gazes at her plate.*) I said she's an old bitch, and should be dead! What's the matter with you? Why don't you leap to her defence!

(CLIFF *gets up quickly, and takes his arm.*)

CLIFF: Jimmy, don't!

(JIMMY *pushes him back savagely, and he sits down helplessly, turning his head away on to his hand.*)

JIMMY: If someone said something like that about me, she'd react soon enough – she'd spring into her well-known lethargy, and say nothing! I say she ought to be dead. (*He breaks for a fresh spurt later. He's saving his strength for the knock-out.*) My God, those worms will need a good dose of salts the day they get through her! Alison's mother is on the way! (*In what he intends to be a comic declamatory voice.*) She will pass away my friends, leaving a trail of worms gasping for laxatives behind her – from purgatives to purgatory.

(*He smiles down at* ALISON, *but still she hasn't broken.* CLIFF *won't look*

at them. Only HELENA *looks at him. Denied the other two, he addresses
her.*) Is anything the matter?

HELENA: I feel rather sick, that's all. Sick with contempt and loathing.
(*He can feel her struggling on the end of his line, and he looks at her rather
absently.*)

JIMMY: One day, when I'm no longer spending my days running a sweet-
stall, I may write a book about us all. It's all here. (*Slapping his forehead.*) Written in flames a mile high. And it won't be recollected in
tranquillity either, picking daffodils with Auntie Wordsworth. It'll be
recollected in fire, and blood. My blood.

Look Back in Anger, 1956

Early in June I asked Pamela to marry me. She accepted at once, warmly
and casually. The problem was a plain one: to get married in secret. The
local registrar was a personal friend of Pamela's father, so the Registry
Office would be barred to us. I was in a vengeful mood but not one reckless
enough to risk horse whips and rioting in the streets of Bridgwater. I knew
nothing about the mechanics of getting married, so I went to the Public
Library and looked up *Whitaker's Almanack*. Pamela and I got on the train
to Wells and bought a special licence to get married within three days. It
cost four pounds, half a week's salary. Holding this, we then went to a local
vicar who scarcely knew Mr Lane and explained the situation. He was
cautiously sympathetic and agreed to marry us on Saturday morning at
eight o'clock, the earliest possible hour, before rehearsal at ten o'clock.

After the Friday evening performance, I broke the news to Bob, asking
him if he would be a witness. He fell to the floor, grasped me by the knees
weeping, and begged me not to do it. My landlady would have had second
thoughts about her lovely boy if she had brought in his supper at that
moment. Earlier I had approached Ivor, the leading man, to be my best
man. He seemed the most appropriate choice and agreed to it almost as
Pamela had done, as an absent-minded conspiracy.

JIMMY: The last time she was in church was when she was married to me. I
expect that surprises you, doesn't it? It was expediency, pure and
simple. We were in a hurry, you see. (*The comedy of this strikes him at
once, and he laughs.*) Yes, we were actually in a hurry! Lusting for the
slaughter! Well, the local registrar was a particular pal of Daddy's,
and we knew he'd spill the beans to the Colonel like a shot. So we had
to seek out some local vicar who didn't know him quite so well. But it
was no use. When my best man – a chap I'd met in the pub that

morning – and I turned up, Mummy and Daddy were in the church
already. They'd found out at the last moment, and had to come to
watch the execution carried out. How I remember looking down at
them, full of beer for breakfast, and feeling a bit buzzed. Mummy was
slumped over her pew in a heap – the noble, female rhino, pole-axed at
last! And Daddy sat beside her, upright and unafraid, dreaming of his
days among the Indian Princes, and unable to believe he'd left his
horsewhip at home. Just the two of them in that empty church – them
and me. (*Coming out of his remembrance suddenly.*) I'm not sure what
happened after that. We must have been married, I suppose. I think I
remember being sick in the vestry. (*To* ALISON.) Was I?

Look Back in Anger, 1956

Apart from the references to Daddy and the Indian Princes, it is a fairly
accurate description of our wedding. The vicar had lost his nerve at the last
moment and rung the Lanes. When we left the church and got to rehearsal
the whole of Bridgwater seemed to know what had taken place. The Saturday morning run-through in the theatre went on without interruption. Our
marriage seemed to have settled the cast's lines and moves wonderfully.
The Costive Slug looked more than ever as if he had been left to drown in a
slow drizzle, and was reported to be stalking the theatre, telling staff and
passers-by that he was about to get his service rifle (reserved, like his occupation, to harass the likes of me) and shoot me. In the event, he shook my
hands and mumbled some congratulations, saying that of course he couldn't
quite approve. I had my rehearsed answer lugubriously ready, which was
that my wife and I were giving him a week's notice. 'So stick your job up
your scoutmaster's arse.' I hope I did say it.

Mr Lane came to the theatre, more weary than angry, insisting that
Pamela and I should have lunch with them at whatever hostelry catered for
the town's Masons and Rotarians. We had pilchard salad and light ale in
almost complete silence apart from an occasional wracking sob from the
mottle-necked Mrs Lane. In the afternoon, we had a matinée and after the
evening performance I saw Pamela back home. To my relief, I was not
invited in. I was overcome with fatigue and the prospect of never-to-be-
consummated excess. When I returned to my digs, the landlady was in the
most motherly tears and told me what a wicked boy I was to have done such
a thing. Pamela and I played the week out. Gratifyingly and, by Saturday,
triumphantly, hardly a word was addressed to us. Well, not to me. The
following Sunday Mr Lane saw us off on the train to Paddington. We spent

our first night alone in a small hotel in the Cromwell Road, patronized by polite impoverished Indian students. We had £20 between us. I was in some kind of excess even if it was not shared.

The good fortune of friendship and the comfort of love

BILL: I am almost forty years old, and I know I have never made a decision which I didn't either regret, or suspect was just plain commonplace or shifty or scamped and indulgent or mildly stupid or undistinguished. As you must see. As for why I am here, I have to confess this: I have to confess that: that I have depended almost entirely on other people's efforts. Anything else would have been impossible for me, and I always knew in my own heart that only that it was that kept me alive and functioning at all, let alone making decisions or being quick minded and all that nonsense about me . . . That I have never really been able to tell the difference between a friend and an enemy, and I have always made what seemed to me at the time to make the most exhausting efforts to find out. The difference. But it has never been clear to me, and there it is, the distinction, and as I have got older, and as I have worked my way up – up – to my present position. I find it even more, quite impossible. And out of the question. And then, then I have always been afraid of being found out.

. . .

I never hoped or wished for anything more than to have the good fortune of friendship and the excitement and comfort of love and the love of women in particular. I made a set at both of them in my own way. With the first with friendship, I hardly succeeded at all. Not really. No. Not at all. With the second, with love, I succeeded, I succeeded in inflicting, quite certainly inflicting, more pain than pleasure. I am not equal to any of it. But I can't escape it, I can't forget it. And I can't begin again. You see?

Inadmissible Evidence, 1964

I felt I had acquitted myself in spite of Pamela's connivance. I was unable to take my eyes off her. I watched her eating, walking, bathing, making-up, dressing, undressing, my curiosity was insatiable. Seeing her clothes lying around the floor (she was hopelessly untidy, in contrast to my own spinsterish habits), I was captive, even to the contents of her open handbag and the few possessions she had brought with her, including her twenty-first birthday present from her parents, a portable typewriter on which I was to type *Look Back in Anger*.

There was little doubt in my otherwise apprehensive spirit that I had carried off a unique prize. It certainly never occurred to me that it might slip away from me. Perhaps I interpreted what might have been bland complacency for the complaisance of a generous and loving heart. Perhaps there is no question to ask. It may be a dull mind which poses unanswerable questions.

We had nowhere to live and little left of the twenty pounds. There was no question of my going to Stoneleigh and none at all of telling my mother that I had married a girl. She had turned Anthony Creighton out of the house after I had written to him in reply to his complaint about the way she was treating him. The landlady of Black Look on Sea had made him stay out during the daytime when he had nowhere to go, and so on. The alternative was her forcible feeding and feigned concern marked down by voracious caprice. In my letter I had made clear, possibly for the first time, my detailed feelings about Nellie Beatrice. Going through his pockets one day, in the way of motherly women, she discovered the letter and read it. Later, she insisted that I had, in fact, written the letter to her. 'When I think of that terrible letter you wrote to me.' 'I didn't write a letter to you. I wrote a letter to Anthony which you opened.' 'I shall remember it as long as I live, that terrible letter. I don't know what your father would have said if he'd read it. He wouldn't have let you say all those terrible things about me.'

After a few days of looking through newspaper advertisements and news-agents' windows ('No Blacks, No Irish' was not yet a preference accountable to tribunals), we decided on one room in a block of flats next to Richmond Bridge. It was a tired, necessary decision. Pamela's opinion was elusive. Mutual indecision might have expressed it all. The occupant was no land-lady but a colonial cast-off who agreed to rent us a room for £6 a week, on the condition that we played mah-jong with her in the evenings. The rent was three times what I had intended to pay, but the Cromwell Road hotel was out of the question for a longer stay. I did something which I had vowed never to do, like asking for unfancy salaries with other unqueer folk: I wrote to a manager called Harry Hanson who was a by-word for tatty, ill-paid, tyrannical, joyless work. He ran about half a dozen companies with queenly ruthlessness and he had a legendary wardrobe of various coloured wigs which he was said to change according to any bout of ill-humour he was indulging.

I had a swift reply and was summoned to the Palace Theatre, Camberwell, where I was interviewed, rather as I had been for *No Room at the Inn*, by a doomed, distracted queen who was later arrested for offences against young men on the train to Deptford and committed suicide before being brought to trial. I was further surprised to find myself hired. Hanson's companies were dreaded as the last funk-hole for any actor, but they were not easy to penetrate. If there was a Hanson kind of theatre, there was a Hanson kind of actor, unpersonable, defeated from the outset and grateful to have any sort of job at all. They were apologetic about themselves, if not among themselves. Equity representatives were unknown to speak, fluffs and dries were entered into a book by the stage director and other misdemeanours, if committed enough times, ensured the sack, administered literally according to the Hanson Book. He was the theatre's Gradgrind and his theatres were administered like workhouses of despair. Binkie would have seemed all Samuel Smiles in comparison. I had to accept and Pamela must cope with mah-jong. Besides, I was convinced that her prospects must be better than mine. To understudy in the West End was the goal, an ambition open to her if not to me.

Working in Camberwell was as unpleasant as I had anticipated and the company were docile, like prisoners without heart or spirit. The repertory of plays was vintage Hanson, consisting of pre-1920s' melodramas, learnt from 'Sides', *Coming through the Rye*, hack adaptations of *Dr Jekyll and Mr Hyde*, *Gaslight*, *Dracula*, *Frankenstein*, *Charley's Aunt* and low, forgotten farces. The audience was noisy and inattentive. Rehearsals were conducted in a guilty kind of haste and the actors were only given moves where not indicated in the script. We committed our lines as if we were sewing mailbags. No one dared fudge them or forget a move.

The journey across London from Richmond to Camberwell involved several changes, including a slow-moving tram from the Embankment to the theatre. The second house ended about eleven o'clock. I had little time for sleep and less for my wife. When my rehearsal finished at one o'clock I would get on the tram across the river to Charing Cross Station and we would sit in the Embankment gardens with a packet of sandwiches she had prepared and a flask of tea. After a couple of hours I made my way back across the river knowing that when I got home to Richmond almost a dozen hours later she must be asleep. In spite of the tram rattle from Camberwell to Richmond, Pamela soon declared herself pregnant. No, she didn't declare it, she mentioned it like a passing comment. Mention seemed all we could offer each other. Anthony's mother sent us a packet of something called Penny Royal pills, with instructions to take these together with gin and a hot bath. Country girl that she was, Pamela followed Mrs Creighton's bucolic wisdom and was rewarded. If she was relieved, she never expressed it, nor I my disappointment.

Dull and boring

'I do believe intensely in the creative value of struggle.' George Devine

I had less time to find work than I had for sex. Three months later the tardy Camberwell trams came to my rescue and I was sacked for being late twice. It probably had little to do with the trams. The Hanson companies operated a policy of spot sacking and I was no doubt selected by the director, in idle depression on the last train to Deptford, as being the most replaceable, and to encourage the others.

Camberwell had been a bleak period but it was over. I thought I knew that green eyes were smiling on me. For one thing, we had left Richmond. Our colonial landlady had decided that she didn't like having lodgers and particularly those who made tea in the kitchen and were unable to play mahjong. Anthony had recovered his downstairs flat in Hammersmith and we moved into one of his two rooms at Number 14 Caithness Road, just off Brook Green where Holst had taught the girls of St Pauls. Our room was dark but friendly. We shared Anthony's comfortable chintzy sitting-room and paid him thirty shillings. It seemed a fine arrangement. For no clear reason, the Labour Exchange abandoned its punitive attitude and urged me to draw the unemployment benefit they had contested for so long. We all talked about work. I dreaded and tried to avoid the journey from Hammersmith to the Charing Cross Road and the agents' offices, but Pamela and Anthony seldom accompanied me, keeping house in Caithness Road in case the telephone should ring.

Noel Coward, who could shoot a cliché between the eyes of a gnat and make it burst into flower about the potency of cheap music, also got it right about certain kinds of love for all kinds of people. 'We were so ridiculously over in love.' It was I who was ridiculously over in love. The melodrama of Bridgwater and the overlapping drudgery of Camberwell were gone. I tried to conceal, I think, I am afraid, successfully, the panic loneliness that gripped me in our pleasant room from day to day. I had never known anything like it and I could think of no way of discovering if she were as untroubled as she seemed.

In the New Year Pamela got herself what seemed, in view of her inexperience, a good job. She went to see an actor-manager, Philip Barrett, who offered her the leading role, Joanna, in a tour of *Present Laughter*. He was well known for having made a small living from touring narcissism, and marrying his leading lady, Eileen Herlie. He was still some improvement on Pat Desmond, and I found myself explaining why she should take the job, which she did. The tour was a short one, I would go on trying to get myself something and we would both save ourselves a little money. In the meantime, I had, so I said, decided to write another play. I had already spent most of my time between the Labour Exchange and the public library where, because of handy radiators, I would sit, write and try to take in the theology of Dante, 'with large sploshes of Eliot', as Jimmy Porter had it. The finished manuscript was written in longhand in three exercise books, which I gave to Pamela. She read it conscientiously and her verdict was characteristically bland, and possibly affectionate. 'Dull and boring'. The three words became a humourless bitter joke between us. If things weren't good, they were 'D and B'. Her own honesty, like so much else, possibly escaped her. My play was indeed Dull and Boring. The two words haunted me.

JIMMY: Thought of the title for a new song today. It's called 'You can quit hanging round my counter Mildred 'cos you'll find my position is closed.' (*Turning to* ALISON *suddenly.*) Good?

ALISON: Oh, very good.

JIMMY: Thought you'd like it. If I can slip in a religious angle, it should be a big hit. (*To* HELENA.) Don't you think so? I was thinking you might help me there. (*She doesn't reply.*) It might help you if I recite the lyrics. Let's see now, it's something like this:

> I'm so tired of necking,
> of pecking, home wrecking,
> of empty bed blues –
> just pass me the booze.
> I'm tired of being hetero
> Rather ride on the metero
> Just pass me the booze.
> This perpetual whoring
> Gets quite dull and boring
> So avoid that old python coil
> And pass me the celibate oil.
> You can quit etc.

No?

CLIFF: Very good, boyo.

JIMMY: Oh, yes, and I know what I meant to tell you – I wrote a poem
while I was at the market yesterday. If you're interested, which you
obviously are. (*To* HELENA.) It should appeal to you, in particular. It's
soaked in the theology of Dante, with a good slosh of Eliot as well. It
starts off 'There are no dry cleaners in Cambodia!'

CLIFF: What do you call it?

JIMMY: 'The Cess Pool'. Myself being a stone dropped in it, you see –

CLIFF: You should be dropped in it, all right.

HELENA: (*To* JIMMY) Why do you try so hard to be unpleasant? (*He turns
very deliberately, delighted that she should rise to the bait so soon – he's
scarcely in his stride yet.*)

JIMMY: What's that?

HELENA: Do you have to be so offensive?

JIMMY: You mean now? You think I'm being offensive? You underestimate
me. (*Turning to* ALISON.) Doesn't she?

HELENA: I think you're a very tiresome young man.

Look Back in Anger, 1956

She played a date near London and I went to see her. She had a playmaker's tailored effective scene in the second act with Philip Barrett who
was taking himself more seriously than those servants of the Master himself. She wore a purple taffeta dress, and her hair and eyes seemed redder
and greener than ever. I could think of nothing like her. She seemed also to
have become a rather good actress, certainly better, more stylish and more
beautiful than Stella had made seem possible to me. Later, I might have
described the impact as her habitual, frenzied torpor. But when the tour was
over she seemed relaxed, reassured and happy. I was delighted to have her
back and, for a while, we achieved some sort of drifting mutual purpose and
made no effort to look for work. Being a leading lady, even to Philip Barrett,
instead of a despised assistant stage manager humping furniture and props
through the streets of her own small town, had exhilarated her, and I told
myself and Anthony that she had acquired a quickening sparkle, or something speakably like it.

I managed to get an odd week's work here or there around London, places
like Hayes and Dartford. On Coronation Day, 2 June 1952, I was performing in a play in Dartford about the Festival of Britain. I came back every

night by train with an actress in the company, committing what President Carter and others unknown were to call Adultery in my Heart. On the eve of Coronation night, after the performance, we arrived at Charing Cross Station which was like the London Underground during the war, covered with slumbering bodies. It was pouring with rain and I had to walk most of the way back to Hammersmith, cursing Her Majesty's loyal lemmings. When I got back to Caithness Road at about four in the morning, Pamela was waiting – was it over-patiently? – for me and gave me my supper tray in bed. She looked agreeably sardonic, unchastening and secure in the belief that I had been committing adultery somewhere between Deptford and Hammersmith, and not only in my rheumaticky heart. If it implied reproof, it might just as well have implied love. I was too tired and depressed to accept either explanation.

My next job was working for the Under Thirty Theatre group at Frinton-on-Sea. Frinton, nearly thirty years ago, was about as untheatrical a town as one could imagine and I don't suppose it has changed. Its immovable feature was its middle-class characterlessness, rather like visiting the reproductions department in a large store. It was full of villas, bungalows and 1930s' concrete bunkers where the *Radio Times* was contained in an embossed leather cover. Nannies went there for the summer with their charges, group captains and admirals retired there and nuns recuperated from vespers. The theatre, which was a small hall, reflected some of this in its own company which seemed to have been selected deliberately by class. Bridgwater, Leicester and Camberwell, especially, had all been made up from lower middle- and working-class actors. If Camberwell never reflected Camberwell, Frinton seemed consciously to reflect Frinton.

I had been in the theatre for less than four years, suddenly I had unknowingly joined a golf club and I knew that I could expect a short stay by that kind of seaside, admitted by a careless secretary. Old ladies arrived in chauffeur-driven Rolls Royces to performances of more or less chauffeur-driven plays. I lasted about three weeks. No reason was given and it would have been bad form and obvious to ask. Like Camberwell, relief set in immediately. The sack was becoming my only feasible work satisfaction. I was replaced by a juvenile straight from RADA and Wellington called James Villiers, who seemed an absolutely Frinton-type of actor, which indeed is what he has successfully become. The last production in rehearsal was *The Deep Blue Sea* and a young actor came down to play the judge, a part for which he was far too young. He was definitely not Frinton, more of a gypsy, I thought. His name was Peter Nichols.

Pamela worked on and off for Philip Barrett, who seemed to respect her as a useful and cheap leading lady for his tours. Pat Desmond sent for me, offering me a part as a sailor and ASM in a tour of *Rain*, with Stella as Sadie. I was hesitant and defensive. I felt wary of Stella. Tenderness is a self-abusing word, implying lesser emotions of gratitude and nostalgia, which is what I more or less felt for her. I was liberated from her but had no wish to demonstrate it. I would have preferred her to think of me as affectionate, as I was, and dependent, which I wasn't, rather than a forgetful little ingrate.

I didn't tell Pamela about Stella 'leading' the company as it was then described. Being a Desmond production, I assumed that there would be no details about it in the *Stage* for Equity to look into. Stella made clear her lack of interest in me but without much pleasure. Similarly, I noted that she was not very good and assuredly never had been. She wore a blonde wig as Sadie, which helped to make a caricature of my remembrance. It was a dull production for all the sounding brassiness of her performance and Pat's billing 'For Adults Only'. Business was poor, morale was low and after a few weeks the tour came to an end.

Stella was impatient to go and I was the least reason. When I got back to Caithness Road, Pat rang me. As ever, he was transparently offhand, a little proud and sadistic as he told me that Stella had had to pack her trunks in a hurry and leave for America. The Inland Revenue men were closing in around the screens and Holloway was no date for someone of Stella's class. When I next saw her in Los Angeles ten years later we hardly recognized each other. She had become an American and, worse, an American blonde. There was no trace of the middle-class English gypsy, if there had ever been any. She regarded me as foreign in the way that only Americans assume, without doubt or suspicion. She might almost have talked about Brighton, England. As it was, she talked about a television programme involving puppets for which she wanted money. I made a pretence of interest which could scarcely have deceived even a foreigner. I couldn't quite bring myself to pretend enthusiasm for puppets, on television or off. As I saw her out, she walked towards a man some twenty years younger than herself, got into her car, an old MG, and drove off. The MG was the only English thing left about her. I am sure we would have both been relieved if I had after all slipped her the few hundred dollars I had ready in my pocket.

I spent the summer of 1953 as Juv. Char. at Kidderminster. The director was a red-veined, boozy poof called Gaston, the men all queer save the character man. I shared an underground dressing-room with the leading man who, like my own family, talked and never listened – in his case, about afternoon tennis and night-time guardsmen, and his prowess at both. The girls were dull on the whole, but better than your average brick walls. Pamela's absence was a sore aphrodisiac. Most companies resisted employing married couples, but I was hopeful. I still thought Pamela was my awarded prize to myself. The unknowing clouds of unwanted detachment faded when we were not together. I was certain that it would not be long before I would get myself into a company like Birmingham or the Bristol Old Vic. Kidderminster courted producers, directors and journalists from Birmingham to come and see us. The leading man in Birmingham was Paul Daneman, who was hailed weekly by the local press as the next Laurence Olivier. Somewhere like Birmingham would pay off, just as Simpson's had paid off in Llandudno.

Kidderminster was sleepily agreeable, quite unlike Bridgwater or Camberwell, but I was incautious enough to think I was worth more than eight pounds a week. The leading man went off to find his guardsmen elsewhere and was unreplaced, leaving me as an accepted but inadequate fill-in. I demanded a rise of £1 which was refused without thought by the management, cheered on by the chairman of the local amateur dramatic society which paid our salary and hated us heartily for it. Pamela went in the autumn to Derby as leading lady. These titles were absurd but contractually definable. The Kidderminster Amateurs made their point easily and I left. Pamela seemed to be doing well at Derby. Like me, she thought that the prejudice against employing married actors could be overcome.

We had spent a little time together before she went up to Derby and a few weeks later she wrote saying that she thought she was pregnant again. Her letter, as always, was hard to interpret. She might have been displeased or dismayed. Delight would have been no less communicable. The Penny Royal pills may have been put to work again but the crisis stole away as it had come. She had scored a success, which was talked of in Derby during the following weeks, as Pamela Tanqueray. At Christmas I was working again at Blythe Road Post Office, as we had both done the Christmas before. Anthony had started work in a debt-collecting organization in Oxford Street.

My separation from Pamela had no consolation now that I was not working. There was no thought of prizes, only loss. I was absorbed in loss, unmistakable loss, inescapable loss, unacceptable to all but gamblers. It still needed the croupier's nod, the bland confirmation from Pamela herself.

She wrote to me saying that Mr Twelvetrees, the director, had agreed to employ me and that I could join her at once. The first night I went up to Derby I watched her play the leading role of Hester in *The Deep Blue Sea*. It was a popular choice in repertory at the time. The prize was there, all right, looking better than ever and I couldn't believe it possible that it might be slipping away. Afterwards, in bed, she said uncomplainingly that she found marriage and a career difficult. Sweet unreason was unanswerable, demoralizing as it did unconfident reason or passion. It was hard to believe that she had even uttered this women's magazine cliché about career and marriage or to guess at the kind of arrangement she had in mind. She had none. Not only weariness made me refrain from asking. Women's Lib was a far-off aberration like Concorde, the Common Market or the National Theatre. The absurdity was patent, but without malice. Almost soothingly, she had absent-mindedly wiped our slate out.

18 John Osborne, Woodfall Street, 1957.

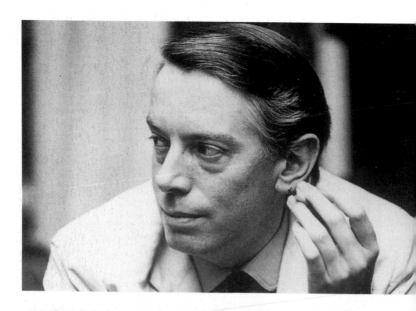

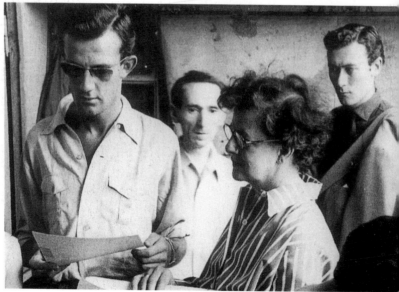

19 Kenneth Tynan.
20 Tony Richardson, Oscar Lewenstein, Margaret 'Percy' Harris and
John Osborne in discussion about the set for the Russian production of
Look Back in Anger.

21 The golden couple: John Osborne and Mary Ure, 1957.

22 Mary Ure in New York's Vegetarian Restaurant, 1957.

23 Elaine Tynan and Mary Ure, Sandy Wilson's flat.

24 Brenda de Banzie and Laurence Olivier in *The Entertainer*,
Royal Court Theatre, 1957.

25 *The Entertainer* at the Royal Court Theatre, 1957: *left to right*, Dorothy Tutin,
Richard Pasco, Brenda de Banzie, Laurence Olivier.

27 Laurence Olivier as Archie Rice in *The Entertainer*.

Royal Court
Theatre

Sloane Square S.W.1

English Stage Company

The Entertainer

by

John Osborne

6"

First performance on Wednesday, April 10th, 1957.

27 Laurence Olivier as Archie Rice in *The Entertainer*.
28 Cover of the original programme for *The Entertainer*.

29 Oscar Lewenstein.
30 Neville Blond.

31 Joan Plowright, George Devine and John Osborne in *The Making of Moo*,
Royal Court Theatre, 25 June 1957.

32 John Osborne and Mary Ure at home.

18. On the Pier at Morecambe

We were rehearsing *You Never Can Tell* in which I was to play the dentist. It was a tedious part and I knew I was giving a wretched performance. After the Monday dress rehearsal, I was unable to think about the opening night at all. I could only watch and listen to Pamela delivering her dull, unfluffed lines. In the hour or so before the performance, she listened to me berating her about Bridgwater, the calumnious testimony of her friend Lynne Reid Banks to her parents, my defeat in the face of such an immovable sense of detachment. She offered no explanation or opinion and a sickening tooth-ache overcame me. She immediately made me an appointment with a nearby dentist, and offered to accompany me. 'I'll come with you,' are truly the words of estrangement. I was to hear them more than once. I found the dentist, unaided. He took out two of my teeth, leaning on my chest and tugging at them as they crunched like rocks in my head. 'You've got teeth like a horse,' he said chattily. Minutes later I was hovering over Shaw's dentist's chair in my white jacket, mouthing his facetious lines with a gum-ful of blood. When I went to sleep that night Pamela read through the play for rehearsal the next day in bed. Most of it was already in her head.

John Dexter was as well known and speculated about in Derby as Pamela in Bridgwater. He visited the theatre every week and would often come round to our digs on Sunday evenings. He seemed always to have just returned from Stratford, the latest opening in London, had read the newest book reviewed in the Sunday papers and got the latest prize hit musical LP over from America. He had no job, lived with his mother and father in a terraced house near the railway where his father had worked all his life as a railwayman. His flaunted indolence, or sponging off his father as it was interpreted, made him unpopular. There were other speculations about him and his companions, the local homosexual mafia. In those pre-Wolfenden days a discreet heavy mob provided the audience for touring theatre. The Ram Gopal and Ballet Nègres companies, middlebrow *Soldiers in Skirts*, were largely sustained by it.

Unlike Blanche du Bois I had never depended upon the kindness of strangers, and I had no more reason to look for it in Derby than Bridgwater. Pamela's star rose like the weekly returns, with the management and the committee in particular. She must have longed for me to go. The committee made an issue out of insisting that the company take coffee with them after the Saturday rehearsal. Pamela, the only member of the company who might carry weight in the face of the bullying board of amateurs, pledged her support to my boycott of this time-wasting imposition. But, like the St Michael's contract, it was only observed by me. My undisguised dissatisfaction was again the reason given for the sack. Pamela was offered and accepted a renewed contract for the next season on better terms. I went alone back to the room in Caithness Road.

> 'She's a very cold woman, my wife, my wife. Very cold. What you might call a moron glacée. Well, I have a go lady, I do, I have a go.'

Pamela went on holiday to Switzerland with the dentist from Derby. Not only was he rich, a member of the Theatre Committee, but, before going to work on my teeth, had, it seemed, made me the town cuckold. Only sphinxes conceal such banal secrets. Dentistry was not then a profession that provoked much gratitude and the events had a logic of sorts.

It was the summer of 1954. Work was hard to come by. The McCarthy trials were at their height and I drove myself to some interest in them, thinking that Pamela must still declare herself. I spent several weeks in the American Library in Grosvenor Square, reading transcripts of the Un-American Activities Committee, taking them back home and going over them with Anthony Creighton. Out of laziness or want of companionship I agreed to write a play with him based on his own melodramatic plot. Perhaps I felt that with my writing and editing of the transcript it could be turned into a superior kind of Patrick Desmond package, specious liberalism sentimentalized like *Because I Am Black*.

We wrote the play quickly. Knowing him to be a publicized victim of the Un-American Activities Committee I sent a copy to Sam Wanamaker at the St James's Theatre, where he was playing in a successful production of *The Country Girl* with Michael Redgrave. He wrote back almost immediately, asking me to go and see him in his dressing-room. I went round to see Mr Wanamaker in his dressing-room, who told me he liked the play very much, that he would dearly like to do it but that he felt the British public was incapable at that stage of accepting something so critical of America. Timidity will go to curious lengths to needlessly explain itself.

I had also sent a copy to Patrick Desmond, who was baffled by the material but impressed by Wanamaker's tepid endorsement. What did concern him were the homosexual inferences. The first thing to do, Pat said, was to make sure the play could get a licence before he could put it on the road as For Adults Only entertainment. We had a stand-up toxic lunch at the Salisbury and proceeded to St James's Palace where we had an appointment to meet the Assistant Comptroller. I was convinced nothing could come of it, knowing I could make out no case for the play, in which I had little belief or enthusiasm. Pat was brimming over with draught Bass and blew Panatella smoke all over the Palace telephonists, who invited defilement like the full page photograph of the week's forthcoming bride in *Country Life*. These girls, faced with consummation from one shire to dubious county, tried to send us off but Pat persisted and we got as far as the amiable Guards Officer who had heard of *someone* reading the play. 'Bloody funny, old boy. We all thought it quite clear: been rodgering her *all* night! I mean, *no* question! Can't do that, I'm afraid.'

In October I went for an audition for the part of Freddy Eynsford Hill in an Arts Council tour of Wales with *Pygmalion*. Before I went in, the stage director told me that the part had been cast already. The director was a Welshman, which discouraged me further, but I read well. He told me immediately that he had already cast the part but was I prepared to stage manage as well? He was a director of the Bristol Old Vic, persuasive, and I was so fired by my own reading that even stage managing again seemed a tolerable alternative to my room in Hammersmith.

The Arts Council took *Pygmalion* through South Wales and the Rhondda. I thought of my father and Pamela. The work was gruelling and soothing, setting up daily in tiny halls and miners' institutes, and the audiences indeed kept a welcome still in the valleys, long after the war and memories of Thorndikes or Greeks. Apart from the St George saturation tour, I had never done one-night stands before but I enjoyed the concert- party idea of it. The Arts Council were hardly the Dinky Doos and the company was dull. Anew McMaster would surely never have employed such actors, who completed the *Daily Telegraph* crossword during rehearsals and would have been always ahead of the queue in the BBC canteen. The actress who played Eliza looked as if she might be anxious to discuss gynaecological mysteries with someone, especially me, but I was able to avoid her even when she invaded my room in Llangollen complaining of ghosts. I had one day off a week from stage management and I enjoyed walking in the Welsh countryside on my own. Playing Freddie was more enjoyable than the snivelling cissy

Marchbanks I had played in *Candida* and I achieved a round of cheap Welsh applause soon after I delivered my first line in the tea-party scene. It was a happier business than playing Shaw's dismal dentist anyway and The Man from The Arts Council seemed pleased.

The play itself was enjoyable to perform and to watch from within. There was an almost cosy feel about it which is scarcely a word one would apply to Shaw, who usually sounds like a giddy spinster or a eunuch who has slipped into something unsuitable when he strives after emotion. Shaw avoided passion almost as prudently as Coward. Frigidity and caution demand an evasive style and they both perfected one. Possibly, the slipper scene in *Pygmalion* is touching in spite of Shaw, but I watched it almost every night. Thrown slippers seem the exactly right comeuppance for a cold pedantic heart. The tour ended, promises about the Bristol Old Vic came to nothing and I found myself working again at Christmas for the GPO.

Anthony had left the debt collectors in Oxford Street and was working as a night-time operator at the telephone exchange, something of a sinecure for unemployed homosexuals. He had told me about two middle-aged women employed at the debt collectors who had both taken a kind of appalling fancy to him and of the crude plot he had worked on around this sickly theme. I supplied the title, *Epitaph for George Dillon*, without much enthusiasm. Collaboration with Anthony was less attractive to contemplate than it had been with Stella but it had the advantage of being undisturbed by sexual emotions, at least on my own part. I left the more tedious playmaking passages (what Stella probably called exposition) which Anthony was eager to do and concentrated on those scenes and aspects which interested me, like the entire Ruth–George scene in the second act and Barney Evans himself. It was cobbled together haphazardly in this way in less than three weeks.

Anthony seemed fired by a Damascus vision of wealth and fame coming from his dalliance with spinsters in Hendon and mums in Croydon. I had thought of him as a dedicated dabbler and his sudden faith and unlikely energy were infectious. We worked together like a pair of weekend decorators, sloshing away happily and separately, intent on getting the job done as quickly and cheaply as possible. The paint ran and the joins showed but it was exhilarating to find oneself doing it all without help from outside playmakers. Besides, I had nothing else to occupy me, and Anthony took my instruction and could never strive to be the kind of man that Stella could become. I could enjoy the rare control of a circumscribed involvement.

Critics were to point out that someone called Anthony Creighton had imposed a discipline on me which I had been unable to exercise on myself in the writing of *Look Back in Anger*. The typing was indisputably all mine and we sent copies to the leading agents, managements and Patrick Desmond. I thought he might have enjoyed Barney Evans as an effective third-act scene-stealer if not as a simple joke against himself. It seemed tolerable playmaking to me, but his response was irritable and dismissive. 'I just don't know what you think you're getting at.' The principal tenet of playmaking being that no one in the world must fail to know what you were getting at, he was losing the patience Stella had abandoned to him. It was discouraging to Anthony's reveries of sausage, mash and diamond tie pins. Few who returned the scripts bothered to point out our mistakes to us, even the odious Henry Sherek, who had made some bizarre cultural reputation by presenting *The Family Reunion*. Stella would never have countenanced my title. Later, Donald Albery, no mean sawbones of the drama, insisted on it being changed before agreeing to transfer it to the Comedy Theatre. The word 'epitaph' was bad box office, he explained. Having little feeling about it, I agreed. Most Americans tell me that it is my best play. They are a trusting race.

One agent who did express insistently cautious interest was Emmanuel Wax. He was forming what he called the Haymarket Group, a collection of would-be playwrights who could meet once every month to discuss their problems. The belief that the mere fatuity of discussion in itself would eliminate or ease problems was not then orthodox as it is now. I went twice to these meetings when we were addressed by two of his clients, Denis Cannan and Christopher Fry, on our craft. The only comfort I can remember is that the audience was left as despondent as myself. Jimmy Wax, who sub-sequently became Harold Pinter's agent, was as morose as the playwrights he discouraged. He practised as a solicitor in the Haymarket and his office was directly opposite Frith Banbury's who seemed to be his only theatrical contact. When I gave him both *Epitaph for George Dillon* and *Look Back in Anger* he said despairingly, 'Well I gave it to Frith and he didn't like it.'

*

Caithness Road,
W.14.

The Dancing Bear: 'Why does the bear dance?' asks the Jew. 'Because he has no wife.'

More than neutrality, and less than enthusiasm.

Christianity makes the most noise. Does it?

Living in the waste we call time, the feeling of inevitable change, even destruc-tion. This is tragic, noble even, this is time – not eternity which is neither.

The disease of mistaking words for things.

He is continually to be seen attending divine lip-service.

He put him in his place all right – but was it the right place?

I commanded the Maharajah's army. How could I fail to be moved as our special train pulled out for the last time, taking us away from the army, the palaces and gardens, and back to the country I had not seen for thirty years.

The present state of WHORECRAFT.

You know ever since I went into the bank as a clerk, I had just one ambition. I made up my mind that as soon as I could afford to, I was going to travel to and from work in a first class carriage every day – and by the time I could afford to, they'd done away with first class carriages on that line. That's your damned Socialism for you.

I could have slept with a score of women and never lost faith with her. She could betray me twice in an hour with a twist of the shoulder or simply a silence.

Her technique is prodigious: when you consider that she is drawing off an account that doesn't even exist. Without deposit, and, in spite of those bent, mean gestures and those insensitive, cautious hands – bingo – she produces the goods. Her acting is not even art; simply a game of bingo. It must be bingo – otherwise one's whole attitude to art collapses. After all, there are Big Bingos and Little Bingos. Eh? One day, she may be in the Big Richard Burton Bingo class, and critics will talk about the tragic mystery behind her eyes.

It convinces because it is detailed *and* outrageous.

Discussing sex as if it were the Art of Fugue.

Humour is a kind of disappointment.

Hanging things up on a wall where there's no hook.

'I must take particular care not to acquire any followers'. *Kyd.*

'The greatest enjoyment of existence is to live in danger.' *Nietzsche.*

'Don't bury me in this vest,' she said. 'You have it.' Lovely drawers she had. Real Wolsey.

'If you die with bedsores, mother, I'll get into trouble if they find bedsores on your body. I'm responsible for your *body*!

'Don't like those glasses she wears.'

'What glasses?'

'Those glasses she wears.'

'Well, they're all the fashion, mother, whether you like them or not.'

'Blondie I've always called her.'

'If you mean her hair's dyed, you're all wrong, mother. It's been like that for years. I've known her for twenty years.'

'You can always tell – the roots.'

'What do you mean – roots.'

'The roots of the hair – they're dark. That's how you can tell.'

'Well, I don't care if she does dye her hair – she's a damn nice girl.'

'Girl – look she's no girl.' Pause. 'She hasn't been a girl for a long time.'

'Well, *I* call her a girl. What do you want me to say – woman?'

You may think I'm a lost cause, but I thought that if you loved me, it wouldn't matter.

I grieve deeply, not that he is dead, but that I cannot feel his loss.

Trivial people suffer trivially.

Pamela: Phoney phrases like: Know that I shall always have a 'loving need for you'. Loving balls! And, of course, 'Deep, polished wood.'

Letter to Pamela, 1 January

My dear,

Thank you very much for the two pounds. A sudden inexplicable fortune out of the blue – I am very grateful indeed.

I say 'inexplicable' because there was no note with the money, and I cannot understand what moved you to send it to me. It's difficult to believe concern for me to be your nature. On the other hand, expensive gestures of contempt are hardly in your line either. However, I suppose I should give up trying to work out your weird emotional processes and content myself with the fact that you were good and kind enough to send me this money.

Perhaps you were irritated because, although I was not too proud to accept your money, I wasn't able to return your rather cosy expression of fraternity in your last letter. Make no mistake – for the money I am sincerely grateful. But your setting up as a kind of emotional soup kitchen to your grubby husband is something else. If you had any understanding or real – and not simulated – feelings at all, you must know what a bitter taste this kind of watery gruel must have. What you may put in a registered envelope and send to me, I accept but spare me the cheesey charity of your feelings. Again, thank you for the money.

She's always so *regal*.

I suspect him of being anxious to avoid giving offence. It is an awful thing to say of anyone, and I hope I am not being unjust.

He is one of those people who answers that the truth must necessarily be unpleasant.

Every time that telephone rings something dies.

Very Important Prig.

The last thing he will give up is his suffering.

Throwing in suffering, to make up for deficiency in emotion.

There are no dry cleaners in Cambodia.

Spineless, cliquish, spinsterly, Pharaisaical and intellectually immodest – [Who could that have been?]

That point at which extreme sensibility becomes vulgarity.

There's a Smoke Screen In My Pubic Hair.

Our imperial preference for each other.

She thinks like a man – a particularly stupid oaf of a man.

Her touch is like a gelding iron.

Her life is the great unsaid. What she dreads most is the terrible, enforced necessity of being articulate.

What makes it pornographic is its lack of either intimacy or passion.

Some people marry for revenge. He's one of them. They both are.

'My dear,
     I must get away. I don't suppose you will understand, but please try. I need peace so desperately, and, at the moment, I am willing to sacrifice anything just for that. I don't know what's going to happen to us, I know you will be feeling wretched and bitter, but try to have patience. I shall

always have a deep, loving need of you.' *Alison*. [Pamela's own words as surely expressed as she had 'dull and boring'.]

With a voice like the death of kings.

In a state of casual FUNK.

He suffers from excessive aspiration. He sweats blood too freely, the stain of endeavour underneath his armpits throws off a constant odour of ideals.

Wet and (plumper), when she's angry, she seems to come down in buckets.

Sex conscious, clothes conscious, music conscious – even radiation conscious. If ever it were possible to be obsessively self-conscious and unconscious at the same time, now is the time all right.

What are they doing to women? The model ideal of superb meanness, a long slink of classical contempt. It begs for defilement.

We are no longer their equals.

The pedantry of indifference.

It is impossible to escape failure.

We cover ourselves by not bothering.

If you haven't bothered, you can't be humiliated.

A worm who has managed to convince everyone that he's got a bird's eye view of what's going on.

Her expression cold; like the school lavatory seat in December.

In playwriting there's some small philosophy.

They criticize me because I don't assume virtues I haven't got.

You can have it, but you're not welcome to it.

We may live in the age of the Common Man, but, my God, how we hate him in ourselves.

The urge to *please* above all. I don't have it and can't achieve it. A small thing but more or less mine own.

The Welfare State: everyone moping about having to bear the burden of everyone else.

Thoughts for 1954

Irresponsible (wage) claims.
Wage restraint.
There are indications that the situation is in hand.
The credit squeeze.

'The nation needs a stronger bit. I did not know the horse was quite so fiery until it saw the oats of freedom.'
'We need to prune our roses to get better blossoms.'
'. . . review . . . and bring into line with present day . . .'
'regain the pioneering spirit with which our ancestors turned barbarous wastes into cultivated land.'
'vigorous imperial patriotism.'
'If I can help somebody . . .'
'We will walk together through the years to come . . .'
'Industrial disputes.'
'Co-partnership schemes.'
'Peace and prosperity.'
'His trying and difficult task.'
'An interesting alternative.'
'He urged that no decision should be taken.'
'A matter for more concern.'
'Would disrupt the agreements between them.'
'Doing our best to sell our jet-bombers in Germany.'
'However great the ideological differences.'
'We must try to live together.'
'The atomic stalemate.'
'I don't seek to deny that at all.'
'You will recall yourself.'
'Solidarity is essential.'
'In a sober mood.'
'Resumption within the framework of.'
'Freedom to sell arms to Germany.'
'Mutual inspection and control.'
'A means of creating contacts between East and West.'
'There's a military and strategic answer to everything.'
'A "get tough" policy.'
'Negotiation.'
'A Climate.'

'Very well received.'
'An atmosphere of freedom.'
'A nuclear and electronic age.'
'Talking point.'
'Ah, *training* for later life.'
'Broad issues.'
'The most important aspect.'
'A grave and growing public resentment.'
'It has been generally recognised.'
'The organisers of planned foolery: the experts.'
'BOOM BRITAIN.'
'Let the full searchlight of opinion be allowed to shine into every dark corner.'
'The paper with a twinkle in its eye.'

The great English virtue, old age.

He prides himself on his horse sense.
It must be the horse I always back.

Happiness means not looking backwards.

Making the other chap feel dowdy and old-fashioned.

Notebook, 1954

*

The entry for 4 May 1955 in my pocket diary reads tersely: 'Began writing *Look Back in Anger*.'
Thursday, May 5th: Vicki [my dog] died.
Friday, May 6th: *Look Back in Anger*, Act 1 finished.
Wednesday, May 11th: Saw *The Boyfriend*.
Friday, May 13th: Went to see *Hedda Gabler*.

This production of *Hedda Gabler* was the first time I saw George Devine. I knew nothing of his reputation, only that he might have done unnecessary damage at the Young Vic to Veronica Wells, already somewhat maimed by a cloying talent. The play was presented at the Lyric, Hammersmith, with Peggy Ashcroft playing Hedda and Micheál MacLiammóir as Judge Brack. The marquee risk of Henry Gibson's name was underwritten by the name of the leading lady, explaining a possible Tennent aberration, and it was difficult to get cheap seats.

Anthony and I had taken in a lodger, a youngish Pakistani businessman. He had knocked on the door one day asking if we had any rooms. He was a desperate man: 'No Blacks or Irish', and Mr Siddiqui passed for black in Hammersmith. We gratefully offered him the room Pamela and I had shared for thirty shillings a week with cooked breakfast, and half our rent was found. He left early and returned late and shivered in unshakeable good humour in his room, never taking off his dark overcoat even in the summer evenings. Like a happy mascot who had wandered in from the street, we soon felt fond and responsive, asking him to listen to the radio with us. Sitting in his hat and overcoat he chuckled joyfully at things like *The Goons* and *Take It From Here.* A pleasure to please is how Nellie Beatrice would have described him. He seemed set to sipping Anthony's gin from Ramadan to Christmas. He had a giggling turn of phrase, full of Raj archaisms and cultural references like, 'Oh, we will be having the most jolly top-hole time, as Thomas Hardy, the author of *Far from the* Maddening *Crowd,* would have it.' He seemed to have decided that the two of us shared sybaritic tastes which differed from Anthony's. He had been occasionally boastful about his textiles. But his wife and children were shrugged off as a burdensome pride. One evening, returning earlier than usual, he clasped me round the shoulder saying, 'Well, John old boy, why do the two of us not go out together tonight? We will go out and get bleeding well drunk like two bloody sailors, and then, by the Jove, we will go up to the Hammersmith Palace of Dancing and pick up a couple of girls. Now what do you say?'

Mr Siddiqui's invitation itself was tempting but not what it promised. Remembering his reference to Hardy, I wondered if H. Gibson might ring some leftover memory implanted by the recent King-Emperor. I suggested that we go out and get somewhat drunk, though not perhaps like sailors at such an early hour, take in the Henry Gibson show, and then go on to the Palace of Dancing and pick up two most top-hole English virgins. English womanhood in Hammersmith that night was uppermost in his mind and I pointed out that one of the finest examples was playing the leading role at the theatre we would visit. He accepted this at once and we set out, dropping into the George Hotel where Veronica Wells was still working part-time with all twelve volumes of Proust still on display behind her for any Irish or Blacks to see. I bought our tickets with his money quickly, and when he settled into the front row of the Lyric Theatre, he looked a little puzzled. Disappointment was forbidden alcohol to him but, even sustained by beer and whisky, he restrained the peevish disappointment he must have been feeling. In the first interval he turned to me and said, 'There are not seeming to be many girls in this performance. When are we leaving? It is most extremely jolly boring.' I assured him that the play would not be lasting very much longer and that the most interesting girls would turn up later at the dance when we would have the time to get really and most truly drunk like bloody sailors. I got him away from the theatre bar and he went back trustingly to his seat.

On Tuesday, 17th May the diary reads: Act II, Scene I finished. Friday, 20th May: Morecambe.

An agent had rung me with an offer of a week's work at Morecambe to play in *Seagulls over Sorrento*. The part was so small that only one day's rehearsal was necessary. However, it did mean £12 and my train fare back to the provinces. I could work on my play, the weather was warm and sunny and the town beginning to fill up. Visiting the theatre for a few minutes in the evenings, I could go down to the end of the pier every morning and spend the day in the sunshine.

On Thursday, 26th of May there is an entry which says: 95 + 85 + 35 – the number of pages I had written in each of the first two acts.
Friday, 27th reads: *Look Back in Anger*. Act II finished. Act III Scene I started.

I would have stayed on the following week but Hammersmith was cheaper than digs. Besides, it was Whit Monday and Morecambe was packed.

Friday, 3 June: *Look Back in Anger* finished.
Thursday, 9 June: *Look Back in Anger*, scripted.

On Monday 13th are marked the names Kitty Black and Pat Desmond. Kitty Black was principal play reader for Curtis Brown, the reputable literary agents. It was a faulty aim at the top and the bottom.
A week or two earlier Anthony Creighton's mother had died and left him a few hundred pounds. Knowing his thriftlessness, I persuaded him to buy an old Rhine barge which was tied up in the Cubitt Yacht Basin in a secluded mooring beside Chiswick Bridge. The mooring fee was only twenty-five shillings a week, calor gas was inexpensive, there was a specially cheap electricity rate and a telephone for ringing agents. Even if it meant enduring the occasional Black Monday, I could surely cadge twelve and sixpence. I had no special hopes of Black or Desmond, but I was in some state of happy grace that the act of writing the play had oddly bestowed on me.
Fifteen years later an inspired annotator in some unreadable book pronounced that *Look Back in Anger* was not originally titled as such but was, in fact, called *On The Pier At Morecambe*. He could have asked me and found out. Perhaps it is as well that he didn't.

19. 'Let Me Know Where *You're* Playing Tomorrow Night and I'll Come and See *You*.'

ARCHIE RICE

M/Y Egret
Cubitt's Yacht Basin,
Hartington Road,
London W.4.
November 1955

NELLIE BEATRICE: So much malice directed at innocence: the yellow pyjamas – 'Those things aren't much good. The narrow trousers make you look thin.' That's how she talks to me. It gets you down when you feel weary and depressed.

'Sit down! What – at eleven o'clock (almost hysterically). I go straight to bed!'

'Funny about Peter getting married. (A sidelong glance.) He was always *girl* mad.' I replied that he was twenty five years old, and that it wasn't surprising that he should be married. She ignored this and started rummaging noisily in her bag for a cigarette.

Those eyes which missed nothing and understood nothing.

'Poor Kid.' Her favourite words. 'I've had enough of down and outs.' Down and outs were two more. 'I've had enough of *him*. Down and out!' Another laugh and then, 'Poor kid.' 'That letter' which became 'the one you wrote to me.'

'It's all right for you – you've got every day off. But it takes the gilt off when you work hard every day. I shall think of this tomorrow. When I'm working. I shall think, well thank God I'm not there, waiting for the bus.'

There is a particular kind of cruelty which she had inherited. She would play off her victim (i.e. – me) to her gallery – of often unwilling spectators – in the bus queue, restaurant or train. When she began to sense my inner rage and the disinterest of others, her nerve fails. 'But he's a good kid though. He thinks I don't know what he's thinking, but I can read John like a book. I can read him like a book.'

Notebook, 1955

Stoneleigh

'*Dear John*, I look at it like this John – I never see or speak to a soul and no one comes to see me. So I think well I might just as well have fresh surroundings as long as there are plenty of people and shops and life about. I don't want to end my days *in this flat*. All I want is 1 Bedroom, 1 Sitting room, Kitchen and Bathroom. I don't want a Dining Room. Small so I can keep it clean: and not much work: I never did like Housework but don't like dirty places . . .

'*Dear John*, I am getting so worked up over my flat in Brighton I am already collecting boxes and washing all china all ready for packing etc. Carpets have been washed and rolled up; blankets all washed, in fact I'm all ready to go and giving a month's notice: am painting odds and ends; washing lace curtains; am enjoying my little self doing all these little things. It's such a great big thrill I am getting even if it doesn't come off; believe me I have enjoyed doing and getting things ready for departure – I hope – . . .

'*Dear John*, Gosh: your beautiful red roses were *so* beautiful, tall graceful and the most lovely coloured red I have ever seen. As Jan. is so on top of Xmas it does get a bit boring getting presents after weeks of Xmas shopping . . .

'*Dear John*, I have not seen a soul or spoken to anyone since I last saw you and it gets a little lonesome at times. My cat Samantha acted rather savage last night which rather frightened me. I was watching the telly all of a sudden she flew for my throat and bit me. I was so surprised I threw her from one side of the room: she had really hurt me: she can be very spiteful also most lovable, now I cover my throat up. I gave her a worm tablet: she is much quieter today. I think I have made too much fuss of her and I'm cross with her: have taken no notice of her all day . . .

'*Dear John*, I am just cooking a nice point Steak, with New Potatoes Coliflower with cheese sauce: Pine apple, Ice cream: wish you were here to share it. Finishing off with a 6d Mars: shall be sick any moment now . . .

'*Dear John*, Queenie is very ill: she stood on a chair and fell but to save herself the poor dear put both hands on the hot boiler and burnt them *very badly* she has a nurse going in daily to attend to her. *I* of course was terribly upset. I sent her a bottle of Brandy. Sid said the dressings are so painful: she is quite helpless as she has burnt both hands and cannot even wash her face. Women do the silliest things – why get on a dam chair when one is so unsteady on those feet as she is. Well: let's hope she will make a speedy recovery: just one of her most unlucky days: the pain must have been awful . . .

'*Dear John*, Stonelcigh is a dead end and shall be glad to get away and make New Friends and New Surroundings . . .

'*Dear John*, Now Queenie *can* write a nice letter: complete with stops, long words and spelt right – but Oh Lord above: so boring and depressing: I could scream. I read them once: give the Cats to play with the pieces. I am worried about my green stamps. I must get them completed before I leave here. I *am* looking forward to my next free gift: my carpet shampoo cleaner for my new flat: how I shall treasure it . . .

'*Dear John*, I hurt my back spring-cleaning its pretty painful at the moment; I washed the ceiling in the sitting room: also I ask my man I usually have how much he would charge to just paint my little bedroom. Well, you know how small it is. He wants £6.10.0. so I got a 10/6 tin of white paint and *did it myself* And honestly John – I don't suppose you will ever see it: but it looks so nice and I feel a little proud of myself. Just had another depressing letter from Queenie: her and Sid had a row – so not on speaking terms: she ask me if I would give her £2 to buy a bird cage for her Budgies: which Mother got her: she said she didn't like to ask Mother for it. I think its an imposition don't you: in view of the fact I sent her a £1 last week to get herself a drink to cheer her up. Oh dear I suppose for peace sake I will send it. Honestly I think they are under the impression I really am in the money. I am always sending her £1s and it all add up. I expect as my back is bad I did not feel very happy with her letter . . .

'*Dear John*, What some of your friends must think of me I don't know: I only realize how kind you have been not to have been ashamed of me. I am not a snob: but I like real nice people . . .

'*Dear John*, I saw my Friend this morning: she has not been very well so looks like death warmed up: I gave her 2/6 to get herself a bottle of beer. In mother's last letter she said '*What do you think of all the Royal babies*. Isn't it wonderful?' I answered *What's so wonderful*: I could not care less: each one has 5 doctors for one baby: good God said I, they ought to give birth to gold mines. Dear Mother – bless her heart.

Always in my thoughts,
Mother

'I'll say that for him – he's never been *ashamed* of me. He's always let me meet his friends – and they're all theatrical people, a good class all of them, they speak nicely.' I am ashamed of her as part of myself that can't be cast out, my own conflict, the disease which I suffer and have inherited, what I *am* and never could be whole. My disease, an invitation to my sick room.

Her letters, her phone calls, our meetings. I would speculate on them for days. What would the first encounter be like? There was no way of telling, but in the first moments, one could precast the pattern of the day – but certainly not the next.

Those hours after he died, when I was dragged back from the corpse, the hatred between us.

Public taste is *created* – never forget that.

They seem to think I'm a sort of juvenile delinquent, the result of an undesirable background. Give him a normal reliable theatrical home, and you'll find he can behave as decently as anyone else.

'His heart is in the right place anyway.'
'Yes, where everyone can see it.'
Concealed, like Rattigan's or Coward's.

'She is beautiful, aristocratic and talented, like one of those superbly mean models who stare from the pages of glossy magazines – "a long slink of classical meanness."'

He writes like a lout and lives like a gentlewoman's companion.
'They put it on as a vehicle for the star.'
If only it were a tumbril.

'The birth of children is the death of parents.' *Hegel*.

Well, she came to see my play, and she didn't even mention it. *Goodnight*.

Don't be afraid of being emotional. You won't die of it.

It's boring living in a world without mortality.

He is generous, understanding, sympathetic and has absolutely no feeling for people.

All I can offer you is the memory of pain.

The book-keepers and chartered accountants who go to plays and tot them up.

Double entry playgoers.

'I enjoyed it. Mind you, I don't think it is one entire and perfect chrysalis.'

Each time he staggers to his feet again, and totters after the woman with glaring eyes. Finally, she is affected, and goes to comfort him. But it is too late. When she is able to give him what he wants, he is no longer able to accept it.

Women never do anything for its own sake.

'My son was killed in the war for the likes of you'.

He suffers the realization: *that there is no real communication with those we love most*.

The common belief that suffering is a form of inferiority.

Even if one is unproductive one provides energy.

He is a tent-peg. He enjoys being knocked into the ground to hold up any old liberal marquee.

'I must create a System, or be enslaved by another Man's.' *Blake*.

Sipping gin and vodka and having visions.

It is better to be a has-been than a never-was. (True then as it is now.)

If I am choleric, I am sanguine also.

'Melancholy men of all others are most witty.' *Anatomy of Melancholy*.

We need more character, instead of *fixed mechanisms*.

What few emotional successes he has, he regards as concessions.

Often neurotics are very irritable, but to prevent themselves from blazing up when provoked, they lapse into an attitude of apathy and become blasé. Alison is no more 'normal' than Jimmy.

People who complain of any character in a play being neurotic, are objecting to the theatrical method.

Critics: those who would send Hedda Gabler to the Marriage Guidance Council.

'If Dad wanted a packet of Woodbines, us kids would have to go without a loaf of bread.'

'He'd black her eyes. I've seen her eyes all swollen.'

Popular song:
'Every day is mother's day to me
Since I was a baby on her knee
For what can take the place
of that care-worn smiling face,
a million angels in her eyes?
Every night I say a simple prayer,
praying she'll never know another care.
The whole wide world will say –
once a year is mother's day,
but every day is mother's day to me.'

'Well, you know, half the people you're insulting, don't know you're getting at them.'

'Don't you see, Dad – they don't want you. People don't wear patent leather shoes any more.'
The old man wears: a stock, patent leather shoes, and spats.

'I belonged to the National Sporting Club, you know.'

'I was bucked to blazes.'

It's better to take the right road, and see the wrong thing.

Even a hunch can be noble.

It contains a large element of fire – incantation.

'My husband – he's had 39 operations but he's always managed to get to a vessel.'

'If I was a man, my balls would hurt.'

'Why are you here – it ain't raining?'

'Are you Jewish?'
'Not necessarily.'

All they do is worry about their balls.

He should have a licence for walking a thing like that round the park. If I see it again, I'll shoot it.

Evading Income Tax.
That isn't British.
No, but it's very Welsh.

Everyone acts in my name without bothering even to ask who I am.

How's your mother's syphilis?

Take my own case: I am governed by fear every day of my life. Sometimes it is the first sensation I have on waking. Even the thought that I have managed to escape death by waking up. Milk bottles. Air raid shelters. Boys in balaclava helmets. Fear in rooms at Kidderminster, at Derby. Money. The dentist's chair and adultery.
Try and make a note of every example of fear you manifest. It should keep you busy.

With creaking smile like a swinging gate.

She can have the top off my egg any day.

Notebook, 1955

I threw myself into painting the boat from stem to stern as if it were a pleasant collaboration in playmaking. Anthony spent most of his time making meals for us and sunbathing unwisely on deck while I splashed away with his Dulux. I received a letter from Kitty Black, which started off something like, 'I feel like the headmistress of a large school in which I have to tell its most promising pupil that he must think again.' It was a blow magisterially struck on behalf of her agency, and the West End. Miss Black said I must think again and Mr Desmond didn't even know what I was thinking about.

Shortly afterwards I had a phone call from Patrick who had arranged a production of the McCarthy play, *Personal Enemy* at Harrogate. I had long lost interest in this and wanted to know what he thought of *Look Back*. He was not simply vituperative but reproachful, as if I had betrayed the treasure of trust that he had put in my flimsy gifts and been almost physically faithless to Stella's memory. He went on for about half an hour. 'You've just got to make up your mind what you think you're going to do. I mean this simply won't do at all.' I listened unhurt. It was the shape of things to come and from the lower depths, the voice of what Sir Peter Hall at the National Theatre later described as his forecasters.

Lying on deck in August, I read in the *Stage* that a new company, the English Stage Company, had been formed with the object of producing new plays and particularly new plays by new writers. By this time I had both Pat's and Miss Black's copies, so I sent one of them to the Artistic Director, expecting a reply within months or an unreturned manuscript. I heard within days. The English Stage Company would pay me twenty-five pounds for an option on my play, and Mr Devine, the Tesman of Mr Siddiqui's disappointment, would like to arrange a meeting. Twenty-five pounds indicated the caution of Jimmy Wax on a day out, but compared to the response I had had from the Headmistress of Curtis Brown, Pat Desmond and Frith-from-just-across-the corridor, it was acclaim.

I rang the number I had been given, hoping for the boyish, enthusiastic tones I remembered from George's Tesman. He seemed to answer the telephone reluctantly, barked for instructions on how to find me on the boat and slammed down the receiver.

On a sunny August afternoon in 1955, the time approached for George to arrive at the boat but there was no sign of him. I had tried to explain that the tides in the basin made it impossible for anyone to come aboard at certain hours of the day. Either I had not made myself clear or, in our very brief telephone conversation, he had not listened. I put on a blazer I'd bought in Derby and a pair of grey flannels and a clubbish-looking tie. The tide rose and the barge bobbed out of access. After two hours, as I was about to take off my Loamshire wardrobe, George appeared through the trees from the river, rowing himself in a small boat. Clambering aboard *M/Y Egret* enthusiastically, in an open-necked shirt and sandalled feet, he sounded just like Tesman again.

There was no question in my mind on that muggy August day that within less than a year – and on my father's birthday – *Look Back in Anger* would have opened, in what still seems like an inordinately long, sharp and glimmering summer.

In 1972 and twelve plays later, *A Sense of Detachment*, a play for which it might be gathered I have some affection, was to be produced in very different circumstances to the climate of wounded bafflement of 8 May. Begrudging rancour had long since been stock-piled, mobilized and had taken up its positions after the disbelief and disarray caused by George's '56 spring offensive. In the interval of that 1972 first night, I met a woman in the foyer who had frequented all my first nights for a time. I called her the Witch of Ongar, and she always said the same thing. 'You've done it this time, Osborne, you've *really done* it to yourself! You've finished it for yourself this time! You've really *done* it.' The Witch of Ongar has not approached me since then and I miss her.

Almost everyone agreed with her, including the *Financial Times*: 'This must surely be his farewell to the theatre.'

VOLUME II
Almost a Gentleman
1955–1966

To Lucy

1. A Palpable Miss

M/Y *Egret*,
Cubitt's Yacht Basin, London W12
12 August 1955

In that midsummer I felt oddly if unaccountably idling-over on some slow charge. It was an unfamiliar feeling, something like a rare intake of heart's ease. I was twenty-five and, for such an importunate soul as I certainly was then, the auguries were discouraging if not downright damning.

Trying to order the chaos of hindsight now, my spirit was partially disabled by diffidence but also fuelled by what was regarded as a reckless, untutored frenzy, a puzzling arrogance, destructive to others and to myself. That seemed to be the implicit impression I created among all those I encountered in my profession. Pamela Lane, my first wife, had confirmed this only a year before, refusing to keep faith with what she saw as a pursuit of distressful disorder. Anyway, I was easily and happily ignorable in those days, when I must have looked most certain to go away. And quite soon.

I didn't feel liberated from Pamela. The prospect of divorce never entered my sometimes wild projections of the future as I moped around the Welsh villages on an Arts Council tour of *Pygmalion*. I would simply resist any approximation to my feelings during those shocked, brooding months after we separated. Writing and finishing *Look Back in Anger* presented no purge or lasting comfort, no justification by either faith or works. I had addressed myself to events in some way. They were particular and personal, but they were not confined to the hulk of my marriage nor even to the wider constraints of general indifference, dislike or mere torpor.

For the first time I had written a play on my own. It had taken me something like seventeen days in all. It had been a sprint. I was apprehensive that anyone might pay attention to my solo dash. 'Don't expect anything. Then you won't be disappointed.' It was the battle-cry of misery of my mother, Nellie Beatrice, a little like the famous wartime catch-phrase, 'It's being so cheerful as keeps me going.' Nothing was so deadly as this sanctimonious, more-cheerful-than-thouness. I continued, then as now, to expect everything, disappointment most of all. It has been a useful mechanism.

I was beholden to no one. Pamela had told me that our three-year-old marriage and her career in the theatre were irreconcilable. She had taken up with a Jewish dentist in Derby. But I began to feel that her all-too-accountable desertion would resolve itself. I began to relish my celibacy. The acceptance of even temporary celibacy a few months before would have seemed like an Establishment heresy, handed down by magistrates, lady journalists, Tory MPs and BBC governors. At that time, the vows of poverty, chastity and obedience were abhorrent. Later, only obedience seemed unthinkable.

Pamela would come back. Our marriage could not be a closed incident, nor an open – or, worse, healed – wound. I felt oddly content to wait on events. Indecision can be a dangerous pawn, but not to those who are set to play an importunate game from the outset. I have seldom failed to rush in, to tread all over the place. But I check the time first very carefully. It is the one gift in which I have almost complete confidence.

Anyway, in that late summer of 1955 I had nowhere to rush in, let alone tread. Pamela was still working at Derby Rep. The telephone hadn't rung for weeks. The sun was shining on the creaky hull of M/Y *Egret* almost every working morning. Painting the length of the boat in nursery-like colours, listening to the Black Box record-player, reading Conrad while Anthony Creighton (my former fellow actor and 'collaborator') messed about with his primitive electronics, there seemed to be a summery, vibrant lull in the air which I hadn't felt much since days in the grass watching frogs and dragonflies as an eight-year-old.

My entitlement to forty-two shillings a week dole money had lapsed, but my expenses were minimal. My half contribution to the weekly mooring fee was ten shillings, Calor gas was cheap for the galley, and we used paraffin oil for the ancient heating-stove. Anthony and I were both vegetarian. I had converted him to a meatless diet not through evangelistic zeal but by practical appeal to our budget.

My own vegetarianism had been prompted by self-interest. I wanted to confound my pitted complexion, implacable daily headaches, throbbing glands, dish-cloth hair and dandruff. That my appearance had marginally improved (though not the headaches) was no doubt due a little to less toxic input. I still lived in some dread of the White Plague that had struck my sister and father and I felt I must be severe with myself at least in this matter of food. I had a superstition that if I could achieve my father's age of thirty-nine, and pass it, I would have managed a kind of pilgrimage into another, less chancy country. Meat could be equated with inner squalor. Vegetarianism might banish that, too.

Just as Pamela and I had consumed mounds of dull but decently cooked cabbage laced with the luxury of half a tin of baked beans, Anthony and I plucked the plentiful nettles from the river bank and stewed them lightly, congratulating ourselves on our homespun ingenuity. They tasted like sweeter spinach and, if you liked spinach, quite pleasant. Combined with the occasional Nuttolene health-shop fantasy like 'Risserole', or the lusty-sounding 'meatless steaks' and as much New Zealand cheddar as we could afford, we just managed to avoid actual hunger.

'If you don't eat it up, you'll grow up to look like Mr Attlee.' After 1945 my grandmother was still telling me that more than one bath a week was 'weakening', that I was outgrowing my strength and that Aneurin Bevin was a wicked man. The GIs, who had never bothered to count their change and left it on the bar counter for my mother to pick up, had gone. If one word applied to that post-war decade it was inertia. Enthusiasm there was not, in this climate of fatigue. Jimmy Porter was hurt because things had remained the same. Colonel Redfern grieved that everything had changed. They were both wrong, but that was hard to see at the time.

The country was tired, not merely from the sacrifice of two back-breaking wars but from the defeat and misery between them. The bits of red on the map were disappearing as the flags came down and the names we knew on mixed packets of postage stamps were erased. Like so much else, it all happened without people being very aware of it. The leaping hare of the Victorian imagination had begun to imitate the tortoise even before 1914, but in that summer of 1955 it was still easy enough to identify what we regarded as a permanent Establishment. The continued acceptance of hanging, the prosecution of homosexuals, and censorship in film and theatre made life easy for the liberal conscience. The Conservative Party could still be stigmatized as figures of fun on their grouse moors; Etonians dominated the Cabinet. The radical spirit would be unprepared for the new middle-class oligarchy when the old Establishment of Law, Church and Parliament was supplanted by neo-Tory grocers, PR men, trainee consultants and Gary and Tracey pink and greasy from a bargain-break on the Costa del Sol.

The physical excitement of writing *Look Back* turned the simplest negative pleasures into overpowering, self-imposed awards. The realization that one can change one's life as easily as shifting the furniture, rehanging a picture or discarding an ugly present has been a recurrent bonus. This has nothing to do with faithlessness or inconsistency; rather it is a natural versatility of spirit, a quality often suspect as frivolous. Perhaps Jimmy Porter did owe a glancing debt, though not much, to my first wife. For the moment, some pride, not altogether paltry, prevented me from contacting her. To be tentative was beyond me. It usually is. Later, after much dubious frenzy, I succeeded rather more with God than I ever did with Pamela.

Something, I felt, was going to turn up – if not God, something.

By early August, the wispy copies of the manuscript of *Look Back*, typed on Pamela's twenty-first birthday present from her parents, had been rejected, often with an exasperated or even gleeful parting cuff or kick, by every theatrical management and play agent I could find listed in the *Writers' and Artists' Yearbook*. The speed with which it had been returned was not surprising, but its aggressive dispatch did give me a kind of baffled relief. It was like being grasped at the upper arm by a testy policeman and told to move on. And not later, but at once. I might, as Kitty Black (then the doyenne of agents) had made clear, be put on a charge. Loitering with intent. Up to no good to anyone, and a particular nuisance to agents.

The play had been finished on 3 June, and only weeks later it was already ragged with over-active policing. The people responding to it in this way were not those to be incensed by mediocrity. Being purveyors of it, this was surely not the quality that had driven them to such quick offence. The implication was that I might have been guilty of an unintended breach of the peace rather than merely writing a dull and untheatrical work. There was a vehement, undisputed judgement: the play was a palpable miss.

The future loomed out of grasp but I had an apprehension of something and, for the moment, I was able and prepared for it to appear in some unforeseeable form. On 12 August it did. George Devine's weighty tread ended the lull undramatically on that summer day, but I knew I detected a difference. If it wasn't hope, which comes from within, it was the shadow of energy, which blessedly sometimes does come from without.

> Born with a contrite heart and a glimmering of sin, opposed to guilt, I came to realize that it is this opposition that divides the religious from the secular spirit.
>
> *Notebook*, 1963

Devine grappled aboard M/Y *Egret* from the rowing-boat he had commandeered. He had disregarded my instructions about how to reach me, avoiding the afternoon tide, and I was already timorously wishing I had persuaded him to let me visit him at his house in Hammersmith's Lower Mall. It was clear that he was determined to scrutinize his unknown author in his own cage. I clumsily hauled him on to the deck.

George was then forty-three, a heavy man, looking larger than he was, though not the huge bear-like figure he had been during his Young Vic days. All his old pupils insisted that some sea-change had taken place in him since then which had altered not only his girth but, more significantly, his personality.

I was not aware of this at the time, being confused by my remembrance of him as an endearing, innocent-seeming Tesman in *Hedda Gabler* and the harsh, terse voice I had heard over the telephone a few days earlier. I was still disconcerted by the way he had banged down the receiver with a peremptory grunt that made me feel I had already taxed his patience before we had even met. Seeing him appear through the trees with his blue open-neck shirt flapping over his trousers and his sandalled bare feet, I felt foolishly and inappropriately dressed in my give-away Loamshire blazer and flannels. I realized that I must look like some vapid juvenile in a Rank comedy about medical students breezing about on houseboats. It was too late to go below and change my absurd costume into some Left-Bank-ish outfit, stale with pastis and Gauloises.

'If I didn't have white hair and smoke a pipe, no one would listen to me,' he was to say later. On that day, he seemed younger and more foxy-nosed than I had expected. Far from being irritated by the delays of getting to the boat, he was amused as if bent on some unexpected scent. We went below while he asked questions and I tried to divest myself of Juv. Char. appearance, removing my clubby tie swiftly to look the more roughed-up serious before the initial image became indelible. The blue blazer, saved for and bought in Bridgwater for all-purpose use in Home Counties comedies, seemed to ring out like a leper's bell, begging radical scorn. It proclaimed my background of provincial hard-tat.

I anticipated a quick merciless viva and merciful dismissal. However little I knew of him, I was certain that George would not only refuse to suffer fools gladly but would make it quickly clear and row away, growling his irritation to the tides. What I had not anticipated was that he was driven by that most blessed of human virtues, abiding and open curiosity. That and unfeigned hope, in the face – most literally and finally – of cigar-wielding lackeys, vocational by-liners and even their voracious stringers.

George was to earn £2,000 a year as the first Artistic Director of the English Stage Company at the Royal Court Theatre. His assistant, Tony Richardson, was paid £14 a week. Neither time nor the imponderabilities of international financial trends in the following thirty years can conceal the fact that subsidy, patronage, loony licence and afraid-and-feigning fashion, disavowing elitism at every turn, have created a cultural system which is no more than democracy gone mad, where every Jack and Jill is better than their patron-person. 'I'm afraid that kind of idealism doesn't exist any longer,' the Chairman of the ESC said to me years later. The Sloane Square red hill-billies beamed.

George sat down on one of the shaky bunks in the main cabin and looked about him. Quickly, I decided that scrutiny was a natural part of his character, that it was not assumed and apparently not censorious. His censure seemed brutal, harsh and intent. His interest was patent and open. Perhaps this spirit led him so eagerly to buy women's magazines, like *Seventeen* and *Honey*, at railway terminals and read them in the pursuit of some small enlightenment on the way to provincial theatres, with more relish and sympathy than he read the playscripts brimming out of his briefcase.

George interrogated me closely, not only about my professional record but about my past and present personal life. It was probing but not prurient. Giving a half-way interesting account of myself had seemed unlikely enough a few hours ago, but his late arrival, and several whiskies burning a sore and acid inside, made me garrulous and even defiant.

It was strange to be examined in this encouraging manner. The Labour Exchange, the National Assistance man and my mother were the only ones who had expressed their cold interest in me during the preceding year. 'When do you think you will get a job?' 'Don't you think it's a funny profession you've chosen?' 'What makes you think you'll get on where all the others haven't?' Pride, for one thing. 'You can't go on like this for ever.' For the sake of forty shillings a week it was politic and fairly easy to agree. For the sake of a few tins of fruit and vegetables, it was neither too contemptible nor humiliating to bear Nellie Beatrice's company on her day off. 'You don't seem very lucky, do you? Poor kid. If only you could have been a barrister or a doctor.' Such Golders Green sentiments from my anti-Semitic mother had their horsefly charm.

Devine, of Wadham (like his associate, Richardson), Old and Young Vic, *gonfalonier* of Copeau, mask and mime, stern brother disciple of Saint-Denis, had come round to the tradesmen's entrance to chat to someone whose entire theatrical experience was below-stairs. Some sour euphoria

lifted me up as I recited, like previous convictions, the reps I had managed
to infiltrate: Kidderminster, Ilfracombe, Bridgwater, Sidmouth, Leicester,
Dartford. Almost a Shakespearian sequence – Talbot, Gloucester,
Hereford, Warwick, Northumberland. 'My Lords, ill news from the north.
Kidderminster is dead and Bridgwater fled.' I asked for other convictions
on number-three tours, twice-nightly and one-night stands to be taken into
consideration. I felt much better. I offered George a drink, but the prospect
of whisky at four o'clock in the afternoon clearly impressed him even less
than the details of my career. Red wine was his day-long tipple, the bouquet
of De Flores, as I found out later. He had a misty, underarm Beaujolais tang,
not entirely unpleasant but a little forbidding, like the odour of black
priestliness.

I ventured to smoke my pipe, but he had the pedantic pipe-smoker's cold
eye for the novice, although I had been smoking one with some discrimina-
tion, I thought, since I was fifteen. An old gentleman in a park in Aberdeen
had even patted me gently on the shoulder, saying, 'It's good to see a young
laddie enjoying the best companionship the world can offer. A pipe's your
friend for life and ye canna say that for man nor woman.'

> There is a fundamental antagonism between tobacco and women. One
> diminishes the other. This is so true that sooner or later men in love
> with women stop smoking because they feel or imagine that tobacco
> has a deadening effect on sexual desire and the sexual act. The fact is
> that love is gross and material compared with the spirituality of a pipe.
>
> *The Goncourt Journal*, 18 July 1868

Years later, I gave George a pair of Dunhill pipes in a case for a Christmas
present. He barely glanced at them and said, 'There's only one place to buy
a pipe and that's Charatan's.' Thereafter I patronized them obediently until
a few years ago I went into Dunhill's in Jermyn Street and bought the most
enjoyable and reliable pipe I have ever owned (an ex-wife having smashed
my previously prized one). I told the gentleman behind the counter of
George's invocation to Charatan. He smiled. 'Oh, yes, sir. But it depends
upon what you *want*.' When I bought my first car, I chose an Austin 110, a
smartish, middle-priced model of the time. Parked confidently outside the
stage door of the Royal Court, I showed it to George. He scarcely glanced at
its creamy roominess and dashing crimson streak. 'Good God!' he growled.
'Why didn't you get an Alfa Giulietta? That's a *grocer*'s car.'

That first August afternoon, he was particularly intrigued by my lunging
performance as Hamlet in Hayling Island. 'We're interested in actors who

are writers.' Or was it writers who were actors? He asked me what else I'd written. I mumbled about my 1950 Huddersfield World Première, luridly titled *The Devil Inside*, but not that I'd written it in collaboration with my mistress, nor that it had limped on for barely a week. Writing a play in tandem seemed a rather folksy enterprise. Anyway, George's somewhat vinegary puritanism was obvious even from the little I knew of his reputation.

Nor did I mention my two verse plays, so succinctly described by Pamela as 'dull and boring'. George's disapproval of Fry, Ustinov and John Whiting was almost startling in its bitterness: 'They're all absolute shit.' It was a little breathtaking. I was only accustomed to this kind of throw-away vehemence from myself.

I cautiously referred to *Epitaph for George Dillon*. Anthony had been characteristically over-excited about George's visit. If not *Look Back*, why not the play we had cobbled together barely nine months before? I hadn't thought of it. I wanted my own thoroughbred, as I saw it, to be paraded in the ring alone, not with a part-owned stable-companion.

From the garbled reports I'd received from Stratford-upon-Avon, then run by Anthony Quayle, I had the strong impression that returning officers and men who were palpably men were the order of the day. Knowing a little of George's war record and believing that men who had experienced killing with their bare hands would not tolerate epicene recruits, I had persuaded Anthony to stay in his cabin and wait for the all-clear invitation to join us. I feared that, fortified by gin, he would lurch in and, literally, queer my uneasy pitch.

George was obviously interested that I was living in this leaky old Rhine barge, only a mile downriver from his own pretty eighteenth-century house. Typically, he asked me closely about the economics of it, the cost of Calor gas, the mooring rental, the special telephone rate. I was forced to say that I was sharing it with another actor, not revealing that the boat actually belonged to him. It was acceptable enough that two young actors should live together in this way without any sexual implications, but I knew that I was dealing with someone of a rather particular generation. I had referred to my marriage to an actress and that we were living apart for the moment. I offered no confidence and none was sought, like the information that the telephone had been temporarily disconnected. It would either be repaired or not.

People often assumed that Anthony and I were lovers. This didn't bother me much but I didn't want this kind of absurdity to cloud my early encounter and cast new meanings upon the play (although they are meted out to this day in dumb textbooks imposed upon children for their A-levels). And my apprehensions were not entirely misguided. The Denville Players of Scarborough had made their conditions of employment brutally laconic: 'No fancy salaries and no queer folk.' It was as uncompromising as the cards then displayed in Hammersmith newsagents' windows: 'No Blacks. No Irish.' We at least knew where we stood.

I don't remember George's words, I doubt if there were any, but the implication was unmistakable. In the newly formed, middle-class-liberal English Stage Company, principles would be applied as rigorously as by the Denville Players. No fancy salaries and the nod that queer folk were not to be considered, certainly not as officer material.

2. Camp Following

The Carlyle,
New York

At last I can write about my particular sins without Lord
Chamberlain-induced sex-change dishonesty, and even without fear of
fussing Aunt Edna overmuch. But my own sins bore me terribly, which
may be the lethargy of old age creeping over me, or just the disinclination to join in the chorus of voices endlessly shouting the love that
once dared not speak its name, from every housetop in every country.
Perhaps I should rewrite *Deep Blue Sea* as it really was meant to be, but
after 20 years I just can't remember why I made all that fuss. 'Emotion
recollected in tranquillity?' What balls! It's just another tranquil non-
emotion, like T.S. Eliot.

    Love,
    Terry

Letter from Terence Rattigan to J.O., 1968

There was a bruised Forgotten Army side to George's antagonisms that was
not always realistic. He was still sounding me out as the light was fading on
the Thames, quizzing me about individual plays. I let slip that I had more or
less admired *The Browning Version*. Realizing my error, I hedged that I had no
high opinion of *Separate Tables*. Before I had time to compound my blunder
on *The Deep Blue Sea*, he cut me short about the patent inadequacies of
homosexual plays masquerading as plays about straight men and women.

Rattigan was later to write me long letters in the small hours from
Bermuda and Paris, bitterly repudiating his deceptions, urging me against
his own example and against becoming a tax exile. In both cases I was
scarcely at risk. I have been upbraided constantly for a crude, almost animal,
inability to dissemble. As for tax exile, not simple patriotism but hubris,
middling xenophobia and dependence on the comforts of history and

homeland make it seem as chilling as the prospect of the bang on the closing gates at the Scrubs.

Like many a lifetime radical of his generation, George was unaware of his own bigotry and sentimentality, which he saw as a harsh endorsement of plain honesty. But if ever an old dog unknowingly gave sanctuary to his fleas it was George Devine, however much he scratched in puzzlement.

As I was to discover, he was torn by so many conflicting instincts. A loveless childhood, abetted by a miserable legacy from his sharp-spined mother and an austere entry into a theatre he disliked, followed by seven bitterly resented years in the Royal Artillery, had left him as suspicious as he was responsive. His private life was dominated by a cold marriage and then by an affair with the designer Jocelyn Herbert (known as 'Brown' because of her addiction to dun-coloured sets) clouded by her self-sacrifice of 'waiting until the children have grown up'.

Perhaps his despondent years in Burma and then the harsh nursery world of the Young Vic had made him a blindfold victim of events, like enduring shell-shock or battle fatigue. He seemed to believe, in a simple-hearted way, that the blight of buggery, which then dominated the theatre in all its frivolity, could be kept down decently by a direct appeal to seriousness and good intentions from his own crack corps of heterosexual writers, directors and actors.

I was never properly privy to all aspects of Royal Court life and procedure. The abiding strength of homosexual strategy is to promote and encourage conspiracy. Only the players grasp the game, and one of its purposes is to make outsiders feel foolish. It was many months of walking in the late hours from George's house in Lower Mall back to the *Egret* before I realized the route was a kasbah for the cavortings of future Royal Court alumni. I did hear squeals and heavy rustling from the towpath but attributed them, rather enviously, to what were still known as 'courting couples'. Courting it was, Royal and male.

Working long into the night, George was equally unaware of this nocturnal scampering only yards from his desk. The love that dared not speak its name was not yet shrilling it from the roof-tops. I doubt if he knew, in those days of wine and Durex, of the supplies of penicillin rushed like plasma to the Dressing Station Upstairs at the Court for crusading veterans to staunch syphilitic wounds in mid-rehearsal. So sophisticated did this Dressing Station become in the mid-sixties that there was a map on the wall charting which swimming-pools and Turkish baths had been recently visited by certain of the theatre's directors. Flags dotted the metropolis for

Royal Court strategic positions just as I had once plotted the course of Montgomery's stalemate and the Ardennes offensive.

George, who wanted at all times to have some idea where he was in a reeling universe, was repeatedly probing the overblown mysteries of camp. I tried without much success to lift one or two veils for him. He would ring me up earnestly: Was *I* camp? 'Now, I think we can take it that Mozart is camp. Or is he really? Then what about Beethoven? Byron, no. Kipling certainly not. What about Tennyson?' And so on.

However, we were not yet at that stage of confidence, if any. Getting there was to take a long time. I suppose we both did little more at that first meeting than throw down hints as if we were strange partners at a card game. But the Devine Grunt – more eloquent than his reluctant attempts at rhetoric – confirmed that I had been offered £25 from the English Stage Company for a year's option on *Look Back in Anger* with a £50 renewal clause. George was unapologetic about the sum but gave the weary impression that it was insufficient. I tried not to appear grateful.

Neither did I know then how deeply his contact with the unsmiling pieties of umbilical Francophilia had wounded and isolated his already lonely spirit. For as long as I could remember the literary and academic classes seemed to have been tyrannized by the French. The 'posh papers' every Sunday blubbered with self-abasement in the face of the bombast of the French language and its absurd posture as the torch-bearer of Logic, which apparently was something to which no one in these islands had access.

Certain writers gave the impression that it was downright indelicate to write in English at all, which is why the *Sunday Times* and the *Observer* were peppered with italics until they sometimes looked like linguistic lace curtains:

JIMMY: I've just read three whole columns on the English Novel. Half of
        it's in French. Do the Sunday papers make *you* feel ignorant?
CLIFF: Not 'arf.

Look Back in Anger

What we all needed was a short, sharp shock of clear-round-the-bend French logic: a dollop of the gynaecological metaphysic of Simone de Beauvoir, a trilogy from Sartre and a slice of melodrama from Camus, cigarette ever a-dangle at the café table, the existentialist Rick of *Casablanca*. Of all the gin joints in the world, Oxbridge men clamoured for a stool at this bar, and George was up there with them. Concepts like Being and Essence sound different with a tongue up your nose.

Concealed mystification of a very lofty sort seemed to prevail. Angus Wilson's stories, *The Wrong Set*, had been greeted like the tide of Elizabethan England, but Waugh and Greene were smirked at. Shaw was still regarded as a serious thinker, an adroit dramatist who had got a bit silly to himself in his dotage. T.S. Eliot was transferred from the then-revered closet of Edinburgh to a bewildered and respectful boulevard public in London. Christopher Fry was received with uneasy relief. Noël Coward was shown the door. He went against received Lit. Crit.

Chesham Place, SW1

I really am very grateful for your letter. It gave me a sharp and much deserved jolt. I absolutely agree that it is unnecessary and unkind to hand out my opinions of my colleagues to journalists. It is also pompous. I know by the grace and firmness of your letter that you will forgive me if I have inadvertently hurt you or even irritated you. I think far too highly of you to wish to do either of these things. I regret very much that since we first met we have known each other so little. This at least can be remedied if you are willing. There is so much that I would like to talk to you about even if our views on plays and playwrights may differ. Please come to lunch with me here either on Monday, Tuesday or Friday of next week or the Monday or Friday of the following week. You see I am pinning you down ruthlessly for the simple reason that I would truly like to see you. Please come. I shall not ask anyone else. What you said in your letter about admiration and respect is entirely mutual. You can telephone me here any morning.

Noël

Letter from Noël Coward to J.O., 1966

George was anxious for me to meet his associate director, Tony Richardson, and asked me along to 9 Lower Mall. Sophie Devine, George's wife, showed me up to his study. He was sitting at a drawing-board, a reassuring sight in itself. Perhaps play-making was an exercise to be worked out on a high stool with T-squares.

He called up the stairs and Richardson appeared. He had the authoritative stoop of a gangler who is born to mastery. In what was to become one of the most imitated voices in his profession he said, 'I think *Look Back in Anger* is the best play written since the war.' He announced himself as its director like a confiding toastmaster.

George sighed. 'You'll have to have an agent, I'm afraid.'

Agents have not changed much since I first became dependent upon them. To be dependent on an agent is like entrusting your most precious future to your mother-in-law or your bookmaker. Most of the females of the species even behave like mothers-in-law, dreaded by many a playwright's wife as she finds her weekends hounded by advice on her spouse's diet, work routine and sexual needs or deficiencies, patent to no one but the agent herself. Like shop stewards, flying pickets or the executive car salesmen of the new Conservative Party, agents despise both innovation and tradition, protecting the laws of deceit, avarice and self-aggrandizement of those they 'represent'.

There were, and may be, exceptions. When I was once threatened with litigation by a Hollywood film producer, and in no position to bargain from any foreseeable strength, Robin Fox advised me: 'Tell him to go fuck himself, dear boy.' It may sound like little enough, but agents are unwilling to bite the hand of their most enduring source of 10 per cent, the manager or the producer.

Thirty years ago, in those days before television and video residuals, matters may have seemed more gentlemanly because the pickings were not so rich. A respectable agent with two or three stage stars and a brace of tried playwrights might earn a comfortable living without his secretary even having to call him to the telephone. Their main preoccupation was that they and their wives were given the best first-night stall seats, where they formed clear pools of indifference or grudging swank.

Even before Lindsay Anderson tried, to the terror of the English Stage Company and the even more craven Arts Council, to exclude critics from the Royal Court in a rather hilarious campaign against some nonentity, I made a similar effort to ban the presence of the bat-like predator-agent from first nights. This time the resistance came, predictably, from the actors. They were appalled at being deprived of what they inexplicably regarded as their 'support'. Fighting cocks may have felt some comfort from their 'supporters'. A dead cock has no supporters.

'They're none of them any good, any of them,' said George that day, 'but I'm afraid you're going to need one. It's a choice of two – Margery Vosper or Peggy Ramsay.' George looked doubtful. 'Ramsay's the best, there's no doubt. But I think you'd be better off with Margery. I can't see you and Peggy putting up with each other for long. Margery's a motherly old thing.'

This proved to be shrewd advice. In the event, Peggy Ramsay turned out to be the best agent I never had, extolling me with a generosity that she sometimes seemed to deny members of her own stable. Her sharpest reproof to me was when she demanded: 'Why do you keep *marrying* these women? I'm sure they can't possibly want to marry you! Oh, well, at least you seem to have given up marrying actresses and married a *real* woman this time. No one should marry an actress, least of all a writer.' It was the second, and last, piece of wisdom I received from an agent.

The following week I made an appointment with Margery, who, like most lady agents of the time, invariably wore a hat. She could be found every day at long lunch-time sessions with her colleagues over sausages and Guinness in the pub opposite the stage door of the Apollo Theatre. Again, George was right about her. She was motherly. She sat behind a desk in her office on Shaftesbury Avenue, three cramped, cheerful rooms like the staff quarters of a small, over-priced school for under-elevens. She rose from it like a welcoming headmistress, as if she were used to putting parents and new pupils at their ease.

In 1955 she was over forty, large-chested rather than breasted, with a flat porkpie-ish hat which, with the addition of a veil, would have done well for a modest wedding, like her navy-blue print frock with its comforting tucks and pleats. It was all reassuring if not stimulating. One of the comforts she could be relied on to dispense was an encouragement to modesty and, most welcome, not to take on too much – 'After all, you've done your bit for a while.'

'*Don't* think we should ask too much, dear. Mustn't look as if we're being greedy.' This homely caution meant being well-nigh supplicant to managers and producers. As Hugh 'Binkie' Beaumont, at the head of H.M. Tennant, and Rank and Associated Pictures would ride on indestructibly during her lifetime, this was perhaps a sensible conclusion. Her star prefects and source of income were the Welsh wizard Emlyn Williams and the husband-and-wife team of Hugh and Margaret Williams, purveyors of fragrant drawing-room comedies. They must have been her bread and butter for a good many years. Ronald Duncan, poet and playwright, was her prize-winner, but Margery was a firm believer in eating up your bread and butter and regarding the jam as a nice little treat to look forward to.

She was a kindly woman and I soon grew very fond of her. It was some twenty years before I was able to bring myself to leave her. When I made the decision she fought it fiercely, still believing that I would, as always, over-reach myself. Although she must have been quite rich, she lived modestly in a dark but pleasant Edwardian flat off Tottenham Court Road. Her holidays were always spent in a pre-war bungalow in a suburban street in Worthing. She was an ace *Times* crossword-puzzler.

Having already turned the play down without explanation, Margery was a little lady-almonerish when she first met me. She was politely surprised by George's endorsement and baffled that the newly formed English Stage Company, with such board members as her own Ronald Duncan (dubbed 'the Black Dwarf' by Devine and Richardson, because of his diminutive height and poisonous spirit) and the Earl of Harewood, should have offered to advance me £25. 'Well dear,' she said. 'I don't think we're going to make much money out of this one, but it'll be very interesting to see what they say. Very interesting indeed.' It was Margery's verdict on everything I ever wrote.

3. May 8th

I am very much more interested in content than in form. I do not think any play is really worth producing if it's not a play of ideas. Literally, the play's the thing.

George Devine, 1956

Tony and George took a monkeyish delight in giving the manuscript of *Look Back* to colleagues and acquaintances so that they could report their unfavourable reactions back to me. They used it as a litmus test of personality and taste, enjoying my unease as much as the aversion of those who read the play. One of the most revered of theatre dames loved it least of all. 'It should be thrown into the river and washed out to sea so that it may never be seen again.' Tony relished every syllable as he repeated her verdict.

During the months before Christmas I spent more and more evenings at Lower Mall. I had never met anyone who could create the expectation of excitement more openly and infectiously than Richardson, the unlikely son of a bookish Yorkshire chemist. From standstill to breakfast time, visitors popped in with a casualness that would have rocked those staid and silent suburban streets of my boyhood in Stoneleigh – Michel Saint-Denis, Glen Byam Shaw, Lindsay Anderson and Karel Reisz, or Bill Gaskill, pale with fatigue from working at the all-night bakery down the road. Angus Wilson and Nigel Dennis came and, later, Ionesco, Beckett, Helene Weigel. French was almost obligatory and German encouraged.

The English Stage Company was to open at the Court in April the following year. The first production would be *The Mulberry Bush* by Angus Wilson, which had been received at the Bristol Old Vic with the unreliable enthusiasm of London critics soothed by an expenses-paid night at a provincial hotel. Nigel Dennis had been persuaded by George and Tony to dramatize his novel *Cards of Identity*. Angus and Nigel were both novelists, both academic, one gregarious, the other reclusive, and both discovered in middle age as the herald voices of the time. George looked to The Novel as the fountainhead for his dream of new theatrical vitality. Angus and Nigel were comic writers in a clear tradition, and neither could be accused of frivolity. Could they and others, like Kingsley Amis and John Wain, be persuaded to bring their weight to bear and light up a theatre which had been intellectually disreputable for so long? Would it now be seriously regarded by the *New Statesman* and the *Observer*?

The original founders of the ESC – Ronald Duncan, Lord Harewood and C.E. Blacksell, a buffoon schoolteacher from Barnstaple – all regarded George's blacklist of writers (prosaic Priestley; clownish, commonplace Ustinov; lightweight Fry; frigid Whiting; middle-brow Mortimer) very seriously indeed. Their original intention had been to mount plays by all of them, a strategy George successfully resisted by a concerted campaign of devious manoeuvring over the next ten years.

He put on two of Duncan's plays (*Don Juan in Hell* and *The Death of Satan*) in the opening season with the unconcealed intention of killing them off as soon as possible. Bile was soon to spurt from the Black Dwarf of North Devon as his work was ruthlessly cut up by George and Tony and turned into a triumphantly unpresentable evening.

I was engaged to join the company as an actor after giving an audition for George at the Palace Theatre, where he was appearing in his own production of *King Lear* with John Gielgud. I gave the rabble-rousing speech by Jack Cade from *Henry VI* and, inexplicably, a piece from a particularly bad play by Sean O'Casey, *The Bishop's Bonfire*. George produced it later, and without me. The audition was soon over and never mentioned by either of us.

The Company Manager, Oscar Lewenstein, contracted me. I was to play as cast and understudy for £12 a week. Tony was directing a BBC crime series called *Tales from Soho* and was able to push a couple of one-liners my way. I became play-reader for £2 a week, taking home nightly some thirty or forty scripts. When I once complained of the burden to Tony, he said, his voice rising to its most imitable pitch, 'But you don't *read* them? Not all *through*?' I ventured some pious pretence about talent being missed through hasty scanning. He picked up a few scripts from my bag and went through half a dozen. Some took him twenty seconds, some half a minute, two minutes at most, a high-pitched, awesome Geiger counter. '*There*, that's how you read a play.'

The plays sent in at the time could be divided into a few recognizable categories. A number of them were written by clergymen's wives. Almost every post brought a play about Mary Queen of Scots, the Virgin Queen,

Queen Victoria and Lady Jane Grey. These were all regular runners, but Mary Queen of Scots was Red Rum to them all. Then there were the plays about literary figures like D.H. Lawrence or Henry James; Loamshire plays; plays set in the past and plays set in the future where lone survivors of the Atomic Holocaust addressed themselves but not each other. Schoolteachers were almost as prolific as clergymen's wives. I read what was probably Robert Bolt's first play, *A Critic on the Hearth*, and recommended it. Tony made it clear that for someone who had written the best play since the war I had a lamentable critical intelligence.

Casting *Look Back* started early in the new year. Finding Jimmy Porter was certain to be difficult. We were seeking something instantly recognizable to us both. Fortunately we were unaware that we were casting what we were to be told weeks later was an unlikely freak and, later still, an archetype. The problem was the practical one of finding not a new archetype but an actor who could face the withdrawal of audience approval and, even, seem to incite it.

Casting is almost always achieved by default and sometimes by calculated compromise. I am not suggesting that selecting Kenneth Haigh was abject. It was a covert Richardson inspiration. The part claimed Kenneth like a stray dog. But then, there were no other takers. Kenneth took it and Tony nodded. Actors are launched by such nods before agents' demands make them unapproachable and reviewers claim to discover them. Tom Courtenay, Rita Tushingham, Albert Finney, Michael Caine, Sean Connery were all given this impeccable auction nod at exactly the right moment of risk by people like Tony, George and Harry Saltzman.

Casting Alison was almost as difficult. The known young stars were a vapid bunch. Actresses and their agents counted the number of Mrs Porter's lines, as well they might, and weighed them against a top salary of £40 a week. The part itself, among other things, was a study of the tyranny of negation. No doubt it was too much to expect anyone to realize that this was the source of its theatrical muscle. Alison's brutal power lay in the puny crackle of her iron. 'Why doesn't she throw the board at him?' The question is still asked by university students, their tutors and bushy-tailed young critics.

A film name, however untried, Rank or Pinewoody, might give some ballast to a cast of unknowns. Tony rang me excitedly to say that he thought he had found our Alison. She was appearing as Ophelia in Paul Scofield's *Hamlet*. She and the production were dreadful, but I must go and see her in a film called *Storm over the Nile*, an appalling remake of *The Four Feathers*, only watchable for the inclusion of the original's second-unit footage by Zoltán Korda.

As it happened I had heard of her. Her name was Mary Ure and I had seen her picture on the front page of *Picture Post* as she bought vegetables at Hammersmith market outside the Lyric Theatre, where she had scored a star-is-born kind of success in *Time Remembered* by Jean Anouilh, again with Scofield. I went to see the film. Mary seemed only more wooden than the other players. 'She looks just like Elsa Lanchester,' I said. Tony had obviously made up his mind. 'I think you're *quite* wrong,' he said. 'I know she can be good. She's a tough little girl from Glasgow.' He made her sound like a sparky barmaid.

I stage-managed all the auditions for the company and received ten shillings for each one. One of the actors selected was Alan Bates and he was among those asked to give readings for Cliff. I favoured Nigel Davenport, but Tony dismissed him. 'Nigel's just like an old *horse*.' John Welsh seemed a fair choice for Colonel Redfern, in spite of his slight Irish accent. George would have been interesting casting, but it might have gone against his terse idea of himself. Glen Byam Shaw was cast almost to type in the film. Nothing seems to become a fierce soldier more than gentleness.

During the weeks of March the core of the company was assembled. Rehearsals for *The Mulberry Bush* took place in a church hall just behind Peter Jones. Those of us not appearing in Wilson's play were expected to go to classes conducted by Yat Malmgren. These consisted of lying on the floor and having your character analysed from your choice of movements. I can't pretend to describe it now as I didn't understand it at the time and found it difficult to take seriously. It was less arduous than PT and more tedious than morning assembly. At least it made you feel that term had started.

As an opening production, heralding the regime of a new company, *The Mulberry Bush* must have been a keen disappointment to George. The indulgent memories of provincial bedrooms often fade on reviewers returning to metropolitan responsibilities. The critics who had already seen the play in Bristol complained that a new company should begin with something untried. It was indeed a tentative start, and timidity, which usually pays such benefits in the theatre, was this time unrewarded. It was calculated caution, but unmistakable caution.

The follow-up, Arthur Miller's *The Crucible*, was more enthusiastically received. Even in Beaverbrook newspapers, McCarthyism could be acknowledged while holdings in South Africa went unmentioned. Besides, Miller was respected, already having saintliness thrust upon him. But the play was still an import, a known quantity, with a distinguished American imprint. No one could have known that my own play was almost consummately handicapped for the following race.

The atmosphere, if I remember it at all, seemed subdued and unspeculative. Rehearsals began in the church hall. Tony made it clear that I was to absent myself from them until I could be of practical help. I was a little surprised but soon grateful for his instinct. When I was permitted to be around, Kenneth was sullen and argumentative. Alan was agreeable and bent on pleasing. Mary was merry as a cockroach in a Kelvinside tea-room. She carped only once at a line about women being noisier than men. It wasn't her experience at all. I tried to point out that it was only the opinion of the character in the play, not mine. For once, I was dishonest in this respect.

Tony's technique of divide and rule was already adept. He kept insisting that I mustn't 'upset' the actors. He must have said the same to them about me. He controlled an iron conspiracy in which no one dared speak to anyone else out of his presence. George and I were mutually intimidated and isolated from each other by this simple ploy for months.

One day I was summoned to the scene of five glum actors. The third act sagged dangerously at the beginning. Tony peered at me bleakly. 'I mean . . . do you think you could *do* something about it? I mean why don't you write a *little song*, or something.' *A little song?* On the Number Nine bus on the way home I took out an envelope from my pocket and started to write my first song.

> Now there's a certain little lady, and you all know who I mean,
> She may have been to Roedean, but to me she's still a queen,
> Some day I'm goin' to marry her,
> When times are not so bad,
> Her mother doesn't care for me,
> So I'll 'ave to ask 'er dad.
> We'll build a little home for two,
> And have some quiet menage,
> We'll send our kids to public school,
> And live on bread and marge.
> Don't be afraid to sleep with your sweetheart,
> Just because she's better than you.
> Those forgotten middle-classes may have fallen on their noses,

But a girl who's true blue,
Will still have something left for you,
The angels up above will know that you're in love,
So don't be afraid to sleep with your sweetheart,
Just because she's better than you . . .

They call me Sidney . . .
Just because she's better than you.

By the time I got to Chiswick Bridge it was finished. When I took it in the following morning I had even improvised a tune. Tony seemed astonished that I had taken him at his word and invited me to sing it. Deeply embarrassed and in front of five sceptical actors, I sang my song to the tune in my head. After I had finished, Tony broke the silence and said, 'Yes, well, we'll *think* about it.' It was his way of saying that he'd made up his mind.

The English Stage Company now employs a full-time press officer and assistant. In 1956 this job was served part-time and just as ineffectively by a man called George Fearon. He was overpaid, but less so than his successors, at £10 a week. Mr Fearon was given a copy of the play and invited me for a drink at a pub in Great Newport Street. He equivocated shiftily, even for one in his trade, and then told me with some relish how much he disliked the play and how he had no idea how he could possibly publicize it successfully. The prospect began to puff him up with rare pleasure. He looked at me cheerfully as if he were Albert Pierrepoint guessing my weight. 'I suppose you're really – an angry young man . . .' He was the first one to say it. A boon to headline-writers ever after. An Angry Young Man. '. . . Aren't you?' I could see no help coming from that quarter.

We had one preview night, nearly unknown then when stars would be expected to clean up automatically for weeks in the provinces before descending on the West End. George and Tony were baffled by the persistent laughter. When the third act opened to discover Helena drooped over Alison's ironing-board, no one could ignore the cheers that applauded the ironing-board's performance. 'But why do you think they're laughing so much?' asked Tony, alarmed. 'Because it's supposed to be funny,' I replied. Neither of them was reassured.

The overnight stardom of the ironing-board was forgotten the following evening, 8 May. The occasion seems to have been confidently documented by the few who were there, but I remember little. I was sitting in the front row of the unfilled dress circle between Oscar Lewenstein and the writer Wolf Mankowitz. Wolf laughed loudly, and alone. Oscar glanced around him like a managing clerk anticipating a disastrous verdict from the jury foreman. Mary dispensed whatever spirit may have prevailed in wartime Kelvinside and pressed champagne on me in her dressing-room. Her unconcern for the play and herself was affecting as the night wore on. By the end of the evening I was very drunk as, for the first time, I went through the playwright's lap of dishonour round the dressing-rooms. This entails fawning upon an actor in front of his hostile and resentful relatives and agents while they look on with contempt for the ordeal you have inflicted on their idol. I was unaware that Binkie Beaumont, most powerful of the unacceptable faeces of theatrical capitalism, had been in the theatre and had walked out in the interval. Or that the critic T.C. Worsley had persuaded Terence Rattigan to stay.

Next morning, I woke in my cabin, still dressed, feeling cold and wondering whether anything had happened at all last evening, the anniversary of my father's birthday. I had a darkened recollection of my creaking bunk and kissing a very friendly plump girl rather older than myself. The taste of vinegary wine, whisky, Mary's champagne and too many Gauloises made me blush at the thought. I crept ashore, across to Mortlake, where there was a newsagent near Lady Hamilton's house. I bought all the dailies and walked back reading them.

There were five reviewers who made the dottle in the Devine pipe bubble with impatience. One was Philip Hope-Wallace, whose maidenly condescension seems to have been mysteriously revered by the less classy bibbers in El Vino. Whatever his possible charm in the bar, it was not on tap to those slogging at the rock-face. The others were Jack Lambert, who seemed to be able to draw off the actual blood of boredom from George, John Barber (whom he had known at Oxford) and Martin Esslin, the Hungarian opinion-maker and BBC mole, burrowing his way into the English air of London clubs. As for someone called Ossia Trilling, another Oxford poltergeist, whose copy flooded German-speaking newspapers and seeped back to chorus boys' magazines like *Plays and Players*, the dottle became positively volcanic.

When I arrived at the theatre, still nauseous from the early-hours drinking, George attempted to brace me up but his own disappointment seemed clearer and more stricken than my own. He told me there was quite a good notice in the *Financial Times*. Tony pretended to be astonished by both of us. 'But what on earth did you *expect*? You didn't expect them to *like* it did you?' His affected scorn was preferable to anyone's encouraging nod. Meanwhile, a gloomy rearguard action was being rehearsed in the foyer by

Fearon. Coining 'Angry Young Man' still pleased him a little, although he could now see no usefulness in it. There was no advance at the box office. He had spoken to a psychiatrist who had seen *Look Back* and assured him that there were clinical examples of young men who behaved and talked like Jimmy Porter. Expert medical evidence might get us through the week.

In the afternoon, Tony held a short rehearsal. The actors were content. No one's performance had been put to any question and their courage in almost overwhelming their material had brought them solicitous attention. Mary was singled out among the victims. 'Mary Ure triumphs over undress.' She chattered on quite beguilingly.

Nellie Beatrice demanded to come to the second performance. I met her at Sloane Square station and she insisted in her usual semi-hysteria on making her way to Lyons for a coffee instead of the drink waiting for her at the theatre. 'I want to keep my head *clear* for the play. I read the *News* and the *Standard*,' she said. 'The write-ups weren't very good were they? I expect you're disappointed, poor kid. Ah, well – perhaps you'll be in the limelights the next time.' It was not unlike getting a girl in the family way, and for no explicable purpose.

During the first interval, people 'passing comments' forced her into the upstairs bar for a drink 'to steady my nerves'. The barmaid confirmed her disquiet. 'They don't like this one, do they dear? They don't like it at all. Never mind, it won't be much longer. We're having Peggy Ashcroft soon. They'll like that. But they don't like *this* one. Not a bit of it.'

There was no reproach or show of unease from George or Tony. There was desultory talk of being 'saved by the Sundays', but if either one of them nursed such hopes he concealed them from me. I watched the play for what must surely be its last performance, and there were almost as many laughs as there had been at the preview. The following day I walked over to the Mortlake newsagent once again and bought the Sunday papers. I read the *Observer* and the *Sunday Times* on a corporation bench in the bright May early morning sunshine.

> *Look Back in Anger* presents post-war youth as it really is, with special emphasis on the non-U intelligentsia, who live in bed-sitters and divide the Sunday papers into two groups, 'posh' and 'wet'. To have done this at all would be a signal achievement; to have done it in a first play is a minor miracle. All the qualities are there, qualities one had despaired of ever seeing on the stage – the drift towards anarchy, the instinctive leftishness, the automatic rejection of 'official' attitudes, the

surrealist sense of humour ... the casual promiscuity, the sense of lacking a crusade worth fighting for and, underlying all these, the determination that no one who dies shall go unmourned ... The Porters of our time deplore the tyranny of 'good taste' and refuse to accept 'emotional' as a term of abuse; they are classless, and they are also leaderless. Mr Osborne is their first spokesman ... I doubt if I could love anyone who did not wish to see *Look Back in Anger*.

> Kenneth Tynan, *Observer*, 13 May 1956

John Osborne is a writer of outstanding promise, and the English Stage Company is to be congratulated on discovering him.

> Harold Hobson, *Sunday Times*, 13 May 1956

I went back to the boat to ring Tony. At noon a dozen of us drank pints of beer outside the pub in Lower Mall. George was grinning at me over his unlit pipe.

The newspapers rang. Kenneth Tynan, then also a script-editor at Ealing, asked me to lunch within days to talk about writing a film. Another call came, this time from the Dorchester Hotel. Would I ring Mr Harry Saltzman – urgently? I was unused to American producers who leave messages for you to ring urgently about most unurgent matters. The call to breakfast with someone passing through the Dorchester or the Savoy was still a quaint myth. I had tea with Harry. He thought *Look Back in Anger* would be a big success in New York if handled properly. He had more flair than to suggest it be translated to Greenwich Village. Harry had just finished making a film called *The Paleface*, which he told me was the only loss-making movie ever made by Bob Hope. His own amusement at this was encouraging. An equally likeable staff writer on *Picture Post* interviewed me and then rushed me off by taxi to be photographed on the deck of M/Y *Egret*.

Mary made the inside of the magazine this time. She was living in Southwell Gardens in Kensington. A single bed in a cold basement suited her own frugal needs. Welsh-Fulham upstarts yearn for sybaritic necessities unknown to Scottish girls from the Clyde, whose cheerful response to a detumescent bedroom was to turn the gas fire up to half-pressure and put on a warm woolly. Spending a night with her meant an assault course of dressing in whispers, coping with the treacherous front-door latch, the landlady's ear ever-open for her returning cat, and then having to persuade a cab driver at 6.00 a.m. to take me outside the eight-mile limit for ten shillings. This was not what I had been used to in the provinces.

In spite of Kenneth Tynan and *Picture Post*, *Look Back* was only playing to moderate business. An effort was made to salvage something from the public confusion of those early weeks by somehow persuading the BBC to present a twenty-five minute extract on television, with an introduction by George Harewood. The response at the box office was immediate and takings went up from £900 to £1,700. A new production was presented at the Lyric, Hammersmith, to make way for the rest of the Court's repertoire.

Donald Albery had summoned me to his office at the New Theatre and offered to transfer the play. He demanded cuts from the passages which he said audiences found most offensive. The most indefensible were the bears and squirrels, which even Tynan had described as 'painful whimsy'. Everyone, said Albery, had been discomforted by them. Surprised by my own coolness, I pointed out that as by this time everyone had been warned against the ending they might feel deprived of it. I didn't try to justify the blackness of my playmaking. We were both pleased not to budge, and *Look Back* waited nine years for its first West End presentation, at Albery's own theatre, the Criterion.

My pocket diary for 1956 is filled with the details of royalties. I took out my last £20 from the Post Office and opened a bank account. I was able to give Nellie Beatrice the largest tip she had seen since her GIs departed. I supplied Anthony Creighton with money and he gave up his agreeable social life at the telephone exchange. The entry for 21 December reads: 'Bank: In – £368. Out – £50. Self – £10.'

I was still earning £12 a week from the English Stage Company. Mary had been given some money by her father, bought herself a small house in Woodfall Street, off the King's Road, and we moved in. It was tiny, with one long narrow sitting-room, a kitchen, bedroom and bathroom and a space as big as a box-room which I could use as my study. She was working again for Binkie, in Arthur Miller's *A View from the Bridge*. We both felt we were doing rather well. Her director, Peter Brook, rehearsed long hours, often till nine or ten in the evening, so I saw little of her. The prospect of having all day to myself in Woodfall Street with a few hundred pounds in the bank was startling in its simplicity, and I had already tried to describe my next play to Tony.

But all these months, I knew that the matter of Pamela could not be left unresolved.

Good nature, or what is often considered as such, is the most selfish of

> all the virtues: it is nine times out of ten mere indolence of disposition.
> William Hazlitt, *On the Knowledge of Character*, 1822

I still had a fugitive hope that Pamela might be the tenth exception, but I was more than fatigued by indolence of disposition and my present modest comfort changed nothing of that. It was clear that I would need the services of a lawyer. I knew nothing about such things, any more than I had about the mechanics of getting married to my twenty-one-year-old bride, having had to look it all up in *Whitaker's Almanack*.

I asked Oscar Lewenstein if he could recommend a solicitor. He knew someone he thought was just the man for me. 'You'll like him,' he said. 'He's rather like you, in fact he's rather like Jimmy Porter.' His office was in Ludgate Hill and his name was Oscar Beuselinck. His secretary and the switchboard girl were both sullen and looked like neglected evacuees, ignorant and ill-fed. The second thing he said to me was, 'You think I'm Jewish, don't you?' And then, grinning all over his face, 'Well, I'm not. You should look at my chopper.'

Oscar was not encouraging about my prospects of divorce, which must involve the risks of collusion. He leered conspiratorially and made it clear that my chances of wheedling any sympathy from a smart-minded judge were remote. I was not yet familiar with how happily lawyers deliver the unhappiest verdict on your life. It is like encountering the Oriental nod which means 'No.' The whole enterprise seemed risky, seedy, indeed criminal. I wasn't intent on marrying Mary, and I was reluctant to go through the business of Pamela being pressed to unwilling action.

While he was rattling off my poor chances, the telephone rang. Cupping his hand over the receiver, he said, 'This is my bank manager. I'm screwing his cashier only he doesn't know that.' He assumed the voice he reserves for posh clients until he put the telephone down. He restored my theatrical faith within seconds. 'No, Johnco, if I don't get it three times a day I feel ill. If I don't get it once a day I feel *physically ill*. I really do. The other night I went home and fucked the wife. Got up, fucked her again. Delia gave me a gobble-job at lunch-time. Then I saw Jenny, that's the bank manager's cashier I was telling you about. Went back and fucked the wife again. *Not bad is it?*' You couldn't help liking him. Like Max Miller. No inner life to hinder. 'Have you ever had it on the kitchen table?' he asked as he saw me out.

Pamela was working in rep in York and I arranged to go up and see her on a Sunday. She met me on the station platform and we went into the buffet. I told her about Oscar and the technical complications of adultery. My train back to London was due in half an hour. I felt I could easily have persuaded her into an unresolving bed. She had heard that I was living with Mary and asked me if we intended to get married. I said, truthfully, that it was possible but not definite. She said nothing to this but told me that she had not been well lately, having had an abortion at a too-late stage, which only she could have contemplated. She saw me on to the train and absent-mindedly kissed me goodbye.

4. 'Take it Orfe'

Despise the things of the world and be indifferent to all changes and events of Providence, but he that creates to himself thousands of little hopes, uncertain in the promise, fallible in the event, and depending upon ten thousand circumstances, shall often fail in his expectations, and be used to arguments of distrust in such hopes.

Jeremy Taylor, *Holy Living*, 1650

During that spring and summer of 1956 I had been as much exhilarated by the prospect of being a company actor as anything else. The days of stage-managing, pushing wheelbarrows of borrowed furniture, calling surly actors and appeasing electricians and flymen seemed to be left behind.

I certainly enjoyed the rehearsals of *Don Juan* and *The Death of Satan*. It seemed like a cheery party in which no one, apart from the author, had any stake. I was aware that I was not any good in my small part (an American businessman in a silver wig) – like so many second-rate actors, I appeared to shine like pinchbeck in flashy roles – but no one else was much better. The Black Dwarf looked as if he was poised to spurt venom on to the stage from his perch in the stalls.

As the only other writer present, I felt some guilt in not sympathizing with his rage: his tiny form almost convulsed with frustration, his long, dark hair sprawled over his pale, papery face. The dress rehearsal took place four days after *Look Back* had opened. The euphoria of the two Sunday notices seemed to infect everyone. Duncan watched helplessly as his unactable double-bill, a rag-bag of Shaw, Eliot and St Augustine, was rolled back unceremoniously like a stack of dusty rugs in a department store. It was a small but cruel revenge on Verse Theatre and Higher Thought. I didn't know how he could have subjected himself to such mockery. Perhaps he still imagined that in performance it would somehow transcend indifferent presentation and reveal itself as a minor masterpiece. Even at my age, I would have been on the Number Nine bus home, demanding my name be ripped from Sloane Square. After four performances it was taken off. Not a friend intervened, not even Harold Hobson with his bent for religious analogy.

Rehearsals then began for *Cards of Identity*. These were altogether different. So was Nigel Dennis. He attended more than Angus had done or poor Ronnie had been permitted. The script, a cobble-job, was sloshed together by Tony, George and Nigel. It was about a hundred pages too long. Sheets of paper were ripped from the actors, who were relieved to have less to say. Nigel wrinkled with pleasure when one of his jokes came off. He would come into the dressing-room and 'chortle' as Edwardian writers would have it. Chortling, like sauntering, was a rare spectacle. He had also struck up a close friendship with George, sadly to end in acrimony over the production of *August for the People*, leaving George with a breakdown, bitterly mourning the loss.

One half of the *Cards of Identity* cast never came across the other. The half I was in included Robert Stephens, Alan Bates and Ernest Milton, an actors' actor like Wilfred Lawson. From the outset it was clear that Ernest was unhappy. He said he was worried about his wife coping with a move to another house. But his part, Father Golden Orfe, was a drunken priest who had a long, self-reviling speech celebrating his loathsome condition which ended with the triumphant cry: 'I *stink* therefore I am!' Ernest, actor and fervent Catholic, had not understood its implications. His caution was correct. The passage caused more offence than any other in the play. When George took over as Orfe he delivered it in dashing fashion and collapsed in my arms before the unbelievers in the stalls started baying out their disbelief.

The first night seemed even more tight-arsed and jacketed than the ones I had already experienced at the Court. Before the long evening was halfway over it was clear that we were not simply playing to a hand-picked Jewish Charity audience but to a hard phalanx of dressed-up ill-wishers. During the last minutes a cloud of resentment and frustration was suspended over the auditorium. I don't think I was the only one to feel a tang of exhilaration wafting over us like cigar smoke at a smart boxing event.

Never having felt 'waves of love' over the footlights, I can only confirm that rollers of hate can be a most warming and stimulating dose of salts. Booing is a strange sound in the theatre, and I had never heard it in such pure form. It was a sound I was to come to know very well during the rest of my career. As my rebellious schoolfriend Mickey Wall used to say, 'If we could package it, it would be worth a guinea a box.'

. . . and who should turn up wearing false, sabre teeth and a hairless dome, but John Osborne . . . ruthlessly funny as the Custodian of Ancient Offices! The Royal Court's captive playwright stands out from an excellent supporting cast.

Kenneth Tynan, *Observer*, June 1956

After a week or two the boos subsided and the audiences became smaller. The stage manager came round to tell me that Mr Devine wanted to see me in his dressing-room. When I got there, a startlingly familiar figure was standing beside him. It was Laurence Olivier with his agent, Cecil Tennant. It seemed that Olivier had been bellowing his strident displeasure about *Look Back* to Tennant, who persuaded him to see the play again. When the curtain rose, they found themselves watching *Cards of Identity*. 'You're my kind of actor,' Olivier told me. 'You like hiding behind make-up.' He said he was preparing a film of *Macbeth* and that I would be very good as the English doctor. I made a note to look it up when I got home. George winked at me.

Almost immediately we started rehearsals for Brecht's *Good Woman of Setzuan*. George had met Brecht during the continental tour of the Gielgud–Noguchi *King Lear* a year earlier. He had been very fired not only by Brecht's achievement but by his presence. The laconic, unmade-bed look, suggesting dark coffee-stained vests, the black and gold teeth, the cheap cigars, the pudding-basin haircut, possibly chopped off by his most official wife, Helene Weigel, with garden secateurs, and the black leather jackets soon to be adopted by another generation of Court directors – all these made an impression on George far removed from elegant theatre managers lunching at the Ivy.

It was a large cast with a lot of small parts, particularly for stoic peasantry. Three hours, fourteen scenes and thirty actors singing, dancing and speaking elliptical folk wisdom to demonstrate that the poor are often a greedy, ruthless and covetous lot. Joan Plowright was a motherly housewife, Nigel Davenport a Chinese policeman, Robert Stephens, Esmé Percy and John Moffatt were gods who descended, shakily. George was a Gradgrind tradesman, Peter Wyngarde an aviator, I was a peasant gardener and Peter Woodthorpe a waterseller. Nightly he goosed me with agonizingly accurate ferocity beneath my worker's rags as he made his entrance: 'I am Wang the Waterseller.' Peggy Ashcroft played a dual role as Shen Te and Shui Ta, one female, one male, adopting masks for the transition and giggling throughout.

The regard for Brecht was then ascendant because of Kenneth Tynan's enthusiasm and the recent visit of the Berliner Ensemble. None of us had any idea of how to begin to tackle him. It seemed to me as daunting as doing a Japanese Noh play in weekly rep. Language, custom, national temperament, training, or lack of it, even physical appearance seemed to doom the effort. The staccato theatrical method was helped tremendously by the German language itself. The new East German state looked like providing a rigour and political bite certainly lacking at home.

I felt like a contented conscript, prepared to do what I might be asked but aware that it wouldn't be much. I was just an underpaid squaddie with a free trip on tour to Brighton. In some vague gesture towards Stella Linden, my older woman, mistress and collaborator, with whom I had spent glorious and instructive months in a flat on the front in 1949, I booked into a bizarre vegetarian hotel. There was no alcohol, it was full of old ladies in half-light and huge portraits of biblical scenes. I soon realized my mistake and switched to the Royal Crescent, then the pros' hotel, where you could be waited on with whisky, wine and sandwiches all through the night.

One of the attractions of the Theatre Royal was its backstage bar which was, literally, on the stage. It was frequented by a more or less cheery collection of has-been bar-flies and Brighton bit-part players. One of these was Gilbert Harding, then at the height of his self-despised reputation as an early TV personality, a take-away Dr Johnson. I had met him once before, at the Savile Club, where he grabbed my knee in almost fatherly affection and demanded, in front of the company of floppy bow-tied waiters, I admit that Jimmy and Cliff were in love with each other and that was what *Look Back* was Really All About. 'Think they're buggers, do you Gilbert?' growled Compton Mackenzie. I hope I wasn't too priggish.

At the Sunday dress rehearsal of *Good Woman* Gilbert didn't recognize me, which was not surprising. He must have been in the stage bar for several hours and in the crusty mood for which he was so admired by a troglodyte television audience. I was sitting in the stalls. Presently, I became aware of old Gilbert slumped beside me and, after a few minutes, I felt a hand on my grey People's Republic knee. The costume was as impenetrable as it was unappealing. I froze, and hoped that the combination of Brecht and afternoon Brighton buzz would at least put the alienation effect to some useful purpose. After a few grumpy fumbles, he turned and growled in a voice immediately identifiable, 'Tell me – are you a boy or a girl?' 'Just a peasant. And I'm nearly on. Excuse me.'

I felt on holiday from events, not only from those of the past half-dozen years but from the persisting strictures of Stella and Pamela, the naked bullying, rabid caution and frozen hearts of Nellie Beatrice and Grandma Osborne who killed pleasure at interminable paces, and from everyone with a brief to diminish endeavour. Of course I was often to feel almost grievously threatened for years to come, but during those summer weeks I had a realization of sorts that I could at least go the full distance, and always would.

The following week in Oxford, Helene Weigel and Paul Dassau, Brecht's composer, came to see us at the New Theatre, and rehearsals began afresh. Aware of our bafflement and keenness to be instructed by visiting Marxist royalty, they were both friendly and encouraging. The interpretation of the songs was particularly difficult. One called 'Chang had Seven Elephants' involved a great deal of snorting, pachyderm stamping and earnest ear-flapping. Hopes were scuppered within minutes. All well-meant attempts to mime died under the Teutonic lash of Weigel and Dassau. To a couple of dozen willing but unequipped Anglo-Saxon actors, Brecht remained little more than the image of a bitten-off haircut and the sprout of a long cigar butt.

My abiding memory of the week is of dining with Peggy Ashcroft and Esmé Percy at an Indian restaurant by the Martyrs' Memorial. They talked entertainingly and Esmé's beloved dog farted incessantly under the table. Peggy grew impatient. 'Don't you think he needs a bit of a clean out?' 'Oh, but I only shampooed him this morning.' 'I meant clean *within*, not without.'

After we opened in London, there was a feeling of genial irresponsibility. It was a little like taking part in an event in some foreign country which hardly anyone understood. Everyone seemed in a good temper and under no pressure to shine. I was back in dressing-room Number Six with Nigel Davenport and Robert Stephens. Down in Number Three, the viper's hell-kitchen, we could eavesdrop on the shrieks of John Moffatt, Esmé and Peters Wyngarde and Woodthorpe. One evening, the peasant Woodthorpe, surrounded by Brecht's pantomime gods, was washing his feet, fresh from a blackened stage and a careless life. Exasperated after days of this thought-lessness, Moffatt, a most fastidious and circumspect man, finally remonstrated: 'I do think, Peter, you might wait for the rest of us to wash our hands and faces before you put your filthy feet in the basin.' The reply drifted gamely up the stairs. 'Oh, come off it, little Miss Muffett. Get off your tuffet!' Like so much else, it was a relief from admired alienation.

Mary had opened in *A View from the Bridge*. We were snapped with

Marilyn Monroe, we had supper with Richard and Sybil Burton at Emlyn Williams' house in Pelham Crescent (where we were announced by a butler). We were photographed in Cecil Beaton's dappled garden. He described me as an elegant camel. I had instruction from Wolf Mankowitz on how to write plays, the genius of F.R. Leavis, good butchering, and how to impregnate a girl and outwit the Inland Revenue. We went to Kenneth Tynan's Mount Street flat to meet Cyril Connolly and Peter Hall, with a gloriously pregnant Leslie Caron.

I was becoming aware that there was a concerted campaign to turn me into a plaything freak of what would now be deadeningly described as the 'media'. It was fairly clear, even to me, what they were up to. It continued quite unrelentingly until the end of the decade, when even Fleet Street could get no more juice from this oversqueezed fantasy. The sub-editors repeated late-night inspirations and looked forward in hope. What is modern society angry about? It seemed that no one could exorcise the whole invention. The inertia, defeatism and conformist suspicion of the despairing years of life in Britain since 1945 seemed to have been injected into some previously armoured nerve.

There was an almost tangible frisson from Lower Mall about the ludicrous attention that both the play and myself were receiving. George and Tony were both genuinely contemptuous of it. I can't pretend that, for me, the absurd spotlight and the feigned friendliness were not invigorating. The abuse, dislike and hell-bent discouragement were also hurtful. I could sense the danger, although none of us spoke of it. I was surely being set up for demolition at a not too late date. Instead of asking George or Tony for loyal advice, I gave interviews and wrote articles on crass subjects ('What's Wrong with Women Today'); I was offered ten times my weekly salary for 700 words which even I had the facility to turn out in an hour or so. Journalism intrigued me as a spur to my brooding, inhibited and ponderous method of working. Apart from the prize-like cheques, I felt an excitement at the carrot of a huge byline. I detected a streak of Wadham spinsterishness in George and Tony's unspoken distaste. It was flattering to be on one's own in this.

Within months of my ticking-off from every agent in London, I was reviewing the collected plays of Tennessee Williams for the *Observer* and writing film and television criticism for the *Evening Standard* and the odd few hundred words for anybody on almost anything from romantic love to favourite dishes. A magazine called *Lilliput*, famous as a beer-and-blazer publication, asked me to choose an item of clothing which they would have made for me if I posed in it. A harmless lark. Thinking of my grandfather's prophecies of becoming either Prime Minister or Bernard Shaw, I decided on a Norfolk jacket. I presented myself to a master and most traditional tailor in Holborn. Looking at my scuffed high-street sports jacket, he didn't bother to smother his scorn. 'What *kind* of Norfolk jacket?' What *kind*? I had assumed it was as identifiable as a hot-cross bun. 'There *are* thirty varieties, sir.'

I was gulled frequently. A journalist from the *Spectator* went through the letters on my mantelshelf while I was out of the room fixing him a drink. The magazine printed the details, including a note from the Inland Revenue. A few weeks later I found myself sitting next to Edith Sitwell. She brandished her great rings at me in welcome, saying that she had sent a protesting telegram from Hollywood to the editor: 'It was always a disgusting paper.' As Laurence Olivier said, 'No one ever won an interview.'

But I had also earned some money. Samuel French, the principal publishers of amateur editions, would offer only £25 for the rights of *Look Back*. I was intrigued to be in the market-place. The first amazing windfall was from Fischer Verlag – £300 for the German rights, more than my annual earnings for years. Unimaginable. I bought the *Encyclopaedia Britannica* with it.

Mary and I spent a week in Spain, south of Tarragona. It was my first trip beyond the Isle of Wight and I was apprehensive of flying and, most of all, being thwarted by language. The clerk at Thomas Cook's was not encouraging. The collapsed lip of the born official expanded into something like near-happiness. 'Oh, not married. Well, I can make the booking for you but I can't, of course, guarantee that you will get a room. Not together, at least. Still, it's up to you.'

Mary was as indignant as a housewife served a stale baptie with her morning coffee. The clerk was unimpressed by her show of Scots womanliness. 'I'm sorry. But there it is.' I almost wished we could go to Margate and Wonderland instead. 'After all, it *is* a Catholic country,' he said as he handed us our vouchers and luggage labels.

As it turned out Mary made the trip very enjoyable. She was fussy, bossy and implacably cheerful. The hotel was perched on stilts directly on the beach. There were a dozen rooms, bright tiles on the floors, a simple restaurant, seafood and champagne at a pound a bottle. It was run by a lady from Manchester who took our passports without a glance for immoral intentions. Mary was one of those unguarded souls who can make themselves understood by penguins or the wildest dervishes. Spanish was no problem. It would have taken a crabbed spirit not to be affected and plunge in with her almost literal carelessness. It was a good time. I was not in love. There was fondness and pleasure but no groping expectations, just a feeling of fleeting heart's ease. For the present we were both content enough.

> *What to do next?* There are too many books, too many plays, too much commentary and clamour. There is no progress only frenzy. There is too much decay of the heart.

Notebook, 1976

As 1956 came to an end, my mood could hardly have been more different from what it was to be twenty years later. Christmas 1956 was the first since 1946 I had not spent working at Blythe Road post office. The year before I had grumpily refused Tony's offer to play a non-speaking sailor in his television production of *Othello*. Apart from pride, I pointed out that my BBC fee would be about half of what I would get by encouraged fiddling and overtime with the GPO. Mary and I spent Christmas quietly together in Woodfall Street.

Salisbury

Dear John,

Once again Xmas has been and gone. We have had a quiet time, nobody to see us but Bessie made it as festive as possible. Please forgive the type as eye operation was not too successful. We were very concerned because your card only arrived on Boxing Day and it worried us. Perhaps I will be more cheerful after I have been in hospital in January. Enjoy yourself John whilst you are young it does not last long believe me.

God bless.
Uncle Jack

Watford

Dear John,

Such lots of thanks for your Xmas parcel. Have put it away and shall drink your health and happiness at Christmas, say 12 o/c. We shall be thinking of you on Xmas Day. Guess you will have a lovely time. We shall just have my sister here and as my other Sister [who] passed away last Jan. had her birthday Christmas Day, we shall no doubt feel a little down.

Lots of love,
Uncle Sidney xxxx

Salisbury

My dear John,

I feel that I did not thank you sufficiently for your Xmas gift. We had a marvellous time. A capon, Xmas pudding, a drink and a piece of roast beef (reminded me of yours). You see with those Harrods hampers you have sent us in the past, you get trivial things, such as mustard, peppers, sauces, we have some 3 years old. We even had two items missing. Do not think I am ungrateful.

God bless.

Uncle Jack

Life in Woodfall Street was oddly settled, almost provincial. We might have been living in Leicester or Harrogate and far from the fiction that was generated about us both. Mary had been fêted by Binkie, fondled by Terry Rattigan, had played Ophelia to Paul Scofield in Moscow, been featured on magazine covers and appeared in two Arthur Miller plays. It was a fairly heady début for a girl who had only intended to be a drama teacher in Glasgow. She treated the whole crowded sequence as if it had hardly taken place.

She took scant interest in her surroundings and, despite her eloquence about her mother's oatcakes, kippers and jams, scarcely cooked at all. I didn't mind. I was quite happy to turn out my vegetarian dishes. The cupboards were bare. When she did cook, as for our first Christmas dinner, the kitchen was blackened. Fortunately, she never apologized. It didn't matter and there was always the Indian at the end of the alley. She would leave the house every day after instant coffee and a slice of toast and reappear in the late afternoon. She would go to her hairdresser (Phyllis Earle in Berkeley Square, grudgingly paid for by Binkie), meet a girlfriend for lunch and then 'go shopping at Harrods'. She rarely bought anything but a bagful of baubles from the make-up counter or a pair of stockings. But she always came back bubbling with happiness.

I was content that I was not making her unhappy in any way. I had no idea what pain I might have inflicted on Pamela and reflected on it daily. I hoped that despair or doubt would never blow on Mary's butterfly spirit. She was no sphinx and concealed no secrets apart from her forays into Harrods. But I still addressed myself to Pamela's motives: had she ever loved me at all; ungiven to gestures, had she married me so casually, withdrawing as quickly from my life and as imperceptibly as she had entered it?

The impression from Fleet Street was that Mary and I were a gilded couple who had won the football pools. She was asked her opinion on cooking, of all things, and the H-bomb. This cut no ice with Grandma Osborne. When I paid her a dutiful visit, she greeted me with as much warmth as she ever mustered and, as ever, asked me not a question. The thin smile was just as wintry and she told me with pride about cousin Tony's job as a probation officer in Macclesfield and cousin Jill's second or third baby. Fleet Street, the wireless and television had no dominion over the *South Wales Argus* and its Births and Deaths columns or the latest Warwick Deeping. I showed her a newspaper photograph of Mary, rising young star. She gazed at it briefly with her ever-painful eyes. 'She seems a pretty little thing.'

Mary, however, had powerful family support from her father and brothers. Her weekly telephone calls made clear how secure she was. The dialogue scarcely changed. 'And how are you?' 'Oh, we're all right. We've all had colds.' Always. 'Is that so? And how's the wee man?' (One of her brother's babies. He'd had a cold, too.) There were calls to her old nanny and reminiscences about sharing their 'sweetie coupons'. Perhaps she should never have set her sights on Dr Johnson's highway into England and the snares of Sassenach show-biz.

5. 'I Have a Go, Lady. I Do. I Have a Go'

Lowndes Cottage,
London SW1

Thankyou. Thankyou for the thrilling and lovely play which will no doubt be in the same Reps Theatre drawer as the Cherry Orchard and The School for Scandal before the century is out. Thankyou for the most deeply engaging part perhaps barring only Macbeth and Lear that I can remember – *certainly* the most enjoyable. I thank you for the play with all my heart, and for the pride it gives me to be in it, and for the joy of playing it. Hope I don't fuck it up for you tonight.

Letter from Laurence Olivier to J.O., 10 April 1957

Journalists insist that I wrote the part of Archie Rice in *The Entertainer* for Laurence Olivier, just as reference books have it that *Look Back in Anger* was originally titled *On the Pier at Morecambe*. These dumb speculations have a way of perpetuating themselves as fact. The true record may not be of much account but it is hard to justify tampering with it.

One evening, when Mary was rehearsing Arthur Miller, I went on my own to the Chelsea Palace. Max Miller was on the bill. Waiting for him to come on, I watched an act, the highlight of which was an impersonation of Charles Laughton playing Quasimodo. I had seen it before. A smoky green light swirled over the stage and an awesome banality prevailed for some theatrical seconds, the drama and poetry, the belt and braces of music hall holding up epic. This, the critics would later tell me, was the Brechtian influence on the play.

Music hall was on its last legs but there were still a few halls in and around London for me to visit, not yet quite defeated by grey, front-parlour television. I made notes for the play. I knew I was on to the problem – remembering George's dictum that all problems were technical ones – and I was even confident enough to give the play a title. I'd been listening to a record by a trumpet-player called Bunk Johnson. He was something of a legend, whose reputation had been revived by a few enthusiasts who had found him working in the Deep South as a truck driver, old and forgotten. They bought him a new set of teeth and he made a short comeback. One of the tunes he recorded was an old Scott Joplin number, 'The Entertainer'. It was graceful and touching and seemed apt for the play.

Sometime in early February 1957, George telephoned me. He was meticulous about not hectoring writers and so I was surprised when he asked, 'How's the play going, dear boy?' 'All right.' 'How far have you got?' This was most unlike him. He knew the powers of my evasion. 'Oh, I've finished the second act. Almost.' 'I see. I hate to ask, but something's just come up. I don't suppose you can tell me if there's a part in it for Laurence?' 'Laurence who?' 'Olivier.'

George persuaded me against all his practice. 'Would you mind awfully if I asked you to let me have the first two acts?' Believing us both wrong, I agreed. Olivier's response was immediate and astonishing. He wanted to play Billy Rice, Archie's father. Letting him read just two acts had confused everyone. A week later I rang Tony and told him I had finished. 'Read me the last page,' he said, and I mumbled Archie's last speech down the telephone to his final line, which Olivier found incomprehensible and made devastating. 'Let me know where you're working tomorrow night – and I'll come and see *YOU*.' It was to be Olivier's face but, I hoped, *my* voice – possibly my own epitaph.

Things moved quickly. Sir Laurence was suddenly 'available' and eager in the way of prized actors who come into season with occasional surprising suddenness and have to be accommodated while the bloodstock is raring. Tony and I were summoned to the Connaught Hotel where, for some domestic reason, the Oliviers were temporarily staying. It is hard to convey what a royal impression these two had made on the press and the public at the same time. In their different ways they had both promoted it.

Seeing Vivien Leigh for the first time, I could only remember watching *Gone with the Wind* as a twelve-year-old recovering from rheumatic fever, sitting in my wheelchair and fainting as she fled from the blood and cries of burning Atlanta. In the flesh, she was strangely robust in a pent-up way, like some threatened animal. Her voice seemed deeper and more rasping than the recollection of Scarlett's 'Great balls of fire' or, even more memorably, Blanche du Bois's 'I have always relied on the kindness of strangers.' I didn't feel she was over-trusting of these two odd-looking young men with their funny old play. Sir Laurence, long regarded by all (including himself) as a bequest to the nation, seemed to be speaking for both of them.

Tony was at his best adroit, northern, breathless-matter-of-factness, and put Larry at his ease a little. The necessity to cast quickly was paramount because of the great man's other commitments. He suggested George Relph to play Billy. It was an unexceptionable choice. There was a 'little actress you may have heard of – Dorothy Tutin'. Tony was keen and, although I wasn't, I felt it was too soon to carp. Then came the question of Phoebe, Archie's wife. Larry came up with a dull selection of H.M. Tennant and Elstree actresses. Suddenly, with dazzling Olivier craftiness, he said, 'Well, now, what about Vivien?'

Tony, Machiavellian and master-technician though he might be, could dissemble no better than myself. The thought of the mouth that once purred through Tara's halls tackling such lines as, 'I don't want to end up in some dead and alive hole' was unthinkable. Before Tony had time to recover, Larry continued: 'I know she's all wrong in a way and far, far too beautiful, but I was talking to Edith the other day about that old woman she played in *Queen of Spades*. It took her five hours in the make-up chair but they put this rubber mask on her, do you see.'

I did see. I had seen the film and enjoyed it enormously, but Edith Evans was not only much older and plainer than one of the acknowledged beauties of stage and screen, she was also playing a woman who was supposed to be at least a hundred years old. *And* it was a film.

After a few minutes it was agreed, without any intervention as I remember from Vivien, that this was, after all, an impractical suggestion, that Vivien was of course far too beautiful and, most unfortunately, the British Public would never accept her as ageing, ugly and common. Larry discarded what was patently being imposed upon him and went on to other possibilities. Now that Vivien was out of the running, we all gratefully agreed to approach Brenda de Banzie, reputed to be trying but powerful, in a very different manner from Blanche du Bois.

When we got to the hotel lobby, Tony tripped out through the revolving door, his breath hitting the cold, late February air. 'What about that!' he whinnied. His gnashing laughter cracked out into Mount Street. 'Rubber masks! Oh, my dear God. Rubber masks!' It was funny enough, but the famous rubber mask was to shadow us for weeks to come, revealing pain, envy, suspicion and dislike.

At the beginning of 1957, the muddle of feeling about Suez and Hungary, implicit in *The Entertainer*, was so overheated that the involvement of Olivier in the play seemed as dangerous as exposing the Royal Family to politics.

There was some relief that an international event could arouse such fierce, indeed theatrical responses, with lifetime readers cancelling the *Observer* and rallies and abuse everywhere. The Korean War had come and gone like a number two touring company: this one would run on well into foreseeable history. The season was open for hunting down deceivers and self-deceivers.

A special meeting of the English Stage Company was convened to make a decision about the production of *The Entertainer*. Left and Right became allies, Lewenstein rooting with Blacksell. Olivier was an undisputed coup, but an embarrassment also. It was decided to drop the play.

Neville Blond, the Chairman of the ESC and its Council, was a Manchester textile magnate and sometime government adviser on transatlantic trade. His wife, Elaine, was a Marks & Spencer heiress. The pair of them promptly issued an invitation to council members for lunch at their flat in Orchard Court to discuss the matter. Over the next few years I attended a few parties at Orchard Court, a gloomy mausoleum block behind elaborate wrought ironwork near Selfridges. These were sumptuous spreads given in the manner of a Christmas party for servants and tenant farmers. Mrs Blond would itemize the value of the pictures on the walls and the price per yard of the upholstery. We were not expected to stay long. She was arguably the most charmless woman I ever met. A few years later she eyed me on the steps of the Royal Court, her cash-register eyes very cold indeed and said, 'Oh – *you're* still here, are you?'

On that first occasion, she told the Council, 'You'd be barmy not to do the play. With Olivier wanting to act in it!' 'You see,' said Neville, less stridently, 'we owe it to the boy.' In the event, George Harewood's casting vote carried the day. *The Entertainer* would go ahead.

I have no record of the cuts imposed on *Look Back in Anger*. The Lord Chamberlain's Office must have misjudged certain elements as for years television critics and provincial newspapers were to complain about the earthy, degrading or even filthy language. The only deletion I can remember was 'as tough as a night in a Bombay brothel and as rough as a matelot's arse'. 'Arm' was substituted for 'arse'.

Lord Chamberlain's Office,
St James's Palace, SW1
20th March, 1957

Sir,

The Entertainer

    I am desired by the Lord Chamberlain to write to you regarding the

above Play and to ask for an undertaking that the following alterations
will be made:—

1) Act I, page 11, alter 'ass-upwards'.

2) Page 29, alter 'clappers'.

3) Act II, page 25, a photograph should be submitted of the nude in
   Britannia's helmet.

4) Page 27 alter 'pouf', (twice).

5) Page 30, alter 'shagged'.

6) Page 36, omit 'Right up to the flies. Right up.'

7) Page 43, omit 'rogered' (twice).

8) Page 44, omit 'I always needed a jump at the end of the day – and
   at the beginning too usually.'

9) Act III, page 3 alter 'wet your pants'.

10) Page 4, omit 'had Sylvia'.

11) Page 6, alter 'turds'.

12) Page 9, alter 'camp'.

13) A photograph of the nude tableau, page 20, should be submitted.

14) Page 21, omit 'balls'.

15) Scene 12, should be submitted in full.

16) The little song entitled, 'The old church bells won't ring tonight
    'cos the Vicar's got the clappers'. Substitute: 'The Vicar's
    dropped a clanger.'

Any alterations or substitutions should be submitted for approval.

Yours faithfully,

Assistant Comptroller

The ESC, the Council and the Lord Chamberlain were contained and we
were in business. It was too late for reservations or quibbling. Olivier had to
fit Archie in during April for five weeks before his summer commitment to
Titus Andronicus. The opening was announced and within a few days every
seat for the short season had been sold. I was happy and unapprehensive.
Whatever the pressures or ill-feeling that might occur during the next few
weeks, there would be little room for manoeuvre, let alone going back.

I was anxious that Olivier should not be tempted into the snare of making
Archie funny. It would have been an understandable mistake for an actor
unused to little less than worship. As it was, people perpetuated the myth
that the character was based on Max Miller. Archie was a man all right and
one which most people, especially maidenly middle-class reviewers, found
unfamiliar and despicable. If they had been baffled that an educated young

man, even an ungrateful graduate of a white-tile university, should *choose* to work at a market sweet-stall, they were mystified by Archie. What could possibly be interesting to the civilized sensibility in the spectacle of a third-rate comic writhing in a dying profession?

Max Miller was a god, certainly to me, a saloon-bar Priapus. Archie never got away with anything. Life cost him dearly, always. When he came on, the audience was immediately suspicious or indifferent. Archie's cheek was less than ordinary. Max didn't have to be nauseatingly lovable like Chaplin. His humanity was in his sublime sauce, Archie's in his hollow desperation. Max got fined £5 for giving them one from the Blue Book and the rest of the world laughed with him. Archie would have got six months and no option.

Olivier took the point from the outset, although he did go and see Miller's fearsome widow. We all paid visits to the remaining London halls. The Chelsea Palace, the Met in Edgware Road and Collins' in Islington were all about to be swept away. When I wrote in the play's published edition that the music hall was dying, I hadn't been aware that the bulldozers and iron balls were poised quite so close to home.

I was especially keen that we should go a few times to Collins', where I had witnessed some of the worst acts imaginable, although the occasional star, like Albert Whelan whistling over his white gloves, Randolph ('On Mother Kelly's Doorstep') Sutton and Ella Shields failing to light her pipe on her sailor's uniform, tottered through their fifty-year-old routines with a kind of detached dignity to a supine audience.

We missed a Scots comedian called Jack Radcliffe who did a very eerie deathbed scene. I thought the spectacle of a 'dying' comic in a sketch about death performed to an almost comatose audience would help an actor who could hardly have witnessed such a farewell to hope and dignity, let alone taken part in it. We did see a more robust act by a Cockney, Scott Sanders, whose signature tune was 'Rolling round the world, waiting for the sunshine and hoping things will turn out right', which he played on a series of pots and pans hanging on a barrow. He was loud, brisk, seldom funny and looked as if he knew it, hurtling through his act hoarsely before retreating to the pub next door. 'Why have you got that lemon stuck in your ear?' 'You've heard of the man with the hearing aid? Well, I'm the one with the lemonade.'

I felt it was important to engage Vivien's support. The rejection of her rubber mask must have added to the rather icy feeling that became clearer during the next few weeks. Once, in Collins', a semen-filled handkerchief was hurled into my lap from somewhere in the dim auditorium. Such an incident would have delighted Lady Olivier. She took to it all, laughing at the dog acts filling the stage with flags, the ventriloquists whose lips flapped like Esther Rantzen on a bad night, the xylophone players with their 'popular melodies'. Unlike the slumped, morose audience around us, Vivien joined in.

One of Olivier's central problems was to persuade audiences that such poetic awfulness could be authentic. The pressure of time was no bad thing and we threw ourselves into what was a unique venture for everyone. Larry was enthusiastic. Tony was at his infectious best. George Relph was clearly going to be splendid as Billy: every flick of his hat or delicate buffing of his fingernails so like my grandfather – and much more agreeable. He had been shot through the throat during the First World War and, having been a successful juvenile, had been forced to become a character man. Brenda de Banzie would hiss in triumph at any old stage-hand or fireman as she came off, 'Look – real tears.' Dorothy Tutin seemed a modest, friendly girl who liked a glass of Guinness and I soon found myself assured that she would give a tougher performance than I had anticipated. Richard Pasco, fresh from playing the second Jimmy Porter, was already a friend.

Jock Addison, the composer, had come with us on our music-hall outings. On these visits he had seemed strangely cautious, but I was unfamiliar with his almost Ben Travers containment. When I suspected he might be bored he was merely worrying over whether to score for two trumpets or one trumpet and a trombone. I was uncertain that he approved of my lyrics. The problem had been to produce something that was identifiably atrocious but good enough to be enjoyable pastiche. Jock set my lyrics in his painstaking way, almost like someone undertaking a set exam piece. The result, with its grasp of the crummy pit orchestra, was not just an accompaniment but an insight into the heart of the play. 'Why should I care?' went unnoticed at the time. When Olivier died, it was on every news bulletin.

Jock's wife, Pamela, was visibly shy and wary of theatrical folk, particularly divide-and-rule men like Tony. The nearest thing to a dramatic experience for her would be an accident in Fortnum and Mason's food hall. Two of the characters in *The Hotel in Amsterdam* are approximations to the Addisons, although I did them small justice. Jock was to score most of the early Woodfall movies, including *Tom Jones*, for which he won an Academy Award. During the next decade, our lives, along with a dozen or so others, spun in a kind of dizzying pattern around Tony and his circle. When Richardson finally said his unfond farewell to England and settled in Los

Angeles for good, the centre didn't exactly fall apart, but the heavens moved to a different rhythm.

In rehearsal there were disturbing rumours about the Oliviers' domestic life. I was not privy to this, although I had the impression that George and Tony knew about the early-morning visits to girls on Thameside house-boats, recriminations and physical vengeance. I hoped that it was not true, for the selfish reason of safeguarding my play and protecting it from pruri-ent interest in Britain's most famous and near-royal couple, which would surely divert attention from what was happening in the theatre itself.

Vivien's watchful presence was the most dangerous threat to the produc-tion's progress, and everyone from George to the ASMs was aware of it. She would drop in without warning and sit in the dress circle with Bernard, her chocolate-uniformed chauffeur, a row behind her. It was usually an unobtrusive entrance, but stardom has no use for tact. Her presence was as distracting as an underwear advertisement at a Lesbians for Peace meeting. She had only recently shouted in protest from the public gallery of the House of Lords about the demolition of the St James's Theatre. What if she should stand up and shout from the dress circle of the Royal Court?

In the event, she always sat quickly and quietly, occasionally asking the chauffeur for a light, intent on Olivier. It was, of course, impossible to know what she was feeling and I could only guess at the pain. It seemed compli-cated, to say the least, that she should be yearning for a rubber mask to turn her into a sort of Brenda – like Niobe, all real tears. Sad also. The clash of feeling made her want to take part in a gamble in which she could hardly have believed, merely to share an act of possible public folly. If Larry was out of his depth now and then, so were we all, but none more so than Vivien, which made her isolation increasingly obvious.

Olivier was relishing his front-of-cloth scenes, attaining an astonishing skill at throw-away business, like a spastic Jimmy Cagney. One Saturday run-through, about midday, he sprang his first realized version of the scene in which Archie sings the blues and crumples slowly down the side of the proscenium arch. The spring sunshine and the noise of the Sloane Square traffic poured through the open door. A dozen of us watched, astounded. Vivien turned her head towards me. She was weeping. I immediately thought of the chill inflection in Olivier's Archie voice: 'I wish women wouldn't cry. I wish they wouldn't . . .'

Before the dress rehearsal, Vivien made a final effort. To do what? I don't know. The production had perhaps become a vehicle containing all her sense of loss to come or already endured. When Tony, George and I were summoned to Number One dressing-room, Olivier was tired, he said little. Like a lioness protective of her energy, she was word-perfect in her complaints and criticisms. Her feverish fury erupted in the cramped room, with its view of the London Transport canteen and the corner of W.H. Smith. After weeks of frustration, watching rehearsals and fuelled by the reception of surely indignant reports back at Binkie's base camp, she lashed out at us all. Finally, edging her fur coat through the door, she said to George, pale but a-puff on his tobacco: 'I was always very fond of you, George. But I could never stand that fucking awful pipe. If you'd been married to me, you would have had to smoke it outside in the garden!'

6. Barwick's Suit

Reticence is called elitism and priggishness passes for compassion . . .
Is it all to do with hatred of the past?

Notebook, 1982

The Entertainer opened on 10 April. On the same day I was due to appear at the Law Courts in the Strand for my petition against Pamela. Months had elapsed since our last meeting, in the buffet on York station. I had gone on hoping I would hear from her. Some vagueness of purpose or even forgetfulness would surely delay the final resort to the court. Mary seemed happy enough in her chirrupy way but I was fairly certain that she would find an obstructive wife too much for her Calvinist morality to accommodate.

She was still largely unaffected by theatrical bohemianism. When I occasionally lapsed into what was then known as 'outrageous camp', she would plead with unsimulated disquiet. 'Oh, do stop it, John. You sound *just* like a queer.' The thought of me making mischief in front of her rugby-playing brothers from Watson's Academy (Scottish camp if ever there was) dismayed her. But, like so many actresses, she found this nonsense perfectly acceptable in crimpers and small-part players. Gordon, her favourite dresser from H.M. Tennant days, was already rather creaky: 'Binkie! Don't talk to me about him. Do you know what I call him? Binkie-Bonkie-Boo-Boo! I do! – Come with me to Woolworth's. I want to buy a lemon shampoo.'

Surely Pamela, sphinx, muddler and arch-procrastinator, could be relied upon to equivocate triumphantly at the last moment? Divorce in 1957 was as risky an adventure and as much a taint on the character as a number of indictable crimes. The concept of guilty and innocent parties was perfectly suited to the avarice and conformism of lawyers, enabling them to encourage their respective clients to go for each other's jugulars like fighting Staffordshires. The implication was that both parties were guilty for having got themselves into such an unthinking mess and, if both dogs died, everyone else got their bets paid.

Divorce, then as now, was concerned almost exclusively with the double-headed monster of sex and money. But worse than physical cruelty or moral indecency was the sin of collusion. The whole masquerade of 'proving' adultery had been lampooned for years by Evelyn Waugh and others. The law remained immune to ridicule. This muddled farce was compounded in my case by Pamela's near-terminal indecision and, more seriously, by the actor we had selected to play the part of co-respondent. I was not sure whether he was the *de facto* party, and tried not to brood about it. He was preferable to the Jewish dentist from Derby, whom I had suggested in some malevolence.

Oscar Beuselinck's clerk, Charlie Barwick, had taken over my case and was even more gloomy about my prospects of success than Oscar, who seemed to regard the whole lengthy business with no more distress than being refused renewal of a dog licence. 'Can't say I think much of your co-respondent, John. Very dodgy. Scruffy cove. Welsh. No collar and tie. We'll have to smarten him up a bit if it does come to it. You may have to buy him some decent clothes. They could go in with our fees.'

As there was no matter of alimony or custody of children, and I had been to all intents and purposes deserted by Pamela, all this dressing-up seemed infinitely frivolous. I had not owned a suit since I joined Harry Hanson's company in Camberwell six years earlier. ('Own Wardrobe and Dinner Jacket.') Bought from a second-hand shop in Vauxhall Bridge Road, it had long ago disintegrated. I went to Aquascutum and fitted myself out with a suitably supplicant-looking outfit: heavy flannel, double-breasted, with a faint concession to dash in a scarcely visible red stripe. On the supposed young scourge of the Establishment it seemed likely to invite suspicion of a hoax.

Before my court appearance, I had one more thing to do. Nellie Beatrice knew nothing of my marriage. I had managed, without much difficulty, to keep it from her. She was now working in a rather disagreeable pub, oddly named the Organ Inn, on the Ewell bypass. I decided to give the plaintiff's suit its first public airing and arranged to meet her in the restaurant of Bentall's store, which she regarded as rather posh. I felt I could not allow her to read about Pamela in the newspapers.

As usual with Nellie Beatrice, I either over- or under-estimated her resilience and cunning. She was surprised, resentful even, that she had not been given the rights of confidence due to a loving mother, but otherwise almost insouciant. She asked no questions about my ex-wife-to-be; the incident could be counted a moral victory and swept into discarded memory. She probably hoped that I would not be silly to myself again and would move in with Anthony Creighton on a steadier basis.

She was in a new rig-out: lemon and cream, coral and brown, all to match. What a telling-off brother Jack was going to get from Uncle Sid; Auntie Queenie kept dropping hints about a pound or two for a drop of brandy; the new barmaid was a common bit of goods; Grandma O. was bedridden above Tesco's. 'Mother, I said, if you don't agree to go into a nice home, I don't know what I'm going to do with you. I said, Mother, if they find you with bedsores, who do you think'll get the blame? I will. And then what will people think. I'm a bag of nerves with it all. My life's been enough rush as it is. You want a bit of peace to buck you up now and again.'

I paid the bill, which irked her slightly, threatening her position of never owing anything to anyone with nothing behind him. 'What's this then? A cheque! I keep telling you. Keep your money for yourself You're going to need it. Fifty pounds! No, I *can't* take that. Suppose I spend it all at once – you know, go on the razzle!'

When I finally got back to Woodfall Street, Mary was in her nightgown watching an Edgar Lustgarten movie about the grim results of criminal miscalculation. 'Thought you were getting rid of her early,' she muttered. That devout wish was not to be consummated for another quarter of a century.

The following day I presented myself at the Law Courts in my Decree Nisi suit and a blue and red Paisley tie I had bought from Burlington Arcade in my teens for good luck at auditions and interviews. Barwick looked like my Great Uncle Lod, the undertaker, before he got his hands on the coffin handles and the mild and bitter. Oscar was pacing up and down cheerfully. He glanced at my suit. 'Not too bad. Can't have you looking like a Teddy boy, son. Not too sure about that tie. Haven't you got anything less flashy? Well, too late now. Remember, you're a famous man. Press is all here.' I recognized a second-string reviewer who was wearing a huge hat suitable for the Royal Enclosure. Joe Jackson, my counsel, seemed pessimistic about the outcome and aggrieved at the dubious brief. He grilled me as if I were a self-confessed double rapist. He turned to Oscar: 'Well, I hope he does a bit better than this in front of the judge.' He walked off, leaving me with the stain of deadly collusion spilled over the suit. A patently irrelevant purchase.

Huddled groups of rather undernourished-looking plaintiffs, defendants and their relatives sat on benches, hankies held at noses, defensive glares and fidgeting chain-smoking fingers. Now and then a scream would ring out from another court, where more than marital life was being dissected, cut short and condemned in the public sight. The other barristers seemed much jollier than my Mr Jackson. Guffaws sounded. They waved at each other like the Hooray Henrys of Woodfall Street running a sporty abattoir.

The suit became heavier and heavier. I felt I would need to be hoisted up like a bandy knight before the field of Agincourt. Mary, who never seemed to have a nerve to crack, had sent me off with a hip-flask as if I were going out for a day with the Quorn. 'For God's sake,' snapped Barwick, 'don't let them see that.' I longed for a cigarette, but no doubt my black Russian Sobranies would be as damning as the flask. The glands in my neck began to throb like a toad's throat. The lunch-time adjournment came and we slipped over to the pub, where Oscar was eating a huge lunch. I ordered a large whisky, and then another. 'Don't get drunk, son. Wouldn't do at all. Especially in your position.' My position was one in which I needed a drink and no more advice. Like most people who disapprove of alcohol, Oscar believed that one sniff of the stuff made you break into the hokey-cokey.

At three o'clock, an usher whispered in Barwick's ear and we were rushed to another court, the hacks close behind. We had been switched. The atmosphere was torpid, long stretches of silence broken by the scratching of pens, carelessly flung briefs and the whispering of clerks slipping in and out of the room. A red-eyed witness in the box was hunched in misery. A mumble came from her chin, pointing down her cheap print dress. An endless pause before the judge looked up. 'What is she trying to say?' 'I couldn't hear, my lord.' 'Neither could I. Would you repeat the question and kindly ask your client to speak so that the court can hear her evidence.' 'I apologize, my lord,' said the pink-cheeked, portly young Woodfall Street reveller. 'As you will have seen, my client is just an ordinary, uneducated woman, and she finds even simple questions hard to answer at times.' 'Yes. I see that. Tiresome. Well, carry on.'

Jackson rose. He seemed wearily confident. Barwick stared down at his feet. My co-respondent was called. He looked decently dressed enough and answered Jackson's questions loudly in a thick Welsh garble. No one asked him to speak up, although I could hardly hear him myself. It seemed all right, although the accent was one I associated with the equivocations of my own family. When I got into the box, my new Simpsons shirt was stuck wet and tight against me. I blundered almost at once. 'Do you or do you not now live at Number Fifteen Woodfall Street, sw3?' Perhaps that wasn't even the question, but I answered 'No.' Wrongly. My counsel gave me a smart Black

Look and the judge smiled. 'I think you mean "Yes" don't you, Mr Osborne?' 'Yes. My Lord.'

Within minutes, a decree nisi was granted without costs, my own adultery being admitted. I was back outside, flanked by Barwick and Oscar. 'No comment, gentlemen, no comment.' No comment was hackneyed enough without having it said for you. Jackson was talking to Oscar as if he had brought off a 10–1 winner. He shook hands with me. 'Hope I don't have to see you again,' he said like an orthodontist showing out a patient who has not been cleaning his teeth properly. 'Yes, one or two nasty moments there,' said Oscar. 'You looked very nervous, son. You'd better go off to your play. You *have* fixed my first-night tickets, haven't you?' It was his first expression of concern all day.

I waved down a taxi. 'This way, John,' the photographers chanted. 'Be a sport.'

When I got back to Woodfall Street, Mary – unlike Oscar – had a large whisky ready for me. It was time to change for the first-night curtain, rid myself of my sodden shirt, toss away my audition tie after my abandoned marriage. I had eaten nothing and felt very sick. As I was throwing up sticky whisky and ginger ale, Mary called: 'Not being *sick*, are you?' Kneeling over the lavatory basin, staring at 'Shanks', I yelled back, 'No.' 'Och, that's all right then.' I felt more lonely than I had for months: the thought of the long evening, so many unfamiliar faces, the stifling scent of such occasions. I never wore the suit again.

In the circumstances, it seemed less deferential to wear a dinner-jacket. I had hardly worn it since the night I had stood on the stage at Bridgwater with my arms clasped shakily round Pamela in her low-dusting-maid's green uniform, waiting for the curtain to go up on *My Wife's Family*. Mary was as cheerful as a bird, as if anticipating the reels at a Highland Ball. I looked around the crowded, tiny foyer. What I had already come to regard as my own theatre was besieged by people who were patently my natural enemies. One voice called out, 'Good luck, John,' and the box-office manager winked at me.

I went through the pass door to find George peering through the curtains in the prompt corner. He was wearing an old velvet jacket and a floppy black tie. I had never seen him dressed up like this before and it was gratifying that he should have taken such unusual trouble. I expected him to be rather grim and soldierly but he was almost gleeful.

'There you are, dear boy, take a look out there.' The serrated rows of sparklers, perfumed earls, belted countesses and the St Michael *mafiosi* in the front of the dress circle were not reassuring. He hugged me and grinned. 'There they are. All waiting for *you*. All of us, come to that. What do you think, eh? Same old pack of cunts, fashionable arseholes. Just more of them than usual, that's all. There's old Harold, thinking about mortal mind. Darlington can't find his ear trumpet. That prick Bessborough. Poor old Neville, that's his mistress, got the same mink on as Elaine. Look at Elaine! Done up like a sofa underneath a Jewish Christmas-tree and twice as prickly. That's what you're up against. That's what we're always up against – *if we're lucky.*'

His fixed-bayonet relish was stunning. I sat at the end of a row seeing little and listening to snatches. I thought idly about other things. Of the people who weren't there. Of Pamela, and Arnold Running ('I wouldn't give him the sweat from my balls'); of my first loves, Joan Turvey, Renee, Stella; and of my father.

The acting is so superlatively good that one could easily be kidded into believing this play to be finer than it possibly is.

Daily Worker

For long stabs it was gin and misery in a show business setting, with no hope in sight for anybody. It's so darned depressing.

Daily Herald

John Osborne is certainly a dramatist of great promise . . . He can write parts for actors . . . He gives Laurence Olivier the chance for a tour de force of impersonation and disguise.

Daily Telegraph

Though maudlin and only partially successful, the new play generates some heat and raw emotion. It is given the immense advantage of being acted by a splendid team of actors led by Sir Laurence Olivier.

Manchester Guardian

The theatrical effect is enormous.

Sunday Times

One of the great acting parts of our age.

Observer

Olivier's presence and the sense of occasion persuaded the notoriously mean management of the Court to allow us the stage and a few bottles of extremely cheap wine for a party. The band played, stage-hands and actors danced and drank. Vivien sang rather sweetly. Mary sang 'Bonny Mary of Argyll.' Richard Pasco and I sang 'Don't be afraid to sleep with your sweetheart', and I forgot the words. Olivier went through his routines from the play. He was happy. He knew he had created a remarkable memory for everyone.

During the early hours, he saw me slumped and buzzed in the stalls. He came over and put his arm around me. 'Whatever you do, dear heart, *don't* ever, ever, get into trouble with the Income Tax Man. Buy certificates.' He sounded like, he still *was*, Archie.

> I was thinking, as we came home, that we all talk about the director, the acting, the theatre but no one ever mentions the *play*. I suppose, lucky us, we take it for granted, like some great tree which just exists and we are all pissing round its base. Anyway, thank you for it, once more –
>
> Best love,
>
> G
>
> Letter from George Devine to J.O.

On the strength of Olivier's defiant act of public slumming, *The Entertainer* had sold out at the Royal Court before its opening. To my delight, he agreed to play another limited season at the Palace in the autumn. In the meantime he and Vivien took the suitably vengeful tale of *Titus Andronicus* on tour to Australia, land of benighted strife, and Mary and I went on holiday to Sicily.

We returned for her costume fittings for the second film under her Rank contract. We were summoned to dinner at the Savoy with John Davis, ex-accountant and new Chairman of Rank Films. I had just filled in for a fortnight as film critic of the *Evening Standard*. I had enjoyed putting a cheerful blowtorch, a kind of hogmanay lark, to a lumpen Davis product called *Campbell's Kingdom*.

At the Savoy Grill, Davis, accompanied by his new wife, Dinah Sheridan, had already ordered the meal for all of us. I spotted that evening's copy of the *Standard* on the chair beside him. 'Mr Bogarde is a very good actor with immense personal charm. For years he has been Britain's most popular screen actor, during which time he has never appeared in a decent film . . . *Campbell's Kingdom* is yet another large-budget British film doggedly maintaining a B-picture standard.'

It hadn't occurred to me that my few cents-worth in a London evening paper could affect anyone's pocket or reputation. I was unprepared for Miss Sheridan's loyal wrath. In my perverse relish for shockable middle-class

It's a Broadway hit! Playwright John Osborne and wife Mary Ure arrive at London Airport after "Look Back in Anger's" New York success

33 John Osborne and Mary Ure arriving at London Airport after the New York success of *Look Back in Anger*, as featured in *Lilliput*.

34 John Osborne, Jamaica, 1958.

35 Francine, 1958.

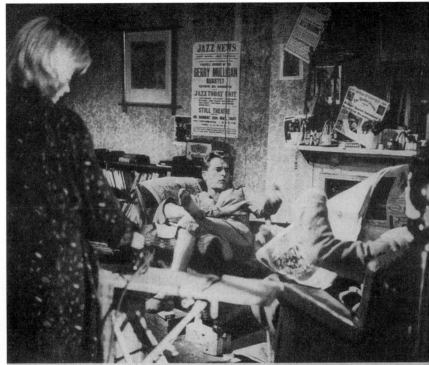

In " Look Back In Anger " Jimmy Porter rages at his wife Alison and their friend, Cliff: " I hate Sundays! Always reading papers; drinking tea; ironing ! "

LOOK BACK
IN ANGER

In scenes from the new film, LILLIPUT captures the sad and eloquent loneliness of one Jimmy Porter. Is he the prototype of a new 'lost generation'?

When Alison finally leaves him, Jimmy consoles himself with Helena, her best friend.

LILLIPUT

26

36 Richard Burton and Mary Ure in scenes from the film version of
Look Back in Anger.

A man's loneliness takes many forms.
With Jimmy it's in the soar of a trumpet.

Jimmy: " This girl's silence twists your
arm off ! I've sat in the dark for hours.
And, knowing I'm feeling as I feel now,
she's turned over and gone to sleep ! "

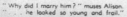

" Why did I marry him? " muses Alison.
" . . . he looked so young and frail."

" There are no good brave causes left to fight " is his epitaph. But Jimmy Porter
knows, here in a clouded jazz cellar, a man can find certainty and a splendour of sorts.

37 *The World of Paul Slickey*, discussions at the Café Royal, 1959: *left to right*, Christopher Whelen, Kenneth McMillan, Jocelyn Rickards and John Osborne.

38 Rehearsals for *The World of Paul Slickey*, 1959: *left to right*, Kenneth McMillan, John Osborne, Christopher Whelen, Jocelyn Rickards.

39 Vivien Leigh in *Look After Lulu*, Royal Court Theatre, July 1959.

40 Jocelyn Rickards, 1959.

girls, I found her rather attractive. I declined the saddle of lamb and asked for an omelette. Mr Davis, brandishing the *Standard*, demanded what I knew about films. I replied that I knew nothing about accounting but had seen four films a week from the age of four. The lamb and the omelette were quickly dispatched. There was little to drink. I began to feel the silent support of the waiters. Mrs Davis threw back her pretty young head: 'More than anyone I've ever met, I'd like to slap your face.' She looked as if she meant it, and in the right circumstances it would have been an intriguing prospect.

The next production at the Court was Ionesco's *The Chairs*, with George Devine and Joan Plowright playing the Old Man and Woman preparing for the arrival of unseen guests and filling the stage with significantly empty chairs. It appealed to George's dogged Francophilia. The curtain-raiser was a piece of Gallic whimsy by Giraudoux called *The Apollo of Bergerac*, in which the young film actress, Heather Sears, told chandeliers and other objects that they were beautiful, in case they didn't already know. When Tony offered me the tiny part of a grumbling gardener, I accepted at once. I had no wish to begin writing another play, although my head was scrambled with what I might do now. The welcome of the past year had been suspicious and had a cannibal relish to it. The cooking-pot was bubbling away. The prospect of putting on another bald-pate wig and streaking my face with lake liner, a drink afterwards with friends and a weekly brown envelope with money inside it was hard to resist.

One lunch-time in the pub next door to the Royal Court, Mary and I were having a drink. The pub was mostly used by Irish labourers, drunks and guardsmen. A hack came over and sat down beside us. 'Hello, John. Mulchrone, *Daily Mail!*' The dirty-mac reporter from Fleet Street still doggedly dressed the part then. 'I understand that you've just come back from a holiday in Sicily. I don't want to spell it out, do I? But the Queen's Proctor might be very interested.'

Mary was genuinely puzzled, having heard of the Procurator Fiscal but not the Queen's Proctor. 'What's he talking about?'

'After all, your decree doesn't become absolute for a few weeks yet, I believe. I've had a word with Mr Beuselinck. You know, public figures, all that, people are bound to be interested. Of course I'd rather be working on the *Manchester Guardian*. Do you think my colleague could take a quick photograph of you together?' said Mulchrone.

'Tell him to fuck off,' said Mary, so caught by her wee-lassie distress that she was trapped into a four-letter comeback.

'You heard what the lady said,' I replied, stoutly.

Nothing did appear in the *Daily Mail*, but I suspected the incident had set Mary on to determining a wedding date as soon as possible, rather than let news of the Queen's Proctor penetrate the north.

The Chairs went into the repertory and was treated with general caution. Giraudoux was more or less ignored, rightly and to my relief. Nigel Dennis had been so excited by *Cards of Identity* that he had written another play especially for George, with parts for Joan Plowright and myself. The gratitude of playwrights for actors is almost as rare as the reverse. Golden eggs have little time for the mucky feathers that cling to them.

Nigel's offering was a sincere response to the shaky iconoclasm of the Court, under constant attrition as it was from its own generals at the rear looking for easy victories and urging swift withdrawal to the dug-out positions of box-office safety. *The Making of Moo* was the first direct product of George's opening campaign. It must have been sweet encouragement for him, coming so unexpectedly from a middle-aged, rather monkish novelist and critic. All the others he pursued had been almost contemptuous of his overtures, making it clear that the Novel and Poetry would continue their ascendance indefinitely.

Moo's theme was unyielding. God was a Bad Thing. It was torch-carrying atheism with small Shavian clowning. It had been tooled up entirely with the object of giving offence. George was happy. Nigel was delighted. My part as George's secretary, an amateur musician set to compose hymns as gruesome substitutes for those Ancient and Modern, was patchy but enjoyable. My Ben Travers training came in useful. The machine itself was endearingly wobbly. The only way to approach it was to jump aboard and hang on before falling off – the kind of pleasure that purists find inexplicable.

There was also the attraction of yet another short tour. Back to Brighton, the Royal Crescent and the stage carpenter's welcome: 'Blimey, not *you* again.' The cast, apart from George, Joan and myself, consisted of Robert Stephens and Anthony Creighton (first and second natives), John Wood, John Moffatt, James Villiers and Esmé Percy. Tony directed. His assistant was John Dexter. I had tried to persuade George and Tony to employ both Anthony and Dexter. In Anthony's case it was in the hope of keeping him out of the Sloane Square pubs at my expense. John, I believed, was possessed with a special talent which, if he would overcome a wounded class pride unsuited to his intelligence and his natural bullying ambition, could become a valuable asset.

Most of us had already worked together for over a year and a half. Robert Stephens and his wife, Tarn, lived a couple of minutes away from Woodfall Street and we spent many evenings together eating heartily at the cheap Indian restaurants at the World's End and drinking late into the night. Robert was a rumbustious jokesmith and had a good line in making his farts explode when exposed to a naked match. Actors from the Court, employed or out of work, dropped in at almost any hour at the Stephens' house in Glebe Place. It must have been hell for Tarn. We probably made as much noise as the Henrys of Woodfall Street. But the Henrys were the ruling garrison, we were bandits from the hills.

The Making of Moo was a short play: 'A History of Religion in Three Acts'. It was a pretty snappy tour of the subject, over in not much more than two hours with a couple of disgruntled intervals to bring relief to the weary observers. Everyone, including Nigel, was aware of its deficiencies. George and Tony promoted a feeling of light-hearted scepticism. We would give ourselves a good time for attempting it at all. There was no question of dragging Nigel down from his Essex cottage and beloved earth-closet, of locking him into a suite at the Grand to rewrite the third act. He came down once during the week and, in the way of authors, laughed shamelessly at his own jokes.

Several of the company decided to go to Brighton on Saturday, move in unhurriedly and spend the evening together. We went out to dinner with Esmé Percy as the unofficial guest of honour. With his glass eye flashing and his old dog farting loyally beneath the table, he became movingly expansive in the way of old men who are astonished by the curiosity of the young. We urged him to remember and coaxed out every detail of Lady Cunard or Colefax's days and nights.

His memory seemed meticulous, waspishly accurate about people and events mostly unknown to us, flowing without pause in his almost castrato, fluting voice. My schoolboy memory of him in wide, sloping hats, astrakhan collars, with jewelled fluttering fingers, was enacted before us. Eventually, he reluctantly pleaded tiredness. It was almost 4.00 a.m. when Robert and I saw him up to his room. He embraced us both. 'What an enchanting evening. I have enjoyed it so much. You are all so sweet. And young. I don't know why you are so kind to me. Thank you, *dear* boys.'

When I went down in the morning to look at my lines on the beach, Robert came along with Esmé's dog on a leash. He had been found snuffling unhappily against Esmé's glass eye, the replacement of the one bitten out by his predecessor. The real eye was closed in death.

Immediately, remembrance felt cruelly treated, and so swiftly. I had hardly known him, but it seemed like a warning shot against careless acquaintance. However, to die in work, with your own farting friend beside you in the Royal Crescent Hotel after a jubilant evening in the affectionate company of younger friends, seems as much justice as most of us would probably wish. Robert, no slouch at breaking wind himself, adopted the dog.

7. 'All Russia is my Garden'

Oh, heavens, how I long for a little ordinary human enthusiasm. Just
enthusiasm – that's all. I want to hear a warm, thrilling voice cry out
Hallelujah! Hallelujah! I'm alive! I've an idea. Why don't we have a
little game? Let's pretend that we're human beings, and that we're
actually alive. Just for a while. what do you say? Let's pretend we're
human.

Look Back in Anger

Shortly after *The Making of Moo* opened in London for a couple of weeks, the
English Stage Company was invited to something called the World Festival
of Youth in Moscow. Trips to Russia were hard to come by and, even under
the dubious sponsorship underwritten by the British Communist Party and
every shade of left-wing dupe, the invitation was irresistible.

Going for the ride, or being taken for one, were Tony, Oscar Lewenstein,
Lindsay Anderson and myself. We flew to Helsinki and then boarded the
train for the twenty-four-hour journey to Moscow. The excitement was
high. Tony muttered at the great landscape, 'All Russia is my garden.'
Oscar, the only card-carrying Communist, looked more smug with every
mile. The train was huge, almost empty, with samovars on the boil at the
end of the corridors and martial music bursting forth as we drew near the
capital. This was the best part.

The official jaunt was a dispiriting affair, zealous but chaotic, possibly
well-intentioned but glum. There were not enough beds, not much food and
we were assigned a guide and interpreter, Marion, with a passion for official
architecture. She responded to our requests for a beer with a blistering, 'I
am not a drunkard!' We spent a few pleasant unofficial hours in Gorky Park,
where some friendly students expressed their affection for Jack London,
A.J. Cronin and J.B. Priestley. We saw a creaky but scenically weighty
performance of *The Sleeping Beauty* at the Bolshoi and I was impressed by a
couple of tough lady claqueurs who I thought I might usefully take home as

a present for George. I swam the width and back again of the River Moskva to aloof disapproval from the natives and was nearly arrested on the train journey home alone.

I had to return to London before the others as *Moo* was due back in the repertory. Despite the Queen's Proctor's mackintosh moles from the *Daily Mail*, my decree absolute was waiting for me, and Mary had begun to make arrangements for our wedding with such determination that I wondered whether she might be pregnant and already in dread of brisk finger-counting-months north of the border. Perhaps to wipe out the stain of Sassenach adultery, like the memory of Glencoe, her father, stepmother, brothers and sisters-in-law, cousins and auld nanny had already been notified, travel and hotel arrangements were organized. She had bought a hat with a veil and a dowdy suit from some madam shop in Baker Street. The Scottish guests would approve, but it would photograph pretty disastrously in the departure lounge.

I was powerless to unscramble this great skein of Scottish knitting. A ready complaisance took me over as it sometimes does when I decide to concede a helpless position and retreat until the ingenuity of time or delayed inspiration will rescue me. Like being trapped in an airport queue or at a nightmare of boredom in the theatre, one can only pretend that it is all happening to someone else and that a ladder from the skies will descend for the execution of a perfect and daring escape.

I persuaded the registrar at Chelsea to open his office on a Sunday morning. Our intention of marriage would not be posted outside until the Saturday evening, when Mulchrone and his clones were unlikely to spot it. The ruse worked until a passer-by tipped off the newspapers for the usual fee. Vivienne Drummond, Mary's friend who had taken over as Helena in *Look Back*, was a witness. The other was Tony, who performed the same office for me five years later in Sussex.

The reception was held at Au Père de Nico, a restaurant in Lincoln Street patronized by the Court. George was there, Robert and Tarn Stephens, Anthony Creighton and others. At least half of the guests came from Over the Border. A genial uncle of Mary's proposed the toast and unmarried Nanny gave the bride advice: 'Remember, lassie, if he ever expects, or wants, well you know what I'm talking about, don't ever *deny* it to him. That's the secret of marriage.'

It had been impossible to exclude Nellie Beatrice from the occasion but I saw to it that she would be hemmed in by the noisiest, less respectable guests and preferably not too near the Lowlanders, who would surely find her barmaid's 'get-up-them-stairs' innuendo as spine-chilling as I had twenty years earlier. Someone had arranged for a Chelsea sculptor to present us with a piece of pottery in the shape of a bear with a honey jar and a squirrel with nuts. It was about eighteen inches high and inscribed:

> The bear has found his squirrel
> The squirrel has found her bear
> Honey will flow, the nuts will grow
> And the anger wasn't there.

Mary seemed to like it but, then, Annigoni was her favourite painter.

During the civic mateyness of the registry ceremony I couldn't help thinking of Bridgwater and of Pamela. The vicar had seemed set upon dinning St Paul into us and with me, at least, he had succeeded:

> So ought men to love their wives as their own bodies. He that loveth his wife loveth himself. For no man ever yet hateth his own flesh; but nourisheth and cherisheth it, even as the Lord the Church . . . For this cause shall a man leave his father and mother, and shall be joined unto his wife, and they two shall be one flesh. This is a great mystery . . . auld Nanny.

> Mummy was slumped over her pew in a heap – the noble, female rhino – pole-axed at last! . . . Just the two of them in that empty church – them and me. I'm not sure what happened after that. We must have been married, I suppose.

Look Back in Anger

So, again, I supposed I was.

Mary's elder brother drove us to Heathrow. Mary burst into tears, even now surprised at Mulchrone's men snapping her Baker Street rig-out. 'This way please, Mary.' There was some misunderstanding about whether she should be going abroad while filming *Windom's Way*. '*I'm* not publicizing that fucking film.' By the time we had boarded she had recovered herself like a toddler rising with bloodied knees. We had made no hotel reservations. 'Just leave it to me,' she said, mopping her face. I did. We got to Nice and moved into the Martinez for the night. Mary thought the prices outrageous. As we were returning in two days it seemed pointless to move, but we did, to a small hotel off the Croisette. The Martinez was too grand.

George's petard had blown a hole that was even harder to fill now that everyone was scrutinizing the success of the first assault. 'What do they expect?' he growled. 'If you can get even two good plays a year, you're bloody lucky. How many passing good novels are there a year? Or paintings?'

But the pressure was on. Revolution had to be pragmatic in those days before the Arts – like Sport – had ministers to support them. The St Michael mafiosi were pleased to have Laurence Olivier in their theatre but not to lose thousands of pounds on plays which carried neither cash nor cachet. Mention John Arden, Ann Jellicoe, Donald Haworth or Christopher Logue and they reached for the blowtorch.

In his first true revival, coming as it did so soon, George had disarmed the slings of amateur know-alls with a brilliant stroke. With the production of *The Country Wife* in December 1956 for his unknown protégée Joan Plowright, he had the proper sense of vulgarity to cast a film star whom he hardly admired, Laurence Harvey. The result was happy for everyone. A fine cast (Alan Bates, Nigel Davenport, George himself and Robert Stephens) and a Jack Hylton transfer to the Adelphi which ran for a year staunched the murmurings of the mafiosi and their moneylenders.

This success also blurred for a time the evidence of a consistently uncommitted public which suited itself capriciously whether or not to attend the next production at the Royal Court. This idea of a 'Court audience' was already attracting deluded enthusiasts. The fact emerged as production followed production that it never existed. Star names might coax the West End punter over to Sloane Square for the right play, as with Harvey in Wycherley, but not for the wrong one, like Ashcroft in Brecht.

In truth, there was no systematic policy except that which engaged the various personalities that grew around the original nucleus assembled by George and Tony. Most of these were, in the mild climate of the time, left of centre, though they would now be regarded as soft-meringue-liberals by the drowsy commissars who have long since taken over. There was criticism that this English approach was damaging and incoherent. It seemed to me human, thoughtful, sympathetic and flexible. It was conviction contained by natural sweetness and not mere aggrandizement. Joan Littlewood had this gift in plenty. George and Tony were perhaps more acerbic: unknowing prophets, but not bullies.

In the midst of such energy, to be accused of being eclectic seemed to be civilized. As I found with the Anglican Church, it would be a rich landscape in which to exercise and refine one's unbelief. 'Choose your theatre as you would a religion,' said George, famously. What he produced was often a comically unbalanced broad Church accommodating anti-democratic works like *August for the People* and the reverential French connection. Now, the bony memory of the arse-aching boredom of many of those evenings helps to send me gasping for the interval air and a succouring drink to ease the pains of past and present.

I think it was Balfour who used to pass out from boredom at political soirées. In the fifties I had more stamina and expectation. I didn't know the form book, either. And, anyway, we were off to America.

There were many understandable reasons why American producers had been reluctant to take *Look Back* to Broadway. There were no stars. Because of the embarrassed sensibilities of Mr Albery over the bears and squirrels, it hadn't been given a West End showing. True, it had aroused almost unprecedented attention, but if it was such a smash why wasn't it still doing boffo or even boffola business? Naturally, it was too long.

In reality, it ran for two hours and forty minutes with two intervals, and even less when Kenneth Haigh used to cut certain speeches on the evenings when he declared that he 'wasn't feeling it'. ('What do you want me to do? Tell the audience a lie?' Yes, by all means, Ken. They won't know the difference.) As many of the London critics had commentated with grim satisfaction, 'It calls out for the knife.' Length is something both reviewers and producers confuse with time. *Hamlet* is too long. So is *Don Giovanni*. So, sometimes, is life.

Another obstacle was language. Although the immigrant populations have all but lost their native tongues, English is still a foreign field to most Americans. Peter Nichols swears that when he was working in Minneapolis, an apparently literate middle-class couple deduced from his speech that he was a foreigner. When he told them that he came from England, they asked, 'Oh, where's that?' 'Well, sort of up on your left from Europe.' 'Is that so, and what sort of language do they speak there?'

So. Could not this piece be transposed successfully from somewhere in the Midlands to Greenwich Village, or even Minneapolis? And a *sweet*-stall? What about a downtown soda fountain? What if they were all Puerto Ricans? None of this reassured Roger Stevens and Alexander Cohen, then reckoned to be the arbiters of New York theatre. The chances of *Look Back* reaching Forty-second Street seemed remote.

I had met David Merrick a couple of times in London. He was one of the many hundreds who later claimed to have been present at the Royal Court on 8 May. A soft-spoken Jewish lawyer, born Margoles, with a mournful moustache and eyes to match, Merrick had an almost sinister obsession with the theatre which made his conversation quickly pall. He had scarcely any small talk except occasional satisfaction at someone else's out-of-town disaster, when the sad-dog eyes would brighten slightly. It was hard to explain his tenacious fervour as he never expressed enthusiasm, rather the opposite: 'I saw it and I hated it'; unimaginable that he should feel affection for a medium so sustained by its own madcap follies, high spirits and occasional generosity. 'It's a bum and so's he.' With his carefully measured evasive manner, dark suits and overcoat, abstemious, non-smoking Merrick would make an ailing bloodhound seem like a cavorting court-jester. He was a most depressing companion and again reminded me of Uncle Lod.

Like all obsessive characters, Merrick was inordinately boring. He was uninterested in books, music, politics, people or, seemingly, even sex. His studied politeness was a mask that must conceal a slow-boiling malevolence. I can't see what he could have responded to in an irrepressible jokesmith like Jimmy Porter. He could squeeze out a frosty smile only when someone like a lovingly hated star collapsed with a coronary. His undisguised antipathy to actors was planned with glum precision. 'You see, I hate *actors.*' He accented the word as a National Front skinhead might spit out 'Jew'. 'Binkie *loves* them,' he added, baffled that so successful an impressario should possess such an aberration. 'But then he hates writers.'

This was undeniable. Binkie Beaumont took great satisfaction in tearing the wings from writers, especially the rich and famous. Rattigan and Coward had both suffered humiliation from his lizard tongue. Merrick, unlike Beaumont, was indifferent to sexual politics. 'Now *I* like *writers,*' he'd say in refutation of Binkie's preference.

He liked writers in the way that a snake likes live rabbits. Unfortunately they were more difficult to dispatch than actors. They could take their plays with them. It could be said that firing actors was his profession, producing plays his hobby. When he sat beside me at a rehearsal, if I made a note or said something to the director, he would turn hopefully: 'What's the matter? You want me to fire him?' Fortunately, rehearsals seemed to bore, even mystify, him. He preferred the out-of-town previews with the backers to appease. 'It's not going to be like *that,* is it?' 'Don't worry, they're working on it.' This evocation of all-night black coffee and weeping actresses in hotel suites would usually comfort the most alarmed angel for a few hours.

Merrick had gained some attention by producing an ill-received musical, *Fanny,* which he managed to keep going by advertising it in the Paris Métro, with the calculation that American tourists would be impressed by seeing a Broadway show touted in such a chic venue. Later, he was to contact subscribers in the New York telephone directory with the same names as theatre critics (Brooks Atkinson, Walter Kerr etc.) and persuade them for a small bribe to put their names to a rapturous quote. 'A stupendous event. An undoubted masterpiece,' Walter Kerr. Walter Kerr was probably an unemployed window-cleaner from 114th Street.

Later, when the *Look Back* business was falling, he hired an out-of-work actor to get up on the stage and strike Kenneth Haigh in a fit of fury. The audience was delighted, a photographer recorded the event for *Time* magazine, and bookings rose. The bewildered leading man got the sock in the jaw that Merrick cherished in his heart for every actor. For $50 it was a stylish investment.

To me, one of his charms was that he cared not at all how much he was disliked. He once inserted a clause into my contract that (a) I should not travel to America by sea and (b) that I should not expect to see my name on any advertising or programme matter. This did seem rather desperate sadism. However, I ignored the first condition and agreed to the second, assuming that an anonymous playwright might prove to be rather more intriguing. In London he would eavesdrop on the interval conversation of critics like a detective shadowing an adulterous wife. He once gave me a detailed account of a collusive dialogue between the critics of the *Daily Telegraph*, the *Spectator* and the *Evening Standard*. It sounded plausible, delivered with the conviction of a finance revenue inspector intent on promotion.

Merrick had no concrete or practical opinions himself, or, at least, he never expressed them. He merely presided like a silent oracle, a broody boatman into a journey of endless ordeal. His advantage was that he was so awesomely unlikeable. One had no misgivings about hurting his feelings. It was as impossible to humiliate him as it was to move him to the merest show of admiration let alone friendship. He produced five of my plays in New York, and I would have chosen no one else.

8. The October Bonfire

An October bonfire opened last night and lit a blaze on Broadway. *Look Back in Anger* by a 27-year-old British playwright . . .

New York Times, 2 October 1957

The waiter rasped it in my ear with urgency, like a conspirator giving the tip-off to George Raft in a speakeasy. He left the first few inches of Brooks Atkinson's galley proof beside my plate and went off muttering, 'More later.'

It was indeed October. October 1957. I was sitting in Sardi's restaurant on Forty-fifth Street, barely aware that Brooks Atkinson was the theatre critic of the *New York Times* or that the *Times*' building backed on to the kitchens of Sardi's and that in a few minutes the trucks blocking the street would be spreading the news of Broadway's bonfire to the rest of the city. Drink appeared. Suddenly, as Arthur Miller said, attention was being paid, and to a small band of British actors unknown outside their own country.

The waiter kept returning to our table with the wet galley pulls from next door. Later these were followed by copies of the *Herald Tribune*. The *News*, the *Post* and *Journal American* would not be on the streets until mid-morning but, with the *Times* and *Tribune* declared, we were a palpable smash. The bonfire, lit by an unknown candidate, had sent up a puff of smoke from the Broadway College of Cardinals. It was a remarkable contrast to the London reception the previous year.

Merrick appeared, his eyes rather less mournful than usual. He had not been able to fire anyone but he had a hit on his hands. The restaurant, which had been half-empty of opening-night rubber-neckers, began to fill up. A few people who had attended the performance pointed out Alan, Mary and Vivienne Drummond. Mary went to the powder room and on her return was greeted by a round of applause. Some of the men rose to their feet when they saw that the star of the evening was a pretty young blonde with an unforced, happy smile. Kenneth Haigh, on witnessing this amazing tribute, went out of the restaurant and made a fresh, more measured reappearance. He received his reward. He may not have been as cute as Mary but he was the man of the hour.

Fellow diners came up to our table in the out-of-towners' ghetto beside the kitchen swing-doors, shaking us by the hand, saying they heard it was just great, couldn't wait to get a ticket. Someone sent over a bottle of wine. More surprising still, Merrick bought some for us. Leonard Lyons, the famous columnist of the *Post*, tracked us down. Sardi's was his first port of call on his all-night round of New York's celebrity spots and here was this unexpected bunch of young British guys making big news almost literally behind his back. Lennie, whose ferrety eyes never missed a face in any gathering however large or noisy, was sharp, shrewd and knew everyone in New York from politicians to actors, writers and gangsters. He managed never to break an implicit confidence and yet still succeeded in writing an entertaining column every day.

Mary, Tony and I had already moved out of our dull hotel and into the Algonquin, where a rather startled management treated us very politely. Accustomed to sober dress and linked for ever to the alleged wits of the Round Table and famous foreigners like Noël Coward, they were particularly baffled by Tony's appearance. Dressed like a bony eccentric from Sunset Strip in his beloved uniform of sneakers, sweatshirt, bowling-jacket and baseball cap, he was very unlike the Englishmen they were used to welcoming. Nearly thirty years later the manager, Andrew Anspach, told me of the dismay we aroused at the time.

The next weeks were headily confusing. Sleep was confined to a snatched hour or two in the late afternoon. The telephone rang constantly, there were piles of urgent messages, there was an invitation to a party at an East Side address which even I could identify as being very grand indeed. From dark horse we had become front runner on the Great White Way. Excitement didn't merely sustain itself, it seemed to increase, unlike the English response to such a tide of interest: 'Jolly good. Any idea what you might be doing next?' It was a shock to realize the containing sea of phlegm that one had to raise one's head above at home.

It was like being called to play oneself in a vast film with settings you had already inhabited in another dream-life from a past that had now become real and present. Here, on the streets themselves, black and white memories from the Essoldos and Odeons of my childhood were transformed into a darting haze in the autumn air, the warm subterranean steam breathing from the sidewalks as though from the nostrils of a vast animal. New York seemed to be alive underneath, raging to burst forth with more energy. Food itself was a street-life spectacular. Smells on every corner; fresh oranges pressed by men in white forage caps, a mystery called root beer, hot dogs, fried onions, bagels, pizzas, chestnuts, Italian sausages, kebabs all the way up and down Fifth and Sixth Avenues.

Here it all was, teeming with affluent squalor, patrolled by oblong-shaped cops, coats buttoned up to the neck, straight from a Cagney film, as Irish as Central Casting could produce. A rush of men looking like unhealthy lumberjacks pushed against ladies inexplicably dressed in hats and wraps as if for a lunchtime cocktail party. Newsboys flashed better teeth than mine. Ragged creatures trussed up in newspapers against doorways; black blind beggars with white canes, rattling tin cups, their guide-dogs slumped beside them on sacks. I began to understand why a flop-house was a flop-house rather than a hostel. A bum was just that, and Skid Row was the gutter he slipped into. Failure, which at home often carried its own distinction of inspired fallibility, was unequivocal here. Irredeemably foreign as I was, I felt myself strangely at home, like a cat sharing a huge household of dogs.

Mary soon seemed to be known to all the salesgirls from Saks to Bloomingdales and in all the coffee-shops from Forty-fourth Street up to Carnegie Hall. 'Why, Miss Uray, we hear you're just wonderful in your show!' She reminded me of the beaming girl of my boyhood who appeared at the wheel of an open car, exclaiming brightly to the naked god beside her, 'Oh, Mr Mercury, you *did* give me a START.' Kelvinist and Calvinist, schoolgirlishly light-hearted, she stood out in Manhattan like a Welsh miner at a bar mitzvah.

We had huge breakfasts in the hotel room with buckwheat cakes, butter and maple syrup to soak up the ninety-proof spirit of the night before as it coursed horribly through gates and alleys of the body never before even noticed. We watched the lines of whores perched in the Astor Bar, where the lady got pinched in the song. We raided all-night record shops like Goody's, where you could choose from an Aladdin's cave of LPs unknown in England. At five in the morning we'd go to Stein's and eat Welsh rabbit, served orange and bubbling in stout, or a selection of sandwiches the size of football boots – the Doris Day (honey, lox and sour cream), the Frank Sinatra (bologna sausage, cheese and dill pickle), the Judy Garland (smoked salmon, honey, cream and nuts) – and a jumbo pack of chocolate to take home.

There were downstairs joints selling thick black-bean soup with huge tankards of beer, or Dinty Moore's for lunch of Irish stew and strange-tasting bottled Guinness. I began going to a barber who was patronized by cigar-smoking men shrouded in towels who emerged purple, manicured and shoe-shined. An hour after my last visit, the windows and mirrors were smashed, the floor covered in a lake of blood and bobbing hair. Albert Anestasia had been rubbed out by a few passing business rivals before he had time to wipe the lather from his chin.

We all made regular visits to the Apollo Theatre in Harlem, where people like Lena Horne were supposed to have begun their careers. Wednesday nights were Amateur Nights and if a contender didn't make it in the first ten seconds he or she was 'given the hook', in the venerable manner of burlesque, by the entirely black audience. It made the first house at the Glasgow Empire seem like a Young Conservatives' dance. White New Yorkers thought we were pretty dumb to venture there, and cab-drivers would leave us at the uptown end of Central Park. I had the fatuous notion that not being a White American I possessed a kind of *laissez-passer*, a foreign passport providing immunity from a switch-blade in the heart.

Mary was not unnaturally beguiled by her new daily round inside the Big Apple, by the lunches with producers, directors and columnists. Now her New York agent began the serious business of launching her into the big time with an apartment in the city and promotion in Hollywood. Yesterday's allegiances – to myself, the Court, London even – were fading. I was pleased to be more or less excluded, like an elderly relative from olden times, but the potential dangers to her and myself were beginning to emerge. Talk of green cards and tax readjustments determined that I should head for home.

I had stopped concealing from myself, if I ever had, that Mary was not much of an actress. She had a rather harsh voice and a tiny range. Her appearance was pleasing but without any personal sweep to it. Binkie had been right to sign her up for his stable of light-comedy fillies. One couldn't imagine her tackling Lady Macbeth, Cleopatra or even Rosalind. Her movie career could lead nowhere very much except to the conventional exile and bondage of a Hollywood 'home', servants, managers and accountants. I would always need a northern bite in my blood if I were to survive the writer's recurrent ailment: exhaustion. A jumbo Judy Garland at five in the morning would not ultimately nourish me as much as a plate of jellied eels in Margate. I felt a stabbing wave of homesickness.

A more disturbing alarm bell was Mary's preoccupation with a new gynaecologist friend. There was, he had told her, no reason at all why Mary and I should not have a baby without any trouble. I had not anticipated any trouble, beyond keeping my fingers crossed. Like most men and women of my generation, I was so accustomed to 'taking risks' that I came to feel I had not only been amazingly lucky for the past ten years but that my potency might be a little haphazard.

Mary took up a regime of counting days and temperatures, applying cold compresses and assuming uncomfortable positions. Her new manual, the gynaecologist's *Good News Bible*, contained numerous illustrations which bore little resemblance to any sexual activity I had known for many a long, uncomplicated and pleasurable hour. It seemed to require all the penitential care of administering a successful enema, only without the aid of soapy water. What had seemed a fairly simple process became a tricky piece of athleticism. The illustrations were daunting. That God, in His infinite wisdom, had come to invent such an all-demanding and capricious object as the clitoris made one wonder if He had nodded off around the same time as He gave us the useless but dangerous appendix.

I began to feel a growing unease which might decline into panic. After six weeks of New York saturation, it *was* time to go home. George rang saying that Anthony Creighton had been injured on his Lambretta. It gave me a small excuse to return, although it confirmed Mary's understandable dislike of Anthony. I said I would be back for Christmas, and landed at London Airport. She had slipped some cheap shirts into my suitcase as presents for her brothers and I failed to declare them, together with some already-worn LPs. I was taken away, stripped and meticulously searched.

Back in Chelsea, the welcome was summary. 'Oh? Did well, did it?' The October blaze had not been sniffed in London. It was rather as if a disgraced school rotter had returned from the Olympics with the old country's one and only gold medal. The fairground fever of the Great White Way quickly receded. Things at home seemed stuffy, unfriendly even, but more serious, light-hearted and normal.

> 5, Norma Villas,
> Town Hall Approach Road,
> Tottenham

Dear Dolly [family name for Nellie Beatrice],

I have written to John thanking him for his kindness. It was kind of you dear to mention me to him it brought tears to my eyes, I have never had anything like that given to me and nobody has ever asked me how I manage to keep this house going.

Well, dear I had a letter from Mum but not one of her nice kind ones, full of Queenie looking her dear old self but said she was still in bed and could not walk. Sidney said different in his letter didn't he. She was full of Jack and Bessie's kindness. I am not answering that letter. All this *kindness* will soon blow over as before. Well, dear my hand is a bit wrong today with Rheumatism so excuse writing and mistakes it is the weather.

Ever your affectionate,
Auntie Min xxxx

[PS from N.B. to J.O.] It looks as though his Lordship is now turning Mother against Auntie, which proves he hates anyone liking me a little but it will blow over, I hope so or else I shall have that on my mind.

Tottenham

Dear Dolly,

Yours to hand. I cannot express my disgust for your so call Brother. He will kill my Sister, it is breaking her heart. He is *bad enough* to stop her coming to me. It worries me, I have had a cry. She is not happy there alone. Cheer up dear God will help us. Don't worry. God pays debts without money.

Affectionately,
Auntie Min.

Tottenham

My dear Dolly,

Your letter just to hand. I certainly cannot understand Mother. I did not think she could be so unkind as to write you those letters. *Do not worry* you will have a Breakdown. I wish I could get about as well as Mum and I am only 88. I have not had a Bed of Roses but I am satisfied, so buck up, do not be downhearted. I will let you know of any trouble at Salisbury.

Love,
Auntie Min xxx

Tottenham

My dear Dolly,

I always thought my Sister such a straight and good living dear. Now she has cast me off. She was always all I had now I am just alone and *not* wanted. This has put the last Nail in my Coffin. Think of me sometimes one thing I have done nobody any wrong.

God bless.

Auntie Min.

PS I have to wait for someone to post this. I would like some new legs.

[PPS from N.B. to J.O.] What a family, I have to laugh really.

                                                     Tottenham

My dear Dolly,

    Mind do not let it worry you, worrying about other people has got me down. I am alone and nobody troubles about me. When I am gone I expect they might send me a few flowers. Hope you are well there is such a lot of illness about.

With love.

Yours affectionately,

Auntie Min xxx

In those pre-breathalyser days, Anthony had driven into the back of a lorry on his way home from the Salisbury in St Martin's Lane, then the chic theatrical gay pub in the West End. There was also a dive called the White Bear where servicemen and young men from the provinces drank black and tans and sipped green chartreuse. It was a few yards from the gents lavatory at Piccadilly Circus, the most famous 'cottage' of the age. Even the heavy tread of the boots of *agents provocateurs* did not deter its visitors. As one was told constantly, the danger and prospect of humiliation were, like the chase, almost as heady as the conquest.

Anthony also spoke with nostalgia of a club in Soho, the Rockingham, which seemed to be a homosexual Athenaeum, a world away from the sweet liqueur squalor of the White Bear or the discreetly camp surroundings of Victorian mirrors at the Salisbury. Pre-Wolfenden, the Rockingham was very exclusive. Although merchant seamen or still-room boys were discreetly welcomed, members were otherwise expected to be most circumspect. Anthony had been there in his bomber-navigator days on leave from missions over the Ruhr and, he said, Terence Rattigan had promised him a job when the war was over.

As the song goes in *Flare Path*:

> I don't want to join the air force,
> I don't want to go to war,
> I'd rather hang around,
> Piccadilly Underground,
> Living on the earnings of a high-born lady . . .

Piccadilly still held its spell for Anthony and with the £20 a week I had
arranged to give him I imagine he had been doing as much hanging about as
£20 could buy in those days. 'Give her a shilling and she'll probably be
willing' had long been overtaken by inflation, but a chartreuse can last an
evening.

Lowndes Cottage was also a world away from the White Bear. When *The
Entertainer* transferred to the Palace, Mary was in America and Vivien
Leigh and I were both spending evenings alone. She would sometimes ring
me up as I settled down in my cupboard-study in Woodfall Street. It was
always a shock to hear her voice. 'What are you doing this evening?' There
was only one answer. 'Why don't we go to the pictures? Come round now
and we'll see what's on.' I dusted down my best suit, best shirt and tie and
VLOI would pick me up.

All sorts of phantom possibilities crossed my mind. Did she expect me to
seduce her? Surely not. The presumption was absurd. I was neither Rhett
Butler, Laurence Olivier, good red meat nor even Peter Finch. Was it a
kittenish plot to involve me as a pawn in a game about which I was ignorant?
I knew that life imitates melodrama more often than not, but my own
profligate and to-hell-with-it nature had not equipped me for this. I had
been foolish to myself for too long to be cast as the spare prick at the demise
of a very public marriage. I felt crass enough *already* for even agonizing over
such self-important guesswork. But the presumption of youth and the sudden appearance of bourgeois caution within me made it all the more baffling
and exciting.

We would look down the list of likely attractions in the *Evening Standard*
and drive off rather late into the West End. On the first occasion we ended
up in the Charing Cross Road watching Sophia Loren. Lady Olivier gave a
running commentary in her pleasing, ginny voice on Miss Loren's physical
and technical deficiencies. It seemed a long ten years since I was sitting in
the circle of the Rembrandt, Ewell, stuck palm-to-palm with Renee.

Afterwards, an autograph signed for the cinema manager, we would glide
round to the White Tower or somewhere similar. She had witnessed my
untutored tussle with an alien artichoke and always helped me tactfully with
good humour over the menu and wine list. Apart from the dressing-room
incident at the Court, I never witnessed those moods of manic caprice for
which she was well known and dreaded by some. 'The only virtue I possess', John Betjeman once told me, 'is hope.' Vivien's virtue, always a prized
one in my book, was enthusiasm, the physical expression of hope, the
antidote to despair and that most deadly of sins, sloth.

On our return to Lowndes Cottage I was unsure whether to go in for a drink or not. I had no wish to be churlish nor – wild projection – to be caught *in flagrante* by Larry after his performance as Archie ('I'm a twice a day man myself'). It was a ridiculously comic notion but events had moved in such a headlong and unlikely sequence for the last few months that almost anything seemed possible. Taking Scarlett O'Hara out to supper might be only a starter.

I could only guess at the state of play between the Oliviers, but theatrical royalty, scandal and heaven knows what scorn were certainly beyond my sophistication. I wasn't, as someone with an acute sense of class and achievement later put it, 'ready for it yet'. I felt a certain loyalty to Olivier. I was also racked by curiosity. In St Augustine's words, 'A Stiff Prick hath no conscience.' Maybe it was a Jacobean plot to damage *The Entertainer*? That seemed too vulgar a device. On the other hand . . . On the other hand what? On the other hand, I wanted nothing to threaten the success of my play.

Not for the first time, I fiercely regretted my indecision in such circumstances. Caution is evil medicine to me, even when it seems to guarantee reward. It was a foretaste of my later conviction that the follies which a man regrets most are those which he didn't commit when he had the opportunity.

In the past eighteen months I had not made the fortune everyone assumed, but it seemed pretty good to me. I need not worry about electricity or telephone bills. I bought new clothes and books and became less nervous of restaurants and hotels. Even Merrick could not whittle down the standard Dramatists' Guild contract in New York. *The Entertainer*'s packed eight-week run at the Palace was earning me almost £900 a week. I still made my £.s.d. entries in my pocket diary and Dr Strach, the accountant who a year earlier had advised me to go back to him when I had a little more to show for myself, was urging me to spend money on a chauffeur, even a valet. He was patently baffled that so much could be earned for doing so little.

Shortly after my return from New York, I took a crash course of driving lessons, passed my test one lunchtime in a deserted Acton High Street and bought the 'grocer's car' so despised by George. Anthony seemed more confused and incoherent than usual. I decided that a short convalescent trip for him would provide me with an excuse not to return to America for two or three weeks before I decided what to do about Christmas. I christened the car by taking him to Wales. It was a fine chance to get back to the provinces.

The choice of Wales displeased Mary. It was, I pointed out, the land of my grandfather's father. (Years later I discovered that my Welsh connection only reached as far back as the early nineteenth century. The Osbornes had been migrant artisans who crossed the Bristol Channel from North Devon.) Why wasn't I going to Scotland? When was I coming back? She was talking about New York as if it were home. I told her Anthony was still a bit goofy, though, I might have added, not much more so than before.

I needed a holiday myself. I could feel her mouth tighten beneath the Atlantic waves. From *what*? There was she slugging it out on Broadway and here was I wandering aimlessly around Wales with a cadging homosexual drunk. Like most actors, she was hysterical when unemployed and resentful when appearing every night to full houses. She also entertained the common belief that a writer is only working when he can be seen head down at his desk. Why are you drinking/dreaming/farting/fornicating instead of making typewriter noises?

After Wales and back in London, time and space in which to manoeuvre seemed to be contracting. I was looking for more air to breath and found it in an unlikely quarter. Harry Saltzman reappeared. He was forty-two, plump, with grey short-cropped hair and large, brown, defensive eyes. He had been in the RCAF and the USAAF during the war, had worked in the circus in Paris before that and spoke perfect argot, dirty-talk French. His suits and shoes were expensive, clinging to him with a sort of Italian fondness. His range of knowledge and reading was impressive for a man whose book on a desert island, apart from the Bible and Shakespeare, would be a bound volume of *Variety*.

Unlike most of the American enthusiasts I had met during the past months, he was friendly but not fulsome. He talked fluently, as if we had grown up together, with a familiarity that was neither intrusive nor objectionable. In spite of massive presumptions, he also had an instinct for reticence. His past experience with the English had alerted him that we were easily scared off by admiration and that praise could make us prance and sweat like horses.

Harry had seen *Look Back* again in New York. He talked engagingly of his wild intentions. He also put them to work. He had an amazing profligacy in his enthusiasms and an energy in withdrawing them, whether it was restaurants, girls or hot properties. 'What do you want to eat tonight?' he'd ask. 'French, German, Italian, Jewish? I know the best Finnish restaurant in town.' One always, rightly, chose the best in town. A week later he might ask the same question. 'Well, that Finnish place was terrific. Why don't we . . .'

He would cut you off like some blundering toddler. 'Forget it. I know a much better place.' I don't think we ever went back to a best-restaurant-in-town.

He dropped ideas for films like restaurants. He wanted to make films of *Look Back* and *The Entertainer*. He wanted to buy, or me to buy, the rights of *A Taste of Honey*. He was going to get *Saturday Night and Sunday Morning* from Joe Janni. We – Harry, Tony and myself – should form a production company. We would call it Woodfall Films. In the meantime, why didn't we go to Paris for Christmas and he'd show me the town. I said I was expected in New York. He brushed this aside like last week's best restaurant. 'I'm going over a week later. We'll go together. Hell, let's go to Paris first and have some fun.'

I found myself in the Hotel Napoléon off the Champs Elysées, eating in the small hours at Les Halles and wondering what I should say to Mary. 'Hell,' said Harry, 'we'll send her a cable.' As if that settled everything. Bemused, I watched him dash it off. 'We love Paris, Paris, Paris. Happy Christmas. See you for New Year. Love John and Harry.' It did not go down well.

9. Broadly Speaking

By thy great mercy, defend us from all perils and dangers of this night.
Third Collect, Book of Common Prayer

My first sighting of Francine was when she made a brief appearance at a party in Harry Saltzman's New York apartment. This was in an anonymous block overlooking the horse-drawn-carriage park round the corner from the Waldorf Astoria. Tony insisted the building was a warren for middle-priced whores. As most New York ladies seemed dressed for the evening long before noon it seemed difficult to tell.

Early in 1958, George came over to America to give a lecture, and it was a relief to have him with me. I had seen little of Tony who, as usual, was pursuing a full day-and-night timetable. Occasionally we would go to the theatre, but we rarely stayed beyond the interval. Like most directors Tony was an appalling spectator, shifting in his seat at the outset like an uneasy colt, head falling forward, jerking back snoring, then snapping into twitching wakefulness.

His boredom was fierce and accusing. He made one feel like a prisoner under escort. 'Are you *enjoying* it?' he would hiss after five minutes. As the play progressed the interrogation mounted, ending with a bristling show of exasperation. 'I mean, do you want to *stay*?' Usually I didn't. Outside, as often as not, he would mutter something about 'having to see someone'. 'I mean, you will be *all right*, won't you?' he'd say doubtfully. Before I had time to answer, he would be striding off down the street. It took me a long time to realize that his schedule for the evening had been fixed implacably long before we had settled into the stalls.

Tony's duplicity was so sinewy and downright that he was able to deceive friends and adversaries effortlessly. His instinct for the strategy of perfidy was immaculately simple. No deception could be too bold. Simple undertakings became mystifying conspiracies. The prospect of arousing his mockery prevented people from comparing notes. Insinuating cabals and strengthening them with discreet misinformation, he was able to gull the most hardened and cynical of spirits. It was a formidable gift and, even as it grew with comic legend, there was always a band of willing eunuchs prepared to sacrifice their interests, sometimes even their destiny, for the promise of his approval.

George and I, spending lazy hours alone together for the first time, began to compare notes on our dealings with Tony. It was clear that we had been manipulated mercilessly, both of us being coaxed into positions of mutual suspicion. By the expedient of scattering distrust and unease between us on a constant feed of innuendo and specific warnings, he had kept us separately stabled like animals in a stud. We had obeyed the handler's instructions submissively with a trust that seemed bovinely unintelligent.

George's tentative attitude to a younger man and my own shyness had been used like blunt instruments to coerce us into avoiding anything like intimacy or confidence. Now, like escaped prisoners, we exchanged anecdotes of our incarceration in the Richardson conspiracy. Inimitable and uninventable phrases tumbled out like mocking Christmas-cracker jokes, suddenly making everything less humiliating and more comic. 'You mustn't speak to Johnny. You know what he's like. You'll only *upset* him!' 'Don't mention anything to George. He's very *sensitive* at the moment. You'll only put him off.' Lie low and leave it to Richardson. Why? His unique perception of two difficult and irreconcilable personalities would preserve a working balance between us. Remonstrance was out of the question. The only remedy was the laughter of self-scorn.

Harry's party was an untheatrical affair, an almost all-male gathering of agents, lawyers and salesmen. Francine's entrance could hardly have been more startling. Every head most certainly turned. She seemed the embodiment of the silliest of American dreams, the Dumb Broad, all in white and glittering, accompanied by a Texas oilman from Central Casting. She was unquestionably a caricature of every snobbish idea of such a girl, almost bursting apart with the effort she had put into her captivating appearance.

A sublimely trashy, brave innocence pervaded the room. If she were a parody of someone striving to give the appearance of a film star, she managed to achieve an odd pouting dignity. Perhaps it was her intrinsic lack of realistic ambition. It worked most effectively, inspiring an atmosphere of instant affection from everyone. So much care to her image, so transparent and so amateur, was a triumph of narcissism. She certainly had the Monroe effect on her audience that night.

Americans invented the dumb broad as the English perfected the gun dog. George drew me aside, 'Now that's the kind of woman you and I could never even hope to get near.' Our agreement could not have been more complete. Inside George's almost anorexic craving for a hang-dog Giacometti posture was a MacGill man in a ballooning red-and-white-striped bathing-suit. If ever there was a bum-and-tit man condemned to a diet of lean pickings it was George Devine. He would pull on his pipe lingeringly at the sight of a pretty girl. His contemporaries might aggressively admire the androgynous beauty of Virginia Woolf or the Plantagenet exoticism of Edith Sitwell, but there were no fine-boned ladies with broad foreheads and drawn-back wispy hair among the rippling nubiles between the covers of *Seventeen* and *Honey*.

'Not a chance, dear boy.' As he said it he put his arm around me with great deliberation. It was a rare gesture and a sure sign of how relaxed his mood must have been. Doubtless a middle-aged English theatre director would scarcely have roused a glimmer of interest in Francine's appraising eyes. Covetousness was a cool gift that seemed to be admired most by its victims. The Great American Broad was never dumb. She had the heart of a snake and the fervour of a prophet. She was a protected species.

A week later I found myself sharing a huge bungalow with Tony and Harry in the Beverly Hills Hotel. I had easily persuaded Mary that my visit could be useful to her. Hollywood was a dream in all our experiences. Harry was handing out fistfuls of dollars. 'Leave it me. We'll settle later.' Settle what, I thought, and then forgot about it. I knew Tony would soon rebel at being hustled along by this genial, impatient courier. We reconnoitred the Polo Lounge, where Harry exuded a feeling of tetchy over-familiarity towards the Praetorian waiters. He bounced us along Wilshire Boulevard to the emptiest, most expensive shops in what appeared to be the most unfrequented street in the world. He waded his way through counters of 'sports' clothes that would have been scarcely saleable on market-day in Derby. Back in the pink and green bungalow, he retired to his bedroom with *Variety*, shouting down the phone to New York, London, Miami, half a dozen other provincial US cities and a few European capitals as well. His fluent French sounded like a union leader addressing a rioting mob.

Then, suddenly, the air-conditioning seemed clattering and cold. It was shivery rather than sunny California and as a subtropical chill settled over the mid-afternoon I felt my first intimations of West Coast dread. When I later described this very particular unease that Los Angeles aroused in me, Christopher Isherwood rasped, 'Oh, you've got the Pacific Blues.' From the twinkle of his eyebrows, he clearly relished those evening shadows which darken both sunshine and spirit.

Tony, sensing my depression, left abruptly, banging the door of his bedroom behind him. Soon he too was screaming into the telephone. I wandered off to the Polo Lounge and on into the 'Pool Area', which was being closed down for the night by those young men in shorts and sneakers who seem to hang from everywhere in California like bats in Indian palaces. I felt as if it was the end of September in Bognor rather than mid-January in Los Angeles.

A slim, dark figure, hair parted familiarly in the middle, came and lay down a yard from me. I remembered a naked girl crashing through a black and white jungle. No longer naked but cool as a cat drying itself in the watery sunshine was Hedy Lamarr. For a few minutes my bungalow gloom vanished. *White Cargo*'s Tondelayo, I learned later, was working as a waitress in a café and was allowed to use the pool when the Real Customers had retired to the Beauty Parlour. She still outshone them all for my one-and-ninepence.

'So, what do you want to do?' Harry was detailing a possible itinerary for the evening, meaning that he had made every arrangement already. Tony eyed us like a parent confronting a pair of dithering children. 'The thing is, Harry. I've arranged to meet someone.' His knee jerked in impatience. He wanted us out. The foot stabbed the air. His voice rose to a tremolo of exasperation. 'I mean, are you going *out*?' 'Sure, sure,' said Harry. 'What time's your party coming?' 'Quite soon.' The banging down of his Cutty Sark marked the end of the discussion.

'I've got to pick up Francine from the airport,' Harry said. 'Coming along, John? I thought we'd take in this guy Shelley Berman . . . Bring your friends if you want.' Tony's glare intensified as if there were squalid implications in this suggestion. 'Who's Francine?' 'The girl in my apartment. John's met her.' Well, hardly. The glare turned on me suspiciously. 'Well, I *might*.' Harry was a hard man to insult, but no one could clear a room so peremptorily as Tony.

Then, to my surprise, he offered a weary explanation, dropping his voice so low that it became all but inaudible. 'Someone's coming to see me I used to know. We've got lots of things to *discuss*.' Things beyond the grasp of the likes of old Johnny and Harry. 'I haven't met up with him for a long time.' He was already adopting German–American prepositions like baseball caps. Strange how eccentrics pick up the trinkets of conformity. 'It's somebody called Gavin Lambert.' He spilled the name out like Shakespeare's being introduced to the unlettered natives. 'The thing is Johnny, you won't *like each other*.' How did he know? This was divide-and-rule by a king-emperor who never allowed his eunuchs to meet.

Francine was even more impressive in her travelling clothes. The tweeds she wore were Paris, France, rather than Harris, Saks. She spoke animatedly in husky French during most of the drive back to Beverly Hills. That would have delighted George. I couldn't remember when I had heard such a joyous range of sound. Playfulness was a quality I cherished more than most. The divine gift of dogs and monkeys, it sometimes seemed as if it were being bred out of my own species, particularly here in Pacific Bluesland, where a mere suspicion of irrationality was subjected to the scrutiny of analysis. She also had a command of hooker's patois, much of it unknown to me, which tripped from her a little incongruously. It was endearing rather than offensive. Her call-girl coarseness sounded, to use one of Nellie Beatrice's favourite words of approval, quite dainty.

At the restaurant, Francine was transformed into the image George and I had reeled at. The pleasure of being seated across the table from the unattainable is that there are no attendant anxieties about the outcome of the evening. The greatest-restaurant-in-town lived up to its reputation so far as I was concerned. Francine seemed studiously unimpressed but her reassumed aloofness was soon cast off. I thought I recognized a depressive of the same kind as myself, eager for persuasion. She and Harry swopped gossip. If they had once been lovers, and I assumed that they had, they appeared to have an affectionate memory of something briefly enjoyable and now a pleasurable, if limited, friendship. A talent for disinterested friendship, especially with a beautiful woman, was not something I would have suspected in Harry.

They reverted from her native Swiss-French to English. I didn't feel she was interested at all in Harry's enthusiastic breakdown of my career or the promise of my future if, indeed, she was listening. However she smiled a kind of dreamy encouragement across at me. It was more than enough and preferable to being asked unctuous questions.

By the time we arrived on the Strip at the club where Shelley Berman was appearing, I was convinced that Harry, Francine and I were destined to be lifelong, valued friends. There could surely be few things more pleasurable than the exhilaration of an attractive woman's company without any constraint of possible seduction. Soaked in a cloud of rarest pragmatism, the Pacific pangs of the afternoon had vanished.

Mr Berman was clearly off-form that particular evening. He wasn't helped by a few witless hecklers. Sitting in a crouch over the microphone, his technique of ingratiating intimacy became more and more wounded and alarmed. Harry chewed on his cigar impatiently. It was a relief when Tony groped his way to our table and sat down like the late arrival at a wedding. Managing a stiff smile at Francine, he glared round him and then at the stage.

Comics often welcome latecomers as a distraction and an opportunity to turn their torment on someone else. Rather to my disappointment, Berman didn't choose to victimize this obvious target and quickly finished his act. The evening had wound down with such suddenness that it might have seemed to Tony that his appearance had dispelled either a dull or an uproarious outing. It had been neither. He had evidently made some effort to find us, and now the party was clearly over. Francine refused a refill, saying she was tired. She made an exit which drew some respectful whistles and applause from Shelley Berman's tormentors.

Its abrupt ending was slightly disappointing but I was not going to let the evening be blighted by either Berman or Richardson. When we got inside our bungalow, its strangeness seemed to affect us all, except for Harry who behaved as if he had lived there all his life. 'Help yourself to a drink.' I was hoping he wouldn't leave the three of us together, hoping childishly that somehow I could be allowed to show my gratitude by rekindling the lights for one more game before we went to bed. But Harry was bushed. We were off to Las Vegas in the morning. 'Get a good night's sleep. It's gonna be a long day.' He slammed the door of his bedroom.

Francine smiled and followed him. There was the sound of good-humoured chatter and laughter. Tony fell on to the sofa, which skidded as if an exasperated ostrich had collapsed on it. 'But what did you *do* all evening?' For once, in the mystery game Tony conducted, I was the banker. Anticipating sullen interrogation, I filled his whisky glass with too much ice, mocking his American affectations rather clumsily. Perhaps I was drunker than I thought.

Francine reappeared, still smiling, and wandered into her own room. The door was unclosed. 'But, I mean, who *is* she?' I told him truthfully what little I had learned. I was about to affect boredom with the subject when she made another entrance. This time she was snuggled into an hotel bathrobe. The back of her hair was glistening and wet from the shower. The whiteness of her robe against her skin, from knees to bare feet, gave an impression of a somewhat larky Tondelayo beneath. She walked over to the sofa and sat beside Tony, curling herself into a comfortable parcel.

Clearly the evening was not yet over. It was a perfect final bonus to the day. She gazed at us, dark smiling eyes and shamingly white teeth, waiting. Waiting for what? There were three of us in the game now. Francine, curious and relaxed, the two of us reluctant to show our hands, let alone start bidding. Tony brought it to a swift close. With the snap of a spastic guardsman, he stamped his feet to the floor. 'Well . . .' he muttered. 'I'll see you all in the morning.' The low conspiratorial tone was there but it could have meant anything, a slipstream of discouraging mystery.

I started questioning her about her Persian ex-husband and her show-biz ambitions, about America and what she hoped to get from it. She made passably funny imitations of her wealthy escorts. 'See here, honey, you and me could make the sweetest music together.' Her contempt was still in control of illusion. Snatches of American Dream dirty-talk somehow emphasized her fastidious foreignness of spirit.

She looked lynx-like and unconcerned beside me until she ran out of cigarettes. Refusing my Gauloises, she went to her bedroom. Her door was partially closed. My provincial musings induced a very shabby-headed feeling: go to bed, wash your face, head on pillow and sweet dreams before the nocturnal gates and alleys bloat up another spasm of the blues. Curbing my suburban instinct to turn off the lights, I crept past her door. 'John?'

We slept very little and, when I did wake, the expected cut and thrust in my head and throat was mild, nothing that a Bloody Mary in the Polo Lounge wouldn't pacify. Francine was sitting up, sheets tucked under her armpits, a packet of king-size Kents balanced on her chest. She began giggling, rather as I used to as a small boy trying to unravel some third-form smut to my patient father. She had evidently interrogated Harry closely about Tony and myself. 'I said, "Jesus Christ, Harry! What are you doing with a couple of English fags?"'

At the airport, Harry greeted us with especial warmth, the immediate past banished by the greater enjoyments to come which, in Vegas, would be lighting up the desert sky. Even Francine abandoned her public languor, smiling broadly at the hostesses who normally would have got no more than a princess's incline of the head. Tony seemed a little detached, squirming less than usual in his seat. 'She seems very charming.' 'Yes.' There was the merest trace of bitterness in his voice as he added, 'She only looked at *you* all evening.' He absorbed himself in a screenplay of Faulkner's *Sanctuary* while I sat speculating on what sleeping arrangements Harry had prepared for us.

At the hotel desk Harry distributed the room keys like spending money

on a school outing. 'That's for you and Francine.' She was already in full
progress behind a procession of bell-hops and flunkeys. 'See you here, 7.30,'
said Harry. 'First show's eight o'clock.'

Francine's application to her evening appearance was a priestly ritual.
After a couple of hours watching her at work, silent before the looking-
glass, I went below. Like an actor on a vast set, I picked my way through
hundreds of intent gamblers, dressed in anything from dude Western
outfits to tuxedos. I felt that if I didn't keep on the move I might be
arrested or whisked away to an outside alley by a couple of hoods and
pinned against the wall. The quiet of European casinos is oppressive
enough but this supermarket roar was worse. I found Francine in one of
the bars, having a drink with Harry. They appeared to be having an
argument.

'Harry's getting Tony a girl,' said Francine. 'I tell him he's stupid. He
wants a girl, let him get a girl. The joint is crawling with them.' Her Swiss
accent had hardened into Hollywood-French, not a playful note to it.
'Aren't I right, darling? Your friend know what he want. Harry must think
he's stupid or something.' Tony appeared, looking confident enough. His
'girl' was a long time coming. Francine grew impatient. 'What the hell,
Harry. Let's go in. I'm hungry. So leave her a message.'

Before he could corral us up for the interminable evening ahead with
Sammy Davis Jr, Tony's partner for the night loomed impassively over us,
indistinguishable from the scores of hefty cactus plants at every turn. Harry
gabbled introductions like a referee instructing a couple of prizefighters.
The two girls assessed each other. Francine barely acknowledged her.
Lorraine-or-Laverne was clearly accustomed to this kind of snub from the
hierarchy of her own sex. Tony scuppered Harry's frantic *placement* so that
I was trapped beside the unconcerned Laverne (or Lorraine).

I expected Tony to leave almost immediately, exposing Harry or myself
to make amends for the other's behaviour. My repertoire of uninspired
questioning palled horribly. 'Do you come here often?' (Yeah.) 'Do you live
here?' (Where else? There was only the desert.) 'Have you see Sammy Davis
before?' A polite, 'Surely.' Francine was flushing angrily and began what
looked like a domestic row, in French once more, complaining unmistakably
about the presence of our guest.

Sammy Davis intervened, seemingly for ever. Harry and Francine continued to argue. Tony remained expressionless. When the performance at
last ended, Harry, hemmed in by the goading glares of Tony and Francine,
was addressed by Laverne/Lorraine. Distinctly, but without reproach, she

uttered her first constructed sentence: 'You know, I understood every word you and this lady were saying. My mother was French.'

Harry's button-brown eyes swivelled, but he recovered. 'C'mon, let's go.' I stood beside Laverne while he reached into his pocket and brought out a deck of Yankee bills. He flipped one out and crumpled it into her palm. 'Thanks, kid. Goodnight.' She slipped the bill into her purse as mechanically as a hat-check girl and walked away without a glance at any of us.

Before I could absorb the facile shame of being privy to such a brutal exchange or her offhand dignity, Francine pounced on Harry. 'How much you give her?' 'Ten bucks. C'mon.' 'You lie, Harry. How much you give her?' 'Twenty.' 'You dumb, Harry. Twenty bucks for nothing.' She made it sound as if it had come from her own purse. 'So what? I felt sorry for the kid. Maybe we gave her a hard time.' 'A hard time? You call that a hard time – for *that* broad!'

10. American Panic

Already Osborne is a professional success here on a big-time scale – almost at the same heights as the grand old days of pre-war Hollywood. And he is also a personal success. I think one reason for this is that he fits into the exaggerated pattern the Americans admire more than anything, the Horatio Alger legend, the boy who rises from rags to riches.

'From the USA', *Daily Express*, 31 January 1958

The Entertainer opened in Boston on 27 January, the anniversary of my father's death, and a week later at the Royale on Broadway, next to the theatre where *Look Back* was still smouldering on.

By this time, I must have agreed to a substantial royalty cut, in the growing custom of mendicant playwrights faced with the option of closure. It would have been impossible, even for Merrick, to extract any concessions from the cast. Mary was earning less than $300 a week, although my New York agent, Harold Freedman, was picking up our Algonquin bill. How the rest of the cast survived, Alan Bates and Vivienne Drummond in particular, was a mystery. Both of them were living in what were little more than red-light apartment blocks in the sleazier streets off Sixth Avenue. Merrick's mask of pain when I suggested he might nudge them just above the New York poverty line was the most frozen expression of pleasure those hard brown eyes and mourning moustache could betray. He looked like an excise man being asked to ignore a false-bottomed suitcase.

The opening of *The Entertainer* was on a different scale. My remembrance of it is little more than a series of sharp images, inconsequential detail, faces, a chaos of narrative. A dream in fact, like most of the coming year, to which I succumbed with a kind of shaky exhilaration and bouts of bleakest disquiet. I was aware of the presence of dangers, of events taking hold of my life, but, as usual, I felt I might ride with them, that I would confront them frantically rather than be driven back or diverted against my will. As in a dream, I was feeling less and less a participant than a bemused spectator.

I left the Algonquin with a good hour to spare before curtain rise. Mary kissed me chirpily at Times Square and disappeared into her own theatre. The sidewalk outside the Royale was already blocked to standstill with familiar-faced Schubert Alley 'fans' and touts reportedly disposing of tickets at $250 apiece, a record price previously held by *My Fair Lady*. Olivier's name had sold out the three-month run weeks earlier. It was a daunting spectacle, the throng voracious and unpredictable like a gathering of anti-hunt supporters. I retreated into the nearby Piccadilly bar, and a few Scotches began to burn comfort into the gape of apprehension within.

A bleep of comic insouciance settled on me, something rather like the moment in so many British films when the senior officer turns his back on a startled wardroom, growling 'Carry On, Number One.' Like Noël Coward, I must Rise Above It. Number One barked a command for another Scotch. I decided that this New York episode would be conducted like a part in a play. It would only be a short run. *Try to enjoy it.* 'Try' was the flaw in that daily injunction to myself.

Sufficiently anaesthetized, I emerged into the bitter February wind-tunnel and picked my way with a sudden rush of agility through a heaving pack of honking cabs and limos, those strangely skinny-looking New York police horses, mink, black ties and Homburgs. By the time I got to the cheerless foyer, smelling harsh and sweet like the cheaper department stores on Sixth Avenue and the flea-pits of my youth, I felt Number One was back on the bridge. There was a wary but elated radar-blip in my head.

The first act seemed pretty cold, similar to one of Mrs Blond's Jewish Charities. Looking around me in the interval, I realized that this was more than exactly what it was. The moody reception lightened a little in the second act. I had already noticed that a number of unwilling husbands felt they had been conned into shelling out $500 for what was little more than a cheap vaudeville show, and a foreign and incomprehensible one at that. But my inner blip scarcely bothered to register this as a scuffle erupted a few rows in front of me. A bulky man was in the throes of a fatal seizure or heart attack, accompanied by anguished moans, suppressed howls and stage whispers that swept through the auditorium and hissed up to the gallery.

What followed was my first experience of American Panic. This exercise in hysteria is so instinctive that it can be set off as immediately by a broken thumb-nail as by an earthquake, preferably in as public a place as possible. A restaurant or an airport concourse is ideal. A packed theatre could not have been more suitable. Everyone was struck with frantic immobility and primal helplessness. No chance here of 'Carry on, Number One': the British may freeze ('Keep calm, old chap'); the Americans explode. They invented a whole genre, the Disaster Movie, based on this national characteristic.

American panic prevented the stage management from bringing down the curtain. There was no officer class backstage to tell them what to do, and even Merrick could not be expected to improvise with sudden death in the stalls. Lowing moans and groaning disbelief grew as the unfortunate corpse was eventually passed from hand to fumbling hand and dragged out of view. The whole business probably lasted only fifteen minutes, but the effect was as onerous as a concertinaed version of the *Ring* cycle.

All this inflamed attention was reluctantly redirected at the intrusive performance on stage But the play was undeniably over so far as the spectators were concerned, the scented air choked with aggrieved impatience. Olivier's crumpling descent against the proscenium arch met with little response from an audience still transfixed by the extra-funereal drama they had just undergone. The applause was thin, irritatingly grateful rather than polite.

I returned to the now-empty Piccadilly bar, reflecting on the possible consequences of the evening. Would Merrick pull one of his tricks? Could he devise a way of depriving me of my share of the advance? A Broadway première where most of the audience were emotionally absent for half of the evening must be some sort of precedent. I went to pick up Mary. She had discarded the Mary Quant dress I had brought back for her and was wearing a middle-aged, flouncy black number from Saks, topped by one of those skull-cap ornaments favoured by American ladies-who-lunch.

There was a first-night party at some ritzy hotel. I was curious to see if American Panic had subsided; if, indeed, any of the guests would turn up. To my surprise, the huge reception room was full. There were some very famous faces, most of whom had visibly risen way above it. Merrick and his henchmen were gathered in a corner, fidgeting like a bunch of bookmakers after the favourite has romped home. David was staring black reproach, his moustache askew like a disarranged toupee.

I turned for escape to a noisy group led by Frederick March who was hugging Olivier and exclaiming, 'You old cocksucker. You *old* cocksucker!' 'Isn't he?' he demanded. His wife, Frances, nodded cheerfully and so did I. The frowning faces of the night were obliterated by a misty collage of Anthony Adverse, Prince Oblonsky, Robert Browning and Willie Loman, a whooping figure hooting hallelujahs. 'You old cocksucker!'

I found myself shaking hands with Greer Garson. She sparkled with an animal energy of gentleness and delight, pre-Raphaelite golden and pale but gloriously animated and unholy. I was drunk enough to have tried to kiss her arm-length glove in adoring gratitude, but she was gone and I was left with at least one smile from heaven, which looked to be the last. As one whose fame or shame lay publicly in the balance, the problem now was how to catch the eye of the drinks waiter.

The blip was quite blurred. As I was seeking an escape from Merrick's Men, Larry grasped me, kissed me and said with a swift tenderness that was like a slap in the face of my near-stupor, 'Darling heart, they're not good. Not good at all.' He meant the reviews, of course. The critics, like the audience, had clocked off half-way through. 'Well, not good for *you* anyway.' He said it without a trace of irony, only concern and healing recompense. 'I shouldn't read them.'

The old cocksucker held me to him, muttering with clear Crispian diction, 'We'll get out of here as soon as we can and go home for a drink together.' So we did. In the small suite at the Algonquin, his actor's energy, damned by hours of concerted indifference, burst forth into gleeful, all-celebrating anecdote. It was like being expelled from school in the company of its brightest star, repudiating the remaining assembly of dross and prudery and isolating them for ever.

Larry sang loudly, to the tune of 'John Peel':

> When you wake in the morning . . .
> Full of fucks and joy . . .
> And your wife's in prison,
> And your daughter's coy . . .
> What's the matter with the bottom
> Of your eldest boy,
> When you wake with the horn in the morning?

Next morning the usually garrulous clerk at the cigar stall in the foyer looked down as I bundled up an armful of newspapers. The knowing desk-clerk, Mr Puley, handed me a few messages absent-mindedly, the Chinese elevator man was uncharacteristically inscrutable and the bell-captain too absorbed with departing baggage to boom his normal daily greeting. They must all have read the reviews. Olivier had been given the respect due to visiting royalty but Archie had struck no responsive chord. There was a dismissive tone throughout: New York had seen it all before in the thirties. Clifford Odets was invoked, a comparison which made me squirm at the taint of being both second-rate and unoriginal, and tardy to boot.

I stumbled on Tony in the chilly gloom of the Blue Bar, where I was downing a couple of cauterizing Bloody Marys. It was like pouring disinfectant and lighted matches into a blocked sink, a form of drastic medicinal chic which I'd convinced myself might be effective in this foreign battlefield of hard liquor. I knew well enough by this time to look for no reassurance from Richardson's stony quarter. 'What did you *expect*?' All his undertakings had the precipitate energy that made closed incidents of them even before completion; failure or fulfilment both produced a fidgety, post-coital unease.

As ever, he was completely informed about everything, having been on the telephone for hours, spoken to Merrick and his Men, and probably arranged his life for the coming year. He was certainly in no mood for reminiscence and leaped to his feet with alarming, uncoordinated speed. 'I've got to go now. I'll talk to you *later*.' He paused in the semi-darkness. 'Why don't we go to Jamaica?' He was gone.

I had a dispiriting lunch that day with my American agent, Harold Freedman, in the harsh light and clatter of Dinty Moore's. He was always most kindly in a polite Judge Hardy manner, but I knew that he was of the same mind as the critics. As a founder-member of the Playwrights' Company, a friend of Odets and those other Broadway luminaries of the thirties, Anderson, Sherwood and Hellman, he must have regarded me as a Limey-cum-lately.

Freedman made it plain that I was expected to clutch at the flimsiest offer Hollywood might see fit to extend. His first offering, which he regarded as a prestigious coup, was a remake of *Blood and Sand*. When I refused, rather unthinkingly, his embarrassed disbelief at my ingrate hubris was almost shaming. He was genuinely hurt. But if I was becoming increasingly confused by my forebodings about New York, my reluctance about being sold into Californian bondage was genuine. Woodfall Films had yet to make its debut. What vague ambitions I may have had about films were resolutely chauvinist. It was a snobbish response which was dominant in England at that time. There was a maidenly horror at the suspicion of corruption, of compromise for either financial or critical advantage. At the Royal Court this obsession was an almost hysterical neurosis. What passed itself off as high-minded scepticism and integrity was often mere prig's timidity, the plain virgin with locked knees.

As I passed the adjoining marquees of my two plays, I half expected that

Merrick might already be gouging out the flashing letters of my name, but they were still there, like a fairground display dimmed by daylight. Back at the Algonquin, Mary had already left for the theatre. I trundled the breakfast trolley into the corridor, flipped up the Do Not Disturb sign. The bathroom was steaming, with trickling taps, a trail of towels, sodden Kleenex, a wet stain of make-up and false eyelashes that looked like a laboratory experiment.

I was free until eleven that evening. The disorder and sheer bloody mess Mary had left behind filled me with a feeling of nauseous regret and failure. My spinsterish response to the state of the room was ludicrous in the face of my own capacity for squalor and error on every scale. The play itself seemed like a blunder. I had possibly, and foolishly, allowed myself to believe in the Alger Hiss theory. At home, I was conditioned to being jostled by suspicion, dislike and hostility, to being regarded as an upstart, a word which had almost no meaning over here. The American Dream had the upstart as hero; Ellis Island was his Golden Gate. My background drilled into me the discipline of low expectations. It was this loveless mockery of flailing endeavour that incited resistance, however blind and ineffectual.

Salisbury

My dear John,

　　As I feel a little better I thought I must write and ask how you are keeping. It is so boring sitting all day doing nothing and cold too. I expect you wish you were in warmer climbs. There is nothing to report, only I have lost the sight of my right eye. Yet there's plenty worse off in the world . . .

　　Uncle Jack

Salisbury

Dear John,

　　We were so grateful to receive your kind letter and think that we put the contents to good effect by buying Dulux paint and redecorated some rooms out, so you can imagine we have been very busy and not without a few aches.

　　God bless.

　　Uncle Jack

Salisbury

My dear Sister,

　　Have enclosed a few snaps of home and hope you will be interested.

Queenie would have loved it and I tried several Charities to get her here. We did not hear of her death until *two months after*. Our letter to her was returned from the hospital where we had arranged to see her. I was sad because Watford did not inform us and think that Sidney should have done. I *have two* letters from her asking that she be cremated with Dad at Putney Vale also saying that Sidney knew all about it and his sister told us that the transport was too dear. In 1945 I got Queen a *free paid up* Cremation Policy No: 13463 from the Cremation Society and *I have her letter* asking the Soc to arrange for Putney Vale. In this letter she said 'I have told Sidney of my wishes.' She paid for that. I thought that you ought to know this dear.

Your ever-loving Brother,
Jack

Salisbury

Dear John,

Shall we ever see you again? I sit about in my chair and think of you and the old times. It always appears my letters are bad news but Bessie's brother died this morning, heart trouble, he was not 70 so you can imagine how it is. I felt I had to tell someone. There is no one to tell and I feel so hopeless and he was such a help and big. He lived at Ringwood. Please forgive me boring you John but I cannot get there in a pushchair.

God bless,
Uncle Jack

Even at the Court, I had been instructed by George and Tony in the guerrilla arts of living off the land, an unyielding landscape patrolled by an enemy that was identifiable and merciless. To have shown feelings of disappointment or expectations of enthusiasm from such battalions as the press, the public or ruling theatrical moguls would be folly and a betrayal of whatever cause we felt we were fighting. It had the excitement of war but also the attrition of wasted energy.

In foreign terrain, I felt untrained and ill-equipped, like a desert soldier suddenly confronted with jungle warfare. The Blue Bar's Bloody Marys were proving ineffective. Lying on the bed, I felt like someone who had foolishly let an undisciplined dog off the lead and watched it hurtle off into an oncoming car.

Harry rang. 'Hi, John, how are you?' He didn't wait for a reply and, to my relief, didn't mention the opening. 'I've spoken to Tony and we think we should all get some sunshine. There's a flight to Montego Bay Saturday night.' I looked up at the ceiling through a tide of tadpoles. Where was Montego Bay? 'Jamaica.' The tadpoles turned into ducks in a shooting-gallery. Jamaica.

I could think of half a dozen reasons why I shouldn't suddenly swoop off to the Caribbean. Mary would most certainly and understandably be displeased at abandonment to the play and the freezing wind-tunnels of New York. I could invent a plausible excuse. I'd done so before. She'd not believed me then and wouldn't do so now. Our relations had never been more than an almost childish game, once pleasurable and now uncontrolled. It was a cruel business.

Could I afford it? Olivier had given me a further lecture about never getting into trouble, like Archie Rice, with the Income Tax Man. As Harry, a natural courier to my anarchy, was rattling off his travel agent's itinerary, my misgivings faded. They were all so bourgeois and cautious. What shall I say to the wife? Can I afford it? Such craven questions should be struck from my record.

For the present I appeared to be caught in a trap of gaudy bungle and sham. I might as well benefit from its enjoyments while I had the opportunity. Gaudy, Bungle and Sham sounded like a firm of solicitors. Recklessness, however dangerous, was preferable to prudence. 'I've booked four tickets,' said Harry. Who was the fourth? 'Oh, Francine's coming. Call you later.' If ever there was a handmaiden to folly, it was surely Francine. Gaudy, yes, perhaps. Certainly a gift-wrapped bungle. A sham, not really. Some certain sadness.

New York seemed a dangerous place in which to pursue an affair which I already regarded as a luxurious, uncomplicated interlude. Francine's currency-wise Swiss soul knew better than to risk the real hard slog of romanticism, but when I arrived at Harry's apartment, she was alone and as excited and apprehensive as I was. Sixth Avenue on that Saturday afternoon was empty and hardly visible under a driving blizzard of snow. I was confident that Harry's arrangements contained some military contingency plan that would see us off to the sun on time, but he rang to say that there was no chance of getting out of the city that day. For thirty-six hours we waited like fugitives for word of escape. Had I blundered into a humiliating, farcical trap? On Monday, Harry rang again. Our flight would be taking off. He and Tony were tied up and would join us in a couple of days. 'Have fun,' he instructed.

So, in the winter of 1958, I found myself the author of two plays running on Broadway, one of them starring Laurence Olivier and the other my wife, staying with a beautiful girl at the Half Moon, Montego Bay. In Glasgow they were all wrapped up in woollies and having colds.

We were the centre of attention among the American tourists, the star honeymoon couple. To my relief, there wasn't an English accent to be heard. Francine spent long mornings on the beach and then would dance under the stars, displaying the most public candle-lit devotion, eyes brimming mournfully across the table. Acting out this cloying pantomime made me think longingly of rain-swept Brighton and anonymous adultery there at Moss Mansions.

Tony would have said, 'I mean, what did you *expect*?' The truth was rather more and a little less. I had not anticipated the leery brutes in Bermuda shorts on the hunt for 'a juicy piece of black ass', their wives cooing over my bride with her 'cute accent', nor Francine's addiction to glutinous Latin love-songs. She would gaze rapturously at the waiters as they warbled '*Amore*' and '*Volare*' into her cleavage. If '*Volare*' could make you blubber, 'Pop Goes the Weasel' must make you weep.

Rescue from 'the boys' in New York was unforthcoming; more pressing things had 'come up'. At least they wouldn't be witness to the spectacle of Montego Bay's most popular young lovers honeymooning the night away to a crass hokey-cokey. I told Harry we'd be cutting it short. I should have known better than to have gone trawling so blindly, but what absurd expectations could Francine possibly have looked for? The heart-melting pramful had become an armful of misery.

Harry met us at the airport. It was the homecoming of a pair of runaways dragged back from a juvenile prank, adulterous but scarcely adult. He didn't throw blankets over our heads but hustled us into a car. He was full of news of the film negotiations for *Look Back*. Everything was fine, fine. Olivier had extended his engagement for another four weeks. That was unexpected. So was the follow-up. 'Mary's telling everyone she's pregnant.' The furry burden stiffened on my shoulder. We drove back to the Algonquin in silence.

'OK then, John, we'll call you tomorrow.' Mr Puley at the desk greeted me with his customary camp eyebrow-lift. 'My, we *do* have an expensive tan.' There was a message from Mary asking me to pick her up from the theatre for supper with Richard and Sybil Burton, Julie Andrews and her husband, Lena (Horne) and Lennie, Rex and Hugh Griffiths, some of them or maybe all of them. I don't remember. When I arrived at her dressing-room, she welcomed me in her absent-minded bubbly way, pouring forth

Broadway gossip, details of her non-buying shopping expeditions, the awfulness of Kenneth Haigh and so on. If Harry's news was correct she made no reference to it. She seemed an untroubled spirit as she tumbled cheerfully into bed.

Mary had accumulated a tight circle of friends. Her immersion in them must have eased the gaping deception of the little time we spent alone together. There was Josephine Premice, a Haitian actress in the cast of Lena Horne's musical *Jamaica*. Witty and articulate, she was as arresting as a Masai chieftain and almost as fearsome. Mary claimed that, whenever I was away, she and Josephine would share the same bed. I wasn't quite sure whether this was the dormitory bravado of the Mount School, York, colonizing Manhattan chic, but pale Quaker Oats curled up beside this blue-black warrior seemed a rather forced sort of lark.

Mary's most attentive escort was Robert Webber, a Broadway actor familiar to most of us through his sharp performance in *Twelve Angry Men* and later in *The Dirty Dozen*. He was an unsubtle but effective performer, a New Yorkerish red-neck sophisticate who had made his reputation in several of Tennessee Williams' plays. He was a close friend of Tennessee and of another, less flamboyant, homosexual playwright, William Inge. Most of his circle were famous queens, and these liberal sympathies must have grated against his insistent balls-flexing stance which was then a stock caricature of widespread sexual unease.

He was a regular visitor to Ziggy's Gymnasium on Broadway and Third and tried to persuade me to join him, to pump some manly iron into my feeble frame, among the ranks of sweating body-boys. His absorption in these gentle giants was expressed in gruff-voiced jokes punched up from profuse testicular powers ('just a bunch of hairy faggots'), but was as full of awed tenderness as derision. I believe that, years later, he did at last emerge, like a snorting bull, from the closet.

Webber, with his butch references to his bed as a work-bench marked with the notches of a hundred grateful maidens, must have earmarked me as an irresistible target for cuckoldry. I was unsure whether he had already succeeded. Mary, feeling herself an object of public neglect, might have found some comfort in private revenge.

I found his company quite endearing in its boisterous way for short periods. At his Eighth Avenue apartment one day, he suddenly began to berate me at the top of his deep-balled voice about my treatment of Mary, the Half Moon expedition and my dumb entanglement with a scheming hooker. His condemnation was accurate enough to be damning and left me helplessly mugged by my own criminal indiscretion. He gave chapter and verse of my behaviour, which was, he said, being openly bruited in Broadway theatres, bar-rooms and the columns of Walter Winchell and lesser gossip-writers. The principal object of his harangue became Francine. I was assigned the role of an innocent alien who had been set up for a messy intrigue with a cheap and tasteless broad.

My own behaviour had been patently wanton and inexcusable, but the assessment of Francine seemed vindictive and extreme, more McCarthyite hysteria than puritan outrage. To compound the evidence of my villainy, he told me of Mary's fierce loyalty at some recent party when, after rejecting a clumsy pass from Elia Kazan, the director had taunted her with the observation, 'I hear your husband's a fag.' It was quite believable. There was a teasing softness of style in the English male that baffled and even outraged these guardians of acceptable mannerism. The ambiguity of English maleness was not merely Un-American but downright provocative. Mary had given Kazan a good Yankee smack in his Armenian face, which turned her into an instant heroine, an exemplar of the fire-power of the frontierswoman.

Webber became more solicitous. 'I should keep your head down for a while if I were you.'

Epitaph for George Dillon, the play I had written in tandem with Anthony Creighton some four years earlier, had just opened to some muted enthusiasm at the Royal Court. Sloane Square suddenly seemed a very friendly, wise and civilized place and even Woodfall Street a pleasant haven from the luxuries of room service and the excitements of all-night New York. I needed to return where I was less regarded and more tolerated.

It was a dismal, cowardly decision but I could think of no other. In writing of one's past, it is an unavoidable pity that there is no one to speak up on one's own behalf. There might be some faint plea of mitigation. Perhaps not. I was born with a contrite heart. This is not a boastful apology, rather it might provide the motive if I have occasionally perjured myself. I hope so.

To the accusation of slovenliness I merely change the plea of guilty to a charge of unremitting and commonplace simpleness. What does it matter? Not very much.

11. 'His own Worst Enemy'

He achieved nothing he set out to do. He made no one happy. No one looked up with excitement when he entered the room. He was always troubled with the void round his heart, but he loved no one successfully. He was a bit of a bore and, frankly, rather useless. But the germs loved him.

Epitaph for George Dillon

I should judge that Osborne has been his own worst enemy. Self-loathing appears to be a driving force of his art. He should control it: he is not as bad as he thinks.

Harold Hobson, *Sunday Times*, 14 April 1958

When I got back to Sloane Square, George had just returned from Buckingham Palace with his CBE from the Queen. He had accepted it 'on behalf of the theatre' and, to ease his misgivings, he would hand around the despised bauble of the Establishment with rather forced mockery, saying, 'Here, feel that, boy. Her Majesty actually touched that.'

It was not a very convincing performance, but his discomfiture was real enough. Her Majesty was, after all, Defender of the Faith and her servant, the Lord Chamberlain (one Sir St Vincent Troubridge), had demanded that twenty-one blasphemous lines be excised from *Endgame*, including Beckett's notorious dismissal of the Almighty: 'The bastard, he doesn't exist.' Moreover, George had dropped the custom of playing the National Anthem before every performance, confining it to first nights to appease the Daimler-and-diamonds brigade.

Apart from the bauble, he seemed in good spirits and a little puzzled by the mild approbation for the opening of *George Dillon*. I had sent him a copy of the play after he first came aboard the *Egret*. He made little reference to it except to imply he found it inferior, and I scarcely thought of it again, although Anthony was disappointed. I was well aware of its deficiencies, in particular the shadows of gauche shabbiness at the heart of it and the impression of irresolute defiance that seemed, even for me, an act of wanton self-denigration, self-manacled Houdini crowd-pulling.

The play's first showing had been a year earlier by the Oxford Experimental Theatre Club, who had written asking if I had an old, unproduced script I might care to let them loose on. On this flimsy proof, George decided to give it an airing at his own theatre. In spite of misgivings, echoing his own verdict, about 'an apprentice work unwisely resurrected', he offered it to the director Bill Gaskill. I was surprised by the choice and, even more, that Bill accepted. I scarcely knew Bill, although I liked him, but felt there must be a natural chasm of taste and temperament between us that would be difficult to negotiate. The low, baiting cruelties scattered all over the piece would surely affront his rather prickly Yorkshire severity. I had been glad to be away in New York leaving him to sort out Anthony's amiable vagaries for himself.

As a result, perhaps for the first and last time, I sat down to watch something of my own with scarcely any apprehension. For once there would be no inner recriminations. The West End triumphs of the day were *The Reluctant Debutante*, *Teahouse of the August Moon*, *South Sea Bubble*, *Sailor Beware* and *The Mousetrap*. I was reassured that *George Dillon* would at least be more stimulating than anything else in London. It was. Bill had cast it extremely well. The curtain line of the first act, 'You stupid-looking bastard,' delivered by Robert Stephens as George Dillon to the photograph of his benefactor's dead son, drew exactly the shocked frisson from the audience I had intended.

Robert was a complex character, exuding actorish high spirits which concealed a deeply divided, embittered soul. Although few could have been aware of this simmering dissatisfaction, it made him an inspired choice. Watching him, I had the needling impression that he might have based his interpretation, consciously or not, on an unflattering observation of myself, even to the extent of physical mannerisms. I didn't brood on it. Robert's innate qualities were more valuable than charm. This letter from him, seven years on, is wholly characteristic:

National Theatre, SE1

My darling, I must say it again I do think *Patriot for Me* truly, truly magnificent! Larry said *he* would give up the National to play it if he were twenty years younger!!! – He said he was *born* to play it!! – And that I was the only other actor who could do it apart from himself! –

So that's two of us who would give an arm and a leg!!! – But apart from all that I think it is immense and deeply affecting and as always makes my hair stand on end.

Hope to see you very soon – and show you my Doug Hayward corduroy suit which is smashing! (not a pinch, I promise).

All my best love.

Always.

Bobby

The year before I had written a piece for a provocatively titled book, *Declaration*. This provided an unexploded package to an eager corps of cultural-disposal experts. The only ones certain to suffer injury were its rash contributors, the eight conspirators in this literary gunpowder prank, who were to find themselves and their pretensions blown up in amateurish ignominy.

Declaration was an early example of instant opportunism, put together by the fluently pushy young publisher Tom Maschler. He trumpeted in the introduction that:

> A number of young and widely opposed writers have burst upon the scene and are striving to change many of the values which have held good in recent years. No critic has succeeded in assessing them or correlating them objectively one to another. This volume aims at helping the public to understand what is happening while it is actually happening – at uncovering a certain pattern taking shape in Britain today.

Maschler had been as shrewd as he was opportunistic in his selection of writers. But his literary clout was marred by his endorsement of Colin Wilson, the trusty Outsider from Leicester and sleeping-bag philosopher of Hampstead Heath, and his two altar boys, Stuart Holroyd and Bill Hopkins. This cranky triumvirate had already been unkindly caricatured as a highbrow Lord Snooty and his scruffy intellectual Pals.

Oddly, they were the only AYM who looked especially young. Wilson, briefly buoyed up by accolades from Cyril Connolly and Philip Toynbee, had the appearance of a sinister, bespectacled swot with a catapult dangling from his threadbare trousers. Their academic simple-mindedness and immature arrogance dashed any possibility of the other benighted essayists receiving a token of sympathetic attention. We were all implicated in their doomed manifesto. Prophetic heroism, proclaimed by self-educated lower-middle-class upstarts, pronounced in English and with dodgy Nietzschean flourishes, never stood a chance. Putting Doris Lessing and Kenneth Tynan, Lindsay Anderson and John Wain alongside Lord Snooty and his Pals was fun but unfair even by the fairground-booth standards of Fleet Street.

At least three of the *Declaration* pieces deserved attention. Lessing's essay, written from the standpoint of an ex-Communist, colonial novelist living in England, was more than realistic about the poetic limitations of working-class heroics. Tynan's was full of fanciful certainties, combative, cool and funny. It would have aroused ill-natured envy wherever it had appeared, especially from those whose mincing, mandarin style Lindsay Anderson nailed in his own essay. My own piece, written hastily over a weekend punctuated by Maschler's deadline calls, deserved some if not most of the scorn heaped upon it.

Party Swoop

A cocktail party for the publication of *Declaration* was banned from London's Royal Court theatre over criticism of royalty by the Angry Young Man author, John Osborne. Mr Reginald Poynter got a telegram from Mr Neville Blond, chairman of the English Stage Company, saying: 'We will not permit the party to be held in any part of the theatre.' He also got a call from Mr George Devine who said, 'Members of the Council are shocked at the John Osborne piece and in particular to the references to royalty. They wish to be disassociated from the book in every way.' Lord Harewood, the Queen's cousin, Lord Bessborough and actress Peggy Ashcroft are members of the Council of ten.

And so the party was held at the Pheasantry, Chelsea. The company included Mr Aneurin Bevan, Mr Michael Foot, Hollywood actor Rod Steiger and the authors.

This is what Osborne wrote in the book. 'My objection to the Royalty symbol is that it is dead: it is a gold filling in a mouthful of decay.'

Daily Herald, 15 October 1957

George had joined the party, so hastily switched to a crumbling, recherché bohemian retreat, and gamely offered to send the bill to the Council. The whole episode must have increased his daily burden with hours of ultimatum telephone calls. He never rebuked me for my part in encouraging the hooligan elements ranged against his own serious efforts. He was already hemmed in by detractors and foresworn enemies. I had merely added to them.

Stuart Holroyd, Lord Snooty's Pal, popped up again the following spring at one of the Court's Sunday-night productions without decor. These were presentations of plays by unknown authors, most of whom were to remain so. But there had been some notable debuts by Michael Hastings, N.F. Simpson and John Arden and, later, Donald Haworth, Wole Soyinka, Edward Bond, Christopher Hampton, Joe Orton and Howard Brenton. They were a little like those turn-of-the-century showings of plays by Ibsen and directors like Granville Barker. The list of actors prepared to rehearse for two weeks for one performance and virtually no money is unthinkable today. Even more fruitful was the recruitment of untried directors including Lindsay Anderson (dubbed by Tony 'the Singing Virgin'), Bill Gaskill, John Dexter, Peter Gill, Robert Kidd and Bill Bryden.

Holroyd's play, *The Tenth Chance*, was directed by Anthony Creighton. How anyone could have countenanced this farrago of talents even as a bad joke on a Sunday night was mystifying. The house was untypically full and there was a discernible impression of assembled factions, including Wilson and his band of apocalyptics dotted among the main body of chafing hostility. The cast included James Villiers (who had replaced me at Frinton Rep and was the object of Anthony's romantic dreams), Bernard Kay, Ronald Fraser and the daily who cleaned Woodfall Street.

The awfulness of the play mounted to a climax, then evened out like the mid-plateau of a hangover before descending into a final tableau of incomprehensibility. Groans and scuffles in the auditorium were drowned out by the superior bombast of Bruckner, which Anthony employed as an extra blanket to throw over the confusion on stage. It was custard-pie anarchy.

I slipped out quickly. Anthony was in the pub next door in high spirits and wearing the Hunting Stewart kilt he favoured when contemplating an evening of seduction. He was surrounded by a group of sympathetic supporters. I decided to leave before any confrontation between the fuming factions broke out. I was too late. There were cries of jubilant aggression from a table in the corner. Colin Wilson, lying in wait for Tynan (who had walked out noisily before the end with his wife, Elaine), pulled the dandy-critic's chair from under him and left him sprawling on the floor.

As I made for the door, a reporter asked me if I had seen anything. I replied that I hadn't. The following morning I read that I had been at the centre of 'an angry young brawl' in a Chelsea pub. It wouldn't have happened at Sardi's.

By 1958 George's adversaries, within and without, could not deny that he had established some kind of bridgehead, however vulnerable. Even the Essenes noted the changes in the desert map of English theatre. The choice of repertory might seem too eclectic for those looking for a clear, doctrinal affirmation of taste, but it conformed to the practical considerations of what was available and possible. It was the application of his insistence that 'all problems are *technical*', a dismal-sounding dictum that might come from a woodwork instructor at an Evening Institute rather than an inspirer of poets. Pondering on it years later, I felt that it was more useful counsel in dealing with women than art. 'There are plays that you do out of passion,' he said. 'There are plays that you do to express your beliefs. And there are plays that you do because the author needs that support at that moment.'

Even if I should wish it, I am not equipped to write a history of the Royal Court. I may have been a participant, but much of the action was going on in other places, other rooms. Rather like a character in Arnold Wesker's *The Kitchen*, I had a fragmented vision of a series of dramas acted concurrently. There was ignorance and indifference to what was going on at the next 'station'. We were too absorbed in our allotted contributions to pay much heed to the troubles of others. The complaints of the vegetable cooks were a hindrance to the pâtissiers. Both were a nuisance to the butcher. Only George had any overall picture. As for the customers, they had no knowledge of the chaos below, and less interest.

So many plays were presented through a system of default, happy and less-happy accidents of fortune: sometimes the stealth of a minority faction, or the apathy of a few, or simply the overnight need to plug up an unforeseeable hole created by a singularly battering disaster. Devine, the Little Dutch Boy of Sloane Square, was obliged to have his finger at the ever ready to thrust into the most shaky of theatrical dykes. John Arden became an in-house joke for box-office disaster. George's triumphant cry at the latest clutch of bad notices was cherished by those below stairs: 'They're worse than *Live Like Pigs*!' Neville Blond, panting for a knighthood, would go white. 'Not *another* Arden, George.'

Arnold Wesker was then living in an LCC block of flats in the Upper Clapton Road with his young wife, Dusty. He had approached Lindsay Anderson outside the National Film Theatre after a showing of Lindsay's film, *Every Day But Christmas*, and entered an early version of *The Kitchen* for the *Observer* play competition, where it received neither prize nor mention. The competition was the inspiration of Kenneth Tynan, whose enthusiasm for working-class theatre was not always helped by his unfamiliarity with the idiom of the man in the bus queue or, in this case, the salt-beef bar. Lindsay reported back to Upper Clapton Road that he thought the play 'Important as well as very *good* . . . Can I send it to George Devine to read for the Court? Of course I haven't any idea what their reaction will be! They are rather incalculable people.'

All creative enterprises, at risk from electricity bills, salaries and box-office caprice, are faced with the inescapable contortion of compromise. In George's case the Wesker plays were a classic example. It was a matter of keeping the right balls in the air. When *Chicken Soup with Barley* fell at his feet, he kicked it straight into touch by offering it to the Belgrade Theatre, Coventry. In exchange for mounting it, there would be a week's showing in Sloane Square. It was the kind of transparent dexterity, limiting financial loss – and loss of face – that cautious impresarios used in similar arrangements with the Court.

The task of directing the play was consigned to John Dexter, then a house guest at the Wesker flat. The two had met on an Aldermaston march, the duffle-coated radical answer to Ascot or Leander-pink Henley. Who knows what ambitions, what plans for plays, novels, between-sheets liaisons and poetry readings were fired on those blustery Easter-weekend route marches? Unlike hot, drowsy pre-1914 summers, Aldermaston weekends were always wet and cold.

JIMMY: Is your friend Webster coming tonight?

ALISON: He might drop in. You know what he is.

JIMMY: Well, I hope he doesn't. I don't think I could take Webster tonight.

ALISON: I thought you said he was the only person who spoke your language?

JIMMY: So he is. Different dialect, but same language. I like him. He's got bite, edge, drive –

ALISON: Enthusiasm.

JIMMY: You've got it. When he comes here, I begin to feel exhilarated. He doesn't like me but he gives me something, which is more than I get from most people.

Look Back in Anger

Webster was one of the twenty-seven off-stage characters referred to in the play who never make an appearance, a breach of the laws of dramaturgy at the time, though for no explicable reason save custom, and often cited as typical of my overall technical ineptitude. Dexter, however, must have been pleased with his non-appearing role because he told everyone *he* was the original Webster. I like to think so, although we never referred to it.

We first met in Derby in 1953. John was no bushy-tailed gay of a later generation and the burghers of Derby had every reason to be resistant to his passing through the stage door of their playhouse. He was a local boy, but he had the mark of metropolitan criminality. He also had a ferocious energy, driven curiosity and a kind of fearful courage which cut little ice in the rink of provincial certainties. His visits were a welcome distraction in Pamela's flat exposed to the year-long chill which swept in from the Dales. Sunday evenings were a dangerous border-crossing of the week, a few short hours infested by my own uncertainties and the usual Sabbath intimations of utter isolation. No one could compound that terror with such finality as Pamela. Oh well, that was another Sunday over. Not much to show for it, and not much promise for the next.

Dexter, like Anthony Creighton, abhorred the mere mechanics of female functioning. No other director could have boomed from the auditorium at a stumbling actress: 'Oh, dear, we know she's got the rags up again, *but* . . .' It was a vengeful, goading shock to bourgeois gentility under a mask of working-class consensus. He once told me that as a fourteen-year-old apprentice he had been gang-masturbated on the factory bench by a bunch of middle-aged housewives in some initiation ritual.

Later, he was infamously charged with various indecencies against a minor during an audition above a pub in Brewer Street. George, summoned to Bow Street to give evidence of good character on John's behalf, had been sick with disbelief at the detail he had been obliged to hear. The magistrate was a renowned queer-hater ('A Hogarthian monster', according to George), but having to listen to the pornographic plod was the worst of it. Dexter received the maximum sentence of six months. George's liberal kindness took a savage mauling. 'I can't tell you the stuff that came out . . .'

In replying to this letter, please write on the envelope: – Number 2952.
Name: Dexter

H.M. Prison,
Wormwood Scrubs,
WI 2

My dear John,
   I think of you back in England now. Hope so, anyway I'll risk a letter finding you. I can't give you many details of life in here, but it's odd:

very cold, not as bad as you expect. So many reforms coming into effect, so many yet to come and the place overcrowded and under-staffed. The screws are in the main, a decent crowd, most of them seem to be aware that things are changing and are happy to change with them: the only people who *hate* any reform are the old lags, but they are all terrible old Tories anyway. The worst thing here is time; it has no feel, no taste, no shape, length, no, nor no bloody brevity neither. Nick is rather like hell: a climate but no situation.

A ghastly rumour has reached me; it is said that I have taken my bird as a punishment for evil and have gone religious!!! This is not true. I have tried to do my time with as much strength and gaiety as I possess. As for religion, what do people think I am for God's sake? I admit I hope to be in Pamplona next year, but that has more connection with bulls than saints. Worry not, I shall never darken your door, whisky-soaked and priest-ridden. I shall bring nothing out with me but experi-ence which I can use, and which is unique. I shan't write a book and as for the strange langue d'oc of the lags, I fear I shall never speak it with ease. No change, in fact, but that which only those who know me best will see.

Now then, on Dec 5th or 6th, I am due for another visit, would you like to come? Tony V knows the routine and will bring you if you wish. Don't for God's sake come if it is going to upset you. But if you think it would interest you I would love to see you. Let me know, and I'll set the wheels in motion.

I am well and half way now and it's going more quickly. Tony and Doris write regularly. I work hard, and time passes. I love you all very much. You must know this, but I didn't know I was loved back!! It makes the world a different shape. Give my love to Tony R and G.D, Mary, Tony C, Oscar B, Jenny, EVERYONE.

For yourself, thanks, gratitude, oh balls! I am going to be a big success, that will be my thank you.

John.

I was there to take him home on the morning when he was released. I later learned he called me 'Sister Mary Discipline'. Fairly amusing. Not very.

Devine, Richardson and Anderson had all been to Oxford and even to the same college, Wadham. Lindsay was known to chant its Latin prayers along with 'The Streets of Loredo' or 'She Wore a Yellow Ribbon'. Among the actors in the original company, there had been a sprinkling of graduates –

Nigel Davenport, Christopher Fettes, Jose Richards – but I was never aware of a conscious clique. Later came Gaskill and Anthony Page. Most of this supposed Oxford bias was little more than pipe-smoking in-filling, like the proscription against homosexuals: it did you no harm and less good. Few of George's playwrights were graduates, with the exception of Arden (Cantab.), Beckett (Trinity, Dublin) and Wally Simpson, who was a teacher. Playwrights who had been to university, let alone Oxford or Cambridge, were then, as now and before, a minority.

As a factor in day-to-day practical considerations, I don't think the 'Oxford' count figured at all. People like Dexter had some reason for feeling intellectually discriminated against, but it was not a substantial one. My own class and credentials were every bit as unpromising as his, or Wesker's, but I didn't detect any evidence of paternalism or impenetrable class chasms between George and myself.

Dexter and George played out their mutual unease in a cross-talk banter, the NCO to the other's Officer. Their shared experience was a bitter dislike of the army. 'Tell me, Dexter, how did you rise from the ranks?' 'I didn't, sir. I stayed on as a staff sergeant because I wanted to be with the boys.' Dexter had looked up the boss's initial assessment in the company files: 'Nice little chappie, not greatly talented, looks like Noguchi.'

Arnold, particularly, found George's presence in the council flat in Upper Clapton Road intrusive and patronizing. I think of George making his way through the gefilte fish dutifully prepared by Dusty. It is a scene rich in comic speculation, but it also makes my heart ache a little. Nothing invites such scorn as good intentions. When George came upon the Wesker's first-born being breast-fed in his office, he delighted all expectations by shouting, 'Get that woman out of my room.' Even the mutual bond of class affinity could be strained, immortalized by Dexter's equally impatient outburst, 'Shut up, Arnold, or I'll direct this play as you wrote it.'

Whether or not directed as written, *Chicken Soup with Barley* opened in Coventry and was received enthusiastically. George honoured his obligation and brought it to the Court, where the phantom audience failed to turn up. A year later *Roots* came in after another success at the Belgrade. Dexter was then able to persuade George and Tony to agree to his Sunday-night staging of *The Kitchen*. Repudiating Tony's verdict that it was 'technically impossible', the result was astonishingly invigorating.

Binkie Beaumont once said as I left the room, 'Well, there goes a million pounds and, probably, good riddance.' George felt much the same about Arnold. Despite Tony's derision and my insularity, there is no doubt that

George's favourites in the 1958 season were the French connection: the Romanian Ionesco's *The Lesson* and *The Chairs* and Irish-Sam's *Endgame* and *Krapp's Last Tape*, known to us all as '*Tape's Last Crap*'.

Appearing with Joan Plowright in *The Chairs*, George was nightly stimulated by the cries of 'surrealist rubbish' and the rows of empty seats in the stalls. Those who knew him from his Young Vic days had never seen him happier. He would puff on his pipe from the window of his dressing-room on to a Sloane Square empty of parked Daimlers and sigh, 'This is what I'm here for.'

12. 'Not at his Best'

> The body of Jonathan Swift, Doctor of Divinity, Dean of this
> Cathedral Church, is buried here, where fierce indignation can no
> longer lacerate his heart.
>
> Epitaph, St Patrick's, Dublin

Donald Albery, who had refused to transfer *Look Back* to the West End
unless the bears and squirrels were given the heave-ho, ran the only
management of any substance to compete against the oligarchy of H.M.
Tennant. Through the patrimony of Sir Bronson he controlled several
key theatres. A tall, chilly figure, he walked with a cane and, in the repertory
of the time, would have been well cast as an embittered ex-officer who
terrorized the small boys in an oppressive prep school.

I was becoming accustomed to condescension, and his was more entertaining than most. It was difficult to believe that he could possibly have
liked *Epitaph for George Dillon* and he presented me with a list of his
'demands' in the matter of cuts and changes. Among these was a stipulation
that the title be changed to '*George Dillon*'. 'Epitaph', with its intimations of
mortality, was a message of death at the box-office. It seemed dull to me but
preferable to his other suggestion, which was to use the mocking title of the
play within the play itself '*Telphone Tart*'.

My compliance didn't seem to give him much pleasure. I was fairly sure
that a few perfunctory clips here and there would be enough to persuade
him, like the critics, that the play had been almost completely rewritten and
become something else. So it was, and continues to be.

I returned to New York, braced to improvise some kind of restraint on
the disorder I was sure to face. Air travel then still had an element of daring
privilege: a twenty-four-hour journey from a large shed at Northolt, cou-
chettes reminiscent of exotic foreign trains (always chivalrously allocated
to ladies), drinks in the cosy bar, the arctic blast of air that ripped through
the aircraft when it landed at Gander, where health inspectors flashed lights

at sleeping passengers as if they were curiosities from a distant world. I drank myself insensible and broke my vegetarian vows by eating something called Cornish Rock Hen.

Wearily sedated against recrimination, I arrived at the Algonquin in mid-afternoon and I was effusively greeted by everyone, including the quizzical Mr Puley, always an accurate wind-sock. Mary, still in her nightdress, was in full-flow of her daily gossip on the telephone. She blew me a cheery kiss and waved at an ice-brimmed champagne bucket on the table beside a gift-wrapped package from Saks. Both resistant to the expensive novelty of transatlantic calls, we had only exchanged a few uninformative letters. If she had received poisonous dispatches from unkindly friends, she showed no sign of suspicion. Her chirrupy ease was almost infectious, even to my wary spirit, and her obsession with the punishing *Kama Sutra* of fertility athletics seemed to have abated.

Algonquin life resumed more or less as I had left it, with the additional hazard of Francine waiting like a mislaid parcel to be reclaimed at Harry's apartment. For the next few months I did no work at all. Margery Vosper, unlike Harold Freedman, had a comfortingly unambitious attitude to advancement. 'I think you've done *quite* enough for the moment, dear,' she would say. With Mary's commitments to Merrick, Fifth Avenue, her girl-friends and the English and Welsh Broadway exiles, I saw very little of her, less than I did of Francine.

If it wasn't a double life, it was an exhaustingly packed double half-life. I could detect a strong undercurrent of displeasure. It genuinely surprised me. I couldn't trace the impulse for it, least of all from a profession which should surely have retained its scorn for anti-bohemian outrage. I was as circumspect as was possible within a square mile of New York. I was observing the most obtuse mechanics of propriety. I was realistic enough to know that to calculate the cost of adultery is like enquiring about the cost of running a private yacht: posing the question defines your inability to afford it. But it wasn't the cost – it never has been – that concerned me. It was the matter of what was justifiable as a caprice of short life and affectionate memory. It didn't seem a great deal to ask.

I continued to have breakfast in the room, then a late lunch at some-where like the Russian Tea Room with Mary, and an early 'Volare' even-ing with Francine at the Little Club, her favourite, most expensive and boring idea of fun. Tinkling pianos, twinkling Manhattan, why should I begrudge such simple upstart pranks? It was minimal consolation for a twenty-eight-year-old dramatist with a play running in London and two on Broadway, and assuredly all over by Christmas.

Merrick summoned me to his office. I knew that I was to be presented with some St Valentine's Day ultimatum. The glum look on the face of his chief hit-man, Jack Schissel, as he ushered me in, confirmed it. He rasped out that *Look Back*'s box-office was slipping, as I already knew from *Variety*. I felt as if I had been found guilty of cheating him in a bootlegging racket on the South Side. What was that object bulging below Jack's left armpit? Merrick agreed, with much show of reluctance, to present *George Dillon* in New York. I would be back in October. *Look Back* would never have survived the steaming New York summer and, with the departure of *The Entertainer*, the exposure of the last nine months looked like becoming a tidily closed incident.

On 8 May, again (my father's birthday, the end of the Second World War, the opening of *Look Back* and, later, the death of Max Miller), Olivier gave a last-night party. He had chartered a private yacht, *Knickerbocker VII*, and welcomed the guests in a Butlin's blazer and yachting-cap to the accompaniment of bagpipes.

Vivien was presumably pining in London. Joan Plowright was tucked among the guests, successfully evading the hovering English journalists. Up the gangplank came Douglas Fairbanks, Henry Fonda, Helen Hayes, Cedric Hardwicke, Ustinov, of course, Denholm Elliott, Eric Portman, Anthony Quayle. And Greer Garson, again. There was a buffet of fish and chips, jellied eels, stout and bottled Bass. As we sailed up the Hudson, I spent most of the night with John Steinbeck, also in a yachting-cap. To Mary's dismay, I gave an extended impression of a typical English faggot to Elia Kazan.

> There are bad times just around the corner,
> There are dark clouds hurtling through the sky,
> And it's no good whining
> About a silver lining
> For we know from experience that they won't roll by.
> With a scowl and a frown
> We'll keep our peckers down,
> And prepare for depression and doom and dread,
> We're going to unpack our troubles from our old kitbag
> And wait until we drop down dead.
>
> Noël Coward, 'There are Bad Times Just Around the Corner'

The following month, Mary and I embarked on an adventure holiday which seemed to be riddled with portent on every hand. I felt she deserved comfort and physical freedom, some recompense for nine months in the poky Algonquin suite and the twenty blocks of exercise yard she had trailed between Forty-fourth Street and the Park. I also felt what Nellie Beatrice would call an 'entitlement' to luxury in the face of the strange and unexpected.

We emerged from the Beverly Hills Hotel and a Cadillac was delivered to the forecourt. George couldn't have described this as a 'grocer's car'. Red and gleaming, it was already warm from the morning sunshine. It was a car for the likes of girls we had decided we would never find ourselves escorting, girls like Francine. Francine would have descended into this eight-cylinder sphinx convertible-absurdity as effortlessly as into a preferred mink stole. Mary looked at it with dismay. This surprised me, as she had taken enthusiastically to American food, clothing and customs without any of my own resistance. Indeed, I suspected, half hopefully, that she might contemplate citizenship. She slumped into the front, clutching an armful of maps and we glided off.

It took me ages to get us out of Los Angeles and on to Highway 1, an operation a Californian eight-year-old could have accomplished in minutes. I soon wished we were in the two-litre grocer's roadster, gazing at the white sands of the West Highland road to the Hebrides, or even back in New York. Out here, Mary was suspicious and fretful in a way I had never seen her before. Where she had been eager and uncomplaining, she was either tentative or disapproving. She discarded the maps. I knew she was capable of navigating a boat on the Clyde without thinking.

For the next six weeks she said less and less, looked at little, the space between us in the rushing wind widening as the mileage clock plunged into four and then five digits of time and distance. If I had any expectations of exhilaration from following the line of the Pacific coast, they were soon dispelled. There was none of the ferocious vastness of the prospect from Falmouth or the enclosed ghostliness from the dereliction of Gateshead. It was monumentally bland.

We stopped at tourist spots like Monterey, where we spent an evening in a perfect Egyptian art-deco cinema, and Carmel, a Disneyish Cornish village, popular with middling phoneys and film actors. Nothing seemed to engage Mary's attention, nor even her disapproval. I felt we should get away from the placid seaboard and strike inland. First stop Reno. From Reno, to the Blackpool of Las Vegas. Then the lunar cities and tiny settlements of Nevada, Utah, Colorado, New Mexico and Arizona. I had never known such parched exposure and banishment in the constant presence of another.

I was increasingly certain that I had been ham-fistedly cuckolded by Robert Webber. The fact that my coltish liaison with Francine had been pre-empted by Mary's conduct with Webber explained her oddly restrained behaviour in New York. Sexual guilt, like jealousy, had never been more than a passing cloud over any of the tumult of the past. Betrayal might end in the bedroom but I found it naïve to assume it necessarily began there.

The one thing which did rouse Mary from her day-long prickly inertia was her motel inspection in the blue-pink light of the late afternoon. The motels varied from lower-middle-class luxury to American-style squalor. We learned that behind the world of Betty Crocker hygiene, of paper-sealed lavatory seats and post-coital showers, there was a continental closet of trash, unlaundered sheets and cockroaches that would make many a Lancashire landlady retch over her scrubbed doorstep. There were times when we found ourselves groping about, after the sun had snapped out in the limitless distance, in ghostly rooms lit by broken lampshades, aired by stale air-conditioning and the presence of the last occupants. The basic rule was never to stay anywhere that was uncarpeted. That could reveal all manner of disagreeable surprises to the most exhausted traveller.

Town after town seemed an exact replica of the one we had just left. The empty diners confirmed Brendan Behan's observation that 'You can tell the richness of a country by its bread and its whores.' In Main Street there would be a general store, a barber's shop, a saddler's, a bar and a sheriff's office. We would retreat to our motel room and hope to make the television work without summoning the Anthony-Perkins-look-alike in reception. No doubt if we had not each been constrained by the listlessness of the other it would have been very different.

One afternoon, late into our venture, after driving in silence through an insanely twisted, cruel landscape, Mary suddenly asked me to stop the car. We were heading for Yuma, the town with the hottest recorded temperature in the United States. The Gila Desert lay to one side and the ridge of the San Bernadino mountains ahead. We had not spoken for hours. 'Can't you wait a bit longer?' 'No. I can't.' Her reply was so terse there was no mistaking its urgency. She got out, scanned the swimming haze of emptiness surrounding us and, without looking at me, snapped, 'I want to be fucked.'

I decided that if it were to be done, it were best done quickly. The back seat looked as if it might start blistering and burst into bubbles. I didn't care for the prospect of an icy lunar night among rattlesnakes and coyotes. I put up the hood. I could have sworn that the sun was actually making sounds as I joined her. It is hard to think of a more unforgiving spot on earth for a loveless coupling, two desert insects locked in the lifeless dust.

Without a word, she got into the front seat and I drove us back on the road to Yuma, thankful that we hadn't trapped the hub-caps. I stumbled into the barber's shop, Mary cooled herself at the soda fountain. The barber looked at my soaking frame. 'You're foreigners, ain't ye? You're from New York.' I nodded and closed my eyes, pounding from the sun and my gasping exertions beneath it. The temperature at noon, he said, had been a record 138 degrees. That was a record. Yup. Even for Yuma.

In the motel it dropped to almost freezing as we climbed into bed in silence and mercifully fell asleep at once.

> To thirst and find no fill – to wail and wander
> With short unsteady steps – to pause and ponder –
> To feel the blood run through the veins and tingle
> Where busy thought and blind sensation mingle;
> To nurse the image of unfelt caresses
> Till dim imagination just possesses
> The half-created shadow, then all night
> Sick . . .
>
> Percy Bysshe Shelley, fragment 'Igniculus Desiderii'

We returned home from New York with Tony and Harry. For most of the flight Mary remained as silent as she had been for the six weeks of our self-capsuled moon-holiday. Going through Customs I was obliged to pay £10 for some trifle. None of us could find the necessary cash, except a hovering reporter who produced a note and said, 'Here, John, have this one on me.' Mary immediately, and to the delight of the spectators, broke into a loud and tearful denunciation of Harry, informing him – and the press – that she might well not agree to appear in the film of *Look Back*.

Harry, fumbling in his pockets, turned to the eager note-flasher, 'Ridiculous. Sure she'll be in it.' 'If I don't appear,' she announced, 'my reasons will be personal. I may have other commitments. Personal ones.' The note-flasher's inevitable next question startled her. She flushed and mumbled, 'No. There's no baby.' I waited for my duty receipt and Harry pushed Tony and Mary away. 'Miss Ure is under contract to Rank,' he puffed. 'I'm trying to borrow her, that's all. We'll have it all sorted out by Monday.'

The four of us drove off in a blanket of sandy silence. No one had been fooled by this toddler's tantrum but it didn't augur well for life in the house from which Woodfall Films took its name. Any hopes I may have had of cauterizing rankling bitterness had vanished in the calcining desert.

During Mary's absence I had acquired Helen Henderson. Anthony had met her when he was working at a debt-collecting agency off Oxford Street and he brought her round for supper. She was small, frail, with a fine, slightly pinched face and a gentle intensity that matched her voice. She made the most ordinary utterance sound like a line snatched from some ancient Scottish ballad. I guessed her to be about fifty and she lived in a small north-London flat with her elder sister. She was also an active and lifelong member of the Communist Party, although she was losing heart. As with every imagined aspect of her life, one longed to offer the simplest comfort but there was none, except silence.

She had an unsickly, still fragility that I had recognized in my father, and I persuaded her away from the sweat-shop job at the agency to become my secretary. In those early days I had not yet learned to throw away and ignore letters or to refuse to answer the telephone. I was still constrained by a doggy amiability and politeness. The prospect daunted her but I hoped it might awaken some new confidence in her. It was a makeshift proposition. I installed her at a toy-like desk in the tiny upper room in Woodfall Street and she insisted that she would improve her typing, learn shorthand in her spare time and cultivate a stern telephone manner.

I was uneasy about Mary's reaction to Helen's presence in the house, but she took to it quite happily. Their common tongue and background made Helen a more suitable lady's companion to Mary than secretary to me and she was a helpful distraction during the few hours we spent in the house together. Mary immediately reverted to her daily routine, Knightsbridge standing in satisfactorily for Fifth Avenue.

Harry had somehow requisitioned Lowndes Cottage, where I had first dined with the Oliviers, which he used as a production office for the film and accommodation for himself and visiting friends. One of these, he implied, was Francine. It was one of his gestures of offhand friendly service, but unhelpful at the time. Mary's hostility to Harry was implacable. Tony and George were busy rehearsing the Ionesco double bill. I saw less of George during the rest of that year. I never even had the opportunity of discussing Francine with him. Perhaps I wouldn't have done so anyway. After the nightly satisfaction of outfacing *The Chairs* audience, there was the beginning of his adventure with Samuel Beckett.

If Ionesco's discordant wilfulness intrigued him, Beckett's temperament inspired him with almost apostolic awe. Even the peremptory sourness of

Brecht couldn't match the incomparably bleached bone of Beckett and his liturgical 'toneless voice'. Uncle Sam had the monstrous good fortune of actually looking like one of his own plays, a graven icon of his own texts. The bristled cadaver and mountain-peak stare were the ultimate purifier that defied all endeavour, pity or hope. If the head of a Balzac or Ionesco or a dozen other sybaritically fleshed-out masters had been put on to the Irishman's torso, the response to the purity of that 'toneless voice' might not have been so immediate. Furthermore, for George, he had the impeccable credentials of French cultural hauteur.

George tried unsuccessfully to persuade Alec Guinness among others to play Hamm in *Endgame*. He was reduced to having to attempt it himself. It was not a happy choice and he knew it. Wrapped up nightly in his rug, cap and blackened spectacles, he would tremble at the enormity of the theatrical task of stepping unfalteringly into emptiness. It was brave but unmoving. It seemed a pretty long chew on a very dry prune. I would never have dreamed of saying so.

Mary was then technically under contract to H.M. Tennant. Binkie Beaumont was still very much the *éminence lavande* and she was awed and enthralled by his undoubted leathery, matinée charm. So when we received an invitation to dine at his house in Lord North Street, she was as flustered as if she had been summoned by a reproving ex-headmistress. The clear purpose was to subject her to a smooth dressing-down for her ingrate behaviour in joining the barbarians and marrying the ugliest voice of them all.

It was an inimitable, taffeta-edged performance: the measured reproach, the hint of avuncular sarcasm and then wise forgiveness. Unlike Merrick, whose greatest pleasure lay in baiting or humiliating actors, Binkie had a consuming itch to make himself indispensable to his actors and, especially, his actresses. They were smothered by his courtesy and discreet air of slightly alarmed concern and admiration. He held out the promise of benign power and sanctuary against the perils of a vulgar, predatory world.

During dinner he was in sprightly command at the head of his table and lobbed several deftly primed grenades in my direction. He had not yet reached that stage when he was to become more or less incoherent after six o'clock. I was made to feel a little like a mud-wrestler being complimented by a duchess.

His housekeeper was a woman called Elvira, who reminded me irrepressibly of the old crone who appears at the top of the stairs in the film of *The Old Dark House* shrieking, 'No beds, no beds!' At one point, as she put a plate in front of me, he turned to her and in an arresting tone said, '*Now*,

Elvira, tell us . . . ' There was a long pre-Pinter pause while he leaned forward. 'Tell me. Mr Brendan Bracken, as you know, has just died, and his house across the road is up for sale. Don't you think . . . it would be *splendid* if Mr Osborne should buy it?' She gave me a gimlet glare and replied emphatically, 'No!' Binkie's lizard lids fluttered beneath the folds of a perennial sunlamp tan. 'But why on earth not, Elvira?' 'Because, 'e's not *ready* for it *yet*!' Game, set and match to Mr Beaumont.

13. 'Letting down England'

Now I have to turn my memory back over thirty years to recapture my first vision of John and Mary as they returned from New York. It is no exaggeration to say they took my breath away, because they did . . . Mary's hair was like corn silk, her skin matt and flawless and, although she was thin, her limbs were exquisitely rounded in an Eighteenth Century fashion . . . A briar rose – natural, honest and wild . . .

The same evening John was a physical Oberon to Mary's Titania, very lean and sunburned, his light hair streaked by the sun and his eyes a truly blazing blue . . . They were both so high with pleasure to be home, competing with each other in their Truman Capote impersonations and, for that evening, they were both full of laughter. I was the only person there unknown to them, but nothing could have blighted their gaiety and pleasure and it left me free to observe and wonder at their outrageous vitality and glamour.

Letter from Don Bachardy to Jocelyn Rickards, 1986

Filming of *Look Back* was due to begin at Elstree in September. Tony and Harry had persuaded Richard Burton to play Jimmy Porter. It was a calculated move on his part to reverse the tide of his career and possibly the last time his shrewd intelligence overrode his duplicity. His most recent films, which had concentrated in Cinemascope on his splendid knees beneath Roman kilts, had failed to establish his surety as an international star. That wouldn't happen until Elizabeth Taylor flipped her Cleopatra's ball from the film scrum into his waiting hands.

He was a huge asset to our modest undertaking, which was regarded with general suspicion from Wardour Street. Burton's presence guaranteed dignity if not commercial success. Harry's principal obstacle in setting up the production, apart from distaste for the play's reputation, was my insistence on employing Tony as director. This was based not on blind loyalty but on my untutored faith in his flair and his being the only possible commander to lead Woodfall's opening assault on the suburban vapidity of British film-making.

Rank had offered me £30,000, which Margery urged me to accept immediately, but insisted on using one of their High Street directors. Eventually, Harry was able to persuade Associated British Picture Corporation to chance its reluctant arm, provided Burton dropped his Hollywood fee to a Celt-chastening minimum, which, in the face of all augury, he did. I was to throw in the rights for nothing except a 'returnable' £2,000.

In spite of the concerted press campaign to transform me into some upstart wordsmith who had inexplicably won the pools ('Osborne mellows now he's on £1,000 a week'), I was not earning great sums from any of the three plays now that two of them had finished their Broadway runs. What had come my way I had largely spent, much of it on travel and the Algonquin, and now I had committed myself to buying the rights of *A Taste of Honey* for Woodfall's next film venture, a considerable gamble and one which was to cost me £30,000.

Although my ambitions for Woodfall and Tony were almost headlong, those for myself were more contained. Film-going had been a secondary education throughout my life, as it was for so many of my unschooled generation, but the technicalities and the organization of it intimidated me, particularly the necessity of becoming an inferior among equals, which is the unacknowledged status of a film-writer. So, in spite of some unenthusiastic prompting to write the screenplay (for nothing), I was relieved when Kenneth Tynan suggested hiring Nigel Kneale and Tony willingly agreed.

Kneale had made a reputation as a skilled writer of science fiction with his creation of the enormously popular *Quatermass* series. It was soon evident that, though he had readily accepted the task, the material was not much to his liking. He and Tony decided to 'open it up'. It seemed to me they were ripping out its obsessive, personal heart. I protested without much authority and Tony agreed to let me rewrite some of the dialogue scenes, particularly those of Ma Tanner, one of the many characters who were discussed but never appeared in the play. We went to the South of France for ten days to – most dread to me of all wasteful activities – 'work on the script' and watch Harry's day-long dealings between plage and pedalo.

Ma Tanner was a treacherously difficult role with almost no immunity against mawkishness, which was the reason I had banished her off-stage early on when writing the play. But working on it with Edith Evans turned out to be one of the few pleasurable privileges film-making ever offered, and between us I think we more or less got away with it. She insisted on going through the text word by word, which she also did later with Miss Western in *Tom Jones*. Her ear was miraculously tuned. 'I have perfect pitch,' she said. '*And*, I am *really* a Cockney.' She took the unresisting costume designer, Jocelyn Rickards, with her round the second-hand shops of the North End Road to choose her costumes, including accessories. Even Tony was unable to argue with that.

From the first moment I met Jocelyn Rickards at Lowndes Cottage, I was intrigued by her. Neither sphinx nor tantrum child, she suggested a passionate intelligence and emotional candour. Small and dark with wide, appraising eyes, she had an almost comic air of uncombative lethargy which I found immediately attractive. It reminded me of Stella's impatience with my own similar affectations of indifference. The ironic temperament always seemed to me the most admirable and bravest of attributes, however little I had managed to achieve it, and an especially English one. Jocelyn was also vulnerably opinionated on almost any subject, as if driven by mischievous dissent. This irritated many people, including Tony, but I found a warmth of irreverence in her drawled commentaries that was reckless and endearing. She knew only too well that she had at least one layer of skin missing when she exposed herself to the cutting edge of adversarial intellects more vain and brutal than her own.

She nurtured, and still does, an immutable affection for men. Her feeling for her ex-lovers was abidingly loyal. As one of them, Graham Greene, observed thirty years on, she has 'an outstanding capacity for friendship – rare in the jealous world of art and letters'. At this time, in the summer of 1958, although I didn't know it, she was attending daily to the needs of Raymond Chandler, dying alone in a basement flat in Eaton Square, where she herself lived with another ex-lover, the photographer Alec Murray.

Along with their friends Loudon Sainthill, the theatrical designer, and his partner Harry Tatlock Miller, Jocelyn and Alec had formed an early advance guard from Australia to a cold, unwelcoming London where they were duly registered with ration books. They soon established themselves with the recidivist ease that is the inheritance of all expatriate Australians. Jocelyn's emergence had been the most leisurely, decorating galleries on commission, painting murals in private houses of the more or less famous, and designing the costumes for a musical which had boasted nine directors before its quite showy collapse.

The professional aspect of her life may have been patchy and tentative, but she had discovered and entered a rather loose fifties-cum-Garsington world of writers, philosophers, painters and eccentrics. The list of her friends in this exclusive – and, to me, suspect – circle was formidable. It made the stern endeavours of Sloane Square seem rather provincial and unworldly. I never really explored it. Although at the age of twenty-eight I had become preposterously famous, I was still partially gagged by the indoctrination of aggrieved lower-middle-class humility. In my work I had not dissembled, I was sure of that, but the nagging inheritance of 'Who do you think you are?' is hard to drown out in the presence of those who seem to have an ironclad awareness of who *they* are.

During the weeks to come, I found myself drawn to the large top-floor flat in Eaton Square at increasingly earlier times of the morning. Jocelyn would put down her paintbrushes and we drank black coffee laced with brandy. I soon gave up the pretence of talking about the film and encouraged her easy flow of energizing gossip. Sometimes she would be interrupted as a visitor passed through to see the occupant of the third bedroom, the ballet critic Peter Williams. Frequently it was a young journalist on the *Daily Express*, later to become drama critic of the *New York Times*, Clive Barnes.

Jocelyn seemed a cliquish, literary-circle kind of name, suitably attached to her namesake Herbert, with her Auntie Virginia Woolf profile, but not to the oddball Rickards. In Australia they had called her 'Joybells'. 'Joy' seemed an acceptable diminutive, so that's what she became.

Look Back began shooting and I went to some of the locations: Stratford East, Deptford Market and Dalston Junction, where I found Oscar Beuselinck and my accountant getting in everyone's way. They seemed to regard it as some expensive game which they had generously allowed us to play. Everyone appeared to be in good spirits. Richard was behaving well, apart from being discovered in his dressing-room *in flagrante* by a startled actress, and the ensuing drama kept Mary happily absorbed. I left earlier than necessary for the opening of *George Dillon* in New York in the first week of November.

Watford

My dear Dolly,

Lots of thanks for your letter I had this morning. Was pleased to hear your Back has eased up a little. I have to see the Chest specialist a week today. I think the trouble was when Queen came home once or twice and would not have a Bed downstairs. I had to take the weight of getting her upstairs on my Stomach and Chest. I used to gasp for breath by the time she was up. All she thought of was herself. For a long time after I met her, I *never* knew she had a mother, father or any relations. I don't mind writing you like this, as I know she was *never* a good Sister to you. No one knows what a life I've had since I married.

I've just done some washing, put in Garden. Thought I would go out in Garden this afternoon, and do a few odd jobs, but the wind is too cold. Do hope dear ole John does *not* overdo things with all the work he has to do. Was pleased to hear you feel better. I felt so very depressed last Sunday night, here alone.

God bless.

Sidney

[PS from N.B. to J.O.] Poor Sid, still washing. I feel sorry for him as they are mad at him for writing me. Good God tell me *what does one have to do not to be hated* like me. I don't feel that *rotten*. Who cares. I *don't* any more. Still, it's not a crime not to come up to others expectations.

Watford

My dear Sister,

I have your letter before me, which I had yesterday mid-day. Sid is upstairs in Bed. He had had all his *bottom* teeth out on Wednesday 5 o/c, they were devils to get out and he had a bad time as they were so large. The Dentist looked as if he'd had a rough time himself.

Ever your loving sister,

Queen

Watford

Dear John,

Lots of thanks for your letter and the suggestion that you will see what you can do from your end, as regards a woman to come in and help. I could get a Home Help here but Queen will *not* agree. You know what the Groves are, just b–obstinate. I also thought of the WVS for meals, but still Queen will not have it. Ah well, why worry. She will not agree to a Bed downstairs, and I have to heave her up and down each night. Have had terrible pains in my stomach. When you write please do not say anything about this as I have to read letters to her.

Love,

Uncle Sidney xxxxx

Uncle Jack and Grandma Grove saw me off at Southampton. As I sat fuddled in a corner of the tender in the midst of a force–eight gale, I was so drunk that I believed I was already aboard the *Isle de France*. The last time I had been in the town was to watch my father's coffin disappear behind the clattering curtains of the crematorium.

The voyage was my first and last glimpse of travel on the grand scale and I loved every moment of it. The setting was operatic and vast and gave me a feeling of liberty and anonymous fame I never experienced again. I dined at the captain's table, surrounded by French aristocrats whose snobbery made that of my own countrymen seem quite matey. There was an elegant Maugham-like character who claimed to be a professional caviare-taster. Like a priestly diviner, he would dangle a small gold instrument over the black slime in its diamond ice-bed and pronounce it acceptable. I was pursued to my cabin nightly by a couple of very rich American widows. They looked like ladies with powerful connections and vindictive appetites. Life was in enough snarl. I might not be exactly a gent, lounging like a deluded film extra in this departing show, but I didn't fancy being leaped on like an Italian waiter.

Anthony Creighton met me in New York with his new American lover, Bernie. They were in a state of ecstatic excitement about the play. The word was around, said Bernie, that it was going to be the biggest hit since *Abie's Irish Rose*. This information steadied my sea legs a little. I liked Bernie and I was glad that he was clearly helping Anthony to enjoy some of the romantic delights denied him since his wartime, high-kicking days in *Boys in Blue*, but I had no trust whatever in his taste. The other source of their excitement was the discovery of Fire Island.

George Dillon opened in Baltimore, going on to Atlantic City, where we played in a 3,000-seat picture-palace of the thirties. It was an Italian palazzo with cypresses and copies of Michelangelo's *David* in every niche. The Royal Court set filled only a third of the surrounding blackness. From the back it looked like a small television set.

The drabness of the Boardwalk made me yearn for Brighton's promenade, Stella, Edlin's bar and cockle stalls. In spite of this, the production was fine. Hurling their performance at a vast amphitheatre, the whole cast preserved a lightness and sublety. Eileen Herlie was a considerable improvement on Yvonne Mitchell. Alison Leggatt was near-perfection and Robert Stephens's performance was quite remarkable. 'What have we heah?' He smirked like an arch-conjuror as he unwrapped the typewriter, destined to tap out a lifetime of 'Telephone Tart' plays. He trapped the audience in a trembling moment of heart's agony.

Atlantic City had been invaded by half a dozen conventions and the hotels were full, so I found myself sharing Robert's motel room. We drank late into the night. His grief and anguish, mingled with a powerful comic intelligence, were terrible to witness. It was truly *endoganoid*, as I believe the Greeks have it, the very style of Philoctetes, an inheritance of creeping malignity. In bed at last, I listened to the sound of his teeth meshing and grinding in the pole-axed death-throes of oblivion. I had never heard such an alarming sound but, then, few ladies possess either the teeth or the temperament for it.

The first night in New York at the John Gorden Theatre was a classic example of Broadway disaster and its comic ritual, which remains unchanged and unchallenged. The astonishment of writers like Arnold Wesker and David Hare when they find themselves its sacrificial victims is hard to understand. It was ever thus. The cab-choked street, the PR men clutching their ulcers, the jewellery displayed like medals on the chest of a Soviet general, the snoozing men from Wall Street, the Sardi's supper entrance. As always, in any enterprise, Americans travel hopefully, fuelled by a thirst for adrenalin not experienced by most Europeans. I felt that the odds were much the same as punting at the Sands' in Las Vegas.

The reception was barely short of rapturous, or so the house manager told me. He hadn't seen anything like it since *My Fair Lady*. Some little whisky-wise worm of instinct told me that we might just be less than a palpable hit. Merrick was glaring. Bernie was weeping copiously, his gaze fixed bravely upwards. 'Well, John,' said my friend Sam Zolotov of the *Times*, 'I'll just read over to you the opening paragraph of Brooks's notice. I'm afraid it's not very good, John.' It was clear that Anthony's dreams of permanent residence in the poofs' paradise of Fire Island were not to be fulfilled.

I decided to go straight to the party at Josh Logan's in Sutton Place, where there must certainly be drink. I felt rather cheerfully exhilarated. A dozen swerving waiters holding champagne-laden trays swooped aside with the nimbleness of a fly-half and whisked their trays further aloft into uncontaminated hands. Mine were leprous with the contagion of failure. I managed to wrench a glass from an unguarded table.

Bill Gaskill had already been there for some time and explained the state of play:

> Josh greeted us at the party like heroes. 'The show is a hit,' he announced. 'I thought you should never say that in New York till the notices came out,' I ventured. 'Look, young man,' he roared, 'when I

say a show is a hit, it's a hit.' . . . Not long after it was noticeable that the room was emptying or rather that there was a mad rush to the door like water running out of a bath. The notices had arrived. I went over to Josh and said, in effect, 'I told you so,' perhaps not the most tactful thing in the circumstances. 'I knew there was something wrong in the third act. You should have done something about it.' 'Why the fuck didn't you say that before?' I wasn't exactly thrown out but I did hit Walter Winchell's column the next morning.

William Gaskill, A Sense of Direction, 1988

To Bill's everlasting credit, he refused to back down in the face of a recriminating gathering, swelled by a bizarre group of British patriots led by Oliver Messel, accompanied by a noisy Danish sailor who shouted at me, 'You've let down England!'

Shortly after this doleful night for the Fire Island heroes, I went for lunch in Sardi's with the Roberts Stephens and Webber, Marty Balsam, Robert Preston, Sam Levene and Christopher Plummer. Apart from Stephens and myself, all were famous faces at the peak of their fame. Marlene Dietrich was at the number-one table, the first banquette on the left. Beside her sat a bald, bearded man who was, I was told, Leo Lehmann, editor of American *Vogue*. The outline of Dietrich's unique profile beneath a small, pointed black hat and short veil outshone even the impact of Greer Garson. As we all tried to direct our attention from one of the century's icons to the menu, a waiter laid down a small salver with a piece of folded paper in front of me. I picked it up. On it, written in a bold hand, were the three words 'Who are you?' Signed, Marlene Dietrich.

I passed it across to Robert, who exclaimed in his George Dillon voice, '*What* have we HEAH?' I craned sideways to see if the sender was still in her place. He passed it round the table to the accompaniment of low whistles and 'Good gods!' He thrust a pen at me and dictated, 'Just write this: "My name is – and may I have the pleasure – no, honour – of meeting you?"'

We dispatched the waiter. I shifted my chair further behind the pillar. If I were about to receive a rejection slip, I had no wish to see the signatory. It returned within minutes. Robert snatched it: 'Any time. Any place . . . My number is . . .' It was a Yukon exchange and I memorized the digits almost at once. I scarcely ate and pondered the next move. The restaurant was almost empty by now. I stepped unsteadily beside Miss Dietrich and announced myself. Her smile was unaffectedly kindly and curious. She said something like, 'Of course, I've heard about you. Forgive me, I didn't know what you looked like.' Lehmann invited me to sit down but I excused myself, never having felt so shamingly inadequate in my life, publicly or privately.

For days, until the last moment before I left New York, I hovered over the Algonquin telephone with the Yukon number beside me. I didn't rise to it, an act of craven timidity that I have regretted ever since. In the words of Binkie's Elvira, 'I wasn't ready for it yet.' Thirty years later I met Lehmann, who confirmed every detail of the occasion. 'She really had no idea who you were. She just admired the look of you.'

When I returned to Woodfall Street Mary greeted me, as I had come to expect, affectionately like an absent-minded parent confronting an off-spring returned from school, suspicious at what it might have been up to but soon losing interest. Shortly after, one night about 2.00 a.m., we were awakened by the sound of laughter and heavy thumpings on the front door. 'We thought we'd drop in,' said Tony, more drunk than I had ever seen him. His countertenor bounced off the cobbles. With him was Robert Shaw, who was reeling. 'Where's poor little Mary?' Poor little Mary was standing at the top of the staircase, startled but not displeased.

'How are you? I mean, are you all right?' She shivered in her nightdress and smiled bravely. 'Robert and I were talking about you and we thought you might like to see us for a drink.' She switched on the bars of the electric fire while I poured whisky for the three of them. They all settled down, Mary happily curled up, knees to chin, pleased as a welcoming dog. I left them and returned to bed. I wasn't angry, mostly surprised that Tony should employ such a clumsy ruse and with such an unlikely carousing companion.

Helen Henderson was left alone for most of the day in Woodfall Street. Mary's attention was fixed between the Knightsbridge daily run and her new *Sons and Lovers* co-star, Dean Stockwell. Jocelyn suggested that she, Alec, Mary and myself should spend Christmas in Rome together. I was astonished when Mary agreed readily. Perhaps she too was keen to avoid the chilly house by the Clyde, her nephews and grim stepmother. Woodfall Street seemed progressively colder and comfortless, a small box that defied decoration or warmth.

We stayed at the Inghilterra in the Via Bocca del Leone. It was delightful. Some of the rooms had terraced gardens overlooking the city. It was warm and sunny, and on Christmas Day we had lunch in the Borghese Gardens in rolled-up sleeves and sunglasses.

Jocelyn was signing off a painful affair with an Italian lover. She returned one evening distraught and tearful from a protracted, nostalgic farewell. She fell on to Mary, who put her to bed, promptly and efficiently sedating her. It was an odd sight, like watching a bossy toddler playing doctors and nurses with a truthfully sick adult for a patient.

For days I sat beside Alec and Jocelyn dreaming that something would summon Mary home alone. Suddenly, she decided that Italy was no place to spend Hogmanay and returned to Scotland to 'first-foot' with her brothers and Auld Nanny.

14. A Night to Remember

When you go out into the world, among the birds and flowers – count your change.

Max Miller

Most of my attention during the following weeks was directed towards securing a licence from the Lord Chamberlain for my next venture, *The World of Paul Slickey*, permanently labelled with the preface 'ill-fated'. Thirty years on, arguments about its worthlessness are of little interest, but the uniform weight of the vituperation it aroused and the hysteria accompanying my own tumbrel ride to the public scaffold in an idiotic and vindictive pantomime still make one pause.

When George padded on to the *Egret* four years earlier, I was tapping away at what I intended to be a modest but amusing 'comedy of manners'. It was titled *Love in a Myth*. I was to find that modesty of intention is never an acceptable mitigation of failure. When vilified for not having achieved something on the scale of the Sistine ceiling, it's useless to plead that you were only attempting a palm-sized miniature.

I decided to question George Goetschius, an American sociologist, eunuch and guru-in-residence at Lower Mall. I liked George very much and knew that he was privy to all that went on politically and emotionally in the Richardson-Devine camp by the river. He told me frankly and helpfully that neither George nor Tony thought much of the play. They were both anxious, he said, not to cause me pain or rouse me to anger, which might be destructive to us all and enduring. I was hurt by their lack of trust in my stability. Perhaps they were right? But I also believed they were wrong, narrow and snobbish. They had confused lightness of heart with frivolity. I was not downcast or aggrieved. Rather to my surprise I was excited.

I can't quite remember why I decided to turn *Love in a Myth* into a musical. Perhaps I had seen so many in New York by this time, good and dull, that the incitement to reach a 'popular' audience was attractive. With the departure of Ivor Novello's highwayman's jinks and lovers-in-lederhosen the English musical had more or less died, although Lionel Bart, booted by the genius of Joan Littlewood into soupy crash-bang-wallop success with *Fings Ain't What They Used to Be* had achieved a knees-up for the nobs, and Sandy Wilson's pastiche *The Boyfriend* flattered its audience into a trance of indulgent sophistication.

The subject matter of *Paul Slickey* was the disagreeable exploits of a newspaper gossip columnist. This nasty species, originating from the snob reportage of obscure landowners, debutantes and duchesses, was almost unchanged since Edward VII had enlivened things with the introduction of royal mistresses, Jewish bankers and upstarts from the Turf. Recently an underclass of mountebanks, including photographers and ballet dancers, American comedians, interior designers and the 'Princess Margaret Set' had proved a new, decidedly 'camp' addition to the Edwardian City and racing fraternity.

Money spoke all right, and no one heard it more clearly than the gossip columnist snooping on the edge of a semi-private world of celebrated non-entities. I was not uninterested in this rising phenomenon and I possibly exaggerated its importance but, like royalty-worship, it seemed to reveal an alarming change in the British character that was cruel and ugly. The most successful agents were William Hickey in the *Daily Express* and the *Mail*'s Paul Tanfield. Each had a coven of malign moles. The title, *Paul Slickey*, had them sniffing for months.

What's Osborne up to behind those locked doors?

Only one thing succeeds more than success in fascinating the entertainers – failure. Which explains the speculation now buzzing in the world of show business over *The World of Paul Slickey*.

This is the John Osborne musical which goes into rehearsal behind closed doors today. Last night he pulled on his Sherlock Holmes pipe and puffed out this definition of his first musical comedy: 'A show about modern archetypes in a schizophrenic setting.'

It is even more. Its fate affects a theatrical phenomenon of the fifties – the Osborne legend. Already Shaftesbury Avenue is asking: 'Is fresh triumph in store for the author of *Look Back in Anger*? Or, switching to a new and more difficult medium, will he stumble in the pitfalls of British musical comedy and come a spectacular cropper?'

Daily Mail, 9 March 1959

George's gnomic throw-away that all problems were technical was especially appealing to me at the time. It implied defiance and cool indifference to almost certain pain. Some simple adjustment, like the use of an old screwdriver or a kick at the faulty mechanism, might turn reversals into triumph. With *Slickey* the first problem was to find a management prepared to be identified with it. The fact that the Royal Court and George, from whose rib I had sprung so unwelcome, were not prepared to endorse it was damning. Even those implacably opposed to the disruptive ambitions of the tiny upstart theatre had been forced to accept that it had made an astonishing impact in little more than a couple of years. Even Beaumont's Bourbons had been shaken by the ugly outbursts of the mob and were now unashamed to nip off the tumbrel and clamber on to a careering bandwagon.

I approached Jack Hylton, the only producer who had ever shown me a hint of geniality. A cheery, popular bandleader of the thirties and a famous Lancashire lecher, he had been a successful producer of gamey twice-nightly plays, variety shows and the abominably popular *Kismet*. More significantly, he had transferred George's production of *The Country Wife* to the Adelphi. He was a happy gambler, read the script and talked about it intelligently. 'I think it's a bit too highbrow for the British public, John,' he concluded. 'I may be wrong and I dare say it's jolly good, but it's too highbrow for *me*.'

So, it was back to Albery, who had taken a short ride on the tailgate with *George Dillon*. He agreed to give his backing, if not his blessing, for an undefined term of trial. His assistant, Ann Jenkins, was as encouraging as her dedication to her boss allowed. He accepted that I should direct the piece myself. This was not surprising, as he must have known that it would be difficult to find anyone of useful reputation to take it on, especially as the score was barely complete.

This was being written in some haste by a young man who had been recommended by Margery. Only my impatience could have persuaded me to consider her judgement seriously. His name was Christopher Whelen. No one, apart from Margery, seemed to have heard of him. He was rather solemn and smoked a pipe in a maidenly, Anthony Creighton manner. But, again, I was grateful prey to a little old enthusiasm, especially as there wasn't much of it about.

It was soon clear that, if the book might be patchy, the music would be more so. However, with the myopic faith that seems to grip people when they get involved in musicals, I chose to assume that the whole process in itself would create an organic mystery. The bit was in my mouth. At last, for the first time since sleeping in crab-infested blankets in the dressing-room at Hayling

Island, living on evaporated milk and biscuits, swanking about as a peroxided Hamlet to an audience of geriatric holiday-makers, I had contrived some sort of personal control over the whole brash enterprise. I would only have myself to blame. The release from benign paternalism was firingly enjoyable.

Auditions were a daily encouragement. Ann Jenkins had no difficulty in assembling an impressive number of actors backstage at the New Theatre, eager to take part in a production for which every augury pronounced disaster. Only two characters really required a fine singing voice, in particular Slickey himself. Slickey also needed someone with a strong sexual presence, or so I thought, as well as the ability to be 'unsympathetic' – not something most actors are prepared to take on. I made a monumental misjudgement by dismissing Sean Connery, who turned up one morning looking like my prejudiced idea of a Rank contract actor. It was a lamentable touch of Royal Court snobbery.

The final choice was a young South African singer called Dennis Lotis, who worked with the better big-name bands and had a loyal following. He had a sweet, lyrical voice, more Mel Tormé than Frank Sinatra. As an actor he was only adequate, but he had grace and a casual sexuality. Perhaps, even in 1959, he was *too* nice and polite to excite admiration, let alone frenzy.

With Dennis, the bet was indisputedly on. To my amazement, I then secured a jewel of Edwardian theatre in Marie Löhr. She embodied everything we could steal from a tradition the piece itself partially mocked. In the dodgy circumstances it looked like a small triumph. Her mere presence would be an asset to the younger actors and, from beginning to end, she behaved with such grace and circumspection that it was difficult to believe my good fortune. It was comparable to having Edith Evans on the team. For the rest, I depended on whim and experience. Philip Locke was one of the Court actors I knew was special and reliable. Harry Welchman was a veteran musical-comedy idol and the original 'Red Shadow' of *The Desert Song*, and Adrienne Corri deserved a chance for sheer profligacy of nerve. In her chaotic way, she managed to inspire a schoolgirl bravura which was helpful at the lower moments to come.

Jocelyn R.'s costume drawings were practical but startling. Through her intervention, Hugh Casson agreed to design the sets. But the happiest and most valuable recruit was the choreographer, Kenneth MacMillan. It was a haphazard choice. I knew nothing about ballet or 'the dance' as it would now be called. I had seen *Swan Lake* at the Bolshoi and used the odd free ticket from the likes of Dexter to touring companies in the provinces or accompanied Anthony on occasional hunting-trips to his favourite Ram

Ghopal Indian ensemble and the more dreaded Ballets Nègres, which brought so much relief to deprived outposts of homosexuality in Streatham and Hammersmith. Faith, as we are supposed to know, is not the same as certainty, and my faith in MacMillan's theatrical genius and originality, notwithstanding my unrepentant ignorance, was as devout as a housewife's in the pin stabbing a racecard.

Asking for trouble

If ever a drumming was invited in advance it is the one John Osborne has taken with *The World of Paul Slickey*. Mr Osborne and his supporters are not in a strong position to resent the discovery that his big guns have the calibre of pea-shooters.

Daily Telegraph, 7 May 1959

There is something I call 'Window-cleaner's Nose'. On a day when every minute is physically unendurable, when in the silent, darkened room even the touch of the sheets feels like a cattle-prod, when you disconnect the telephone and curl up like an exhausted louse to oblivion, that will be the day when the window-cleaner's nose twitches and summons you to the front door. His untroubled spirit whistles and hums as he clatters his buckets and ladders, asking for an extra cloth, some more warm water. He hounds despair with his optimism and health, making retreat even more furtive and ashamed.

Will it be a signal for others to come sniffing at the entrance to the burrow? The lady from the Conservatives ringing doorbells which refuse to be disobeyed? The old man with his tray of Remembrance Day poppies? A briefcased gauleiter from the Social Services tracking down your unkept records for thirty years past? Or, worst of all, Archie's Income Tax Man?

There must be a saint assigned to this happy army of window-cleaners, blessing their gift of intrusion into the blackest dates of the calendar. Albery had been endowed with the nose, if not the innocence, and had a magical knack of appearing at rehearsals on the darkest of days. It must have been one of them that finally decided him to withdraw from the management. A fresh look up at the surrounding hills of antagonism gave no further sign from whence any help might come. But come it did, and indirectly through my connection with Merrick.

David Pelham was an improbably effusive, red-haired young man, who had worked as one of Merrick's 'assistants'. He came to London to exploit the experience he had gained as one of Schubert Alley's hired hit-men, wrapping leading ladies in concrete-lined mink coats and slipping them into the East River. I was sceptical at first. He had little familiarity with the West End. But English managements, with their gentile caution and suspicion of shameless enterprise, might gain from an injection of mobster strategy. In my present circumstances there seemed little to lose.

Pelham's enthusiasm was unquestionable. His reactions to everything were shrewd and thoughtful. His grasp of the immediate 'technical problems' was impressive. He delivered his first coup by persuading Emile Littler, licensee of the Palace theatre, to promise a booking in May. In *Who's Who*, Littler listed himself as 'Theatrical producer, racehorse owner and play-doctor'. Sawbones and butcher would have been nearer the mark. Even Margery, most generous fudge of playwright's enemies, felt constrained to down an extra Guinness and gin-chaser before telephoning him.

Then, most vitally and almost overnight, Pelham persuaded three backers to invest in the production. One of these was a rather mysterious but affable Russian with an undistinguished entrepreneurial past in films and theatre; another was a Jewish furniture manufacturer who had no showbiz connections at all.

> Mr Osborne is a figure of anxious speculation at the moment. Like someone silhouetted on a cliff-edge one gets a sudden feeling he is going to jump over. He is as fascinating as a firework on November 4. Tense as a photo-finish. His new musical will either be the biggest fallen hope since airships, or such a success they'll start selling Anger on the Stock Exchange. Mr Osborne has been playing with fire too long not to get his fingers not simply burned but amputated – if he's lost his touch.
>
> In the chill dark of the auditorium as he comes on-stage, sits his most vulnerable audience. The backers of the play. He stands, back to the footlights. His is a narrow, leaning figure that he props up like a ladder against light and shadow.
>
> The chief of the angels comes forward to be presented to the young man who has become one of the portents of our time. The angel is wearing that becoming and unmistakable indication of wealth – a tan. He is rich. But he is shy. And it is difficult to know *what* to say to the brilliant and wicked Mr Osborne.
>
> He proffers the kindest, meekest, best-meaning phrase he can remember from his schooldays. 'Very promising,' he tells Mr Osborne, encouragingly.
>
> Anne Sharpley, *Evening Standard*, 11 April 1959

A budget was agreed almost on the nod. Even by the deflated standards of the time it was bone-spare. With a cast of twenty-four actors, ten dancers, a musical director, a choreographer, set and costume designers and an orchestra of a dozen or so, Pelham proposed an astonishing budget of £20,000 with a £5,000 overcall. Today the cost would be terrifying.

The Russian and the Jew kept an anxious, respectful distance. The third backer, Gilda Dahlberg, responsible for the possible overcall, was not so easily corralled. A rich New York widow and former chorus girl, she was reputed to have been engaged to the English director Anthony Page and saw herself as the successor to Irene Selznick, who had produced *A Streetcar Named Desire* in America. Short, plump and teetering, she would clop down the aisle at rehearsals in open-toed lamé shoes with shimmering matching pants topped off by a mink coat. She caused some comic diversion but her flabby fidgeting and incessant notebook-scribbling soon became irksome. Merrick would have had her efficiently dispatched in the direction of the East River.

I was summoned to her Dorchester suite. Pelham was an untried mountebank bumming a few thousand pounds from a prominent widow. I was a jumped up bus-boy, or whatever the British called it, with a couple of questionable Broadway hits behind me. I agreed to most of her objections, but she wasn't to be taken in by my Limey smooth talk and when she discovered I had ignored every one of her instructions her neckless head slumped in fury as she clattered to the exit doors.

She struck back by turning spy and informer to our most eager enemy, the press. Excited reporters waited outside the Dorchester and delightedly set down her complaints of our ineptitude. She was the only passenger on board shouting 'Iceberg!', and the captain was pouring garbage on her. Pelham tried to persuade her that if anything guaranteed us sinking it was her own renegade campaign. But she was content. She had achieved her ambition and become an overnight celebrity. The more the Slickeys scribbled, the more detailed her invention. She had brought with her a considerable wardrobe for her role as star impresario and was photographed at first nights and night-clubs. She was a miraculous gift, a rival to Lady Docker, Zsa Zsa Gabor and the Princess Margaret set.

Will success pacify John Osborne?
No post-war musical has been awaited in London with such excited speculation as Osborne's *The World of Paul Slickey*. Will *Slickey*

succeed and consolidate Osborne's soaring reputation? Or will it – together with its adventurous author – come a cropper in the West End, following other off-beat song-and-dance offerings into Flopsville?

Well, we shall have the answer in a month or so. Meanwhile Britain is not lacking in prophets waiting to display a gloating glee if Osborne this time encounters a disaster. He has, after all, sired three major successes in a row. And this is, in some ways, an ungenerous land which resents uninterrupted triumphs and finds satisfaction in witnessing a downfall . . . Many of my Fleet Street colleagues when they interview Osborne inevitably tabulate his cars, suits, shoes and other evidence of wealth. As though, somehow, they were corrupting influences. As though, somehow, nobody that angry has any right to luxury.

'It's impossible in this business to do anything interesting without making enemies,' he said. 'Too many people want to be loved, you see.' He lit another cheroot and looked very sad.

Herbert Kretzmer, Daily Sketch, 8 April 1959

Apart from Gilda, rehearsals became increasingly encouraging. Dennis was still irredeemably sweet-natured, but there was a month or so to fit him with a set of fangs. MacMillan, Jocelyn and I spent many evenings together, partly to work and also for pleasure. Mary was in Nottingham filming *Sons and Lovers*, scripted by Tony's mysterious visitor in Beverly Hills, Gavin Lambert. Late at night in Woodfall Street we discovered that one of those yellow fogs had descended on London, thick beyond Hollywood legend. Kenneth, hardened by the workhouse discipline of his profession, decided that he could find his way home. Jocelyn sensibly refused to set out in these Captain Oates conditions and stayed.

It was mid-morning before she returned to Eaton Square. Alec Murray was waiting for her with a laconic open eye. 'Oh, Jocelyn, you bloody fool.' She limped off to bed. She told me, 'All I could say was: "Don't nag, Alec. I don't exactly feel full of wisdom, but no one's going to get hurt."'

> I'm just a guy called Paul Slickey,
> And the job that I do's pretty tricky,
> I'm twenty-eight years old
> And practically everybody, anybody, anything
> You can think of leaves me
> Quite completely

Newspaper neatly,
Quite, quite cold.

The World of Paul Slickey

I was braced for a rough opening in Bournemouth. Famed for its wheelchair garrison and huge Conservative catchment, it seemed a disastrous choice. The air itself was notoriously enervating. Half of Fleet Street had made the journey. I recognized many faces feigning friendship. 'Hello, John,' they trilled, like men bellowing at a badger cornered in its sett.

Dennis began the show with a brisk number called 'Don't think you can fool a guy like me.' His voice was confident and subtle and the audience responded quite gratefully. There were two and a half hours for them to lose patience. Marie's magisterial entrance was greeted as if she were about to wind up the Proms; Harry, the 'Red Shadow' of many a Bournemouth bosom, was applauded for his nervous stumblings. At the interval there was a general reaction of enthusiastic relief. Kenneth, Jocelyn and I could scarcely look at each other for our disbelief.

The second act was a minefield of what had been prophesied as monumental bad taste. The high – or low – point was a scene in which Philip Locke as Father Evilgreene led a satanic dance which would, we were assured by Hickey and Tanfield, enrage the most agnostic sensibilities. It didn't. Even 'Bring back the axe,' drop-kicked at the groin of feminine Toryism, got an odd cheer from the shrine of primitivism. Half-way through the curtain calls, I heard the sound of 'Author, author!' It was so unfamiliar, I thought it was 'Off with it! Off with it!'

That Musical

And what did respectable Bournemouth think of John Osborne's first musical which opened there last night?

Lady Cobham, wife of Sir Alan Cobham, who lives at West Overcliff Drive said: 'I thought the whole thing was dreadful. Not at all artistic. It is shocking to put on anything like that and call it entertainment . . . The ballet where the parson sings hymns and there is all that rock'n'rolling reminded me of the reptile house at the Zoo. Give me the potted palms of Bournemouth to these Angry Young Men.'

Mr Philip Tridmore, manager of the Norfolk Lodge Hotel told me: 'I didn't think it was so bad. After cutting it could be slick.' Finnish Baron Godot Wrede, who was staying at Norfolk Lodge, said: 'It is very nice to see in England something naughty, like we see in France.'

I am sure Mr Osborne is delighted to have disturbed the still Bournemouth air.

The Star

Shocker

While columnists sat in the lounge of the Royal Bath Hotel, Bournemouth, discussing John Osborne's musical, he was sleeping soundly upstairs. He didn't care what they said about him, or his effort. 'I am surprised that more people didn't walk out.' Only three years ago Osborne filled in his income tax return: 'No income. No tax.'

Evening News

Mr Osborne Sprays Weed Killer

Mr Dominic Elwes, in the only dinner jacket I saw, and his wife Tessa, represented the biceps of society. Mrs Gilda Dahlberg was there in jewels, and Mr David Pelham in a sports coat. But they are financially involved. And any masochistic gossip writers who made the trip had to buy their seats.

Evening Standard

Slickey Makes Them Seethe

Christopher Whelen, composer of the music for *The World of Paul Slickey*, John Osborne's controversial play now running at the Pavilion, has had a nervous breakdown. He is at present being looked after in the Parkstone home of his mother, Mrs W.E. Whelen. She told *Bournemouth Times*, 'Christopher always gets like this after a first night. This time he has not slept for four days and has hardly eaten anything.'

Bournemouth Times & Directory

The effect on the company's morale was tangible – even the Equity representative looked happy. Leeds, the next week, was even more encouraging. They laughed knowingly at the jokes Bournemouth missed. But I was apprehensive about Brighton. We were playing the old variety house, the Hippodrome, home of Max Miller. There was an elegant, glass-enclosed bar at the back of the stalls. It must surely attract a better class of audience. They turned out to be a little rowdy and unpredictable. Towards the end of the week a strong claque of local queens dominated this bar promenade with scattered bouts of sniggering barracking. They were being urged on and orchestrated by Patrick Desmond, Stella's ex-husband.

All-time Low

Sir: – In my opinion the British Theatre sinks to an all-time low with this week's offering at the Brighton Hippodrome. I consider John Osborne's so-called musical comedy to be blasphemous and disgusting – an insult to decent-minded and intelligent theatre-goers.

Evening Argus

Why Does Slickey Make Them Froth?

So this was *Paul Slickey*. Before I saw John Osborne's calumnied, castigated and near-crucified piece, about 25 people had described it to me in terms ranging from atrocious to zymotic. Certainly Osborne leaves nothing out; nothing is sacred. But I must admit I cannot understand the vitriolic, bitchy, almost unbalanced opposition the thing has aroused . . . Mr Osborne's startler is far from being the horror it is painted. *Expresso Bongo* was much worse.

Worthing Gazette

We were to open at the Palace in London on a Tuesday. On Monday we had an all-day run-through. Emile, play-doctor and horse-fancier, sent one of his minions to tell me that, unless certain adjustments and cuts were made, Mr Littler would not allow the performance to take place the following night. Robin Fox's invaluable advice came to mind. We went on rehearsing, waiting for the house lights to be snapped out and the doors barred. They weren't.

> Such night in England ne'er had been, nor e'er again shall be.
> Thomas Babington Macaulay, 'The Armada'

I must be the only playwright this century to have been pursued up a London street by an angry mob. Like most battle experiences, my own view was limited by my vantage point at the back of the stalls. There was an inescapable tension in the house. The theatre itself took on a feeling of rococo mockery and devilment, too hot, a snake-pit of stabbing jewellery, hair-pieces, hobbling high heels, stifling wraps and unmanageable long frocks.

First nights brought out duchesses in those days. I had never seen so many black ties. The public-relations girl insisted on letting me know who was trooping in: the Duke of Bedford, Lord Montague, the Marquess of Milford Haven, 'Bubbles' Harmsworth, Cecil Beaton, Noël Coward, Jack Hawkins, John Mills, Michael Foot and the Profumos. Worst of all, George, on his own. Whatever the outcome, it could only bring him grief.

These occasions were made more hazardous by the now-defunct 'Gallery First-nighters'. This group of self-appointed deputies queued for hours for the fifty or sixty gallery seats of most London theatres. They were organized and hierarchical. Their leader was Nellie (another one). Surrounded by carrier-bags, sandwiches and flasks, she would loll over the edge like a poised gorilla. Nellie was the final arbiter. Thousands of pounds, investors' sleep, actors' careers were in ransom to her sticky thumbs. Her supporters were as intimidated by her as the managements.

Nellie set off a few exploratory skirmishes. Dennis had the misfortune to utter the line: 'God in heaven, it's like a pantomime.' 'Hear, hear,' roared the First-nighters. 'What we want is a return to commonsense.' Nellie and her henchmen rose in applause. The dowagers' humps settled back in comfort to enjoy the sound and smoke of battle. In the redoubt of the pit, the MD whipped the orchestra into a thunderous barrage. It was magnificent, and war. The cast faced front and hurled their lines like grenades.

At the curtain-call, John Gielgud was booing, not waving. So was Coward. Adrienne shouted a scarcely audible, 'Go fuck yourselves.' The cast was sheepishly elated. Marie embraced me regally. '*What* a silly audience.' She boomed at Pelham, 'Where *did* you find them?' 'Take no notice, my dear,' she said to me. 'They can't stand originality in one so young.'

I wandered on to the stage, looked up at Nellie's firing-position and then at Casson's set, shivering in the stare of the working light. A photographer, concealed in the curtains by an exit door, snatched a flash picture. It appeared in the *Evening Standard* the following day, captioned 'Lonely Moment'. The front of house seemed the only likely exit for dignified escape. But the foyer doors were still open, flooded with light. There was no question of retreat. I hoped I wouldn't lose my balance from a hefty punch or whisky vision. I could hear cries of 'Tripe' and 'Bloody rubbish'. I tried not to hurry up Charing Cross Road but the footsteps were coming nearer and I broke into a halting run. I imagined a few public-school scrum-forwards who would bring me down in a flying tackle before Foyle's.

Astonishingly, a taxi-driver threw open his door. I hopped in and he revved off like a bank robber. Fists banged on the window. Woodfall Street was dark, silent and empty. It was very cold. I switched on the electric fire and opened a gift-bottle of champagne. I fell asleep and dreamed of lying half-clothed with Stella at Moss Mansions, the sea roaring beneath the girders of the Palace Pier. I fancied she might have had some sympathy with the audience at the Palace Theatre. I awoke, shivering. Mary and Jocelyn were helping me upstairs.

Mary must have had a difficult evening but she said very little. Helen Henderson arrived early to deal with the continuous telephone calls, Mary's polemics about Albert Finney's cruel behaviour towards his wife and child and Charles Laughton's misery and trepidation at the reception of his forthcoming Lear. She was returning to Stratford that afternoon. I clutched the edges of the lavatory basin, feeling as if the inside of my head had been scrubbed with a rusty cheese-grater.

> The high and low spot of my London visit was the opening night of John Osborne's musical *Paul Slickey* at the Palace. Never in all my theatrical experience have I seen anything so appalling, appalling from every point of view. Sad lyrics, dull music, idiotic, would-be-daring dialogue – interminable long-winded scenes about nothing and above all the amateurishness and ineptitude, such bad taste that one wanted to hide one's head.
>
> *The Noël Coward Diaries*

15. Surprised by Joy

He Should Have Known Better!
The first night audience at the Palace seemed to be about equally divided between those who loathed it politely and those who hated it audibly ... The final curtain came down to the most raucous note of displeasure heard in the West End since the war.

Milton Shulman, *Evening Standard*

Extraordinary dullness ... manifest failure ... vulgar mockery ... lack of skill ...

The Times

An evening of general embarrassment ... three boring hours ...

Manchester Guardian

Osborne has been his own worst enemy ... *Slickey* isn't slick enough ... everything is out of proportion ...

Observer

It has almost every fault.

New Statesman

> I want to hear about beautiful things
> Beautiful things like love
> I don't want to hear of emotional wrecks
> Of people who practice peculiar sex
> I want my love to be pure
> My income secure
> I don't wish to wallow in a spiritual sewer.

The World of Paul Slickey

Gilda was having a field day with her press boys. 'Sipping orange juice in her seventh-floor suite at the Dorchester, 52-year-old, 4′ 10″ Mrs Dahlberg said, "I've never known a show take such a terrible beating from the critics but, believe me, the beating was well deserved. I put thousands into the show."' Not yet, she hadn't, nor did she. '"I was meant to be the associate producer. I made notes and notes on every page of the script. *Now* perhaps they will listen to my suggestions."' One of her pals from Fleet Street left the Dorchester with a couple of mink stoles, valued at £2,000 each. Ten days later, Gilda moved into the London Clinic, suffering from 'nervous exhaustion'.

There seemed little point in hanging on in London for any possible reprieve. The cast were cheerful enough. They had received praise and unaccustomed offers, and Pelham had promised to keep things going for a minimum of six weeks. Mary was immersed in the daily domestic routine of Stratford. Jocelyn R. and Alec had been invited to stay in Graham Greene's villa and so, a couple of days later, I picked Jocelyn up at Eaton Square. In my new racing-green Jaguar XK150, unobserved by Fleet Street's 'has-been' spotters, we swept into the tiny concourse of Lydd Airport and drove the car on to the ferry-plane, *en route* for a leisurely journey to Naples and then Capri.

Moving south slowly down the secondary roads of France through the horizon points of the poplar trees, Jocelyn was the perfect companion. She possessed that most powerful antidote to opinion, joyful curiosity. With the hood down, the squalor and play-acting of the past year blew away as we drove from long lunches at tiny inns along empty, unbending avenues. We dined early, falling sated and inflated with food, wine, folly and fresh air into a goose-feathered well of forgetfulness. We were halted for a week by a fierce, enclosing storm in a fishing-village on the Camargue coast. The shutters clattered ill-temperedly for hours but the respite from driving was welcome and the sunny stillness that followed, with bowls of bougainvillaea and platters of lobster, almost convinced me that the French could be likeable, when they were off-guard.

By the time we snaked our way along the Côte d'Azur and into Italy I began to feel that the wind, sun, garlic, even the angry *mistral*, had flushed out all the poisons of ill-nature I had absorbed. For the past ten days, life had been marked out in Michelin spoons and it doubtless showed, but as we crossed the Italian border, I felt as young as only the old can remember feeling: lean, lithe and swift. In Rapallo we drove up to an Edwardian wedding-cake of an hotel and were welcomed like milords on the Grand Tour. Beaming over my passport, the concierge declaimed, 'Oh, Signor Osborne – the World of Paul Sickly!'

In Rome we joined Alec at the Inghilterra. The English press had been seeking us out and Mary seemed to have dealt with their descent on Stratford with blindfold skill. Paul Sickly it was indeed.

> While John Osborne was moving towards Paris with his friend Jocelyn Rickards, his actress wife Mary Ure talked to me about this latest in the line of unusual theatrical holidays. Mr Osborne is driving Miss Rickards, *Slickey*'s costume designer, while Miss Ure is stuck with the rigours of a season at Stratford. 'John is utterly exhausted. He's got the feeling, you know, when one simply has to get out of England'. With Miss Rickards? 'Jocelyn is my oldest, dearest friend,' said Miss Ure. 'She and John and I have known each other for years. She was going to Paris – so John said he could give her a lift.'
>
> *Daily Express*, 18 May 1959

It was all very game. I couldn't make out whether she was being blithe or brave and it seemed mean not to give her the benefit of the doubt.

The *Express* continued:

> 'This is one of those theatrical holidays where one partner goes on holiday – I'm afraid I can't join him – I'm up to my neck in it in Stratford.' Mr Osborne's holiday will keep him away from the première of his film *Look Back in Anger* at which he was due to meet Princess Margaret.

This set the features editors to work: 'Does Show Business Have its own Marriage Code?'

> In show business married couples taking their holidays apart is not an eyebrow-raising experience. Not since those well-known style-setters, the Oliviers, did it a couple of years ago. But the Osborne-holiday-alone raises rather an interesting issue. Supposing Osborne wasn't a successful playwright but a milkman? And supposing his wife Mary wasn't a successful actress but a secretary? Would we be so ready to accept the situation where the milkman suddenly takes a Continental holiday while his wife stays at home sharpening her pencils and taking dictation? How many people go along with the Oliviers, the Trevor Howards and the Osbornes?
>
> *Daily Mail*, 1 June 1959

It was still 1959.

Long before I was confronted with the task of giving witness to it, I regarded my childhood as not so much unhappy as devoid of happiness.

'What you've never had you'll never miss,' was a calumny on my life. Myth is just as admissible as history, and my sense of lost inheritance was as powerful as any downright deprivation. Happiness when it did come, snatched from the air in provincial corners, was so rare and irreversible it could survive every avenging assault upon it. I decided not to ring Mary and hear the latest progress of Finney's marriage. That could wait most contentedly. Its postponement was an additional spice to the happiness that had sped past in the fugitive progress south.

As the three of us drove on the autostrada to Naples, I nudged the needle past the 100 m.p.h. mark for the first and last time in my life. The misty rain, mingled with the scent of the countryside, slammed into our faces in the open Jaguar. Jocelyn's question to Alec, shrieked above the wind, was as characteristic as his reply. 'Isn't the wild thyme marvellous?' 'I don't know,' he said, knees clenched and teeth clamped on his cigar. 'We're travelling faster than the speed of smell.'

We spent the next two weeks at the Villa Rosario, Greene's house high up in Anacapri. They had both stayed there before and knew the locals. The house was low, bare and full of light, the perfect fortress against the infelicities we had left behind. We lay in the sun, reading and staring out over the bay of Naples, lunching simply at a restaurant in the square, occasionally bathing from the rocks below Gracie Fields' swimming-pool. Nino, an Italian friend of Alec's, joined us and in the evenings we would sit in the opera-house setting of the piazza and watch the new arrivals, their luggage trundled up by flamboyant porters, or the black-tie set bawling from the yachts moored at the Marina Grande, a gaggle of sound from well-goosed Wentworth-Brewsters.

On our last evening, Alec suddenly rose and drawled, 'Time we were leaving.' His professional ear had picked up the click of a Sickly camera. Grabbing Jocelyn's hand, he sauntered away. The following day dozens of pictures of them appeared in the London newspapers, strolling like a pair of dozey lovers. You could see Nino's head in the rear and most of my legs.

When we returned to London, Eaton Square was staked out with waiting reporters. Jocelyn managed to dash through the front door. I was less lucky. Woodfall Street was jammed from its entrance in Smith Street to the brick wall at the end. I parked the Jaguar, battered by alpine rocks, at the corner and made my way to the front door. 'Come on, John. Be a sport, John.' I fumbled with my keys and was photographed as if I were caught breaking into my own house. Helen was upstairs looking panicked and frightened. Jocelyn was on the telephone. She sounded pretty shaken herself.

Angry Young Man's Mother Pulls Pints

The charming lady I found pulling pints at the Spring Hotel, Ewell, laughed and said, 'I don't work as a barmaid because I'm hard-up. I like doing it. My son makes me a very generous allowance indeed.' Mrs Nellie Beatrice (Bobby) Osborne does not look her 66 years . . . 'I never did stand in John's way. He was never a strong boy – he survived double pneumonia, double hernia, double this and double that. But I never thought he'd end up a down and out. I thought he might be a barrister or something.'

Mrs N.B. Osborne, *Empire News*, 3 July 1959

On my way to Stratford, I noticed in my mirror a large Rolls Royce of the same royal vintage as the Oliviers' VLO 1. As we emerged from the usual crawl through High Wycombe, it began to make bold attempts to pass me. It was TR100 and behind its impassive chauffeur were lounging Terence Rattigan and Mr Beaumont. I was determined not readily to be overtaken by such lordly opposition and I managed to keep in their eyeline all the way to the Memorial Theatre, where my satisfaction was slightly spoiled by Peter Hall's Jaguar, identical to my own, parked importantly outside.

Mary had already opened in Hall's production of *A Midsummer Night's Dream*, in which she played Titania to Robert Hardy's Oberon, with Charles Laughton as Bottom and Vanessa Redgrave and Albert Finney romping away listlessly as the juveniles. It had been an earthbound, schoolmasterly business, unhelped by Laughton's unease. He was a useful addition to Mary's corps of self-kneecapped wounded; a most suitable case for her busybody brand of concern. Thirty years on, she would have made an admirable 'counsellor'.

Laughton was one of the most pugnaciously morose men I had ever met. His huge talent seemed to endorse his implacable resentment. His Caliban self-portraiture must have been further agonized by being incarcerated, like so many of his unhappy generation, in that closet which dared not speak its name. Even his large collection of Klees and Kokoschkas was displayed as trophies of martyrdom rather than joyful plunder.

After the absorbent tranquillity of Capri, the return to Woodfall Street had a head-on impact of instantly returning fatigue. However, I could scarcely avoid the brick wall of Mary's first night as Desdemona. Tony had directed it. He and Oscar Lewenstein had winkled Paul Robeson from his McCarthyite bondage to play Othello. His legendary appearance with Peggy Ashcroft twenty-five years before ensured that expectations were running high. Loudon Sainthill had designed the sets, and Tony provided one of his proscenium menageries of hooded birds and Great Danes. The expectant energy that a rising curtain bestows even on the likes of myself quickly wilted. Robeson, the beloved volcano, rumbled thrillingly, but the eruption was choked back, the fire gone cold, banked down by age and the extinguishing weight of neglect and cruelty.

Mary was unimpressed by my mother's Cockney gush. She and Nellie Beatrice disliked each other and they were both too artless to be capable of pretence, let alone artifice. In a mood of idle vengeance, I invited my mother to stay. Mary's rented house in Stratford was bright, Edwardian and airy, but the days were stifling now that she was no longer rehearsing. The town had the unfriendly, philistine air that most centres of tourist culture seem to radiate. We had less than ever to say to each other, and I was straining to try to work. Mary had made few friends, apart from Jane Wenham, Finney's wife, and her newly born son, both objects for counselling and homely comfort. We went to the twenty-first-birthday party of an attractive young bit-part player, Diana Rigg.

I took Nellie Beatrice to see *Othello*. Afterwards Robeson joined the three of us upstairs for supper. Perhaps it was as well that my mother was not wearing her favourite outfit, what she might have described to him as her coral and nigger-brown rig-out. We waited apprehensively for his appearance, a handsome but exhausted giant. Nellie Beatrice was genuinely admiring, in awe of this massive, Blakean figure, possibly wondering why he wasn't clad in one of Lord Sandy's left-over leopard skins.

She hardly spoke until we came to the main course, when she piped up in her most ingratiating-the-head-waiter voice, 'Oh, Mr Robinson,' she said, 'it's such an honour for us to meet you.' Mr Robinson acknowledged this sweetly. 'Especially for my son. He's such an admirer of yours. You see . . .' She looked around the restaurant, graciously drawing her audience, then said with deferential confidence: 'You see, Mr Robinson, he's always been very sorry for you *darkies*.' A large, gentle smile spread over his face. In those days, innocent of racial policing, cheerfulness did have a way of breaking in on simple prejudice.

After *Othello* Tony was to direct Vivien Leigh in Noël Coward's translation of the Feydeau farce, *Occupe-toi d'Amélie*, retitled *Look After Lulu*. The combined force of Vivien, Noël, Binkie Beaumont and Citizens Devine and Richardson was prickly and suspicious from the outset, as doomed an attempt to contradict the emnity of history as an allegiance between France and Albion.

Tony rang me from Nottingham, where *Lulu* had opened in an atmosphere of divisive conspiracy and recrimination. 'You've *got* to come up.' I
was accustomed to this kind of urgent pleading when he was merely bored
with his present company or wanted another hand at bridge. But I was
curious to be an observer of the whole explosive enterprise. It also provided
me with an acceptable excuse to get away from Stratford and the aimless
defeated days Mary and I were spending together. As usual she was
unconvinced and possibly relieved, and cheerfully waved me off without
any pressure on when I should return.

I picked up Jocelyn and we set out north to watch the progress of the
faltering Grand Alliance. We booked into the Turk's Head where Tony was
waiting, enjoying every moment of intrigue and sub-plot. 'Thank God
you've come. I think I'm going mad. Vivien's gone to pieces because of
Joan, George is in a *state*, and Noël insists on being fucking *witty* all the
time.'

A supper had been arranged after the performance and Tony insisted
that we must be present. Binkie presided over the table that included
Vivien, George, Meriel Forbes (Lady Richardson), who was also in the
cast, Noël and a posse of Vivien's reinforcements, among them the preposterous agony-journalist, Godfrey Winn, who had been hearing her lines and
comforting her as she sat by the telephone waiting for Olivier to call from
Stratford, where he was about to open in *Coriolanus*. There was common
anxiety about her health and state of mind. She had been in an almost
unbroken condition of shock ever since Larry had peeled off his Archie
Rice eyebrows in the Palace dressing-room and, addressing her image in the
mirror said, in a reversion to Coward-like delivery, 'Of course, you know
I'm in love with Joan Plowright, don't you?'

Coward himself, though increasingly impatient with what he considered
to be a vulgar circus of tedious procrastination, was possibly more helpful
than anyone. His cold eye saw quite correctly that Vivien must somehow
reconcile herself to the divorce Olivier was set upon. His anxiety was
prompted by fears for his leading lady's endurance, but also by his loyalty
and affection for them both. Unlike most of the spectators to the whole
miserable indignity of their situation, including Larry's forced hole-in-
corner dalliance with Plowright, he appeared not to stoop to the silliness of
'taking sides'.

I found myself at the far end of the table, next but one to Coward.
Perhaps this *placement* was Binkie's way of demonstrating Elvira's assessment of my social standing. Listening to this undaunted ornament of the

century, born in the same year as my father, I remembered Binkie throwing a few chips of encouragement to me as he said with a gleam of disaffection, 'Of course, Noël's *quite* uneducated.' Whether it implied that the Master was as unashamedly ignorant as myself, expelled and barely literate at fifteen, condemned to a fixed condition of 'not being ready for it yet', I hadn't resolved. It merely seemed a piece of clumsy treachery, a fair example of the reverence for academic skill and a classic misapprehension of its link with creative imagination. Even Binkie, from his own more distinguished productions, could have deduced that from Shakespeare to Shaw a little Latin and less Greek, or none of either, did no damage to untutored dramatists.

I could see what Tony meant about Coward's compulsion to be 'fucking witty' all the time. Fortunately, Jocelyn, with her salon experience of abstruse table talk and literary gossip, was adroit at stirring the vanities of opinionated celebrities into the illusion of making conversation rather than dominating it. She asked him intelligent questions about himself which he answered amusingly, pinning down each one with an exact date, place and relevance to the Coward calendar of first-night triumphs and occasional disasters. I was tempted to ask him about his own confrontation with Nellie of the first-nighters, but decided against it. The evening ended amiably.

As we went to bed, I suggested to Jocelyn that it might have been trying the Master's patience to run her fingers over his head as we left. She said she was so overcome with affection that she couldn't resist his careful crewcut. 'I loved him so much.' 'Oh well,' I said. 'I suppose you *are* Australian.'

Lulu continued acrimoniously in Nottingham and then opened at the Court, where it enhanced no one's reputation and drew rather gratuitous scorn for the incompatibility of the two theatrical factions. It must have seemed to Vivien that we, George, Tony, even myself, were the instruments of her present misery and Larry's disavowal of the whole courtly progress of the legend surrounding their love and lives. However much one sympathized with Olivier's desperation to escape the destruction of her magic alchemy, it was impossible not to be affected, like Coward, by the pain cascading over both of them.

The most generous assessment of the whole miserable enterprise came from Harold Hobson in the *Sunday Times:* 'The trouble is that Mr Coward is too witty and Miss Vivien Leigh is too beautiful. For the kind of play that *Look After Lulu* is, beauty and wit are as unnecessary as a peach Melba at the North Pole.'

Vivien's presence ensured *Lulu's* transfer to the West End, justifying

George's derided intention of using the proceeds to pursue his own theatre's proper course. Whether or not the rewards of his pragmatism were worth so much hysteria, he was running a corner shop which demanded speedy turnover, improvisation rather than adherence to fixed principles. Some people never forgave him for it. Perhaps they were already dreaming of airport-like buildings whose very existence would create a sacrosanct brotherhood of public 'funding'.

Even Tony's resilience had been tested by Tennant's battalions and he insisted that we should go off to Ischia to work on the screenplay of *The Entertainer*. It was a kind of second-time-around bonus. The chance to return so quickly to the Naples skyline and a further reprieve from Stratford was welcome. It was out of the question to take Jocelyn with me. The flat landscape of Ischia provided less chance of concealment than the lush hillsides of Capri. Apart from a fairly attractive secretary, who might be an amusing decoy, there would be no female accompaniment. Another respite.

We stayed at a barely opened new hotel overlooking the sea. We seemed to have it almost to ourselves. Ten years later it was overrun by huge Germans grunting and wallowing in the volcanic mud baths. In the mornings we sat by the pool chatting, working swiftly. I scribbled while Tony's knees jerked in reflex to his own inspirations. One jab for yes, three jabs for no. Before noon, we would have a drink, perhaps an unwise Negroni, and wander off to the veranda of a simple beach restaurant nestled in a cove round the corner. We would lunch on fruit, smoked meats and pasta with a couple of carafes of the local wine. Apart from a few noisy Teutons blubbering away in blue-black wells of mud by the rocks, we were undisturbed. I would write up what we had discussed in an agreeable haze before a cool snooze.

Most evenings we took a rattling scooter-taxi across to Porto d'Ischia, twinkling with lights but fairly deserted. Our fellow diners were usually groups of Englishmen in blazers and striped socks, all oppressively self-conscious, shouting at each other to keep up morale. Their unresponding audience were middle-aged couples, retired soldiers, housemasters or husband-and-wife authors of children's tales. To Tony and me, both in relaxed humour, their performances were open to infinite speculation and salacious fantasy.

One night we had to pick our way through crowds to the courtyard entrance, revealed by the lights of a fiesta, the Victorian bandstand sparkling in the square and white-uniformed musicians tootling out Verdi. Euphoria and grappa flowed upward into the shimmer of the Neapolitan night.

There was a newcomer at one of the café tables. He was flabby, debauched and was being fêted by a group of New York faggots and the local passing trade. Tony stared at him with a kind of repelled excitement. It was Chester Kallman, long-time companion to W.H. Auden. Not for the first time, I found myself leaving Tony at a street corner and going back to the hotel alone. All the same, the days that followed were probably the most careless and stimulating that I was ever to spend with him.

Grand Hotel, Ankara

My dear John,

I am sorry you feel so bitter. I feel bitter in some ways too but they're not the most important ones.

The trouble is that you have a one way morality as far as films are concerned. You don't really like writing them, you don't give of your whole self and heart but you expect other people to treat what you do as if it was one of your own plays. You don't really value the writing in the same way but you can't bear others not to.

I'm sure this probably won't help our relationship only exacerbate it because I feel increasingly that what you want from a friendship is not real loyalty which is based on truth or on knowing each other but sycophancy and adulation which I can't give, and despise anyway.

I hope your present feelings will change soon. Whether they do or not they won't change mine. I love you.

Tony

Letter from Tony Richardson to J.O., 1966

16. Viva Mexico!

I am a worm and no man, a byword and a laughing stock.
Crush out the worminess in me, stamp on me . . . I am alone,
I am alone, and against myself.

Luther

When I was in New York for the opening of *George Dillon* in November
1958, I had seen very little of Francine. Robert Webber made a somewhat
sinister reappearance to tell me she was 'a mess, bloated with booze' and
spending all day in Harry's apartment on Eighty-second Street with the
blinds drawn. He was not exaggerating. When she opened the door to me,
she was in her underwear, barefoot, with a glass in hand. Her face was puffy,
her body had a stiff, swollen look and the apartment was thick with an
accumulation of tobacco and marijuana. She seemed bewildered.

After a while she had settled against me, comforted and tearful, then
chattering as if she had spoken to no one for weeks. I rang Harry, who was
sympathetic but unsurprised. 'Give the kid a good time, if you can.' I
couldn't think what I could do to ease her fragile mood. The only thing
which seemed to give her pleasure was dancing the night away in deafening
night-clubs. After which she would spend the next few days in the apartment, clutching a glass and rolling joints, her eyes brimming as she listened
to numbing Spanish love-songs in the darkened room.

I tried to coax her into recapturing her high-spirited playfulness, but,
whatever had taken place, she was reluctant to talk about herself any longer.
She was still disarmingly affectionate, but the tiny pearl of innocent lustre
she had preserved beneath the mink-and-diamond drag had gone. She was
intelligent and realistic enough to know that there was no chance of or even
desirability in continuing our affair for long.

I was anxious to get back to England, to the filming of *Look Back* and my
headlong fling with *Slickey*, but I felt wretched leaving her curled up in the
smoky pool of light by her bed listening to some mawkish variant on *Volare*.

I knew little about her or how little there might be to know. If her heart-strings had cracked slightly, they might also have hardened. I felt as if I was already something half-forgotten.

When I got back to London I instructed my accountant to send her some money, not in expiation but because she would expect it. The size of the cheque might reassure her of my small-time English stinginess. With true accountants' insight, he observed, 'I think you've got off very lightly, John.' I would not see her again for almost a year, and then in circumstances so surprising they confirmed all my instincts about her Swiss resilience.

The film of *Look Back* opened in June 1959 and was fairly politely received. Someone wrote, 'In essence, it doesn't amount to a row of beans eaten with a knife straight out of the tin.' There was some carping about Burton's age and 'very unlovely people living jaded and appallingly crude lives in the filth of a Midland garret'. And, more damning, it was described as 'beautifully made', a certain euphemism for dull and arty.

Harry had tried unsuccessfully to bribe the organizers of the Cannes Film Festival to accept Woodfall's first-born in competition. He had hosted an elaborate dinner for the French dignitaries, headed by the Chef du Festival, Fauvre LeBret, and afterwards dealt out pound notes like a croupier to the gaiety of a circle of outstretched hands. He was pipped at the post by *Room at the Top*. As some sort of recompense, in November we were invited as the official British entry to a film festival in Acapulco, of all places.

This was a banana-republic fiesta with no cultural pretensions. It was organized to provide the President with the company of desirable foreign actresses. Dozens of countries sent representatives, directors, producers, starlets and that army of vagrants who can sniff out free food and carousing from across continents. Most of the films 'entered' in the non-competitive 'festival' were already commercial or artistic failures. Or both. Each was awarded a prize.

Tony and I had been attracted by the comic possibilities of the event and the agreeably tangible prize of freeloading Mexican sea and sunshine. Apart from the Rank and ABPC front-office boys, Sandy McKendrick was there and Peter Brook, preparing his film of *Lord of the Flies*. The President entertained at his hacienda in furious El Gatsby style, the gardens, beach and palm-trees popping with female flesh of all nations and ringed by a detachment of the army, all armed to their gold teeth.

The films were shown at midnight under the stars in the courtyard of a disused fort as little more than an afterthought to the principal proceedings. The British participation was sulkily mismanaged by the Rank contingent.

Perhaps because of this, Tony decided he must make a speech from the platform on the night of *Look Back*'s presentation. A Mexican interpreter was coaxed into translating it into phonetic Spanish which Tony would learn by heart. As she rehearsed him in delivery and pronunciation, she kept repeating, 'Maria! He can't say that. He can't!' It seemed he was in danger of being badly mauled or even lynched. She would accept no responsibility for his safety. As I was to appear with him, I would be in danger of the national wrath myself.

Under the spotlight of a bright moon, I stepped forward, bowed and acknowledged the audience's mild applause. Then Tony thrust himself forward and launched into his strangled Spanish harangue. They were silent throughout the whole arm-waving, uncoordinated mime, until he came to a shrill crescendo, proclaiming with clenched fist: '*Gracios muchos. Viva Mayheeho! Viva Mayheeho*. And – *Viva Buñuel!*' At this, everyone in the courtyard stood, whistling and booing, and the interpreter dragged us off into some dark passage in the fortified walls. 'I told you not to mention Buñuel.'

Whether it was the Mexican sun, day-long parties or his headlong determination to master water-skiing, Tony was in an odd mood. Our next brush with physical danger was by the pool of the El Presidente Hotel. In an idle moment, I mentioned to Tony and Oscar Lewenstein (another Woodfall free-rider) that I was thinking of writing a play about Martin Luther. Oscar immediately bristled with Marxist certainties. Tony said he felt I was ill-equipped to pay enough attention to the historical and social background of the bloody events which took place and changed the face of Europe. My heart went cold within me as we sat under the bruising sunshine. Apart from my own hesitancies about belief and doctrine, I began to feel that I was embarking on something which would have been better left for a few years, when my own confusion might have resolved itself into some coherence.

The conversation turned to the matter of Luther's undoubted anti-Semitism, a favourite weapon used against him by his detractors. I had planned to avoid this aspect of his character, from artistic rather than moral timidity. My own crude perception is that the Jews, rather like the Irish, are essentially a cold-hearted race. Sentimentality, which they both have in abundance, is the sugar-armour of the hard of heart.

I relapsed into silence by the pool. Oscar, as usual, was waiting for someone else to make something happen. Tony raised his shiny beak and fixed us with a peregrine stare. He has spent a lifetime thrusting his face provocatively at the sun. Suddenly, in a castrato shriek which bounced back across the Olympic-size pool, he bellowed at Oscar: 'Sometimes, Oscar, when I look at you . . .' Oscar stiffened as the inflection rose skyward. 'When I look at you, I think Hitler was right . . .' The flight straightened out into counter-tenor, then ascended. 'You fucking little Jew.'

The pool-side silence seemed interminable, cigar butts drooped limply. Oscar frowned, more in irritation at gratuitous frivolity than at intention to wound. 'Oh dear, oh dear. You really shouldn't say things like that, Tony. You really shouldn't.' Tony was uneasily exhilarated. The silence around us had not yet broken. I decided it was time to leave and strolled off as unhurriedly as I could. Tony's outburst seemed like some prankish madness, a device to cause instant pain and disarray. It had certainly worked.

Tony had hired a water-skiing boat on a daily basis from one of the many plying beachboys. He selected José, beautiful, about nineteen, with the kind of rippling iron-spare body that few of us ever glimpse outside an athletic stadium. He was unquestionably the noble savage among the others. He spoke little English but he seemed free and independent, breathing out the air of sanguine, grave delight. Watching him made one feel like an unwholesome face-flannel.

José would pick us up about eleven and we'd go round the bay. Learning to water-ski with a careless driver at the wheel can be a painful business. Half an hour of this bone-pounding keel-haul was enough for Oscar and myself, but Tony snapped and catapulted into the foaming wake for hours until he reluctantly agreed to pause for lunch. We went to the same restaurant each day, a dark hut with an ill-stocked bar which served delicious langoustines, octopus and shellfish. They had a reviving effect after the morning's buffeting. We suggested to José that he might take us somewhere else, cleaner and with a less restricted menu; he smiled charmingly and continued to take us back each day. The sullen owners were his relations. Apart from a few ferocious-looking locals, we were the only customers.

After a week of listening to Tony's scornful analysis of my athletic disabilities ('You look like some old porpoise'), I was beginning to get bored with all this obsessive effort for such intermittent excitement. José revved up at furious speed towards Acapulco's inner harbour; as we bumped and crashed over the water, Tony asked him where we were going. He throttled up, shouting into the wind, 'You see. I take you someplace else.' We weaved in among the moored fishing-boats, missing them by inches.

José brought the engine down to a croak and the boat's nose back to the water. We were heading for a beach crowded with Mexican faces. Screaming children splashed and waded. It was palpably not a tourist beach and our arrival aroused some lethargic curiosity. It was the shanty-*sur-mer* end of town. As we approached the jetty, I saw a figure waving a ritual greeting. She was wearing a bikini. Even a hundred yards away, it was apparent that she would have been more than acceptable in Cannes. An abandoned tourist? As we staggered ashore, aided by the beaming José, she walked towards us, unhurriedly and gracefully. It was Francine.

Her skin, naturally dark, glistened like a coco-bean sheath, not quite what Nellie Beatrice called 'nigger brown' but a shade darker than José's, her eyes marbling an almost independent life of their own. Her teeth seemed to foam with the bright, hardening polish of the sun. There could be no doubting her pleasure at seeing us. I was so astonished to see her on that dirty, native beach that it was a while before I realized that her delight was as much centred on Tony as on myself. I had never seen her so unguarded and free or, indeed, so beautiful. I felt a wave of happy relief, almost of justifiable pride. When we had last been together, she had been so broodingly despairing. It was difficult to reconcile that with this bounding, uncautioned creature.

She took us by the hand and led us to a primitive beach café which also turned out to be run by José's relatives. Francine's tone changed when she addressed orders to them, as if she were the proprietor and they disorderly children. They were in grudging awe of her, their Latin torpor broken by her Swiss proficiency. She had retreated from the hooker's gutter to this tiny, peasant dominion.

A plump, barefoot, middle-aged woman banged down some bottles of wine. She was probably not much older than Francine. Her flesh was wizened and hung in folds beneath her knees and armpits like a lizard's throat. She pushed her belly forward as if she might bite the bottle-tops off with her yellow teeth. Francine watched her with open distaste. 'This is José's mother. Hey, Maria. Say hello to my friends from England.' Maria ignored her. Francine snapped at her in Spanish. She responded by pulling her stained dress up to her face and wiping it. José flashed a proud smile. Francine's disgust mounted. 'She's my mother-in-law too. Yes. My little old mother-in-law. Aren't you?' She turned away. 'Don't you think me and José are lucky to have such a creature to look after us?'

Tony pressed her with questions. Yes, she had married José six months ago. The boat was hers. 'He's pretty, my little monkey boy. He's beautiful, don't you think?' She looked over at him as if she might leap astride that powerful body. 'So strong, so beautiful, not like American men.'

Tony persuaded her to take us to their house. 'Is nothing to see, I tell you.' It was true. Their married quarters were a few streets from the harbour, a pedestrian run of sleeping drunks, black pigs and chickens. Their home was like all the others, little more than a mud-and-stone-built hut bleached in the sun. An antique oil-lamp burned all day, the floor was covered in rush matting and the furniture consisted of a large divan and a couple of peeling armchairs. But Francine's dressing-table, covered by a large Mexican shawl, was prominent, laid out with huge bottles of expensive scent and all the working tools of an expensive courtesan. Where could she keep her wardrobe? Her furs, her scores of shoes? What about her jewellery? Perhaps she had sold them all to buy the boat, the cafés. And José.

The others left. 'What have you done with all your smashing things?' I asked. 'No worry. I keep. They're around.' She winked. 'I'm quite a smart, Swiss girl. All those dumb Americans were wrong, weren't they, darling?' She slipped her arms round me and kissed me unhurriedly. It could swiftly have become a case of grievous bodily pleasure. I disengaged myself with some difficulty. I had no wish to confront the iron-willow power of her young brown god, nor his vengeful relatives.

She smiled a mock-reproachful smile. 'You no want me no more?' 'Of course I do. Still, you *are* married.' 'So what? I take care of José. He's like a child.' I felt a tremendous relief. It was the assurance that in spite of her surroundings, she was in control of her life, perhaps as she had never been before. She was redrawing her lipstick in the gloom. 'José, he's sweet. Can't read or write. None of them can. I teach him English. Just enough.' She kissed me again, less avidly but assuringly, like a flimsy but tender seal.

Francine and José came to dine at El Presidente. He was in a swamping borrowed suit, she was quite startling in white with long gloves and a pricey-looking evening-purse. Dozens of heads, fresh baked from the beauty parlour, turned to study this incongruous couple. We ordered several bottles of horribly sweet American champagne. 'José left. 'He's OK,' said Francine. 'He's gone out to play with the boys.' She was slightly drunk but fired with craving energy. 'You all look so miserable. This place . . . . ' she addressed the other diners, '. . . all these mother-fuckers from Hicksville. C'mon. I take you someplace else interesting.' She rounded us up into a taxi.

After twenty minutes we found ourselves in the outer suburbs. There was no street lighting and the few prosperous houses disappeared as we swept up a dusty track and stopped outside a small, bare fortress. There were figures of rifle-toting soldiers – or policemen – silhouetted at various vantages. Francine went over to the entrance to talk to a couple of lounging guards. Presently, she waved us to one of the dozen or so tables scattered around the forecourt. A plump moustachioed girl waddled towards us and laid down a tray with a bottle of Spanish whisky and a muddy-looking carafe of what might have been orange juice. Apart from a slumped body in a sombrero, we were the only customers.

Francine filled our glasses. 'Well, guys? OK? What you think?' A cluster of girls emerged to lean over the low balcony. The doors behind them opened and more appeared, singly and in groups. Tony sniggered rather loftily. 'Well, it's obviously a *brothel*!' His mocking falsetto cackle echoed out into the chilly stillness. Oscar looked more like the Gandhi of Threadneedle Street than ever before. We were being observed closely both by the soldiers and by the girls above. Some of them wandered down in pairs, stared at us and sprawled at the other tables.

Francine grinned. 'They want you should buy them a drink.' She immediately anticipated suspicions that she had lured us into an enterprise in which she had a percentage stake. 'Don't worry. I see you not cheated. You have a good time. You afford it.' She had adopted a pidgining of her English as phoney as the strangled Americanization of Tony's Shipley vowels. She waved at the girls, stabbing her cigarette-holder like a farmer at a sheep-pen. 'What you think, eh?' She was beginning to sound like an auctioneer. 'Yeah, well these are pretty much all dogs.' She shouted across to the soldiers in the porch. 'He says all the good things inside. I show you.'

A very bored madam or head girl led us into a whitewashed cave strewn with large cushions, low tables, chairs and rush matting, with bare coloured bulbs slung across the walls. It smelt of cigars, stale spirits, a glutinous sweet scent and things I thought it better not to identify. She went over to a rickety bamboo bar and opened several bottles of something masquerading as champagne. Francine was concentrating on the girls who paraded in and out, naked except for what were then called 'baby dolls'. Open at the top and transparent below in pubic-catching, greasy nylon, they concealed nothing.

I half expected Francine to be incensed by our undissembled, absurd dismay. Instead, she turned her thwarted fury on the head girl, 'Don't you worry. I take care of her.' They screamed at each other, fingernails flashing, noses almost locking. I feared we should all be rifle-butted. She broke off breathlessly. 'We make a mistake. However, she say she show you something.'

The girl led us upstairs into a bare pink cell containing a large bed covered by a rumple of grey sheets. A broken lamp glowed on a wooden orange-box, a hole in the wall led into what was presumably some kind of washroom. There was a large crucifix above the bed and a low bench beside it. A baby doll, reading a film magazine, watched us sourly as we were pushed down on the bench, scarcely long enough to accommodate the three of us. Another baby doll, red-haired, plump and even less wholesome than the first, was hustled into the room. She crawled reluctantly on to the bed, lugging her leg over the other girl outstretched beside her.

The raw squalor and enslaved inertia of the pantomime that followed were quite literally paralysing. Admittedly the local whisky and champagne were flailing my inside like a blunt propeller and I concentrated on the thought of the gleaming haven of the washbasin at the El Presidente Hotel. I looked straight ahead. I thought of the English Stage Company Council watching the three of us cramped together in silence confronting the heaving bed.

Francine, exasperated by the girls' sloth, became an hysterical ring-master. 'For Christ's sake, go down on her! No, not that, *do* something. Whistle the Marseillaise in her. *Viva Mexico*, you bitch! What's the matter with you? You think we pay money for *this*?' She was almost collapsing with rage, prodding and punching them. Fortunately, it ended as quickly as it had begun. 'Let's go. We finish the shitty champagne and go someplace else.' We stumbled downstairs, Oscar shaky and muttering in appeal, 'Oh, dear. Oh, dear. It's so degrading. So degrading.' An Artistic Director of the Royal Court, its most profitable playwright and a highly regarded West End producer sat in silence on the journey back to the El Presidente.

For a few more days we met José at an appointed place, water-skied and had lunch at Francine's beach café. But Tony had begun to show impatience with her, and Oscar was increasingly wary. She made some effort to be amusing but we had intruded on her life and it had unsettled her. I began to feel that she would not be sorry when we went.

The day before we left for New York, as we were dropping her off at the harbour, she embraced me, the sea dragging her away by the knees. She whispered, 'I'm not saying goodbye tomorrow. Bye, l'il monkey! I see you sometime. Don't forget José. See Tony don't cheat him.' She ran up the beach, turned, waved and disappeared among the crowd.

There were rumours later that she had left José, clutching the proceeds from the sale of his boat, and moved back to New York or, possibly, Paris. For some years I looked out for her in likely migration places, Cannes, Geneva, Venice. But I never saw or heard of her again.

17. Pushing Thirty

The glass is falling hour by hour, the glass will fall for ever,
But if you break the bloody glass you won't hold up the weather.

Louis MacNeice, 'Bagpipe Music', 1937

Woodfall had raised the money for *The Entertainer*. In spite of Olivier, it was to be a tightly budgeted film. His recent attempts to make a movie of *Macbeth* had been humiliatingly rejected. We were offered the alternative contenders of the English-speaking French star Eddie Constantine and James Cagney, who turned it down on moral grounds.

Tony and I had gone to Rottingdean to persuade Brenda de Banzie to repeat her stage performance. Her put-upon husband, employed as one of Binkie's stage-managers, and her aspiring-pop-singer son listened obediently as minuscule drinks were poured and she made her demands. Her Gilda-like 'suggestions' centred on the importance of 'developing' the part of Phoebe. We readily agreed. Tony shot most of her embellishments with a camera empty of film. He later played the same costly trick with Laurence Harvey in *The Charge of the Light Brigade*.

The rest of the casting was cautiously agreed by the principal investors, British Lion, headed by Sir Michael Balcon. Tony cast Roger Livesey as Archie's father. I would have preferred a less cold actor with fruitier, pre-1914 resonance. Not wishing to add to the splashing waters of unease, I didn't pursue this. Shirley Ann Field, a young actress who had attracted attention for her alleged association with Frank Sinatra, was to play Olivier's girlfriend, a part which didn't exist in the play. Thora Hird, Morecambe's most famous daughter, would be her pushy mother.

The only choice that was certain to incite fatuous controversy was that of Archie's daughter, Jean. There was a consensus that the part was underwritten. In fact, Jean is herself a somewhat insubstantial girl, expending her vapid emotions on cloudy universal concerns rather than the comfortless tragedy of isolated hearts. She had an obstinate, docile earnestness which,

twenty years on, would have led her to the barbed-wire theatricals of
Greenham Common. Beneath those woolly hats beat conforming, mousy
hearts. The image of Jean prefigured them all.

It was tricky ground. Joan Plowright, already agreed upon by Tony and
Olivier, would fire the gossip columnists' tedious speculations still further.
All those concerned gathered in a viewing-room in South Audley Street to
look at Tony's rushes of the tests made for Geraldine McEwan and Joan.
Geraldine had taken over the part at the Palace after Joan, who herself had
succeeded Dorothy Tutin, and in my opinion she had been the best of the
three.

The lights went up to the usual apprehensive silence that hangs over
these occasions when Talent is kept waiting at the tradesman's entrance of
Power. Balcon growled bad-temperedly. Harry looked sweaty and anxious.
Tony was poised in one of his defensive knots. Geraldine was pregnant
and an insurance liability but she had no scandalous or even kitchen-sink
associations. I was certain that Balcon would plump for her. He did, quite
vigorously, adding, 'That other girl simply won't do.' In the hush that
followed came Jocelyn Rickards' puzzled drawl, 'Why are you against her,
Sir Michael? She's a marvellous actress, will play well with Olivier and
won't be intimidated by him. Why don't you settle for her?'

I managed to scoop Jocelyn off to the American Bar at the Dorchester,
leaving Balcon to rage at Harry. 'Who is that girl?' he demanded. 'I won't
be spoken to like that by anyone.' 'Jesus Christ, Michael,' Harry pleaded.
'She's the costume designer. And it's not just that – she's the author's
mistress.'

When we all went up to Morecambe to scout for locations, a more signifi-
cant rift appeared, the first of many that marred, and finally ended, my
Woodfall partnership with Tony. We booked into the unwelcoming art-deco
Midland Hotel. I was looking forward to wandering round the empty
Winter Garden theatre and the rep where I had appeared in *Seagulls over
Sorrento* while scribbling the end of *Look Back* in a deck-chair on the pier.

At dinner, talk again returned to the matter of the Plowright casting,
which I had by then accepted as a *fait-accompli* in the complicated Olivier
circumstances. Argument seemed to have become a daily exercise and it was
not a stimulus I sought in friendship. I had little taste for public bickering
and I looked to my friends for the balm of complaisance. I heard Jocelyn's
voice, blown like a distracting smoke-ring. Tony's reply seemed too swift to
disguise his eagerness to wound. 'You're employed to design the costumes,
not to intrude your opinions on the rest of the film.'

It was an arguably deserved rebuke, but delivered with such satisfaction that I instantly took the blade as directed at myself. We all hastily agreed to meet at the Palais de Dance. In our room, Jocelyn said she would stay behind. 'You must go, but I'm not. Nor am I going to work on the film.' I was angry and didn't argue. Downstairs, Tony was waiting. 'I had to stop Jocelyn.' He sounded like a schoolteacher who has broken up a fight in the playground. 'She does go too far, you know. I mean, you must agree.' I didn't, not with the manner in which it was done, and said so.

Harry took me over to the Palais. Tony persuaded Jocelyn to join us. A lone couple were dancing under the green flashing light of the ballroom. I thought of the Gaycroft School of Dancing in North Cheam, Mrs Garrett who had set me on the road to Morecambe Pier and Renee whose only expressed preferences were in the matter of Bravington rings.

I was puzzled by the fearfulness of Harry's anxiety. My own contribution to the film was virtually finished and replacing Jocelyn wouldn't be more than slightly irksome. But he looked as if the whole venture had collapsed. We travelled back to London in icily separate compartments. When we got to Lowndes Cottage, Tony made the best show of contrition he could manage. He said he had allowed his love for us both to degenerate into jealousy. He asked me to persuade Jocelyn to stay on the film. Harry poured out a rare vintage. Jocelyn agreed to carry on. But the inducements to drift in and out of Morecambe in expectation of fun and irresponsibility during the filming were effectively withdrawn.

If diffidence is the weakness of right-thinking men, I had it in abundance. However it may have appeared at the time, especially to myself, my inability to act decisively and put an end to the charade of marriage to Mary was not sustained by timidity or inertia. The debilitation of petty dissembling was humiliating and the indulgence of guilt was repugnant. My behaviour had been idiotic rather than wicked, a drift into a state of gracelessness rather than palpable sin.

Vainly, I assumed that the pains of inadequacy chafed more heavily on myself than on Mary, whose most serious wound was pride. My instinct was that if I presented the proposition to Mary that our life together was fraudulent it would only stiffen her obstinacy. Procrastination, wasteful though it was, might precipitate her into grabbing at a dignified and happier alternative. If there were other Roberts, Shaws or Webbers, cluttering up the wings, she was at least free to cue them in without loss of face.

For the time being, she still derived pleasure from presenting our faces together, particularly if they could be caught in the light of social worthiness rather than show-biz frivolity. The marriage of true minds, brains and beauty, exemplified in the Miller-Monroe honeymoon visit two years earlier, still lingered in some simple imaginations. A unique medium for its expression appeared in the recruiting exploits of the Campaign for Nuclear Disarmament, which declared itself in mid-September.

Mary determined that we should be seen together in the vanguard. The fact that our propagandist value must be negligible eluded her. She was committed to joining the public picket of Downing Street. Refusal to be alongside would be interpreted as marital disloyalty, a politicized act of adultery. Convenience was more persuasive than conviction and I agreed. Tramping up and down Whitehall, strapped to a sandwich-board, on a Saturday was preferable to an empty weekend in Stratford. We were photographed parading past the Cenotaph, sportily dressed, looking penitential and foolish, caparisoned in our message to humanity. I had once applied unsuccessfully for a job as a sandwich-board man for London Transport's Lost Property Office, and I wished I was touting cheap umbrellas and briefcases rather than self-consciously hawking peace.

I suppose each generation has its quota of prominent prigs and dupes. The learned, the gullible, the senile and vainglorious stride out to be counted. It is unsurprising that a previous generation should have responded so numbly to the contributors to *Declaration*, or that my own should feel a rheumatic chill at the giddy praise heaped upon today's *nouveaux naïfs*. But some of us, like those who preceded us, had fugitive gifts discernible to those whose principal commitment was to literature, poetry and drama rather than to pamphleteering politics.

From 1956 I had abused my intelligence and, more seriously, instinct with frolicking priggism. After 1961, came an abstemious hangover. By 1968 I was quite reformed and vilified by the priglets as 'Tory Squire'. 'Mellowed blimp', they exclaimed wittily. But, for the meantime, I played the fool fairly prettily and consistently.

> The Committee of 100 held its first meeting in Friends' House on Saturday. Those present had responded to Lord Russell's invitation to come forward to form a committee that would sponsor acts of civil disobedience . . . From all accounts, its deliberations were inconclusive. The first disappointment was that there were not more well-known names among those present. Lindsay Anderson, Reg Butler, Alex Comfort, Doris Lessing, Christopher Logue, John Osborne and Arnold Wesker were there. [Not yet a first eleven. Reinforcements

were promised.] Alex Comfort objected that there were not enough scientists; Rev Michael Scott was sorry there were no other clergymen and Reg Butler thought the list lacked very important people in general. [Lindsay, Arnold and the likes of myself, who had put ourselves forward as openers, were insignificant.] It was decided that the list should be longer and more impressive before any names were released for publication. [I decided to accept a half-hearted invitation to Scotland from Mary's parents, after all.] But many ideas were put forward. It was suggested that there should be direct action against military installations and centres of authority – even the Houses of Parliament. Others thought of disrupting official functions such as the Opening of Parliament or the Trooping of the Colour, or capturing the Chancellor of the Exchequer on Budget Day, or jamming the BBC and setting up pirate radio stations. The collection of funds is said to have gone well.

Manchester Guardian, 25 October 1959

This is when I should have left, hands firmly in my pockets. Once again, diffidence and ingenuous belief in some organic flexibility of human spirit led me to the same wasteful inaction with which I was conducting my personal life. But I'd no intention of associating with lunatics intent on disrupting theatricals like the Trooping the Colour, still less of throwing myself beneath the well-trained boots of British squaddies.

Mary's father, Colin, was a retired engineer and had recently moved into a mullioned, stained-glass Edwardian house on a hill above the Clyde in a suburban outpost of Glasgow called Kilcreggan. It was the coldest house in which I had ever stayed and made more comfortless by the stewardship of Mary's stepmother, a Scots Mrs Danvers, who decreed that no fire should be lit before 6.30. If you were cold you 'put a woolly on'.

Colin Ure had made a great deal of money from the manufacture of concrete pipes, had no interest in the theatre and, happily, seemed quite unaware of newspaper gossip or anything published outside the *Glasgow Herald*. His wife was scarcely friendly to me but then, like Grandma Osborne, withholding approval was one of her principles, bestowing it only on the dead or barely living. She more or less ignored me, recognizing at once a shivering southern upstart. She reserved her asperity for her stepdaughter. This reached its apex when she discovered us rising from bed in the morning wrapped in overcoats, something I hadn't done since Stella and I shared a room in Scunthorpe. Mary fumed over this domination of her father and the breach it had caused between them. However, he seemed content and waved us off cheerfully on our journey following Dr Johnson's Hebridean route.

In the same way that we had set off up Highway 1, I had no idea of any objective. I entertained some vague notions of her being comforted and invigorated by the return to familiar landscapes, that it might reassure and recharge the resilience, as I saw it, of her Scottishness. But, as we drove towards Loch Ness and Fort William, she seemed just as indifferent to the soft white beaches, inviting and protective, as she had been to the hostile glare of Nevada and Colorado. We relapsed into a misty, narcotic progress up to Oban, where Mary decided that that was enough of Scotland and we returned to Woodfall Street.

1960 began unpromisingly enough with my submitting a commissioned television play, called *A Subject of Scandal and Concern*, which was turned down with peremptory haste by Granada and resold almost immediately to Associated Television. Mary accepted the offer of replacing Claire Bloom in Christopher Fry's adaptation of Giraudoux's *Duel of Angels*, opposite Vivien Leigh and opening in Boston in late February. It was an opportunity to shine in New York and regain American interest which had not yet resulted in anything concrete in Hollywood. It was an almost perfect temporary arrangement, offering us respite from the attrition of our present pretence and Mary access to the trappings she had come to covet.

> Were it not for imagination, Sir, a man would be as happy in the arms of a chambermaid as of a Duchess.
>
> Samuel Johnson, 9 May 1778

It seemed inappropriate to go on living in what lawyers call, in their charmless way, 'the marital home', especially if I should feel constrained to invite anyone to stay. It was a prospect that offended every canon of taste. Even more important was the realization that Helen was becoming increasingly unhappy working for me. Her affection and loyalty were inviolable, but it was evident that the pressure and squalor of so much that had taken place in the preceding year had troubled her to the extent that it was affecting her health. She had become so frail-looking that I found myself feeling guilty for thrusting her into a world of such bewildering chaos and vulgarity. I could feel her pining for release like a dog.

Jocelyn had found a flat in Lower Belgrave Street and we agreed it seemed sensible for both of us to move into it. When I put this to Helen she responded as I knew she would, saying that she didn't feel able to join us. I knew that she was motivated not by dislike of Jocelyn or moral disapproval, but by relief at being offered an outlet from a burden that had become a nightmare.

She had made some practical provisions for herself. Her sister had retired from the Civil Service with a pension comfortable enough to keep them both. So she told me, and it would have been hard to disbelieve anything she ever said. My accountant devised a legal hand-out (less than sympathetic-ally, as there was no sex involved) and I could supply her with whisky, untipped cigarettes and theatre tickets. It was a tearful parting for us both, one of those death in-life leavings. I felt wretched watching her patter up Woodfall Street for the last time. How differently my throat had cleared as Mary disappeared through the flight-gate to New York. How bitter is love-lessness both to suffer and to inflict. More than anything I have dreaded the despair of its remembrance and the threat of its repeat.

The flat in Lower Belgrave Street consisted of a tall, windowed drawing-room adjoining the dining-room, which looked on to a terrace garden which Jocelyn soon filled with climbing roses, honeysuckle and clematis. It was only a few yards from Ebury Street but it was quiet enough to lunch in during the early spring days to come. Above the kitchen were a large study and a smaller one for an incoming secretary. I had few possessions and Jocelyn left most of hers in Eaton Square, so the move was like little more than changing digs. It was extremely cheerful and we settled in gratefully.

It was the first time I had shared this kind of domestic comfort with anyone, and the next six months were the most uninterruptedly private I had known since the year at Arundel Terrace in Brighton with Stella. Jocelyn cooked huge, elaborate lunches, which were followed by long, lazy afternoons. Occasionally we went to the theatre, the cinema or a restaurant, but we ventured out rarely and there were few visitors. Most evenings Jocelyn would curl up with Henry James while I worked or turned on the television, which she resolutely refused to watch.

The rare visitors were usually figures from her recent past. I liked most of her male friends and ex-lovers. Her taste in female companions seemed to me pretty execrable. None of them appeared to exhibit any of her gener-ous gifts of affection and loyalty. Most of them seemed snobbish, avid, calculating star-fuckers. Women who are encouraged to complain of 'harass-ment' have never felt the nasty draught that whistles round a man subjected to female scrutiny. The masculine leer at least is warmed by the breath of inquisitive lust. It may be tedious, even offensive, but it must be preferable to the rubber-glove approach of the female National Health Medical: one's brains as well as balls are up for grabs. However, I could always escape and walk down the street to Lowndes Cottage for a drink and a chat with Harry or Tony.

One visitor who didn't drive me from the house was Barbara Skelton, ex-wife of Cyril Connolly and George Weidenfeld and ex-mistress to King Farouk, a hat-trick whose taste alone aroused mild curiosity. She would arrive at midday looking as if she had been aroused by the all-clear siren after a night crouched in an air-raid shelter. Jocelyn has described a typical ensemble: a pair of man's striped flannel pyjamas, a cashmere pullover covered by a djellaba and several shawls, thick woolly socks and fur-lined slippers, the lot topped off by a sheepskin-lined suede coat and a pair of mittens. It was the perfect outfit for weekending with the Ures at Kilcreggan.

Barbara would fall, bleary-eyed, through the front door and make directly for the kitchen, muttering, 'My God, I'm ravenous.' Once in there, she would open the refrigerator and methodically finish off all the leftovers. She was an upper-class version of the woman in N.F. Simpson's *One Way Pendulum*, who 'came in' daily to 'clear up' the debris of food left behind from the previous night. Like Simpson's lady who 'did' for food, she was undaunted by bulk. Refusing to acknowledge defeat by a surviving jar of pickles, she'd say, 'I'll come and finish them up for you tomorrow.' In spite of this vacuum-cleaning talent she was always Jack-Sprat lean. I found her amusing in her remote fashion, although too thin for my fancy. I was unquestionably not fat or worldly enough for her own.

The male exception to my acceptance of Jocelyn's drop-ins was Professor Freddie Ayer, who would invite himself to lunch from time to time. It was simple enough for me to find an alternative engagement; my presence would have been intrusive and indelicate. I had nothing to contribute to their trips down the groves of memory and could only inhibit something that both of them wished to preserve. It was a principle of continuity that I thoroughly endorsed, even though I felt it was misplaced in this case. I was in no position to pass judgement on such inexplicable lapses.

After one of these extended lunches I found Jocelyn, her face streaked with tears, more upset than I had ever seen her. It confirmed my view that Ayer was possibly the most selfish, superficial and obtuse man I had ever met, spitting out his commonplace opinions to an audience mystified by the tricks of manipulated sleight-of-mind. He had announced that he was contemplating marriage to an American, but was undecided whether the match fulfilled his standards of wisdom and self-esteem. He offered his ex-mistress a two-card choice: he was prepared to marry the American unless

Jocelyn should feel impelled to offer herself as an alternative. Anyone less kindly would have kicked this pear-shaped Don Giovanni down the stairs and his cruel presumption with him. She could find nothing to say except, 'But, Freddie, it's too late.'

Meanwhile, back on the Rialto, Woodfall's activities began to attract attention, although it was not until the release of *Saturday Night and Sunday Morning* that the attention became friendly.

> Woodfall is *British*. The brains behind it belong to John Osborne and Tony Richardson, men who are willing to sink their last sixpence – and their hearts – into the films they make. [Willing to sink my last sixpence, alas, and stupidly.] When rebellion is in the air, Osborne is pretty sure to be in on the act.
>
> Alexander Walker, *Evening Standard* 27 October 1960

It's surprising how patriotism is bestowed on commercial success, particularly when it looks like penetrating the foreign market. Before this our Britishness went for very little. *The Entertainer* was dogged by rumour and auguries of disaster. Negotiations with the censor, John Trevelyan, dragged on for three months. He hobbled us with an X-certificate – 'a borderline case, not as X-ish as some' – which ensured that it would be turned down as the entry for the Royal Film Performance, which might have helped its general release.

Then there was the matter of 'those bloody seagulls'. A legend had grown, encouraged on both sides of Wardour Street, that whole sequences of dialogue were inaudible – a calumny against deserting the studios for location shooting. Finally, there was a newspaper invention that Olivier had confiscated the print because he refused to allow Tony to supervise the soundtrack. Even Oscar Beuselinck managed to bring a successful libel action against that one.

A Taste of Honey ended its West End run and, mercifully, my own disappearing supply of all-British sixpences. We were free at last to start casting the role of the young girl in the film version. Several hundred were auditioned and we were obliged to test all the unpromising starlets who were under contract. There were plenty of talented young actors worthy of a calculated gamble but there was a dearth of actresses. There was no equivalent of the so-called 'northern' school of young men spilling out of drama schools or slogging away unseen in remote reps.

As it was, the part found the right candidate, a young, inexperienced seventeen-year-old from Liverpool. Her name was Rita Tushingham. As with Albert Finney, the money-men went into a frenzy: 'Jeez, you can't put that up over the marquee.' Film financiers have an illiterate belief in the power of words. But we had some fun out of their useful publicity: 'Kitchen Sink men discover their Ugly Duckling.'

18. Off the Peg

A Gentleman is one to whom discourtesy is a sin and falsehood a crime.

Richard Brathwaite, *The English Gentleman*, 1641

The spring and summer of 1960 passed even more pleasurably and uneventfully than the days splashing about on the deck of the *Egret* five years earlier. There was an almost sybaritic sense of siege comfort in Lower Belgrave Street and my first taste of the pleasures as well as the constraints of a sustained domestic regime.

I had to overcome my natural indolence and start writing again, to prove to myself that my nerve was only faltering not failed. Martin Luther was with me still. I wanted to write a play about the interior religious life. I was not yet reconciled to an inheritance of the perpetual certainty of doubt. This effort alone linked easily with the uncertainty of faith, and Luther's explosive revelation of its precedence over good works was irresistible.

Justification by faith and not works, the notion that good intentions are not enough, seemed like a justification for any anarchy I might have imposed on my own actions, some key to plunder. Applied, or reduced, to daily experience, it might be a case for the supremacy of imagination over doing good, of sceptics over the 'carers', of the undissembling over the radical pharisees. It pointed the way to resolving the severest doubt of Christian faith, which, to me, was its taint of insurance, of guarantee. In whatever form faith revealed itself, it was emphatically not the same as certainty. 'Oh, Lord, help thou my unbelief.' A modest request, surely, reasonable and dignified.

I managed to discard some of my natural engaged unease, working quite robustly on the play, my head buzzing with visual images as much as history and argument – the frightening *Garden of Earthly Delights* of Bosch and Bach. It was essential to find a replacement for Helen Henderson, and an efficient one. I wasn't sure of the kind of secretary I was seeking. Certainly not one who could be smooth-talked on the telephone, intimidated by pressmen or saddened by the vagaries of my personal life.

Jocelyn came up enthusiastically with a girl lately off the boat from Melbourne. I liked her immediately and took her on. Joy Parker was frank, funny and strangely friendly for a native of that suspicious, benighted land. I think I was the only pom she spoke to apart from bus conductors and the man who read the gas meter in the flat she shared with three compatriots in Earls Court. At work there were Jocelyn and Alec, whose remembrance of and attachment to their homeland were very separate.

It was an arrangement that worked well for all of us. After Helen's granite gentility, there was heady pleasure in employing such a cool bouncer; Joy could blow the Slickeys off the telephone within seconds.

She spent most non-hairwashing evenings at the Down Under Club. From here, she introduced me to Fosters lager and the early records of Barry Humphries and I immediately took to them both. It intrigued me that she should have responded so heartily to Humphries' material, which mocked girls like her who had got on the P&O liner and wrote home complaining letters before it had left the shadow of the Suez Canal about the unbelievable price of lamb chops and the Brits' hygiene – or neglect of it.

In 1969 I was asked by some intermediary to write a programme note for the sleeve of Humphries' latest recording. I couldn't think of any reason for the invitation but, partly as a tribute to that early discovery made for me by Joy, I sent it off. It was used, although I never received any acknowledgement from Humphries. The Australian mystic turned megastar was then, as now, a true son of his native land.

> Writing their parts has too often been like serving a puffed-up actor, [or] bedding a plain woman out of kindliness rather than lust . . . It only excites their fury and revenge.
>
> Handel, in *God Rot Tunbridge Wells*

The whips and scorns to be expected by an unknown playwright are nothing to those endured by those who discover that neither reputation, success nor standing will prevent them being sandbagged frontally, publicly, privately or from behind. The unexpected blow from a stranger is more easily dismissed than some young Hal you once caroused with giving you the frozen lip from beneath his critic's crown, clutching his orb of Nomination as he plants a passing whack from Bankability's sceptre. Actors bear the ceremony without forfeiting the heart's ease those that serve them must forgo. Inside every playwright there is a Falstaff, gathering like a boil to be lanced by his liege employers – fashion and caprice. That discovery was still to come.

> John Osborne is being unusually quiet just now. What is he up to? I'm told he has a new play on the stocks – a play about Martin Luther.
>
> *Evening Standard*, 11 March 1960

> John Osborne has been tuning himself both spiritually and physically . . . a visit to the Community of the Resurrection at Mirfield at the invitation of Father Trevor Huddleston. He has also become a regular visitor to a London gymnasium where he spends about an hour weight-lifting and skipping. He is expected to surface in a couple of weeks I am told.
>
> *Daily Express*, 6 April 1960

How anyone had come by these two unremarkable items was a little puzzling and depressing. Edward Bolton, the proprietor of the gymnasium, had befriended George after a recent illness and helped him in his recovery. Oxford-educated and reticent, he seemed rather austere to me and not the kind of man who would discuss his clients with gossip columnists. I could see that his soft manner and monkish gravity would be persuasive and comforting to George. In the face of the ever-open beaks of the young Royal Court company and the dying battle-fatigue of life with Sophie coming to an end in Lower Mall, he looked for more gentle affinity among the male, middle-aged and stoic.

The gym attracted other acolytes, like Olivier and Robert Stephens. Keen to undergo some reasonable spiritual and physical rigour, perhaps to penetrate the clouds of unknowing thickening above my head and scourge the spreading flesh from Jocelyn's afternoon-long lunches, I set out a couple of times a week in the early morning for my solitary work-out against flab of form and spirit. The exercises, mostly pulling weights, emphasized strengthening the spine against all the strain the world imposed on it. They seemed admirably lucid, but extremely punishing. On my return, I would grasp at Jocelyn's remedy of black coffee and brandy. Both flesh and spirit were stubbornly unwilling as well as weak.

Bolton told me that my frame and size demanded more muscle, more strength to sustain their engagement in an alien space. I could believe it. The evidence seemed only too obvious. After several weeks I seemed to feel minimally less ill, with undiscovered muscle appearing on my neck and chest. My collar size changed from 14½ to 16. No longer Aubrey Beardsley on a crash diet, I looked bloated without and felt coarse within. I decided that whether it was a mutual allergy of conflicting psychic temperament and physical metabolism, the combination of gym and Jocelyn was inimical. A flirtatious American reporter told me that I reminded her of a quarterback for the Chicago Bears. It was back to Jocelyn but never again to the gym.

I also met Trevor Huddleston through George's intervention. I can't remember the exact circumstance that brought them together, but Huddleston was the very sort of radical populist the Court's few followers and many detractors wished to see sweeping up the steps of Sloane Square. South Africa and apartheid, that golden gift to the radical conscience, were among the company's pet obsessions. Oscar Lewenstein raised no smiles when he pronounced that hotels should replace the Gideon Bible in their bedrooms with Genet's *The Blacks*. I had placed an embargo on productions of my own work in South Africa, to the chagrin of Margery Vosper and the dubious cultural deprivation of Capetown and Johannesburg.

Huddleston had roused attention with *Nought for your Comfort*, a best-selling polemic about his adopted homeland. He was a member of the Anglican Community of the Resurrection and a commanding figure even to foot-slogging unbelievers like George. I almost wrote 'even to Christians'. He was very much an emergent figure of that time when the tide of secular absorption was beginning to submerge the Church of England. Glamour was one of his most seductive credentials as an acceptable front man for the humanitarian infantry impatient to break heads in Whitehall. He was handicapped by elitist vows of poverty, obedience and chastity, but his physical appearance and demeanour enabled him to achieve that gift for universal ministry which became identified as 'charisma'.

It also helped to explain George's response to such vulgar appeal. Like Beckett's, Huddleston's persona of saintliness, even more than his undoubted gifts and sincerity, had been blessed by his very facial sculpture. The turbulent priestly head might have been cast from the same block as Sam's, cropped, scarred to the bone of suffering, with the same unblinking gaze of fallen sainthood, gouged by anguish, impervious even to grace. It was the mask of transparent nobility. Few masks of virtue can have been so miraculously fashioned, and George knew all about the uses and authority of the mask. He had been preaching its potential for integrity and power for twelve years.

At this time Huddleston was Prior of the London house of the

Community in Holland Park. He was about to return to Africa to take up the bishopric of Masai. He invited George to dinner, and George suggested I might like to come with him. We had an excellent soufflé, salad and, I think, red burgundy. Like many priests, most bishops and all politicians, Huddleston, it seemed to me, was possessed by a driving vanity. Such a frailty underlined rather than diminished his inhuman perfection. Perhaps it even justified the technique of George's comic half-mask, which transformed the inner persona of vanity into an equally valid expression of saintliness, a convincing case of the right actor having found the exact mask. It was not such a preposterous speculation, even if it illuminated George's theatrical apprehension of character rather than the nature of charismatic priests, which was occupying me at the time.

Huddleston had been Novice Master at Mirfield and suggested I might care to stay there. I took the train to Huddersfield and for the next week relished a kind of indolence in a setting of minimal rigour. It was a brief respite from the languor I had been enjoying in Lower Belgrave Street, an invigorating outer world that was also a state of retreat.

The house, built by some Victorian iron-master, was dark with wide rooms and long corridors and overlooked a fiery, smoky landscape of scarred hillsides and forests of satanic mills jostling the Community's Dunsinane. Its prospect was a shivering rub-down of the senses. Only plainsong rose above the muffled wind of croaking birdsong. The silence observed in all communal rooms was broken by the sounds of sandalled feet on stone, utensils on wood and the single bell ringing the offices of prime, terce, sext, none and compline. It was as bracing as the view from my small window.

In the mornings I would read and wander around the grounds, where it was permitted to speak to those working in the gardens. One especially garrulous novice showed me the open-air theatre he was building in a grotto. I would walk over the moors, descend on pubs tucked away in hillsides and listen to the Priestley, non-priestly conversation of the customers, smoking my pipe in a corner and drinking enough of the local brew to ensure a decent snooze on my narrow iron bedstead.

After the opening prayer at supper the restrictions of the day broke. Fifty or so straining tongues slipped their lips into a noise that gave fresh resonance to the very onomatopoeia of 'chatter', a mixed Babel of high table, saloon bar and chorus boy's dressing-room. The palpable sense of relief created an instant conviviality. Some of the visitors were incense-queens and Mary-fetishists who came on holiday to Mirfield from one-room lodgings in towns like Rochdale, where they lived surrounded by ecclesiastical kitsch, vestments and assorted liturgical campery. Affectionately known as the Walsingham Matildas, their annual pilgrimages were a source of kindly amusement. In return for a few simple tasks they enjoyed an ecclesiastical breakaway comparable to an alcoholic weekending in a brewery.

One was merely required to put anonymously what one could afford in the box. I assisted one of the brothers twice with the washing-up, which was all chatter and no hardship. On leaving I stuffed £50 into the Guest Master's receptacle, which seemed about right for the best value I could remember.

The only office I attended was compline. This end to the day seemed to invoke not only rest but a sense of soothed watchfulness, which I might do well to remember, as in the antiphon to the *nunc dimittis*:

> Take ye heed, watch ye all and pray, for ye know not when the time is. Watch thee, therefore, because ye know not when the Master of the house cometh, at even, or at midnight, or at cockcrow, or in the morning; lest coming suddenly, peradventure, he should find you sleeping.

> Tedious, mostly class-conscious stuff . . . Osborne, the acknowledged head of the Angry Young Man school (or racket) of dramatists . . . Ought to have had the kind of education which encourages people to think for themselves: all this blether about the Wicked Establishment is the new, off-the-peg clothing of the mind.

Reader's report on *The Entertainer* to the British Board of Film Censors

The film of *The Entertainer* opened at the end of July at the Odeon, Marble Arch, not exactly a prime site for a film starring Laurence Olivier. The general impression was that we were lucky to be tucked in at all at the wrong end of Oxford Street. The notices were predictable. 'How did Olivier get mixed up in this farrago?' 'Not even Olivier can make this entertaining.' The posh papers, even when polite, couldn't be described as money-notices. 'The film is gloomy. Gloom is not my cup of tea. Osborne is not my plate of biscuits,' said the *Observer*. 'But I think it's a film that should be seen.' Thank you, Miss Lejeune.

The film was either too close to the original or not removed enough. 'Mr Osborne is at once too Brechtian and not Brechtian enough.' As my school-friend Mickey Wall used to favouritely quote: '*Ira furor brevis est*' – 'Anger is a short madness.' I had begun to learn that George's half-mask, the comic one, was more effective than the full tragic one.

I am not interested in the past but only in the future. But I do believe in the inspiration of tradition.

George Devine, New York lecture, 1960

It is invariably those who have detested or distrusted your work from the outset who complain most vehemently of their sense of betrayed disappointment at your subsequent efforts. Having begun to assimilate this rule, I was in no hurry to finish *Luther* and press it on George. As ever, he was meticulous in concealing any hint of anxiety or impatience. Margery, for different reasons, was almost discouraging me to present myself again after the garish indignities of *Slickey*.

My prevarication in completing the play was only partly encouraged by a determination not to be goaded into a precipitate denial of the popular rumour of my creative death. I was excited by the way in which I had, I believed, resolved the 'technical problem'. I was at least certain that I had infused some vitality into that moribund genre, the English 'historical' play. I was confident that it had enough brawn of language. I forgot that no one *listens*. Fry and Eliot almost got away with it until their 'language' was exposed as the cumbersome armoury of the feeble warrior-poet. It was not my writing arm that was holding me back from the lists but my exposed inner and religious uncertainties.

In May, Vivien had issued a press statement revealing that Olivier had asked for a divorce in order to marry Joan Plowright. Later she had appeared on television looking pale and ill, wearing the fullest mask of Betrayed Wife *and* idolized Star. There was no reason to believe that the grief behind it was dissembled. Her rabid devotion to Larry, however ruinous, was incontrovertible.

When Olivier and Plowright opened in Ionesco's *Rhinoceros* at the Court they were hemmed in by newsmen within minutes. Joan went immediately to a 'safe house' and left the play. It was understandable but undignified to be driven into hiding. George and Tony were deeply immersed in the ensuing public melodrama, almost comparable to the abdication of Edward VIII. 'What's that coming down the street?/ Mrs Simpson's ugly feet.'

Of course, I was intrigued, and also concerned for Larry, whose glimpse of freedom from Vivien's mounting madness was blighted by the vulgar furore which enveloped his hubristic sense of National Dignity as much as his hopes of deliverance from years of guilt and unhappiness. This was clear when I visited him in his temporary foxhole in Glebe Place. He confided little that was not public knowledge, but even the unease of his more trivial preoccupations, like royal esteem, were consumed with wild, terrible pain. It was as if Nelson had been caught with his hand in the Admiralty till.

By the end of the summer it was inescapable that I should break my retreat in Lower Belgrave Street, that I would have to summon some sort of resolution to pump out the blocked drain of matrimony. I braced myself for what must surely be an acrimonious and wounding encounter with Mary in America. There had been little communication between us since she joined the cast of *Duel of Angels*, where she was in harness with the famously wronged Vivien. I was concerned that she would try to adopt the same tragic mask. She could not hope to match Vivien's authentic effect but it would be disagreeable and, although remarriage was not in my mind, would cause Jocelyn mischievous distress. I could already hear Beuselinck: 'No, son, I'm afraid she's got you by the short and curlies there!'

The run of *Duel of Angels* in New York had been interrupted by a strike of technical workers. The management decided to send it on a national tour, starting in Los Angeles. Mary had accepted Tony's invitation to stay with him at the house he had rented from Zsa Zsa Gabor in Westwood Village. George and Jocelyn Herbert were also there. George was badly in need of respite from the tit-swingers at the Court and was shortly to lecture in New York and give master-classes in Restoration acting.

Tony had contrived a deal with Merrick which only he could have achieved. In the evenings he would rehearse *A Taste of Honey* in Los Angeles and open there before a brief tour and its Broadway première. During the day George would deputize while Tony was filming *Sanctuary* for Fox. It was impossible to think of any New York producer contemplating such a split commitment, let alone Merrick. Persuasion was Richardson's most deadly gift.

As always with his urgent invitations, one's flattered delusion that they were an exclusive mark of favour, seductively revived in the soil of past-remembered chaos, was immediately dispelled on arrival. It was further confounded by *his* half-mask of injured astonishment, protesting that all other guests, like Joan Plowright, who was playing the lead in *A Taste of Honey*, were self-invited. 'I mean I don't know *why* he's/she's here! They just *arrived*. They won't say when they're *going*!'

He had assigned Mary the master-bedroom overlooking the swimming-pool. Joan was obliged to swelter in a tool-cupboard beside the boiler-house. In the August humidity, it can't have been much fun. George and the terminally tired Jocelyn Herbert had been packed off elsewhere. Jocelyn's 'tiredness' was a refinement of her mask of 'saintliness'. It assumed, and still does, a Goya expression of inner suffering.

Zsa Zsa's house – 110 Montana Street, West Los Angeles – was the kind of Hollywood 'home' that always surprises outsiders like myself by its suburban scale. There was the obligatory bar in the drawing-room and just enough room to accommodate a baby grand. Visitors wandered in and out at all hours. They were mostly tanned young men from Malibu or Muscle Beach in uniform T-shirts, white shorts and sneakers. 'Hi, John,' they would say politely. 'Pleasure to meet you. I'm Don.' Or Bob. Or Rick. Or Dick.

Regulars round the pool included Zachary Scott, a saturnine young actor called Tom Tryon who later turned up as Tony's companion at the Broad way opening of *A Taste of Honey*, Yves Montand and Simone Signoret. Montand was appearing in *Sanctuary* and was about to co-star with Marilyn Monroe in *Let's Make Love*. Signoret was present to keep a very cold, Gallic eye on him. This simmering drama fired Mary with excitement and loyal indignation. It also deflected any immediate attempts to rationalize our own less starry dilemma.

Tony's more intellectual friends tended to 'drop by' around midnight. This was unusual in Los Angeles even then. Hollywood's Cinderellas had to be up for make-up at six o'clock or back at the rewrite desk by eight-thirty. Only the Ugly Sisters could stay up drinking. These were headed by Christopher Isherwood and his long-time companion the portraitist Don Bachardy, unkindly dubbed 'the Frozen Madonna' because he rarely spoke above a breathy whisper. I enjoyed Christopher's company, and his predator's gaze and impish, schoolboyish enthusiasms, although his reminiscences of England and Berlin were more intriguing than his anticipations of the 'gay rights' crusade.

A stranger arrived during one of Christopher's visits. He was tall, wearing high-heeled expensive cowboy boots and matching hat. His name – Lyall Flewitt – was as striking as his appearance. As he listened to Christopher's fancies, his disapproval became clear. When he left, he drawled feelingly: 'Well, it sure has been something, listening to this goddam bunch of English liberals. Guess you none of you know what the fuckin' hell you're talking about. Goodnight to you all, *gentlemen*.' Tony recrossed his tireless legs and gave out that shrill neigh of disbelief. 'Well, what about *that*!'

It transpired that Lyall Flewitt, far from having dropped in straight from Dodge City, was a highly rated Wall Street financier, which might have accounted for Tony's current fascination with stocks and bonds. He turned up later in the role of Master of the Horse in the film of *The Charge of the Light Brigade*, another recurring figure in the Magical Mystery Life of Tony Richardson.

I decided to delay any confrontation with Mary until *Duel of Angels* moved to San Francisco. On the Sunday evening before her departure we attended the technical dress rehearsal of *A Taste of Honey*. It was the usual stop–go process of seemingly insoluble hold-ups and delays, abetted by American panic. After about ten hours, Tony went backstage to give 'poor little Joanie' her notes. He suggested that the four of us should meet in a nearby bar. I explained to Mary that it would be better to leave them alone, but her sense of rivalry was intense. She had her own 'notes' about Joan's hair-style, skirt length and cack-handed use of Leichner, and she was intent on delivering them.

Increasingly drunk, she did so, ignoring Tony's pumping foot and Nellie-Beatrice black stares. Finally, I hustled her out of the bar into the dawn of downtown Los Angeles. She shrieked like a Kelvinside housewife resisting rape as I pulled her across a drab square littered with slumbering wrecks. She wrenched away, screaming with a cry which almost rivalled Olivier's legendary Shylock shriek of a mink with its tongue frozen to an ice-cap. On she plunged, fortunately in the direction of Westwood Village, scattering astonished early-risers on their way to work.

I walked back slowly in the clearing smoke. Tony was already home, drink in hand, revved up by the hysteria of others. Poor little Joanie had gone to sleep in the taxi and was safely tucked in beside the boiler. Mary was in the bedroom. '*Well!* And how are *you*?' We began talking about the play. I assumed that tears, rage and drink had done their trick, until Mary appeared at the doorway, quite naked, and waddled with drunken delibera-tion across the room and out on to the patio. Tony shot me one of his astonished head-jerks. We went on talking.

There was a resounding splash from the pool and then silence. We lis-tened. 'What do you think she's doing?' he said in his accused-fascination tone. 'No idea. Can't say I care.' 'I mean, do you think she's *drowning* herself?' 'Quite possibly.' There was no sound at all from the pool. 'I mean, don't you think *you* should *do* something?' 'No.' Then. 'I mean she's not swimming.' 'Maybe she's just waving.' 'Don't you think you should go and see?' 'No.' 'Perhaps she's gone *under*!' 'Let her drown. Have another drink.'

It did begin to seem a long time since that one peremptory splash. Tony snapped his legs together and strode out into the garden. The sound of furious splashing came through the French windows. Tony reappeared with Mary's dripping, apparently unconscious body in his arms and stumbled with it into the bedroom. I could just make out her gasping voice, and then it became silent again. 'She's gone to sleep,' he said, as if an exhausting day had ended happily.

When I went to bed she was sleeping heavily, thumb in mouth, curled up beneath a towel. In the morning I was woken by her cheerful chirruping as she splashed in the pool. As I fumbled towards the Gabor bar to mix the first Bloody Mary of the day, I glimpsed her smiling indulgently at little Joanie, who was engrossed in dipping bread into a huge plate of kidneys bubbling beneath the noonday haze spread over sweltering Westwood Village.

19. Never to be Seen Again

I lived a very long time in a very flattering, very artificial, very insincere kind of world – the world of an actress.

Vivien Leigh in Tennessee Williams's, *The Roman Spring of Mrs Stone*

It is indeed depressing about the play & it has been a horrid time but I am sure the decision not to bring it to London is the right one. It is not John Osborne, darling ... I think John Osborne would be very surprised if this particular play were attributed to him!!

Vivien Leigh in a letter to her first husband, Leigh Holman,
on appearing in *La Contessa*, by Paul Osborn

I stayed in Los Angeles a few days longer for the opening of *A Taste of Honey*, while Mary went on to San Francisco. When I rejoined her there, I found she had booked into a very scruffy hotel near the port, partly for reasons of economy but also because it had a Scottish-sounding name. It was the sort of place where it was always night-time in the lobby and the desk-clerk looked like Elisha Cooke Jr. For me, luxury had become an easeful necessity against foreignness and especially the suicidal anxiety which the West Coast induced in me. I had a dread of collapsing in some bar with no one to supervise the handling of my corpse on to a British plane home. I could easily imagine Richardson's satisfaction as he watched me being lowered into the Californian sod. 'The trouble with you, Johnnie, is that you're so fucking British.'

When Mary saw my genuine dismay at the prospect of spending the next three weeks in such a dismal dump, she telephoned Vivien, who immediately sent someone round for our luggage and booked us into a suite in her own hotel, the Huntingdon. Vivien was installed there with her twenty pieces of luggage, her Siamese cat, a Renoir, a Picasso and the bewildered man in her life, the actor Jack Merivale, who was also appearing in the play.

My panic at the idea of death or divorce in the Hotel-of-Scottish-origin subsided and I set out quite cheerfully for the performance of *Duel of Angels*. I have a tendency to allow myself to become over-affected by the nature of audiences. Their pleasure enflames my prejudice, their indifference stirs my rage. I remember George's words: 'Look at them! *That's* what you're playing to.' This piece of French puffery had been sprinkled with fairy dust by the director Robert Helpmann, and at least the San Francisco audience responded to his unmistakable signposts. The Los Angeles promenaders regarded any visit to the playhouse as a gruelling intellectual marathon.

Kenneth Tynan, who had described Leigh's Blanche du Bois as 'a Hedda Gabler of the gin palaces', had mounted a crude campaign to belittle her frail gift and prove that she was personally hobbling Larry's flight into giant destiny. He mocked her Lady Macbeth as 'more niminy-piminy than thundery-blundery ... quite competent in its small way'. Olivier never forgave him for this kindless strategy. He feared such attempts to drive a wedge into their royal status would exile her permanently to Harley Street and make his own desperate attempts more exhausting and damaging than ever. When Tynan proposed himself to Olivier as the National Theatre's dramaturge, Larry passed the letter from his prospective Duke of Clarence to his new wife rasping, 'How shall we slaughter the little bastard?'

Except as Blanche, it had always seemed to me that Vivien adopted a breathy, lisping intimation of comic gentility which transformed her from the lass-unparalleled into an enunciating doll. Her Cleopatra at the St James's had sounded less like flutes than like a pussy-cat purring through the treble end of a mouth-organ. She sounded like Violet Elizabeth Bott as she mouthed, 'If it be love indeed, tell me how much.' She threatened to scream and scream until she made herself sick.

Now, she appeared to have undergone a transformation. The pitch had given way from kittenish wheedling to the slicing, raw-throated buzz of her off-stage natural voice. She strode the stage, a reborn Scarlett with the fires of Atlanta and despised love within the eighteen-inch waist newly let out. It was defiant, desperate and moving as she swathed her way through the fog of French bombast and twaddle. She almost redeemed it by naked personal courage.

Vivien was revelling in the hospitality and privileges accorded to a monarch-in-exile. It gave her an opportunity to enjoy her gifts as a hostess and 'leader of the company'. She took them out on fishing and sailing trips, picnics in the redwoods. She bought an open white Thunderbird, upholstered in black, and, to the horror of her agent, gave it to Jack Merivale, much to his embarrassment. In daylight she covered her rather thin hair and part of her face from the brutality of the light with a scarf, Blanche-like. After the performance, she would drop the scarf and organize a party at a restaurant.

One night she took us, Saltzman-style, to the grandest Chinese in town. It overlooked the bay in a fishing village called Sausalito, an American attempt at St Ives and a hive of every imaginable full-time phoney. It confirmed all Vivien's enthusiasms. We sat down at a large table, exquisitely decorated, in the middle of which a tower of dishes revolved. She set it on a happy roar. Suddenly bedlam broke out among the diners, hitherto silenced by the spectacle of the banqueting glitter of Scarlett's court. I identified the sounds of American panic: splashes, screams and sounds of drowning. Waiters, hat-check girls and the restaurant 'captain' were about to jump ship like the crew of a doomed Italian liner.

There was a long bout of utter confusion. The police and fire department jammed the foyer. Vivien's men stood firm and British, trying to order drinks from the distraught barman. A searchlight finally picked up two figures floundering in the water. I half expected Merivale to nonchalantly strip off his dinner-jacket and plunge in. The police looked gun-happy.

The fire department dumped two wet bodies distastefully on to the floor like a pair of palpitating fish. Downing her drink, Vivien – followed obediently by Mary – parted the awed spectators and, with the dexterity of trained nurses, peeled the clothes off the two gasping survivors. Vivien ordered her wrap and Mary's coat. They covered the bodies with mink and tweed. They rubbed the limbs of these local illicit lovers until the woman came round, screeching, 'That's *my* man! You *leave* him.' Mary and Vivien returned to the bar to some scattered, guilty applause. Merivale muttered, 'Bit like the Battle of Britain, eh? That kind of style's pretty foreign to them.' He took Vivien's sopping mink from her with a casual kiss.

One of her current enthusiasms was a young stand-up comedian called Bob Newhart. She was infectiously elated at the prospect of introducing us to her new discovery and took a large party to a place called the 'Button Down Club'. Since her last visit, a new act had been inserted before Newhart's. I was sitting beside her. Presently, to great applause, a young man appeared dressed as Archie Rice. He proceeded to give an atrocious parody of Olivier in *The Entertainer*, ending up with a grotesque version of 'Why Should I Care?' I could feel her frame tighten. When the act came to a merciful close, Vivien, defying any expectation that she might justifiably walk out, politely joined in the rather puzzled American reception. It was like presenting a mother with her dead child. I grasped her hand. When Newhart appeared, she sat throughout the performance she had brought us to share, attempting to laugh with so many eyes on her, pressing her fingers deeply into my palm.

Back at the Huntingdon, I found myself alone with Helpmann in the drawing-room of Vivien's suite. From the bedroom there were sounds of genuine hysteria and Merivale's soothing tones. Helpmann offered me a drink and spread himself in a pouting pose of balletic elegance. Possibly the demands of his craft had reduced him to a thin bloat of spiderishness. His many-ringed fingers stabbed at me. The huge, swivelling eyes spat out distrust as he made it plain that it was my own presence that was mostly responsible for Vivien and Jack's distress. It had been a cheap attempt at ill-disguised seduction.

As I tried to restrain my anger, he shifted his target to Larry with a series of anecdotes illustrating his pathetic delusions of grandeur and his gratuitous cruelty to Vivien. I knew all of them to be distortions but, before I had time to escape this invidious web, he sent a fluttering little boomerang into my lap, which must have been directed to the next room. 'I hear from everyone – that you've got . . .' bristling pause – 'a huge – cock.' He went on accusingly, 'Well, that's what *everyone* tells me. Of course, you know, Larry's got a *very* small one. I've slept with both of them.' The bedroom door was closed by now.

When I saw Vivien the following evening it was as if the incident at the Button Down Club had never taken place. A few days later, she gave a farewell party for Mary, who was leaving the show at the end of the San Francisco run. She kissed me goodbye with unfeigned affection and asked me to come and see her when she returned to London. I was glad that she might want to see me, I couldn't believe that she would dissemble, but I suspected it was an unlikely eventuality. I was right. I never saw her again.

English Stage Company

To: CO Jewish Rifles.
From: CO Jewish Brigade.
Priority: Most immediate.
Classification: Slightly less than most secret but more secret than most.
Subject: Great news. Stop. Refer Corinthians 2 chap 3 verse 7 and keep your muzzles repeat muzzles clean. In other words, I was thrilled to hear you had got it down so quickly. We ought to be able to get it on

41 John Osborne, Lower Belgrave Street, 1959.

42 John Osborne, Nuclear Disarmament Week, September 1959.

43 The first Aldermaston March passing through Kensington; the banner is carried by Christopher Logue (*left*) and George Devine (*right*).

44 Tony Richardson, Rita Tushingham and John Osborne at the première of the film *A Taste of Honey*.

45 The 1961 protest at the Royal Court Theatre against the arrest of Wesker, Bolt and Logue: *left to right*, Keith Johnstone, Bill Gaskill, Miriam Brickman, Pauline Melville, Anthony Page and Derek Goldby.

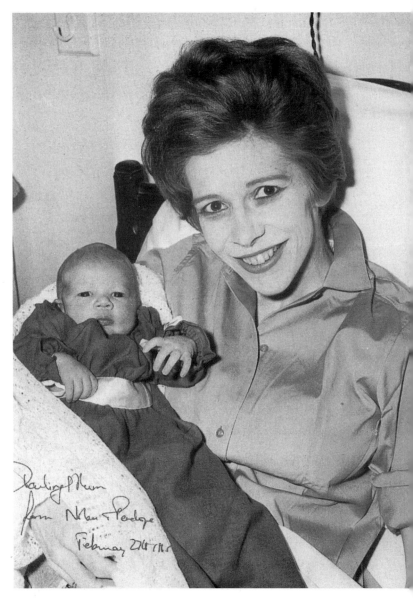

Darling Mum
from Nolan + Penlope
February 26th 1965

46 Penelope Gilliatt and Nolan, 1965.

47 Jill Bennett.

48 Jill Bennett as Countess Sophia Delyanoff in *A Patriot For Me*,
30 June–14 August 1965.

49 Ferdy Mayne as Judge Advocate Jaroslav Kunz and George Devine as
Baron Von Epp in *A Patriot For Me*, 30 June–14 August 1965.

50 John Osborne the day after the opening of *A Patriot For Me*, 1965.

as scheduled if we can have the script as soon as possible. Longing to read it, 'peculiar' or not.

Love,
George

George, returned from champagne receptions and ovations in New York, found himself quickly deflated by renewed assaults on his stewardship. The newspapers sniffed out the merest signs of setback and disaffection. The *Daily Mail* typified the pitch: 'The Royal Court is in the hands of a clique. Good playwrights are being squeezed out by the policy of badly written left-wing plays which belong to the 1930's.'

Luther, which I had finished weeks earlier, was all set for production, but Albert Finney, who was seemingly indispensable to its commercial success, could not be released from his contract with Lewenstein in the long-running production of *Billy Liar*. George's plans for a European tour of seven countries had also collapsed after the British Council's bland withdrawal of financial support. It was a bleak homecoming for him.

His only two fancied runners for the coming year were staked on Finney and, now, Rex Harrison, whom George had persuaded to star in Nigel Dennis's eagerly awaited special baby, a 'dark', misanthropic comedy called *August for the People*. Mary, cast out of work in mid-November, was left loose in Woodfall Street and Harrods until she began rehearsing with Tony for *The Changeling* in the New Year. I decided to accept an 'insistent' invitation from British Lion to take part in the pre-publicity campaign in New York for the première of *The Entertainer*. I was growing weary of this expedient transatlantic commuting, wanting more than anything to return to the slothful calm of Lower Belgrave Street. Gripped, temporarily at least, by catatonic procrastination, I went back to idle away the rest of 1960 between the Algonquin and Broadway or somewhere, although it was made clear that I should have to return dutifully for Christmas at Woodfall Street with Mary.

Before I left, I had a farewell meeting with Harry, who had decided that it was time to end his association with Woodfall. I hoped he hadn't regretted it and I don't believe he did. But Tony and I had become like last week's greatest restaurants. Tony may have been instrumental in persuading him to make newer, more lucrative discoveries. I was a little sad. I had enjoyed Harry's company when he was at his effervescent best, before marriage tamed his bravado. Without him Woodfall would never have got started. He had fairground flair and uncanny taste. *Saturday Night and Sunday Morning* and *A Taste of Honey* both saw the light in Harry's bustling brown eyes. He never disowned the rest, although failure to make money was the most damnable sin of his trade.

He told me, shoulders twitching with excitement, about his next big venture. 'I've bought the Bond books,' he declared. I had just about heard of James Bond and scarcely of Ian Fleming. 'All of them. Who do you think I've got as Bond?' I tried to be interested. 'I don't know. James Mason?' 'Hell, no.' 'David Niven?' 'For Christ's sake.' Harry paused. 'Sean Connery.' 'Harry, he's a bloody Scotsman. He can hardly read!' I think my reaction pleased him. So much for my gifts of prophecy.

> But you, gods, will give us
> Some faults to make us men.
> > William Shakespeare, *Antony and Cleopatra*, v i

The year drew to a close. Among those who had died in the past twelve months was my friend from the Savile and Brighton, Gilbert Harding, as well as Clark Gable, Vivien's bad-breathed Rhett Butler, Aneurin Bevan, Oscar Hammerstein, Edwina Mountbatten, Lewis Namier, Melanie Klein, A.E. Matthews and Dornford Yates. Peter O'Toole had 'set the Avon on fire' with his Shylock and Petruchio. By October *Saturday Night* had become the first Woodfall film to be in profit. In December the Oliviers were divorced. On New Year's Eve Mary and I went round to Robert Stephens's house and Mary got as wholeheartedly drunk as she had been *chez* Gabor. I supported her back to Woodfall Street and managed to get her to bed, where she sat up briefly and brightly told me that she was pregnant. She then went to sleep.

I awoke with an Algonquin-sized hangover and crouched in front of the electric fire feeling sour and very feverish. I was half-convinced that Mary's announcement was no more than a piece of drunken bravado, like her plunge into the pool. When she came to in the late afternoon, she clearly had almost no remembrance of her first-footing capers the night before. It was soon obvious that we were both stricken with not only hangovers but severe 'flu. I took our temperatures, which confirmed the diagnosis.

Apart from a general feeling of physical defeat, I had not yet been lucid enough to marshal the facts denying my possible responsibility for her condition. I made a dazed consultation of my diary, laboriously comparing dates of the previous months with my absences in New York, and the likelihood of my having fathered her child seemed far-fetched if not impossible. I needed a woman's expertise in these matters and could only conjecture uncertainly until I consulted Jocelyn. If my suspicions were well founded, it was at least to my advantage as far as determining my next and overdue course of action. I was in no position to take up any stance of outrage, but it facilitated the task of choice, existential or not, considerably. I also knew that Mary was certain to maintain a course of ambiguity and evasion.

Remembering the small-hours descent on Woodfall Street by Tony and Robert Shaw, it was not difficult to hazard the beginnings of some makeshift plot which had led up to the present dilemma and its consequences. Mary's apparent connivance also clarified her restraint over my affair with Jocelyn, adding the thrill of retribution to whatever other satisfactions she gained from Shaw. I dosed us with hot whisky and a couple of sleeping-pills. It seemed the only practical way of facing the first onslaught of the New Year. We were both asleep long before midnight.

A few hours later I was woken by the sound of barking. Snoopy, our lively but neurotic dachshund, was thumping his paws on my chest. The bedroom was thick with smoke. The well of the staircase was consumed with flames taller than a man. I grabbed Mary, who was still asleep, thrust a pillow into her hands and dragged her to the study, opened the window and perched her on the sloping roof. She clung there dazed but fairly calm while I picked up the telephone, which was miraculously still working.

Within minutes we could hear the bells of the fire-engines entering the street. Then there was a delay and a great deal of shouting below. A fleet of Hooray sports cars blocked the approach. Snoopy's barking had stopped and flames were visible beneath the door. Suddenly a figure appeared through the smoke, flipped Mary over his shoulder and covered her in a blanket. I clutched the window-frame, burning from the heat behind and wondering if I should resign myself to jumping and the certainty of a broken limb or two. A helmeted figure scampered up a ladder at astonishing speed, held out a strong arm and guided me down.

I was bundled into a waiting police-car where Mary was crouched unhurt, crying for Snoopy. It seemed unlikely he could have survived, but he was found later curled up beneath her dressing-table and returned to us at the Goring Hotel, where we were efficiently installed. It was almost light when we sat down in our Edwardian suite, congratulating the dog and drinking coffee laced with whisky.

It turned out that Woodfall Street had not been seriously damaged but it would be uninhabitable for weeks. During the morning I tried to persuade Mary to acknowledge the practical realities of the immediate situation, at least as it appeared to me. I had established a stable base of loyalty and affection in Lower Belgrave Street which I had no intention of abandoning because she found herself pregnant by persons unknown. I was prepared for her to insist on my fatherhood of the child, even vehemently to deny the existence of any other liaison, to declare her commitment to our wedlock and launch into a bout of self-righteous reproval for my own callous conduct. On the other hand, she might come clean, confirm my calendar notes and, more important, acknowledge the utter sterility of our masquerade marriage. It was too much to expect. She did neither and adopted an ice-fairy bland chillness. She would admit nothing, not even her own possible pain.

I rang Joy Parker asking her to gather some clothes together so that I could at least walk the hundred yards or so round to Lower Belgrave Street. Mary said nothing until the telephone rang. It was the costume designer for *The Changeling*. She became immediately elated, explained her predicament, nakedness, poor Snoopy's gallantry and asked him round for a costume fitting for both stage and street. Joy sent up a parcel of clothes and, while I put them on, Mary returned to bed, absorbed in the 'notices' of our fire in the evening papers. I slipped out and walked back to Jocelyn, who was happily preparing a welcome-home celebration.

The following day, Neville Blond gave his annual lunch for the press and critics at the Savoy. I was feeling especially spiky because of the obtusely vicious reception they had given to Shelagh Delaney's second play, *The Lion in Love*, then playing to poor houses at the Court. It was a classic example of a second play being demolished on the grounds of feigned admiration for a first play's privately resented success. None of the women playwrights who followed Shelagh possessed a fraction of her four-square plain gifts and poetic realism. Yet, at the age of twenty, she was savaged with such deliberation and spite that her successors would have run howling to some lunatic Equal Opportunities Tribunal.

I had been tempted to skip Neville's lunch, but his bemused loyalty to George persisted against all the aggrieved mutterings and threats from the Zionist heavies, especially from his wife Elaine, who regarded us as a bunch of down-and-out opportunists cynically manipulating Neville's naïvety, despising his happy philistinism and using his secretary and mistress as a Mata Hari to manipulate his decisions between enseamed sheets. Neville resisted even Elaine's scorn, although he still blanched at the whispered name of 'Arden'. I had grown very fond of him as each renewed blow from the front-of-house returns diminished his dreams of knighthood. Knowing that the straight road to the Honours List was the simple foot-slog of charity, he pleaded apologetically for the English Stage Company's survival as if it were a respectable community centre for recidivist Jewish youth.

In his address to the critics, Neville spluttered his testimonial to our unimpressed judges and George, in full curmudgeonly mendicant style, spelled out the company's disputed achievements and tersely announced the details of the coming season with the grudging correctness of a captured prisoner of war giving only name, rank and number. The fume of reproach would have been chastening to an audience of minimal sensibility; it produced no more than an air of sour defensiveness. A Savoy lunch with port and cigars, the cost of which would have matched the loss on Shelagh's play, brought a shaky, sulking truce.

Luther was palpably George's ace in the hole, its ambitious production might be the company's urgent 'financial saver'. His rumbustious excitement when he read the play was not the gruff Devine demeanour of everyday. He lifted his arms aloft at the open window of Lower Belgrave Street and cast a fine growl down at the passers-by. 'By God, boysie. You've done it! You've done it again!' I never saw him so thoroughly justified and joyful, like a man acquitted by a torn jury. 'I always say to them: it may take time and a lot of sweat but when Johnny finally does bring one out, he really *shits* it out!' He was the only person whom I could forgive for using the diminutive of my name.

I went on my own to see Mary in *The Changeling*. Tony had assembled a fierce cast. Apart from Mary and Robert Shaw, it included Jeremy Brett, Mary's rival Zoë Caldwell, Annette Crosbie, Alan Howard, Charles Kay, Robin Ray and Norman Rossington. All of them were excellent except Mary, who seemed out of her depth in the midst of all this Jacobean tooth and claw, which Tony had directed with chilling power. During the run there were prominent announcements, together with smiling pictures, of Mary expecting a baby in the summer, one of them posed in a night-club with her friend, the kitsch royal-portrait painter, Annigoni.

I suggested that we should meet now that she had moved into her new house in Cliveden Place. It was eccentrically shaped, like a triangle, and one of its 'features' was a rather unwelcoming hall designed with original Eric Gill frescos. It reminded me of the foyer of Broadcasting House and seemed to demand a saluting commissionaire.

Mary looked vibrantly healthy and glowed in the spring sunshine pouring through the uncurtained windows of the bedroom. She chattered without pause about how much she had enjoyed working with Tony, the awfulness of Zoë, her visits to the doctor, her decorating plans, her confinement in Welbeck Street and then, to my astonishment, about Shaw, his latest novel *The Sun God*, how he had introduced her to *Middlemarch* and, finally, his considerable prowess as a lover.

Beginning to undress, she added, smiling, 'Not as good as *you*, dear,' and turned down the lilac-coloured nylon sheets. I followed her obediently, feeling that the whims of an expectant mother should be indulged without quibbling over matters of propriety and taste. I had never made love to a pregnant woman before and she seemed impatient with me in an amused way. Her usual practicality and doggedness made it briefly pleasurable. She leaped up to go to the bathroom. I noticed a letter, several pages long, on the bedside table. A quick glance revealed it to be a very explicit and erotic love-letter from Shaw, full of excitement about the baby and the mechanics of quickly following it up with another one.

It was the first time I had read a letter addressed to someone else. When Mary returned to the room and got back into bed, still quite naked, I slipped it into my trouser pocket while I dressed. If she noticed, she said nothing. I had been in the house for less than an hour. She sat up comfortably, putting on a shawl, as I leaned down and kissed her goodbye. She said not another word and waved as she settled down to read her magazines. It was as if I had dropped in to hang the new bedroom curtains.

I never saw or heard from her again, except through her solicitors and accountants. The acrimony she displayed through them and publicly at the divorce surprised me after the casual circumstances of our parting. She repeatedly refused to return the postcards so sweetly drawn by my father and sent to me as a child and which I treasured alone among my belongings.

She died ten years later, choking on her own vomit in the hotel room she was sharing with Shaw after opening in a mediocre thriller in the West End.

Some time earlier, I had been apprehended by Shaw in the Savoy Grill. As he rolled and roared across the floor in the early hours, a fascinated group of waiters circled round us and he launched into a blundering apology for having calculatedly seduced my wife, who was about to ring him from their home in Spain. I told him to think nothing of it, but he persisted, berating himself for having since impregnated her too often or too quickly. Blessedly, Mary's call came through and I never saw him again either.

When he died in 1978 of a massive heart attack, leaving ten children, four of them Mary's, I broke the news to Nicol Williamson, who was staying in my house, as I took him his breakfast. He paled. He had an envious respect for Shaw's commercial stardom and his athletic drunken ambition. He proceeded to execute a persuasive mime of the manner of his death as he strode from his Rolls Royce into the Spanish sun to be struck down by a pitiless god.

It didn't seem such a waste as that of Mary, whose destiny dragged her so pointlessly from a life better contained by the softly lapping waters of the Clyde.

20. 'Do your Nuns Decline?'

Sometimes I have to console myself with the fact that he who has lived a lie loves the truth.

Ingmar Bergman, *The Magic Lantern*, 1988

How much do we believe of these memories? How much does it matter? All autobiography is fiction to a greater extent.

J.O. reviewing *The Magic Lantern* in *New York Review of Books*, 27 October 1988

I was grateful to be installed in Lower Belgrave Street, but I soon began to find myself disturbed by dangerously incontinent flushes of restlessness. I don't know whether Jocelyn detected this itch. I suspected she did, although she said little, for which I was grateful. She had an almost witch-like prescience, shrewd rather than suspicious, and I imagine I was a poor dissembler. Apart from a natural resistance to emotional coercion, I was in a mood of prickly assertion of my independence. It was not long before she exercised her 'ethic of frankness' and sent up a few warning flares, in a tone of amused knowingness, about my jay-walking urge.

We had struck up some sort of acquaintance with Roger and Penelope Gilliatt at Tynan-like gatherings in their flat in Lowndes Square. He was a rather stern, saturnine neurologist, who had become an overnight celebrity on account of the reluctant part he played in the melodrama that had been created when it was sniffed out by a creepy hack that Tony Armstrong-Jones's best man at his wedding to Princess Margaret, Jeremy Fry, had once been involved in a youthful homosexual scandal. The subsequent clamour of outraged morality was deafening, threatening to become an issue of constitutional proportions.

Fry was dumped overnight and replaced with desperate haste by Roger, whose respectability was ironclad. Penelope, a staff writer on *Vogue* and, later, *Queen*, achieved some popular fame as Wife-to-the-Best-Man at this most gaudy royal occasion, a living seal of irreproachable official hetero-sexuality. The only mark against Roger was that he was a Roman Catholic, albeit a lapsed one. However, there was no time to cast about.

Penelope had acquired a repertoire of Wedding anecdotes, from the early-morning vigil in the Abbey to the scenes behind the balcony at Buckingham Palace. Roger looked a little uneasy at these mocking breaches of confidence, but she told them well enough to set smart, radical tables a-titter. They were genuinely amusing: speculations about the travail suffered by the mighty but incontinent trapped in the nave without hope of escape for hours; of the magnificently uniformed Master-at-Arms barking at a rigid young lifeguard, 'Don't *breathe* on the GLADIOLI! You're turning 'em YALLER!'; and the old Duke of Gloucester, absenting himself hun-grily from the waving chorus line on the balcony to munch through a plate of cucumber sandwiches, finally enthusing, 'Bloody good sandwiches you get here. Real *butter*! Only get margarine at 'ome.'

Jocelyn's hostility to Penelope's demeanour and ambitions was soon plain. If she had any doubts about the likelihood of inciting defensiveness on Penelope's behalf instead of my assumed disinterest, her temperament disallowed caution. The decorative style of the Lowndes Square flat, which was very much Penelope's own, came in for instant scorn. '*Nothing* to displease the eye, like Syrie Maugham's, all white on white.' As did her clothes ('Unpressed azalea-coloured chiffons') and her catering, which admittedly was only adequate: 'Curling bits of smoked salmon and watery pools of scrambled egg.'

Jocelyn's strictures were justifiable, but I was dismayed and then irritated by this insistent venom expended on such trifles. What seemed far more important was Penelope's exhilarating display of two qualities I prized most highly: energy and, yes, like J. Porter, enthusiasm. And there was also her fierce curiosity, always titillating to those who find themselves its object. As someone put it less kindly, 'Penelope always greets you as if you had just suffered a grievous loss.' Like Susan Sontag, as described by Gore Vidal, she was 'awesome in her will to understand'. What I admired as divine vitality, Jocelyn and others damned in a single word – gush.

I had met Penelope for the first time five years earlier and saw her quite frequently at gatherings which must have had connections with what she called 'London's Intellectual Life'. Later, when she complained of the working and social pressures which were hindering her development as a novelist and short-story writer, I suggested the solution might be to move away from them physically and live in the country. My uncouth naïvety tried her forbearance terribly; her eyes and tongue snapped together, 'You mean – give up London's *intellectual life*!'

Muddle-headed Johnny, as she cared to call me in the hearing of first-class minds, had no idea of what she could be talking about. Her impatient reply reminded me of the old joke about the dismay of the circus worker who, informed by his shivering, wet, starved and miserable colleague that he could no longer endure the prospect of more years spent scooping up elephants' droppings and was finally quitting, cried out, in disbelief, 'What! You mean quit! And give up Show Business!'

Our first meeting was in a small pub in Lower John Street, just off Hanover Square, where Penelope was making her early mark in the cultural show-ring at the offices of *Vogue*. *Look Back* was about to open and George Fearon, amazed at his own persuasive powers in arousing interest from what he regarded as a classy publication, had arranged an interview with one of *Vogue*'s brightest young stars. Being judged 'terribly bright' as a lady journalist was the equivalent of the thumbs-up from the casting-couch. If anyone was prepared to shovel up brightness by the bucket, whatever the circus privations, it was surely Penelope.

When I arrived around noon in the empty pub, she was crouched over the bar, caught in the light like an insect dropped on to a lampshade. I was unused to being quizzed by journalists, and by ladies not at all, but public houses were the only place where, as the son of a performing licensed victualler's assistant, I felt a certain advantage, particularly over an attractive middle-class young woman. Since parting from Pamela, celibacy had seemed almost a soothing comfort of mourning rather than a further imposition on pain and confusion. It was not so much chastity that troubled me, but the withdrawal of feminine intimacy. And, now, here I was, giving a routine interview to a young, animated woman, seemingly very informed and quick to laugh. The twinge of a limb so recently lost insisted that a significant part of me was not yet dead after all.

By the time we left the pub to go round the corner to *Vogue*, where Richardson was joining us for a photo-session, I suppose I was already engaged by the prospect of mild and easy flirtation. I hadn't marked Penelope down in any appraising way as a future sportive fancy, but I had always been addicted to flirtation as a game worth playing for itself. Unconsciously, perhaps, I calculated that this was someone whose path I would cross more adroitly when I was in a more robust state of health.

Penelope was a redhead, as was Pamela. In my fanciful projections, I took red hair to be the mantle of goddesses and priestesses who craved not obedience, like Ayesha, but a siren enjoining flight up into the firmament of life itself. It was the copper-headed helmet of destiny of those who would hurl their challenge against the very centre of creation and, having struck, plummet and explode upon a disbelieving world. It was lifted by the winds from the north-east, breathing like warspite Hotspur. It was the shade of the imagination's crimson twilight, punitive and cleansing, the colour of communing voluptuaries, of pre-Raphaelites, Renaissance princes, of Medicis and Titians, of Venice and Northumbria, of bloodaxe and vengeance, Percy and Borgia, of Beatrice – Dante's and Shakespeare's – of hot pretenders and virgin monarchs. A red-haired Doris Day was unthinkable.

Robert Webber, who had recently seduced a young, auburn-haired English actress, was emphatic that even the most vapid redhead possessed an entirely different set of biological, sexual, neurological and glandular responses. In specific circumstances of fear or passion they gave off an acrid, foxy smell, sweet to the discerning and repellent to others. A few years on, I brought up this theory with Penelope's obstetrician, himself married to a copper-haired beauty, who solemnly confirmed my dubious theory, adding that they also possessed a lower pain-threshold than their fair or brunette sisters. Whenever I have sought the view of the 'sisters' on this, it has always been greeted with either outrage or laughter.

Six years later, during those early months of 1961, I was infused with that mixture of redemptive joy and apprehension that almost always anticipates a new production, a gale of dayspring from within and on high to contain, and I had until June to snort and stamp all this reined-in starting-gate eagerness. I was straining with the sense of speed and power. I felt the leap of it not simply from on high but even within my eye. Walking down Cork Street one afternoon, I astonished myself by entering the Waddington Gallery, which was given over to an exhibition by Elisabeth Frink. On display in the window was a figure of either a Cock or a Fallen Man, I can't remember which, but either would have been an appropriate subject of interest, and I was intrigued.

Inside, the room was empty and still, I felt like an interloper in one of those madam's shops that used to post a single hat in the window like a challenging sentinel. Retreat was beyond me now and I was handed a catalogue, which, to my instant relief, had the prices pencilled in. If any one had carried an additional nought, I would have been daunted but unsurprised. There was the sound of laughter from downstairs. I had never bought a painting, let alone a piece of sculpture, and I knew almost nothing about either. But these objects seemed to match my own mood with hammering ferocity. I wandered from one to another, and then again, beginning to feel a creature of some bronze myself.

I rejected the Cock after a while. Perhaps there was too much bombast in its poised stride, and that was not how I was feeling at all. It would have to be the Fallen Man or the eighteen-inch-high Harbinger Bird, a bandit creature, swooped for attack or sudden flight. It seemed full of mystery and mockery. The Fallen Man writhed like a shattered bolt from the sky. I wanted both, which seemed like a costly compromise, and I could scarcely afford one. A hundred and fifty pounds was more than I had spent on anything in my life. For the first time, I would buy myself a gift, a consolation against whatever soot and abuse might be hurled down my chimney at the play's opening, a tangible tribute to myself. If I had nothing else pleasurable to retain from the experience, I would at least have this fearsome trophy as remembrance. Like the play, it would be my own.

I paced between Man and Bird. I settled for the bird. I checked again that I had got my noughts right and announced my decision. Miss Frink, it seemed, was downstairs and would be delighted. Would I like a glass of champagne? No, I had an urgent appointment with my dentist. Just a moment, I'll ask her up. Damn it, I wanted to pay and get out. She would spot me as a footloose philistine and mark me as having chosen her own least favourite piece. She would feel affection for her runt but despise its buyer.

She appeared immediately, like someone summoned to an accident, authoritative and comforting. There could be no question that this big-boned, warrior-faced young woman was the right arm in the creation of these fables. 'Which one have you bought?' I nodded towards Harbinger IV. The response was immediate. 'Oh, good.' She turned to Leslie Waddington. 'He's chosen the right one.'

Caught in my present flight, I had already invited myself round to the Gilliatt flat to talk to Penelope alone, but chastely. I interpreted her avidity as high spirits, like my own. But a small, wormy voice was saying, 'If not you, who else?' One day, ascending the Lowndes Square staircase, I met Penelope arm-in-arm with a most famous academician bearing an immovable post-coital smirk on his face. She furiously denied any reason for his well-being; such secrecy and recklessness increased her attraction.

She admitted to an evening spent with another ill-concealed scalp, 'Freddie' Ayer, Juan Don, in his rooms at New College. She described his appearance as he divested himself of his trousers while she sat at the dining-table finishing her College Pudding, *and* the condition of his underpants – the kind of confidence I had only known from homosexuals in the dressing-room hours of reminiscence. It seemed as if I was making a habit of climbing into the Juan Don's still-warm sheets. As a sought-after cocksman, Ayer had one unenviable advantage: a cold heart. If a stiff prick hath no conscience, the dirty don when detumescent had scarcely more. His organ-grinder's monkey brain was an undoubted aphrodisiac. It was hard to believe that Penelope would have refused the offer of such a coveted college sweetmeat.

Jocelyn insisted later that she had never watched anyone make such a concerted, unadorned play as Penelope did for me. During the admittedly unappetizing dinners at Lowndes Square her intent was plain. Even Roger, creased with fatigue from a galley-slaving day at the Middlesex Hospital, must have noticed it, as inexorable as one of his EEG readings. I was in a mood of importunate bravado. The fact that I was not yet in love and fearful of rejection, nor apprehensive of causing anguish, pumped my confidence. Sadly, the comforts and unfamiliar domesticity Jocelyn had provided incited rather than restrained me. If Penelope was culpable, selfish and ruthless, I was no better.

One bright morning, the page proofs of *Luther* arrived. Excited, as always, by this tangible confirmation of work done, the transformation of my scribbled shorthand notebooks into authenticated, irrefutable *existence*, I rang Penelope. For no reason, I assumed not only her interest but her pleasure. I invited myself over for a celebratory drink. As usual, she was crouched on the floor. I began the badly fluffed masquerade of reading passages aloud from the play. I had never before committed adultery beneath the cuckold's own roof. I had an alarming vision of Roger appearing at the door, haggard from a night-and-day session at the Middlesex. Penelope seemed unconcerned and I committed myself to the magical hands of the eternal redhead of my spellbound dreams. As I walked back to Lower Belgrave Street, I practised contorting my face into the most unsmirklike post-coital half-mask I could devise.

Penelope's behaviour and my own during the weeks that followed were probably grotesquely indefensible. I am no more able to interpret mine now than I was at the time, caught in a narcotic flight of conviction that I could soar above the groundlings who dare not leap at the abyss and be borne up triumphantly. No doubt my hindsight judgement of her Icarus intentions, that they were a trial run for a similar sequence of frantic expeditions fuelled by a kind of spastic ambition, is uncharitable. However, her succeeding journalistic and personal careers, which were not always separable, do seem to bear this prejudice out, notwithstanding pussyfoot feminist apologists.

Her series of 'pieces' or interviews with the likes of Jean Renoir, Buster
Keaton, Tati, Hitchcock and Nabokov and, most famously, her plagiaristic
interview with Graham Greene seem pretty convincing testimony to this
driving avidity wearing the full mask of critical appreciation. Later, these
pieces, presented as exercises in creative insight in well-paying magazines
like the *New Yorker*, extended themselves into domestic involvement.
Penelope, flattering as she was to her hosts, became the Critic Who Came to
Dinner, most especially in the cases of Mike Nichols and Edmund Wilson. I
was even privy to her selection of Nichols as an essential weapon of her
ambition, although I was not aware of it at the time. Oddly, almost all her
icons were old men with ravaged reputations, ancient oaks standing in lofty
isolation, waiting for the preserving skill of an ingenious tree-surgeon.

Jocelyn told me that she had never seen me so out of control of my
life. Even the recent record of my mishandling of events with Mary and
Francine might have alerted her to the fact that I often confronted problems
like an improvising chimpanzee faced with the dashboard of a jumbo
jet. What she did not grasp was that old muddle-minded Johnny was
trying, above all else, in a spirit of life-long caprice, to re-establish his own
authority and get his simian claws on the levers.

It seemed essential that Penelope and I arrange an uninterrupted weekend away, a bargain-break from Roger's looming presence and the gloomy
intuitions around the corner in Lower Belgrave Street. To this purpose,
Penelope, by now the film critic of the *Observer*, invented the Folkestone
Film Festival. The Slickeys were still alerted for the merest sniff of
indiscretion; we settled on a small, unstarred hotel in Sandgate.

It faced the beach and was indifferent rather than unwelcoming. Encouraged by its overbearing anonymity, we went straight up to the cold bedroom. There was an air of practical discomfort that could only promote
instant sexual revival between the sheets. The bed was our single necessity
and, united in intent, we swooped into it, shivering but well pleased. We
were interrupted within minutes by a loud banging on the door. Penelope
sat up smartly, impervious to the springtime chill off the Kentish coast. A
lugubrious voice announced that there was an urgent call for Mrs Gilliatt
from the *Observer*. Grabbing a tactically placed kimono, she scrambled
barefoot out of the room.

There had been some queries about her proof. She slipped back into bed.
From her frowning expression, it seemed that the problem was not quite
resolved. I was slightly puzzled that she had given the number to her
high-minded employers. Twenty minutes later the asthmatic porter was

thumping on the door again. She sprang away. After an even longer interval, I masked my nibbling exasperation and asked what could be so important for the *Observer* to ring her so close to the time when the paper was put to bed, and frustrating our own similar endeavours. Her patient smile implied that it was something I shouldn't bother my fluffy little head about. Our own presses had begun to roll again when her head drew back, fixed by the sound of the porter's plod up the corridor. Before the *interruptus* knock, she was out of bed and gone.

When she returned, she was exultant as she threw off the kimono. 'How was it for you?' I was tempted to ask. She had achieved a climactic triumph over a disputed spelling and a couple of colons. In trying to affirm autonomy on my rights to chaos, I was scarcely helped by these Feydeau incursions. It was my first close intimation of her manic pedantry. It was only a review of a fairly commonplace film, which was unlikely to be scrutinized for stray commas by somnolent Sunday-morning readers. Semi-copulation seemed a disproportionate price for a couple of colons, but not, patently, to the *Observer*'s fearless film critic.

As the room took on an early summer chill, we ventured out for an evening in festival Folkestone to the local repertory theatre and Benn Levy's comedy *Clutterbuck*. The whole apparatus of clandestine festival seemed, suddenly, comically worthwhile and physically promising. We huddled together in enjoyment, even Penelope seemed confident that all arts editors and libel lawyers would be settled in their unadulterous beds, leaving us with a bottle of whisky between damp sheets.

We returned to London on Sunday evening. I was in a state of some dread at the thought of Jocelyn's catechism. Penelope was terse, detached and determined. She instructed me to appraise the state of play in Lower Belgrave Street. She would wait outside for ten minutes. Jocelyn was pale, drink in hand, smoking one of her cheroots. She concentrated with the authority of a referee just openly fouled by the players. 'I've had Roger on the phone for hours,' she drawled in that Australian uprise that Nellie Beatrice called her 'beautiful speaking voice'. 'Where's Penelope?' 'Outside.' 'I think you'd better ask her in.' Adding, in an it's-going-to-be-a-bumpy-night inflection, 'She's going to need a drink.'

In the scene that followed, I was a silent spectator, a spare prick at the funeral as Jocelyn and Penelope squared up as if they had been rehearsing the match for weeks. I remember Penelope, propped up against the mantel, unusually erect, her brown eyes eclipsed into black as she spat out, 'You've both got to realize the fact that – John and I are in love.'

Like a spectator in a dream, I found myself following her downstairs and arranging to meet her the following day after her morning film-showing. I watched her stride crablike towards the corner of Eaton Square, where she turned to wave and disappear, thinking how fortunate I was to remain with Jocelyn's tear-stained complaisance while she confronted Roger's cadaverous outrage. He'd had the whole weekend to assemble epithets, and 'jade' and 'Jezebel' were the very first. So she said the next day, and I didn't disbelieve her.

Later that year, in November, Tony and I decided to accept another invitation to Acapulco's film festival. Penelope was eager to come along. By this time we were being swarmed on by the British press from all sides. To my dismay, I discovered that she had arranged to file a 'piece' on the festival. She spent the afternoons tapping away at a report for London on a film festival that was only a little less spurious than the one she had created in Folkestone. I began to wonder if Francine was still in residence with José.

Tony erupted in a fury of boredom. He insisted that the three of us go to Yucatan to inspect the ancient Mayan ruins. The athletic agony we could hear from the room next to ours, which he was sharing with Diane Cilento, may have driven him to move on. The prospect of a back-breaking archaeological tramp didn't appeal to my lazy spirit of historical enquiry, but the thought of remission from Penelope's clattering machine persuaded me to go along.

After a bone-bruising drive to Yucatan, we arrived at a filthy hotel where, for the second time in my life, I was stricken by a plague of crabs, which were in full training session on the trampoline blankets of our bed. These Slickeys of the microbe world, first encountered in Hayling Island, do not simply squat and observe vigil in the pubic parts, but dig their vampire gums into the merest hirsute sprout on the body, from a few clusters on the chest to the fuzz of an inner ear. For days, Penelope and I shampooed, scrubbed and impaled these bleeding-mouthed creatures, clenched to every follicle. It was the kind of shared physical squalor, like childbirth, which, some people claim, bestows a definitive lifetime bond; relinquishing all pretence of fastidious secrecy, true love is established for ever. Or not.

Itching from earhole to crotch, we rose at dawn before the full humidity of the peninsula enveloped the day and obediently clambered behind Tony's leaping figure up the steps of the ceremonial towers of the ancient Mayan civilization. Cursing myself for my indulgence of the overbearing whims of others, whether writing idiotic reports of a fatuous festival or alleviating sexual panic through archaeological exploration, I barely listened to the querulous lilt of our Mexican interpreter. Penelope, panting behind him, considered his every word. As we all paused for breath above the Courtyard of the Holy Virgins, she closed in on him with a question of syntax of that lost world.

'Tell me, señor . . .' What could she possibly want to know? Tony glowered from the cruel steps beyond. 'Señorita?' 'Tell me, how do your nouns decline?' An expression of desperate fear clouded the guide's sweating face. 'No, señorita,' he pleaded. '*Our* nuns do not decline.' Tony turned upwards, his cackling echoing below in the ruins. 'Nuns! Decline!' Penelope's eyes clouded with impatience. 'It's a perfectly proper question.'

I should have interpreted the signs then. Or earlier, back in out-of-town Sandgate.

21. Holy Moses

For a writer, success is always temporary. Success is only failure –
delayed.

Graham Greene, 1963

Protest is easy. Grief must be lived.

Notebook, 1980

Will it be a *success*, George?

Neville Blond – any time

George must have known that the part of Staupitz in *Luther* had not exactly
been written for him but was a tentative tribute to a possibly romanticized
account of our relationship, or my own view of it. The point was never
made, but I felt that he had immediately responded to the intimate reso-
nances drifting from the exchanges between the young Luther and the
Vicar-General of the Augustinian Order as they strolled arm-in-arm – as
George and I had often done in Sloane Square – around the garden of the
Eremite Cloister in Wittenberg. The mentor's combination of sympathy
and rigour spoke through Staupitz in a clear voice.

STAUPITZ: I've never had any patience with all your mortifications. The
only wonder is that you haven't killed yourself with your prayers,
and watchings, yes, and even your reading too. All these trials and
temptations you go through, they're meat and drink to you.

During rehearsals and the run of the play, Staupitz's admonition to
Luther – 'Don't think that only you are right' – became a running gag in
the company, to be used whenever a disagreement was in need of speedy
defusing. It worked unfailingly.

Rehearsals for *Luther* could not begin until June, when Lewenstein
released Finney from *Billy Liar*. It was frustrating for me, each passing
week seeming to shorten the breath of what had been brought to life with

such difficulty. I was not yet accustomed to this extended period of limbo after a work's exhausting struggle to achieve existence, the half-life of anxiety before its lusty proclamation of health and survival in production. These are the playwright's heaviest days, when the play seems poised between life and death, remote and still-born. I had been unusually lucky with *The Entertainer*, when both star and director were on stand-by to slap it into life almost before it emerged.

However, the delay did provide valuable time to protect *Luther*'s hope of eventual life against the unexpected threats of the Lord Chamberlain. Neither George nor I had anticipated such a stern renewal of opposition, particularly as the comic activities of theatre censorship were now widely ridiculed, even in the popular press. It seemed as if a high-ranking decision had been made that the principle of censorship was the strategic redoubt of the Establishment, to be defended at all cost and certainly not to be abandoned in the face of a barrage of laughter.

In March, George sent me the list of cuts demanded by the other side's commander, Sir Norman Gwatkin. There were fourteen of them, none disastrous, but, having gained some ground in public opinion, it appeared faint-hearted to concede without furious resistance. I was reluctant to impose on George the added burden of yet another foray with Lewenstein into St James's Palace, but all our past struggles would have been dishonoured if we abandoned the small advantage we had gained. I dispatched a letter to George, a bluffing ultimatum, in which I said that I found the proposed concessions unacceptable '*under any circumstances*', and refused to agree to any substitutions on the questionable grounds that they were 'severely damaging to the structure, method and interest of the play'. Piling self-righteousness upon rhetoric, I claimed that the principle involved was too important for me to be influenced by the possibility that the English production might be indefinitely postponed. 'I don't write plays to have them rewritten by someone else . . . I am quite prepared to withdraw the play from production altogether.' George tucked the letter into his folder for presentation at the Palace, doubtless with a weary sigh, and set off for another clash with the guardians of morality and, now, religion.

To everyone's surprise, the Assistant Comptroller relented almost at once and passed all but four of the passages he had banned two weeks earlier. Remaining obstacles were reduced to: 'convent-piss', 'piss-scared', 'monk's piss' and, most wondrous of all, the 'Balls of the Medicis'. I was able to refer to references to 'piss' in Shakespeare – 'Master, I do smell all horse piss' (*The Tempest*) – and, in response to the helpful suggestion of substituting 'testicles' for the heraldic balls of the original, to the historical fact that balls of bronze were the famous emblem of the Medici family. It was a swift capitulation, although it offered little encouragement for the future.

I didn't attend many of the rehearsals for *Luther*. After the dread ritual of the first read-through, I kept away. These obligatory occasions are detested by everyone involved but no one seems to have come up with a satisfactory alternative. They have to be endured like the Opening of Parliament and tolerated as a piece of theatre in itself, like Black Rod knocking on the door and the Lord Chancellor stamping up the steps to the Queen on her dais. It is an official opening of proceedings, a bit of low pageantry before the real work begins. The ceremony invariably starts late, actors greet familiar faces with relief, something passed off as coffee is handed round by ASMs, trembling or surly. Someone calls out, 'Right, shall we make a start?' and hopes of a quick dash to the pub are abandoned. Then, unless a self-important management or administrator decides to open the batting, the director addresses an uneasy company.

For *Luther*, neither George nor Oscar took advantage of this opportunity. In Oscar's case it was just as well. A St Crispian call from Lazarus, looking as if he was undecided about his own revival let alone the prospects of the production, would have sent the cast rushing to the stage-door telephone to contact their agents, begging for release. George, the indisputable leader of the gathering, properly decided to cede the kick-off to Tony, who mowed down suspicion and lived up to his genius for summoning up enthusiasm. He gave a brilliant account of the play, its intentions so far as anyone could know them, the historical background and so on. The rather wan group laughed nervously in more or less the right places and the reading began with the NCO production staff at a long trestle-table and the actors facing them.

When it all ended, I felt quite happy to leave them to it. I could feel Tony willing me to disappear so that he was free to go through the masquerade of wilful tampering with my work. I knew that he was implacably protective of it, watching for signs of disaffection from any querulous actor. Besides, I had George there to act as warder to my interests.

Many people, other playwrights in particular, are sometimes puzzled by my infrequent attendance at rehearsal, suspecting it to be indolence or even indifference. In America especially, where such trust in the company would indeed be folly, I am asked, 'But don't you *care* about your play?' The answer is that I care more than inordinately, being the only one who has lived, possibly for years, in the travail of bringing it forth, bloody and bawling. I also know when my presence at its nurturing is unnecessary and even intrusive. My experience with Tony on *Look Back* and *The Entertainer* had set an unusual and exhilarating precedent of directorial *in loco parentis* that would have been impossible without fierce mutual confidence.

Putting a director on his honour can be chastening in itself. Most playwrights at rehearsals are of as much use as a father, all masked-up and sterilized, at the delivery of a child. 'All you want to do is sit there fretting over your fucking old golden words,' Tony would say to me. It was an unjust accusation, but many writers do sit in the stalls drooling over their precious syllables, inhibiting and even antagonizing the faltering actors with their proprietorial scrutiny.

Very few playwrights possess personal experience of the practical problems confronting an actor. The same can be said of many young directors, fresh from university where amateur excess is more highly prized than technical precision. Most of them haven't enough improvisatory experience to *demonstrate* to a bemused or maladroit player how to cope with an intractable doorknob or make a clean exit. A minority of writers *are* capable of interpreting their work better than anyone else, including Pinter, Beckett and Coward. But they are the masters of their own meticulous notation. In Harold's case, he has the irreplaceable advantage of having worked in the kitchen as an actor, making do with inferior, tame material and giving it life. Most playwrights should observe the same constitutional rights as the Queen: to be consulted, to advise and to warn.

I knew the play was good. That it could have been better was certain, a routine assumption that would be unhelpfully seized upon by the advocates of the 'Flawed Masterpiece' school of creative thinking: a blemished jewel, suitable for sale, but knocked down as 'slightly soiled'. There's no satisfying some punters, and there's no point in trying. Berating someone for failing to achieve what they never set out to do is one of the most elementary gambits of criticism.

My own view has always been that a play that is susceptible to crucial rewriting in rehearsal should never have reached that stage. Some people, particularly Americans, regard a 'finished' script as a contradiction, little more than a blueprint for the cast, director, backers and any bossy busybody to transform into a demonstrably complete product. The model for this creative approach was Moss Hart and the legend of his all-night pit-stop repairs in out-of-town hotel rooms. These were executed in deference to the producers' timidity, the terror of the angels and, above all, the dubious taste of the audience, whose every cough was slavishly monitored. This was the revered Broadway-bespoke method of playmaking, and it had its less capable practitioners in England. Texts were measured, pins-in-mouth, against the intransigent dummy of the imaginary audience. The most miniscule indication of an ill-fit demanded immediate attention:

> *They*: definitely get restive round about that line.
> *They*: don't understand the joke.
> *They*: aren't prepared.
> *They*: are offended.

Such is the skill of turning out comfortable 'hits'.

As I see it, from the doubtless despotic view of the one and only architect and tailor, democracy goes out of the door the moment the writer has thrown his pen through it. You don't launch a ship with a leaking hull, however much fun it may be for those who've clambered aboard at the last moment. Tony, in spite of his mischievous teasing, understood this very well. He had assembled a fine cast, exemplifying the kind of gritty actor the Court had already made its own: Finney, Peter Bull, fearsome as Tetzel the bovine, bullying indulgence salesman, John Moffat, all silky first-class mind as the Papal Legate, Julian Glover as the Knight and Charles Kay, a rakish Charles V.

For once, Tony's scatterings of plainchant, drums, banners, falcons and Afghan hounds were not cosmetic flourishes disguising unease but a blast of exuberance. He had coaxed Jocelyn Herbert to throw her famous brown paint over the peasants' costumes instead of the scenery. Gauzes, pinched Gothic arches, a lowering figure of Christ, twisted and broken, shadows banished by scalding light, luminous colours, rich red and orange courtly dress were all manipulated with gripping fluency just as I had indicated, usefully for once, in the extended stage directions: 'The medieval world dressed up for the Renaissance, in the brightest sunshine of colour, bold, joyful . . .'

I was slightly sorry that Jocelyn H. had not followed my pointers towards the sickly, frightening nightmares of Bosch, but even so the result burst upon the cramped, versatile stage of the Court, beckoning the spectator with a dazzling garden of earthly delights. My head buzzed with the physical demonstration of my rehabilitated imagination. Not only did it work, it palpably took flight. Instead of dreading Tony's peremptory summonses to rehearsal ('You've *got* to talk to Peter Bull. He's terribly *upset*. He's very *shy* and, because Tetzel's such a beetling shit, he thinks nobody likes *him*!), I longed to be consulted, advise and warn.

Because of this growing absorption, I agreed with Penelope that, after the melodrama of our Folkestone outing, we should give some pause to our regular meetings. Roger's righteous anger was certain to abide for some time, and was most likely to be permanent. In the meantime, they maintained a kind of bitter truce beneath the same roof. Further Scandinavian discussions in the forenoon at Lowndes Square were out of the question. Jocelyn R.'s constraint was chastening enough to deter me from further isolated acts of offensive, ill-bred behaviour, at least for the moment. I could no longer bring myself to concoct contemptible, puny lies about my whereabouts, but I stubbornly rejected any obligation to submit myself to probing catechism. It seemed best to let the air clear itself before entering into any charged debriefings. Penelope and I arranged to make our next rendezvous in Paris, where *Luther* had been invited to play at the International Festival of Arts.

Meanwhile, Jocelyn and I travelled to Nottingham, where it opened at the Theatre Royal. Once again, we stayed at the Turk's Head, scene of the ill-tempered clash-alliance between the Binkie-Coward-Vivien brigade and the disorderly Court guerillas. Tony was as taut as a whippet outgrowing his strength. He greeted me with a huge, bony grin: 'We've cut *whole* passages. I wonder if you'll notice where they are.' I would have been alarmed by this opening shot in earlier days, but this time I was fairly sure it was prompted by irrepressible euphoria rather than sharpshooting sadism.

As I watched the performance, the reason for his outburst became clear. Like the play, it was an endorsement of justification by faith rather than works. Of course I spotted his tinkerings with the text, even anticipating their exact location before they unfurled. Afterwards, when their gnomish intent had made such small impact, he even restored some of the tampered passages.

The following morning I faced Tony's routine note-giving to the company quite free of any qualms about cautionary back-tracking that often emerge from these occasions. The cast responded eagerly to his unique gift of incitement. Only Oscar Lewenstein rose predictably, Lazarus-like, to offer a dissenting note. He was twitching rabbity glances of anxiety in my direction. As we passed through the darkened front of the theatre into the sunshine, he came out with it: 'Have you seen the *Manchester Guardian*?' 'No.' 'It's not very good.' 'Fuck the *Guardian*.' He looked at me with pained disbelief as we walked in silence to the bar of the Turk's Head, where I presented him with a consoling orange juice and ordered a large whisky for myself. I was sure that Harbinger Bird IV had better news to provide than a provincial stringer from the *Guardian*.

Happily, the actors were as unaffected as myself by those auguries from the north that cast Oscar into such gloom, and by the time we reached Paris the general mood was unchanged. I had never seen George in such joyous form. Sitting at café tables, Jocelyn H. beside him, he was massively relaxed, liberated from the tit-swingers of Sloane Square. 'If this doesn't go, we can't pay the actors,' he growled from ear to ear. 'You'll have to find your own way to Amsterdam [the following date].' Once more, he was a lounging player among players. Some of the actors were astonished by their first glimpse of this concealed expansive core within him. Paris had revived his old French fevers and, as I watched him setting the café on a roar, I felt a stab of gratitude that I was partly responsible for this discarding of the half-mask of responsibility.

After the snooty inertia of the first-night festival audience, Jocelyn R. seemed genuinely tired and elected to go back to the hotel and bed. Whatever intimations she may have had of my plans, she accepted my decision to stay up with the others, drinking into the night and listening to Albert Finney's whore-hunting adventures. I saw her into a taxi and kissed her, my conscience well fortified by the reasonableness of the actors having a prior call on my attendance. The pre-planned liaison with Penelope seemed an after-irrelevance at this stage.

We were all heady with battle-readiness and the bravado that so often infects actors on the road and binds their disparate temperaments, even the gloomiest, into a temporary, headlong bout of high spirits. It is one of the occasional joys of my profession, scattering all my ungregarious inclinations. If it is incompatible with my other longing for perfect containment within the daily domestic stimulus of a woman's entrenched presence, it is equally essential. Unlike those who pursue the thing they declare they most cherish and are left still unfulfilled by its attainment, I thought I at least knew the nature of the two things that could provide me with a working wholeness of spirit and enterprise. That night in Paris, I had a refreshed affirmation in the supremacy of my sanguine powers over the disabling inheritance of bloody melancholy.

There was a pink ridge of first daylight over the skyline when I finally left the café, the others still sitting, cheerily immune to the early chill. It took me a while to find a taxi and the driver refused to believe in the existence of the address I gave him. When I eventually arrived at Penelope's hotel and was admitted by a surly concierge, it was almost daylight. I realized with some pride that it was to be a night without sleep. And so it was. Penelope was in bed when I knocked at her door but she rallied with no show of reproach. To my surprise, she seemed to regard my dutiful carousing as a holy obligation rather than eager participation in a thumping good time with the lads.

It was mid-morning when I set out into the street, dappled with sunshine that must have warmed even the surliest Parisian a little. I strode to the nearest *tabac*, revelling in my energetic step after the renewing exertions of the night, bought the English Sunday newspapers, sought out a sunny bench and began to read them.

Oddly enough, no reviewers from London had been sent to Nottingham to report pre-emptive disaster. They had all come to Paris like an official British delegation. Their reports back home on the prowess of our boys abroad were loyal, almost glowing, at least in the *Times*, *Observer* and *Telegraph*, which were the only ones of sidelong interest or influence. I thought of Harry's ill-received cable to Mary: 'We love Paris, Paris, Paris.' I didn't love it any more now than I did then, but it had provided me with the most freely happy evening I could remember. A strategic dream of delights.

Sometimes, it might seem that I conducted my life, or steered its lurching progress, rather in the manner of my overboisterous rendering of Hamlet on Hayling Island. Why now, 'e that was mad and gone into France, was set to return to Denmark, sicklied o'er by the pale cast of muddle-headed thought.

> Moses has my great respec's,
> For up his rod he grabs
> And, getting lip from Pharaoh Rex,
> He scourges him with crabs.
>
> For flight and freedom then he bids,
> The Red Sea route he chooses,
> Shakes off ten tribes of fucking Yids,
> Three cheers for Holy Moses.
>
> From the poetic works of Ben Travers

Back at the Court, it was bruited that expectations were high. In other words, malign speculation was growing to the accompaniment of unstifled yawns. Cavalier and Roundhead joined forces to identify and condemn the misguided alliance with Brecht, to protest against the deployment of insufficient historical data and, of course, the dearth of 'explanation'. They may

have regarded such an over-extended production as a last chance to repel
and crush George's unfortified outpost of rebellion. But they seemed to
have lost heart, even if they didn't exactly turn and run.

> Perhaps someone will be bold enough to suggest that Mr Osborne has
> added pretentiousness to his shortcomings as a dramatist, though
> there is a risk of being blinded by Tony Richardson's brilliant direction
> and Albert Finney's most moving performance. [Par for the course.]
> But let us be fair. [Why?] There are long speeches and brief flashes of
> theatre in *Luther* showing a sense of beauty and a depth of intelligence
> of which I admit I did not think Mr Osborne capable.
>
> W.A. Mitchell, *Press & Journal*, 5 August 1961

Slings and arrows with added riders. Others shifted the blame for the evening's failure to Tony, implying that he had travestied a play they didn't like
anyway. T.C. (Cuthbert) Worsley, who had surprisingly taken up arms on
behalf of *Look Back* in the company of Binkie and Rattigan on the first
night, delivered a schoolmasterly reproof for the ineffectiveness of the ending, but acknowledged 'the anguish which Mr Osborne has known and felt'.
Perhaps it wasn't the Teddy boy's con-trick after all.

> The seal on *Luther*'s excellence is Osborne's language. No one in the
> English theatre can write prose like him, dramatic prose designed for
> the voice and the ear, and he has now proved what an adaptable
> instrument that prose is.
>
> Bamber Gascoigne, *Spectator*, 7 July 1961

So, it wasn't the concerted output of a million simian fingers tapped out in a
flashpast thousand years.

> The seemingly effortless fluency of Mr Osborne's writing has its effect
> not only in the great set pieces . . . We at any rate can be certain that
> *Luther* in terms of pure theatre (in the widest sense of the phrase)
> enriches Mr Osborne's reputation and our stage.
>
> Bernard Levin, *Daily Express*

> Every stage picture seems to have been cut from a frame in the Uffizi,
> and set into motion. Just so should the Afghan hounds stand beside
> Pope Leo. It is a mistake for Osborne to tell us too much too often in
> explanation of his hero. [Now, that's an odd retreat.] Still, it remains a
> hammer-blow of an evening.
>
> Alan Brien, *Sunday Telegraph*

Tynan, in the *Observer*, sounded his proprietary incantation to Brecht:

> In form, the play is sedulously Brechtian, an epic succession of
> tableaux conceived in the manner of *Galileo*. [Too Brechtian, or not
> Brechtian enough? Anyway:] ... the prose, especially in Luther's
> sermons, throbs with a rhetorical zeal that has not often been heard
> in English historical drama since the seventeenth century, mingling
> gutter candour with cadences that might have come from the pulpit
> oratory of Donne.

It began to seem that some people had actually listened to the old golden
words. Harold Hobson in the *Sunday Times* was almost alone in recognizing
that the piece was concerned with religious experience rather than political
history, and chided the other reviewers:

> They will fail to notice the astonishing fact that this play leaves as the
> last thing in the audience's mind the words of Christ, 'A little while
> and ye shall not see me, and again a little while and ye shall see me,'
> finishing, actually finishing, with a tender and timid hope of
> immortality.

So it did. All that concerned our more immediate hopes was the fact that
the production was booked out for the season at the Court and the transfer
to the Phoenix in September was guaranteed. We were home, if not
altogether dry.

Stoneleigh

Dear John,

Well, *what do you know* at last my Luther has made it – how
delighted I was when it came over on the 7 o/c news yesterday morning and the 10 o/c official. *I was so happy* as I had always adored
Luther and must try and see it again, once was *not* enough to see such a
wonderful play. Full marks again for the reward you certainly deserve.
It said '*that it is the first British play to ever have received the Oscar in
New York*'. What an honour. Just off to the hair-dresser so forgive my
haste. Weather *not* too bad – but it could be *better*.

Always in my thoughts,

Mother xxxx

22. Grey-haired Youth

All that is personal soon crumbles away and to this destitution one has to submit. This is not despair, not senility, not coldness and not indifference: it is grey-haired youth. *Only by this means* is it finally possible to survive certain wounds.

> Alexander Herzen, *My Past Lives and Thoughts*, 1891

If you can get through the twilight, you will live through the night.

> Dorothy Parker

I am rather tired of democracy being made safe for pimps and prostitutes, the spivs and the queers.

> Sir Cyril Osborne, MP, in the House of Commons debate on theatre censorship, 9 June 1967

During the six years that had followed my first meeting with Tony up in George's workroom on Lower Mall, my love for him had grown into something taunting, mysterious and quite inexplicable. In spite of all my regular outraged efforts to repudiate and expunge it in the bitter course of a lifetime, I was slowly forced to concede that this was a phantom which had penetrated my heart inexorably and, however fiercely I tried to banish it, I would never be finally rid of its implant. So it has proved and remains in the present silence between us now, thirty-six years on.

Utterly dissimilar to my passionate friendship for George, it is a chaste, severe love circumscribed by some mutually agreed attachment of alienation. It is cool, circumspect, and no exchange of mockery or disillusion can dislodge its binding brace of respect. No one has inflamed my creative passions more tantalizingly than Tony, nor savaged my moral sensibilities so cruelly. Whatever wayward impulse of torment he inflicted, his gangling, whiplash courage, struggling within that contorted figure, was awesomely moving and, at the last, unimpeachable. The rewards are recorded in scars rather than the stars, but I shall never regret one moment in his company, nor our scabrous *mariage blanc*.

After *Luther*'s opening it seemed the most logical solution, or easement of our separate constraints, that we should spend the summer in each other's company and in some sort of luxuriously managed isolation. Jocelyn R., with her invaluable access to the upper as well as the intellectual classes, had negotiated the rental of what seemed the perfect retreat, a secluded farmhouse in Valbonne, perched in the dusty hills between Nice and Grasse.

> There was little I could do except watch. Whenever he [J.O.] entered a room or spoke to her, she [Penelope] would light up like a one-armed bandit when someone hits the jackpot. Quite funny, though at the same time totally humourless, she was absolutely determined, come hell or high water, to secure John for herself. It was as pre-ordained as night following day.
>
> I couldn't pretend that I didn't know what was going on. Her behaviour was too blatant. I had told John that I would not, indeed could not, be manoeuvred into leaving him; if my leaving him were to be done it would not be done by me. I was still in love with him and had no feelings of pride, no matter how much the rest of me might hurt.
>
> Jocelyn Rickards, *The Painted Banquet: My Life and Loves*, 1987

Such was Jocelyn's perception, and I doubt that if she had expressed it so plainly at the time it would have diverted me from the course I had stabbed out for myself. I had no clear, ultimate intent, only a wilful determination not to be thwarted. At first she insisted that she would prefer to remain behind on her own in Lower Belgrave Street. I felt that she deserved the least reward of a few weeks of Riviera sunshine, the company of those she liked and some respite from the flights, uncertainties and harassments of the last year, all of which she had endured on my behalf. I didn't express it as kindly as that. 'I'm fed up with your mute attrition. I've been waiting for you to say that. Don't be so ridiculous, you need a holiday and you shall have it.' So she reported my friendly persuasion, and I don't disbelieve her. With a canny forbearance, she responded with constraint more chastening than any reproach or demands for clarification she might justifiably have thrown at me. Gracefully, she agreed to come.

According to my finger-counting calculations, Mary's baby would arrive by the end of the following month, when Lower Belgrave Street would come under press siege once again. However Valbonne might turn out, it must surely provide Jocelyn with some refuge from that dismal doorstep vigil. With this in mind, we set off in something like hopeful heart in my newly acquired, custom-built Alvis, which even George must surely approve for its Swiss Graber-designed body. Fortified inside fifteen hundredweight of Park-Ward, Armstrong-Siddeley blue coachwork, hood down and open to the wind, we lurched south, white leather gleaming in the sunshine. A grocer's car it was not: an upstart's *bella macchina*, almost a gentleman's motor. It is the only car for which I ever felt affection, and I have it still.

When we arrived at Valbonne, we must have both been in a state of triumphant fatigue, like a pair of bandits locating their mountain retreat. *Luther*, Mary's baby, even Penelope, had been nimbly eluded as the barriers of privilege, astutely planned, closed behind us. The Alvis pitched its weight against the rugged drive that led for the last half-mile up to the house. Hemmed in by a dozen acres of pinewood, La Beaumette was almost buried among grapevines, olive-trees and an overhang of dry greenery, heavily sweet and scented, surrounded by a hedge of lavender. It seemed like the dream of a secret place, but any fugitive fancy I may have held of inaccessible seclusion was smartly dispelled. Tony was already installed, impatient and full of plans for forestalling the threat of isolation or boredom.

Jocelyn and I settled gratefully enough into our bedroom overlooking the swimming-pool, wondering how we might best organize ourselves against whatever regime Tony had set in train. For the rest of the summer, well into September, a succession of his hapless or voracious guests (they came in two categories, we decided) bumped up the lane, usually in the drowsy late afternoon, bewildered, ill-tempered or both. Tony's response to their arrival was ever the same, shrill astonishment. 'I don't know *why* they're here! Do *you*?' How long will *they* be staying? 'How should *I* know? I mean, *you*'ll have to find out. Jocelyn will have to make the arrangements. I don't know *where* we're going to put them . . .' Jocelyn, of course, did, swinging into an extremely proficient partnership with the resident housekeeper, Mme Voisin.

Oscar Beuselinck turned up, all chippy and confident that he had established some kind of bridgehead into our chaotic lives. He strutted around the pool in the early morning, slapping his belly, bellowing, 'Well, what are we going to do today?' He brought with him his teenage son, later to become a television star, Paul Nicholas. George arrived later with Jocelyn

H., saintly-weary as ever, followed by her three teenage children. The middle one, a boy, was quiet, solicitous and very agreeable, but the two girls were, with the restless torpor of youth, openly peevish that they were obliged to share the pool and the sunshine with a bunch of battle-scarred convalescents in their thirties, even forties.

George was clearly in a very bad way over the miserable humiliation of *August for the People*, over Rex Harrison's brutal superstar behaviour and, most woundingly, over the bitterness of his rejection by its author, Nigel Dennis. It was hideous to witness his agony at being accused of treachery by one of his most loved writers. The pantomime of events had been cruelly familiar. Caught between the actor's famous vanity and the author's indignation, George as director had more or less given up. In the face of their implacable strategies, he had lost his nerve, turning for solace from the acrimony of rehearsals into the evening's comfort of his part as kindly, integrated Staupitz. 'He fled into that like a wife who can't face the washing-up,' was Dennis's sour observation.

After a fractious opening in Newcastle, *August for the People* stumbled on mutinously to Edinburgh, where Kenneth Tynan denounced it as the 'dead duck' of the Festival. This should have been consistent with the whole tradition of George's fingers-up cameraderie. The production arrived in Sloane Square with the sort of pre-opening reputation associated with most of his past offerings. In spite of the first-night diversion of Lindsay Anderson bearing a banner demanding the release of three newly gaoled CND-affirming Court playwrights and the inevitably grumpy reviews, thanks to Harrison there was no reason for the play not to continue its sell-out run.

Dennis sulked in his earth-closet in Essex; Harrison's irascible panic mounted. His time and costly talent had been squandered by a bunch of dithering amateurs, and he announced his intention of leaving the play in mid-run. He had been offered the part of Caesar in the Burton–Taylor epic *Cleopatra*, and Twentieth Century Fox and its legal battalions happily bought out his contract from the cock-a-mamie Royal Court. George pleaded with Harrison, the finest light comedian of his generation. Sexy Rexy, international star, refused to budge.

The cupidity of rich actors is usually tinged with self-righteousness, but Harrison was too stylish to apologize for claiming his portion of the greed and disloyalty the peaks of his profession might bestow. George knew only too well that no contract is enforceable and that his only course was to take the silver Fox dollars, hand them to Neville Blond and cancel the run.

Dennis, in his turn, pleaded with George to take over Harrison's part. Only a contemptuously abandoned playwright would fail to see that this was an impossible demand. George could only refuse, and the rancour between them was sealed for ever.

When George arrived in Valbonne in the midst of the Herbert contingent and adolescent clamour, he collapsed into fits of uncontrollable weeping. The atmosphere at La Beaumette was already strained with Jocelyn's personal uncertainties, my own, the rapacious behaviour of our guests and the parching, dusty heat of the Côte d'Azur in August. Even the shade from the overhanging vines created a mood of chill unease.

So it was perhaps wise of Tony to cordon George off into a kind of quarantine for the next ten days. It was managed with his usual swift skill, successfully and even physically dividing his friends and ensuring his own control. When I protested at George's summary whisking-away into Tony's intensive care, he accused me of insensitivity. 'You've got to be reasonable, Johnny. I mean, you only *upset* him.' It seemed presumptuous to suggest that I might have done the opposite. 'He doesn't want to see anyone. And, besides, the doctor says he's got to rest completely.' I was out-manoeuvred and inflamed that Tony should appropriate responsibility so blandly. I also knew there would be no appeal to Jocelyn H.

Pitched into this swelter of variously aggrieved feelings, there was the daily irritant of registered 'express' letters from Penelope. Each morning, either from timely effort or accident, Jocelyn – mine own, then – would sign for them, tip the *facteur* and mockingly deliver them to me. I took to leaving them around unenveloped. It was a shabby gesture but then the circumstances were wearisomely vulgar, like the whole venture, the South of France, August, even George's breakdown and, above all, myself. I could persuade myself I had been uncommonly goaded.

Worse came later. My secretary rang in what I presumed to be innocence and told Jocelyn the whereabouts of the bank where I could collect the *lire* I should need the following month when I met Penelope at the Venice Film Festival. This time, Jocelyn abandoned all mime and pursued me deadly to the pool. 'If you're going to Venice, you must talk to me.' 'I don't *have* to talk to anyone,' I know I must have snarled back, diving into the pool, and so she says I did.

Afterwards, like Rex Harrison, I made no apologies for my conspiracy, only exacting a promise from her to remain at La Beaumette until I returned. It was an astonishing request and, astonishingly, she agreed. Tony, naturally, sniffed all this out of the air, when he didn't actually witness the melodrama. He asked Jocelyn about the letters. 'You mean the Collected Letters of Mrs Gilliatt,' she replied. He then told her that he had already asked Penelope to marry him.

Two figures appeared mercifully at this stage in the Valbonne farce: Christopher Isherwood and Don Bachardy. Their arrival could scarcely have been more timely. They had a nicely sanitized Californian detachment from the incestuous, provincial preoccupations of their English friends, so trivially inspired in comparison with the earnestness of West Coast campus matters. And they both had the hardest heads for alcohol I have ever encountered. Even Robert Stephens was a mere corporal to these gentlemen.

One early morning, I discovered them both fresh and dazzling beneath the vines, shaven, in white sneakers and as well groomed as their upstanding healthy heads of cropped hair. I could just remember that the three of us – at some time earlier, hours or days before – had disposed of at least three bottles of Ralph Richardson's favourite tipple, Marc-de-Bourgogne. He gave me a bottle of it as a present for the publication of the first volume of this book. It was – once more – the last time I saw him.

Feeling almost euphorically ill, I found myself blurting out eagerly an urgent yet insignificant secret I had told no one, not even Jocelyn. I was feeling driven by indecision about everything in view, my choice of work, where I should direct my energies, both seething and troublesome. The nag of disquiet and all the inescapable forebodings with which I had been born were so rooted that they couldn't be dismissed by the pleasure, the luxuries, the companionships and liberations that I felt I should have been enjoying at this point in my life.

One thing, however, did divert me and obviated some of this fever of tedium and apprehension. It was a small thing, not yet mine own and little more than a figment. It was no more than the impression in my head for a scene in a play which I knew would have to bide its time before it was written. Beneath the trees, in the early coolness of the morning and that oddly pharmaceutical smell of French breakfast coffee, I outlined to Christopher and Don the Drag Ball scene in *A Patriot for Me*.

The hangover pulse hammered away at my neck glands and the frictions of La Beaumette receded as I tried to describe the pattern and the setting of the ball and its slow effect on the audience as the gloriously dressed characters revealed themselves to be exclusively male. Christopher's animated response was rewarding, especially from a homosexual novelist who didn't seem suspicious about an 'outsider' poaching territory he might have regarded as his own.

He remembered the grand drag balls of the thirties, including annual occasions presided over by the famous performing aesthete Bunny Rogers. George told me he had attended one during his Oxford days when his companion was the actress Hermione Baddeley, a jewel of campery hotly pursued by his fellow undergraduates of all persuasions. 'What did you go as?' I had asked him. 'Nelson,' he growled. It seemed a tasteful compromise and I consequently wrote a Nelson into the final stage directions of *Patriot*. He was played by Ferdy Mayne. 'It is a measure of my love for you, dear boy,' said George later, 'that I consented to appear on the same stage as one of my least favourite actors.'

Christopher went on to talk about the scene's implications. 'You know,' he said, 'it reminds me of the other night. Know what I mean, Don?' Don smiled beatifically. 'It was in the Negresco. In Terry Rattigan's suite. The company could all have been characters in your play. It was quite a glittering cast: Terry, Cuthbert Worsley, Binkie Beaumont, Michael Redgrave, John Perry, Don and myself. And *then* there were the bit players. Lots of them. Oh, and of course, Tony. Quite a tableau for you, don't you think?' So that was why Tony had made one of his unexplained trips immediately after dinner, roaring down the drive alone in his careering Thunderbird.

It was an oddly encouraging footnote, a small omen, and I felt I could safely put the play away in custody at the back of my head for a couple of years, when I might be 'ready for it'. But not yet.

In August the Cold War escalated with the Berlin Crisis, and the proliferation of nuclear weapons seemed certain.

A Letter to my Fellow Countrymen

This is a letter of hate. It is for you, my countrymen. I mean those men of my country who have defiled it. The men with manic fingers leading the sightless, feeble, betrayed body of my country to its death. You are its murderers, and there's little left in my own brain but the thoughts of murder for you . . . My hatred of you is almost the only constant, satisfaction you have left me. My favourite fantasy is four minutes or so non-commercial viewing as you fry in your democratically elected hot seats in Westminster, preferably with your condoning democratic constituents . . . You have instructed me in my hatred for 30 years. You have perfected it and made it the blunt, obsolete instrument it is now. I only hope it will keep me going. I think it will. It may sustain me in the last few months. Till then, damn you England. You're rotting now, and quite soon you'll disappear. My hate will outrun you yet, if only for a few seconds. I wish it could be eternal . . .

Your fellow countryman,
John Osborne
Valbonne, France

Tribune, 18 August 1961

I had written intemperate declarations of this kind before and, indeed, have done since. Usually, I tuck them aside, soothed by the quick expectorating exercise itself. 'Damn you, England' was written without pause, as it plainly shows, when I sat beneath the vines sipping my forenoon Ricard. I knew it to be a slovenly, melodramatic misuse of my so-called gift for 'rhetoric'. Unfortunately, I libelled my own passionate confusion by omitting any grace notes of rigour or irony. I foolishly hoped that a few perceptive souls might recognize the naked outrage at the heart of its posturing self-dramatization. If I had not believed that it partially reflected my overwhelming mood of agitated disaffection, I would never have popped it in the post.

The style was deliberately overheated because I knew that would be the only way to gain attention, to adopt a different tone from the tame blandness of left-wing journals like the *New Statesman*. If this tone was misjudged, it was because my soft-headed liberal analysis of the political realities of international Communism was pitifully naïve. My duped perceptions exactly matched the sentimental orthodoxy that has since shifted its bleeding heart from Atomic Destruction to even dreamier preoccupations like rainforests, United Nations resolutions, the Third World (happy hunting-ground of the eternal liberal) and, lately, the holy relic of the cardboard box.

I had sent the letter to *Tribune* because I knew it was the only journal which would even consider publishing such a seditious piece. What I had not expected was that the editor, Richard Clements, would present it as a message delivered in self-exile from a sybaritic retreat in the south of France, with my address at the bottom. There would be no doubt that I had undergone some kind of brainstorm, to the delight of many and the dismay of my friends. Muddle-headed Johnny had hurled his marbles in the air and, this time, on a bridge far, far too far.

Only a few days after the Glorious Twelfth the Silly Season in England exploded into life and banged on well into September. For weeks holiday-makers opened their airmail editions of the *Telegraph* and more popular papers to find selections of pro- and con-Osborne correspondence (surprisingly weighted one against the other), editorial comment, cartoons and pronouncements of respected journalists like Peregrine Worsthorne, who gave discursive judgements on the present state of the nation and myself. His interpretation of the letter and the flood of response to it covered almost the whole centre page of the *Sunday Telegraph* on 20 August:

> I have an uneasy suspicion that Osborne speaks for far more people than we care to recognize . . . For his hatred of Britain is much more than a mere personal idiosyncracy. The murderous language, of course, is personal, but the feeling behind it is shared, I believe, by a frighteningly large number of his fellow countrymen. The truly significant conflict today is not between the rich and poor but between those over thirty-five and those under . . . The friction it causes at periods of acute crisis – such as the present – when the young feel that their fate is in the hands of men whose values they do not share, gives rise to precisely the feeling of passionate despairing resentment which John Osborne so virulently articulated in *Tribune*. Here is the driving force of deep social bitterness – a basic conviction in the young that the established order neither reflects their faith nor protects their lives.

That same Sunday, the *Sunday Times* carried its own 'Critics and Disciples':

JOHN BRAINE: I agree with every word Osborne writes.

HUGH TREVOR-ROPER: I never read things written in that kind of language. I think I might read it if it were translated into English.

JOHN BRATBY: I can't think why he's written it at all. It can only damage his reputation.

J.B. PRIESTLEY: I haven't read the whole thing, but is it all that important?

SHELAGH DELANEY: John has had the courage to say something a lot of people have been thinking.

ARNOLD WESKER: I know what he feels and so do hundreds of thousands of others.

JOHN WHITING: I thought John Osborne's letter was very funny. The

MAILBAG

HAVING read John Osborne's "attack" I want to say how much I and most mothers I know agree with it.

I have two small children and another baby on the way. I go to bed every night, my heart filled with fear for their future. I'm not brave. I'm frightened to death, but most of all I'm frightened of it for my children.

I, too, wish to God that all the statesmen of the world would get blown up if it meant the end of the Bomb and the fear of our children's destruction.

MARJORIE DENT.
Keighley.

WRONG BASIS

JOHN OSBORNE was right to voice his feelings about warmongers and public apathy. But he has done a poor service to the cause of peace by expressing himself in terms suggesting the hysterical ravings of a psychopath.

He does not speak for the true pacifist element in this country, which is based on reverence for life and not on corrosive hate.

ISABEL SUTHERLAND.
London.

HE'S HONEST

MAY I suggest that all those who, like John Osborne, want us to lay down our arms and surrender should be equally honest?

It is far easier to respect a man who confesses to being afraid than one who hides his fear behind a smoke-screen of sanctimonious hypocrisy.

DESMOND ALLHUSEN.
Beaminster.

PITY HIM

WHAT a pitiable state John Osborne is in ! Little left in his own brain but thoughts of murder, and fearing death, but clinging wretchedly to life !

(Mrs.) B. JACKSON.
Goole.

SO RIGHT

THANK you for John Osborne's brilliant and much-needed attack on our tin-pot, grouse-hunting politicians' handling of the Berlin crisis.

He expresses so correctly the feelings of the younger generation.

K. Q. KING.
Pentraeth.

Daily Mail, 21 August 1961

whole thing was a bit overwritten and sending it from the South of France wasn't exactly tactful.

RICHARD HOGGART: Oh, dear!

The *Mail*, obviously taken aback by the weight of response and surprised that its readers were by no means unanimously condemning, delivered a ponderous leader on 23 August:

> John Osborne's letter of hate reads like that of a betrayed lover . . . This is the cry of the individual who feels powerless to affect the world he lives in. But nobody can change the destiny of the world by going to a village in the South of France and crying 'The Game's Up!' Osborne should be shouting in his own country . . . Men like Osborne should be speaking in Trafalgar Square, as Bertrand Russell does. They could be arguing in the columns of newspapers or on television. They could be standing for Bristol South East . . .

The principal beneficiary from all this nonsense was *Tribune*.

> Every true Socialist should roar with applause at Osborne's letter. We five navvies have not read anything like it since Nye Bevin's 'vermin' speech. Hell's bells, you're a *great* newspaper to print it. In the name of God, wake up, wake up, you weak-kneed, sheep-brained sons and

daughters of a land that has never cried out so loud in its history for salvation, and has never appeared such a stupid and cowardly shower. All our hate, along with Osborne's.

Jack Jones and the Four Navvies.

Tribune, 21 September 1961

23. 'Don't Cry for Me, Nicaragua'

Everyone in the world has as much as they can do in caring for themselves and few have leisure to really think of their neighbour's distress, however they may delight their tongues in talking of them.

Samuel Johnson, 1783

A mistress should be like a little country retreat near the town, not to dwell in constantly, but only for a night and a day.

William Congreve

> Fly if your pigtail catches fire,
> Dive down the nearest sink,
> Remember if you wash a pancake,
> Its underwear is sure to shrink.
>
> How do I live? On the Parish.
> Where do I sleep? In a tomb.
> I was born in a sardines' graveyard,
> Where treacle and sausages bloom.
>
> What does it matter if rock cakes rock,
> And pineapples fly in the air?
> 'Cos at death I shall cheerfully cry,
> But he'll say Pontoons only, 'I'm sticking'.

Billy Bennett, 'Devil-May-Care', 1926

Major Colin de Vere Gordon-MacLean (retired), thirty-three years old, who had served in the British Army as a regular soldier in Germany, Hong Kong and Malaya, arrived on the doorstep of La Beaumette with his yellow labrador, Simla, and a rifle under his arm.

He had had to negotiate our next-door neighbours, a rather louche nudist colony, and make his way on foot up the dusty, broken drive for a mile or two. He was lightly dressed in an open-necked white shirt and a pair of old bags, as fresh and eager as when he set out. In the breathless buzz of the airless August afternoon, he must have felt that the farmhouse was deserted. No doubt the plains of Salisbury and Hanover had taught him how to kick up some action from entrenched local inertia during a hot siesta. Sure enough, he discovered Jocelyn R., nodding over Henry James. Major Colin de Vere Gordon-MacLean knew how to sum up a situation smartly and act on it at once. He instructed Jocelyn to seek me out. 'Just tell him I've come to accept his apologies to Britain – at once.'

Jocelyn, in a drowsy state of late-afternoon Calvados, Henry James and the sight of Simla, the Major and his rifle, found me asleep by the pool. 'He's got a gun and a sweet labrador. And he wants you to apologize to England.' 'Tell him to fuck off, or we'll tell the gendarmerie we've got an armed foreign intruder trespassing on the Glenconners' property.' She pottered back happily to deliver this message.

After a while, when she hadn't reappeared at the pool, and there had been no sounds of shots or scuffle, I decided to go and look for myself. The Major had proceeded to reconnoitre the interior of the house while she returned to her bowered hammock and left him to it. He set up a tactical observation post in the drawing-room. What followed could have been nicely worked up by that intrepid farceur Ray Cooney and performed by the splendid Donald Sinden. I acted true to all the conventions of the game. Assuming the golden Simla would spot it at once, I scribbled on a piece of paper and slipped it beneath the door. It read: 'I am tied up at present. Please go away.'

Not a particularly defiant response to a demand for unconditional surrender, but I felt that the Major had made his point for England and would feel no dishonour in accepting such a mild entreaty. Jocelyn pattered back with the major's reply. 'We progress, it seems. I wanted to let you know what many people feel about your disgraceful outburst. I have taken some pains to find you in order to do so.' 'Tell him to fuck off. If he's a British officer, he's not likely to take his rifle butt to an unarmed lady.' 'Well, Simla's frightfully friendly.'

Colin de Vere Gordon-MacLean was a product of the modern post-war British army. He conducted a careful debriefing operation from the Post Office in Valbonne.

OSBORNE: You are a complete stranger. Why should I receive every lunatic who comes beating at my door?

MAJOR: I am not a lunatic.

OSBORNE: I didn't say you were. You are probably an intelligent person.

You no doubt are. But what makes you think you have the right to come to my house and expect me to greet you?

MAJOR: When a gentleman calls on another gentleman, he ought to be received at least.

OSBORNE: You've come bursting into my life.

MAJOR: I didn't burst in. I wanted to discuss these sweeping statements you have made about the British people. What do you think their reaction is?

OSBORNE: I know what the public reaction is. I am not interested in your reactions. I am losing my temper.

MAJOR: A lot of people are losing their tempers – with *you*. Are you sincere or not?

OSBORNE: That's impertinent. I'm a writer.

MAJOR: Writer? Writer? You use a lot of hackneyed phrases like hanging out dirty washing. You are a disgrace. You seem to like hiding behind pencil and paper.

From then on the house was in a state of intermittent siege from stray local stringers of British newspapers and phone calls which Jocelyn R. dutifully answered. Tony said nothing, but his cool, quizzical glances only made me more furious with myself for having visited these squalid indignities on what should have been a healing gathering of friends, all tired, fretful but united in their concern for each other.

A week later, on 31 August, Mary gave birth to her son, Colin, in a Regent's Park nursing-home. Tony came back from his morning foray into Cannes and scattered the English newspapers on the floor, along with his own preferred copies of *Le Monde* and the *Herald Tribune*. There were huge blow-ups of Mary looking more radiantly effervescent than she had done even during our Roman Christmas. The headlines and stories were almost as uniform as the accounts from the Mad Major. 'For Mary Ure – a son. While Osborne stays Abroad.' 'John Osborne is a Shy Dad.' 'A New Son for Osborne – but he stays away.' 'The Strange World of John Osborne – He stays on holiday in France as his son is born in London.' Mary herself was being almost chillingly circumspect, as were her unfortunate parents.

During the evening of the following day, the three of us – Tony, Jocelyn and myself – dined indoors for the first time. The damp, evening chill had begun to set in, driving us inside as well as within ourselves. It was a dispiriting occasion, all nuances confused but oppressive. It was as if each one of us wished to escape the others. Jocelyn's gossiping fluency was almost stilled, and even Tony's spinning core of energy seemed depleted. A heavy pall of leave-taking, a sense of vague misadventure, hung over the table. There was none of the pursued frivolity or wanton speculation of the previous weeks we had spent in each other's company. I could detect a sense of repressed bafflement and disappointment from both of them.

Almost at once, we became aware that we were being observed at very close quarters. In the overhanging foliage of the terrace we began to make out a twilight Tenniel-like vision of faces and the steely reflection of camera lenses trained on the table. As we rose together, the trees erupted into little flashes of white light. We had been ambushed like bandits in a mountain fortress. Paparazzi of all nations hung like bats from the branches. Tony and I shook the trees and they dropped to earth, squealing, clutching their cameras, and disappeared into the darkness. Tony left early the next morning for the airport to oversee the transfer of *Luther* to the Phoenix Theatre and the West End première of *A Taste of Honey*.

I didn't know whether he was aware of my own intended departure and arranged rendezvous with Penelope at our next shared film festival, in Venice. Nor did I really want to. His relief at extricating himself from a steamy mess of emotions must have been profound. Left alone together, Jocelyn and I lapsed into a grateful armistice of humane reticence. During the late siesta, I rose, dressed and packed little more than a change of clothes in a bag. I hoped I was being discreet, not furtive. I also hoped that she would wake with a long, drowsy intake of relief when she found that I had gone.

I don't think I ever asked Penelope why she had chosen Folkestone for a fictitious film festival and the *venue* (in popular tradespeak) for our opening bound into adultery. But, arriving at the tiny Da Vinci airport, I felt as inexplicably in control – at least in the principle of choice – and powerful and lusty as the winged lions of St Mark's. I was as aware of this seizure of euphoria as I was of the blast of concrete heat and the mist from the lagoon.

Penelope was waiting for me behind the barrier at the concourse, a smudge of bright yellow in her frock, northern pale, the large brown eyes bleached from any black. Her hair out-Titianed the arrival gate to Venice. What others would nail as her greeting gush felt to me on that September morning more like the embrace of a voluptuous goddess. It is tempting to deride and disown what may have been howling fits of delusion. But the abandonment of sense and judgement cannot honestly repudiate it, just as my passion for Pamela had been a folly and, most demonstrably, a delusion. That one took more than thirty years before she stamped on it finally with her own authority.

Penelope had booked us into a discreet, that is to say cheap, room at the Europa Hotel on the Grand Canal, almost opposite the magnificently baroque Santa Maria della Salute. It was Germanic, efficient, anonymous – if anonymity is possible in Venice. Unlike Folkestone, Venice's festival showed films, hundreds of them, an astonishing number of which Penelope was determined to attend. As film critic of the *Observer* she felt constrained to present herself at press showings, press conferences and general promotional junketings. The giddy romantic lustings of the Europa paled in comparison.

The piazzas and palaces of Venice were not merely coursing with the international lava of tourists but, as every September, were bobbing with the flotsam of film-reviewers, show-biz columnists, gossips, commentators, stray stringers, baggage-trailers, photographers, directors, producers, actors, starlets and their minders – the hungry international train which followed and scavenged off the whole calendar of festivalizing for a living and as a way of life.

It was an almost blind dementia of hopefulness for the newly respected film critic of the *Observer*, wife of Dr Gilliatt, most publicly approved and vetted best man, and John Osborne, angry young playwright, notorious less for his plays than for his spoiled, intemperate attacks upon his own country, to contemplate the possibility of enjoying lunch unseen together at the Fenice restaurant or Torcello, mingling in the crush at Harry's Bar or sipping midnight coffee at Florian's and traipsing through the pigeons hand-in-hand. And yet we managed it.

I spent long periods on my own at the Europa, either asleep in our bedroom or drinking on the terrace while Penelope toiled across to the Lido to load herself with an armful of bumph from the festival press office. After the grapplings of a long night, I did not want to set out before breakfast to watch ideological dramas about peasant passions among Romanian villagers at the turn of the century or Kurosawa's latest, *Yojimbo*.

Penelope, however, was hell-bent on appeasing her critical conscience by attending everything on offer. I chose to excuse this as quaint dedication rather than undiscriminating avidity. At this stage, I was still able to stifle my irritation at her rigid priorities which gave misty art-screenings precedence over the tangible passions smouldering in our hotel room. For my own part, I was in no mood to squander precious hours of proven delight by enduring boredom-until-death with a thousand frames of prize contenders for that year's Golden Lion like *L'Année Dernière à Marienbad*.

Of course, I should have spotted the phoney gambler then, weeks before I heard the call 'Do your Nuns Decline?' Yet when I heard affections like 'I shall never, never have to look for anyone again,' the deepest nerve within me was shot through. No one, not even Stella, had seemed to proclaim themselves with such joyous effrontery. Cheap music it may have sounded in other ears, but in my ravenous condition it had the clangour of Mahler, full of frenzy and, here in Venice, a tragic preoccupation with longing and joy in the shadow of the Salute.

I was in the grip of an abiding resolution that I would reject nothing that might be thrown at me, however inadequate my resources. My five years at rest with the Court had provided me with an escape from the wilderness, and I had a premonition of some certainty that the most recent sequence of absurdities and illusions was entering a new stage of haunted apprehension. There was no way I could be rid of it. I could only obey what I must accept as my nature, put my head down and God Rot them all, either to fade or to survive. Redemption of some sort might even break in cheerfully now and then.

Penelope and I left each other at the airport. She went on the 9.00 a.m. plane to London. My flight to Nice had been 'delayed', and I was sweetly told by the nubile Alitalia girls at the desk that it would not take off until four o'clock in the afternoon. I had no money at all. I had given my change to Penelope for her cab fare from London airport. This was in the days before jumped-up clerks and salesmen affected 'executive' calling-cards along with their armoury of briefcases, faxes, lap computers, ties, pens, even homes. 'Lifestyle' had yet to be coined for the man utterly bereft of style. There was therefore no 'executive' lounge. I settled down for the next seven hours on a sweaty leatherette sofa in a hut perched on the marshy edge of the most glorious commercial outpost in the world. Where on earth was I? Perhaps it was God's off-hand reproof for the folly of Folkestone.

Two years later, just after Penelope and I were married, we returned to Venice, accompanied by my mother, Nellie Beatrice, who complained of the city's sparse amenities and its mysterious lack of pubs and Mackeson's cream stout. Penelope, who made an elaborate pretence of liking her and called her 'Mum', was insistent that it would be such a good thing if 'Mum' could be shown that there were other horizons beyond Margate and more enriching alternatives to the Laundry's Day Out on the coach.

My own mock forbearance, as so often, provided me with scope for manoeuvre I might not have been able to exploit had we been alone together. Roving Posh Paper critic, hitched to muddle-headed but acceptable playwright, having drilled lovable old working-class Mum into the cross-over family-shared experience of a publess town, might be put off by the simple bureaucratic difficulties of dragging her unwillingly to the next Resnais or Truffaut press showing. Old Mum's reluctance would give me an excuse to stay away.

One afternoon, after lunch at the Fenice, when old Nellie Beatrice had demanded to know the price of every dish so that she could compare it with her remembrance of the wartime bill at the Strand Palace Corner House, we were on our way back to the hotel. Quite suddenly, Penelope made a crabwise leap through the crowds outside St Mark's and disappeared. For once, I reacted fairly quickly. 'Wait here,' I said to Nellie Beatrice, black-looked and sweating irritably. One of the advantages of being an Englishman in Italy, and certainly in the Basilica, is that you can see above the heads of everyone else.

I shoved my way through the final set of doors leading into the church, looked down the nave and spotted Penelope's copper head bobbing above a sprawling ruck of gawpers and church officials. Everywhere there were signs in five languages requesting ladies not to enter with bare arms or uncovered heads. Penelope had sprinted down the nave bereft of necessary covering. She was tackled by several vergers like a pack of floor-waiters arresting a shoplifter in the food hall. Caught up in the crush were dozens of sightseers, all bawling in the full throat of American panic.

Mercifully, a cool, calm, mid-Western voice could be heard. 'Come on, my dear. Can't you see? There are notices everywhere. You have to cover your head inside this beautiful place.' 'Go and fuck yourself.' 'Come my dear, you must be reasonable. It isn't much to ask of you. Here, cover yourself with this.' A scarf was thrust under her nose. 'Fuck off. Fuck off. All of you.' By this time she was in the grasp of five panting officials of the Basilica, who looked like frog-marching her through the crowd. 'Now, be reasonable, my dear. Surely you can read. It's only ordinary politeness . . .' 'Fuck off, all of you.'

Like the firemen who had raced through Woodfall Street to snatch Mary from my side, I plunged through a cordon of people some twenty deep, grabbed Penelope's bare upper arm and wrenched her from the grasp of the Basilica's men. In the Piazza, Nellie Beatrice looked on almost approvingly as I dragged Penelope towards the safety of the Inghilterra.

Stoneleigh

My dear John,

I promised to drop you a few lines, after I got home made a cup of tea and went to bed as usual thinking of all the nice things there were instilled in my mind. First thank you for my nice lunch and drinkies – also for helping to put right the mess I got myself into through misunderstandings.

How right you were when you said I was wicked. I have known this for a long time, and selfish and self-pitying, you have only confirmed what my brother told me long ago: but I was too much of a coward to admit it this afternoon. There is no crime in being any of these things. It's beyond my control to adjust myself. I have tried – its failed, so please don't ask me to do the impossible. The truth is I'm afraid, *really afraid*; and must face up to my own selfish stupidity and fight this out alone. Somehow. I ask for no forgiveness or make any excuse for my bad behaviour. You come from fine stock, The Osbornes, gentle – sweet and kind: hold on to these . . .

Dear John,

I know how you feel towards me: and you have reason to dislike me so – and I have never been much of a Mother; and so only deserve and to know how you have felt towards me for a long time now. I make no excuses; only ask you not to be bad friends. I feel terribly sad and unhappy but I deserve to be. Please try to forgive me. I think I have been punished enough. I am not self-pitying myself its the guilt that lays within that makes me realize what a horrible person I have been and am.

My dear,

How are you: I think of you so much. I don't blame you for hating me so much for the hurt I have caused you. I *hate* myself too; believe me – I have suffered so much. I'm nearly going mad knowing that you have cut me out of your life. Please John I beg of you to help me in my great distress, I know it is unforgiveable, and it is a big thing to ask of you . . .

My dear dearest John,

What a relief to get your letter. Oh God so understanding, how rotten can a mother feel. My dear boy I feel so dreadful, you will never know how cheap: selfish to know I treated you so cruelly I cannot offer any excuses. It's unbelievable one's utter selfish and cruel temper. I have indeed suffered and quite rightly too, John, nearly gone mad thinking what for God sake have I done to hurt you so much. I can't ask you to forgive me, it is too much to expect for the cruel treatment I have given you. Moods are so hard and difficult to explain. I hardly know what to say to your kind and sad letter. I am now crying. Oh dear God do understand and believe I do not mean to hurt you: it just boils down to the truth lets face it: I am and feel the most horrible creature alive cheap and low: here I am living on luxury by your brains and in return you receive such cruel and unkind treatment. It sounds so dam stupid and does not make sense. Hughie Green was on television last night. He was out in India and showed us the picture of a beautiful temple. He said it was the loveliest thing he had ever seen. I thought of you . . .

Your loving,
Mother

24. Crimson Twilight

Voltaire, who was in a torment of envy for the universal esteem in which Congreve was held by men of all parties, felt irritated by the Playwright's disclaimers for his gifts as a poet of the theatre. When he had called on Congreve, the Englishman declared that his plays were trifles, produced in an idle hour, and begged Voltaire to consider him merely as a gentleman.

'If you had been merely a gentleman,' said Voltaire, 'I should not have come to see you.'

Notebook, 1957

DORN: (*alone*) I don't know, maybe I don't understand anything, maybe I've gone off my head, but I did like that play. There is something in it. When that child was holding forth about loneliness, and later when the devil's red eyes appeared, I was so moved that my hands were shaking. It was fresh, unaffected . . . Ah! I think he's coming along now. I feel like telling him a lot of nice things about it.

Dr Dorn in Anton Chekhov's *The Seagull**

Jocelyn R. met me at Nice Airport. We decided to let the evening Croisette cut-up chariot race abate a little and had a drink in the shade of the roof-terrace bar. We were pleased to see each other. She said not a word of reproach, implying that she had enjoyed having La Beaumette to herself without the daily flood of letters from Penelope.

I was able to relate news from the Rialto, quite literally, and provide her with a few choice ends of gossip which gladdened the eager spite we shared towards certain figureheads in films and journalism. I had enough malicious

*Produced by the English Stage Company at the Queen's Theatre, March 1964, directed by Tony Richardson, with a cast including Peggy Ashcroft, Ann Beach, Mark Dignam, Peter Finch, Rachel Kempson, Philip Locke, Peter McEnery, Vanessa Redgrave and George Devine as Dr Dorn.

scraps of disasters, clowning, tales of aborted narcissism and duplicity gone awry to keep her stocked with the pleasure of several weeks of dinner-party recounting. Open, ill-natured gossip was one of our devout bonds. Although much of my stay in Venice had been spent in idle hours in the bedroom at the Europa on my own, I had been too preoccupied to read the newspapers or take account of what had been going on at home. Jocelyn filled me in on the confrontation in Berlin, the Oder-Neisse line, and the prospect of imminent nuclear destruction.

It was well into the second week of September 1961 and the Committee of 100's campaign for a mass sit-down in Trafalgar Square on Sunday the 17th had been shrewdly stage-managed. The preliminary meetings I had attended were overlorded by experts in dissidence, those who would have been most at home in the days of Babylon, locked in canonical disputation and Deuteronomical intrigue among the tribes of Israel.

The beginning of the fanaticism that was to expand and impose itself on every aspect of life – from the anti-smoking lobby to animal rights – was stirring, a rabid, venomous and neurotic collection of factions, united by their frightening brand of righteous ruthlessness. I had never believed it could take such hold among my temperate, lazy-hearted countrymen.

Like many others at the time, and for many years to come, I had a sentimental, indulgent attitude towards the adherents of CND and even its militant wing. It was the popular view of a substantial minority of high-minded folk driven to unremitting extremity by their sense of helplessness in the face of the wickedness of those who had seized dominion of their lives. The familiar image was of well-humoured, peaceable folk, pushing the prams of a doomed generation and singing their gentle defiance to the accompaniment of a jolly marching jazz-band.

The reality was somewhat different. The inner heart of the movement was cynical, sophisticated and rigidly political. The simple, idealistic, apocalyptic visions it aroused among the mass of good-hearted adherents were ruthlessly engineered and exploited by professionals who were dedicated, born enemies of their own country. They used all their fanaticism and skill at arousing panic and dissatisfaction among the ranks of decent, respectable, dim liberals who were genuinely dismayed and alarmed by the way the world seemed to be heading for hideous destruction.

In the week before I returned to Valbonne, the government's alarm at the rising tide of feeling, which could no longer be ignored, began to make itself plain. Embarrassment at the revelations of incompetence on a grand scale at the George Blake trial in April and, particularly, its effect on American confidence, was still biting hard. The economic situation, grim enough at the Budget, had worsened still further during the summer. Unemployment, running at the then 'unacceptable' figure of over a million and a half, had remained static and, by mid-July, the Chancellor of the Exchequer, Mr Selwyn Lloyd, had been forced to increase taxation by £70 million before a shot had been fired on the Glorious Twelfth.

All of this was as meaningless as usual to most of us, immersed in peccadilloes at film festivals from Folkestone to Venice, but the climate of panic seemed clear to all, and it might have been this that prompted Mr Harold Macmillan to make one of his grandiose pronouncements at the end of July, that his government had decided officially to apply for full membership of the EEC. It didn't seem to have much effect on the public mood, even to those who were happily contemplating a new era of frantic common enterprise, accompanied by the civilizing influence of French cuisine and German poetry.

Nearer to the homely realities of our own lives, Tony had rung Jocelyn R. to report on the opening night of *Luther* when it transferred to the Phoenix. British Prime Ministers are not remembered for their enthusiasms for literature or drama, although Macmillan was already highly regarded as an Edwardian eccentric with his addiction to bedtime with Trollope. He seemed to have gone out of his way to be present at the opening, taking his young grandson with him. The newspapers were mystified. Was this not an unlikely gesture from a Premier burdened with the gravity of the developments in Berlin, economic pressures at home, sustained unemployment, the unease of the trade unions at his government's disputed intrusion into the negotiation of wage agreements?

Not at all, he had said to amazed reporters during the interval. Just the thing to take his grandson to see. But what about the play, Mrs Lincoln/Mr Macmillan? Written by the author of an infamous letter, damning his own countrymen? 'I thought the play was wonderful,' he said. Whether he did or not, Tony confirmed his public reaction, having been cornered by him in the bar. 'I mean, it was very weird, Jocelyn. He just went on and on very emotionally. All Johnny's old Edwardian wilderness stuff, and then the young men dying in the trenches, the dole queues, the soup-kitchens. I mean, Johnny would have loved it.'

The subsequent declaration of the government's intentions over the proposed Trafalgar Square demonstration was not so benign. A couple of forgotten mid-Victorian Acts relating specifically to public order and vagrancy had been winkled out of the statute-books and, by the invocation of these, summonses were served on several of the most prominent Committee members, including the stridently frail Chairman, Bertrand Russell, and playwrights Arnold Wesker, Robert Bolt and Christopher Logue. They had all duly appeared at Bow Street and been required to enter into recognizance not to breach the peace on the big day in question. All of them refused and were sentenced to a month in gaol in Brixton.

Jocelyn had a copy of the report of the proceedings in one of the more ponderous dailies. When I finished reading it, she said very simply and with no satisfaction, 'You'll have to go back, won't you?' Her restraint was as helpful as everything else she had said while we sat in the noise and glare of the Aeroport Côte d'Azur. 'I was hoping you'd say that,' I replied.

For once, there was no room for equivocation, which made my next act, even its physical execution, strangely easy. The following day, in the taxi from Heathrow to Lower Belgrave Street, we stopped at traffic lights beside Chesham Place, where Penelope had moved. I opened the door unhurriedly, in those days of unlocked cabs which didn't thank you for not smoking, got out and said, 'I'm sorry, my darling. I'm afraid I'm going to behave rather badly yet again.' It was odiously expressed and odiously executed. Perhaps I felt too numb even for self-disgust. I could only think of Sir Henry Irving's legendary desertion of his wife in a brougham after the first night of *The Bells*. 'Are you going on making a fool of yourself like this all your life?' Lady Irving asked him. Jocelyn might have justly repeated the question.

Meeting Penelope again in the thirtyish nastiness of her new mansion-flat was as dispiriting as joining a long bus queue in the airless mid-September heat. She seemed suddenly remote after the stifling closeness of our room at the Europa. She was not taking part in Sunday's pantomime and made dutiful noises about joining me. But I would have done my best to dissuade anyone from going near the whole ludicrous event. Her relief at being absolved was so clear that I couldn't possibly hold it against her, any more than her prepared defence of Kenneth Tynan's alibi, that he was supervising a filmed television account of this momentous event in popular British politics.

'Of course, he feels so awful,' said Penelope, 'not being in there with you and everybody else.' Sensible, crafty old Ken, I thought. They would probably cuddle up together while I spent the night in the nick. It was just enough, the way things go among the birds and flowers.

The morning of 17 September seemed very long indeed. Penelope and I slept late, until noon, but the day still seemed like early morning. There was a breathy, aluminium haze over the London sky that I couldn't remember before. Like every other reluctant bit-player that day, I assumed that within twenty-four hours I should be starting a gaol term of at least twelve months. There was no reason to think otherwise. Both government and press had made it very clear that none of us could expect any quarter and that the public was impatient to see us all dispatched and forgotten for a decent period of time and the whole incident properly contained by firm action. Ordinary, right-thinking people had been imposed upon enough by presumptious, self-advertising 'intellectuals' and other odd folk. That was indeed becoming my own view.

By one o'clock, the rain had begun to drizzle down. Of the few clothes I had brought from my Valbonne wardrobe, I laid out my raincoat and filled the pockets with packets of Cojene, for my palpitating head-glands, to smuggle somehow into the Scrubs (John Dexter would have been too spry to get caught up in this amateur nonsense), some pious small book and a half-bottle of whisky.

Penelope and I walked through Belgravia, on to Hyde Park Corner and down Piccadilly. London was not then blighted by tourists but, even so, Piccadilly Circus itself was almost empty and the resonant hum that every great city must contain at any moment of the day or night seemed to be stilled. Somewhere opposite the Garrick Theatre, we went into an empty Italian restaurant and poked at some pasta, which seemed to have been reheated repeatedly for weeks, with a bottle of Post-Office-inky wine. She went on about how 'Ken' was going to keep tabs on where I was and how I ended up. Soon we were both longing for me to go.

By 2.30, ignoring Penelope's solicitous irrelevancies, I had many times gone through in my mind the ritual mime of handing over my watch, keys, money, lowering myself into a humiliating, uncleansing bath and so on. Imprisonment seemed as inescapable as death or despair. Penelope continued to twiddle her spaghetti. I began to anticipate the pleasure of being locked up against the petty legal harassment we would both face from the newly maternal Mary and the righteously vengeful Dr Gilliatt – the naming of names, the closing in for costs. *She* would have to sort that out on her own while I was pressing shirts in the prison laundry.

With hung-over fatigue from Valbonne and Venice, I kissed her farewell in the north corner of Trafalgar Square, Sir Henry Irving keeping a watchful eye on the right, and the hopping lust of barely a fortnight earlier almost forgotten. Trafalgar Square seemed vast in expectation and emptiness. I skipped up the steps to the National Gallery. Inside, the faces upturned to the famous paintings were almost all equally famous. We were like figures in an old spy thriller. All-night companions were pretending not to recognize each other. It was a dumb-show of bizarre, conspiratorial behaviour.

I spotted the vague, unfocused stares of Bill Gaskill, Anthony Page, Lindsay Anderson, Keith Johnstone and Ann Jellicoe, and then of John Arden, John Berger, Shelagh Delaney, John Neville, Alan Sillitoe, George Melly and Vanessa Redgrave. And these were only the people I knew personally. I was beginning to wonder what my next instructions were and where they would come from. Should I be wearing a buttonhole and carrying the *Daily Telegraph*?

Then I spotted Doris Lessing poring over an Impressionist painting. I knew her a little and was extremely fond of her. She possessed an extraordinary delicacy and eroticism which touchingly discounted all her White Rhodesian liberal tedium. I knew she wouldn't disown me with a vague smile but that she would embrace me, which she did. As we joined arms and descended the steps into the Square, I felt as if I had selected a bride. I cannot think of a public entrance more cheekily stage-managed or carried off with such enjoyment. Doris looked so innocent and sweet underneath that charmless sky that I would happily have married her there on the spot. I half expected one of the chief inspectors to ask, 'Bride or groom?'

Within minutes, Doris and I were sealed off and settled in among the damp patches below Landseer's lions. A pall seemed to descend, distorting sound and sight, a very little like battle without danger, blinded and deafened without knowledge of what is happening. In the throng around us I could identify Arden, Sir Herbert Read, in his seventies and clearly suffering pain from a kidney disorder, a very worried Lady Read, Sillitoe and, somewhere beyond Doris, Vanessa. They were talking about deadlines on various commissioned works until the surrounding roar and thrust put paid to the pretence. Doris and I consigned ourselves to a mime of passionate public intimacy.

Young men in leather jackets fell on us, shouting instructions to make a thrust down Whitehall. A cry went up: 'They've got Vanessa!' I think I saw her being passed, hand over hand, like a plank, above the edges of the inner circle around the lions, and on towards a surge trying to charge its way to Downing Street. By around 6.30, the mob had made some kind of breakthrough as sounds of shouting receded. Around the lions it was comparatively quiet. Strutting pigeons had returned and, rather to my relief, most of my disconsolate companions had dispersed, including Doris. I sat it out, as instructed, and no one took the slightest notice, neither patrolling policeman nor preening pigeon.

The air seemed heavier than ever, mixed with a sickly sense of torpor and anticlimax. It only needed more rain to make the remnants of the demonstration even more despondent. The clamorous folly of it all, the gritty pounding of my eyeballs and an enormous thirst tempted me to walk away. But I decided against it. Arrest seemed certain, but I'd no wish to precipitate it. The police were busy rounding up the hard-liners at the front. They would leave the defeated core for the time being. I settled down with the half-bottle of whisky I had rather meanly kept in reserve for myself.

The glum consensus in the Royal Court barracks, before we showed our colours, had been that we could all expect to be treated much more severely than the unfortunate Wesker, Bolt and Logue. If they had been sent down for a mere month, it was certain that the Heavy Brigade could expect no mercy from Macmillan's merry magistrates and were assured of a minimum of six months. Did one get remission on such a short sentence? I tried to remember if Dexter had served his full term. I might even find myself up before the theatrical-hating Sir Laurence Dunne, VC, who had dismissed George's testimony to John's good character with such Hogarthian loathing.

My speculations became gloomier as I swigged the whisky. I thought of poor Oscar being jeered on the platform of Clapham Junction on his way to the treadmill at Reading Gaol. Sodomy began to seem genuinely brave, even romantic, compared to sitting down wanly on a wet London pavement. I lay beside the lions, growing chilled in my thin south-of-France finery, my thigh-bones bruised from the damp stone, wondering how I – with the pride of my cold view of simple faiths – could ever have let myself be gulled as any other fat-headed seeker after true happiness. I made an almost formal vow to myself never to do so again.

By the time I heard the midnight chimes from St Martin-in-the-Fields, the effects of the whisky and ten hours without food had brought me to that condition of near narcosis which I used to induce to persuade myself that I was not actually taking part in something disagreeable, like a double period of maths, a bad play or an aircraft flight. It was all happening to someone else. I was fading into a buzz when I heard a voice over my head.

'Mr Osborne?' I saw an extremely dapper police superintendent wearing gleaming leather gloves and sporting a silver-headed cane under his arm like an RSM pausing on parade. 'Mr Osborne?' The voice was quiet and polite. 'Yes.' I began to raise myself up, until I was lifted with careful firmness by about half a dozen silent constables. I had the pleasant sensation of being gently suspended and carried away. Looking up at the stars, I felt mild irritation at having been disturbed, however discreetly, and then a flood of relief. When should I look up at the stars again?

I heard a voice, surely Alan Sillitoe's. 'They've got John.' It was Alan. Other voices, friendly and excited, took up the cry. 'They've got John! Good luck, John. Good old John.' As an exit, it was a very exhilarating curtain-call. After fifty yards of being borne up like Hamlet on the stage at Hayling Island, only more expertly, we reached a waiting police van and I was lowered to the ground as carefully as I had been lifted. 'Now, Mr Osborne, do you want us to put you in the van or will you walk into it?' I struggled with cramp. 'Oh, I'll walk. Certainly.' I clambered into the empty van and they left me, the doors still wide open. Perhaps Mr Macmillan had enjoyed the play after all.

I waited for twenty minutes, when some policemen arrived with more arrests, young men, kicking and yelling. They refused to 'walk' aboard and each landed with a hefty thump on the floor beside me. I huddled in the shadows. They were full of pretty-fair hatred for the rest of the world, peace-lovers or not. I tried to will myself into a further trance. The police returned with more struggling passive-resisters and threw them in a heap among us. When the van was full, the door slammed and we moved off at speed.

Past a few streets, and we were bundled aboard a waiting coach with other detainees. For the next hour or so, we stopped off at police stations all over the West End as a few weary protestors were led off to be charged and booked for the night. It must have been around dawn before we drew up in a tiny street at the back of John Lewis. The station looked like a rather cosy Victorian cottage with a dinky blue gas-lamp outside.

I found myself standing beside John Calder, the distinguished English publisher of Samuel Beckett. He looked as grim and dour as I felt myself. Inside it was not so pretty, and the police at the desk were tired and bad-tempered after a leave-cancelled weekend. When I had been booked, I was shoved into a windowless cell. Again, I was happily alone. There was nothing on the extremely cold floor, so I bunched up my raincoat once more and tried to sleep.

Presently, there was a great deal of scuffle outside, the door opened and three or four wild-looking men were shoved with extreme force into the cell. They shouted abuse at our captors through the door. They spat out eyewitness accounts of monstrous acts of police brutality past and present. Their credentials as veteran peace-protestors were immaculate. As their professional euphoria wore off and a tiny sliver of light appeared, peace-loving grunts and snores rumbled in the shadows. They were all in their early twenties, wearing expensive leather items. They looked like a group of Millwall supporters, tired out from a happy afternoon smashing up the away team.

The door was opened at about nine o'clock. By this time, my tongue was clamped to my palate and I asked the desk sergeant if I might have a cup of traditional police-station tea. His expression implied that I had possibly committed a further chargeable offence. I didn't press it. I glanced at his copy of the *Daily Express*. It was headlined in huge type: '1,140 ARRESTED INCLUDING JOHN OSBORNE [top billing], FENNER BROCKWAY, VANESSA REDGRAVE, SHELAGH DELANEY AND CANON COLLINS TOO . . . THE WEARY POLICE VICTORIOUS AND NELSON DEEP IN DEBRIS.' No wonder I didn't merit a cup of orange-coloured tea.

I was finally disgorged into a huge room below the court in Bow Street. To my dismay, Oscar Beuselinck came waddling over, with his clerk, Charlie Barwick, beside him. Trying to look grave, his familiar vindictive manner made me instantly suspicious. 'Just plead guilty, son. Just plead guilty.' Twenty-four hours spent on stone surfaces had eroded my patience. 'What else would I do, you cunt.' 'Come now, come now, language,' he rebuked in his avuncular voice. 'You're in a police court now.' 'No, I'm not. I'm in a fucking police cell.' He looked around as if he expected me to be arrested and charged all over again.

I found myself speedily in the dock before I had to suffer much more of Oscar's puffed-up gravity. The magistrate, Mr Bertram Reece, looked more like Rob Wilton's music-hall magistrate, Mr Muddlecombe, than a Hogarthian bully. 'This is a court of justice, not a court of politics,' he muttered amiably. Within minutes my turn came and I pleaded guilty.

Mr Reece smiled at me over his half-lenses, like any competent character actor. 'Fined. Twenty shillings.'

25. Bad, Sad and Mad

> We loved, sir – used to meet;
> How sad and bad and mad it was –
> But then, how it was sweet.
> > Robert Browning, 'A Death in the Desert'

> I tell you, hopeless grief is passionless.
> > Elizabeth Barrett Browning, *Sonnets* – 'Grief'

> Sir: – The *Daily Telegraph* was always a footman's paper. Since its
> amalgamation with the *Morning Post* it seems to have progressed as far
> as 'What the Butler Saw'.
> > Nancy Harrison, Dulwich (letter to the *Spectator*, 13 October 1961)

Earlier in that summer, on a stifling day just after *Luther* opened at the
Court, Jocelyn R. and I drove down to Sussex in the open-topped Alvis,
buzzing with morning hope, clear sky and sunshine. I was intent on finding
a place in the country where I could spend most of my time and work
without hindrance. I felt that even an hour's drive away from London
would discourage people assuming access to my life. Up to a point, I was
right. I knew that the ultimate decision of where to park my bones permanently in England would probably take years of searching to achieve. When I
asked John Betjeman to suggest the most perfect resting place, he snapped
back with utmost seriousness and good faith, 'Middlesex.'

Fired by the symbolic attributes of having acquired Frink's Harbinger
Bird, I was convinced that somewhere, in the no-man's present, I would
find a place that would be more than a temporary refuge against all the
froth, sham and enmity that had pursued me for the past few years. I had no
clear idea of whether Jocelyn or anyone else should want to share it with me.
I craved solitude but I didn't want to be alone.

I remembered that Vivien Leigh's last retreat had been Tickerage Mill, at
Blackboys in Sussex, only about five miles from another mill-house which I

had seen advertised. The Old Water Mill at Hellingly, near Hailsham, just off the main Eastbourne road, was about an hour and a half's drive from London. It was attractive enough for my purposes, within my West End playwright's grasp at a price of £10,000, and Jocelyn, whether or not she was considering the likelihood of moving in with me, was enthusiastic about its possibilities.

The property was contained within a few acres of fairly wild but tameable garden and enclosed by two running streams of the River Cuckmere. The main house was small and mid-Victorian, with a happy, reassuring feel about it even though it was functioning as a simple boarding-house for stray geriatrics. There was a cluster of outbuildings – always a special attraction to unpropertied townies like myself – that included an eleventh-century mill recorded in Domesday Book which had been active up until the early thirties, a large, unused granary and a rather twee little cottage by the mill-race. They could all be easily and modestly converted.

I immediately rang Beuselinck and tried to impress on him that the security of my immediate future depended on his instantly acquiring the Old Water Mill for me without any petty lawyer's haggling. By the end of the month, and to my great surprise at having my simple wishes executed so swiftly, contracts were exchanged, the owners moved out, the place was empty, waiting and my own.

Penelope's choice of a flat in Chesham Place as what journalists like to call a 'love-nest' was not a happy one. Its Belgravia location alone confirmed the squalor of the course in which we had trapped ourselves. I was anxious to clear my presence from Jocelyn in Lower Belgrave Street, and Penelope was yearning for her portion of the Gilliatt library in Lowndes Square, her small wardrobe and the tools of her voracious trade.

Within a week of the Trafalgar Square sit-down we had made arrangements with Jocelyn and Roger to extricate both our lives and simple props from their own. Jocelyn took herself off for the afternoon while my secretary and her husband stripped Lower Belgrave Street of my books and few belongings. Reluctantly, I then accompanied Penelope to an empty Lowndes Square where she went through her own larger and more disputed inventory.

Anthony Creighton had borrowed a small van from one of his fellow late-night workers at the Chiswick telephone exchange. Penelope and I spent hours puffing up and down the adulterous stairway of Lowndes Square, clutching her collection of review copies, and thankfully filled the van before Dr Gilliatt returned, when he would most surely have contested her claims of total ownership. By the time she had finished, the flat looked whiter, more Swedish and too bare to be habitable without a great deal of refurnishing and book-buying. It was almost midnight. Anthony went on ahead in the van with his driver-telephonist companion and, after a reviving hour of drinks at Chesham Place, Penelope and I set off for Sussex in her new, snappy Triumph Herald.

As is usually the case with the mere mechanics of this kind of strategic withdrawal and domestic disintegration, the dreaded process had proved more swift, simple, almost satisfying, than anyone could have hoped. Penelope drove through the night, showing off her pointless double-declutching skills, and we arrived at Hellingly in a mood of triumphant relief at our nimble resourcefulness.

This was immediately dispelled as we nosed into the narrow lane that was the only approach to the house. Our path was blocked by dozens of cars; we were dazzled by battalions of light from all directions. Had we suddenly come upon a huge film-crew engaged in an ambitious night set-up? Figures and faces advanced on the little roadster. Hemmed in by cameras, microphones, flashlights, notebooks, we stumbled our way across the creaky, narrow bridge that straddled the stream beside the Mill. We were pelted with questions by a couple of dozen reporters and cameramen. Having only visited the place once before on a blazing afternoon, I was just able to guide Penelope to what I remembered as the back door.

The house seemed drab, deserted and much smaller than my dim recollection of it. When we stumbled into the kitchen, all the doors and curtainless windows were open. Every room seemed to have been invaded by shouting, joking journalists. Anthony reeled towards us like a drunken host welcoming a pair of deprived late-comers. He had invited the press unit inside and they had gratefully presented him with cases of drink which they were all joyfully knocking back downstairs, upstairs in the geriatrics' bedrooms and in shadowy corners of the garden. It took the better part of an hour to persuade, cajole and bully his guests from the house and then the garden and, finally, the lane. We managed to avoid saying anything, and least of all 'no comment', to the hundreds of light-hearted enquiries after our health, domestic intentions, personal and professional plans for the future.

I would have lost my temper with Anthony, but he was soon blissfully collapsed in the protective arms of some equally sodden hack. When the last car sprinted away up the pitted lane and the morning light began to show up the dirt and debris on the floorboards, the stained markings of pictures past on the walls, Penelope and I were left feeling equally soiled and derelict, as if we had been burgled, defiled and humiliated.

I half expected her to make a crablike Lucia di Lammermoor descent down the bare, creaking stairwell, presaging her mad dash to the altar of St Mark's. Her eyes were flecked black beneath the bare light-bulbs. Perhaps the sheer volume of pressing hysteria had restrained her own. We retrieved an old blanket to shield the upstairs window of a room containing an abandoned mattress. We dropped down on it and fell asleep.

Shortly, we woke, fully clothed and shivering in the smoky light of a late September day. Piled up with tea-chests and scattered piles from the Lowndes Square library, the otherwise empty, unheated rooms were stung with the first winter chill. Sidling up to the windows, like holed-up gang-sters in a remake of a classic French movie, we peered out. Dozens of cars and vans had returned, scattered all over the lawn. Reporters and cameramen were wandering through the garden or lolling beside the stream.

Anthony's press party had re-established itself during our short bout of unconsciousness. Having discovered Penelope's hoard of coffee, he was already busy in the kitchen greeting his guests through the window. Blessed with a toxin-proof head as impenetrable as Christopher Isherwood's or Robert Stephens's, he had shaved with great care and sprinkled himself with Old Spice. He was as skittish and lively as he must have been playing one of Terry Rattigan's famous fairies in *Boys in Blue* during the war.

There seemed little to be done except keep out of eye-line and make sure that we had enough food and drink to get through the day. Most urgently, Penelope needed the assurance of seeing her byline in the *Observer*. Only Anthony could run the gauntlet thrown round us. He was more than eager to do so, having scored a huge personal success, as he saw it, which over-shadowed all the triviality of my own marital mess. Having sworn him to speak to no one, not even the most godlike young reporter, I sent him off down the lane with a fistful of money and instructions to buy all the news-papers, cigarettes, two bottles of whisky for us and a bottle of gin for himself.

A couple of hours later he returned, explaining that he had dropped in at a nice little place down the road called The Wheatsheaf, where he had been obliged to have a couple of drinks with a few chaps who were actually quite decent and hated hanging around and being a nuisance but had a job to do, however much they disliked it. One of them, like himself, had been in Bomber Command and had also flown Halifaxes.

For the next few days, indeed weeks, life was once again measured out in column-inches rather than coffee-spoons. There was an odd compulsion to read them, not from squeamish vanity but to find out what we had apparently been up to. That first Sunday, it was spelled out that every movement we had made during the past twenty-four hours had been observed and noted down for what the Press Council had just announced a 'Warrant of Public Right'. Anthony Creighton's van had been followed, the Triumph Herald had been followed and an inventory had been compiled of goods removed from assorted residences around Belgravia. It could hardly have interested those that read it, and probably not even those who recorded it.

The following Friday, 29 September, Cyril Ray in the *Spectator* and Francis Williams in the *New Statesman*, gurus to the cleverer classes, made things clear about the press handling of a case of commonplace adultery. What emerged, to those who might care, was the louche behaviour of the footman's newspaper. Mr Ray, although himself of the Left, summed up for the Right:

> When I refer to the sensational gossip-mongering papers, let it be clear as to which they are. The *Daily Express* gave the story seventy-nine lines and one single-column photograph of the lady concerned, and the *Daily Mail* gave it sixty-nine lines, a similar single-column picture and a small photograph of Mr Osborne. The *Daily Telegraph* gave it 162 lines on its middle page, opposite the leading articles, a bigger picture of Mr Osborne (across two columns) and one of the lady.
>
> I have always thought that one measure of a newspaper's dignity is whether *any* of its stories could have been undertaken by *any* member of its staff without his feeling ashamed of himself and his calling. I wonder how the *Telegraph*'s editor or political correspondent, say, would have liked to hang around Mr Osborne's house, asking him impertinent questions about his marriage that elicited the answer, 'I do not wish to discuss these matters,' and about his friendship with another lady which forced him to say that, 'All I want is some peace and quiet.' I cannot believe that the high-minded Peter Simple would have enjoyed chasing the unhappy lady in question from cab rank to railway station or that the urbane Peterborough would have relished snooping around Mrs Osborne's front door, making an inventory of the furniture that was being removed. I should have thought that a paper with the *Telegraph*'s pretensions to gentility would have hesitated before exposing even the lowliest of its staff to having to report that he was told, 'She doesn't want to talk to you. Nor do I. Now go away.'

The Spectator's readers the following week joined in:

> Sir: – Cyril Ray's sneer at the *Daily Telegraph* is not justifiable. John Osborne has recently sought, and obtained, wide publicity for a virulent attack on the morals of his fellow-countrymen. For a proper evaluation of his opinions, it is a matter of public interest that his own morals should be under equally close scrutiny.
>
> W.I.D. Scott, Chester

> Sir: – The gossip-mongering papers, which Cyril Ray had the courage to list, have now stooped to a new level of prying that almost defies satire. It brings to mind Oscar Wilde's comment: 'In centuries before ours the public nailed the ears of journalists to the pump. That was quite hideous. In this century journalists have nailed their own ears to the keyhole; that is much worse.'
>
> B.R. Jones, Chelsea

More surprising was the spirited response of that week's *New Statesman*, which, apart from Cuthbert Worsley's schoolmasterly critical attentions, had always ignored my existence:

> The *Sunday Pictorial* [tame equivalent of today's *Sun*] was the first to answer the call of 'the public right'. Determined that no one should be able to accuse it of being 'faithless to its trust', it announced on its front page in large white type on a black background, 'John Osborne and Friend in Mystery Midnight Move'. This was flanked by a four-column picture of 'Playwright John Osborne and his wife Mary' and a two-column picture of 'Dr Roger Gilliatt and his wife Penelope'. 'John Osborne, Britain's bomb-squatting playwright, has made a sudden moonlight move from London to his new country home down by an old mill by the stream in Sussex.'
>
> The story by *Pictorial* reporters opened dramatically. 'Just after midnight yesterday, he drove down to Hellingly in Sussex accompanied by a beautiful woman in a light coat'. He was, 'a dark-haired woman who said she was Mr Osborne's secretary' explained, in a phrase that deserves to go down in history, moving from London 'to get away from all the publicity'. He evidently misjudged the high ideals of public service that animate Fleet Street; he should read *The World of Paul Slickey* some time. The *Pictorial* was on his tail.
>
> Indeed, it seems to have had reporters lurking behind every third lamppost for hours while fast cars stood by. At all events, every move-

ment of Mr Osborne, his secretary, Mr Anthony Creighton (his friend) and a small removal van were watched by *Pictorial* men, who followed the van in a fast car. Eventually they reached the Old Water Mill, where their vigil was rewarded: 'An hour later, Mr Osborne drove up. With him in his hard-topped sports car was the beautiful woman wearing a light coat.' End of First Episode . . .

So that was what had happened.

. . . On Monday the story was taken up in the *Daily Mirror*, the *Daily Express* and the *Daily Mail* and, somewhat surprisingly, the *Daily Telegraph*. One had tended, apparently wrongly, to assume that the *Telegraph* governed its affairs by somewhat different standards. Not so. Only *The Times* and the *Guardian* took the strange view that the private life of a well-known playwright is his own affair and not a matter for hour-by-hour journalists playing the part of disreputable private detectives.

The *Mirror* took up where the *Pictorial* left off. By Thursday Mr Osborne and Mr Creighton were finally persuaded to appear . . .

Thank God, in his enthusiasm for the venture, Anthony had forgotten to pack his kilt.

. . .'I have nothing at all to say,' said Osborne, 'and neither has Mrs Gilliatt. Now go away.' Go away indeed. Hadn't he heard about the freedom of the press? Who does the man think he is? Neither the *Telegraph* nor the others were prepared to stand for this sort of nonsense. The *Telegraph* man spoke out straight and proper for the right of the press to poke its nose where it wishes. 'I asked him', he proudly informed *Telegraph* readers, 'about the future of his marriage'. Also, 'had Mrs Gilliatt left her husband?' Osborne – an uncooperative man if ever there was one – while remaining polite but firm (why he should have been polite I do not know) – actually refused to answer. If he is not careful he will be making an enemy of the press.

No doubt the Press Council will in due course explain to us the 'warrant of public right as distinguished from public curiosity' that governed this operation. I can only say that this seems to me to be one of the most disreputable and degrading examples of what passes in some parts of Fleet Street for newspaper enterprise I have come across in years. I consider the editors, news editors and reporters involved showed themselves in this matter a disgrace to journalism. I should like to think that in due course they will feel a little ashamed themselves. But that, I am afraid, is too much to hope.

28 SEPTEMBER: The entrenched guardians of press freedom and purveyors of news to footmen of the gentry were startled by the appearance of a demonstration by local residents outside the Old Water Mill.

During the morning a car drew up, driven by Captain Vivian Hancock-Nunn. Major Colin de Vere Gordon-MacLean may have felt unable to put Simla into quarantine in order to join him, but the captain was accompanied by his wife, Mrs Eileen Hancock-Nunn, who was described as a 'prominent Sussex personality' residing at Lealands, Hellingly. Also with them in the car was Mr Fred Livingstone, a scientific and technical writer, together with his wife, Mrs Florence Livingstone, of South Lodge, Lealands.

Led by the 'snuff-taking' Mr Livingstone, each produced large placards in a dignified demonstration before the front gate. The placards, displayed for the benefit of the photographers present, read: 'DAMN YOU OSBORNE', 'HELLINGLY'S ANGRY OLD MEN OBJECT' and 'HELLINGLY WANTS MARY URE.'

Mrs Hancock-Nunn, whose placard supported Mary Ure, told reporters, 'I think a man who says "Damn You England" deserves anything.' Mrs C.C. Brunning, of Little Gates, Hellingly, wholeheartedly agreed with her. They had planned to sit down in the road but decided against it, although Mrs Brunning had brought a raincoat just in case. Mr Livingstone added that they were in a public place, were entitled to protest and were prepared to call the police. Then they climbed back into their cars and drove off.

4 OCTOBER: One or two newspapers report that Robert Shaw – Dan Tempest of the television series *The Buccaneers* – 'is being cited in the divorce petition being brought against Mary Ure by her husband, John Osborne. Mr Shaw is in New York, where he is about to open in Harold Pinter's *The Caretaker*.'

Two days later, the *New Daily* comments, 'How little the newspapers know about Osborne's life is shown by the fact that it is he who has filed a petition for divorce against his wife, citing Robert Shaw.'

13 OCTOBER: Only the *Scottish Daily Mail* carries the story that Robert Shaw – old Dan Dare – has become a father for the fourth time. His wife, Jennifer, has given birth to a daughter in Charing Cross Hospital.

14 OCTOBER: Mary Ure flies to Philadelphia with her seven-week-old baby, Colin, and a nurse. She is travelling under an assumed name, 'Mrs Fisher',

and is met at the airport by a cordon of photographers. Asked why she has come to America, she replies, 'For a rest.' Refusing to say if she would be meeting Robert Shaw, she came out of the airport alone, leaving the baby with its nurse, and leaped into a taxi which took her to an hotel. After two hours, she left in a black, chauffeur-driven car, headed towards New York.

26 OCTOBER: Tony Richardson announces Woodfall Film's £500,000 production of Henry Fielding's *Tom Jones*, which he'd read at Oxford. It seems a wonderful opportunity to get away from the kitchen sink and a chance to work with friends, practically a Royal Court camp.

1 NOVEMBER: Mary Ure reveals her intention to reply to allegations of her adultery and will defend the suit.

11 NOVEMBER: Dr Roger Gilliatt files a petition against his wife, Penelope, citing John Osborne as co-respondent.

18 NOVEMBER: John Osborne best man at Oscar Beuselinck's wedding.

30 NOVEMBER: John Osborne and Penelope Gilliatt, attending the Acapulco Film Festival with actresses Mary Peach, Billie Whitelaw and Diane Cilento, are photographed on the beach. A cameraman from the *Daily Express* attempts to punch Mrs Gilliatt.

2 DECEMBER: Mary Ure cross-petitions, alleging Osborne's adultery with three women and denying that he is not the father of her child.

8 DECEMBER: After an investigation into John Osborne's friendship with Mrs Gilliatt, *Tribune* declares: 'It would be difficult to think of any more impertinent and disgraceful intrusion into the private life of two individuals than the pursuit of these two people by certain gallant gentlemen of Fleet Street.'

And then the *New Statesman*, again: 'These stories were unique even in the annals of popular slime for their piling up of detail and in their reports of every movement of the two individuals to whom it had been decided to give the full treatment.'

10 DECEMBER: Osborne, returning from New York and unaware of the existing strike by technicians, appears on the arts programme *Tempo* and is immediately expelled from Equity.

25 DECEMBER: My mother comes to stay at Hellingly with Penelope, her sister Angela and myself for Christmas.

Laurence Olivier rings up from Brighton to ask us over for a drink in Royal Crescent, where he and Joan have just moved. I use Nellie Beatrice, whom he has met once, as an excuse not to go. He won't hear of it, and insists we bring 'Mum' along.

During the celebrations, he opens a huge jar of the most luscious, oily caviare. I watch Nellie Beatrice as she takes a portion from him. Instead of refusing it politely, she executes a dextrous mime, watched by all, and Joan in particular, during which she slowly and slyly deposits a creamy black stream of finest Beluga on to the newly laid, purple-pristine carpet.

She slowly grinds it in with sole and heel. The Oliviers watch this performance with well-mannered horror. Nellie Beatrice enlivens the whole pantomime by looking down at the lake-sized stain and blaming Penelope's sister. The Oliviers will remind me of the incident for another decade.

31 DECEMBER: A more than usually large number of public figures seem to have died. They include Gary Cooper, Peter Dawson, George Formby, Bransby Williams, Thomas Beecham, Ernest Thesiger, Percy Grainger. All of them had some special meaning for me. And then, of course, there were others who left a resonance of one kind or another: Hemingway, Moss Hart, Jung, Augustus John and James Thurber, whom I used to talk to in the lift at the Algonquin.

Worse, 1961 had seen the introduction of the New English Bible. It had condemned even 1 Corinthians 13 as irrelevant 'to modern minds and a changing world':

> Though I speak with the tongues of men and of angels, and have not charity, I am become as sounding brass, or a tinkling cymbal. And though I have the gift of prophecy, and understand all mysteries, and all knowledge; and though I have all faith, so that I could remove mountains, and have not charity, I am nothing.

No longer. So much for the marvel of language.

In the New Year, Penelope and I took a flat in Hertford Street, around the corner from Woodfall's offices in Curzon Street, while the builders made Hellingly habitable.

26. Then Whom Have I Offended?

And I will put enmity between thee and the woman, and between thy seed and her seed; it shall bruise thy head, and thou shalt bruise his heel.

Genesis 3:15

I am troubled; I am bowed down greatly; I go mourning all the day long . . . I am feeble and sore broken: I have roared by reason of the disquietness of my heart . . . My lovers and my friends stand aloof from my sore; and my kinsmen stand afar off. They also that seek after my life lay snares for me: and they that seek my hurt speak mischievous things, and imagine deceits all the day long.

Psalm 38:6–12

I believe the notion of a 'love-nest', so beloved of Fleet Street's hackettes, was first coined during a sexual scandal involving America's President Harding. I had always coveted one, ever since I heard the phrase as a young boy. My image of it had been quite precise. It was subterranean and windowless, with child-size furniture, a huge open fire and a patchwork bed. The floors billowed with brightly coloured eiderdowns for bare feet to tread. It was eternally tea-time, and vague doctors-and-nurses games went on all day in this enchanting Mrs Tiggywinkle whore-house.

The service flat Penelope and I rented in Hertford Street was, alas, not like that. It was built and furnished in tawdriest fifties style, the kind of place where lesser executives from the North-Western Area branch would reel back with a hostess after a night at a Shirley Bassey cabaret. The wife would be propping up the cocktail bar alone in the lounge of her ranch-style home in a select suburb of Walsall.

What we remember is what we become. What we have forgotten is more kindly and disturbs only our dreams. We become resemblances of our past. So Sam Beckett appears as an ancient bird, like the one in the Apocryphal

Book of Tobit, who dropped a good large mess in the eye of those who
dared to look upwards to heaven. Perhaps it was the onset of a new pattern
of daily constraints and fresh habits, but the events that took place after we
moved into the Love-Nest remain with me very clearly.

We had only just begun to test the novelty when Tony Richardson rang
me early one evening from Lower Mall. He sounded openly distressed, a
most unusual concession to plain dealing. He was also, just as rarely, almost
incoherent. What became evident was that he and Goestschius, the American sociologist and genial guru with whom he shared a flat overlooking the
river, had just had a violent clash of wills. I knew that he was most unlikely
to confide any of the details, but I was relieved and flattered that he had
been constrained to ask for my practical assistance.

Did I know of anywhere he could stay? 'I mean immediately, now, this
moment!' His insistence was so urgent and as he was such a profligate spirit,
I wondered why he didn't take the most obvious course and book into a
hotel. I hesitated. The Walsall executive's love-nest would surely make
Tony's lip curl up like a goosed caterpillar. Yet the sudden helplessness of
his appeal was so insistent. 'Well, there *is* a spare room here, but it's tiny and
I don't think you'd care for it. It's pretty tawdry.' 'That sounds absolutely
marvellous. I'll be half an hour.' And he was. I had a drink ready for him
from our own cocktail cabinet, a huge, glistening affair like a mini cinema
organ. He was seemingly unaware of the hideousness of the room. He
didn't confide in me any further and went around the corner to Woodfall's
offices.

During the days that followed, Penelope and I scarcely saw Tony for
more than a few minutes, although we would hear him return late at night
and crash into the bed in the room beside our own. He was always an early
riser and usually left in the morning before we were awake. I expected him
to move on soon, for both room and bed were very small and scarcely
comfortable. However, he continued to come and go mysteriously. One
Wednesday, after Penelope's last midweek film screening – most probably a
compelling study of peasant passion in pre-revolutionary Slovenia – we
decided to brave the draughts, noise and discomforts imposed by the
builders and spend a long weekend at the Old Water Mill, this time without
the company of Anthony and his new-found Fleet Street admirers.

When we returned early on Monday morning, in time for Penelope's
next weekly offerings from the Art of Film, the morose porter was waiting
at Hertford Street. 'Oh, Mr Osborne, I must ask you to accompany me
upstairs to your flat.' He sounded like a police inspector going through the

official proceedings before making an arrest. 'And *Mrs* Osborne, of course.' He knew full well that she wasn't. We followed him into the lift and ascended the three flights to our perch, where the front door was open and the housekeeper was waiting with buckets, mops and an assortment of cleaning equipment.

'Mr and Mrs Osborne have returned,' the porter boomed. 'I should like you to take a look at your flat . . . before witnesses.' We went in. The reason for all this gravity and preamble was plain. There was undeniable evidence of concerted damage of a rather haphazard nature, obviously not executed with the vindictive fury of a frustrated burglar.

'Allow me to show you,' he said, pointing a finger in the direction of the debris. A pane had been smashed in the French windows; a length of curtain was hanging loosely as if a chimpanzee had gone for a swing. The ugly iron-framed glass dining-table was chipped and cushions were scattered everywhere, some stained with a murky coffee-like substance. There were cigarette burns on the uncut-moquette of the drab three-piece suite, and a G-plan coffee-table had collapsed. Bottles of Cutty Sark and Moët et Chandon were strewn around, some of them half-full. In the kitchen there was similar chaos. The porter ushered us solemnly into the small bedroom. It looked as if it had been serviced by a tribe of Sumo wrestlers. Our own room was quite untouched.

He finally pointed to his prize exhibit, several piles of juicy dog-shit. 'Well, Mr Osborne?' 'We've been away since Wednesday.' 'I know, I know.' 'Burglars?' 'Burglars! Burglars with *small* dogs?' As a professional dog-walker, he doubtless knew about this kind of thing. 'I tell you, Mr Osborne. This is an inside job.' He was beginning to grow slightly hysterical. 'There has been an orgy in this flat. Most definitely an orgy.' He pronounced the word with a hard 'g', which for some reason made it seem very funny.

I decided that polite sympathy, some indignation and a small bribe were necessary or he would detain us all day. I made puzzled noises, offered – naturally – to pay for the damage, and slipped him £20. Penelope went off to her movie and I began to clear up the wreckage. Going into Tony's bedroom, I noticed that all over the sheets and scattered among the pillows was a large quantity of hairpins. Tony's favourite brand of whisky was Cutty Sark, but he never smoked. The flat had indeed become a love-nest, and a very soiled one. And what about the little dog?

Later that morning, I called in at Curzon Street. Oscar Lewenstein was bleating anxiously about my tardiness in delivering the full *Tom Jones* script and Tony's foot was wagging furiously behind his desk. It had quite a punch. I decided to ask no questions. But I was still intrigued about the hairpins. In Acapulco, Tony had shared a room with Diane Cilento. He had been greatly taken with her for a long time, insisting on a general deference to her. I very much liked her broken-glass Aussie coarseness, but she didn't strike me as a girl who'd bother with hairpins. As I sat there, listening to Oscar's strictures and watching Tony's foot pumping perilously near the pretty Georgian window, the penny finally dropped from the very heaven of incongruity.

Vanessa Redgrave, hereinafter known as Big Van, had just made her debut as Rosalind. It had been received with a tumult of rapture. I had first come across her in the 1959 Stratford season, when she had played along-side Mary in Peter Hall's Hamley's-window-display production of *A Midsummer Night's Dream*. Her hoydenish-netball capering was no worse than Mary's tinny-toylike Titania in this resolutely un-magicked evening. Her Tory innocence and pro-Suez passions had afforded the rest of the company some amusement, and Tony especially.

The following year I caught Vanessa in a collector's item for hard-hearted dealers in theatrical folklore. It was a delightfully fatuous piece called *Look on Tempests*. She played a young bride who discovers that her husband is homosexual. It was the work of a Lady Playwright in joined-up writing, and it was common knowledge, even outside the profession, that the innocent bride's wilful naïvety exactly matched Big Van's perception of her own father, Sir Michael. Art was rapidly imitating life all right.

Later the same year, I went with Jocelyn R. to see her in Robert Bolt's *The Tiger and the Horse*. Jocelyn, in one of her opinionated pitches for inspired speculation, turned to me and said, 'Mark me, that girl is going to be a very, very big star.' I wasn't sure whether I was appalled by her forecast or troubled by her descent into feeble-mindedness. But then, if I had been asked to take a flier on the future of Coca-Cola, I would probably have been the single vote against it.

Later on, with great difficulty and faint hope of changing my mind about the rising star's sorcery, I hustled a couple of lowly seats for *As You Like It*. I spotted Tony a few rows in front of us. He was on his own. The evening was exactly as I had expected. Afterwards, Penelope hurtled us into the basilica of Big Van's dressing-room. Robert Bolt was seated by her dressing-table, like a presiding elder, leaning on it almost in an attitude of contemplation, as if he had been there all evening.

I scarcely knew Robert but, like many, or some, of the people who live by the same trade as myself, I had always felt a kind of arm's-length affectionate regard for him. I had a feeling that, even if one would never become close friends or enjoy the clash of personal disagreement, one's isolation would never be quite total while he and others existed at the same time in the same world, however uncontacted and even remote.

Tony glared round the door. Two men face to face: one whom I knew so well and understood so little and the other known hardly at all but perhaps more understood. Robert rose politely, 'I'm Robert Bolt,' he said, looking like a prosperous farmer from the Dales. At least they're both Yorkshire-men, I thought. 'I know,' said Tony. There was a silence which Tony could sustain for ever. 'Taking Vanessa out for supper then?' Bolt could almost have been a Victorian father sounding out a young whipper-snapper and his intentions towards his daughter. Tony ignored this and looked at me, as if I should do something. Robert continued in his alderman's plain manner: 'I understand – people tell me – that you don't care overmuch for my work.' It was expressed as a matter of reportage. He could just as well have said, 'I understand you've just come up on the train from Brighton.'

When Big Van appeared, Penelope looked set to gush for two, if not even for England. But Rosalind was still trailing clouds upon clouds of Arden. She let out one of her breathy, deflating sounds like the slumbrous yawn of some waking beast, a kind of mooing acknowledgement. She embraced Tony and stared above my head, perhaps at some departing dreaming lyricism. Penelope shifted into overdrive.

Tony had a tight vice on Vanessa's arm and was swivelling her firmly towards the door. It was only then that I realized that Vanessa's attention had switched to a shivering bundle at her breast, a beribboned miniature Yorkshire terrier, no bigger than an animated pen-wiper. Soon all three of them disappeared. If she was wearing pins, they were firmly fixed in her upswept hair.

A few days after the pillage of Hertford Street, Tony invited us to join them both for supper. It was a disarming gesture, quite out of keeping with his customary methods of manipulating his friends and isolating them from each other. Perhaps he wanted openly to declare his new obsession for all the world to see. The following day he summoned me to Woodfall and suggested that the four of us leave that 'horrible little place of yours' and move into a cute little house he had leased in Eaton Mews North. I sug-gested that he and Vanessa might be happier alone together, but, with his usual tortuous powers of persuasion, he presented the move as a huge adventure, one that Penelope and I would be very dowdy not to join in.

They were a bizarre couple. Similar in some tangled physical way, they seemed to compound a piranha-toothed androgynous power within each other. The prospect of sharing a small mews house with them sounded less an adventure than a punishing military exercise. But Penelope was most eager, and I didn't want to jeopardize my friendship with Tony by allowing him to expose my true feelings about his weird trophy. With luck, it might be re-awarded before long.

The reality was worse than muddle-headed melancholy could have envisaged. The house was small enough for two, normal-sized, co-ordinated people. Life shared within its walls was not easy. In the use of the one minute bathroom, Tony and Vanessa both had the marauding skills of German tourists bagging early-morning deck-chairs. They could sprint to it in a quarter of a second, barricade themselves in for hours and emerge leaving a sodden wreckage of uncapped toothpaste tubes, every item of toiletry dripping, dropped to the floor or lying in moist clusters among a slimy compost of towelling. Both bath and basin would be overflowing with grey, tepid water.

I resigned myself to bathless days on my trips to London, which became less frequent. Sloane Square was only a ten-minute walk away and I could shave and clean my teeth at the Royal Court Hotel. Penelope chose to regard it all as the prerogative of the godlike and gifted. To me it seemed like middle-class dedication to good old Number One.

They had assumed the whole bag of flailing adolescent romance – all whirlwind love, locked eyeball-to-eyeball overfond gazing, kissing, fondling, fumbling – and all played out in a full-frontal, embarrassingly athletic public show. It was as sentimental as the doggerel on a Christmas card.

Worse was their determination to perform a comic double act. They had decided that they were the real-life counterparts of the characters in the recent Truffaut film *Jules et Jim*, a pair of Gallic, custard-pie, cerebral comics. Tony Laurel and Vanessa Hardy. One evening, Penelope and I arrived late and they insisted on giving us the full cabaret. In the course of it, they piled up a trail of damage very similar to the one in Hertford Street.

A few weeks later, long after I had decided that the builders' trannies and day-long rock music in Sussex were preferable to life among the godlike and gifted, Tony met me at the Woodfall office with an indignant solicitor's letter. Our landlady, who was rather grand and a figure at Court (Buckingham Palace, not Sloane Square), had visited her house and been outraged at its condition and the breakages, which included her most cherished Coronation chair – a splendid memento of the crowning of George VI, which she claimed was beyond repair – and an entire floor of fitted carpet which had been sprayed indelicately by the Yorkshire pen-wiper.

'I mean, don't you think it's a disgrace?' 'No, I don't. The damage you've done to her little house would sound impossible to achieve. You've had a right old orgy.' I pronounced it with a hard 'g'. 'And you must pay up.' 'What do you mean – Augie!' 'I mean, my dear friend, that you and Vanessa should live together in a brick underground shelter with wall-to-wall rubber sheeting.' He looked astonished and angry. We had a frosty script conference.

I was prepared to dissemble shamelessly over my feelings for Big Van after their marriage the following year, determined that a wedge of such banality would not come between Tony and myself. Newly married women sometimes conduct a scorched-earth policy on their spouse's past, and previous wives, lovers and male friendships are the first targets for annihilation, especially if there is the merest hint of sexual ambiguity. I knew that Tony's acute perception of his friends' weaknesses might also allow him to accept their feigned complaisance at its face value.

Shortly after their first child, Natasha, was born, he invited Penelope and me to dinner at the marital home in St Peter's Square, a lofty house in a row built for Wellington's officers returning from Waterloo. It was elegant and spacious, but inhabited by Tony, Big Van, Natasha, a ferocious toucan, South American parakeets, bush babies and an assortment of lizards, it was even more in need of wall-to-wall rubber sheeting than Eaton Mews North.

Two of Tony's pre-set explosive devices had been primed to enliven the evening. Staying with the Richardsons was the Broadway actress Kim Stanley, who had worked with Tony in New York. From the battery of coded glares I was receiving from my host, it was clear that I was being instructed to fawn on her. She was in some state of apparent distress, and I refused to be bullied into accepting responsibility for it. I had no idea what had driven her to such fondness for the hard stuff – in American panic-speak, her alcohol 'problem' – but I wasn't going to be snared into a conspiracy of collective guilt for her condition. Brendan Behan, Wilfred Lawson, Trevor Howard, all so-called 'hell-raisers', might become tedious during the course of a long and entertaining evening, but they had the redeeming grace of charm.

Before the meal had ended, Tony pushed his first button. Big Van undid her shirt and clamped the young Natasha to her bosom. 'I shouldn't do that in front of Johnny, Vanessa. I mean, he's very *peculiar* about that kind of thing.' Indeed I was, and didn't deny it. Momentarily wrenched from permanent self-absorption, she glanced at me pityingly, gathered up the hungry infant and left the room. Game and set uncontestably to Richardson *père*.

Penelope, who would never have subjected herself to what she regarded as the ignominy and female subjection of breast-feeding, looked on in embarrassment at old Muddle-Head's crude prejudice. I was probably the only one present who found the idea of non-evangelistic suckling quite erotic. Conducted in private, that is.

Tony's next fuse looked set to activate itself prematurely as Miss Stanley prowled around the room whenever the conversation at table veered away from her own preoccupations. She was one of those women I was rarely to meet who set up an instant wave of magnetic, mutual dislike between themselves and me. She turned up an Edith Piaf record to full volume and began dancing to it, like Blanche du Bois gripped in a bad fit of the Isadoras, wailing in a whisky baritone, '*This* is the real me! This is *my* life!' Resistant to the plight of the famous Parisian sparrow, I was encouraged to shout above the noise, 'You're dead right.'

Tony's prepared booby-trap might well blow up in ugly melodrama. With some relish, I noticed that he was looking rather alarmed. The pinched fear on Penelope's face was stimulating, too. I prepared to pick up the grenade and lob it back at him, but he intervened swiftly, grasped the stumbling star in his arms and bore her away, protesting, upstairs. When he returned, his mouth was tight and reproachful, his anger, for once, unsimulated: 'The trouble with you, Johnny, is that you will never understand the rawness and sensitivity of a creature like Kim.' 'You're right,' I said, 'I won't.' And we left.

When the Richardsons' second daughter, Joely, was born, Tony took a villa for the summer outside St Tropez. Ostensibly it was a recompense for the trials his wife had suffered during the birth. In fact, it was another annual diversion, an auditorium where his friends could be put through their paces like so many performing dogs. Penelope and I were among the early contestants.

We were met at the airport by Jan, Woodfall's driver and Tony's personal valet, nanny and hit-man. He was Polish, an ex-prisoner of war to the Germans, bearer of hideous personal suffering, great-hearted, sweet-natured and a dedicated lecher. His dedication to Tony's needs was passionate and his loyalty total. Less ardent but indisputable was his affection for myself. In Los Angeles he went to great trouble to entertain me with blue movies he had 'borrowed' from the Police Department. In London he would take me along to his Polish club in South Kensington, introduce me to his friends and charge me with the endless sweet and potent liqueurs of his native land.

However, his sweeping affections were by no means undiscriminating and he could nose out suspect enemies and anyone inimical to our well-being. No one ever demonstrated so eloquently the invocation of the Prayer Book's Second Collect of the Day: 'To serve is perfect freedom.' On the journey from the airport, he made his allegiance clear. 'Oh, Mister Osborne, is so good you are here. Mister Richardson, he so unhappy. I never seen him like it before. He need you so badly, but he never bring himself to tell you. He loves you, but he can't say that. Mister Osborne, please help him, is only you can do it.' He was on the edge of tears and hesitated in the darkening track leading to the house. 'That woman, she is a bitch, Mister Osborne, she is not a kind person and she makes Mister Richardson so unhappy.'

He had not exaggerated. The atmosphere in the pre-war bungalow was poisonous and Tony was unmistakably in the grip of it as he went through an abstracted mime of semi-relieved welcome. Big Van smiled vaguely *à la* Giaconda at the Alpes Maritimes somewhere above our heads. Once again, I cursed myself for letting myself be gulled. 'I mean, it'll be such *fun*, all of us together.'

We went out for dinner that evening because Vanessa was 'so tired'. Jan drove, the Richardsons beside him, the Osbornes in the back. No one spoke. As Jan took us down the rocky path towards St Tropez I settled into a numb apprehension which was broken by Tony and Big Van punching each other at close quarters. Jan crouched beside the wheel as the protagonists ejected themselves from the car. The three of us sat in silence while the Oscar-winning lad from Shipley and his adulated wife slugged it out. They returned without a word, and Jan drove on.

The following morning, Tony cornered me. 'You've *got* to talk to Vanessa.' 'Why?' 'She thinks you don't like her.' I couldn't believe he thought I might be taken in by such a disingenuous appeal, but he did. So, for days, I tried to talk to her, to arouse her curiosity or vanity, to engage her in any way. It was no use. I cast not a shadow on her awareness of the world outside herself.

A stream of visitors descended. We left our enseamed, unchanged sheets to be inherited by Jock and Pamela Addison. Three months later I was helping Pamela across the north-west corner of Sloane Square. 'You know I'm pregnant again,' she said. No, I didn't. They already had five children, which seemed enough. 'It's all your fault,' she went on. '*Your* sheets. Tony and Vanessa were so beastly to us we stayed in that bed all day simply to get away from it all.'

Life at Hellingly took on a pattern which I had not expected, but then I had not given it much thought. I had assumed that, having moved in, Penelope and I would spend most of our time there. She had given me the impression that her job as film critic of the *Observer* was more or less a part-time commitment which could easily be adapted to accommodate the principal thrust of her life, which included me. It wasn't so. At first, she went up to London for the first two days of the week, returning early on Tuesday evening. That seemed reasonable enough. But the reality turned out to be something else; another central-European peasant passion would be scheduled for Wednesday afternoon. Her working life in London became permanently extended.

She was understandably tired and also abstracted. Thursday was referred to as '*Observer* Day'. At eight in the morning she would take a pot of coffee over to the granary and stay there until almost midnight to finish her 'piece'. On Friday morning she delivered it to Polegate Station. It would be put on the train for Victoria, where it would be collected by an *Observer* messenger. On Friday afternoon her proofs arrived by the same system in reverse.

The next twenty-four hours would be taken up, as I had discovered in Folkestone, with editorial telephone calls, queries, arguments with the libel lawyers and so on until the paper was finally put to bed. But on Saturday evening she would still fret about what she might have omitted. The shadow of this anxiety often persisted well into Sunday, when she would go over her own piece repeatedly and then spend hours poring over the efforts of others.

In other words, it was effectively a seven-day week, with little time or inclination to divert to other pleasures or relaxation. I tried to point out that it seemed an inordinate amount of time and effort to expend on a thousand-word review to be read by a few thousand film addicts and forgotten almost at once. She was immovable and denied, in the face of the week's passing, that a two-and-a-half-day job had become a seven-day obsession. She was the grotesque adult embodiment of that properly despised schoolboy creature of fretful, incontinent ambition, a swot.

Wherever we went, the albatross typewriter followed. Every fresh absorption was concentrated on something like a script, uncommissioned, of a film which would never be made, or a dashed-off novel which should, and could, have been worked on without hurry. For someone who insisted that work was so important, it seemed a strangely unserious approach.

Penelope shared the public's illusion that writing is something that you sit down and do at prescribed sittings, and not that it is something that must be lived daily amid preoccupations that have nothing to do with putting together sentences – ordinary activities like cooking, going to the races, walking the dogs, seeing a bad movie and *not* writing about it, reading only for pleasure, going to pubs, the seaside, church. Not for her: an embassy supper was obligatory, the church fête a tiresome frivolity.

She was to become increasingly obsessed with fripperies and titles. She insisted on writing 'FRSL' after her name, a negligible bauble which she wore like a banner. She took to calling herself 'Professor Gilliatt' when she answered the telephone or replied to letters. She told me she had received an honorary doctorate from Oxford. In Debrett's *People of Today* she awards herself an exhaustive bunch of unperformed plays and operas. All this was yet to come. But muddle-headed Johnny, with his primitive talents, would clearly provide only a limited diversion for her questing spirit.

When our daughter was born, she was rather eccentrically christened Nolan, after the wild captain who delivered the fatal order to Lords Lucan and Cardigan at the head of the Light Brigade. When the child was older, her mother told her that she had been named after a character in an essay by James Joyce. There's intellect for you.

27. All the Day Long

Deliver me from blood-gatherers, O God,
Thou art the God of my health.
The sacrifice of God is a troubled spirit;
A broken and contrite heart, O God, shalt Thou not despise.

> 'A Commination', Book of Common Prayer

Why do sinners' ways prosper? and why must
Disappointment all I endeavour end?

> Gerard Manley Hopkins, 'Thou Art Indeed Just, Lord'

1962

17 FEBRUARY, HELLINGLY: Well, Osborne, where is your lustre now? I am increasingly alone. These whole Thursday *Observer* days. Penelope beavering lather in the granary, pints of coffee and whisky and nothing else, all for 900 words about a biblical epic, another western or some pharisaical French tosh. Despite it all, *Plays for England* are done: *Blood of the Bambergs* and *Under Plain Cover*.

Bambergs is simply a broadly satiric account of one of the permanent fixtures in English life, a Royal Wedding. It's quite affectionately based on Anthony Hope's superb invention of Ruritania and the familiar plot of *The Prisoner of Zenda*. It seems a good idea to match the shuffling pantomime of contemporary royal fantasy with the real, romantic thing. *Under Plain Cover* is equally circumspect, a light *cadenza* on the clash of public prurience and private innocence.

No one will want them, but they'll be better than anything else on offer. One must be allowed – no, encouraged – to indulge these sportive fancies. Penelope *not* keen on *Plays for England*. Thinks I should do something more *ambitious*. ('You've got it *in* you, darling.') She wants experiment . . . 'But don't go *too* far, darling.'

1 APRIL, ROYAL COURT: *Plays for England*. John Dexter will do *Bambergs*. But he's terrified of *UPC*. Which is OK. Heterosexual sex scares the shit out of him. Jonathan Miller agrees to do *UPC*. No one else wants it. It might still be fun. You never know.

George bemused by St James's Palace lack of response to the repetition of 'knickers' some forty-five times in less than an hour. Penelope is impressed by Dr Miller. London's Intellectual Life. She's not much time for Dexter, Derby's son, although he's infinitely cleverer and, in rehearsal, it shows.

18 JULY, ROYAL COURT: *Plays for England*. Dress rehearsal. Not brilliant but it will do. Not much of a lark for anyone. *UPC*: I'm glad I've kept away from J. Miller. No chance of much contact there. The striving fluency of the Hampstead nanny's boy is deceptive and occasionally plausible. With its cultural allusions and cross-references to other disciplines, it is the gab-gift of someone to whom English is an adoptive tongue. Intellect does terrible things to the mind. As a director, he's an Armenian carpet-seller, although the cast is decent enough – Anton Rogers in particular, and little Annie Beach.

Bambergs: John Dexter *has* provided a few larks, though the actors are afraid of him. As George says, a born NCO. *Not* officer material. Oh, well, it'll soon be over.

I am already fired up into the future with *Inadmissible Evidence* and, maybe, *A Patriot for Me*. (I *am* good at titles, if little else.)

Inadmissible: I read a letter in a newspaper from a woman who was distraught at the spectacle of her husband, a man she admired and respected, being slowly isolated by the dislike and suspicion he aroused in other people. For all his tangible good and honour, she watched others recoil from his presence, until it overcame their children and, finally, even herself. Bill Maitland was born. It was an overpowering image of desolation.

Working away for hours in the Mill on *Inadmissible* was technically absorbing, but left me feeling so permanently despoiled that, at the end of a day, it called out for respite, some consuming recompense of fire. I found it at once in *Patriot*, which, by now, was like an old friend, and even an acquaintance to others, like Christopher Isherwood, to whom over the years I had confided its future.

Where *Inadmissible* was a banged up, irreversible journey, *Patriot* was a grand, operatic venture, all aria, history, sweep and grandeur. One made the other bearable. Alfred Redl and Bill Maitland demanded to be born across the half century of the terrible, Old Testament perils of the time. Anyway, it made sense to me, and that's how I did it.

19 JULY, ROYAL COURT: *Plays for England*. Well, we opened. They didn't like it. Princess Melanie (Vivian Pickles) was magnificent as the Bride in *Bambergs* when she said, 'I'm so bored'; Alan Bennett, too, as the Archbishop. Jocelyn R. shrieked, maddeningly, at all my Australian jokes.

1 NOVEMBER: Mary sues for divorce.

14 DECEMBER: She *gets* it. Names poor Francine, Jocelyn, and Penelope. Admitted own adultery (who *dates* wins!). Brave smiles all round. Costs to me. Beuselinck: 'Got off lightly there, son.' Fancy! How lawyers and accountants gloat over the defeats of the likes of myself.

1963

8 MAY: Max Miller, the great priapic God of Flashness dies. 'There'll never be another.' As old John Betjeman says, an English genius as pure gold as Dickens or Shakespeare – or Betjeman, come to that. Max's last words: 'Oh, Mum,' to his wife. There is so much to dread.

25 MAY, HELLINGLY: Penelope and I are married. Tony is best man (again). Penelope's sister, Angela, another witness. The Addisons come and Pamela complains about the dog-shit on the lawn. George arrives, Jocelyn H., too. Big Van sends a typical telegram: 'I wish I could write an epithalamium for you.' Bet she thought I wouldn't know what that was. Oh, but Penelope would. She did.

1964

4 JANUARY, 'DAILY CINEMA': *Tom Jones* longest running picture at London Pavilion. Over six months. Grossed record-shattering £100,000 plus. In thirteenth New York week broke all-time house record.

5 JANUARY, HELLINGLY: Nellie Beatrice's birthday. Why does Penelope pretend to *like* her? To irritate me? Surely not. What made me take her to Venice (merry St Marks!) of all earth's wonders? Let alone New York. Barbados, now she liked that. Well, she would. One day, the cunning and the unteachable, like N.B., will run the show and give no quarter.

27 FEBRUARY: *Tom Jones* nominated for ten Oscars.

16 MARCH, QUEEN'S THEATRE: The English Stage Company's West End season, in conjunction with Binkie, opens with *The Seagull*. Everyone is moved by George's performance as Dorn. In his white suit and hat, he looks almost dapper – well, jaunty at least. During his speech about what he'd like to say to Konstantin about his play, to *tell* him that he liked it, my eyes felt like pin-cushions at the beautiful autobiography of it.

And then, when he is left to bring down the curtain. 'How distraught they all are! How distraught! And what a quantity of love about. It's the magic lake. [*Tenderly*] But what can I do, my child? Tell me, what can I do? What?'

He was *really* asking a question. As always. And daring for an answer.

20 MARCH: Dear Brendan Behan dead. I remember him banging on our door at the Algonquin. 'Is there anyone at home in this fuckin' cat house?' Strangely *un*cruel for an Irishman (IRA, at that).

24 MARCH, HELLINGLY: All hell's been going on at the Queen's Theatre. Big Van is in the club and the season of *The Seagull* and *St Joan of the Stockyards* has been put on especially for her! Binkie insists she have an abortion. T.R. quite lost control. Siobhan McKenna might take over from her. Lindsay Anderson brought in to deal with the hysteria. *He* can't cope either. Up to George now. I think Binkie's right!

7 APRIL, HELLINGLY: *Inadmissible Evidence*. I am rid of Bill Maitland. Last night I dragged myself into the Mill with a bottle of champagne – later, at about 5 a.m. came back for more – and *finished* the play. Penelope full of pity for primitive man at work. Sister Angela playing Bach fugues all night – or motets, or something. She's *still* mooning on about the death of Dag Hammarskjöld.

Anyway, with *Inadmissible* I've done new language things for the first time. *No* one will notice. Still, that's not what the enterprise is about. Whole of Maitland's opening speech is a parody of Harold Wilson's at Scarborough. All that bullshit about technology . . .

(FAST FORWARD: When the play was revived in 1978, the audience laughed, as intended. By then they had seen the Wilson future and *knew* it didn't work.)

21 APRIL, INDIA: On holiday. This is the only way to avoid United Artists shipping me off in handcuffs to the Oscars ceremony. Edith [Evans] will do

it for me, perfectly. The actors saved that film. Jock's music covered up some holes too . . .

Penelope glowing and in quite mischievous mood. *Suggests* getting pregnant. In India . . .? Typewriter clattering from Bombay to Rajasthan for what . . .? She saved my life last week after an attack by wasps in a temple. Too hot for sex – let alone work.

2 JUNE, ROYAL COURT: *Inadmissible Evidence*. Auditions. For Bill Maitland we need someone with the periscope view of an Olivier, scanning the ocean-ic grip of squalor from the secret, submerged depths in an echoing chamber of hollowness. All my suggestions – good actors all – a disaster.

At the end of the afternoon, Anthony [Page, the director] brings on his dark horse: Nicol Williamson. Nicol is in *costume*. He's *it*. Somehow the play rises. It takes flight. This twenty-seven-year-old, pouting, delinquent cherub produced the face to match the torment below the surface. He's much too young, but no matter. He is *old* within.

(FAST FORWARD: Addition to the John Gielgud Anthology of Dropped Bricks. During dinner in his house, he stopped in mid-flight: 'That actor – oh dear me – young, Scottish, *most* unattractive . . . He was in that long, terribly dull, boring play. Oh, dear God, of course, you wrote it.' That was *Inadmissible*.)

12 JULY, COVENT GARDEN: Crush Bar. Penelope is wearing a full-length frock made from raw silk stuff we got in Kashmir. 'Well,' she says, 'you're going to be a dad.' *No* excitement. Grandma O. on Boxing Day. In the Crush Bar. '*No one* must be told. *Only* Angela.' Brown eyes gone to black, with what – fury, disappointment? I feel sick with the contemptuous repudiation of it. There is an obdurate malignity in this? God, I hope not.

13 AUGUST, BRIGHTON: *Inadmissible Evidence*. We open at the Theatre Royal. The stage carpenter says, again: 'Not *you* again!' We have a lovely night at the pub where all the actors are staying. John Hurt shaking with lust and banging on Ann Beach's bedroom door. Can't blame him. Funny girl . . .

9 SEPTEMBER, ROYAL COURT: *Inadmissible* opens.

43, Cloth Fair, EC1

My dear old Top,
Here, in the calm of the morning, I affirm what I said last night to you
– that is a tremendous play. The best thing you – yes, even you – have

ever written. Apart from the sentiments in the diatribe – which I heartily endorse – it is the most heart-rending and tender study of every man who is not atrophied. We want to avoid giving pain and we want to be left in peace. Love makes us restless and we resist it. I felt increasingly that the play was about *me* and that is what all the great playwrights and poets can do for their watchers and readers.

Oh, my dear boy, I can't exactly *thank* you for such an agonizing self-analysis. I can only reverence the power and generosity in you which makes you write such a shattering and releasing piece. Once more my warmest congratulations on a mighty achievement – Oh, hell, what words are there to express myself? I feel as though I am writing to the elements.

Love from,

Bill Maitland-Betjeman

1 OCTOBER, CALIFORNIA: Chez Richardson. Fly to LA to talk to T.R. about *Patriot* and when he will be able to direct it. Neil Hartley, his assistant on *The Loved One*, meets me at the airport. He was Merrick's henchman for twenty years (an amazing testimonial to toughness and endurance) and T.R. shrewdly seduced him away during *Luther*'s run in New York.

Not, as expected, a taciturn bespoke-tailor of concrete overcoats, but a tall, handsome man from North Carolina, might have been a thirties' film star himself. Immaculate manners, good humour, diplomatic skills. Almost a parody of a Southern gent. The prospect of a new, permanent friendship.

T.R., three months into the shooting of Waugh, has set up an impregnable GHQ in a collection of Hollywood Tudor buildings recently vacated by Rex Harrison. There's the main house, surrounding the pool, and several bijou bungalows occupied by various adjutants, 'writers' and assistants in obligatory shorts and sneakers. Neil wryly assures me that the majority of staff officers have been flushed out in anticipation of my arrival. He has the impeccable gift of confiding in me without compromising his loyalty to T.R.

I am summoned to a location in a depressing street in Watts. T.R. is shooting a scene in a clapboard hovel in which Mr Joyboy, improbably played by Rod Steiger, cooks an orgiastic meal and stuffs his bullfrog, bed-ridden mother with tureens of spaghetti, meatballs, haunches of fat pork and offal. I stand at the back of the suffocating little room all the morning, feeling sick. I have never seen such a venomous, uncoordinated assault, such a crowing repudiation of the female species and distortion of its physicality.

I escape into the smoggy street and wait for the lunch break. T.R. arrives, exhilarated, bubbling with the results of the morning. Suddenly, slamming down this flow of self-excitement, he turns to the script of *Patriot*. 'I read this last night. Frankly, Johnny, I'm a bit mystified. I mean, you'll have to *explain* it to me. I mean, what's it all *about*?'

I had never thought he would put such a question to me. I handed him a letter from Penelope, which she had rightly trusted me not to open. I suspected it was some garbled rationalization of her pregnancy. He opens it and flips through it, leg stabbing virulently. He throws it aside and fixes the messenger with a hostile stare, as if I am some accosting beggar.

'I mean, *what*'s it about?' I feel even more sickened and humiliated. I can't think of anything to say. We look at each other in fixed alienation.

He begins to pour mock surprise scorn on Evelyn Waugh, who has evidently heard news of the savage mutilation of his novel. 'Don't you think he's being very *peculiar*?' The final result was to be one of the most ill-judged films ever perpetrated. He tried to appal me further with descriptions of the morgue and corpses hanging from their ears in neat plastic bags.

There is no point. I must face it: it is unarguable that he dislikes *Patriot* and won't do it. I shall have to look elsewhere. I decide to flee, before I myself die in that terrible place, suspended like a bundle at the dry cleaners.

22 OCTOBER, ROYAL COURT: *Cuckoo in the Nest*. Back on to the boards again in the blessed Ben Travers masterpiece. *He* thinks we are all marvellous! Arthur Lowe certainly is. Penelope not pleased by her exclusion from my vagabond life, once again. But absorbed in spending my money on massive renovations on the house we have bought in Chester Square, her refuge against the country, complete with copper dining-room doors and Swedish experiments in the drawing-room.

1965

1 JANUARY, SAVOY HOTEL: George, ground down by illness and the tit-swingers of Sloane Square, has decided that he will step down, after ten years, as director at the Court in September. I dread Neville Blond's annual lunch for the critics. They are prickly and oleaginous, full of pique and ill-feeling. This time, most of all, I dread George's retirement speech.

'When a man begins to feel he is part of the fixtures and fittings it is time he left. I am deeply tired. The weight of this edifice had driven me up to my neck like poor Winnie in *Happy Days*. I should have passed the job on years ago. I am getting out just in time.'

There was a vote of thanks from some nonentity, as if we had just heard the Chairman of the local Rotary Club turning it in. Chairs started to crunch. That was it then. Those ten years . . . Rage and impatience. Suddenly, we hear the voice of Lindsay Anderson: 'I cannot let this occasion go by so unrewarded.' Some honour was plucked from the shoddy moment.

5 JANUARY, HELLINGLY: Nellie Beatrice's birthday. The Lord Chamberlain gives *Patriot* the full thumbs down. No quarter. It's now clear that if the Council agrees to turn the Court into a club for the play – which *terrifies* them – they'll make *me* stump up at least half. Budget £15,000 at present. J.O.: £7,000. After all the money *I've* earned for them. This place would have closed five years ago if it wasn't for me.

12 JANUARY, CHESTER SQUARE: *Patriot*. Marge Vosper for lunch. Wonders if the Lord Chamberlain might not just be right, after all, dear. The public *will* only take *so* much and *you* have given them quite enough to be getting on with all these years. *We mustn't expect too much.* (I never do. And I never get it.) Dear old Marge. Still hasn't got over *UPC*, and all those unnecessary jokes about knickers. Ewan (her husband) hated it so much he had to go to bed. Yet he tells all those filthy jokes about Robert Burns:

> His breeks were doon,
> His airse was bare,
> His balls were swinging in the air.
> If he nae was nae fucking
> I was nae there.

Cultured Scottish gentility, I dare say.

4.30, WOODFALL OFFICES: *The Charge of the Light Brigade*. Cecil Woodham-Smith, author of *The Reason Why*, has slapped an injunction on us. Oscar Beuselinck is relishing it. How he hates people who create things. He thinks everyone steals. *I've* plagiarized no one. Only myself, in the style of G.F. Handel (never stopped, and who better to steal from?). Beuselinck declares triumphantly that it's going to cost us £12,000 to buy off Laurence Harvey, who owns Woodham-Smith's rights. I hear T.R. has already offered him 'my part' as the Russian prince.

19 JANUARY, ENGLISH STAGE COMPANY: *Patriot*. Elaine Blond more surly and charmless than ever. Blacksell, the redundant schoolteacher from Devon, drones on about 'Young People'. When *I* was Young People, they treated us like dirt. Didn't matter. Now, not to be reverential about the little

bastards is regarded as a logical extension of anti-Semitism. Dear Greville Poke looks and behaves more like Ralph Lynn than ever, spats and all. Perhaps I should give him a monocle for the opening of *Patriot*. But would he wear it?

21 JANUARY, WOODFALL OFFICES: *Patriot*. We are *summonsed* by T.R. to Curzon Street. He sits there, the papal legate from Shipley. We crouch on nasty Swedish-Gilliatt-style chairs. Marge Vosper is mystified, Anthony Page is sweaty *and* shifty, Maximillian Schell is polite.

T.R., however, is in Machiavellian form: 'I mean, the thing is, well, it's so embarrassing, but when Johnny [don't!] brought his play to me in Los Angeles, I had to tell him I couldn't do it – because of, ah – commitments. [Too windy, you mean.] Well, the thing is: *now*, it appears I can, after all. Do it. *That*'s the situation.'

I don't know what he expected. Old Marge didn't know what to say. Page looked like a Wykehamist about to deny he'd fiddled his New College viva by offering up his body. Max was very good, already very Colonel Redl, I thought.

T.R. was smirking at this display of full house. Bang down went my royal flush. Expressed with most circumspect, triumphant piety. I'm sorry, Tony. But while you were away in California, I've spent a great deal of time with Anthony [Page, none of it very enjoyable, spitting food all over me]. We've worked on the casting, the sets, the music. He's been down on the usual run to St James's Palace. I couldn't change horses in mid-stream.

Collapse of long, thin party. I shall cherish his leg arrested in mid-thrust, the old Shipley jaw wrenched back like a pulled-up stallion.

It will never happen again!

22 JANUARY, WELBECK STREET: Saw Dr Hemans (Penelope's gynaecologist). Too wise for that job. Saw *Divorce Me, Darling*. Blimey. It's *still* 1956. Maybe always will be.

29 JANUARY, ENGLISH STAGE COMPANY: Another meeting. Usual stuff about ladies' lavatories. Elaine seems to spend so much time in there, why doesn't she just whip out her chequebook and buy us a new ballcock. God, the rich are tight-fisted. How they *live* money.

30 JANUARY, COVENT GARDEN: *Arabella*. Now, that's more like it. Old Strauss does for ladies' voices what oats does for horses. He *invented* another human sound. I looked rather pretty in my black waistcoat, which may be why a lavendery Loamshire gent said, 'I suppose *you're* our Verdi.'

[Popular? No. Vulgar and hummable, I suppose he meant.] 'No,' said his companion, 'Mozart.' That's pitching it a bit too high. Berlioz would do. Vaughan Williams really best of all.

2 FEBRUARY, ROYAL COURT: *Patriot*. Anthony does waffle on. I *do* dislike greedy people. He's at the peanuts, stuffing his face, all the time. Gluttony *really* is a sin. Lust can constrain itself. He's intent on getting a Continental lady for the Countess. Now, it's (no!) Delphine Seyrig (model) and old Swedish black-looks, Liv Ullman. I do tell him there are plenty of our own girls at hand. Jill Bennett, he suggests. Not keen. I saw her being very patronizing to her husband, Willis Hall, one night in Beoty's. We'll see.

3 FEBRUARY, PAMELA'S FLAT: 11.30 a.m. Once again, easy slide between sheets. Very cosy Tiggywinkle Kilburn basement. Bland still upon bland, but quite affectionate. Says the weekly sums she got from her piece of *Inadmissible* have kept her going. Quite a large sum when I think of it – £200 a month at least. No, more. And then there'll be America.

16 FEBRUARY, WOODFALL: *The Charge of the Light Brigade*. T.R. is hell-bent on making an anti-war film. Oscar Lewenstein looks as glum as he did in the Acapulco brothel. I am losing heart. T.R. is tampering with history – all there in Kingslake's classic account of the battle, minute by minute. I think they should forget me and get in Charles Wood. He's not only a proper writer but a professional soldier – Seventeenth/Twenty-First Lancers. War? Loves it, abominates it.

17 FEBRUARY, OLD VIC: *Much Ado*. Zeffirelli's with Robert and Margaret Stephens. Loved all this wog nonsense. He's a clever bugger.

Penelope insists she writes it up for Friday. Proofs on Saturday. She looks thin and ghostly. Baby due on Wednesday. And no one has a clue that she's pregnant. Well, she's done it. *Not* very flattering to me. Calculated disavowal. Nolan will be born with a proof in his/her mouth.

18 FEBRUARY, CHESTER SQUARE: Went to a factory in Sevenoaks to get Penelope her harpsichord to celebrate the birth. I hope she'll be pleased. Not just to perfect her Bach, but a bit of Fats Waller, Hoagy Carmichael. I fancy not. Nicol Williamson might hot it up a bit. Or Jock Addison.

24 FEBRUARY, WELBECK STREET NURSING HOME: Nolan Kate Conner –! Osborne born, 9.05 a.m. Saw her at 9.15. Not at all red and nasty. Caesarean swank, I suppose. Quite pretty. By 4.00 p.m. Penelope is in a state of rage

about some hooray friend of the family whose own wife was in a prolonged state of labour in the room next door and talked about the possibility of 'putting the ferrets up her'. Standard coarse upper-class joke I'd have thought.

She wants to go home *tonight*! Uncorrected Proofs. Even she conceded she couldn't make it. Perhaps she'll start eating again now.

26 FEBRUARY, ROYAL COURT: *Meals on Wheels*. Corporal Charles Wood has sent the Court a bizarre comic extravaganza of such inventiveness that nobody understands it. None of the tame resident directors will risk it, which is a disgrace. *I* don't 'understand' it either, but so what? It's clearly very good. Told George I'll direct it.

WELBECK STREET: Penelope still in a rage about the ferrets. She rails about the food (which *is* terrible). She has to be *thin*. George and Jocelyn H. bring her some fish and chips, which she pretends to enjoy. Her eyes black again with outrage, ill-use. A drop of milk splashes from her breast to her knee. She throws up. That same *obdurate malignity*. It is. Don't.

26 MARCH, ST JAMES'S PALACE: *A Patriot For Me*. The Lord Chamberlain stands firm. So, it will have to be the Club Theatre, £7,000 out of my own money, working for nothing, and the plod of policemen's feet. And all on account of this. They've sent it back, confirmed:

Cuts and alterations requested by the Lord Chamberlain

I–I 'His spine cracked in between those thighs . . . All the way up.'
I–I This scene must not be played with the couple both in bed.
I–4 From: 'She moves over to the wall . . .' To: . . . Presently he turns away and sits on the bed.'
I–5 Reference to 'clap' and 'crabs'.
I–9 Reference to 'clap'.
I–10 Omit the whole of this scene.
II–II Ditto.
III–I From: 'You'll never know that body like I know it . . .' To: '. . . you've not looked at him. You never will.'
III–I From: 'Your turn, Stefan, . . .' To: '. . . . than any ordinary man'.
III–2 Omit: 'You were born with a silver sabre up your whatsit.'
III–4 Omit: 'Tears of Crisst'.
III–5 Omit: the whole of this scene.

And, of course, the Drag Ball. OMIT THE WHOLE OF THIS SCENE.

And put half the queens of Chelsea out of a job? Poor George. What grief I bring him.

19 APRIL, ROYAL COURT: *Meals on Wheels*. Usual dismal first reading. Comic actors are even *worse* on these occasions. At least the stage management laughed. Frank Thornton knows his stuff. Very good. That's over. I equivocated very prettily. Well, *I* thought so.

ST JAMES'S PALACE: *Meals on Wheels*.

Page 24:   'She never knew the Duke of Windsor', substitute 'She never knew Leslie Howard'.
Page 25:   'Duke of Windsor', substitute 'God Bless the Prince of Wales'.
Page 61:   'Because you looked like the Duke of Windsor', substitute 'Because you looked like him'.
Page 63:   'I can't help looking like the Duke of Windsor', substitute 'I can't help what I look like'.

There will, of course, be no attempt to impersonate the Duke of Windsor.

6 MAY, PALLADIUM: In an attempt to lift the *Meals on Wheels* cast into the higher realm of Corporal Wood's imagination, I take them to see Ken Dodd.
Once again, Betjemanesque divine genius. 'This morning I woke up with Miss Givings' . . . 'Grandad used to stand with his back to the fire. We had to have him swept.' Don't know what they made of it.

9 MAY, ROYAL COURT: *Meals on Wheels*. Despondent rehearsal. I dread facing one of the actors, Lee Montagu, first thing. He smokes a pipe at 10 o'clock. He actually *looks* for the few difficulties we *haven't* got. His wife always seems to have had an *idea* in bed the night before. I pretend to listen . . .

They keep on asking does it (whatever) mean *this* – or – that? I reply: 'I suspect . . . it's both.' They stare at me resentfully. 'We'll ask Charles when he comes up from Bristol.' He does. 'Well, Charles,' I say, feeling a shit for not protecting him, 'what does it mean?' With a fine soldier's simplicity, he replies, 'Both.'

20 MAY, ROYAL COURT: *A Patriot For Me*. 'Victory or Westminster Abbey!' First reading. George *very* grumpy. Don't blame him. It's beyond belief that Page should have made him *audition*, and twice, for the Baron. He is going to be magnificent, I know. Everyone is agog at the prospect. In his dressing-room, he tells me what 'girls have to go through for tights and

mascaras'. He is fondling his wig and gloves as if they were the rarest objects. All this with legs wide *open* and a pipeful of Edgeworth blasting out into Sloane Square.

26 JUNE, ROYAL COURT: *Patriot*. Dress rehearsal. George says to me, 'I thought people *hated* Tony Richardson in this theatre – until I saw Anthony Page at work.'

30 JUNE, ROYAL COURT: *Patriot*. Opening night.

> My dear Friend,
>
>   Don't know quite how to express myself tonight. It is a great night and must be viewed as such, although it seems the end of a period and all that. But these things are what we make them. The essentials remain – and the way our friendship has grown over these years is vastly important to me.
>
>   Love, ever.
>
>   George

9 AUGUST, ROYAL COURT: *Patriot*. Sloane Square stifling. Theatre sweltering after matinée. George collapses with heart attack in full gear. Oh, God. Taken to St George's Hospital.

14 AUGUST, ROYAL COURT: *Patriot*. Last night. Audience told George is recovering. I suppose he is. But the thought of his spirit stifling in that dreary ward hangs over the whole theatre. Scene after scene; his memory seems to pierce everything, the costumes, the words and, of course, the Drag Ball . . . a silk shirt, an ancient Greek ring. George, our play, our world, coming to an end. I could scarcely bear to watch it.

There am I, tears streaming from every orifice and some dumb accusing creature accosts me during the second interval. She had, she tells me smugly, been deeply hurt by the play, and found it most offensive. Her mother is one of the Sloane Square Zionists. Life *is* offensive, I say, hardly able to see for the disintegration of my own world. All those painful anti-Semitic remarks? That's how it was in 1912 Vienna, I suggest. She nods in disbelief at my insensitivity. 'You don't understand.' I do, lady, I do.

>   St George's Hospital, SW1
>
>   (Just been told I can feed myself. Get that for progress.)
>
> My dear John,
>
>   I thought of you this morning when I remarked to the nurse that we hadn't had any new casualties since I came in on Saturday. 'Oh, yes, we

have,' she replied rather snootily. 'There's the gentleman down the end in No. 24 who passed out watching the changing of the Queen's Guard!'

What a shock, without any warning at all, I really thought I'd had my chips that night, but about fifty miles behind my head I was obstinately hanging on, answering their questions with an angry resentful snarl. I was in an oxygen mask and my speech was distorted so when I heard one cry, 'How old is he?' 'Oh, about 57 or 58,' I lashed out 55 with great venom . . .

Above all, John, your card meant the most. I can't help thinking I made a balls of it by collapsing. I suppose I should not have gone on on Saturday night, but the thought of all the flap and Anthony Royle in *my* costume and that packed house and one's innate vanity . . . However, it was, thank goodness, no more than a pity.

Let's talk about a trip somewhere later. Would love that.

From the Baron who went too far.

1 SEPTEMBER, ROYAL COURT: George officially retires as Artistic Director. Bill [Gaskill] takes over. Well, that's Good.

13 OCTOBER, HELLINGLY: *Charge of the Light Brigade*. Finished. Hooray.

31 OCTOBER, NEW YORK: *Inadmissible*. Back to the Algonquin for the Broadway production.

9 NOVEMBER, PHILADELPHIA: *Inadmissible*. American tour begins. Anthony Page is no good at handling gangsters like David Merrick. Showdown backstage tonight with Merrick and Nicol Williamson squaring up to each other like old-time fairground pugilists. Merrick told Williamson, 'Page is fired.' Williamson replied, 'You can't fire the fucking director without telling me.' They are both quivering with fear. St Valentine's Day Massacre. Nicol discovered next morning at the Railroad Depot singing 'Mammie'. Merrick tells me to fuck off. Back to England and my Queen. Point out an unlikely welcome from either.

12 DECEMBER, HELLINGLY: My birthday. Spiffing note from John 'Maitland' Betjeman. What did Trollope say – muddle-headed Johnny? It's deep honesty that distinguishes a gentleman. *He's* got it. He knows how to *revel* in life and have no expectations – and fear death at all times.

CHRISTMAS, HELLINGLY: A meticulous fuck-up. Penelope in filthy mood. Insisted Jock and Pamela Addison come. Fine! With their five children.

No. Compromise. They come for Boxing Day without their children. 'Christmas is *for* children,' Pamela admonishes. I said it's too good for them. Penelope also insists on asking Jill Bennett. 'She's lonely now that Willis has left her in that little house.' I'm sure she doesn't want to come here. Penelope gets her way.

BOXING DAY, HELLINGLY: Penelope makes everyone go off to the Devonshire Park Theatre for the pantomime. *She* stays at home with Nolan. Pamela cheers up a bit. I think J.B. *quite* enjoyed it. I loved it.

28. Vale Nora Noel

By the pricking of my thumbs
Something wicked this way comes.
Macbeth, III. i

The mind is its own place and in itself
Can make a heaven of hell, a hell of heaven.
John Milton, *Paradise Lost*, Book One

Keep thou my feet; I do not ask to see
The distant scene; one step enough for me.
I loved the garish day, and spite of fears
Pride ruled my will; remember not past years
And with the morn these angel faces smile
Which I have loved long since and lost awhile.
'The Pillar of Cloud', *Lead Kindly Light*, 1833

FAST FORWARD: *Notebook, 7 October 1990*: Nora Noel Jill Bennett committed suicide yesterday. Except, of course, that she didn't, merely perpetrating a final common little deceit under the delusion that it was an expression of 'style', rather than the coarse posturing of an overheated housemaid.

Reading through the glib newspaper cant of today, it appears that only I know what should have been apparent to even the most crass journalist: that she was a woman so demoniacally possessed by Avarice that she died of it. How many people have died in such a manner, of Avarice? Of pride, sloth, gluttony and, most publicly, of lust. But to die of Avarice takes driving of the will, some low, scheming ingenuity. However, there it is, she did actually contrive to polish herself off with the deadly draught. This final, fumbled gesture, after a lifetime of glad-rags borrowings, theft and plagiarism, must have been one of the few original or spontaneous gestures in her loveless life.

I don't think she would have been too pleased with her notices this morning, in spite of the corn-drivel phrases from the lady hacks, who are simply relieved to find that they're a bit more on top of their own plundering avidity. But she would have been satisfied with the poor Silly-Jilly gush spewed up by the gay faithful and hairy show-biz sob-sisters. The power of popular sentimentality does wonders with invention.

B.A. (Freddie) Young tootles on in the *Financial Times* (she deserved a rave review there – money was her undisputed reason for living): 'Petite [he can't even remember what she looked like] and charming, she was always an active outdoor woman.' He must have been at the Garrick port a little too late in the afternoon. Something's certainly fevered his muddy old remembrance. She could have tucked little Freddie under her 'glitzy, up-market armpits' (*Daily Express*).

During the nine years I lived beneath the same roof with her, she spent half the day in bed. There was a short period when she took dressage lessons, that most intensive course in aids to severe narcissism, but in an *in*door school. She *was* intermittently athletic. She could throw a weighty punch or kick, *and* sustain it for hours on end. My friends can give you a guided tour of the scars around my head.

'At the Court, she played the Russian Countess in *A Patriot for Me*, a part she adorned beyond its proper worth.' Wrong, Freddie. Petite and charming as a rattle-snake before breakfast, she got the part by default, and it was later truly 'adorned' with considerable power, grace and charm by Sheila Gish and June Ritchie in the 1983 revival. Apart from their superior gifts, they managed to speak the text without sounding like a puppy with a mouthful of lavatory paper.

During the long nights of hearing her lines, which only laziness prevented her from getting down unassisted, I did everything I could to scrub up her diction, but it never improved. Indeed, after we separated and she was consigned to lesser parts, it became even worse. During a television series in which she stooged to Maria Aitken, lamentable even by the pier-end standards of sit-com, she was quite incomprehensible and cried out for sub-titles.

Perhaps it was Tony's declaration that she was the 'worst actress in England' and Anthony Page's capitulation to little Jilly's tiresome refusal to give a reading that persuaded me to give her the Countess nod. For once, Mary McCarthy was uncommonly perceptive when she pronounced the performance 'common and strident'. It was straight from life.

More of today's 'tributes': 'Former screen sex symbol' (the *Sun*, couldn't remember who she was); 'Tempestuous, ritzy star' (*Express*, again). Star she never was, even by the saloon-bar tally of the *T.V. Times*. All those lies she fed out *ad nauseam* are here again: of J.O. having gone off with her 'best friend', who was never more than a lunchtime acquaintance; of *her* sheep-dog – mine – which *I* had destroyed. I loved him and saved him from her vicious neglect. And so on – the perpetuation of this whole rotting body of lies and invention which was her crabbed little life.

At least some of them have rumbled her real age. Poor Willis had years of grilling with immigration officials infuriated by her amateurish efforts to change her birth date. As so often, the provincial papers were on to it first.

> Marguerite Vernon, 81, of Sidford in East Devon, was Jill's cousin, and closest surviving relative. 'When she became famous, contact was broken. We went to see some of her plays but were fairly coldly received. [I'll bet.] She was a good actress, but extrovert, noisy and loud.' [Come, Mrs Vernon, don't you mean 'witty and vulnerable, warm-hearted, feline, wonderfully droll and naughty, instinctive and hard to please'?] Mr Vernon is also convinced that Jill, who won best actress award in 1968 for her part in John Osborne's *Time Present*, kept a secret of her real age.
>
> Western Morning News

But what of her 'diamond sparkle which made her so irresistible and so wonderful in *Hedda Gabler*' (Patrick Procktor, painter of her portrait and a friend of twenty-five years)? Well, he didn't have to hump her through her lines. Wasn't it her 'essential quality of intelligence and lack of sentimentality which made her Hedda so remarkable' (Anthony Page)? Sentimentality she had in abundance; feeling none.

'She was eighteen years younger than my wife,' Mr Vernon continues, 'which would make her sixty-three and not fifty-nine as she claimed.' No matter, Mr Vernon. The producer Thelma Holt recalls her 'wit and larky sense of fun. Even in recent times, when her career and personal life were sometimes in the doldrums, she maintained her essential elegance and stoic brightness.' I remember the tragic actress's stoic brightness very well, Ms Holt. I remember the shit and the vomit on the sheets and calling out my friend Patrick Woodcock every other month with his little black bag. I know how carefully she knew the practical drill of suicide and how many times she rehearsed it:

ESSENTIALS Thirty or forty sleeping pills of maximum strength. 30mg Carbitol, for instance. At least half bottle of brandy. Half a loaf of moist brown bread. Most important: make sure that you will not be accidentally disturbed. An anonymous, second-rate hotel, booked in on Friday with the Do Not Disturb notice put up at once. The Cumberland at Marble Arch is ideal.

My cheap joke about calling her 'Adolf' has followed her to Putney Vale. Even those who might consider themselves her admirers took to using it.

How do I know that Adolf didn't intend to kill herself? Very simple. Her body contained hardly a trace of alcohol. She was relying on someone 'coming on her' sufficiently comatose for a good night's sleep but not enough to feel the brush of angels' wings. But her dog-walker failed to return and the millionaire stockbroker whose bed – and fortune – she coveted, was on business in Hungary and could not be summoned.

The sound of 'I left my heart in San Francisco' will waft across Putney Vale, and that distinguished film director Michael Winner will pronounce: 'She was a bit of a sexpot. One of the kindest, nicest people you could ever meet!'

Dogs home left £½m by actress

By A J McIlroy

THE ACTRESS Jill Bennett, former wife of John Osborne, the playwright, left more than £500,000 to Battersea Dogs Home in her will.

Miss Bennett, who died last October, left estate valued at £582,530 net (£596,978 gross). The will bequeathed the residue of her estate to her mother but stipulated it should go to the dogs home should her mother die before her.

There were bequests of £5,000 each to the Theatrical Ladies Guild of Charity and her long-standing secretary and companion Mrs Linda Drew. Had her mother not died the dogs home would also have received £5,000.

Jill Bennett: always had dogs around

Daily Telegraph, 27 May 1991

NOTEBOOK, 27 MAY 1991: Adolf has left half a million to Battersea Dogs' Home. She never bought a bar of soap in all the time she lived with me. Always she cried poverty. 'Poor Jilly, she's got no money.' All the time she was bursting with krugerrands, cast-iron stocks and bond she inherited from her wise old dad, Randle, to say nothing of the £157,000 old mother Nora left her. Ever since those days in 1947 when I used to pass her front-of-house photograph outside the Vaudeville in the Strand on my way from Benn Brothers to pick up Renee, she had been piling up the heftiest assets of any actress since Lily Langtry.

I must have been more profitably 'touched' than most, but all her gay boyfriends, clamouring for AIDS charities, can't be well pleased. She left them only her contempt. Half a million pounds. To the Dogs' Home.

It is the most perfect act of misanthropy, judged with the tawdry, kindless theatricality she strove to achieve in life. She had no love in her heart for people and only a little more for dogs. Her brand of malignity, unlike Penelope's, went beyond even the banality of ambition. It had its roots deep in a kind of bourgeois criminality. Her frigidity was almost total. She loathed men and pretended to love women, whom she hated even more. She was at ease only in the company of homosexuals, whom she also despised but whose narcissism matched her own. I never heard her say an admiring thing of anyone. Her contempt was so petty and terrible. Everything about her life had been a pernicious confection, a sham.

I have only one regret remaining now in this matter of Adolf. It is simply that I was unable to look down upon her open coffin and, like that bird in the Book of Tobit, drop a good, large mess in her eye.

29. Philadelphia Story

23 JANUARY 1966, *Observer*

The Pioneer at the Royal Court

In my own life, January seems to have a gratuitous trick of springing cruelty. Perhaps it is a personal illusion that life at the beginning of the year, like life at the beginning of the day, is harder to bear or contemplate. For me a year hardly begun that springs the death of George Devine is a harsh one to face. It is a bleak week in the English theatre.

I don't think many people really knew him well. I believe I did. I would like to think I had been able to get at least one foot inside that surprising and moving personality. Like many men blessed with a gift for friendship, he was not easily accessible, although he appeared to have an almost comically natural Socratic persona.

He could appear harsh to outsiders, especially know-alls, and, like most profoundly modest and self-critical people, he could seem most arrogant when he was self-denigrating and felt himself being merely realistic. If he could have dissembled with even a little jauntiness, his career might have been more apparently successful and certainly easier. But he despised flattering and wheedling, which is probably why the relations of the Royal Court with the Press were usually a trifle prickly, to say the least of it.

Brush-off

George was a natural teacher. This was because he longed to respect his pupils and learn from them. And he was always fiercely unpatronizing, except to the over-ambitious, dewy-eyed or expedient. On these occasions his contempt could be chilling. He was unfailingly watchful and suspicious of opportunism, ambition, caution and timidity.

People think of the Royal Court as having been a forcing-house for younger writers, but this was not a matter of systematic policy. George made consistent efforts from the very beginning to bring older, established writers – novelists and poets whom he admired – into what people assumed to be a charmed circle of youth. The lack of response from his own generation disturbed him. It seemed like a lordly brush-off of the art he loved.

He was incapable of sentimentality, and I think it is important to stress that this was especially true of his dealings with younger people. What was so formidable was his nose for sham in art and people. I think perhaps the friendships he prized most were with those more or less his own age – Beckett, Michel Saint-Denis, Glen Byam Shaw; only three weeks ago he made a very special effort to entertain Ionesco. It seemed to me he also had a very rare attitude among men – he genuinely and eagerly admired and respected gifted women.

In ten years as artistic director of the Royal Court, George Devine was almost solely responsible for its unique atmosphere, which anyone who knew him knew to be a reflection of his own unique temperament. Some people with their hatred of what they believe to be a self-congratulatory theatrical in-life may think that this became cosy. It never did. It was very English in its approach – empirical is a respect-able word for it, I suppose – unsystematic, non-manifesto.

In the end he was worn down by the grudging, removed attitude to decent and sustained effort that is such a recurrent and depressing aspect of English life. No one can surpass the Englishman's skill of maiming with indifference. Viewed from outside his ten years in Sloane Square may have seemed wonderfully rewarding and exciting, as indeed they often were for him. But this peculiar native climate of critical attrition chilled, bit into him and wore him down. I can imagine his special, amused shrug at the crass newspaper headlines which described him last week as 'kitchen sink director'.

If I give an impression of George Devine as someone disappointed or embittered, I would be quite wrong. His disappointment was mini-mal, in fact, because his expectation was relentlessly pruned. This, combined with his prodigious, hopeful effort, seemed to make his stoicism heroic and generous, rather than a pinched, carping austerity. These were exactly the qualities he admired and saw in the work of personalities as different as Beckett and Brecht. Perhaps it was a kind of reticence. Strength, gaunt lines and simplicity always excited him. During an earlier illness he used to enjoy making furniture and it always expressed this passion in a very touching way.

Thanks Due

The sort of people who were dismissive about George Devine's work were the ones who were aware of the Royal Court only when a star or a fashionable revival appeared there. In spite of that dim support he did make its name a household word. Only a tiny minority actually sampled any of its goods, but most people had at least heard of his work.

The two big subsidized companies – the National and the Royal Shakespeare – owe a debt to him that is incalculable. Their existence is directly due to him. Hundreds of writers and actors owe their present fortunes and favour to him. I am in the greatest debt of all. It seems extraordinary to have been quite so fortunate.

J.O.

FAST FORWARD: *Notebook entries 1972*: Oh, yes, after railing on about her historic performance as Hedda for yet another four hours, J.B. said:

'I was written out.' Very likely. I dare say. She's helping.

'Disliked by everyone at the Court.' – That's me again.

'Always a hopeless fuck.'

'Even the queens don't fancy me because my eyes are very Welsh and too close together.'

'Can't think *how* I earned my money' . . . Me neither.

I, the whole while being a sort of Stoneleigh Oscar Wilde again. Why did I listen? No drink. Wanted the bed. Utterly alone. Too tired. Fitzgerald's 4.00 a.m. crack-up time . . . Oh, yes, she's excited about the opening [*Hedda Gabler*] and Lufer, the sheepdog, which *I* shall have to care for and clean up after. Poor little devil. God protect me, but I can't protect you.

'You only remember the bad things.' What are the good things?

She's obsessed about getting over 40 (surely, already!). What can *I* do? She's attractive sometimes. To me, she's just a pretty scalpel.

I don't think I can last much longer. Dusty, doctoring, disapproving death. I can feel thy sting only too well at the moment. All these books to *read* and can't see the pages. I *am* like a mooching scruffy bear(!) curled up in the dirty corner of the cage he paces. No lustre, no life, only dullish dread. Drew up a list in my pacing head, sweating out the names of *all the people I no longer see* . . . What a *long* list.

Not a drink for seven days. Last night was the most difficult, surprisingly. Saw the Addisons, affectionate but, of course, undercurrent of alarm . . .

Two more plays – *if* they get produced. I see no future. Not even a different one. This is over and it's a relief. Could I learn to fish? Doubt it . . . I don't think I can face *managements* – even though I am so much stronger(?). This is *not* the time for God! Except in its inconsequences and wrangling squalor.

Woke at 10.30. Took too many pills: one, was it two, Carbitol. And one 10mg Valium. J.B. having one of her secretive – or secr*ee*tive as she says – lunches. One of the Pouf Boswells clinging to her wit and, of course, vulnerability. I imagine pterodactyls were vulnerable but still pretty nasty till they got nature's come-uppance. J.B. is clearly going to be a great personal success as Hedda. I hope so, I do – though she says I am willing it to *fail*. Dear God . . .

Try not to be serious. I don't like guttering out much. As Lytton Strachey said on his deathbed: 'If this is it, I don't think much of it.' I look awful and that I don't care about. J.B. has brought her own strategy of ineffable emotional swindling to the play and made it possibly better than we all thought. My notes to A. Page on the acting were rather good. *She* immediately suspected conspiracy. Her own métier. Anyway, she deserves the bravos. I wouldn't know what to do with them. Some hope. Why so hurt? Perhaps that is ceasing too. Thank God, no children, no kiddies, above all no goddam *grand*children. How grisly grandparents are – all that slobbering pride.

More a.m. hours about Hedda and myself when the Carbitols haven't worked off her evening adrenalin of Ibsen. This time:

The staff hate and despise me. Mutual, on the whole.

Alan, the driver. Don't believe it.

Sonny, the housekeeper. Possibly, more like indifference. Too busy thinking up his next frock for his Shirley Bassey appearance at the Gay Ball in Grosvenor House.

My secretary. Most likely. Her office is becoming like a coven for the two of them.

The dogs. Natch.

Nolan. Partly assisted by P.G., I suppose.

Rotten actor. Not altogether true. I could have persevered.

Bad skin. True.

Taken in by 'intellectual codswallop'. – *Me*! Muddle-headed J.O.

Usual stuff about P.G.

Sex not much bother. Scarcely at all. The girls can't fancy me and I don't seem to go overmuch for them . . . After all this, I suppose I shall buy her an overpriced first-night present on Monday. Only one thing I *couldn't* dismiss. After I turned out the light, I thought she was asleep. 'Oh, yes! Even George Devine didn't like you. Do you know why? What he said about you? Because you were always being *sick*!'

1966

2 JANUARY, OPERA HOUSE: I went to a party given for the Friends of Covent Garden. Intellectuals up from the shires and a very Penelope sort of occasion which I would normally have talked or rowed myself out of attending, but I had an incidental reason for going without argument. Robert Stephens had persuaded me to take the part of the Narrator in a crash tour of Stravinsky's *The Soldier's Tale*. He was playing the Devil, Derek Jacobi, whom I knew slightly from the National and liked, was the Soldier, and the Girl was Sally Gilpin, wife of the dancer John. The director was John Cox.

The venture consisted of three or four dates around Tyneside, ending up with a Sunday-night charity performance at the Royal Opera House. The thought of projecting up into the heavenly regions of that vast auditorium was daunting, and something most actors presently at the Court would find beyond their television-mike-trained capabilities. However, Robert's clownish gifts of persuasion won me over. Besides, it was another January and I could feel the noontime chill of midwinter casting its shadow over everything I confronted. The prospect of a.m. hours of hotel-lounge conviviality on the road again and in Robert's company was irresistible. Penelope's plain annoyance at a link with the life of my profession, which seemed to be claimed by a past no longer open to me, added conviction to my decision. It seemed worth risking my negligible reputation as a performer for the sake of a few nights of provincial touring-larks away from the sober constraints of Chester Square's intellectual life.

In the event, I did find rehearsals rather gruelling, which I decided was probably all the more effective as a chastening retort to my numb apprehensions of the Winter Blues. The conductor, an awesomely young, waspish Canadian Jew, who was administrator of the Northern Sinfonia and drove a splendid vintage Rolls, was a merciless disciplinarian. As I spluttered and stumbled, very aware of Robert's grinning relish, he would bang down his baton crossly. 'Mr Osborne, don't you recognize a *downbeat* when you see it?' 'Actually, I don't think I do. In fact, I don't. Perhaps you could give me a signal?' 'That's what I'm *doing*!'

On 17 January, I had a note from George:

> 6, Rossetti Studios
> Flood Street

My dear boy,
Excuse the type-written letter. I was so delighted to receive a copy of *Patriot*. I can't think of any better person to approach the grave with than Baron von Epp.
My best love.

On 19 January we organized a threesome train call and Robert, Jacobi and I had a merry journey up to Newcastle, where we booked in at the Station Hotel. I already wished the tour could go on for weeks. Our opening date was a late-afternoon performance at, I think, Middlesborough Town Hall, a severe Victorian building with the lofty air of a Methodist Chapel. The stage was little more than an open platform but the band made Stravinsky's harsh, hectoring music sound exciting. Robert was an ideal devil-comedian, Jacobi attractively bewildered, Mrs Gilpin performed prettily and the eager audience seemed delighted. Even Doctor Downbeat looked pleased.

We drove back happily in his Rolls to the hotel and I was more giddily and, yes, autonomously joyous than I had been for a very long time. We arranged to meet for a protracted evening of celebration, dinner and then whatever Newcastle after dark had to offer. There was a message from Mrs Gilliatt to ring her urgently. Not from Mrs Osborne. As I put the key in the door, the telephone was ringing. It was my wife, Mrs Gilliatt. 'Darling, I've been trying to get you all afternoon.' 'I've been giving my all to the burghers of Geordieland.' It was a world which excluded and even intimidated her. 'Your compatriots. They were very good, even if we weren't.' 'Darling – George is dead.'

I scarcely heard a word after that. She went on breathlessly, without pause; there was no need to respond. Presently, I became aware that her urgency was mounting as she kept reverently repeating the words *Observer* and its Arts Editor, Richard Findlater. Dragging up attention, I listened. They were *so* anxious that *I* should write George's obituary for the paper on Sunday. Could I do it? Could I? Did it matter? I couldn't write 'Wish you weren't here' on a postcard. I sensed she was becoming impatient with muddle-headed Johnny's sluggish grasp of the situation. This was the kind of professional contingency where her own critical, scalpel skills could bring some intellectual light to bear on an undoubted tragedy for the English theatre.

'Darling,' she said, like someone addressing a geriatric trundling a walking-frame, 'do you think you'll be able to manage it? I know how you must be feeling.' True, I had neither the detachment nor the skills, nor even, possibly, the grammar for the swift construction of a suitable prose tribute in a posh paper, the very phrase I had, in innocence, invented. 'I'll manage.' 'I mean, if you can't do it, everyone will understand. I'm sure Richard will.' Fuck Richard. 'But I do think it should be someone *close* and not just an outsider. Poor Georgie.' Fuck the *Observer*. Still getting no response from old muddle-brain, she persisted like a physiotherapist working on a recalcitrant limb. 'The thing is, darling ... would you like me to do it *for* you? I mean, I know it won't be the same, but George would understand.' How did she *know*? If George could point his pipe at some medium below, he would surely have chosen some other eager Madame Arcarti to interpret his 'understanding'.

'So what do you want me to do, what shall I say to them?' 'I'll do it.' 'Oh, are you really sure you can? It doesn't give you much time.' 'When do they want it?' 'About eleven at the latest. I could phone it through to the copy-takers for you.' Yes, and tidy it up for the discerning *Observer* readership. 'What time does your train get in?' '8.15.' 'I'll have it ready.' 'Are you absolutely sure?' 'Yes.' 'Oh, darling. Poor, darling Georgie. Are you all right?' 'Yes.'

I ordered a bottle of whisky. It was early evening, I had about twelve hours to get my 900 words together and I needed all the aids I could get. I walked out into the night and soon found myself in darkened squares and narrow alleys. Wherever I was, it felt well above the tide and bitterly exposed to the rising sweep of icy air from the North Sea. I was wearing a thick overcoat and woolly scarf and have never felt so cold. Men were already reeling out of pubs and, caught in the light of street corners, streams of ale spewed on to the pavement. I had had no idea where I was going or what I should do next, but the streets were clearly going to become even colder and more hazardous. I remembered the days I had wandered in a daze of adolescent abandonment when Stella had left me to close the windows and turn off the electricity in Brighton. How soft and southern even that summer pain and beach breeze seemed compared to this scalding northern night.

I found myself outside a cinema, newly refurbished. It was showing *The Sound of Music* for the fifth month. In Newcastle. If only Woodfall could manage five months in a back-street picture palace. The box-office was closed but a young man and a girl were making up the evening's takings.

Unable to sell me a ticket, they called a departing usherette and urged her to let me in. I don't know how I may have appeared to them but something made them act quickly and together, and all three hustled me inside. The usherette, a motherly seventeen, told me she had seen the film a hundred and twenty-three times and skilfully flashed a light on what must have been the only empty seat in the house.

For the next couple of hours I watched the trials of the unrelentingly brave Von Trapps climbing every mountain through eidelweiss and unstinting sorrow. I tried not to disturb the rapt couple beside me as I shook silently, shouting down the cry of loss with sounds alive to the tinsel of Hollywood music. My friends, to say nothing of the good readers of the *Observer*, might have been puzzled to witness England's angry not-so-young playwright sitting in a packed northern cinema watching Julie Andrews in alpine flight, blinded by tears.

I blundered out before they started the National Anthem stampede, back into the night, dodging the vomit pools and broken glass. I hadn't eaten since breakfast but felt drained enough by tears and the Von Trapps to sit down with my whisky and a wedge of British Rail writing-paper and start scribbling my 'piece'. As always, a flicker of determination popped up from the flames of alcohol and that nauseous resolve that sometimes goes with it.

By eight o'clock in the morning, I had got down what I calculated in my amateurish way to be around 900 words. Fuck it – like *Luther*, or indeed anything else I had ever sweated over to the indifference of others, they were lucky to get it. So, even, was George. I began weeping again, but it was gone by the time Penelope appeared in the doorway, crabwise and concerned at about 8.30. She took in my fuddled condition at once and expectantly went through my scribbling. Whether it was more coherent than she expected I didn't know and was well past bothering. I lay on the bed and drifted into a painful sleep while she spoke to Findlater and then began the tedious process of dictating to the copytaker. It seemed to take hours and wasn't helped by her on-the-spot setting-to-rights of my personal syntax and punctuation. I thought them both superior to her own affectations, but protest in the face of dumb pedantry was beyond me. I wanted to disappear not proof-read.

With the lead given to her by the London to Newcastle timetable, Penelope was able to take over the arrangement of George's funeral. No one objected, including Jocelyn Herbert, who seemed glad to be relieved of the task of tasteful interment. As in her early days on *Vogue*, Penelope went at it as an inspirational challenge to 'creative enterprise'. Beneath the grim

Golders Green towers of dispatch, it was a triumph of farce and circum-stance. As Bill Gaskill said, none of us knew how to behave. Fortunately, the only decision I felt constrained to make was which suit to wear. I knew I could rely on Penelope to behave for me. Bill arrived at the crematorium with Keith Johnstone – and Sam Beckett in a taxi. All of them had forgotten the address. 'Hoop Lane', Beckett suggested.

> We waited in a dreadful little room until the door opened and a for-mally dressed figure beckoned us. It was Olivier, looking like an under-taker; he always knew how to transform himself. Inside we had to endure some boring piece of the *War Requiem* [Penelope's insistence], which seemed wholly inappropriate for George but it was not quite the thing to play the Modern Jazz Quartet, which we did later at a tribute on the stage of the Court. There was added tension because Sophie, George's wife, and Jocelyn, his mistress, were both there and we felt that where we sat in the chapel was a declaration of our loyalties.
>
> William Gaskill, *A Sense of Direction*, 1988

Three weeks later, Sophie Devine, designing a film for Polanski, was dead of cancer.

Something was most certainly over and irrecoverable, although even I was not yet aware of the bleak landscape that beckoned, or that loveless times would manifest themselves so swiftly and in such succession, and continue and consolidate for the best part of the next ten years. But I already knew that there would never be a place for me to start again. My Court days were over. It was clear enough as I walked away from the concrete and red roses of the crematorium. Yet I hung around Sloane Square, bereft of intent, for another decade or so before I was chucked out. 'Grateful as we are and mindful of your unique contribution to the theatre in general and this building in particular . . .'

On 17 February the House of Lords agreed to review one of the lesser contributors to George's death at fifty-five, the matter of stage censorship. A committee of enquiry was projected, with representatives from both Houses, to look into its application with 'regard to Law and Practice'. Along with Emile Littler, Peter Saunders, Kenneth Tynan and Peter Hall, I was invited to give evidence. The following day there was a memorial meeting, chaired by Lindsay Anderson with a skill I could not fault after his touching defence at George's farewell luncheon barely more than a year earlier. From the stage, I remember only two faces looking up from the stalls: the *Times* critic (what *could* he be doing there?) and Alec Guinness.

Ennismore Gardens Mews, sw7

Dear John Osborne,

I hope you won't feel this note an intrusion or an impertinence. I knew George fairly well for over thirty years, though of course not as intimately as you during the past decade, and I just wanted to tell you how beautifully you evoked him at the memorial meeting at the Court yesterday. All you said was riveting and pleasing and your choice of reading superb. I am sure it would have made George chuckle in that harsh voice as much as it touched many of us in the audience.

Alec Guinness

But there was committee-life after death, and on 8 April, I found myself in the cramped upstairs bar of the theatre announcing the institution of the George Devine Award for Promising Playwrights. I managed to choke my way through that, and subsequently presented a fat cheque to some graceless recipient. Only the once.

For the past four years I had been encouraging Penelope to concentrate her creative yearnings for novel-writing and a stream of short stories and to suppress her obsession with the petty consolation of a weekly by-line. Suddenly, she agreed to take off a few weeks to write her first novel, *One by One*. I rented her a villa in Positano, from a reassuring figure in London's intellectual life; she packed her typewriter and books and was gone, leaving the departure lounge of Chester Square bare. Apart from my sporadic dalliance with J.B., which, like everything else, felt as if it were happening under water, there was little to do.

A short time passed and then, after a series of manic telephone calls, when she exploded as she had done at the Basilica in St Mark's, I decided I had better join her. When I arrived at Positano, she greeted me more effusively and more absorbed than ever. It was clear that, consumed with suspicion as she undoubtedly was, nothing could deflect her from the task of creation. The villa was comfortable and delightful, with a jolly Italian cook-maid to spare her any distracting chores and bring up the fuel to light the fire during the chilly evenings. Penelope spent all day and most of the evenings tapping at her machine. She said very little and was exceptionally secreetive over her manuscript, which she hid away at the end of each day's toil. I read, walked and listened to Dave Brubeck, which pleased her as she insisted on accepting it as a nostalgic tribute to our life together.

When it was time for me to return to London, she accompanied me on the headlong taxi-ride to Naples airport and said not a word. Her head was buried in the manuscript as she scribbled her corrections. She finished, quite literally, as we drew up at embarkation and thrust the script at me, barking simple instructions and kissing me in a kind of crippled passion. She returned to the cab and sped back to the creative eyrie over the Bay of Naples.

I don't remember the circumstances of her return to Chester Square. The summer of 1966 is all but lost to me.

At Easter in 1985, after watching *God Rot Tunbridge Wells*, an affectionate account of George Frideric Handel I had written for television, I looked at the quaintly peevish reviews of it in the Sunday papers, had a few more glasses of champagne and went into a prolonged coma. I emerged from it not cowed by the brush of the fearful angel's wing but angry and astonished at my determination not to go gentle into any good night in Tunbridge Wells or anywhere else. Unconscious in intensive care, I experienced a vivid succession of images that were comparable to the impressions I retained while more or less conscious during the summer of 1966. All I can retrieve of the cloud of events, scraps of a dream in magical inconsequence, is the following:

Firstly: a physical, nursery brawl in Chester Square, while Penelope tried to prevent me dragging a suitcase down the staircase . . .

Escaping to the Park, finding a shady tree near the Albert Memorial and falling asleep with the suitcase as my pillow . . .

Then: rising in the early mornings, sitting alone downstairs in J.B.'s mews flat, drinking brandy from the bottle . . .

Seeing *Trelawny of the Wells* at the Old Vic, where J.B. had replaced another actress, and weeping not at her but at Pinero's lament for our calling ('What a rotten profession!') and at Robert Stephens's performance as Tom Robertson, most surely based on my own imminent degradation . . .

Lastly: having dinner at the Ivy with J.B., Svoboda, the most fashionable Czech stage-designer – all plunging staircases – Doris Lessing, who had adapted the play under discussion (Ostrovsky's *The Storm*), and Dexter, who was directing it at the peak of his energy in his early days at the National.

At some point I must have decided not to inflict on others whatever behaviour increasing oblivion was imposing on me. Knowing that the housekeeper in Sussex was away on holiday, I got myself down to Hellingly and settled in alone with my Great Dane, Western. There was plenty of tinned food in the kitchen, the house was warm and there was a wide selection of drink, although I confined myself to a hangover cocktail, recommended to me by Robin Fox, of iced Fernet Branca and *crème de menthe*. I drank it pre-emptively, obviating the in-between cause of hangover. Western curled up with me on the bed and must surely have slept for a very long time, although I know I did feed her once and she reluctantly went out for a pee.

Ringing Jocelyn R.: I must have because I saw her, beside the bed, with her new husband, looking down at me. I heard nothing. It was intensive care without wiring up.

Next: Penelope getting into bed beside me before driving me to this place, the Regent's Park Nursing Home, and kissing me on the forehead.

A very cheerful nursing sister kept giving me pills and urged me not to swallow too much water. A lanky psychiatrist, a night-club Jonathan Miller, came in now and then, palpably madder than I could be in whatever clinical extremity. He pumped Pentothal into me.

J.B. came, carefully got-up for the occasion and looking as concerned as she could manage but more honestly vexed and resentful. 'I wish *I* could afford a nervous breakdown … The psychiatrist thinks you should be married to a farmer's wife.' It didn't sound such a bad idea.

Tony came with the sort of book he thought might entertain a sickly blimp, *The Washing of the Spears*, a fascinating account of the Zulus' heroic resistance to the British Army, and a rather tame volume of erotic poetry. I was still in the thrall of Pentothal, Largactil and other little sweeties, and my insistent flow of chatter must have alarmed or bored him off smartly.

The day after my arrival, I suppose it was, a telegram arrived from Penelope postmarked Philadelphia. My muddle-headedness was only exacerbated by 'Philadelphia', celebrated for ever by W.C. Fields, to whom I was feeling close. The sister read it out to me in rotund Irish style:

> SLEEP AND SLEEP STOP PRETEND THE NUNS ARE MEN IN DRAG STOP TAKE GREATEST CARE OF YOURSELF AND GAIN SPACE AROUND YOURSELF STOP MIKE IN HIS OWN WAY IN NEED OF MY LOVE AND SUPPORT HERE STOP WILL THINK OF YOU ALL THE TIME HOPE YOU ARE WELL AND NOT IN PANIC WITH ALL MY HEART – YOUR WIFE

She followed Mike Nichols's pre-Broadway tour. The next prestigious date to be marked by another batch of telegrams was Boston, Mass. I can't remember the name of the play that necessitated her presence nor, indeed, if it was a palpable Broadway hit. It seems most likely. Anyway, I think that her telegrams from the real world helped my recovery and sent the neurologists packing.

In early September, Noël Coward invited – no, ordered me – to have supper, *à deux*, as he might have said. He was making his last and successful appearance in his own plays, *Suite in Three Keys*. I arrived promptly, I thought, after curtain-down. Coley opened the door. 'The Master is waiting,' he said. I was being reprimanded. Noël, however, was brisk and welcoming.

We had a simple but delicious soufflé and salad. He began to interrogate me, almost as if he knew I had been released so recently from the Bin. His second question was, 'How queer are you?' If I myself had small talent to amuse, I could at least make an effort to please. 'Oh, about twenty per cent.' 'Really! Are you? I'm ninety-five.' He went on. 'I understand you've been a very silly boy. You must never trust a woman.' 'But you've so many women friends,' I protested. More than I had. 'No matter. Never trust 'em and never, never marry them. Which you appear to do.'

His own tiredness and my weariness of such close confinement with myself for a whole summer prevented me from confiding in him. I excused myself and rose to go, feeling frail and afraid of the threatened effort of intimacy. He gave me my card of departure. 'You're *very* melancholy, aren't you?' 'Yes. Very. But I'm also sanguine when I'm able.' 'I'm glad to hear it.' He embraced me quickly and I left, grateful for his circumspection and, for once, my own.

Envoi

The prince of darkness is a gentleman . . .
>Edgar in William Shakespeare, *King Lear*, III. iv

Whatever else, I have been blessed with God's two greatest gifts: to be born English and heterosexual.
>*Notebook*, 1964

When Nolan was about six, Penelope was paying one of her rare visits to London from New York and, after a great deal of prolonged negotiation, agreed that I might come round to Chester Square and spend an hour or so in my daughter's company.

The nanny opened the door and ushered me upstairs to the airport lounge where Penelope was sprawled on the floor, much as she had been at our first unchaperoned encounters in Lowndes Square. With her was an Israeli film-director and they were going through a loud demonstration of young film-director being fired by distinguished critic-turned-writer Oscar nominee. Nolan was seated in a corner of the open-plan, L-shaped room and I tried to have some sort of conversation with her.

Penelope attempted to include me as a professional outsider privy to the problems presented by her script, which seemed to have something to do with life in England during the last war. Muttering something about only working when I was paid in advance, I felt I had endured enough crude humiliation, and took my leave.

She followed me to the front door, past the sixteen-foot-high copper doors to the dining-room which had cost me a ransom. As I said goodbye to her, her mouth slid to one side, the piercing brown of her eyes eclipsed into the black fury I had seen so often. 'Goodbye, then.' She raised her face to kiss me, drew back against the porch and contemplated me. 'You've really fucked your life up, haven't you?'

I walked past the Royal Court, down the Kings Road and back to J.B. It was hard not to agree with Penelope. There was no escaping from it. It was an irreversible judgement, the irrefutable evidence of a visible cirrhosis of my spirit.

> I will not refrain my mouth, I will speak in the anguish of my spirit, I will complain in the bitterness of my soul.

Job, 7:11

I wanted to shout out and for someone to hear me. 'I am not yet dead.'

> Today I went for lunch at the Garrick. Leaning against the bar was a young man in his late twenties perhaps, not a member but a guest. He began asking me questions about myself and I made a slight effort to answer them politely. Finally, he stretched himself to his full height to follow his host-member downstairs to lunch and said very loudly, 'Of course, you *did* go through a bad patch, we know. However, I've no doubt you'll recover!'

Notebook, 1972

Such certainty, like mediocrity, can be unbearably enviable. In particular, to a life overruled by passion.

Index

Abbott and Costello, 45, 198
Abie's Irish Rose, 398
ABPC, 427
Acapulco, 427–33, 474, 523, 528
Ackerley, J. R., 225
Ackers Street, Manchester, 174
Actors' Church Union, 172
Addison, Jock, 321, 533, 545, 549, 558
Addison, Pamela, 321, 533–4, 549, 550, 558
Adelphi Theatre, 338, 405
The Adventures of Robin Hood, 5, 52–3, 58
Aga Khan, 16
Aitken, Marie, 552
Aladdin, 231–2
Albery, Donald, 255, 302, 339, 384, 405
Aldington, Richard, 91–2
American Library, Grosvenor Square, 252
Amis, Kingsley, 294
Anderson, Lindsay, 290, 293, 335, 376–9, 381, 437, 438, 489, 511, 539, 543, 564
Anderson, Maxwell, 366
Andrews, Julie, 370, 563
Anestasia, Albert, 345
Angel Pavement, 133
Angela (Penelope Gilliatt's sister), 523, 524, 538, 539, 540
Anglican Community of the Resurrection, 447
L'Année à Marienbad, 502
Annigoni, 337, 463
Anouilh, Jean, 296
Anspach, Andrew, 343
The Apollo of Bergerac, 331

Apollo Theatre, Harlem, 345
Apollo Theatre, Shaftesbury Avenue, 291
Arabella, 544
Arden, John, 338, 377, 378, 382, 511
Argosy, 153
Ariel, 91
Armstrong-Jones, Anthony (later Lord Snowdon), 466
Arnold, Edward, 79
Arthur, Uncle, xv, 9, 16
Arts Council, 253, 254, 277, 290
Arundel Terrace, Brighton (No., 7a), 201, 205, 210, 211, 212, 213, 440
As You Like It, 528
Ashcroft, Peggy, 261, 300, 307, 309, 338, 376, 420, 506n
Askey, Arthur, 73
Associated British Picture Corporation, 394
Associated Pictures, 291
Associated Television, 439
Atkins, Miss (actress), 171, 175, 176
Atkinson, Brooks, 341, 342, 399
Atlantic City, 398–9
Attlee, Clement, 153, 159, 193, 207, 279
Auden, W. H., 425
August for the People, 306, 339, 459, 489–90
Augustine, St, 305
Ayckbourn, Alan, 191
Ayer, Professor Freddie, 441–2, 470–71

Bach, Johann Sebastian, 444, 539, 545
Bachardy, Don, 393, 452, 491, 492
Baddeley, Hermione, 492

Baker, Hylda, 168
Balcon, Sir Michael, 434, 435
Ballet Nègres company, 251, 407
Balsam, Marty, 400
Banbury, Frith, 255, 271
Banks, Lynne Reid, 220, 221–3, 251
Barber, John, 299
Baring-Gould, Sabine, 77, 158
Barker's (John Barker & Co. Ltd),
     Kensington High Street, 29
Barnes, Kenneth, 220
Barrett, Philip, 245, 246, 248
Barrett, Reginald, 216
Barry O'Brien Productions, 167
Bart, Lionel, 404
Barwick, Charlie, 325, 326, 327, 328, 514
Basil, Uncle, 105
Bates, Alan, 296, 297, 306, 338, 342, 362
Bates, Queenie Phoebe Adelina Rowena
     (née Grove; JO's aunt), 13, 17, 18,
     20–24, 29, 32, 36, 46, 81, 106, 107,
     109–10, 145–6, 169, 194, 203, 265–6,
     326, 347, 368, 396–7
Bates, Sidney (JO's uncle), 21–3, 24,
     106–7, 145–6, 194, 203, 266, 312, 326,
     347, 368, 396–7
Baxter, Beverley, 40
BBC, 78, 86, 198, 199, 294, 299, 312, 438
Beach, Ann, 506n, 537, 540
Beardsley, Aubrey, 447
Beaton, Cecil, 310, 413
Beatrice (actress), 195
La Beaumette, Valbonne, 488, 490, 491,
     497, 506
Beaumont, Hugh 'Binkie', 136, 203, 207,
     243, 291, 299, 302, 313, 323, 324, 340,
     345, 382, 391, 392, 401, 405, 420–23,
     434, 481, 484, 492, 539
Beauvoir, Simone de, 288
Beaverbrook, Lord, 16
Because I'm Black, 212, 215, 252
Beckett, Samuel, 293, 382, 390–91, 447,
     479, 513, 525–6, 557, 564
Bedford, Duke of, 413

Beecham, Sir Thomas, 524
Behan, Brendan, 388, 531, 539
Belgrade Theatre, Coventry, 379, 382
Bell, Mary Hayley, 222
The Bells, 16, 509
The Bells of St Mary's, 146
Benn, Sir Ernest, 150, 154, 160
Benn, Glanville, 150, 154, 157
Benn, John, 150, 154, 157
Benn Brothers, 150, 154–7, 159, 161, 168,
     213, 555
Bennett, Alan, 538
     review of *A Better Class of Person*
          xii–xvii
Bennett, Billy, 497
Bennett, Jill, 160, 163, 545, 549–55,
     558–60, 566, 567, 569
Bennett, Nora, 555
Bennett, Randle, 555
Benson, Frank, 229
Berger, John, 511
Bergman, Ingmar, 466
Bergman, Ingrid, 145
Berliner Ensemble, 308
Berlioz, Hector, v, 545
Berman, Shelley, 356, 357–8
Bernie, 398, 399
Bert (stage carpenter), 170, 171, 172, 177,
     194
Bessborough, Lord, 376
Bessie, Auntie, 104, 105, 109, 312, 347
Betjeman, John, 349, 515, 549
A Better Class of Person (reviewed by Alan
          Bennett) xii–xvii
Betty (dancing teacher), 166
Beuselinck, Oscar, 303, 304, 325–8, 331,
     396, 442, 451, 488, 514, 523, 538, 543
Bevan, Aneurin, 193, 279, 376, 460
Bevin, Ernest, 495
Billy Liar, 459, 476
Birmingham, 249
The Bishop's Bonfire, 294
Bishop's Park, Fulham, 9, 25
Black, George, 28

Black, Kitty, 263, 270, 271, 280
The Blacks, 447
Blacksell, C. E., 294, 318, 543
Blake, George, 507–8
Bliss, Sir Arthur, xvi, 147
Blithe Spirit, 166
Blond, Elaine, 318, 363, 462, 543, 544
Blond, Neville, 318, 376, 378, 462–3, 476, 489, 542
Blood and Sand, 366
Blood of the Bambergs, 536, 537, 538
Bloom, Claire, 439
Blore, Eric, 79
Blue Angel, 215–16
The Blue Lagoon, 166–7
Blundell, Mr (teacher), 60, 61, 65, 66
Bob (actor at Bridgwater), 234, 237–8, 239
Bogarde, Dirk, xix, 330
Bognor, 82–6, 98, 99, 145, 147
Bolshoi Ballet, 335, 406
Bolt, Robert, 295, 509, 512, 528–9
Bolton, Edward, 446
Bond books (Fleming), 460
Bond, Edward, 377
Bosch, Hieronymus, 444, 480
Bottomley, Horatio, 12
Bourne Hall, Ewell, 50
Bournemouth, 194, 204, 411
The Boyfriend, 404
Boys in Blue, 398, 518
Bracken, Brendan, 392
Bradford Drive, Ewell (No. 39), 70–71, 84, 90, 100, 104
Bradlaugh, Charles, 77
Braine, John, 494
Brambell, Wilfred, 214
Bratby, John, 494
Brathwaite, Richard, 444
Brecht, Bertolt, 20, 307, 308, 309, 315, 338, 390–91, 483, 485, 557
Brenton, Howard, 377
Brett, Jeremy, 463
Brideshead Revisited xv

Bridgwater, Somerset, 233, 234–40, 247, 251, 281, 328, 337
Brien, Alan, 484
Brighton, xiii, xv, xvii, xx, 13, 108, 197, 199, 200–201, 203–7, 212, 308, 332, 333, 370, 398, 412, 460, 524
Brighton Hippodrome, 412, 413
Bristol Old Vic, 253, 254, 293
British Council, 459
British Gas Corporation, 150
British Institute of Fiction Writing Science, 152–3, 207
British Lion, 434, 459
Brockway, Fenner, 514
Brompton Hospital, 9, 25, 26–7, 60, 164, 203
Brook, Peter, 20, 302, 427
Browning, Elizabeth Barrett, 515
Browning, Robert, 515
The Browning Version, 286
Brubeck, Dave, 565
Bruce, Edgar K., 215, 216
Brunning, Mrs C. C., 522
Bryden, Bill, 377
Buffen, Joan, 54–60, 66, 70, 81, 86, 89, 94, 102, 103, 109, 119, 139, 171
Buffen, Mrs, 54–5, 56, 67, 103, 117
Bull, Peter, 480–81
Buñuel, Luis, 428
Burns, Robert, 543
Burton, Richard, 235, 310, 370, 393, 394, 427, 489
Burton, Sybil, 310, 370
Butler, Reg, 437, 438
Button Down Club, 457, 458

Caddie, Auntie, 20, 21, 145
Cagney, James, 344, 434
Caine, Michael, 295
Caithness Road, Hammersmith (No. 14), 244, 247, 252
Calder, John, 513
Caldwell, Zoë, 463, 464
Camberwell, 243, 244, 247, 325

Cambridge, 177–8
Campaign for Nuclear Disarmament (CND), 437, 489, 507
Campbell's Kingdom, 330
Camus, Albert, 288
Candida, 254
Cannan, Denis, 255
Cannes Film Festival, 427
Capote, Truman, 393
Capri, 419, 424
Cardiff, 170, 172
Cards of Identity, 293, 306–7, 332
The Caretaker, 522
Carfax Hotel, St Lawrence Halt, Isle of Wight, 88, 89, 90, 92, 93, 103
Carmichael, Hoagy, 545
Caron, Leslie, 310
Carroll, Lewis, 75
Carroll, Madeleine, 79, 129
Carson, Sir Edward, 16
Carters Seed Factory, Raynes Park, 30, 96, 107
Casablanca, 288
The Case for Conservatism, 76
Casson, Hugh, 406, 414
Cecil, Uncle, 105
Central Casting, 344, 354
The Chairs, 331, 332, 383, 390
Chamberlain, Neville, 86
Champion, Harry, 33
Chandler, Raymond, 395
The Changeling, 459, 462, 463
Chaplin, Charlie, 45, 74, 200, 320
The Charge of the Light Brigade, 434, 453, 543, 545, 549
Charley's Aunt, 243
Cheffie, xiii, 108, 112, 118, 144, 160, 193, 209
Chekhov, Anton, 506
Chelsea Palace, 315, 320
Cherry, Mr (grocer), 231, 232–3
Chichester, 83–4, 98–9
Chicken Soup with Barley, 382
Chips, 73

Chiswick Empire, 107
Church of England, 447
Churchill, Sir Winston, 12, 235
Cilento, Diane, 474, 523, 528
The Citadel, 21
Citizen Kane, 80
Clandon Close, Stoneleigh, 31–4, 37, 41, 43, 46, 72, 82, 87, 94, 95, 103, 116, 193
Clarence, Duke of, 12
Clarendon pub, Hammersmith, 17, 33
Clark's College, xii, 144, 161
Clements, Richard, 493
Cleopatra, 489
Club Theatre, 546
Clutterbuck, 473
Cobham, Sir Alan, 411
Cobham, Lady, 411
Cohen, Alexander, 339
Coleman, Mrs (landlady), 179
Colindale Sanatorium, 25
Collins, Canon, 514
Collins' Theatre, Islington, 320–21
Comedy Theatre, 255
Comfort, Alex, 437, 438
Coming Through the Rye, 243
Committee of, 100, 507
Confessions of an English Opium Eater, 24–5
Congreve, William, 497, 506
Connaught Hotel, 316
Connery, Sean, 295, 406, 460
Connolly, Cyril, 310, 375, 441
Conservative Party, 171, 279, 290
Constantine, Eddie, 434
La Contessa, 455
Contraception, 57
Cooke, Elisha, Jr, 455
Cooney, Ray, 498
Cooper, Gary, 524
Copeau, Jacques, 228, 282
Coriolanus, 422
Cornwall, xvi
Coronation Street, 79
Corri, Adrienne, 406, 414

Cotter, Mr (teacher), 97, 118, 120
The Country Girl, 252
The Country Wife, 338, 405
Courtenay, Tom, 295
Coward, Noël, 77, 120, 191, 204, 209, 244,
    254, 267, 289, 340, 343, 363, 386, 413,
    414, 415, 421, 422, 423, 479, 481, 568
Cox, John, 560
Creighton, Anthony, 219–26, 228–33, 242,
    244, 249, 252, 254, 261, 262, 263, 270,
    278, 279, 284, 302, 326, 332, 346,
    348–51, 372, 373, 374, 377, 380, 398,
    405, 516–19, 521
Creighton, Mrs, 229, 243–4, 263
Cripps, Sir Stafford, 151
Criterion Theatre, 302
A Critic on the Hearth, 295
Crompton, Richmal, xvi, 63
Cronin, A. J., 335
Crookham Road, Fulham (No., 2), 8
Crosbie, Annette, 463
Crosby, Bing, 145
The Crucible, 296–7
Crystal Palace, 11
Cuckoo in the Nest, 542
Curtis Brown, 263, 271
Customs and Excise, 227–8, 230–33

Dahlberg, Gilda, 409, 410, 412, 416–17
Daisy, Auntie, 104, 105, 109, 128, 193,
    201
Dallas, Uncle, 105
Dalton, Miss (theatre company manager),
    176, 194–5, 197
Dancing Years, 28
The Dandy, 73
Daneman, Paul, 249
Daphne (of Elmsleigh Road School), 96,
    98, 118, 119, 121, 133
Dassau, Paul, 309
Davenport, Nigel, 296, 307, 309, 333, 338,
    382
Davis (actor), 172, 195
Davis, Bette, 79

Davis, John, 330, 331
Davis, Sammy, Jr, 360
Dawson, Les, 110
Dawson, Mrs (landlady), 110, 112, 114,
    119
Dawson, Peter, 33, 128, 524
de Banzie, Brenda, 317, 321, 434
de Havilland, Olivia, 113
de Quincey, Thomas, 24–5
Death of a Hero, 91–2
The Death of Satan, 294, 305
Declaration, 375, 376, 437
The Decline and Fall of the West, 158
The Deep Blue Sea, 247, 250, 286
Deeping, Warwick, 38, 40–43, 74, 80, 193,
    314
Delaney, Shelagh, 462, 463, 494, 511,
    514
Dennis, Nigel, 293, 294, 306, 332, 459,
    489
Denville Players, 285
Derby, 249, 250, 252, 278, 380
Derby Day, Epsom xx
Derby Rep, 278
Derry and Toms, Kensington High Street,
    29
The Desert Song, 406
Desmond, Patrick, 186, 201, 205, 207,
    211–12, 220, 222, 223, 225, 227, 230,
    232, 245, 253, 263, 271, 412
    produces *No Room at the Inn*, 189
    and the Granville Theatre, Walham
      Green, 191–2
    marriage, 197
    produces *The Devil Inside*, 198, 211, 216
    and *Because I Am Black*, 212, 215
    finds JO a job in Leicester, 213
    produces *Blue Angel*, 215, 216
    produces *Rain*, 248
    dislikes *Epitaph for George Dillon*, 255
    and *Personal Enemy*, 270
    reads *Look Back in Anger*, 270–71
The Devil Inside, 197–8, 211, 216–17, 284
    see also Resting Deep

Devine, George, xxi, 40, 184, 220, 226, 244, 261, 271, 272, 280–81, 284, 293–4, 310, 315, 354, 368, 376–7, 381, 382–3, 422, 447, 449–50, 560
  appearance, 281
  character, 281, 355
  and English Stage Company, 282
  early life, 287
  and *Look Back*, 288, 293, 298, 299, 300
  on agents, 289, 290, 292
  blacklist of writers, 294
  and Richardson's divide and rule technique, 297
  and *August for the People*, 306
  and *Cards of Identity*, 306
  in *The Good Woman of Setzuan*, 307
  and JO's journalism, 310
  and *The Entertainer*, 316, 322–3, 328, 330
  and Vivien Leigh, 322
  in *The Chairs*, 331
  and *The Making of Moo*, 332, 333
  and *The Country Wife*, 338
  lectures in America, 353, 451
  receives CBE, 373
  and *George Dillon*, 373, 374
  and *Declaration*, 376
  and *Chicken Soup*, 379
  and John Dexter, 380
  and Beckett, 390–91
  and *Paul Slickey*, 403, 405, 413
  and *Lulu*, 421, 424
  and Edward Bolton, 446
  and Trevor Huddleston, 447, 448
  and *Luther*, 450, 463, 476, 477, 478, 484
  friendship with JO, 486
  in Valbonne, 488–90, 539
  in *The Seagull*, 506n, 539
  attends JO's marriage to Penelope Gilliatt, 538
  resigns as director of Royal Court, 542
  and *Patriot*, 546, 547, 548, 561
  has heart attack, 548
  death, 556, 561
  debt of Royal Court to, 556–7
  JO's obituary, 556–8, 561–3
  JO addresses memorial meeting at Royal Court, 564–5
Devine, Sophie, 289, 564
Devon, 123, 132, 139
Devonshire Park Theatre, 550
Dexter, John, 251, 332, 377, 379–82, 406, 506, 510, 512, 537
Dickens, Charles, 186
Dietrich, Marlene, 400–401, 538
Dignam, Mark, 506n
Diplock, Mr and Mrs, 234, 236, 238
The Dirty Dozen, 371
Divorce Me, Darling, 544
Docker, Lady, 409
Dodd, Ken, 547
Don Giovanni, 339
Don Juan in Hell, 294, 305
Donat, Robert, 21, 79
Donerail Street, Fulham, 9
Donne, John, 485
Dorset, xvi, 114, 117
Double Indemnity, 139
Douglas, Lord Alfred, 12
Douglas-Home, William, 160
Down Under Club, 445
Dr Jekyll and Mr Hyde, 243
Dracula, 243
Dramatists' Guild, 350
Drummond, Vivienne, 336, 342, 362
Dryden, John, 170
Duckworth, Reverend, 177–8
Duel of Angels, 439, 451, 453, 456
Duet for Two Hands, 222, 223
Duncan, Ronald ('the Black Dwarf'), 291, 292, 294, 305, 306
Duncannon pub, off St Martin's Lane, London, xv, 13, 19
Dunne, Sir Laurence, VC, 512
Duryea, Dan, 79

Earle, Phyllis, 313
East Cheam, 44, 55

East Grinstead, 223
Eastbourne, 194, 204
Edinburgh Festival, 489
Edward VII, King, 404
Edward VIII, King (later Duke of Windsor), 16, 450
Eliot, T. S., 205, 289, 305, 450
Ell, Grandma (JO's great-grandmother), xv, 10, 11
Ell family, 10–11, 12
Ellerby Street, Fulham, 9
Elliott, Denholm, 386
Elliott, G. H., 174
Ellis, Mary, 234
Ellis, Mrs (landlady), 178
Elmsleigh Road School, Stoneleigh, 95–8, 99, 102–3, 112, 114, 118, 119, 121
Elstree Studios, 317, 393
Elvira (Beaumont's housekeeper), 391–2, 401, 422
Elwes, Dominic, 412
Elwes, Tessa, 412
Empire, Kingston, 184, 187
Empire, Sunderland, 178, 179
Endgame, 373, 391
English Stage Company (ESC), 271, 282, 285, 288, 290, 292, 293, 294, 298, 301, 302, 318, 319, 335, 376, 433, 463, 506n, 539, 543, 544
The Entertainer, xv, xxi, 8, 15, 20, 315–24, 328–30, 349, 350, 362–6, 386, 477, 479
The Entertainer (film), 352, 424, 434–6, 442–3, 449, 459
Epitaph for George Dillon, 179, 184–6, 231, 254–5, 284, 372, 373–4, 384, 386, 396, 398–9, 405, 426
Epsom, Surrey, 51, 58, 70, 73, 83, 163, 203, 223
Epsom Choral Society, 77
Epsom College, 59
Epsom Cottage Hospital, 145, 164
Equity, 172, 177, 184, 203, 228, 230, 231, 243, 248, 523

Eric (a spiv), 109, 116, 117, 118, 120, 161
Essex pub, Strand, 25
Esslin, Martin, 299
Evans, Edith, 317, 394–5, 406, 539
Every Day But Christmas, 378
Ewell, Surrey, 35–6, 37, 50–52, 60, 80, 90, 93, 100, 103, 108, 118, 152
Ewell Boys' School, 51, 60–67, 84, 88
Ewell Castle School, 50, 121
Ewell Parade, Ewell (No. 2), 51, 71

Fairbanks, Douglas, 386
The Family Reunion, 205, 255
Farouk, King, 441
Farrell, Charlie, 107–8
Farrell, Mrs, 108
Faulkner, William, 359
Fearon, George, 298, 299–300, 468
Felpham, near Bognor, 82, 84, 85, 98
Fettes, Christopher, 382
Feydeau, Ernest, 421, 473
Field, Shirley Ann, 434
Field, Sid, 198, 223, 232
Fielding, Henry, 523
Fields, Gracie, 419
Fields, W. C., 567
Film Fun, 73
Financial Times, 272
Finch, Peter, 349, 506n
Findlater, Richard, 561, 562, 563
Fings Ain't What They Used to Be, 404
Finlay Street, Fulham, 9
Finlay Street Infants School, Fulham, 9, 26
Finney, Albert, 295, 415, 419, 420, 421, 443, 459, 476, 480, 482, 484
First World War, xiv, 87
Fischer Verlag, 311
Fitzherbert Court, Rottingdean, 208, 209–11
Flanagan and Allan, 232
Flare Path, 218–19, 348
Fleming, Ian, 460
Flemyng, Robert, 201

Flewitt, Lyall, 452–3

Flynn, Errol, 5, 53

Folkestone Film Festival [fictitious], 472, 500, 508

Fonda, Henry, 386

Foot, Michael, 376, 413

Forbes, Meriel (Lady Richardson), 422

Formby, George, 33, 120, 524

Formby, George, Senior, 174

Forster, E. M.: 'Racial Exercise', 6

The Four Feathers, 58, 79, 295

Fox, Robin, 290, 413, 567

Francine, 353–61, 369, 370, 372, 385, 387, 388, 390, 426–7, 430–33, 472, 474, 538

Frank, Great Uncle, 104, 105, 122–3

Frankenstein, 243

Fraser, Ronald, 377

Frayn, Michael, 50

Freedman, Harold, 362, 366, 385

Freethinker, 77

Friends of Covent Garden, 560

Frink, Elisabeth, 469–70, 515

Frinton Rep, 377

Frinton-on-Sea, 247

Fry, Christopher, 255, 284, 289, 294, 439, 450

Fry, Jeremy, 466

Fulham, xv, 8–9, 25, 26, 30, 108, 118, 235

Furness-Bland, Ronald, 126, 128–30, 132, 197

Gable, Clark, 460

Gabor, Zsa Zsa, 409, 451, 452, 460

Galileo, 485

Gandhi, Mahatma, 16

Garnsey, Rita, 168, 170, 176, 177, 184

Garrett, Elizabeth, 161, 166, 167, 212, 436

Garrick Club, 570

Garson, Greer, 365, 386, 400

Gas Council, 151

Gas World, xvii, 150–55, 156, 158

Gascoigne, Bamber, 484

Gaskill, Bill, 293, 374, 377, 382, 399–400, 511, 549, 564

Gaslight, 243

Gaston (director in Kidderminster), 248

Gay, Maisie, 234

Gaycroft School of Dancing, North Cheam, 161, 165, 166, 168, 169, 436

Gaynor, Janet, 51

Gem, 51, 73, 101

General Election (1945), 76

Genet, Jean, 447

George VI, King, 530

Gideon, Melville, 33

Gielgud, John, 294, 307, 414, 540

Gill, Eric, 463

Gill, Peter, 377

Gilliatt, Penelope, 466–75, 481, 482–3, 490–91, 500–503, 506, 509, 510, 516–18, 520, 521, 523–32, 534–40, 542, 544, 545, 545–6, 555, 559, 560, 561, 563–70

Gilliatt, Roger, 466, 467, 471–4, 481, 501, 510, 516–17, 520, 523

Gilpin, John, 560

Gilpin, Sally, 560, 561

Giraudoux, Jean, 331, 332, 439

Gish, Sheila, 552

Glasgow, 173

Glasgow Empire, 345

Gloucester, Duke of, 467

Glover, Julian, 480

Glyn House, Ewell, 51

Glyn, Sir Arthur, 51

God Rot Tunbridge Wells, 445, 566

Goetschius, George, 403, 526

Gone with the Wind, 113–14, 316

The Good Companions, 133

The Good Woman of Setzuan, 307–8

Gopal, Ram, 251, 406–7

Gordon-Maclean, Colin de Vere, 497–9, 522

Grainger, Percy, 524

Granada, 439

Granville Theatre, Walham Green, 9, 192, 197

Granville-Barker, Harley, 377

Green, Hughie, 505

Greene, Graham, 289, 395, 417, 419, 472, 476

Gregg, Betty, 139

Gregg, Jane, 139

Griffiths, Hugh, 370

Grimm Brothers, 75

Grimsby, 173–4, 220, 234–5

Grisewood, Freddy, 96

Grove, Adelina Rowena (née Ell; JO's maternal grandmother), 9, 10, 12–14, 17, 19, 22, 33, 35, 36, 78, 102, 103, 105–6, 169, 194, 203, 266–7, 346–7, 397

Grove, Jack (JO's uncle), 22, 24, 105–6, 203, 312, 313, 326, 347, 367–8, 397, 504

Grove, John Henry ('Jack'; JO's uncle), 13

Grove Park Hotel, Ilfracombe, 220–21, 223

Grove, Peter (JO's cousin), 24

Grove, Vi (JO's aunt), 24

Grove, William Crawford (JO's maternal grandfather), 9–13, 15, 16, 17, 35, 46, 76, 102, 103, 108, 131, 169

Grove family, 16–17, 19, 46, 47

Guinness, Alec, 391, 564–5

Gwatkin, Sir Norman, 477

Hackney Empire, 187

Haigh, Kenneth, 295, 297, 339, 341, 342–3, 371

Hall, Sir Peter, 271, 310, 420, 528, 564

Hall, Willis, 545, 550, 553

Hamilton, Michael, 167, 168, 186–7, 195, 213

Hamlet, xiii, xx, 229–30, 295, 339

Hammarskjöld, Dag, 539

Hammersmith Palace of Dancing, 262

Hammerstein, Oscar, 460

Hampton, Christopher, 377

Hancock-Nunn, Eileen, 522

Hancock-Nunn, Captain Vivian, 522

Handel, George Frideric, 543, 566

Hanley, 194, 197, 220

Hanson, Harry, 242–3, 244, 325

Happy Birthday, 204–7

Happy Days, 542

Harbord Street, Fulham, 9, 10, 12, 16, 18, 24, 46, 87, 102, 108, 109

Harding, Gilbert, 308, 460

Harding, Warren, 525

Hardwicke, Cedric, 386

Hardy, Robert, 420

Hare, David, xviii–xxii, 399

Hare, Robertson, 214

Harewood, 7th Earl of, 292, 294, 302, 318

Harmer, Dolly, 168

Harmsworth, 'Bubbles', 413

Harrison, Nancy, 515

Harrison, Rex, 166, 187, 195, 459, 489, 490, 541

Hart, Moss, 190, 479, 524

Hartlepool, 220

Hartley, Neil, 541

Hartley Wintney, 223

Harvey, Laurence, 338, 434, 543

Harvey, Martin, 172

Hastings, Michael, 377

Hawkins, Jack, 413

Haworth, Donald, 338, 377

Hay, Ian, 92

Hay, Will, 120

Hayling Island, 224–5, 283, 405–6, 474, 483, 513

Hayling Island School of Dancing, 231, 232

Haymarket Group, 255

Hazlitt, William, 302–3

Hedda Gabler, 261, 281, 553, 558

Hellingly (The Old Watermill), near Hailsham, 516, 517, 520–24, 526, 534, 537, 539, 549–50, 566

Hellman, Lillian, 366

Helpmann, Robert, 456, 458

Hemans, Dr, 544
Hemingway, Ernest, 524
Henderson, Dr, 27
Henderson, Helen, 390, 401, 415, 419, 439, 444
Henry, Uncle, 11
Henry VI, 294
Herbert, Jocelyn, 287, 451–2, 480, 482, 488, 490, 546, 563
Herlie, Eileen, 245, 398
Hertford Street flat, 524, 525–7, 529, 530
Herzen, Alexander, 486
Hi Gang, 112
Hickey, William, 404, 411
Hippodrome Theatre, Bristol, 172
Hird, Thora, 168, 434
Hitchcock, Alfred, 472
Hitler, Adolf, 86, 429
Hobson, Harold, 301, 306, 373, 423, 485
Hogg, Quintin, 76
Hoggart, Richard, 495
Holborn Empire, 198
Holman, Leigh, 455
Holroyd, Stuart, 375, 377
Holt, Thelma, 553
Homedale, Stoneleigh (No. 8), 49, 50, 51
Hope, Anthony, 536
Hope, Bob, 301
Hope-Wallace, Philip, 299
Hopkins, Bill, 375
Hopkins, Gerard Manley, 536
Horne, Lena, 345, 370, 371
The Hotel in Amsterdam, xv, 23–4, 321
Hotel Metropole, Beaulieu, 68
Hotel Metropole, Brighton, 207
House of Lords, 564
Houston, Donald, 167
Howard, Alan, 463
Howard, Leslie, 166, 195
Howard, Trevor, 531
Huddersfield, 216, 217, 284, 448
Huddleston, Father Trevor, 446, 447–8
Humanity (music-hall sketch), 19
Humphries, Barry, 445

Hunter, N. C., 204
Hurt, John, 540
Huxley, Aldous, 180
Hylton, Jack, 195, 338, 405

I Have Been Here Before, 165–6
Ibsen, Henrik, 261, 559
Ilfracombe, xvii, 130, 139, 218, 233, 238
In Which We Serve, 77
Inadmissible Evidence, xii, xxi, 122, 241, 537, 539, 540, 545, 549
India, 540
Inge, William, 371
Instow, 139
International Festival of Arts, Paris, 481
Ionesco, Eugene, 293, 331, 383, 390, 450, 557
Irving, Sir Henry, 16, 509, 510
Isaacs, Rufus, 16
Ischia, 424
Isherwood, Christopher, 355–6, 452, 491–2, 518, 537
Isle of Wight, 87–94, 145
ITMA, 112

Jackson, Freda, 167
Jackson, Joe, 326, 327, 328
Jacobi, Derek, 560, 561
Jacobs, Naomi, 234
Jamaica, 368–70
Jamaica, 371
James, Henry, 295
Jan (Woodfall driver), 532–3
Janni, Joe, 352
Jellicoe, Ann, 338, 511
Jenkins, Ann, 405, 406
Jenkins, Frank, 79
Jenny (Eric Pepper's niece), 139–40, 141, 144, 178
Jews, 19–20, 50, 109, 126, 428, 429
Jill (JO's cousin), 44, 45, 55, 115–16, 193, 314
John, Augustus, 524
John Gorden Theatre, New York, 399

John, Uncle, 44, 45
Johnson, Bunk, 316
Johnson, Dr Samuel, 190, 439, 497
Johnstone, Keith, 511, 564
Joint Stock theatre company xx
Jones, B. R., 520
Jones, Mr (headmaster), 36, 60–61, 66, 68, 69
Joplin, Scott, 316
José (in Acapulco), 429, 430, 431, 433, 474
Joyce, James, 535
Jules et Jim, 530
Jung, Carl Gustav, 524

Kallman, Chester, 425
Kay, Bernard, 377
Kay, Charles, 463, 480
Kazan, Elia, 372, 386
Kean, Edmund, 223
Keaton, Buster, 74, 472
Kempson, Rachel, 506n
Kensington High Street, 29, 203
Kerr, Walter, 341
Kidd, Robert, 377
Kidderminster, 175, 248–9
King, Diana, 170
King Lear, 294, 307, 315, 569
King's Arms, Newport, 39
King's Head pub, Fulham, 25
Kingslake, Alexander, 545
Kingston, Surrey, 73, 147, 163, 164, 203
Kismet, 405
The Kitchen, 108, 209, 210, 378–9, 382
Klein, Melanie, 460
Kneale, Nigel, 394
Knox, Collie, 40
Korda, Zoltán, 296
Krapp's Last Tape, 383
Kretzmer, Herbert, 409–10
Kurosawa, Akira, 501

The L-Shaped Room, 220
Labour Movement, 76
Labour Party, 77, 152, 153, 159, 171, 205

Lamarr, Hedy, 356
Lambert, Gavin, 356–7, 410
Lambert, Jack, 299
Landseer, Sir Edward, 511
Lane, Mr, 237, 238, 240, 241
Lane, Mrs, 237, 238, 240
Lane, Pamela (JO's first wife), 249–50, 280, 284, 309, 313, 328, 329, 337, 380, 468, 500
  and *Look Back* xv
  playing in her home town, 235
  appearance, 236
  JO's instant obsession, 236, 241–2
  Somerset accent, 238
  marries JO, 239
  pregnancy, 243–4
  tour of *Present Laughter*, 245, 246
  in Derby, 249–52
  marriage breaks down, 250, 252, 277, 278, 284, 302–4
  and JO's court appearance, 324, 325
Langtry, Lily, 555
Lansbury, George, 76
Larkin, Philip: 'Coming' xiv
Laughton, Charles, 315, 415, 420
Laurel and Hardy, 45, 73
Lawrence, D. H., 77, 295
Lawson, John, 19, 168
Lawson, Wilfred, 306, 531
Layton and Johnstone, 33
Leatherhead, Surrey, 165
Leavis, F. R., 310
LeBret, Fauvre, 427
Leeds, 181, 412
Leggatt, Alison, 398
Lehmann, Leo, 400, 401
Leicester, 213–15, 247
Leigh, Vivien, 316, 317, 320–23, 330, 349, 386, 390, 421, 422, 423, 439, 450, 451, 455–8, 460, 481, 515
Lejeune, Miss (critic), 449
Lessing, Doris, 376, 437, 511, 566
The Lesson, 383
Let's Make Love, 452

Levene, Sam, 400
Levy, Benn, 223, 473
Lewenstein, Oscar, 294, 298–9, 303, 318,
   335, 420, 428, 429, 433, 447, 459, 476,
   477, 478, 481–2, 527–8, 545
Lewisham, 178
The Lilac Domino, 28
Lilliput magazine, 310–11
Lily (of the Rembrandt Cinema), 193
Lily (stage carpenter's wife), 171
Linden, Stella, 193–6, 209, 210, 211,
   212–13, 219, 220, 223, 225, 232, 246,
   248, 254, 255, 271, 308, 309, 329, 395,
   398, 414, 502
   in No Room at the Inn, 186–9
   reads Resting Deep, 189–90
   encourages JO to write, 191–2
   affair with JO, xvii, 196, 197, 206
   in Brighton, 201, 203, 207, 440
   and The Devil Inside, 197–8, 216–17
   and Happy Birthday, 204–7
Linguists' Club, 77
Linklater, Eric, 228
The Lion in Love, 462, 463
Lisbon Story, 28
Littler, Emile, 408, 413, 564
Littlewood, Joan, 338
Live Like Pigs, 378
Livesey, Roger, 434
Livingstone, Fred, 522
Llandudno, xvii, 196
Lloyd, John Selwyn Brooke, 508
Lloyd, Marie, xv, 13, 17
Locke, Philip, 406, 411, 506n
Lockwood, Margaret, 208
Lod, Uncle, xv, 10–11, 326, 340
Logan, Josh, 399–400
Logue, Christopher, 338, 437, 509, 512
Löhr, Marie, 406, 411, 414
Lombard, Carole, 79
London, Jack, 335
London Hippodrome, Leicester Square,
   28, 119
London Library, xvi, 75

London Palladium, 547
London Pavilion, 538
Lonsdale, Frederick, 191
Look After Lulu, 421, 422, 423–4
Look Back in Anger, xiv, xxi, 5, 15, 190,
   236–40, 242, 245–6, 255, 261, 263,
   270–71, 277, 279–80, 288, 289,
   291–2, 293, 295–302, 305, 307, 308,
   311, 315, 318, 335, 336, 337, 339, 341,
   342, 351, 352, 362, 379–80, 384, 386,
   389, 435, 468, 479, 484
Look Back in Anger (film), 296, 370, 393–6,
   418, 426, 427, 428
Look on Tempests, 528
Lord of the Flies, 427
Loren, Sophia, 349
Lotis, Dennis, 406, 410, 411, 414
Love in Albania, 228
Love in a Myth, 403
The Loved One, 541
Lowe, Arthur, 542
Lower Belgrave Street flat, 439, 440, 444,
   451, 459, 462, 463, 466, 472, 473, 487,
   516
Lowndes Cottage, 349, 350, 390, 395, 436,
   441
Lulu, Auntie, 44, 45, 55
Lustgarten, Edgar, 326
Luther, xxi, 12, 426, 428, 444, 446, 450,
   459, 471, 476–85, 487, 488, 500, 508,
   515, 541, 563
Lynn, Ralph, 544
Lyons, Leonard, 343
Lyric Theatre, Hammersmith, 261, 262,
   296, 302
Lyttelton Theatre xiii

McAndrew, Renee, 106, 107, 145
Macbeth, 307, 315, 434, 551
McCabe, Father, 78
McCarthy, Mary, 552
McEnery, Peter, 506n
McEwan, Geraldine, 435
McKendrick, Sandy, 427

McKenna, Siobhan, 539
Mackenzie, Compton, 308
MacLiammóir, Micheal, 261
McMaster, Anew, 172, 180, 196, 253
Macmillan, Harold, 508, 512, 513
MacMillan, Kenneth, 406, 407, 410, 411
McMurray, Fred, 139
MacNeice, Louis, 434
McTaggart, Mr and Mrs, 213–14
The Magic Lantern, 466
Magnet, 51, 73, 101
The Making of Moo, 332–3, 335, 336
Malmgren, Yat, 296
Manchester, 174
Mankowitz, Wolf, 298, 310
March, Frances, 364
March, Frederick, 364
Margaret, Princess, 409, 418, 466
Margate, 5, 31, 49–50, 145, 194, 345, 502
Marples, Ernest, 151
Maschler, Tony, 375, 376
Matthews, A. A., 460
Matthews, Jessie, 33, 234
Maugham, Syrie, 467
Maurois, André, 91
Mayne, Ferdy, 492
Meals on Wheels, 545, 547
Melly, George, 511
Memoirs (Berlioz) v
Menton, 5, 81
Merivale, Jack, 455, 456–7, 458
Merrick, David, 339–43, 350, 362, 364–7,
    385, 386, 391, 399, 407, 409, 451, 541,
    549
Messel, Oliver, 400
Metropolitan Theatre, Edgware Road, 320
Middlesbrough Town Hall, 561
A Midsummer Night's Dream, 139, 420
Milford Haven, Marquess of, 413
Miller, 155, 156, 158
Miller, Arthur, 296–7, 302, 313, 315, 342,
    437
Miller, Harry Tatlock, 395
Miller, Jonathan, 537

Miller, Max, xx, 120, 198–200, 232, 303,
    315, 319, 320, 386, 403, 412, 538
Mills, John, 222, 413
Milton, Ernest, 306
Milton, John, 551
Min, Auntie, xv, 10, 346–8
Minehead, xvii, 222, 223, 233
Miracle in the Gorbals, xvi, 147
Mirfield, 446, 448–9
Mitchell, W.A., 484
Mitchell, Yvonne, 398
Modern Jazz Quartet, 564
Moffatt, John, 307, 309, 332, 480
Mon Abri, Isle of Wight, 90, 92, 93
Monroe, Marilyn, 310, 354, 437, 452
Monson and Petty (Newport solicitors), 94
Montagu, Lee, 547
Montague, Lord, 413
Montand, Yves, 452
Moore, Thomas, 96
Morecambe, 263, 435, 436
Mortimer, John, 294
Moss Empire, 168, 186
Mountbatten, Edwina, 460
The Mousetrap, 374
Mozart, Wolfgang Amadeus, 545
Mr Skeffington, 80
The Mulberry Bush, 293, 296
Mulchrone, John, 331, 336, 337
Murray, Alec, 395, 401, 402, 410, 417, 419,
    445
My Past Lives amd Thoughts, 486
My Wife's Family, 235, 328

Nabokov, Vladimir, 472
Namier, Lewis, 460
National Advertising Benevolent Society,
    83, 87, 94, 114, 119, 121, 123, 145,
    150
National Film Theatre, 378
National Gallery, London, 510–11
National Service, 158–9, 160, 162, 164
National Theatre, xiii, 130, 250, 271, 374,
    456, 558, 560, 566

Neville, John, 511
New English Bible, 524
New Statesman, 493
New Theatre, 302
New Theatre, Oxford, 309
Newcastle, 176–7, 489, 561, 562
Newhart, Bob, 457, 458
Newport, Monmouthshire, 5, 43, 94, 104
Nicholas, Paul, 488
Nichols, Beverley, 40
Nichols, Mike, 472, 567
Nichols, Peter, 247, 339
Nietzsche, Friedrich Wilhelm, 158
Night Must Fall, 223, 227
No Room at the Inn, 167–8, 169, 172,
    186–8, 189, 212
Noel, Conrad, 76
Noguchi, 307, 382
Noh plays, 308
Nonsuch Park, 38, 50, 52, 53, 56, 58, 60,
    66, 161
Norman, Mr and Mrs, 57
North Cheam, 161, 166
Northern Sinfonia, 560
Notebook, 201–2, 260–61, 264–5, 267–70,
    280, 312, 324, 476, 506, 551, 555,
    558–60, 569, 570
Nottingham, 422, 481
Nought for your Comfort, 447
Novello, Ivor, 21, 28, 404
Now Barabbas, 160
Now Voyager, 80
Nursery World, 155, 157

O'Brien, Barry, 195
O'Casey, Sean, 294
Occupe-toi d'Amélie, 421
Odeon Cinema, Marble Arch, 449
Odets, Clifford, 365–6
The Old Dark House, 391
Old Vic, 209, 235, 249, 545, 566
Olivier, Laurence, 229, 307, 311, 315,
    316–23, 329, 338, 350, 363, 364, 365,
    370, 374, 386, 390, 420, 422, 423, 434,

435, 442, 446, 449, 450–51, 456, 457,
    460, 524, 540, 564
On the Kitchen Front (radio programme),
    96, 97, 107
One by One, 565
One of Our Aircraft is Missing, 139
One Way Pendulum, 441
Orton, Joe, xii, 377
Orwell, George, 76
Osborn, Paul, 455
Osborne, Annie (JO's paternal
    grandmother), 7, 12, 31–43, 45–8, 55,
    64, 70, 71, 74, 78, 79–80, 83, 87, 92–5,
    103–4, 105, 109, 121, 144, 193, 201,
    213, 309, 314, 326, 438, 540
Osborne, Fay (JO's sister), 29, 164, 279
Osborne, Harry (JO's great-uncle), 43
Osborne, Helen xviii
Osborne, Jim (JO's paternal grandfather),
    13, 25–6, 31, 36–40, 42, 43, 64, 93, 94,
    103, 122–3
Osborne, John
    dancing lessons, 161
    at Clark's College, xii, 144
    ill-health, xii, xvi, 14, 20, 26–7, 46, 78,
        83, 88, 93, 112–13, 133, 134, 145, 152,
        164, 420, 566–8
    convalescent home in Dorset, xvi,
        114–18
    death xviii
    character, xix, 14
    birth, 8
    education, 9, 20, 26, 36, 51, 60–67, 88,
        89, 92–3, 95–8, 102–3, 119–43
    move to Stoneleigh, 30
    first girlfriend, 54–60
    starts to write, 73, 169–70
    love of the cinema, 77–80
    on the Isle of Wight, 87–94, 146
    father's death, 93–4
    appearance, 122–3, 278–9, 393
    influenced by Mr Prentiss, 127
    starts work at Benn Brothers, 150
    correspondence course, 152–3

engaged to Renee, 163
army medical, 164
becomes an ASM, 167
marries Pamela Lane, 238, 239
vegetarianism, 278–9
divorce proceedings, 324–8, 523, 538
Russian trip, 335–6
marries Mary Ure, 336–7
on New York, 343–5
visits Wales, 350–51
first sees Francine, 353, 354
his 'damn you England' letter, 492–6, 499, 508
marries Penelope Gilliatt, 502, 538
arrested and fined, 510–14
buys the Old Water Mill, 516
expelled from Equity, 523

Osborne, Lottie (JO's great-aunt), 43, 44
Osborne, Nellie Beatrice (née Grove; JO's mother), xvii, 10, 14, 16–21, 25–33, 36, 38, 39, 41–51, 55, 56, 57, 59–62, 67, 70–73, 81–2, 84, 85, 86, 105–11, 118–19, 128, 141, 143, 144, 145, 148, 160, 161, 173, 209–10, 213, 233, 264–5, 278, 302, 357, 523, 543
appearance, xiii–xiv, 28
character, xiii, 27–8, 37, 55, 309
and her husband's death, xiv, 93–4
marriage, xiv, 25, 30, 32, 49
and JO's theatrical career, xix, 169, 193, 229–30, 282
moves to Stoneleigh, 31
on the Isle of Wight, 88, 90–93
JO first hates, 94
and the Lisbon incident, 94–5
in the Second World War, 101–2, 107, 109
letters to JO, 105–6, 169, 202–3, 265–7, 485, 504–5
and JO's rheumatic fever, 112–14
and JO's engagement, 163, 165, 180
Mondays with JO, 202, 203
JO's letter to Anthony, 242
attends Look Back, 300

meets JO before his divorce proceedings, 325–6
at JO's marriage to Mary Ure, 336–7
Empire News interview, 420
and Mary Ure, 421
and Luther, 485
in Venice, 502–3
at the Oliviers, 524

Osborne, Nolan (JO's daughter), 535, 545, 550, 559, 569
Osborne, Sir Cyril, 486
Osborne, Thomas Godfrey (JO's father), xiv, 5, 17, 25–6, 36, 38, 44, 48, 51, 52, 56–7, 66, 73, 84–5, 87, 114, 119, 121, 141, 178, 202, 253
appearance, xiv, 6, 26, 47, 123, 166
death, xiv, 93–4, 117, 362
influence on JO xiv
marriage, xiv, 25, 30, 32, 33–4, 49
short stories, xiv, 148
holiday in Margate, 5, 49–50
ill-health, 5, 9, 25, 26, 34, 61, 62, 81, 82, 86, 88, 93, 164, 279
in Menton, 5, 81, 82
takes JO to the theatre, 8–9
moves to Stoneleigh, 31, 32–3
the Lisbon affair, 34, 47, 83, 94
on the Isle of Wight, 87–94
'Crawshay-Bailey Had an Engine', 152–3
'Mouse Pie', 153

Osborne, Tom (JO's great-uncle), 43–4
Osborne family, 7, 19, 46–7, 202, 351, 504
Ostrovsky, Alexander, 566
Othello, 420–21
O'Toole, Peter, 460
Oxford Experimental Theatre Club, 374

Page, Anthony, 382, 409, 511, 540, 544, 547, 548, 549, 552, 553
The Painted Banquet: My Life and Loves, 487
Palace Theatre, 330, 349, 350, 408, 413, 414, 415, 416, 435

Palace Theatre, Camberwell, 243, 294
The Paleface, 301
Palette, Eugene, 79
Palmer, J. Wood, xvi, 146–9, 178, 234
Parker, Dorothy, 486
Parker, Joy, 445, 462
Pasco, Richard, 321, 330
Patrick, Gail, 79
A Patriot for Me, xvi, xxi, 127, 374–5, 491, 492, 537, 541–8, 552
Payne, David, 224, 225, 227, 231
Peach, Mary, 523
Pelham, David, 407–8, 409, 412, 414, 417
Penzance, 145–9
Pepper, Eric, 120–21, 123–4, 126–7, 129, 131, 132, 137–43, 144, 148, 150, 154, 157, 195
Perchance to Dream, 28
Percy, Esmé, 307, 309, 332, 333–4
Percy, Uncle, 105
Perry, John, 492
Peter Pan, 167
Phoenix Theatre, 485, 500, 508
Piaf, Edith, 532
Pickles, Vivian, 538
Pinero, Sir Arthur Wing, 190, 191, 197, 566
Pinocchio, 98
Pinter, Harold, 479, 522
Playhouse Theatre, Brighton, 201, 206
Plays for England, 536, 537, 538
Plays and Players, 299
Playwrights' Company, 366
Plowright, Joan, 307, 331, 332, 338, 383, 386, 422, 435, 450, 451, 453, 454, 524, 528
Plummer, Christopher, 400
Point Counter Point, 77
Poke, Greville, 543–4
Polanski, Roman, 564
Ponting's store, 29
Ponting's store, Kensington High Street, 29

Porter, Harry (JO's uncle), xv, 10, 11, 31, 37–8, 43, 104
Porter, Nancy (JO's aunt), 31, 37, 39, 47, 94, 103
Porter, Tony (JO's cousin), 7, 31, 39, 41–4, 104, 193, 314
Portman, Eric, 386
Positano, 565
Powell, William, 79
Poynter, Reginald, 376
Premice, Josephine, 371
Prentiss, Mr (teacher), 126, 127, 151
Present Laughter, 245
Press Council, 519, 521
Preston, Robert, 400
Priestley, J. B., 133, 165, 204, 294, 335, 494
Principia, Act One, 190
The Prisoner of Zenda, 79, 536
Procktor, Patrick, 553
Profumo, John, 413
Puley, Mr (desk-clerk), 270, 365, 385
Pygmalion, 253–4, 277

Quayle, Anthony, 284, 386
Queen of Spades, 317
Queen's Theatre, 506n, 539

RADA, 215, 219
Radcliffe, Jack, 320
Rain, 248
Ramsay, Peggy, 290–91
Rank Films, 291, 330, 389, 394, 406, 427
Rathbone, Basil, 53
Rationalist Press Association, 77
Rattigan, Terence, 191, 201, 203, 218, 219–20, 267, 286, 299, 313, 340, 348, 420, 484, 492, 518
Rawalpindi (P&O liner), 89
Ray, Cyril, 519, 520
Ray, Robin, 463
Raymond (Isabel Sells' fiancé), 89, 92, 103
Read, Lady, 511
Read, Sir Herbert, 511
The Reason Why, 543

Rebecca, 38
Redgrave, Lady, xii, xiii, 136
Redgrave, Sir Michael, 252, 492, 528
Redgrave, Vanessa, 420, 506n, 511, 514,
    528–34, 539
Reece, Bertram, 514
Regent Palace Hotel, 28, 119
Reisz, Karel, 293
Relph, George, 317, 321
The Reluctant Debutante, 374
Rembrandt Cinema, Ewell, 67, 79–80, 113,
    144, 193–4, 349
Renoir, Jean, 472
Resnais, Alain, 503
Resting Deep, 179, 181, 189–90, 197
    see also *The Devil Inside*
Rhinoceros, 450
Richards, Jose, 382
Richardson, Joely, 532
Richardson, Natasha, 531
Richardson, Ralph, 491
Richardson, Tony, 282, 292, 294, 302, 338,
    368, 377, 381, 395, 401, 455, 486, 492,
    526, 527–8, 539, 548, 567
    and English Stage Company, 282
    and *Look Back*, 289, 293, 295–8, 300,
        393–4, 479
    divide and rule technique, 297, 321,
        357, 529
    and play reading, 294
    and *Cards of Identity*, 306
    and JO's journalism, 310
    and *Othello*, 312, 420
    and *The Entertainer*, 316, 317, 322–3,
        424, 435, 436, 442, 479
    settles in Los Angeles, 321–2
    and *The Apollo of Bergerac*, 331
    and *The Making of Moo*, 332, 333
    in Russia, 335
    at JO's weddings, 336
    appearance, 343
    and Woodfall Films, 352, 523
    character, 353–4
    and Saltzman, 355, 356

and Francine, 358, 359
and *The Kitchen*, 382
and *Paul Slickey*, 403
and *Lulu*, 421, 422
writes to JO (1966), 425
and Acapulco, 427–33, 474, 528
and Mary Ure, 451, 453–4, 463
and *A Taste of Honey*, 451, 500
and Flewitt, 452–3
and *The Changeling*, 463
and *Luther*, 478, 480–81, 484, 500, 508
nature of friendship with JO, 486–7
in Valbonne, 488, 490, 499, 500
and *The Seagull*, 506n
and Vanessa Redgrave, 529–34
and *Patriot*, 541, 542, 544
on Jill Bennett, 545, 552
and *The Charge of the Light Brigade*,
    543, 545
Devine on, 548
and JO's breakdown, 567
Richmond, Surrey, 242, 244
Rickards, Jocelyn, 395–6, 402, 406, 410,
    411, 414, 417, 418, 419, 423, 435, 436,
    439–42, 445, 446, 447, 451, 461, 462,
    466, 467, 471, 472, 473, 481, 482, 487,
    488, 490, 491, 498, 499–500, 506–9,
    515, 516, 528, 538, 567
Rigg, Diana, 421
Ritchie, Julie, 552
Robeson, Paul, 33, 420–21
Robey, George, 33
Roc, Pat, 208
Rockingham club, Soho, 348
Rogers, Anton, 537
Rogers, Bunny, 492
The Roman Spring of Mrs Stone, 455
Rome, 401, 417–18
Room at the Top, 427
Roots, 382
Rose, Auntie, 11
Rossington, Norman, 463
Royal Court Theatre, xiv, xix, 5, 223, 282,
    287–8, 290, 293, 302, 306, 307, 318,

322, 329, 330, 333, 336, 338, 339, 349, 366, 368, 372, 377, 378, 379, 382, 398, 405, 406, 423, 433, 446, 450, 451, 459, 462, 480, 481, 483, 485, 489, 502, 512, 515, 523, 537, 538, 542, 543, 546–9, 552, 556–8, 564, 565
Royal Opera House, Covent Garden, 560
Royal Shakespeare Theatre, 558
Royale Theatre, New York, 362, 363
Royle, Anthony, 549
Running, Arnold, 155–9, 161, 163, 169, 213, 329
Running, Mrs, 157
Russell, Bertrand, 437, 495, 509

Sabu the Elephant Boy, 58
A Safety Match, 92
Saffron Walden, 98, 223
Saga Repertory Company, 218–24
Sailor Beware, 374
St Boniface's School, Ventnor, 89, 103
St Denis, Michel, 226, 228, 282, 293, 557
St George, Clive, 218–25, 233
St James's Palace, 253, 477, 537, 544
St James's Theatre, 252, 322, 456
St Joan of the Stockyards, 539
St Michael's College, North Devon, 119–43, 145, 150
St Tropez, 532–3
Sainthill, Loudon, 395, 421
Saki (Hector Hugh Munro) xvi
Salisbury inn, St Martin's Lane, 224, 253
Saltzman, Harry, 295, 301, 351–61, 368–71, 385, 390, 393, 394, 426, 427, 435, 436, 459–60
Samuel French, 311
Sanctuary, 359, 451, 452
Sanders, Scott, 320
Sandgate, 472
Sartre, Jean-Paul, 288
Saturday Night and Sunday Morning, 352, 442
Saturday Night Music Hall (radio show), 144, 459–60

Saunders, Peter, 564
Savile Club, 308
Sayers, Dorothy L. xii
Schell, Maximillian, 544
Schissel, Jack, 386
Scofield, Paul, 295, 296, 313
Scott, Rev Michael, 438
Scott, W. I. D., 520
Scott, Zachary, 452
Scunthorpe, 438
The Seagull, 506, 539
Seagulls over Sorrento, 263, 435
Sears, Heather, 331
The Second Mrs Tanqueray, 190
Second World War, 5, 76, 78, 86–90, 97–8, 100–102, 107, 109, 110, 112, 139, 141, 142, 143
Sells, Isabel, 89, 90, 92, 93, 103, 119, 145
Sells, Mrs, 89, 91, 93
Selznick, Irene, 409
A Sense of Detachment, xii, xiii, xvii, 135, 136, 182–3, 196–7, 226–7, 271–2
Separate Tables, 286
Seyrig, Delphine, 545
Shakespeare, William, 168, 216, 229, 460, 477, 538, 569
Shakespeare Memorial Theatre (later Royal Shakespeare Theatre), Stratford-upon-Avon, 420, 528
Shanklin, Isle of Wight, 90
Sharpley, Anne, 408
Shaw, George Bernard, 16, 74, 147, 251, 254, 305, 311
Shaw, Glen Byam, 293, 296, 557
Shaw, Jennifer, 522
Shaw, Robert, 401, 461, 463, 464–5, 522, 523
Sheffield, 194
Sheila (actress), 171, 178, 180, 181, 183–4, 186, 187, 189, 192, 195, 197, 225
Sheila (Eric Pepper's niece), 139–40
Shelley, Percy Bysshe, 76, 77, 158, 389
Shepherd's Bush Empire, 25
Sheppard, Reverend Dick, 29

Sherek, Henry, 255
Sheridan, Dinah, 330–31
Sherwood, Robert, 366
Shields, Ella, 320
Shinwell, Emanuel, 151, 153
Shippard, Mr, 162, 163, 169, 172, 178, 180, 181, 193
Shippard, Mrs, 161, 162, 163, 165, 166, 169, 173, 177, 178, 180
Shippard, Renee, 160–66, 169, 170, 171, 177–80, 187, 235, 329, 349, 436, 555
Shippard family, 164, 165, 186, 187, 213
Shropshire xviii
Shulman, Milton, 416
Siddiqui, Mr (lodger), 261–2, 271
Sidmouth, 21
Signoret, Simone, 452
Silcox, Mr (Editor-in-Chief of *Gas World*), 150–57, 163, 195
Silcox, Primrose, 150–51, 153, 154, 156
Sillitoe, Alan, 511, 513
Simmons, Jean, 166
Simpson, Mrs Wallis (later Duchess of Windsor), 16, 450
Simpson, N. F., 377, 441
Simpson, Wally, 382
Simpson's store, Piccadilly, 187, 196, 249
Sinatra, Frank, 142, 434
Sinden, Donald, 498
Sitwell, Edith, 311, 355
Skelton, Barbara, 441
The Sleeping Beauty, 335
Smith, Dodie, 204
Socialism, 76, 205, 256, 495
Soldiers in Skirts, 175, 212, 219
The Soldier's Tale, 560, 561
Sons and Lovers, 401, 410
Sontag, Susan, 467
Soul of Man under Socialism, 76
The Sound of Music, 562, 563
South Sea Bubble, 374
Southend, 162, 163
Southport, 172
Soyinka, Wole, 377

Spengler, Oswald, 158
Spotted Horse pub, Putney, 25
Spring Hotel, Ewell, 51, 420
Springtime for Henry, 223, 227, 232
The Stage, 213, 218, 224, 225, 248, 271
Stanley, Kim, 531, 532
Stanwyck, Barbara, 139
A Star is Born, 51
Steiger, Rod, 376, 541
Steinbeck, John, 586
Stephens, Margaret, 545
Stephens, Robert, 306, 307, 309, 332, 333, 334, 336, 338, 374–5, 398, 399, 400, 446, 460, 491, 518, 545, 560, 561, 566
Stephens, Tarn, 333, 336
Stevens, Roger, 339
Stockwell, Dean, 401
Stoneleigh, Surrey, 30–31, 35, 37, 44, 80, 100, 160, 165, 186, 217, 223, 233, 235, 266, 293
Stoneleigh Hotel, 30–31, 33, 35, 38, 50, 71, 101, 107, 108, 112, 201, 213
Stoneleigh Park Road, Stoneleigh (No., 68), 31, 32, 48, 49
Stopes, Marie, 57
Stoppard, Tom, 191
The Storm, 566
Storm over the Nile, 295–6
Strach, Dr, 350
Strachey, Lytton, 559
Stratchey, Lytton, 76
Stratford-upon-Avon, 284, 415, 417, 418, 422
Strauss, Richard, 544
Stravinsky, Igor, 560, 561
A Streetcar Named Desire, 409
A Subject of Scandal and Concern, 439
Suite in Three Keys, 568
Surbiton, 144
Surrey, xiii, xvi, 30, 37
Sutton, Randolph, 320
Svoboda, 566
Swan Lake, 406
Swift, Jonathan, 184

Tales from Soho, 294
Tanfield, Peter, 3, 411
Tapper, Terry, 165
A Taste of Honey, 352, 394, 442, 451, 452,
    453, 455, 460, 500
Tati, Jacques, 472
Tauber, Richard, 33
Taylor, Elizabeth, 393, 489
Taylor, Jeremy, 305
Teahouse of the August Moon, 374
Temple, Joan, 167
Tempo (arts programme), 523
Tennant, Billy, 96
Tennant, Cecil, 307
Tennant, H. M., 291, 317, 324, 384, 391,
    424
The Tenth Chance, 377
Theatre Royal, Brighton, xviii, 136, 308,
    540
Theatre Royal, Cardiff, 170
Theatre Royal, Hanley, 197
Theatre Royal, Huddersfield, 198, 216
Theatre Royal, Leicester, 213, 214
Theatre Royal, Nottingham, 481
Thesiger, Ernest, 524
They Call It Cricket, 12
The Thinker's Library, 77–8
The Thirty-Nine Steps, 79
Thomas, J. B., 76
Three Stooges, 45, 74, 198
Thurber, James, 524
Tickerage Mill, Blackboys, Sussex, 515
Tiffins School, Kingston, 72, 74, 94, 103,
    119, 124, 153
The Tiger and the Horse, 528
Time Present, 553
Time Remembered, 296
Titus Andronicus, 319, 330
Toby Jug pub, Tolworth, 71
Tom Jones, 321, 395, 523, 527, 538
Tormé, Mel, 406
Torquay, 194
Tottenham, 11, 46
Tottenham Crowd, xv, 10, 12, 202

Toynbee, Philip, 375
Tracey, Arthur, 33
Travers, Ben, 204, 332, 483, 542
Treasure Island, 201
Trelawny of the Wells, 566
Trevelyan, John, 442
Trevor-Roper, Hugh, 494
Tridmore, Philip, 411
Trilling, Ossia, 299
Trocadero Restaurant, 27–8
Trollope, Anthony, 508, 549
Troubridge, Sir St Vincent, 373
Truffaut, François, 503, 530
Tryon, Tom, 452
Tucker, Sophie, 67
Turk's Head pub, Nottingham, 422, 481–2
Turnham Green, 106, 107
Turvey, Joan, 329
Tushingham, Rita, 295, 442–3
Tutin, Dorothy, 317, 321, 435
Twelve Angry Men, 371
Twelvetrees, Mr (director), 249–50
Twentieth Century-Fox, 451, 489
Tynan, Elaine, 377
Tynan, Kenneth, 300–301, 302, 307, 308,
    310, 376, 377, 379, 394, 456, 485, 489,
    509, 564

Ullman, Liv, 545
Un-American Activities Committee, 252
Under Plain Cover, 536, 537, 543
Under Thirty Theatre group, 247
United Artists, 539
United Nations, 493
An Unsocial Socialist, 147
Ure, Colin, 438–9
Ure, Colin (Mary's son), 499, 522, 523
Ure, Mary, 295–7, 299–304, 309–15, 326,
    328, 330, 331–2, 336, 342–6, 349, 351,
    352, 355, 362, 363, 364, 369–72, 385–
    91, 393, 396, 401, 402, 410, 415, 417,
    418, 420, 421, 422, 436–40, 451–5,
    457, 459–65, 472, 487–8, 499, 510,
    520, 522–3, 528

Ure, Mrs, 83, 87, 94, 114, 119, 144
Ustinov, Peter, 228, 284, 294, 386

Valbonne, 487, 491, 498, 507
Vaudeville Theatre, Strand, 160
Vaughan Williams, Mrs Ralph, 77
Vaughan Williams, Ralph, 545
Venice, 502–3, 507
Venice Film Festival, 490, 500–502, 508
Ventnor, Isle of Wight, 87, 90, 103
Verdi, Giuseppe, 544
Vernon, Marguerite, 553
Vernon, Mr, 553
Victoria Inn, North Cheam, 161
Victoria Theatre, Hayling Island, 224
Vidal, Gore, 467
A View from the Bridge, 302, 309
Vile Bodies, 128
Villiers, James, 247, 332, 377
Viper Gang Club, xix, 72, 73, 74, 76, 121
Vogue, 466, 468, 563
Voisin, Mme (housekeeper), 488
Voltaire, 506
Vosper, Ewan, 543
Vosper, Margery, 290, 291–2, 385, 405,
    408, 447, 450, 543, 544

Waddington, Leslie, 470
Wain, John, 294, 376
Walker, Alexander, 442
Wall, Alan, 72, 85
Wall, Edna, xvi, 69, 71–2, 81, 85, 100
Wall, M. Geoffrey (Mickey), xvi, 63,
    66–77, 80, 85, 87, 94, 98–101, 103,
    109, 112, 119, 124, 140, 144, 148, 153,
    158, 159, 160, 165, 306, 449
Wall, Mr, 69, 70, 74, 81, 87
Wall, Mrs, 69, 85
Wall family, 81, 82, 109, 116, 169
Waller, fats, 545
Wanamaker, Sam, 252, 253
War Requiem, 564
The Washing of the Spears, 567
Watch it Come Down, xiii, 221

Waters, Elsie and Doris, 168
Watling, Jack, 215
Watson, Greville Pelham Monserrat, 121,
    132, 134, 136, 138, 218
Waugh, Evelyn, 289, 325, 541, 542
Wax, Emmanuel, 255, 271
Webber, Robert, 371–2, 388, 400, 426, 469
Weidenfeld, George, 441
Weigel, Helene, 293, 307, 309
Welch, Denton xvi
Welchman, Harry, 406
Wells, H. G., 74, 83
Wells, Veronica, 220, 222, 223, 224, 261,
    262
Welsh, John, 296
Wenham, Jane, 421
Wesker, Arnold, 108, 209, 378, 382, 399,
    437, 438, 494, 509, 512
Wesker, Dusky, 378, 382
West, Mae, 82
Westcliff, 162–3
Western Approaches, 139
Whelan, Albert, 320
Whelen, Christopher, 405, 412
Whelen, Mrs W. E., 412
White Bear, Piccadilly Circus, 348
White Cargo, 214–15, 356
Whitelaw, Billie, 523
Whiting, John, 284, 294, 494
Wilde, Oscar, 11–12, 16, 75, 76, 157, 512,
    520
William books, xvi, 31, 63
Williams, Bransby, 524
Williams, Emlyn, 223, 291, 310
Williams, Francis, 519
Williams, Hugh, 291
Williams, Margaret, 291
Williams, Mrs (landlady), 95, 100, 101, 110
Williams, Peter, 396
Williams, T. B., 134, 139
Williams, Tennessee, 310, 371, 455
Williamson, Nicol, 464–5, 540, 545, 549
Wilson, Angus, 289, 293, 294, 296, 306
Wilson, Colin, 375, 377

Wilson, Edmund, 472

Wilson, Harold, 539

Wilson, Mr (school secretary), 129

Wilson, Mrs (school matron), 129, 130

Wilson, Sandy, 404

Wilton, Rob, 514

Wimbledon, 178, 203

Winchell, Walter, 372

The Wind and the Rain, 214

Windom's Way, 337

Windsor, 154

Winn, Godfrey, 422

Winner, Michael, 554

Winnie, Auntie, 11

The Winslow Boy, 191

Wolverhampton, 179

Wood, Charles, 545, 546

Wood Green, north London, 197, 201

Wood, John, 332

Wood, Wee Georgie, 168

Woodcock, Patrick, 553

Woodfall Films, 321, 352, 366, 390, 394, 427, 428, 434, 435, 442, 459, 460, 523, 524, 526, 529, 530, 532, 543, 545, 562

Woodham-Smith, Cecil, 543

Woodthorpe, Peter, 307, 309

Woolf, Virginia, 355

Worcester Park Road, Worcester Park (No. 120), 95, 101, 110

World Festival of Youth, Moscow, 335

The World of Paul Slickey, 403–15, 416–17, 426, 450, 520

Worsley, T. C. (Cuthbert), 203, 299, 484, 492, 520

Worsthorne, Peregrine, 494

Wrede, Baron Godot, 411

The Wrong Set, 289

Wycherley, William, 338

Wyngarde, Peter, 307, 309

Yates, Dornford, 460

Yojimbo, 501

You Never Can Tell, 251

Young, B. A. (Freddie), 552

Young Vic, 219, 220, 222, 261, 287

Yucatan, 474–5

Yvette (kitchen worker), 213

Zeffirelli, Franco, 545

Zolotov, Sam, 399